Greenhill Books

A HISTORY
OF THE
PENINSULAR
WAR

A HISTORY OF
THE PENINSULAR WAR

Volume I: 1807–1809
From the Treaty of Fontainebleau to the
Battle of Corunna

Volume II: January to September 1809
From the Battle of Corunna to the End of the Talavera
Campaign

Volume III: September 1809 to December 1810
Ocaña, Cadiz, Bussaco, Torres Vedras

Volume IV: December 1810 to December 1811
Masséna's Retreat, Fuentes de Oñoro, Albuera,
Tarragona

Volume V: October 1811 to August 1812
Valencia, Ciudad Rodrigo, Badajoz, Salamanca, Madrid

**Volume VI: September 1, 1812 to
August 5, 1813**
The Siege of Burgos, The Retreat from Burgos, The
Campaign of Vittoria, The Battles of the Pyrenees

Volume VII: August 1813 to April 14, 1814
The Capture of St. Sebastian, Wellington's Invasion of
France, Battles of the Nivelle, The Nive, Orthez and
Toulouse

A HISTORY
OF THE
PENINSULAR
WAR

Antonio Carnicero lo dibuxó   Juan Brunetti lo grabó 1800

CARLOS IIII.

REY DE ESPAÑA.

A HISTORY
OF THE
PENINSULAR
WAR

Volume I: 1807–1809
From the Treaty of Fontainebleau
to the Battle of Corunna

SIR CHARLES OMAN

Introduction by
Colonel John R. Elting, USA, Ret.

Greenhill Books, London
Stackpole Books, Pennsylvania

Greenhill Books

This edition of *A History of the Peninsular War*, volume I
first published 1995 by
Greenhill Books, Lionel Leventhal Limited, Park House,
1 Russell Gardens, London NW11 9NN
and
Stackpole Books, 5067 Ritter Road, Mechanicsburg,
PA 17055, USA

British Library Cataloguing in Publication Data
Oman, Sir Charles
History of the Peninsular War. – Vol. I: 1807–08: From the
Treaty of Fontainebleau to the Battle of Corunna. – New ed
I. Title
940.27
ISBN 1-85367-214-9

Library of Congress Cataloging in Publication Data
Oman, Charles William Chadwick, Sir, 1860–1946.
A history of the Peninsular War / by Charles Oman
720 p. 22 cm.
Includes index.
Contents: v. I. From the Treaty of Fontainebleau
to the battle of Corunna
ISBN 1-85367-214-9 (hc)
1. Peninsular War, 1807–1814. I. Title.
DC231.05 1995
946'.06—dc20

PUBLISHING HISTORY
A History of the Peninsular War, volume I, was first published
in 1902 (Oxford), and is reproduced now exactly as the original
edition, complete and unabridged, with the addition of an
Introduction by Col. John R. Elting (USA, Ret). The original
maps have been represented by John Richards, in the
interests of clarity.

Printed and bound in Great Britain.

INTRODUCTION

CHARLES William Chadwick Oman (1860–1946) began his teaching and writing career in 1883 when he was elected a fellow of All Souls College, Oxford.[1] He was a man of strong and varied interests, which ranged from classical Greece and Rome through the Middle Ages and into the nineteenth century, and included such odd subjects as Welsh castles, British coinage, and the *code duello* as practised by British army officers. As a result he was ignored by the Oxford School of History, whose dons thought that no one who wrote on such an unspecialized collection of subjects – and especially nobody who presented history as stories of times past, rather than writing in professionally phrased academic style – could be considered a true scholar and respectable historian. Today Oman is probably better remembered than any of them.

Oman's first book (1888) was his *History of Greece*. It was followed by works on medieval England and a *Short History of the Byzantine Empire* (1892). His *A History of the Art of War in the Middle Ages* (1898) was the first English-language study of that subject; originally well-received, it gradually proved to be unreliable. (A man who made some conscience of his work, Oman brought out an extensively revised second edition in 1924, which still has considerable value as a general survey of its subject.)

Apparently it was Oman's discovery of the papers of Sir Charles Vaughan, left to gather dust in the All Souls archives, that inspired him to begin his history of the Peninsular War. (Vaughan, an adventurous British diplomat, had served in Spain during most of that conflict and had collected masses of material on all possible aspects of it.)

The major work on the subject at that time was William F. P. Napier's *War In the Peninsula and the South of France, From the Year 1807 to the Year 1814* (5 vols.: 1834–1840), a vivid, contentious work by a distinguished officer who had gone through the war as a regimental commander, admired Napoleon, did not admire various English generals and politicians, and had the old-soldier characteristic of calling a spade a "bloody" shovel. Oman's intention obviously was to produce a history that would update and correct Napier's version, utilizing the large amounts of reference material that had become available since its publication. He would also extend its scope, covering the campaigns which Napier had omitted or merely outlined, as not being a part of his own service, and would avoid Napier's occasional flare-ups of personal bias (Oman did not exactly admire Napoleon). He succeeded admirably in his first two objectives and quite well with the third.

Oman was a skilled researcher with an excellent knowledge of possible source material. He used everything available and then looked for more – memoirs, diaries, and unpublished papers of both officers and enlisted men; Wellington's published dispatches; the general orders of the British and Portuguese armies; Foreign Office and Admiralty records (the latter, for some reason, held all documents concerning French prisoners of war); Parliamentary papers; newspaper files; and the French, Spanish, and Portuguese archives. Whether by skill or luck he made discoveries such as the 1813 "morning states" (strength returns) of Wellington's army, which had been mislaid in the Record Office for over sixty years. When working with personal memoirs Oman was careful to check them against official reports and other reminiscences of the same events. To all this he added one basic qualification of the true military historian – he attempted to walk over the battlefields he was to describe and to trace out the important roads and topographical features.

His first volume, which covered the causes of the Peninsular War and ended with the withdrawal of Moore's army from Corunna, was published in 1902 (in which year Oman also produced *Seven Roman Statesmen*); Volume II came out a year later, dealing with Wellington's early campaigns and the battle of Talavera. The effect of these volumes was considerable, not the least result being that they moved several descendants of Peninsular veterans to make their papers available to him. During Oman's subsequent exploration of the Portuguese frontier districts, the boy-king Manuel II placed an automobile (then a rare item) and a military guide at his disposal.[2] Volume III (1908) continued with Masséna's 1810 campaign, ending with Wellington's withdrawal into the lines of Torres Vedras. Volume IV (1911) followed with Masséna's retreat from Portugal and the battle of Albuera. (These volumes did not receive Oman's whole attention: in 1906 he wrote *The Great Revolt of 1381*; in 1910 he published one of his major works, *A History of England Before the Norman Conquest*.) In 1913, using information left over from his history of the Peninsular War, Oman finished *Wellington's Army*, a useful work that contains some of his best writing. A year later, Volume V carried the Peninsular War forward to Wellington's crucial 1812 victory over Marmont at Salamanca. Oman was now receiving advice from John W. Fortescue, author of the authoritative nineteen-volume *A History of the British Army*, who had recently become a lecturer at Oxford. (It can be helpful, while studying Oman's Peninsular War, to consult the concurrent portion of Fortescue's History.)

World War I interrupted Oman's writing; too old to serve in any military capacity, he worked in Whitehall as a civilian official. Then in 1919 he was elected to Parliament as Oxford's representative – Conservative, naturally – which position he held until 1935. Despite the requirements of this new post, Oman managed the publication of Volume VI of the Peninsular War history, covering the decisive Vittoria campaign, in 1922 (Oman apologized for its comparative lack of maps, which post-war prices had made extremely expensive). This was followed (1926) by an antiquarian's delight, his *Castles*, "the result of two most interesting, if rather laborious journeys" in Wales, Cornwall, and southeast England, which is illustrated by his son's photographs. Next came *Studies in the Napoleonic Wars* (1929) an odd-lot, thrown-together book which contains considerable misinformation, including Oman's almost-comic delusion that the United States' 1812 declaration of war against Great Britain was a dastardly bit of deliberate conniving between President Madison and Napoleon. Volume VII was published the next year, bringing the series to an end. It can only be called monumental.

Oman continued writing into 1945, his principal book during this latter period being *The Art of War in the Sixteenth Century* (1937). His work had brought him many honours, including that of Knight Commander of the Order of the British Empire in 1920.

Like any work of such magnitude and detail, *A History of the Peninsular War* inevitably contains debatable material and some errors. An appreciable amount of new information has become available since 1930. Sources such as Gleig and Miot de Melito, whom Oman considered quite reliable, have proven less so; others, like Thiebault whom he used with care, are now known be totally untrustworthy. Also, Oman's evaluations could be affected by a certain contrariety between author and subject. A life-long academician, he could draw on neither personal military education nor experience [3] – and war is an incredibly complex, chancy and messy business that will not fit itself into neat academic concepts. A scrupulous researcher, Oman found and studied large amounts of new material, but the knowledge he thus amassed was not leavened by a thorough understanding of the organization, command systems, and tactics of the contending armies. Quite possibly he did not comprehend their importance. This was especially true of the French aspects. It may be that his knowlege of "military French" was imperfect, or that he worked at his French sources too hurriedly. He listed "marines" and an "Irish Brigade" – neither of which existed in the French armed forces – as units of the French armies in Spain, and he certainly made mistakes in his translations of Marbot and Pelet. His limited comprehension of those military basics led him into one major, long-enduring error – that the Peninsular War was largely a matter of French columns vainly attacking British lines.

Notwithstanding these criticisms, it must be acknowledged that Oman strove to be completely impartial in his writing – a standard he usually achieved as far as was consciously possible for an English gentleman and Oxford Fellow in Britain's high days of empire. If he normally gave his countrymen the benefit of any doubts, that is only to be expected: he was writing for them concerning the deeds of their fathers, grandfathers, and uncles. But he seldom failed to acknowledge an enemy's skill or valour, whether it was the perfectly controlled fighting withdrawal of Reille's veteran infantry amid Vittoria's howling rout, or the garrison of San Sebastian, coming out of their defences under fire to rescue the helpless wounded, left on the beach after an unsuccessful British assault, from drowning in the incoming tide. He had a proper Victorian horror (based on incomplete information) of Masséna's character, but unhesitatingly acknowledged his talents as a general.

Just as important, and essential to a complete history of the Peninsular War, was Oman's coverage of England's allies. He was the first to make a proper study of and describe Beresford's recreation of the Portuguese Army, and to give due credit to its service as an essential part of Wellington's forces. Similarly he tried to show the full extent and value of the Spanish military effort – not only its usually hapless major armies and the much-glamorized guerrilla bands, but also the minor regional forces which sometimes gave the French more trouble than either of these. Before Oman, British historians – like Napier – had concerned themselves largely with Wellington's own operations: apart from some mention of guerrillas, their coverage of Spanish forces was generally limited to those armies which were supposed to operate in conjunction with Wellington's – and, unfortunately, had been noted for little except an obstinacy, inefficiency, and cowardice that taxed the English language's available vocabulary of opprobrious expression. In presenting the Peninsular War as a whole, Oman demonstrated how events in one corner of Spain might drastically influence operations hundreds of miles away across the country (especially how French efforts to concentrate sufficient strength against Wellington's dangerous small army might leave their forward bases and communications too weakly garrisoned to handle sudden attacks by local Spanish forces) and how Wellington depended on the Spaniards for such diversionary efforts and for information as to the strength, location, and movement of those French forces that were beyond the reach of his own outpost patrols and scout officers. Oman made it plain that without this cooperation, uncoordinated and indeed accidental as it   frequently was, the liberation of Spain and Portugal from French occupation would have been a most uncertain   business.

In all his work Oman displayed his gift of telling a story clearly and concisely. In fact, few military men can surpass his ability to describe the setting, development, and decisive moment of a complex, fast-moving action. Napier's writing stands out for its compelling feeling of personal participation, with hardship and danger experienced at first hand, but Oman has the advantage of freedom from the strong personal prejudices that sometimes twist Napier's recollections of battles fought and sieges lost or won. And if his judgements are those of a life-long academic, "smelling" (so Napoleon would have put it) of lamp-oil and not gunpowder, they are based on considerable study and honestly intended.

We now know a good deal more of the Peninsular War and especially of the armies that waged it, than was possible for Oman, roughly three-quarters of a century ago. His work can be supplemented by those of competent later historians such as Donald Horward, Richard Glover, Jac Weller, S.P.G. Ward, and Juan Priego López. But it unquestionably is still the most complete and generally reliable multi-volume history of that war in the English language – and probably in any language. There is no substitute for it. As a homely comparison, it is like a grand living Christmas tree, on which we may hang any number of new ornaments, replacing those which may have lost their lustre, as the years pass by. But it is the tree itself that gives them place and pertinence.

John R. Elting
Col. USA, Ret.
1995

1. Oman was born in India where his father was a planter. As customary, he was sent "home" to England for his education.

2. Unfortunately, Manuel (king from 1908 to 1910) was forced into exile by a naval mutiny. His republican successors lacked his generosity.

3. Although he did marry the daughter of a general of the Royal Engineers.

PREFACE

IT is many years since an attempt has been made in England to deal with the general history of the Peninsular War. Several interesting and valuable diaries or memoirs of officers who took part in the great struggle have been published of late[1], but no writer of the present generation has dared to grapple with the details of the whole of the seven years of campaigning that lie between the *Dos Mayo* and Toulouse. Napier's splendid work has held the field for sixty years. Meanwhile an enormous bulk of valuable material has been accumulating in English, French, and Spanish, which has practically remained unutilized. Papers, public and private, are accessible whose existence was not suspected in the 'thirties; an infinite number of autobiographies and reminiscences which have seen the light after fifty or sixty years of repose in some forgotten drawer, have served to fill up many gaps in our knowledge. At least one formal history of the first importance, that of General Arteche y Moro, has been published. I fancy that its eleven volumes are practically unknown in England, yet it is almost as valuable as Toreño's *Guerra de la Independencia* in enabling us to understand the purely Spanish side of the war.

I trust therefore that it will not be considered presumptuous for one who has been working for some ten or fifteen years at the original sources to endeavour to

---

[1] I need only mention the diaries of Sir Harry Smith, Blakeney, Shaw, and Tomkinson on our side, and Foy's private diary and the Memoirs of Fantin des Odoards, St. Chamans, and Thiébault on the French.

summarize in print the results of his investigations; for I believe that even the reader who has already devoted a good deal of attention to the Peninsular War will find a considerable amount of new matter in these pages.

My resolve to take in hand a general history of the struggle was largely influenced by the passing into the hands of All Souls College of the papers of one of its most distinguished fellows, the diplomatist Sir Charles Vaughan. Not only had Vaughan unique opportunities for observing the early years of the Peninsular War, but he turned them to the best account, and placed all his observations on record. I suppose that there was seldom a man who had a greater love for collecting and filing information. His papers contain not only his own diaries and correspondence, but an infinite number of notes made for him by Spanish friends on points which he desired to master, and a vast bulk of pamphlets, proclamations, newspapers, and tables of statistics, carefully bound together in bundles, which (as far as I can see) have not been opened between the day of his death and that on which they passed, by a legacy from his last surviving relative, into the possession of his old college. Vaughan landed at Corunna in September, 1808, in company with Charles Stuart, the first English emissary to the Central Junta. He rode with Stuart to Madrid and Aranjuez, noting everything that he saw, from Roman inscriptions to the views of local Alcaldes and priests on the politics of the day. He contrived to interview many persons of importance—for example, he heard from Cuesta's own lips of his treasonable plot to overthrow the Junta, and he secured a long conversation with Castaños as to the Capitulation of Baylen, from which I have extracted some wholly new facts as to that event. He then went to Aragon, where he stayed three weeks in the company of the Captain-

General Joseph Palafox. Not only did he cross-question Palafox as to all the details of his famous defence of Saragossa, but he induced San Genis (the colonel who conducted the engineering side of the operations) to write him a memorandum, twelve pages long, as to the character and system of his work. Vaughan accompanied Palafox to the front in November, but left the Army of Aragon a day before the battle of Tudela. Hearing of the disaster from the fugitives of Castaños's army, he resolved to take the news to Madrid. Riding hard for the capital, he crossed the front of Ney's cavalry at Agreda, but escaped them and came safely through. On arriving at Madrid he was given dispatches for Sir John Moore, and carried them to Salamanca. It was the news which he brought that induced the British general to order his abortive retreat on Portugal. Moore entrusted to him not only his dispatch to Sir David Baird, bidding him retire into Galicia, but letters for Lord Castlereagh, which needed instant conveyance to London. Accordingly Vaughan rode with headlong speed to Baird at Astorga, and from Astorga to Corunna, which he reached eleven days after his start from Tudela. From thence he took ship to England and brought the news of the Spanish disasters to the British Ministry.

Vaughan remained some time in England before returning to Spain, but he did not waste his time. Not only did he write a short account of the siege of Saragossa, which had a great vogue at the moment, but he collected new information from an unexpected source. General Lefebvre-Desnouettes, the besieger of Saragossa, arrived as a prisoner in England. Vaughan promptly went to Cheltenham, where the Frenchman was living on parole, and had a long conversation with him as to the details of the siege, which he carefully

compared with the narrative of Palafox. Probably
no other person ever had such opportunities for
collecting first-hand information as to that famous
leaguer. It will please those who love the romantic
side of history, to know that Vaughan was introduced
by Palafox to Agostina, the famous 'Maid of Saragossa,' and heard the tale of her exploit from the
Captain-General less than three months after it had
occurred. The doubts of Napier and others as to her
existence are completely dissipated by the diary of this
much-travelled Fellow of All Souls College.

Vaughan returned to Spain ere 1809 was out, and
served under various English ambassadors at Seville
and Cadiz for the greater part of the war. His papers
and collections for the later years of the struggle are
almost as full and interesting as those for 1808 which
I have utilized in this volume.

I have worked at the Record Office on the British
official papers of the first years of the war, especially
noting all the passages which are omitted in the printed
dispatches of Moore and other British generals. The
suppressed paragraphs (always placed within brackets
marked with a pencil) contain a good deal of useful
matter, mainly criticisms on individuals which it would
not have been wise to publish at the time. There are
a considerable number of intercepted French dispatches
in the collection, and a certain amount of correspondence
with the Spaniards which contains facts and figures
generally unknown. Among the most interesting are
the letters of General Leith, who was attached to the
head quarters of Blake; in them I found by far the best
account of the operations of the Army of Galicia in
Oct.—Nov., 1808, which I have come upon.

As to printed sources of information, I have read all
the Parliamentary papers of 1808–9, and the whole file

of the *Madrid Gazette,* as well as many scores of memoirs
and diaries, French, English, and Spanish. I think that
no important English or French book has escaped me ;
but I must confess that some of the Spanish works
quoted by General Arteche proved unprocurable, both in
London and Paris. The British Museum Library is by
no means strong in this department ; it is even short of
obvious authorities, such as the monographs of St. Cyr
and of Cabanes on the War in Catalonia. The memoirs
of the Peninsular veterans on both sides often require
very cautious handling ; some cannot be trusted for
anything that did not happen under the author's eye.
Others were written so long after the events which they
record, that they are not even to be relied upon for facts
which must have been under his actual observation.
For example, General Marbot claims that he brought to
Bayonne the dispatch from Murat informing Napoleon
of the insurrection of Madrid on May 2, and gives
details as to the way in which the Emperor received
the news. But it is absolutely certain, both from the
text of Murat's letter and from Napoleon's answer to
it, that the document was carried and delivered by a
Captain Hannecourt. The aged Marbot's memory had
played him false. There are worse cases, where an eye-
witness, writing within a short time of the events which
he describes, gives a version which he must have known
to be incorrect, for the glorification of himself or some
friend. Thiébault and Le Noble are bad offenders in
this respect : Thiébault's account of some of the incidents in Portugal and of the combat of Aldea del
Ponte, Le Noble's narrative of Corunna, seem to be
deliberately falsified. I have found one English authority who falls under the same suspicion. But on
both sides the majority of the mistakes come either
from writers who describe that which did not pass under

their own eyes, or from aged narrators who wrote their
story twenty, thirty, or forty years after the war was over.
Their diaries written at the time are often invaluable
correctives to their memoirs or monographs composed
after an interval; e. g. Foy's rough diary lately published by Girod de l'Ain contains some testimonials to
Wellington and the British army very much more
handsomely expressed than anything which the General
wrote in his formal history of the early campaigns of
1808.

I hope to insert in my second volume a bibliography of
all the works useful for the first two years of the war.
The inordinate size to which my first volume has swelled
has made it impossible to include in it a list of authorities, which covers a good many pages.

It will be noticed that my Appendices include several
extensive tables, giving the organization of the French
and Spanish armies in 1808. For part of them I am
indebted to General Arteche's work; but the larger
half has been constructed at great cost of time and
labour from scattered contemporary papers—from returns to be found in the most varied places (some of the
most important Spanish ones survive only in the Record
Office or in Vaughan's papers, others only in the *Madrid
Gazette*). No one, so far as I know, had hitherto
endeavoured to construct the complete table of the
Spanish army in October, or of that of the exact composition of Napoleon's ' grand army ' in the same month.
I hope my Appendices therefore may be found of
some use.

More than one friend has asked me during the last
few months whether it is worth while to rewrite the
history of the Peninsular War when Napier's great work
is everywhere accessible. I can only reply that I no
more dream of superseding the immortal six volumes of

that grand old soldier, than Dr. S. R. Gardiner dreamed of superseding Clarendon's *History of the Great Rebellion* when he started to write the later volumes of his account of the reign of Charles I. The books of Napier and Clarendon must remain as all-important contemporary narratives, written by men who saw clearly one aspect of the events which they describe; in each the personal element counts for much, and the political and individual sympathies and enmities of the historian have coloured his whole work. No one would think of going to Clarendon for an unprejudiced account of the character and career of Oliver Cromwell. But I do not think that it is generally realized that it is just as unsafe to go to Napier for an account of the aims and undertakings of the Spanish Juntas, or the Tory governments of 1808–14. As a narrator of the incidents of war he is unrivalled: no one who has ever read them can forget his soul-stirring descriptions of the charge of the Fusilier brigade at Albuera, of the assault on the Great Breach at Badajoz, or the storming of Soult's positions on the Rhune. These and a hundred other eloquent passages will survive for ever as masterpieces of vigorous English prose.

But when he wanders off into politics, English or Spanish, Napier is a less trustworthy guide. All his views are coloured by the fact that he was a bitter enemy of the Tories of his own day. The kinsman not only of Charles James Fox, but of Lord Edward Fitzgerald, he could never look with unprejudiced eyes on their political opponents. Canning and Spencer Perceval were in his ideas men capable of any folly, any gratuitous perversity. Castlereagh's splendid services to England are ignored: it would be impossible to discover from the pages of the *Peninsular War* that this was the man who picked out Wellington for the

command in Spain, and kept him there in spite of all
manner of opposition.   Nor is this all : Napier was also
one of those strange Englishmen who, notwithstanding
all the evidence that lay before them, believed that Napoleon Bonaparte was a beneficent character, thwarted
in his designs for the regeneration of Europe by the
obstinate and narrow-minded opposition of the British
Government.   In his preface, he goes so far as to say
that the Tories fought the Emperor not because he was
the dangerous enemy of the British Empire, but because
he was the champion of Democracy, and they the
champions of caste and privilege.   When the tidings
of Napoleon's death at St. Helena reached him (as
readers of his *Life* will remember), he cast himself down
on his sofa and wept for three hours !   Hence it was
that, in dealing with the Tory ministries, he is ever a
captious and unkind critic, while for the Emperor he
displays a respect that seems very strange in an enthusiastic friend of political liberty.   Every one who has
read the first chapters of his great work must see that
Bonaparte gets off with slight reproof for his monstrous
act of treachery at Bayonne, and for the even more
disgusting months of hypocritical friendship that had
preceded it.   While pouring scorn on Charles IV and
Ferdinand VII, the silly father and the rebellious son,
whose quarrels were the Emperor's opportunity, Napier
forgets to rise to the proper point of indignation in
dealing with the false friend who betrayed them.   He
almost writes as if there were some excuse for the
crimes of robbery and kidnapping, if the victim were
an imbecile or a bigot, or an undutiful son.   The prejudice in favour of the Emperor goes so far that he
even endeavours to justify obvious political and military
mistakes in his conduct of the Peninsular War, by
throwing all the blame on the way in which his marshals

executed his orders, and neglecting to point out that the orders themselves were impracticable.

On the other hand, Napier was just as over-hard to the Spaniards as he was over-lenient to Bonaparte. He was one of those old Peninsular officers who could never dismiss the memory of some of the things that he had seen or heard. The cruelties of the Guerrillas, the disgraceful panic on the eve of Talavera, the idiotic pride and obstinacy of Cuesta, the cowardice of Imaz and La Peña, prejudiced him against all their countrymen. The turgid eloquence of Spanish proclamations, followed by the prosaic incapacity of Spanish performance, sickened him. He always accepts the French rather than the Spanish version of a story, forgetting that Bonaparte and his official writers were authorities quite as unworthy of implicit credence as their opponents. In dealing with individual Spaniards—we may take for example Joseph Palafox, or the unfortunate Daoiz and Velarde—he is unjust to the extreme of cruelty. His astounding libel on La Romana's army, I have had occasion to notice in some detail on page 416 of this work. He invariably exaggerates Spanish defeats, and minimizes Spanish successes. He is reckless in the statements which he gives as to their numbers in battle, or their losses in defeat. Evidently he did not take the trouble to consult the elaborate collection of morning-states of armies and other official documents which the Spanish War Office published several years before he wrote his first volume. All his figures are borrowed from the haphazard guesses of the French marshals. This may seem strong language to use concerning so great an author, but minute investigation seems to prove that nearly every statement of Napier's concerning a battle in which the Spaniards were engaged is drawn from some French source. The Spaniards' version is ignored.

In his indignation at the arrogance and obstinacy with which they often hampered his hero Wellington, he refuses to look at the extenuating circumstances which often explain, or even excuse, their conduct. After reading his narrative, one should turn to Arguelles or Toreño or Arteche, peruse their defence of their country-men, and then make one's ultimate decision as to facts. Every student of the Peninsular War, in short, must read Napier: but he must not think that, when the reading is finished, he has mastered the whole meaning and importance of the great struggle.

The topographical details of most of my maps are drawn from the splendid Atlas published by the Spanish War Office during the last twenty years. But the details of the placing of the troops are my own. I have been particularly careful in the maps of Vimiero and Corunna to indicate the position of every battalion, French or English.

I am in duty bound to acknowledge the very kind assistance of three helpers in the construction of this volume. The first compiled the Index, after grappling with the whole of the proofs. The second, Mr. C. E. Doble, furnished me with a great number of suggestions as to revision, which I have adopted. The third, Mr. C. T. Atkinson, of Exeter College, placed at my disposition his wide knowledge of British regimental history, and put me in the way of obtaining many details as to the organization of Wellesley's and Moore's armies. I am infinitely obliged to all three.

C. OMAN.

ALL SOULS COLLEGE,
March 31, 1902.

CONTENTS

SECTION V

THE STRUGGLE IN CATALONIA

SECTION VI

THE CONSEQUENCES OF BAYLEN

SECTION VII

NAPOLEON'S INVASION OF SPAIN

SECTION VIII

THE CAMPAIGN OF SIR JOHN MOORE

APPENDICES

MAPS

PORTRAITS

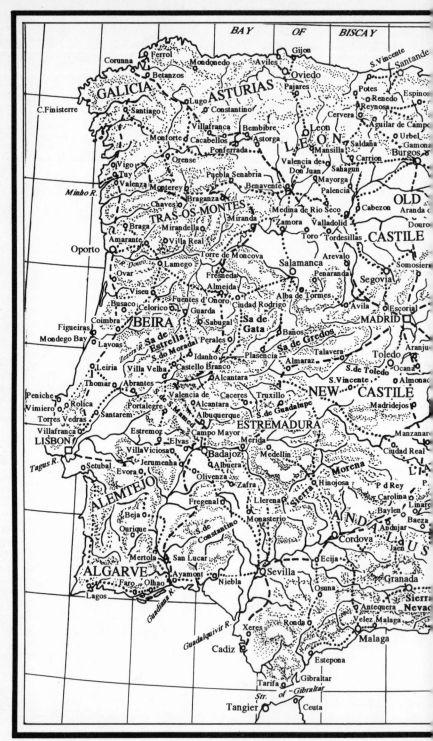

Spain and Portugal,

showing Physical features and roads.

Main Roads   Other Roads

Engl.Miles 100   0   100

The Oxford Geographical Institute

SECTION I

NAPOLEON AND THE SPANISH BOURBONS

CHAPTER I

THE TREATY OF FONTAINEBLEAU

'I AM not the heir of Louis XIV, I am the heir of Charlemagne,' wrote Napoleon, in one of those moments of epigrammatic self-revelation which are so precious to the students of the most interesting epoch and the most interesting personality of modern history [1]. There are historians who have sought for the origins of the Peninsular War far back in the eternal and inevitable conflict between democracy and privilege [2]: there are others who—accepting the Emperor's own version of the facts—have represented it as a fortuitous development arising from his plan of forcing the Continental System upon every state in Europe. To us it seems that the moment beyond which we need not search backward was that in which Bonaparte formulated to himself the idea that he was not the successor of the greatest of the Bourbons, but of the founder of the Holy Roman Empire. It is a different thing to claim to be the first of European monarchs, and to claim to be the king of kings. Louis XIV had wide-reaching ambitions for himself and for his family: but it was from his not very deep or accurate knowledge of Charlemagne that Napoleon had derived his idea of a single imperial power bestriding Europe, of a monarch whose writ ran alike at Paris and at Mainz, at Milan and at Hamburg, at Rome and at Barcelona, and whose vassal-

---

[1] He works out the idea in his letter to Talleyrand of May 16, 1806.

[2] Such is the main thesis of chapter I of Napier's *Peninsular War*.

princes brought him the tribute of all the lands of the Oder, the Elbe, and the middle Danube[1].

There is no need for us to trace back the growth of Napoleon's conception of himself as the successor of Charlemagne beyond the winter of 1805–6, the moment when victorious at Austerlitz and master for the first time of Central Europe, he began to put into execution his grandiose scheme for enfeoffing all the realms of the Continent as vassal states of the French Empire. He had extorted from Francis of Austria the renunciation of his meagre and time-worn rights as head of the Holy Roman Empire, because he intended to replace the ancient shadow by a new reality. The idea that he might be Emperor of Europe and not merely Emperor of the French was already developed, though Prussia still needed to be chastised, and Russia to be checked and turned back on to the ways of the East. It was after Austerlitz but before Jena that the foundations of the Confederation of the Rhine were laid[2], and that the Emperor took in hand the erection of that series of subject realms under princes of his own house, which was to culminate in the new kingdom of Spain ruled by ' Joseph Napoleon the First.' By the summer of 1806 the system was already well developed : the first modest experiment, the planting out of his sister Eliza and her insignificant husband in the duchy of Lucca and Piombino was now twelve months old. There had followed the gift of the old Bourbon kingdom of Naples to Joseph Bonaparte in February, 1806, and the transformation of the Batavian Republic into Louis Bonaparte's kingdom of Holland in June. The Emperor's brother-in-law, Joachim Murat, had been made Grand-Duke of Berg in March, his sister, Pauline, Duchess of Guastalla in the same month. It cannot be doubted that his eye was already roving all round Europe, marking out every region in which the system of feudatory states could be further extended.

At the ill-governed realms of Spain and Portugal it is certain that he must have taken a specially long glance. He had against the house of the Bourbons the grudge that men always feel against

---

[1] It is curious to note how often the name of Charlemagne occurs in Napoleon's letters during the early months of 1806. It is especially common in his correspondence about the relations of the Papacy and the Empire.

[2] The negotiations for the Confederation were completed in July, and it was formally constituted on Aug. 1, 1806.

those whom they have injured. He knew that they could never forgive the disappointed hopes of 1799, nor the murder of the Duc d'Enghien, however much they might disguise their sentiments by base servility. What their real feelings were might be guessed from the treacherous conduct of their kinsmen of Naples, whom he had just expelled from the Continent. The Bourbons of Spain were at this moment the most subservient and the most ill-used of his allies. Under the imbecile guidance of his favourite Godoy, Charles IV had consistently held to the league with France since 1795, and had thereby brought down untold calamities upon his realm. Nevertheless Napoleon was profoundly dissatisfied with him as an ally. The seventy-two million francs of subsidies which he was annually wringing from his impoverished neighbour seemed to him a trifle. The chief gain that he had hoped to secure, when he goaded Spain into war with England in 1804, had been the assistance of her fleet, by whose aid he had intended to gain the control of the narrow seas, and to dominate the Channel long enough to enable him to launch his projected invasion against the shores of Kent and Sussex. But the Spanish navy, always more formidable on paper than in battle, had proved a broken reed. The flower of its vessels had been destroyed at Trafalgar. There only remained in 1806 a few ships rotting in harbour at Cadiz, Cartagena, and Ferrol, unable even to concentrate on account of the strictness of Collingwood's blockade. Napoleon was angry at his ally's impotence, and was already reflecting that in hands more able and energetic than those of Charles IV Spain might give aid of a very different kind. In after years men remembered that as early as 1805 he had muttered to his confidants that a Bourbon on the Spanish throne was a tiresome neighbour—too weak as an ally, yet dangerous as a possible enemy[1]. For in spite of all the subservience of Charles IV the Emperor believed, and believed quite rightly, that a Bourbon prince must in his heart loathe the unnatural alliance with the child of the Revolution. But in 1806 Bonaparte had an impending war with Prussia on his hands, and there was no leisure for interfering in the affairs of the Peninsula.

---

[1] See, for example, the very interesting story told by Marshal Jourdan in his *Mémoires* (p. 9) of the long conversation which the emperor had with him at Verona on June 16, 1805 : ' Tant pour l'affermissement de ma dynastie que pour la sûreté de France,' concluded Napoleon, ' un Bourbon sur le trône d'Espagne est un voisin trop dangereux.'

Spain, he thought, could wait, and it is improbable that he had formulated in his brain any definite plan for dealing with her.

The determining factor in his subsequent action was undoubtedly supplied in the autumn of 1806 by the conduct of the Spanish government during the campaign of Jena. There was a moment, just before that decisive battle had been fought, during which European public opinion was expecting a check to the French arms. The military prestige of Prussia was still very great, and it was well known that Russia had not been able to put forth her full strength at Austerlitz. Combined it was believed that they would be too much for Napoleon. While this idea was still current, the Spanish king, or rather his favourite Godoy, put forth a strange proclamation which showed how slight was the bond of allegiance that united them to France, and how hollow their much vaunted loyalty to the emperor [1]. It was an impassioned appeal to the people of Spain to take arms *en masse*, and to help the government with liberal gifts of men, horses and money. 'Come,' it said, 'dear fellow countrymen, come and swear loyalty beneath the banners of the most benevolent of sovereigns.' The God of Victories was to smile on a people which helped itself, and a happy and enduring peace was to be the result of a vigorous effort. It might have been pleaded in defence of Charles IV that all this was very vague, and that the anonymous enemy who was to be crushed might be England. But unfortunately for this interpretation, three whole sentences of the document are filled with demands for horses and an instant increase in the cavalry arm of the Spanish military establishment. It could hardly be urged with seriousness that horsemen were intended to be employed against the English fleet. And of naval armaments there was not one word in the proclamation.

This document was issued on Oct. 5, 1806: not long after there arrived in Madrid the news of the battle of Jena and the capture of Berlin. The Prince of the Peace was thunderstruck at the non-fulfilment of his expectations and the complete triumph of Napoleon. He hastened to countermand his armaments, and to shower letters of explanation and apology on the Emperor, pointing out that his respected ally could not possibly have been the 'enemy' referred to in the proclamation. That document had

---

[1] For the full text of this bombastic appeal see Appendix, No. I. Godoy speaks throughout in his own name, not in that of his master.

reached Napoleon on the very battlefield of Jena, and had caused
a violent paroxysm of rage in the august reader[1]. But, having
Russia still to fight, he repressed his wrath for a moment, affecting
to regard as satisfactory Godoy's servile letters of explanation.
Yet we can hardly doubt that this was the moment at which he
made up his mind that the House of Bourbon must cease to reign
in Spain. He must have reflected on the danger that southern
France had escaped ; a hundred thousand Spaniards might have
marched on Bordeaux or Toulouse at the moment of Jena, and
there would have been no army whatever on the unguarded
frontier of the Pyrenees to hold them in check. Supposing that
Jena had been deferred a month, or that no decisive battle at all
had been fought in the first stage of the struggle with Prussia, it
was clear that Godoy would have committed himself to open war.
A stab in the back, even if dealt with no better weapon than the
disorganized Spanish army, must have deranged all Napoleon's
plans, and forced him to turn southward the reserves destined to
feed the 'Grand Army.' It was clear that such a condition of
affairs must never be allowed to recur, and we should naturally
expect to find that, the moment the war of 1806–7 was ended,
Napoleon would turn against Spain, either to dethrone Charles IV,
or at least to demand the dismissal from office of Godoy. He
acknowledged this himself at St. Helena : the right thing to have
done, as he then conceded, would have been to declare open war
on Spain immediately after Tilsit[2].

After eight years of experience of Bonaparte as an ally, the
rulers of Spain ought to have known that his silence during the
campaigns of Eylau and Friedland boded them no good. But his
present intentions escaped them, and they hastened to atone for
the proclamation of Oct. 5 by a servile obedience to all the orders
which he sent them. The most important of these was the
command to mobilize and send to the Baltic 15,000 of their best
troops [March, 1807]. This was promptly done, the depleted

---

[1] 'Je jurai dès lors qu'ils me la paieraient, que je les mettrais hors d'état de
me nuire,' said Napoleon to De Pradt, eighteen months later (*Mémoires sur la
Révolution d'Espagne*, p. 16). The archbishop's story is amply borne out by
the repeated allusions to this unhappy proclamation in Napoleon's official
justification of his conduct in Spain. The Spanish ambassador at Berlin,
Don Benito Pardo, was told by Napoleon at the time that he had forgiven the
Proclamation, but could not forget it.

[2] *Correspondance de Napoléon*, xxxii. 59.

battalions and squadrons being raised to war-strength, by drafts of men and horses which disorganized dozens of the corps that remained at home[1]. The reason alleged, the fear of Swedish and English descents on the rear of the Grand Army, was plausible, but there can be no doubt that the real purpose was to deprive Spain of a considerable part, and that the most efficient, of her disposable forces. If Godoy could have listened to the interviews of Napoleon and Alexander of Russia at Tilsit, he would have been terrified at the offhand way in which the Emperor suggested to the Czar that the Balearic Isles should be taken from Spain and given to Ferdinand of Naples, if the latter would consent to cede Sicily to Joseph Napoleon[2]. To despoil his allies was quite in the usual style of Bonaparte—Godoy cannot have forgotten the lot of Trinidad and Ceylon—but he had not before proposed to tear from Spain, not a distant colony, but an ancient province of the Aragonese crown. The project was enshrined in the 'secret and supplementary' clauses of the Treaty of Tilsit, which Napoleon wished to conceal till the times were ripe.

It was only when Bonaparte had returned to France from his long campaign in Poland that the affairs of the Iberian Peninsula began to come seriously to the front. The Emperor arrived in Paris at the end of July, 1807, and this was the moment at which he might have been expected to produce the rod, for the chastisement which the rulers of Spain had merited by their foolish proclamation of the preceding year. But no sign of any such intention was displayed: it is true that early in August French troops in considerable numbers began to muster at Bayonne[3], but

---

[1] The demand was made in the most peremptory fashion, and in almost threatening language. Napoleon writes to Talleyrand that the Spanish division in Tuscany, which was to form part of the expeditionary corps, must march in twenty-four hours after receiving its orders. 'If they refuse, everything is at an end,' a most sinister phrase (Napoleon to Talleyrand, March 25, 1807).

[2] This was Article IV of the Seven 'Secret Articles' of the Treaty of Tilsit. See for this proposal the notes in Vandal's *Napoléon et Alexandre Ier*, vol. i.

[3] The first notice of the 'Corps of Observation of the Gironde' is to be found in a dispatch of Masserano, the Spanish ambassador at Paris, dated July 30, which gives notice of the approaching concentration at Bayonne. But the quiet movement of troops in this direction had begun long before the Russian war was over.

Bonaparte openly declared that they were destined to be used, not against Spain, but against Portugal. One of the articles of the Peace of Tilsit had been to the effect that Sweden and Portugal, the last powers in Europe which had not submitted to the Continental System, should be compelled—if necessary by force—to adhere to it, and to exclude the commerce of England from their ports. It was natural that now, as in 1801, a French contingent should be sent to aid Spain in bringing pressure to bear on her smaller neighbour. With this idea Godoy and his master persisted in the voluntary blindness to the signs of the times which they had so long been cultivating. They gave their ambassador in Lisbon orders to act in all things in strict conjunction with his French colleague.

On August 12, therefore, the representatives of Spain and France delivered to John, the Prince-Regent of Portugal (his mother, Queen Maria, was insane), almost identical notes, in which they declared that they should ask for their passports and leave Lisbon, unless by the first of September the Regent had declared war on England, joined his fleet to that of the allied powers, confiscated all British goods in his harbours, and arrested all British subjects within the bounds of his kingdom. The prince, a timid and incapable person, whose only wish was to preserve his neutrality, answered that he was ready to break off diplomatic relations with England, and to close his ports against British ships, but that the seizure of the persons and property of the British merchants, without any previous declaration of war, would be contrary to the rules of international law and morality. For a moment he hoped that this half-measure would satisfy Napoleon, that he might submit to the Continental System without actually being compelled to declare war on Great Britain. But when dispatches had been interchanged between the French minister Rayneval and his master at Paris, the answer came that the Regent's offer was insufficient, and that the representatives of France and Spain were ordered to quit Lisbon at once. This they did on September 30, but without issuing any formal declaration of war.

On October 18, the French army, which had been concentrating at Bayonne since the beginning of August, under the harmless name of the 'Corps of Observation of the Gironde,' crossed the Bidassoa at Irun and entered Spain. It had been placed under the orders of Junot, one of Napoleon's most active and vigorous officers, but not a great strategist after the style of Masséna, Soult, or Davoust. He was a good fighting-man, but a mediocre general. The reason that he received the appointment was that he had already some knowledge of Portugal, from having held the post of ambassador at Lisbon in 1805. He had been promised a duchy and a marshal's bâton if his mission was carried out to his master's complete satisfaction.

It is clear that from the first Napoleon had intended that Portugal should refuse the ignominious orders which he had given to the Prince-Regent. If he had only been wishing to complete the extension of the Continental System over all Southern Europe, the form of obedience which had been offered him by the Portuguese government would have been amply sufficient. But he was aiming at annexation, and not at the mere assertion of his suzerainty over Portugal. The fact that he began to mass troops at Bayonne before he commenced to threaten the Regent is sufficient proof of his intentions. An army was not needed to coerce the Portuguese : for it was incredible that in the then condition of European affairs they would dare to risk war with France and Spain by adhering too stiffly to the cause of England. The Regent was timid and his submission was certain ; but Napoleon took care to dictate the terms that he offered in such an offensive form that the Portuguese government would be tempted to beg for changes of detail, though it sorrowfully accepted the necessity of conceding the main point —war with England and the acceptance of the Continental System. The Prince-Regent, as might have been expected, made a feeble attempt to haggle over the more ignominious details, and then Napoleon withdrew his ambassador and let loose his armies.

Shortly after Junot had crossed the Bidassoa there was signed at Fontainebleau the celebrated secret treaty which marks the second stage of the Emperor's designs against the Peninsula. It was drawn up by Duroc, Napoleon's marshal of the palace, and Eugenio Izquierdo, the agent of Godoy. For the official ambassador of Spain in Paris, the Prince of Masserano, was nct taken into the confidence of his master [1]. All delicate matters were conducted by the favourite's private representative, an obscure but astute personage, the director of the Botanical Gardens at Madrid, whose

[1] Talleyrand declares in his *Mémoires* (i. 349) that Napoleon kept Champagny, his own minister of foreign affairs, in equal darkness.

position was legitimized by a royal sign-manual giving him powers to treat as a plenipotentiary with France. 'Manuel is your protector: do what he tells you, and by serving him you serve me,' the old king had said, when giving him his commission.

The Treaty of Fontainebleau is a strange document, whose main purpose, at a first glance, seems to be the glorification of Godoy. It is composed of fourteen articles[1], the most important of which contain the details of a projected dismemberment of Portugal. The country was to be cut up into three parts. Oporto and the northern province of Entre-Douro-e-Minho were to become the 'Kingdom of Northern Lusitania,' and to be ceded to a Bourbon, the young King of Etruria, whom Napoleon was just evicting from his pleasant abode at Florence. All Southern Portugal, the large province of Alemtejo and the coast region of Algarve, was to be given as an independent principality to Godoy, under the title of 'Prince of the Algarves'[2]. The rest of Portugal, Lisbon and the provinces of Beira, Estremadura and Tras-os-Montes were to be sequestrated till the conclusion of a general peace, and meanwhile were to be governed and administered by the French. Ultimately they were to be restored, or not restored, to the house of Braganza according as the high contracting parties might determine.

Instead therefore of receiving punishment for his escapade in the autumn of 1806, Godoy was to be made by Napoleon a sovereign prince! But Spain, as apart from the favourite, got small profit from this extraordinary treaty: Charles IV might take, within the next three years, the pompous title of 'Emperor of the Two Americas,' and was to be given some share of the transmarine possessions of Portugal—which meanwhile (treaties or no) would inevitably fall into the hands of Great Britain, who held the command of the seas, while Napoleon did not.

It is incredible that Bonaparte ever seriously intended to carry out the terms of the Treaty of Fontainebleau: they were not even

---

[1] See the text in Appendix, No. II.

[2] In the curious exculpatory memoirs which Godoy published in 1835-6, with the aid of d'Esménard, he endeavours to make out that he never desired the principality, and that Napoleon pressed it upon him, because he wished to remove him from about the person of Charles IV. 'The gift of the principality of the Algarves was a banishment' (i. 54). This plea will not stand in the face of the fact that Godoy had solicited just such preferment as far back as the spring of 1806 ; see Artèche, *Guerra de la Independencia*, i. 148. His real object was to secure a place of refuge at the death of Charles IV.

to be divulged (as Article XIV stipulated) till it was his pleasure. Godoy had deserved badly of him, and the Emperor was never forgiving. The favourite's whole position and character (as we shall presently show) were so odious and disgraceful, that it would have required an even greater cynicism than Napoleon possessed, to overthrow an ancient and respectable kingdom in order to make him a sovereign prince. To pose perpetually as the regenerator of Europe, and her guardian against the sordid schemes of Britain, and then to employ as one's agent for regeneration the corrupt and venal favourite of the wicked old Queen of Spain, would have been too absurd. Napoleon's keen intelligence would have repudiated the idea, even in the state of growing autolatry into which he was already lapsing in the year 1807. What profit could there be in giving a kingdom to a false friend, already convicted of secret disloyalty, incapable, disreputable, and universally detested?

But if we apply another meaning to the Treaty of Fontainebleau we get a very different light upon it. If we adopt the hypothesis that Bonaparte's real aim was to obtain an excuse for marching French armies into Spain without exciting suspicion, all its provisions become intelligible. 'This Prince of the Peace,' he said in one of his confidential moments, 'this mayor of the palace, is loathed by the nation; he is the rascal who will himself open for me the gates of Spain[1].' The phantom principality that was dangled before Godoy's eyes was only designed to attract his attention while the armies of France were being poured across the Pyrenees. It is doubtful whether the Emperor intended the project of the 'Principality of the Algarves' to become generally known. If he did, it must have been with the intention of making the favourite more odious than he already was to patriotic Spaniards, at the moment when he and his master were about to be brushed away by a sweep of the imperial arm. That Napoleon was already in October preparing other armies beside that of Junot, and that he purposed to overrun Spain when the time was ripe, is shown in the Treaty itself. Annexed to it is a convention regulating the details of the invasion of Portugal: the sixth clause of this paper mentions that it was the emperor's intention to concentrate 40,000 more troops at Bayonne—in case Great Britain should threaten an armed descent

---

[1] 'Le Prince de la Paix, véritable maire du palais, est en horreur à la nation. C'est un gredin qui m'ouvrira lui-même les portes de l'Espagne' (Fouché, *Mémoires*, i. 365).

on Portugal—and that this force would be ready to cross the Pyrenees by November 20. Napoleon sent not 40,000 but 100,000 men, and pushed them into Spain, though no English invasion of Portugal had taken place, or even been projected. After this is it possible to believe for a moment in his good faith, or to think that the Treaty of Fontainebleau was anything more than a snare?

Those who could best judge what was at the back of the emperor's mind, such as Talleyrand and Fouché, penetrated his designs long before the treaty of Fontainebleau had been signed. Talleyrand declares in his memoirs [1] that the reason for which he was deprived of the portfolio of Foreign Affairs in August, 1807, was that he had disliked the scheme of invading Spain in a treacherous fashion, and warned his master against it. No improbability is added to this allegation by the fact that Napoleon at St. Helena repeatedly stated that Talleyrand had first thought of the idea, and had recommended it to him 'while at the same time contriving to set an opinion abroad that he was opposed to the design.' On the other hand, we are not convinced of the Prince of Benevento's innocence merely by the fact that he wrote in his autobiography that he was a strenuous opponent of the plan. He says that the emperor broached the whole scheme to him the moment that he returned from Tilsit, asseverating that he would never again expose himself to the danger of a stab in the back at some moment when he might be busy in Central Europe [2]. He himself, he adds, combated the project by every possible argument, but could not move his master an inch from his purpose. This is probably true; but we believe it not because Talleyrand wrote it down—his bills require the endorsement of some backer of a less tarnished reputation—but because the whole of the Spanish episode is executed in the true Napoleonesque manner. Its scientific mixture of force and fraud is clearly the work of the same hand that managed the details of the fall of the Venetian Republic, and of the dethroning of Pope Pius VII. It is impossible to ascribe the plot to any other author.

[1] Talleyrand, *Mémoires*, i. 308–329.
[2] Ibid., i. 378, 379.

SECTION I: CHAPTER II

THE COURT OF SPAIN

Junot's army was nearing the Portuguese frontier, and the reserve at Bayonne was already beginning to assemble—it was now styled 'the Second Corps of Observation of the Gironde'—when a series of startling events took place at the Spanish Court. On October 27, the very day that the treaty of Fontainebleau was signed, Ferdinand, Prince of the Asturias, was seized by his father and thrown into confinement, on a charge of high treason, of having plotted to dethrone or even to murder his aged parent. This astonishing development in the situation need not be laid to Napoleon's charge. There have been historians who think that he deliberately stirred up the whole series of family quarrels at Madrid: but all the materials for trouble were there already, and the shape which they took was not particularly favourable to the Emperor's present designs. They sprang from the inevitable revolt against the predominance of Godoy, which had long been due.

The mere fact that an incapable upstart like Godoy had been able to control the foreign and internal policy of Spain ever since 1792 is a sufficient evidence of the miserable state of the country. He was a mere court favourite of the worst class: to compare him to Buckingham would be far too flattering—and even Piers Gaveston had a pretty wit and no mean skill as a man-at-arms, though he was also a vain ostentatious fool. After a few years, we may remember, the one met the dagger and the other the axe, with the full approval of English public opinion. But Godoy went on flourishing like the green bay-tree, for sixteen years, decked with titles and offices and laden with plunder, with no other support than the queen's unconcealed partiality for him, and the idiotic old king's desire to have trouble taken off his hands. Every thinking man in Spain hated the favourite as the outward and visible sign of corruption in high places. Every patriot saw that the would-be statesman who made himself the adulator first of Barras and then of Bonaparte, and played cat's-paw to each of them, to the ultimate

ruin and bankruptcy of the realm, ought to be removed. Yet
there was no sign of any movement against him, save obscure
plots in the household of the Prince Royal. But for the interference of Napoleon in the affairs of Spain, it is possible that the
Prince of the Peace might have enjoyed many years more of
power. Such is the price which nations pay for handing over their
bodies to autocratic monarchy and their souls to three centuries
of training under the Inquisition.

It is perhaps necessary to gain some detailed idea of the unpleasant family party at Madrid. King Charles IV was now a
man of sixty years of age: he was so entirely simple and helpless
that it is hardly an exaggeration to say that his weakness
bordered on imbecility. His elder brother, Don Philip, was so
clearly wanting in intellect that he had to be placed in confinement and excluded from the throne. It might occur to us that
it would have been well for Spain if Charles had followed him
to the asylum, if we had not to remember that the crown would
then have fallen to Ferdinand of Naples, who if more intelligent
was also more morally worthless than his brother. Till the age
of forty Charles had been entirely suppressed and kept in tutelage
by an autocratic father: when he came to the throne he never
developed any will or mind of his own, and remained the tool
and servant of those about him. He may be described as a good-
natured and benevolent imbecile: he was not cruel or malicious
or licentious, or given to extravagant fancies. His one pronounced
taste was hunting: if he could get away from his ministers to
some country palace, and go out all day with his dogs, his gun,
and his gamekeepers, he was perfectly happy. His brother of
Naples, it will be remembered, had precisely the same hobby.
Of any other tastes, save a slight interest in some of the minor
handicrafts, which he shared with his cousin Louis XVI, we find
no trace in the old king. He was very ugly, not with the fierce
clever ugliness of his father Charles III, but in an imbecile fashion,
with a frightfully receding forehead, a big nose, and a retreating
jaw generally set in a harmless grin. He did not understand
business or politics, but was quite capable of getting through
speeches and ceremonies when properly primed and prompted
beforehand. Even his private letters were managed for him by
his wife and his favourite. He had just enough brains to be
proud of his position as king, and to resent anything that he re-

garded as an attack on his dignity—such as the mention of old
constitutional rights and privileges, or any allusion to a Cortes.
He liked, in fact, to feel himself and to be called an absolute king,
though he wished to hand over all the duties and worries of kingship to his wife and his chosen servants.   Quite contrary to Spanish
usage, he often associated Maria Luisa's name with his own in
State documents, and in popular diction they were often called
' los Reyes,' ' the Kings,' as Ferdinand and Isabella had been three
hundred years before.

The Queen was about the most unfit person in Europe to be
placed on the throne at the side of such an imbecile husband.
She was his first cousin, the daughter of his uncle Don Philip,
Duke of Parma—Bourbon on the mother's side also, for she was
the child of the daughter of Louis XV of France.   Maria Luisa
was self-confident, flighty, reckless, and utterly destitute of conscience of any sort.   Her celebrated portrait by Goya gives us
at once an idea of the woman, bold, shameless, pleasure-loving,
and as corrupt as Southern court morality allows—which is saying
a good deal.   She had from the first taken the measure of her
imbecile husband : she dominated him by her superior force of
will, made him her mere mouthpiece, and practically ruled the
realm, turning him out to hunt while she managed ministers and
ambassadors.

For the last twenty years her scandalous partiality for Don Manuel
Godoy had been public property.   When Charles IV came to the
throne Godoy was a mere private in the bodyguard—a sort of
ornamental corps of gentlemen-at-arms.   He was son of a decayed
noble family, a big handsome showy young man of twenty-one—
barely able to read and write, say his detractors—but a good singer
and musician.   Within four years after he caught the Queen's eye
he was a grandee of Spain, a duke, and prime minister !   He was
married to a royal princess, the Infanta Teresa, a cousin of the King,
a mésalliance unparalleled in the whole history of the house of
Bourbon.   Three years later, to commemorate his part in con-
cluding the disgraceful peace of Basle, he was given the odd title
of ' Prince of the Peace,' ' Principe de la Paz': no Spanish subject
had ever before been decorated with any title higher than that of
duke [1].   In 1808 he was a man of forty, beginning to get a little

[1] The princes that occur in Spanish politics, e.g. Eboli or Castelfranco,
were holders of Italian, generally Neapolitan, titles.

plump and bald after so many years of good (or evil) living, but
still a fine personable figure.   He had stowed away enormous
riches, not only from the gifts of the King and Queen, but by the
sale of offices and commissions, the taking of all sorts of illicit
percentages, and (perhaps the worst symptom of all) by colossal
speculations on the stock exchange. A French ambassador recorded
the fact that he had to keep the treaty of peace of 1802 quiet for
three days after it was signed, in order that Godoy might complete
his purchases 'for a rise' before the news got about[1].   Godoy
was corrupt and licentious, but not cruel or even tyrannical:
though profoundly ignorant, he had the vanity to pose as a patron
of art and science.   His foible was to be hailed as a universal
benefactor, and as the introducer of modern civilization into Spain.
He endeavoured to popularize the practice of vaccination, waged
a mild and intermittent war with the Inquisition, and (a most
astonishing piece of courage) tried to suppress the custom of
bull-fighting.   The last two acts were by far the most creditable
items that can be put down to his account: unfortunately they
were also precisely those which appealed least to the populace of
Spain.   Godoy was a notable collector of pictures and antiquities,
and had a certain liking for, and skill in, music.   When this has
been said, there is nothing more to put down in his favour.
Fifteen years of power had so turned his head that for a long
time he had been taking himself quite seriously, and his ambition
had grown so monstrous that, not contented with his alliance by
marriage with the royal house, he was dreaming of becoming
a sovereign prince.   The bait by which Napoleon finally drew
him into the trap, the promise that he should be given the
Algarves and Alemtejo, was not the Corsican's own invention.
It had been an old idea of Godoy's which he broached to his
ally early in 1806, only to receive a severe rebuff.   Hence came
the joy with which he finally saw it take shape in the treaty of
Fontainebleau[2].   When such schemes were running in his head,
we can perfectly well credit the accusation which Prince Ferdinand
brought against him, of having intended to change the succession
to the crown of Spain, by a *coup d'état* on the death of Charles IV.
The man had grown capable of any outburst of pride and ambition.

---

[1] Foy, *Guerre de la Péninsule,* ii. 267.

[2] See the proofs from papers in the Spanish Foreign Office, quoted in
Artèche's *Guerra de la Independencia,* i. 148.

Meanwhile he continued to govern Spain by his hold over the imbecile and gouty old king and his worthless wife, who was now far over fifty, but as besotted on her favourite as ever.   It was his weary lot to be always in attendance on them.   They could hardly let him out of their sight.   Toreño relates a ridiculous story that, when Napoleon invited them to dinner on the first night of their unhappy visit to Bayonne, he did not ask the Prince of the Peace to the royal table.   Charles was so unhappy and uncomfortable that he could not settle down to his meal till the emperor had sent for Godoy, and found a place for him near his master and mistress [1].

The fourth individual with whose personality it is necessary to be acquainted when studying the court of Spain in 1808 is the heir to the throne, Ferdinand, Prince of the Asturias.   Little was known of him, for his parents and Godoy had carefully excluded him from political life.   But when a prince is getting on for thirty, and his father has begun to show signs of failing health, it is impossible that eyes should not be turned on him from all quarters.   Ferdinand was not an imbecile like his father, nor a scandalous person like his mother ; but (though Spain knew it not) he was coward and a cur. With such parents he had naturally been brought up very badly. He was ignominiously excluded from all public business, and kept in absolute ignorance of all subjects on which a prince should have some knowledge : history, military science, modern politics, foreign languages, were all sealed books to him.   He had been educated, so far as he was trained at all, by a clever and ambitious priest, Juan Escoiquiz, a canon of Toledo.   An obscure churchman was not the best tutor for a future sovereign : he could not instruct the prince in the more necessary arts of governance, but he seems to have taught him dissimulation and superstition [2].   For Ferdinand was pious with a grovelling sort of piety, which made him carry about strings of relics, spend much of his time in church ceremonies, and

---

[1] Toreño, i. 86.   The story is confirmed by Savary, in his *Mémoires*, ii. 221.

[2] That Escoiquiz was a clever man, and not the mere intriguer that he is often called, is (I think) shown not only by the impression which he made upon Napoleon (who called him, in jest, *le petit Ximénès*) and on De Pradt at Bayonne, but still more by his work, the *Conversation avec Napoléon*.   If he invented it, he must have been a genius, so well has he caught the Emperor's style ; if he only reproduced it he was at least an admirable and picturesque reporter.

MARIA LUISA

REYNA DE ESPAÑA.

(as rumour said) take to embroidering petticoats for his favourite image of the Virgin in his old age.

The prince had one healthy sentiment, a deep hatred for Godoy, who had from his earliest youth excluded him from his proper place in the court and the state. But he was too timid to resent the favourite's influence by anything but sulky rudeness. If he had chosen, he could at once have put himself at the head of the powerful body of persons whom the favourite had disobliged or offended. His few intimate friends, and above all his tutor Escoiquiz, were always spurring him on to take some active measures against the Prince of the Peace. But Ferdinand was too indolent and too cautious to move, though he was in his secret heart convinced that his enemy was plotting his destruction, and intended to exclude him from the throne at his father's death.

To give a fair idea of the education, character, and brains of this miserable prince it is only necessary to quote a couple of his letters. The first was written in November, 1807, when he had been imprisoned by his father for carrying on the famous secret correspondence with Napoleon. It runs as follows:—

DEAR PAPA[1],

I have done wrong: I have sinned against your majesty, both as king and as father; but I have repented, and I now offer your majesty the most humble obedience. I ought to have done nothing without your majesty's knowledge; but I was caught unawares. I have given up the names of the guilty persons, and I beg your majesty to pardon me for having lied to you the other night, and to allow your grateful son to kiss your royal feet.

(Signed) FERNANDO.

San Lorenzo (The Escurial), Nov. 5, 1807.

It is doubtful whether the childish whining, the base betrayal of his unfortunate accomplices, or the slavish tone of the confession forms the most striking point in this epistle.

But the second document that we have to quote gives an even worse idea of Ferdinand. Several years after he had been

---

[1] Observe 'Papa Mio' instead of 'Padre Mio.' The Spanish text I have printed as Appendix 3 of this volume. Some say that Godoy dictated the wording of the letter, and did not merely insist that a letter of some sort must be written to secure a pardon. In any case the terms were such as no self-respecting person could have signed. The sentence 'pido à V. M. me perdone por haberle mentido la otra noche,' the most vile in the whole composition, are omitted by the courtly De Pradt when he translates it into French.

imprisoned by Napoleon at Valençay, a desperate attempt was made to deliver him. Baron Colli, a daring Austrian officer, entered France, amid a thousand dangers, with a scheme for delivering the prince : he hoped to get him to the coast, and to an English frigate, by means of false passports and relays of swift horses. The unfortunate adventurer was caught and thrown into a dungeon at Vincennes [1]. After the plot had miscarried Ferdinand wrote as follows to his jailor :—

'An unknown person got in here in disguise and proposed to Señor Amezaga, my master of the horse and steward, to carry me off from Valençay, asking him to pass on some papers, which he had brought, to my hands, and to aid in carrying out this horrible undertaking. My honour, my repose, and the good opinion due to my principles might all have been compromised, if Señor Amezaga had not given proof of his devotion to His Imperial Majesty and to myself, by revealing everything to me at once. I write immediately to give information of the matter, and take this opportunity of showing anew my inviolable fidelity to the Emperor Napoleon, and the horror that I feel at this infernal project, whose author, I hope, may be chastised according to his deserts.'

It is not surprising to find that the man who was capable of writing this letter also wrote more than once to congratulate Joseph Bonaparte on his victories over the 'rebels' in Spain.

It had been clear for some time that the bitter hatred which the Prince Royal bore to Godoy, and the fear which the favourite felt at the prospect of his enemy's accession to the throne, would lead to some explosion ere long. If Ferdinand had been a man of ordinary ability and determination he could probably have organized a *coup d'état* to get rid of the favourite, without much trouble. But he was so slow and timid that, in spite of all the exhortations of his partisans, he never did more than copy out two letters to his father which Escoiquiz drafted for him. He never screwed up his courage to the point of sending them, or personally delivering them into his father's hands. They were rhetorical

---

[1] There is a very black underplot in the story of Baron Colli. When he was caught the French police sent a spy with his credentials to Valençay, to see how far the persons about Ferdinand could be induced to compromise themselves. But the prince's terror, and abject delation of the supposed baron, stopped further proceedings.

compositions, setting forth the moral and political turpitude of Godoy, and warning the King that his favourite was guilty of designs on the throne. If Charles IV had been given them, he probably could not have made out half the meaning, and would have handed them over for interpretation to the trusty Manuel himself. The only other move which the prince was induced to make was to draw out a warrant appointing his friend and confidant, the Duke of Infantado, Captain-General of New Castile. It was to be used if the old king, who was then labouring under one of his attacks of gout, should chance to be carried off by it. The charge of Madrid, and of the troops in its vicinity, was to be consigned to one whom Ferdinand could trust, so that Godoy might be check-mated.

But the Prince of the Asturias took one other step in the autumn of 1807 which was destined to bring matters to a head. It occurred to him that instead of incurring the risks of conspiracy at home he would do better to apply for aid to his father's all-powerful ally. If Napoleon took up his cause, and promised him protection, he would be safe against all the machinations of the Prince of the Peace: for a frank and undisguised terror of the Emperor was the mainspring of Godoy's foreign and domestic policy. Ferdinand thought that he had a sure method of enlisting Bonaparte's benevolence: he was at this moment the most eligible *parti* in Europe: he had lost his first wife, a daughter of his uncle of Naples, and being childless was bound to marry again[1]. By offering to accept a spouse of the Emperor's choice he would give such a guarantee of future loyalty and obedience that his patron (who was quite aware of Godoy's real feelings towards France) would withdraw all his support from the favourite and transfer it to himself. Acting under the advice of Escoiquiz, with whom he was always in secret communication, Ferdinand first sounded the French ambassador at Madrid, the Marquis de Beauharnais, a brother-in-law of the Empress Josephine. Escoiquiz saw the ambassador, who displayed much pleasure at his proposals, and urged him to encourage the prince to proceed with his plan[2].

---

[1] Godoy had the impudence to propose to the prince that he should marry Donna Luisa, the younger sister of his own unfortunate wife, and the cousin of the King. Ferdinand found courage to refuse this alliance.

[2] The intrigues of Escoiquiz had begun as early as March, 1807, the month in which the letters to the King against Godoy were drafted. The negotiation

The fact was that the diplomatist saw profit to his own family in the scheme: for in default of eligible damsels of the house of Bonaparte, it was probable that the lady whom the Emperor might choose as Queen of Spain would be one of his own relatives—some Beauharnais or Tascher—a niece or cousin of the Empress. A wife for the hereditary prince of Baden had been already chosen from among them in the preceding year.

When therefore Escoiquiz broached the matter to the ambassador in June, 1807, the latter only asked that he should be given full assurance that the Prince of the Asturias would carry out his design. No private interview could be managed between them in the existing state of Spanish court etiquette, and with the spies of Godoy lurking in every corner. But by a prearranged code of signals Ferdinand certified to Beauharnais, at one of the royal levées, that he had given all his confidence to Escoiquiz, and that the latter was really acting in his name. The ambassador therefore undertook to transmit to his master at Paris any document which the prince might entrust to him. Hence there came to be written the celebrated letter of October 11, 1807, in which Ferdinand implored the pity of 'the hero sent by providence to save Europe from anarchy, to strengthen tottering thrones, and to give to the nations peace and felicity.' His father, he said, was surrounded by malignant and astute intriguers who had estranged him from his son. But one word from Paris would suffice to discomfit such persons, and to open the eyes of his loved parents to the just grievances of their child. As a token of amity and protection he ventured to ask Bonaparte for the hand of some lady of his august house. He does not seem to have had any particular one in his eye, as the demand is made in the most general terms. The choice would really have lain between the eldest daughter of Lucien Bonaparte, who was then (as usual) on strained terms with his brother, and one of the numerous kinswomen of the Empress Josephine.

Godoy was so well served by his numerous spies that the news of the letter addressed to Bonaparte was soon conveyed to him. He resolved to take advantage to the full of the mistake which

with Beauharnais began in June. These dates are strongly against the idea that Bonaparte was at the bottom of the whole affair; his hand does not appear till July–August. Indeed he was far away in Eastern Germany when Escoiquiz began his interviews with the ambassador.

the prince had made in opening a correspondence with a foreign power behind the back of his father. He contrived an odious scene. He induced the old king to make a sudden descent on his son's apartments on the night of October 27, with an armed guard at his back, to accuse him publicly of aiming at dethroning or even murdering his parents, and to throw him into solitary confinement. Ferdinand's papers were sequestrated, but there was found among them nothing of importance except the two documents denouncing Godoy, which the prince had composed or copied out under the direction of his adviser Escoiquiz, and a cypher code which was discovered to have belonged to the prince's late wife, and to have been used by her in her private letters to her mother, the Queen of Naples.

There was absolutely nothing that proved any intention on the part of Ferdinand to commit himself to overt treason, though plenty to show his deep discontent, and his hatred for the Prince of the Peace. The only act that an honest critic could call disloyal was the attempt to open up a correspondence with Napoleon. But Godoy thought that he had found his opportunity of crushing the heir to the throne, and even of removing him from the succession. He caused Charles IV to publish an extraordinary manifesto to his subjects, in which he was made to speak as follows :—

'God, who watches over all creation, does not permit the success of atrocious designs against an innocent victim. His omnipotence has just delivered me from an incredible catastrophe. My people, my faithful subjects, know my Christian life, my regular conduct : they all love me and give me constant proof of their veneration, the reward due to a parent who loves his children. I was living in perfect confidence, when an unknown hand delated to me the most enormous and incredible plot, hatched in my own palace against my person. The preservation of my life, which has been already several times in danger, should have been the special charge of the heir to my throne, but blinded, and estranged from all those Christian principles in which my paternal care and love have reared him, he has given his consent to a plot to dethrone me. Taking in hand the investigation of the matter, I surprised him in his apartments and found in his hands the cypher which he used to communicate with his evil counsellors. I have thrown several of these criminals into prison, and have put my son under arrest in his own abode. This necessary punishment adds another sorrow to the many which already afflict me; but as it is the most painful of all, it is also the most necessary of all to carry out. Meanwhile I publish the facts: I do not hide from my subjects the grief that I feel—which can only be lessened by the proofs of loyalty which I know that they will display'[1] [Oct. 30, 1807].

Charles was therefore made to charge his son with a deliberate plot to dethrone him, and even to hint that his life had been in danger. The only possible reason for the formulating of this most unjustifiable accusation must have been that Godoy thought that he might now dare to sweep away the Prince of the Asturias from his path by imprisonment or exile. There can be no other explanation for the washing in public of so much of the dirty linen of the palace. Ferdinand, by his craven conduct, did his best to help his enemy's designs: in abject fear he delated to the King the names of Escoiquiz and his other confidants, the dukes of Infantado and San Carlos. He gave full particulars of his attempt to communicate with Napoleon, and of all his correspondence with his partisans— even acknowledging that he had given Infantado that undated commission as Captain-General of New Castile, to come into effect when he himself should become king, which we have already had occasion to mention. This act, it must be owned, was a little unseemly, but if it had really borne the sinister meaning that Godoy chose to put upon it, we may guess that Ferdinand would never have divulged it. In addition the prince wrote the disgusting letter of supplication to his father which has been already quoted, owning that 'he had lied the other night,' and asking leave to kiss his majesty's royal feet. It is beyond dispute that this epistle, with another similar one to the Queen, was written after a stormy interview with Godoy. The favourite had been allowed by his master and mistress to visit Ferdinand in prison, and to bully him into writing these documents, which (as he hoped) would ruin the prince's reputation for ever with every man of heart and honour. Godoy was wrong here: what struck the public mind far more than the prince's craven tone was the unseemliness of publishing to the world his miserable letters. That a prince royal of Spain should have been terrified by an upstart charlatan like Godoy into writing such words maddened all who read them.

Napoleon was delighted to see the royal family of Spain putting itself in such an odious light. He only intervened on a side issue

---

[1] The manuscript of this decree was in the handwriting of Godoy himself.

by sending peremptory orders that in any proceedings taken against the Prince of the Asturias no mention was to be made of himself or of his ambassador, i. e. the matter of the secret appeal to France (the one thing for which Ferdinand could be justly blamed) was not to be allowed to transpire. It was probably this communication from Paris which saved Ferdinand from experiencing the full consequences of Godoy's wrath [1]. If any public trial took place, it was certain that either Ferdinand or some of his friends would speak of the French intrigue, and if the story came out Napoleon would be angry. The mere thought of this possibility so worked upon the favourite that he suddenly resolved to stop the impeachment of the prince. In return for his humiliating prayers for mercy he was given a sort of ungracious pardon. 'The voice of nature,' so ran the turgid proclamation which Godoy dictated to the old king, 'disarms the hand of vengeance; I forgive my son, and will restore him to my good graces when his conduct shall have proved him a truly reformed character.' Ferdinand was left dishonoured and humiliated: he had been accused of intended parricide, made to betray his friends and to confess plots which he had never formed, and then pardoned. Godoy hoped that he was so ruined in the eyes of the Spanish people, and (what was more important) in the eyes of Napoleon, that there would be no more trouble with him, a supposition in which he grievously erred. After a decent interval the prince's fellow conspirators, Escoiquiz and Infantado, were acquitted of high treason by the court before which they had been sent, and allowed to go free. Of the dreadful accusations made in the Proclamation of Oct. 30 nothing more was heard.

The whole of the ' Affair of the Escurial,' as the arrest, imprisonment, and forgiveness of Ferdinand came to be called, took place between the twenty-seventh of October and the fifth of November, dates at which it is pretty certain that Napoleon's unscrupulous designs against the royal house of Spain had long been matured. The open quarrel of the imbecile father and the cowardly son only helped him in his plans, by making more manifest than ever the deplorable state of the Spanish court. It served as a useful plea to

---

[1] Cf. Foy and Toreño, who agree on this point. Napoleon insinuates as much in his letter to Ferdinand of April 16, 1808 : ' I flatter myself that I contributed by my representations to the happy ending of the affair of the Escurial' (*Nap. Corresp.*, 13,750).

justify acts of aggression which must have been planned many
months before. If it had never taken place, it is still certain
that Napoleon would have found some other plea for sweeping out
the worthless house of Bourbon from the Peninsula. He had
begun to collect armies at the roots of the Pyrenees, without
any obvious military necessity, some weeks before Ferdinand was
arrested. When that simple fact is taken into consideration we
see at once the hollowness of his plea, elaborated during his exile
at St. Helena [1], that it was the disgraceful explosion of family
hatred in the Spanish royal house that first suggested to him the
idea of removing the whole generation of Bourbons, and giving
Spain a new king and a new dynasty.

NOTE TO CHAPTER II

It may perhaps be worth while to give, for what it is worth, a story which
I find in the *Vaughan Papers* concerning the causes of the final quarrel between Godoy and the Prince of the Asturias, ending in the arrest of the latter
and the whole ' Affair of the Escurial.' Among Vaughan's large collection
of miscellaneous papers is a long document addressed to him by one of his
Spanish friends, purporting to give the secret history of the rupture ; the
narrative is said by the author to have been obtained from the mouth of
the minister Caballero, who would certainly have had the best means of
gaining court intelligence in October, 1807. The tale runs as follows : ' The
Queen had for many years been accustomed to make secret visits to Godoy's
palace under cover of the dark, escorted only by a lady-in-waiting and a
single body-servant. The sentinels round the palace had been designedly
so placed that none of them covered the postern door by which her majesty
was accustomed to pass in and out. One night in the autumn of 1807 the
whole system of the palace-guards was suddenly changed without the Queen's
knowledge, and when she returned from her excursion she ran into the arms
of a corporal's guard placed in front of the privy entrance. The men, fortunately for Maria Luisa, did not recognize the three muffled figures who fell
into their clutches, and allowed them to buy their way in for an *onza d'oro*,
or gold twenty-dollar piece. But when Godoy and the Queen talked the
matter over, and found that King Charles had ordered the inconvenient alterations in the sentinels, they came to the conclusion that Ferdinand had
deliberately induced his father to change the posts of the guard, with the
object either of stopping his mother's exits or of making a public scandal by
causing her to be arrested at this strange place and hour. The Prince
chanced to have had a private conversation with his father on the previous
day, and this might well have been its result.' In high wrath, the story

[1] Las Cases, ii. 206.

proceeds, the Queen and the favourite resolved to crush Ferdinand at once, and to get him excluded from the succession. They chose the very inadequate excuse of the letter of the Prince to Napoleon, of which they had perfect cognizance from the very moment of its being written. But, we are assured, they were quite wrong in their suspicions, the originator of the movement of the sentries, which had so disconcerted them, having been Baron Versage, the newly appointed colonel of the Walloon Guards. He had got the King's leave to rearrange the watching of the palace, and going round it had spied the private door, which he had blocked with a new picquet, quite unaware of the purpose for which it had been used for so many years. This Versage, it will be remembered, served under Palafox, and was killed in Aragon during the first year of the war. I should imagine the whole tale to be an ingenious fiction, in spite of the name of Caballero cited in its support : of that personage Napoleon wrote [*Nap. Corresp.* 14,015] 'il a une très mauvaise réputation ; c'est tout dire que de dire qu'il était l'homme de confiance de la Reine.' But the story was current in Spain very soon after the alleged adventure took place.

SECTION I: CHAPTER III

THE CONQUEST OF PORTUGAL

THERE is certainly no example in history of a kingdom conquered in so few days and with such small trouble as was Portugal
in 1807. That a nation of three million souls, which in earlier
days had repeatedly defended itself with success against numbers
far greater than those now employed against it, should yield without
firing a single shot was astonishing. It is a testimony not only
to the timidity of the Portuguese Government, but to the numbing
power of Napoleon's name.

The force destined by the Treaty of Fontainebleau for the invasion of Portugal consisted of Junot's 'Army of the Gironde,' 25,000
strong, and of three auxiliary Spanish corps amounting in all to
about the same numbers. Of these one, coming from Galicia [1], was
to strike at Oporto and the Lower Douro; another, from Badajoz [2],
was to take the fortress of Elvas, the southern bulwark of Portugal,
and then to march on Lisbon by the left bank of the Tagus.
These were flanking operations: the main blow at the Portuguese
capital was to be dealt by Junot himself, strengthened by a third
Spanish force [3]; they were to concentrate at Salamanca and Ciudad
Rodrigo, and make for Lisbon by the high-road that passes by
Almeida and Coimbra.

The Army of the Gironde crossed the Bidassoa on October 18:
by the 12th of November it had arrived at Salamanca, having covered
300 miles in twenty-five days—very leisurely marching at the rate of
twelve miles a day. The Spaniards would not have been pleased
to know that, by Napoleon's orders, engineer officers were secretly
taking sketches of every fortified place and defile that the army
passed, and preparing reports as to the resources of all the towns
of Old Castile and Leon. This was one of the many signs of the

[1] Composed of 6,500 men under General Taranco, marching from Vigo.
[2] Composed of 9,500 men under Solano, Captain-General of Andalusia, and
marching from Badajoz.
[3] Composed of 9,500 men under Caraffa.

Emperor's ultimate designs.   On the 12th of November, in consequence we cannot doubt of the outbreak of the troubles of
October 27 at the Spanish court, Junot suddenly received new
orders, telling him to hurry.   He was informed that every day
which intervened before his arrival at Lisbon was time granted to
the Portuguese in which to prepare resistance,—possibly also time
in which England, who had plenty of troops in the Mediterranean,
might make up her mind to send military aid to her old ally.
Junot was directed to quicken his pace, and to strike before the
enemy could mature plans of defence.

For this reason he was told to change his route.   The Emperor
had originally intended to invade the country over the usual line
of attack from Spain, by Almeida and Coimbra, which Masséna
was to take three years later, in 1810.   But when the events at
the Escurial showed that a crisis was impending in Spain, Napoleon
changed his mind : there was the fortress of Almeida in the way,
which might offer resistance and cause delay, and beyond were
nearly 200 miles of difficult mountain roads.   Looking at his
maps, Napoleon saw that there was a much shorter way to Lisbon
by another route, down the Tagus.   From Alcantara, the Spanish
frontier town on that river, to Lisbon is only 120 miles, and there
is no fortress on the way.   The maps could not show the Emperor
that this road was for half of its length a series of rocky defiles
through an almost unpeopled wilderness.

Orders were therefore sent to Junot to transfer his base of
operations from Salamanca to Alcantara, and to march down the
Tagus.   The Spaniards (according to their orders) had collected
the magazines for feeding Junot's force at Salamanca and Ciudad
Rodrigo.   But for that Napoleon cared little.   He wrote that the
army must take the shortest road at all costs, whatever the difficulty
of getting supplies.   'I will not have the march of the army
delayed for a single day,' he added ; '20,000 men can feed themselves anywhere, even in a desert.'   It was indeed a desert that
Junot was ordered to cross : the hill-road from Ciudad Rodrigo
to Alcantara, which hugs the Portuguese frontier, has hardly a
village on it ; it crosses ridge after ridge, ravine after ravine.   In
November the rains had just set in, and every torrent was full.
Over this stony wilderness, by the Pass of Perales, the French army
rushed in five days, but at the cost of dreadful privations.   When
it reached Alcantara half the horses had perished of cold, all the

guns but six had been left behind, stranded at various points on the road, and of the infantry more than a quarter was missing—the famished men having scattered in all directions to find food. If there had been a Portuguese force watching Alcantara, Junot must have waited for many days to get his army together again, all the more so because every cartridge that his men were carrying had been spoiled by the wet. But there were no enemies near; Junot found at the great Tagus bridge only a few Spanish battalions and guns on the way to join his army. Confiscating their munitions to fill his men's pouches, and their food to provide them with two days' rations, Junot rushed on again upon the 19th of November. He found, to his surprise, that there was no road suitable for wheeled traffic along the Tagus valley, but only a poor track running along the foot of the mountains to Castello Branco, the sole Portuguese town in this part of the frontier. The march from Alcantara to Abrantes proved even more trying than that from Ciudad Rodrigo to Alcantara. It was through a treeless wilderness of grey granite, seamed with countless ravines. The rain continued, the torrents were even fuller than before, the country even more desolate than the Spanish side of the border. It was only after terrible sufferings that the head of the column reached Abrantes on November 23: the rear trailed in on the 26th. All the guns except four Spanish pieces of horse artillery had fallen behind: the cavalry was practically dismounted. Half the infantry was marauding off the road, or resting dead-beat in the few poor villages that it had passed. If there had been even 5,000 Portuguese troops at Abrantes the French would have been brought to a stop. But instead of hostile battalions, Junot found there only an anxious diplomatist, named Barreto, sent by the Prince-Regent to stop his advance by offers of servile submission to the Emperor and proffers of tribute. Reassured as to the possibility that the Portuguese might have been intending armed resistance, Junot now took a most hazardous step. Choosing the least disorganized companies of every regiment, he made up four battalions of picked men, and pushed on again for Lisbon, now only seventy-five miles distant. This time he had neither a gun nor a horseman left, but he struggled forward, and on the 30th of November entered the Portuguese capital at the head of 1,500 weary soldiers, all that had been able to endure to the end. They limped in utterly exhausted, their clothes in rags, and their cartridges so soaked through that they could not have fired a shot had they been attacked. If the mob of Lisbon had fallen on them with sticks and stones, the starving invaders must have been driven out of the city. But nothing of the kind happened, and Junot was able to install himself as governor of Portugal without having to strike a blow. It was ten days before the last of the stragglers came up from the rear, and even more before the artillery appeared and the cavalry began to remount itself with confiscated horses. Meanwhile the Portuguese were digesting the fact that they had allowed 1,500 famished, half-armed men to seize their capital.

While Junot had been rushing on from Salamanca to Alcantara, and from Alcantara to Abrantes, Lisbon had been the scene of much pitiful commotion. The Prince-Regent had long refused to believe that Napoleon really intended to dethrone him, and had been still occupying himself with futile schemes for propitiating the Emperor. Of his courtiers and generals, hardly one counselled resistance : there was no talk of mobilizing the dilapidated army of some 30,000 men which the country was supposed to possess, or of calling out the militia which had done such good service in earlier wars with Spain and France. Prince John contented himself with declaring war on England on the twentieth of October, and with garrisoning the coast batteries which protect Lisbon against attacks from the sea. Of these signs of obedience he sent reports to Napoleon : on the eighth of November he seized the persons of the few English merchants who still remained in Portugal ; the majority had wisely absconded in October. At the same time he let the British Government know that he was at heart their friend, and only driven by brute force to his present course : he even permitted their ambassador, Lord Strangford, to linger in Lisbon.

In a few days the Regent began to see that Napoleon was inexorable : his ambassador from Paris was sent back to him, and reported that he had passed on the way the army of Junot marching by Burgos on Salamanca. Presently an English fleet under Sir Sydney Smith, the hero of Acre, appeared at the mouth of the Tagus, and declared Lisbon in a state of blockade—the natural reply to the Regent's declaration of war and seizure of English residents. Other reasons existed for the blockade : there had lately arrived in the Tagus a Russian squadron on its homeward way from the Mediterranean. The Czar Alexander was at this time Napoleon's eager ally, and had just declared war on England ;

it seemed wise to keep an eye on these ships, whose arrival appeared
to synchronize in a most suspicious way with the approach of Junot.
Moreover there was the Portuguese fleet to be considered : if the
Prince-Regent intended to hand it over to the French, it would
have to be dealt with in the same way as the Danish fleet had been
treated a few months before.

Lord Strangford retired on board Sydney Smith's flagship, the
Hibernia, and from thence continued to exchange notes with the
miserable Portuguese Government. The Regent was still hesitating
between sending still more abject proposals of submission to
Bonaparte, and the only other alternative, that of getting on
board his fleet and crossing the Atlantic to the great Portuguese
colony in Brazil. The news that Junot had reached Alcantara
only confused him still more ; he could not make up his mind
to leave his comfortable palace at Mafra, his gardens, and the
countless chapels and shrines in which his soul delighted, in order
to dare the unaccustomed horrors of the deep. On the other
hand, he feared that, if he stayed, he might ere long find himself
a prisoner of state in some obscure French castle. At last his
mind was made up for him from without : Lord Strangford on
the twenty-fifth of November received a copy of the Paris *Moniteur*
of the thirteenth of October, in which appeared a proclamation
in the true Napoleonesque vein, announcing that 'the house of
Braganza had ceased to reign in Europe.' The celerity with which
the paper had been passed on from Paris to London and from
London to Lisbon was most fortunate, as it was just not too late
for the prince to fly, though far too late for him to think of
defending himself. Junot was already at Abrantes, but during
the four days which he spent between that place and Lisbon
the die was cast. Abandoning his wonted indecision, the Regent
hurried on shipboard his treasure, his state papers, his insane
mother, his young family, and all the hangers-on of his court.
The whole fleet, fifteen men-of-war, was crowded with official
refugees and their belongings. More than twenty merchant
vessels were hastily manned and freighted with other inhabitants
of Lisbon, who determined to fly with their prince : merchants
and nobles alike preferred the voyage to Rio de Janeiro to facing
the dreaded French. On the twenty-ninth of November the
whole convoy passed out of the mouth of the Tagus and set sail
for the West. When he toiled in on the thirtieth, Junot

found the birds flown, and took possession of the dismantled
city.

Junot's Spanish auxiliaries were, as might have been expected
from the national character and the deplorable state of the
government, much slower than their French allies. Solano and
the southern army did not enter Portugal till the second of
December, three days after Lisbon had fallen. Taranco and the
Galician corps only reached Oporto on the thirteenth of December.
To neither of them was any opposition offered: the sole show
of national feeling which they met was that the Governor of
Valenza closed his gates, and would not admit the Spaniards till
he heard that Lisbon was in the enemy's hands, and that the
Prince-Regent had abandoned the country.

Junot at first made some attempt to render himself popular and
to keep his troops in good discipline. But it was impossible to
conciliate the Portuguese: when they saw the exhausted condition
and comparatively small numbers of the army that had overrun
their realm, they were filled with rage to think that no attempt
had been made to strike a blow to save its independence. When,
on the thirteenth of December, Junot made a great show out of
the ceremony of hauling down the Portuguese flag and of hoisting
the tricolour on the public buildings of the metropolis, there broke
out a fierce riot, which had to be dispersed with a cavalry charge.
But this was the work of the mob: both the civil and the military
authorities showed a servile obedience to Junot's orders, and no one
of importance stood forward to head the crowd.

The first precautionary measure of the French general was to
dissolve the Portuguese army. He ordered the discharge of all men
with less than one and more than six years' service, dissolved the
old regimental *cadres*, and reorganized the 6,000 or 7,000 men left
into nine new corps, which were soon ordered out of the realm.
Ultimately they were sent to the Baltic, and remained garrisoned
in Northern Germany for some years. At the time of the Russian
War of 1812 there were still enough of these unhappy exiles left to
constitute three strong regiments. Nearly all of them perished in
the snow during the retreat from Moscow.

Further endeavour to make French rule popular in Portugal was
soon rendered impossible by orders from Paris. The Emperor's
mandate not only bade Junot confiscate and realize all the property
of the 15,000 persons, small and great, who had fled to Brazil with

the Prince-Regent; it also commanded him to raise a fine of 100,000,000 francs, four millions of our money, from the little kingdom. But the emigrants had carried away nearly half the coined money in Portugal, and the rest had been hidden, leaving nothing but coppers and depreciated paper money visible in circulation. With the best will in the world Junot found it difficult to begin to collect even the nucleus of the required sum. The heavy taxes and imposts which he levied had no small effect in adding to the discontent of the people, but their total did little more than pay for the maintenance of the invaders. Meanwhile the troops behaved with the usual licence of a French army in a conquered country, and repeatedly provoked sanguinary brawls with the peasantry. Military executions of persons who had resisted requisitions by force began as early as January, 1808. Nothing was wanting to prepare an insurrection but leaders: of their appearance there was no sign; the most spirited members of the upper classes had gone off with the Regent. Those who had remained were the miserable bureaucrats which despotic governments always breed. They were ready to serve the stranger if they could keep their posts and places. A discreditable proportion of the old state servants acquiesced in the new government. The Patriarch of Lisbon issued a fulsome address in praise of Napoleon. The members of the provisional government which the Regent had nominated on his departure mostly submitted to Junot. There was little difficulty found in collecting a deputation, imposing by its numbers and by the names of some of its personnel, which travelled to Bayonne, to compliment Bonaparte and request him to grant some definite form of government to Portugal. The Emperor treated them in a very offhand way, asked them if they would like to be annexed to Spain, and on their indignant repudiation of that proposal, sent them off with a few platitudes to the effect that the lot of a nation depends upon itself, and that his eye was upon them. But this interview only took place in April, 1808, when events in Spain were assuming a very different aspect from that which they displayed at the moment of Junot's first seizure of Lisbon.

SECTION I: CHAPTER IV

THE FRENCH AGGRESSION IN SPAIN: ABDICATION OF CHARLES IV

THE 'Affair of the Escurial' added some complications to the situation of affairs in Spain from Napoleon's point of view. But there was nothing in it to make him alter the plans which he was at this moment carrying out: if the Bourbons were to be evicted from Spain, it made the task somewhat easier to find that the heir to the throne was now in deep disgrace. It would be possible to urge that by his parricidal plots he had forfeited any rights to the kingdom which he had hitherto possessed. In dealing with the politics of Spain he might for the future be disregarded, and there would be no one to take into consideration save the King and Queen and Godoy. All three were, as the Emperor knew, profoundly unpopular: if anything had been needed to make the nation more discontented, it was the late scandalous events at the Escurial. Nothing could be more convenient than that the favourite and his sovereigns should sink yet further into the abyss of unpopularity.

Napoleon therefore went steadily on with his plans for pushing more and more French troops into Spain, with the object of occupying all the main strategical points in the kingdom. The only doubtful point in his schemes is whether he ultimately proposed to seize on the persons of the royal family, or whether he intended by a series of threatening acts to scare them off to Mexico, as he had already scared the Prince of Portugal off to Rio de Janeiro. It is on the whole probable that he leaned to the latter plan. Every week the attitude of the French armies became more aggressive, and the language of their master more haughty and sinister [1]. The tone

---

[1] It is impossible to doubt that Napoleon's scheme was already in progress as early as October. On Nov. 13 he sent orders for the secret arming and provisioning of all the frontier fortresses of France (*Nap. Corresp.*, 13,343). On Nov. 24 he directed his chamberlain, De Tournon, to spy out the condition of Pampeluna and the other Spanish border strongholds, and to discover the

in which he had forbidden the court of Spain to allow any mention of himself or his ambassador to appear, during the trial of Prince Ferdinand and his fellow conspirators, had been menacing in the highest degree.   After the occupation of Portugal no further allusion had been made to the project for proclaiming Godoy Prince of the Algarves.   His name was never mentioned either to the Portuguese or to the officers of Junot.   The favourite soon saw that he had been duped, but was too terrified to complain.

But it was the constant influx into Spain of French troops which contributed in the most serious way to frighten the Spanish court.   Junot had entered Lisbon on Nov. 30, and the news that he had mastered the place without firing a shot had reached the Emperor early in December.   But long before, on the twenty-second of November, the French reserves, hitherto known as the 'Second Corps of Observation of the Gironde,' which had been collected at Bayonne in November, crossed the Spanish frontier.   They consisted of 25,000 men—nearly all recently levied conscripts—under General Dupont.   The treaty of Fontainebleau had contained a clause providing that, if the English tried to defend Portugal by landing troops, Napoleon might send 40,000 men to aid Junot *after giving due notice to the King of Spain*.   Instead of waiting to hear how the first corps had fared, or apprising his ally of his intention to dispatch Dupont's corps across the frontier, the Emperor merely ordered it to cross the Bidassoa without sending any information to Madrid.   The fact was that whether the preliminary condition stated in the treaty, an English descent on Portugal, did or did not take place, Bonaparte was determined to carry out his design.   A month later the Spaniards heard, to their growing alarm, that yet a third army corps had come across the border: this was the 'Corps of Observation of the Ocean Coast,' which had been hastily organized under Marshal Moncey at Bordeaux, and pushed on to Bayonne when Dupont's troops moved forward.   It was 30,000 strong, but mainly composed of conscript battalions of the levy of 1808, which had been raised by anticipation in the previous spring, while the Russian war was still in progress.   On the eighth of January this army began to pass the Pyrenees, occupying all the chief towns of Biscay and Navarre, while Dupont's divisions pressed on and cantoned themselves in Burgos,

exact distribution of the Spanish army (13,354).   Such moves could have but one meaning.

Valladolid, and the other chief cities of Old Castile. They made no further advance towards Portugal, where Junot clearly did not require their aid.

The Spanish government was terror-stricken at the unexpected appearance of more than 60,000 French troops on the road to Madrid. If anything more was required to cause suspicion, it was the news that still more 'corps of observation' were being formed at Bordeaux and Poitiers. What legitimate reason could there possibly be for the direction of such masses of troops on Northern Spain? But any thought of resistance was far from the mind of Godoy and the King. Their first plan was to propitiate Napoleon by making the same request which had brought the Prince of the Asturias into such trouble in October—that the hand of a princess of the house of Bonaparte might be granted to the heir of the Spanish throne. The Emperor was making an ostentatious tour in Italy while his forces were overrunning the provinces of his ally—as if the occupation of Castile and Biscay were no affair of his. His most important act in November was to evict from Florence the ruling sovereign, the King of Etruria, and the Regent, his mother, thus annexing the last surviving Bourbon state save Spain to the French crown. He wrote polite but meaningless letters to Madrid, making no allusion to the boon asked by Charles IV. The fact was that Napoleon could now treat Ferdinand as 'damaged goods'; he was, by his father's own avowal, no more than a pardoned parricide, and it suited the policy of the Emperor to regard him as a convicted criminal who had played away his rights of succession. If Napoleon visited his brother Lucien at Mantua, it was not (as was thought at the time) with any real intention of persuading him to give his daughter to the craven suitor offered her[1], but in order to tempt her father to accept the crown of Portugal—even perhaps that of Spain. But Lucien, who always refused to fall in with Napoleon's family policy, showed no gratitude for the offer of a thorny throne in the Iberian Peninsula, and not without reason, for one of the details of the bargain was to be that he should divorce a wife to whom he was fondly attached.

It was only after returning from Italy in January that the Emperor deigned to answer the King of Spain's letter, now two months old,

---

[1] Note on this point Talleyrand's *Mémoires*, i. 333, and *Nap. Corresp.*, 13,402 (Napoleon to Joseph Bonaparte, Dec. 17, 1807).

in precise terms. He did not object to the principle of the alliance, but doubted if he could give any daughter of his house to 'a son dishonoured by his own father's declaration.' This reply was not very reassuring to Godoy and his master, and worse was to follow. In the end of January the *Moniteur*, which the Emperor always used as a means for ventilating schemes which were before long to take shape in fact, began a systematic course of abusing the Prince of the Peace as a bad minister and a false friend. More troops kept pouring across the Pyrenees without any ostensible reason, and now it was not only at the western passes that they began to appear, but also on the eastern roads which lead from Roussillon into Catalonia and Valencia. These provinces are so remote from Portugal that it was clear that the army which was collecting opposite them could not be destined for Lisbon. But on February 10, 1808, 14,000 men, half French, half Italians, under General Duhesme, began to drift into Catalonia and to work their way down towards its capital—Barcelona. A side-light on the meaning of this development was given by Izquierdo, Godoy's agent at Paris, who now kept sending his master very disquieting reports. French ministers had begun to sound him as to the way in which Spain would take a proposal for the cession to France of Catalonia and part of Biscay, in return for Central Portugal. King Charles would probably be asked ere long to give up these ancient and loyal provinces, and to do so would mean the outbreak of a revolution all over Spain.

In the middle of February Napoleon finally threw off the mask, and frankly displayed himself as a robber in his ally's abode. On the sixteenth of the month began that infamous seizure by surprise of the Spanish frontier fortresses, which would pass for the most odious act of the Emperor's whole career, if the kidnapping at Bayonne were not to follow. The movement started at Pampeluna: French troops were quartered in the lower town, while a Spanish garrison held, as was natural, the citadel. One cold morning a large party of French soldiers congregated about the gate of the fortress, without arms, and pretended to be amusing themselves with snowballing, while waiting for a distribution of rations. At a given signal many of them, as if beaten in the mock contest, rushed in at the gate, pursued by the rest. The first men knocked down the unsuspecting sentinels, and seized the muskets of the guard stacked in the arms-racks of the guard-room.

Then a company of grenadiers, who had been hidden in a neighbouring house, suddenly ran in at the gate, followed by a whole battalion which had been at drill a few hundred yards away. The Spanish garrison, taken utterly by surprise and unarmed, were hustled out of their quarters and turned into the town [1].

A high-spirited prince would have declared war at once, whatever the odds against him, on receiving such an insulting blow. But this was not to be expected from persons like Godoy and Charles IV. Accordingly they exposed themselves to the continuation of these odious tricks. On February 29 General Lecchi, the officer commanding the French troops which were passing through Barcelona, ordered a review of his division before, as he said, its approaching departure for the south. After some evolutions he marched it through the city, and past the gate of the citadel; when this point was reached, he suddenly bade the leading company wheel to the left and enter the fortress. Before the Spaniards understood what was happening, several thousand of their allies were inside the place, and by the evening the rightful owners, who carried their opposition no further than noisy protestations, had been evicted. A few days later the two remaining frontier fortresses of Spain, San Sebastian, at the Atlantic end of the Pyrenees, and Figueras, at the great pass along the Mediterranean coast, suffered the same fate: the former place was surrendered by its governor when threatened with an actual assault, which orders from Madrid forbade him to resist [March 5]. Figueras, on the other hand, was seized by a *coup de main*, similar to that at Pampeluna; 200 French soldiers, having obtained entrance within the walls on a futile pretext, suddenly seized the gates and admitted a whole regiment, which turned out the Spanish garrison [March 18] [2]. It would be hard, if not impossible, to find in the whole of modern history any incident approaching, in cynical effrontery and mean cunning, to these first hostile acts of the French on the

---

[1] In *Nap. Corresp.*, 13,588, will be found the orders to General D'Armagnac to get possession of the citadel by menaces if he can, but if he cannot, by the actual use of force. 'S'il arrivait que le commandant-général de Navarre se refusât à rendre la citadelle, vous employeriez les troupes du Maréchal Moncey pour l'y forcer.'

[2] It will hardly be believed that Napier, in his blind reverence for Napoleon, omits to give any details concerning the seizure of the fortresses, merely saying that they were 'taken by various artifices' (i. 13). It is the particulars which are scandalous as well as the mere fact.

territory of their allies. The net result was to leave the two chief fortresses, on each of the main entries into Spain from France, completely in the power of the Emperor.

Godoy and his employers were driven into wild alarm by these acts of open hostility. The favourite, in his memoirs[1], tells us that he thought, for a moment, of responding by a declaration of war, but that the old king replied that Napoleon could not be intending treachery, because he had just sent him twelve fine coach-horses and several polite letters. In face of his master's reluctance, he tells us that he temporized for some days more. The story is highly improbable : Charles had no will save Godoy's, and would have done whatever he was told. It is much more likely that the reluctance to take a bold resolve was the favourite's own. When the French troops still continued to draw nearer to Madrid, Godoy could only bethink himself of a plan for absconding. He proposed to the King and Queen that they should leave Madrid and take refuge in Seville, in order to place themselves as far as possible from the French armies. Behind this move was a scheme for a much longer voyage. It seems that he proposed that the court should follow the example of the Regent of Portugal, and fly to America. At Mexico or Buenos Ayres they would at least be safe from Bonaparte. To protect the first stage of the flight, the troops in Portugal were directed to slip away from Junot and mass in Estremadura. The garrison of Madrid was drawn to Aranjuez, the palace where the court lay in February and March, and was to act as its escort to Seville. It is certain that nothing would have suited Napoleon's plans better than that Charles IV should abscond and leave his throne derelict : it would have given the maximum of advantage with the minimum of odium. It is possible that the Emperor was working precisely with the object of frightening Godoy into flight. If so his scheme was foiled, because he forgot that he had to deal not only with the contemptible court, but with the suspicious and revengeful Spanish nation. In March the people intervened, and their outbreak put quite a different face upon affairs.

Meanwhile the Emperor was launching a new figure upon the stage. On February 26 his brother-in-law, Joachim Murat, the new Grand-Duke of Berg, appeared at Bayonne with the title of ' Lieutenant of the Emperor,' and a commission to take command

---

[1] *Memoirs of Godoy*, i. 122.   Cf. Arteche, i. 251.

of all the French forces in Spain. On March 10 he crossed the Bidassoa and assumed possession of his post. Murat's character is well known: it was not very complicated. He was a headstrong, unscrupulous soldier, with a genius for heading a cavalry charge on a large scale, and an unbounded ambition. He was at present meditating on thrones and kingdoms: Berg seemed a small thing to this son of a Gascon innkeeper, and ever since his brothers-in-law Joseph, Louis, and Jerome Bonaparte had become kings, he was determined to climb up to be their equal. It has frequently been asserted that Murat was at this moment dreaming of the Spanish crown: he was certainly aware that the Emperor was plotting against the Bourbons, and the military movements which he had been directed to carry out were sufficient in themselves to indicate more or less his brother-in-law's intentions. Yet on the whole it is probable that he had not received more than half-confidences from his august relative. His dispatches are full of murmurs that he was being kept in the dark, and that he could not act with full confidence for want of explicit directions. Napoleon had certainly promised him promotion, if the Spanish affair came to a successful end: but it is probable that Murat understood that he was not to be rewarded with the crown of Charles IV. Perhaps Portugal, or Holland, or Naples (if one of the Emperor's brothers should pass on to Madrid) was spoken of as his reward. Certainly there was enough at stake to make him eager to carry out whatever Bonaparte ordered. In his cheerful self-confidence he imagined himself quite capable of playing the part of a Machiavelli, and of edging the old king out of the country by threats and hints. But if grape-shot was required, he was equally ready to administer an unsparing dose. With a kingdom in view he could be utterly unscrupulous[1].

On March 13 Murat arrived at Burgos, and issued a strange proclamation bidding his army 'treat the estimable Spanish nation as friends, for the Emperor sought only the good and happiness of Spain.' The curious phrase could only suggest that unless he gave this warning, his troops would have treated their allies as enemies.

---

[1] That Murat did not dream of the Spanish crown is, I think, fairly well demonstrated by his descendant, Count Murat, in his useful *Murat, Lieutenant de l'Empereur en Espagne* (1897). But that after once reading the dispatches, *Nap. Corresp.*, 13,588 and 13,589, he failed to see that his brother-in-law's intention was to seize Spain, is impossible.

The scandalous pillage committed by many regiments during February and March quite justified the suspicion.

The approach of Murat scared Godoy into immediate action, all the more because a new *corps d'armée*, more than 30,000 strong, under Marshal Bessières, was already commencing to cross the Pyrenees, bringing up the total of French troops in the Peninsula to more than 100,000 men. He ordered the departure of the King and his escort, the Madrid garrison, for Seville on March 18. This brought matters to a head : it was regarded as the commencement of the projected flight to America, of which rumours were already floating round the court and capital. A despotic government, which never takes the people into its confidence, must always expect to have its actions interpreted in the most unfavourable light. Except Godoy's personal adherents, there was not a soul in Madrid who did not believe that the favourite was acting in collusion with Napoleon, and deliberately betraying his sovereign and his country. It was by his consent, they thought, that the French had crossed the Pyrenees, had seized Pampeluna and Barcelona, and were now marching on the capital. They were far from imagining that of all the persons in the game he was the greatest dupe, and that the recent developments of Napoleon's policy had reduced him to despair. It was correct enough to attribute the present miserable situation of the realm to Godoy's policy, but only because his servility to Bonaparte had tempted the latter to see how far he could go, and because his maladministration had brought the army so low that it was no longer capable of defending the fatherland. Men did well to be angry with the Prince of the Peace, but they should have cursed him as a timid, incompetent fool, not as a deliberate traitor. But upstarts who guide the policy of a great realm for their private profit must naturally expect to be misrepresented, and there can be no doubt that the Spaniards judged Godoy to be a willing helper in the ruin of his master and his country.

Aranjuez, ordinarily a quiet little place, was now crowded with the hangers-on of the court, the garrison of Madrid, and a throng of anxious and distraught inhabitants of the capital : some had come out to avoid the advancing French, some to learn the latest news of the King's intentions, others with the deliberate intention of attacking the favourite. Among the latter were the few friends of the Prince of the Asturias, and a much greater number who

DON MANUEL GODOY
PRINCE OF THE PEACE
AT THE AGE OF 25

sympathized with his unhappy lot and had not gauged his miserable disposition. It is probable that as things stood it was really the best move to send the King to Seville, or even to America, and to commence open resistance to the French when the royal person should be in safety. But the crowd could see nothing but deliberate treason in the proposal : they waited only for the confirmation of the news of the departure of the court before breaking out into violence.

On the night of the seventeenth of March Godoy was actually commencing the evacuation of Aranjuez, by sending off his most precious possession, the too-celebrated Donna Josepha Tudo, under cover of the dark. The party which was escorting her fell into the midst of a knot of midnight loiterers, who were watching the palace. There was a scuffle, a pistol was fired, and as if by a prearranged plan crowds poured out into the streets. The cry went round that Godoy was carrying off the King and Queen, and a general rush was made to his house. There were guards before it, but they refused to fire on the mob, of which no small proportion was composed of soldiers who had broken out of their barracks without leave. In a moment the doors were battered down and the assailants poured into the mansion, hunting for the favourite. They could not find him, and in their disappointment smashed all his works of art, and burnt his magnificent furniture. Then they flocked to the palace, in which they suspected that he had taken refuge, calling for his head. The King and Queen, in deadly terror, besought their ill-used son to save them, by propitiating the mob, who would listen to his voice if to no other. Then came the hour of Ferdinand's triumph ; stepping out on to the balcony, he announced to the crowd that the King was much displeased with the Prince of the Peace, and had determined to dismiss him from office. The throng at once dispersed with loud cheers.

Next morning, in fact, a royal decree was issued, declaring Godoy relieved of all his posts and duties and banished from the court. Without the favourite at their elbow Charles and his queen seemed perfectly helpless. The proclamation was received at first with satisfaction, but the people still hung about the palace and kept calling for the King, who had to come out several times and salute them. It began to look like a scene from the beginning of the French Revolution. There was already much talk in the crowd of the benefit that would ensue to Spain if the Prince of the Asturias, with whose sufferings every one had sympathized, were to be entrusted with some part in the governance of the realm. His partisans openly spoke of the abdication of the old king as a desirable possibility.

Next day the rioting commenced again, owing to the reappearance of Godoy. He had lain concealed for thirty-six hours beneath a heap of mats, in a hiding-place contrived under the rafters of his mansion; but hunger at last drove him out, and, when he thought that the coast was clear, he slipped down and tried to get away. In spite of his mantle and slouched hat he was recognized almost at once, and would have been pulled to pieces by the crowd if he had not been saved by a detachment of the royal guard, who carried him off a prisoner to the palace. The news that he was trapped brought thousands of rioters under the royal windows, shouting for his instant trial and execution. The imbecile King could not be convinced that he was himself safe, and the Queen, who usually displayed more courage, seemed paralysed by her fears for Godoy even more than for herself. This was the lucky hour of the Prince of the Asturias; urged on by his secret advisers, he suggested abdication to his father, promising that he would disperse the mob and save the favourite's life. The silly old man accepted the proposal with alacrity, and drew up a short document of twelve lines, to the effect 'that his many bodily infirmities made it hard for him to support any longer the heavy weight of the administration of the realm, and that he had decided to remove to some more temperate clime, there to enjoy the peace of private life. After serious deliberation he had resolved to abdicate in favour of his natural heir, and wished that Don Ferdinand should at once be received as king in all the provinces of the Spanish crown. That this free and spontaneous abdication should be immediately published was to be the duty of the Council of Castile.'

SECTION I: CHAPTER V

THE TREACHERY AT BAYONNE

THE news of the abdication of Charles IV was received with universal joy. The rioters of Aranjuez dispersed after saluting the new sovereign, and allowed Godoy to be taken off, without further trouble, to the castle of Villaviciosa. Madrid, though Murat was now almost at its gates, gave itself up to feasts and processions, after having first sacked the palaces of the Prince of the Peace and some of his unpopular relations and partisans. Completely ignorant of the personal character of Ferdinand VII, the Spaniards attributed to him all the virtues and graces, and blindly expected the commencement of a golden age—as if the son of Charles IV and Maria Luisa was likely to be a genius and a hero.

Looking at the general situation of affairs, there can be no doubt that the wisest course for the young king to have taken would have been to concentrate his army, put his person in safety, and ask Napoleon to speak out and formulate his intentions. Instead of taking this, the only manly course, Ferdinand resolved to throw himself on the Emperor's mercy, as if the fall of Godoy had been Napoleon's object, and not the conquest of Spain. Although Murat had actually arrived at Madrid on March 23, with a great body of cavalry and 20,000 foot, the King entered the city next day and practically put himself in the hands of the invader. He wrote a fulsome letter to Napoleon assuring him of his devotion, and begging once more for the hand of a princess of his house.

His reception in Madrid by the French ought to have undeceived him at once. The ambassador Beauharnais, alone among the foreign ministers, refrained from acknowledging him as king. Murat was equally recalcitrant, and moreover most rude and disobliging in his language and behaviour. The fact was that the Grand-Duke had supposed that he was entering Madrid in order to chase out Godoy and rule in his stead. The popular explosion which had swept

away the favourite and the old king, and substituted for them
a young and popular monarch, had foiled his design.   He did
not know how Bonaparte would take the new situation, and meanwhile was surly and discourteous.   But he was determined that
there should at least be grounds provided for a breach with
Ferdinand, if the Emperor should resolve to go on with his
original plan.

Accordingly, he not only refused to acknowledge the new king's
title, but hastened to put himself in secret communication with the
dethroned sovereigns.   They were only too eager to meet him halfway, and Maria Luisa especially was half-mad with rage at her
son's success.   At first she and her husband thought of nothing
but escaping from Spain : they begged Murat to pass on to the
Emperor letters in which they asked to be permitted to buy a little
estate in France, where they might enjoy his protection during
their declining years.   But they begged also that 'the poor Prince
of the Peace, who lies in a dungeon covered with wounds and
contusions and in danger of death,' might be saved and allowed to
join them, 'so that we may all live together in some healthy spot
far from intrigues and state business [1].'

Murat saw that the angry old queen might be utilized to dis-
credit her son, and promised to send on everything to Napoleon.
At the first word of encouragement given by the Grand-Duke's
agent, De Monthion, Maria Luisa began to cover many sheets with
abuse of her son.   'He is false to the core : he has no natural
affection : he is hard-hearted and nowise inclined to clemency.
He has been directed by villains and will do anything that ambition
suggests : he makes promises, but does not always keep them [2].'
Again she writes :—'From my son we have nothing to expect but
outrages and persecution.   He has commenced by forgery, and he
will go on manufacturing evidence to prove that the Prince of
the Peace—that innocent and affectionate friend of the Emperor,
the Duke of Berg, and every Frenchman !—may appear a criminal
in the eyes of the Spanish people and of Napoleon himself.   Do
not believe a word that he says, for our enemies have the power
and means to make any falsehood seem true [3].'   In another letter
she says that the riots of Aranjuez were no genuine explosion of

---

[1] See the letters of March 22–7 in Toreño, Appendix, i. 436–45.
[2] Letter of March 27, in Toreño, Appendix, i. 441.
[3] Ibid., p. 436.

popular wrath, but a deliberate plot got up by her son, who spent
countless sums on debauching the soldiery and importing ruffians
from Madrid.   He gave the signal for the outburst himself by
putting a lamp in his window at a fixed hour—and so forth [1].

Finding the Queen in this state of mind, Murat saw his way to
dealing a deadly blow at Ferdinand : with his counsel and consent
Charles IV was induced to draw up and send to Bonaparte a formal
protest against his abdication.   He was made to declare that his
resignation had not been voluntary, but imposed on him by force
and threats.   And so he ' throws himself into the arms of the great
monarch who has been his ally, and puts himself at his disposition
wholly and for every purpose [2].'   This document placed in
Napoleon's hands the precise weapon which he required to crush
King Ferdinand.   If the Emperor chose to take it seriously, he could
declare the new monarch a usurper—almost a parricide—the legality
of whose accession had been vitiated by force and fraud.

As a matter of fact Bonaparte's mind had long been made up.
The revolution of Aranjuez had been a surprise and a disappointment to him : his designs against Spain were made infinitely more
difficult of realization thereby.   While he had only the weak and
unpopular government of Godoy and Charles IV to deal with,
he had fancied that the game was in his hands.   It had been more
than probable that the Prince of the Peace would take fright, and
carry off the King and Queen to America—in which case he
would, as it were, find Spain left derelict.   If, however, the emigration did not take place, and it became necessary to lay hands on
Charles and his favourite, Napoleon calculated that the Spaniards
would be more pleased to be rid of Godoy than angry to see force
employed against him.   He was so profoundly ignorant of the
character of the nation, that he imagined that a few high-sounding
proclamations and promises of liberal reforms would induce them
to accept from his hands any new sovereign whom he chose to
nominate.   It was clear that the accession of a young and popular
king would make matters far more difficult.   It was no longer
possible to pose as the deliverer of Spain from the shameful predominance of Godoy.   Any move against Ferdinand must bear
the character of an open assault on the national independence of
the kingdom.

[1] Letter of March 26 in Toreño, i. 439.
[2] The Protest of Charles IV will be found printed in Appendix No. 4.

But Bonaparte had gone too far to recede: he had not moved 100,000 men across the Pyrenees, and seized Pampeluna and Barcelona, merely in order that his troops might assist at the coronation ceremonies of another Bourbon king. In spite of all difficulties he was resolved to persevere in his iniquitous plan. He would not recognize the new monarch, but would sweep him away, and put in his place some member of his own family. But his chosen instrument was not to be Murat, but one of the Bonapartes. He knew too well the Duke of Berg's restless spirit and overweening ambition to trust him with so great a charge as Spain. And he was right—with only Naples at his back Joachim was powerful enough to do his master grave harm in 1814. The tool was to be one of his own brothers. It was on the night of March 26 that the news of the abdication of Charles IV reached him: on the morning of the twenty-seventh he wrote to Amsterdam offering Louis Bonaparte the chance of exchanging the Dutch for the Spanish crown. The proposal was made in the most casual form —' You say that the climate of Holland does not suit you. Besides the country is too thoroughly ruined to rise again. Give me a categorical answer: if I nominate you King of Spain will you take the offer; can I count on you?[1]' Louis very wisely refused the proffered crown: but his weaker brother Joseph, tired of Naples and its brigands, made no scruples when the same proposal was laid before him.

This letter to Louis of Holland having been written on the first news of the events at Aranjuez, and four days before Murat began to send in his own plans and the letters of protest from the King and Queen of Spain, it is clear that the Emperor had never any intention of recognizing Ferdinand, and was only playing with him during the month that followed. It was not in mere caution that Beauharnais, the ambassador, and Murat, the military representative, of France, were bidden never to address the new sovereign as king but as Prince of the Asturias, and to act as if Charles IV were still legally reigning until they should have specific directions from Paris[2].

---

[1] *Nap. Corresp.*, xvi. 500; see also in *Documents historiques, publiés par Louis Bonaparte* (Paris, 1829), ii. 290.

[2] It is scarcely necessary to say that the letter which Napoleon is said to have sent Murat on March 29, and which is printed in the *Mémorial de Ste-Hélène*, is (as Lanfrey and Count Murat have shown) a forgery composed by

This state of semi-suspended relations lasted for a fortnight, from Ferdinand's arrival in Madrid on March 24, down to his departure from it on April 10. They were very uncomfortable weeks for the new king, who grew more alarmed as each day passed without a letter from Paris ratifying his title, while French troops continued to pour into Madrid till some 35,000 were assembled in it and its suburbs.

A very few days after his accession Ferdinand was informed that it was probable that Napoleon was intending a visit to Madrid, and was at any rate coming as far as Bayonne. He immediately sent off his eldest brother Don Carlos (the hero of the unhappy wars of 1833-40) to compliment his patron, and if necessary to receive him at the frontier [April 5]. Two days later there appeared in Madrid a new French emissary, General Savary— afterwards Duke of Rovigo—who purported to come as Bonaparte's harbinger, charged with the duty of preparing Madrid for his arrival. He carried the farce so far that he asked for a palace for the Emperor's residence, produced trunks of his private luggage [1], and began to refurnish the apartments granted him. That he bore secret orders for Murat we know from the latter's dispatches, but this was only half his task. Napoleon had confided to him verbal instructions to lure Ferdinand to come out to meet him in the north of Spain, among the French armies massed in Biscay and Navarre—if possible even to get him to Bayonne on French soil. In his St. Helena memoirs Napoleon denies this, and Savary in his autobiography also states that he did not act the part of tempter or make any promises to the young king: the journey to Bayonne, he says, was a silly inspiration of Ferdinand's own. But neither Bonaparte nor Savary are witnesses whom one would believe on their most solemn oath. The former we know well: the latter had been one of the persons most implicated in the shocking murder of the Duc d'Enghien. When we find the Spanish witnesses, who conversed with Savary during his short stay in Madrid, agreeing that the general promised that Napoleon would recognize Ferdinand as king, give him an imperial princess as wife, and take him into favour, we need not doubt them. It is not disputed

Napoleon himself long after. It is quite inconsistent with the offer to Louis Bonaparte, and with other letters to Murat of the same week.

[1] It is said that they afterwards turned out to be full of smuggled goods, a private speculation of Savary or his underlings.

that Savary, unlike Murat and Beauharnais, regularly addressed his victim by the royal title, and it is certain that he started in his company and acted as his keeper during the journey[1].   The move that he at first proposed was not a long one: the general said that according to his advices the Emperor must be due at Burgos on April 13: it would be time enough to start to meet him on the tenth.   Burgos lies well inside the frontiers of Castile, and if it was packed with French troops, so was Madrid: one place was no more dangerous than the other.

Exactly how far the perjuries of Savary went, or how far he was apprised of his master's final intentions, we cannot tell, but it is certain that on April 10 he set out from Madrid in the King's company: with them went Escoiquiz, Ferdinand's clerical confidant, Cevallos the minister of foreign affairs, and half a dozen dukes and marquises chosen from among the King's old partisans.   To administer affairs in his absence Ferdinand nominated a 'Junta' or council of regency, with his uncle Don Antonio, a simple and very silly old man, at its head[2].

On reaching Burgos, on April 12, the party found masses of French troops but no signs of Napoleon.   Savary appeared vexed, said that his calculation must have been wrong, and got the King to go forward two more stages, as far as Vittoria, at the southern foot of the Pyrenees [April 14].   Here Ferdinand received a note from his brother Don Carlos, whom he had sent ahead, saying that Bonaparte had been lingering at Bordeaux, and was not expected at Bayonne till the fifteenth.   Ferdinand, always timid and suspicious, was getting restive : he had nothing on paper to assure him of Napoleon's intentions, and began to suspect Savary's blandishments.   The latter doubted for a moment whether he should not have the court seized by the French garrison of Vittoria, but

---

[1] Savary, in his mendacious autobiography, denies that he persuaded Ferdinand to start for Bayonne.   But he is refuted by two contemporary documents.   The young king, in his letter of adieu to his father, states that Savary has convinced him of the necessity of going ; while Murat in a dispatch to Bonaparte says that ' Savary has in no small degree contributed to induce the new court to quit Madrid ' [April 8].

[2] For Don Antonio's habits we have on Talleyrand's authority some very curious stories.   He spent most of his time of captivity at Valençay sitting in the library, mutilating illustrated books with his scissors, not to make a scrap-book, but to destroy any engravings that sinned against morals or religion !

finally resolved to endeavour to get a letter from his master, which would suffice to lure Ferdinand across the frontier. He was entrusted with a petition of the same cast that Napoleon had been in the habit of receiving from his would-be client, full of servile loyalty and demands for the much-desired Bonaparte princess.

The four days during which Savary was absent, while the royal party remained at Vittoria, were a period of harassing doubt to Ferdinand. He was visited by all manner of persons who besought him not to go on, and especially by Spaniards lately arrived from Paris, who detailed all the disquieting rumours which they had heard at the French court. Some besought him to disguise himself and escape by night from the 4,000 troops of the Imperial Guard who garrisoned Vittoria. Others pointed out that the Spanish troops in Bilbao, which was still unoccupied by the French, might be brought down by cross-roads, and assume charge of the king's person halfway between Vittoria and the frontier, in spite of the 600 French cavalry which escorted the cavalcade. Guarded by his own men Ferdinand might retire into the hills of Biscay. But to adopt either of the courses proposed to him would have compelled the King to come to an open breach with Bonaparte, and for this he had not sufficient courage, as long as there was the slightest chance of getting safely through his troubles by mere servility.

On April 18 Savary reappeared with the expected communication from Bayonne. It was certainly one of the strangest epistles that one sovereign ever wrote to another, and one of the most characteristic products of Napoleon's pen. It was addressed to the Prince of the Asturias, not to the King of Spain, which was an ominous preface. But on the other hand the Emperor distinctly stated that ' he wished to conciliate his friend in every way, and to find occasion to give him proofs of his affection and perfect esteem.' He added that ' the marriage of your royal highness to a French princess seems conformable to the interests of my people, and likely to forge new links of union between myself and the house of Bourbon.' The core of the whole was the explicit statement that ' if the abdication of King Charles was spontaneous, and not forced on him by the riot at Aranjuez, I shall have no difficulty in recognizing your royal highness as King of Spain. On these details I wish to converse with your royal highness.' This was a double-edged saying : Napoleon had in his pocket Charles's protest, complaining that the abdication had been forced upon him by fears

for his personal safety: but Ferdinand was not aware of the fact;
indeed he so little realized his parent's state of mind that he had
written to him before quitting Madrid in the most friendly terms.
If he had fathomed the meaning of Napoleon's carefully constructed sentence, he would have fled for his life to the mountains.

These were the main clauses of Napoleon's letter, but they are
embedded in a quantity of turgid verbiage, in which we are only
uncertain whether the hypocrisy or the bad taste is the more
offensive. 'How perilous is it for kings to permit their subjects
to seek justice for themselves by deeds of blood! I pray God that
your royal highness may not experience this for yourself some day!
It is not for the interest of Spain that the Prince of the Peace
should be hunted down: he is allied by marriage to the royal house
and has governed the realm for many years. He has no friends
now: but if your royal highness were to fall into similar disgrace
you would have no more friends than he. You cannot touch him
without touching your parents. You have no rights to the crown
save those which your mother has transmitted to you: if in trying
the Prince you smirch her honour, you are destroying your own
rights. You have no power to bring him to judgement: his evil
deeds are hidden behind the throne. . . . O wretched Humanity!
Weakness, and Error, such is our device! But all can be hushed
up: turn the Prince out of Spain, and I will give him an asylum in
France.'

In the next paragraph Napoleon tells Ferdinand that he should
never have written to him in the preceding autumn without his
father's knowledge—'in that your royal highness was culpable;
but I flatter myself that I contributed by my remonstrances in
securing a happy end to the affair of the Escurial.' Finally
Ferdinand might assure himself that he should have from his ally
precisely the same treatment that his father had always experienced
—which again is a double-edged saying, if we take into consideration
the history of the relations of Charles IV and France.

The King and his confidant Escoiquiz read and reread this
curious document without coming to any certain conclusion:
probably they thought (as would any one else who did not know
the Emperor thoroughly) that the meeting at Bayonne would open
with a scolding, and end with some tiresome concessions, but that
Ferdinand's title would be recognized. Savary's commentary was
reassuring: Spanish witnesses say that he exclaimed 'I am ready to

have my head taken off if, within a quarter of an hour of your majesty's arrival at Bayonne, the Emperor has not saluted you as King of Spain and the Indies. . . . The whole negotiation will not take three days, and your majesty will be back in Spain in a moment [1].'

On April 19, therefore, the royal party set out amid the groans of the populace of Vittoria, who tried to hold back the horses, and to cut the traces of the King's coach : on the twentieth they reached Bayonne. Napoleon entertained them at dinner, but would not talk politics : after the meal they were sent home to the not very spacious or magnificent lodgings prepared for them. An hour later the shameless Savary presented himself at the door, with the astounding message that the Emperor had thought matters over, and had come to the conclusion that the best thing for Spain would be that the house of Bourbon should cease to reign, and that a French prince should take their place. A prompt acquiescence in the bargain should be rewarded by the gift of the kingdom of Etruria, which had just been taken from Ferdinand's widowed sister and her young son.

The possibility of such an outrage had never occurred to the young king and his counsellors : when something of the kind had been suggested to them at Vittoria, they had cried out that it was insulting to the honour of the greatest hero of the age to dream that he could be plotting treachery [2]. And now, too late, they learnt the stuff of which heroes were made. Even with Savary's words ringing in their ears, they could not believe that they had heard aright. It must be some mere threat intended to frighten them before negotiations began : probably it meant that Spain would have to cede some American colonies or some Catalonian frontier districts. Next morning, therefore, Ferdinand sent his minister Cevallos to plead his cause : Napoleon refused to bargain or compromise : he wanted nothing, he said, but a prompt resignation of his rights by the Prince of the Asturias : there was nothing left to haggle about. It was gradually borne in upon Ferdinand that the Emperor meant what he had said. But though timid he was obstinate, and nothing like an abdication could be got out of him. He merely continued to send to Napoleon one agent after another

[1] Cevallos, p. 36.

[2] It was the Duke of Infantado who made this exclamation. See Urquijo's letter to Cuesta in Llorente's collection of papers on the Bayonne business.

—first the minister Cevallos, then his tutor and confidant Escoiquiz, then Don Pedro Labrador, a councillor of state, all charged with professions of his great readiness to do anything, short of resigning the Spanish throne, which might satisfy his captor.   Cevallos and Escoiquiz have left long narratives of their fruitless embassies. That of the latter is especially interesting : he was admitted to a long conference with Bonaparte, in which he plied every argument to induce him to leave Ferdinand on the throne, after marrying him to a French princess and exacting from him every possible guarantee of fidelity.   The Emperor was ready to listen to every remonstrance, but would not move from his projects.   He laughed at the idea that Spain would rise in arms, and give him trouble. 'Countries full of monks, like yours,' he said, ' are easy to subjugate. There may be some riots, but the Spaniards will quiet down when they see that I offer them the integrity of the boundaries of the monarchy, a liberal constitution, and the preservation of their religion and their national customs [1].'

When such were Napoleon's ideas it was useless to argue with him.   But Ferdinand refused to understand this, and kept reiterating all sorts of impracticable offers of concession and subservience, while refusing to do the one thing which the Emperor required of him.   Napoleon, much irritated at the refusal of such a poor creature to bow to his will, has left a sketch of him during these trying days.   'The Prince of the Asturias,' he wrote, 'is very stupid, very malicious, a very great hater of France. . . . He is a thoroughly uninteresting person, so dull that I cannot get a word out of him.   Whatever one says to him he makes no reply. Whether I scold him, or whether I coax him, his face never moves. After studying him you can sum him up in a single word—he is a sulky fellow [2].'

As Ferdinand would not budge, Bonaparte had now to bring his second device to the front.   With the old king's protest before him, the Emperor could say that Charles IV had never abdicated in any real sense of the word.   He had been made to sign a resignation ' with a pistol levelled at his head,' as a leading article in the *Moniteur* duly set forth.   Such a document was, of course, worth nothing : therefore Charles was still King of Spain, and might sign

[1] Escoiquiz, p. 318.   Every student of Napoleon should read the whole of the wonderful dialogue between the Emperor and the Canon of Toledo.

[2] Napoleon to Talleyrand, May 6, 1808.

that surrender of his rights which Ferdinand denied. Napoleon promptly sent for the old king and queen, who arrived under a French escort on April 30, ten days after their son's captivity began. At Bayonne they rejoined their · dearly-loved Godoy, whom Murat had extorted from the Junta of Regency, under cover of a consent sent by Ferdinand to Napoleon from Vittoria two days before he crossed the frontier.

Charles IV arrived in a state of lachrymose collapse, sank on Napoleon's breast and called him his true friend and his only support. 'I really do not know whether it is his position or the circumstances, but he looks like a good honest old man,' commented the Emperor. 'The Queen has her past written on her face—that is enough to define her. As to the Prince of the Peace, he looked like a prize bull, with a dash of Count Daru about him.' Godoy and the Queen had only one thought, to avenge themselves on Ferdinand: after what had taken place they could never go back to rule in Spain, so they cared little what happened to the country. As to the King, his wife and his favourite pulled the strings, and he gesticulated in the fashion that they desired. The Emperor treated them with an ostentatious politeness which he had always refused to the new king: at the first banquet that he gave them occurred the absurd scene (already mentioned by us), in which Charles refused to sit down to table till Godoy had been found and put near him.

Two days after their arrival Napoleon compelled Ferdinand to appear before his parents: he himself was also present. The interview commenced by King Charles ordering his son to sign a complete and absolute renunciation of the Spanish throne. Bonaparte then threw in a few threatening words: but Ferdinand, still unmoved, made a steady refusal. At this the old king rose from his chair—he was half-crippled with rheumatism—and tried to strike his son with his cane, while the Queen burst in with a stream of abuse worthy of a fishwife. Napoleon, horrified at the odious scene, according to his own narrative of it, hurried Ferdinand, 'who looked scared,' out of the room.

The same night [May 1], Ferdinand's advisers bethought them of a new and ingenious move—we need not ascribe it to his own

---

[1] Of this interview we have the version of Napoleon himself in a dispatch to Murat, dated May 1 ; another by Cevallos, Ferdinand's minister ; a third by De Pradt (afterwards Archbishop of Mechlin), then present at Bayonne.

brains, which were surely incapable of the device. He wrote to King Charles to the effect that he had always regarded the abdication at Aranjuez as free and unconstrained, but that if it had not been so, he was ready to lay down his crown again and hand it back to his father. But the ceremony must be done in an open and honourable way at Madrid, before the Cortes. If his parent personally resumed the reins of power, he bowed to his authority: but if his age and infirmities induced him to name a regent, that regent should be his eldest son.

This proposal did not suit the Emperor at all, so he dictated to the old king a long letter, in which the Napoleonesque phraseology peeps out in a score of places. Charles refuses all terms, says that his son's conduct had 'placed a barrier of bronze between him and the Spanish throne,' and concludes that 'only the Emperor can save Spain, and he himself would do nothing that might stir up the fire of discord among his loved vassals or bring misery on them [May 2]. Ferdinand replied with an equally long letter justifying at large all his conduct of the past year [May 4].

When things stood at this point there arrived from Madrid the news of the bloody events of the second of May, which we have to relate in the next chapter. This brought Napoleon up to striking point, and once more he intervened in his own person. He sent for Ferdinand, and in the presence of his parents accused him of having stirred up the riot in the capital, and informed him that if he did not sign an abdication and an acknowledgement of his father as the only true king by twelve that night 'he should be dealt with as a traitor and rebel.' This is Napoleon's own version[1], but Spanish witnesses say that the words used were that 'he must choose between abdication and death[2].'

To any one who remembered the fate of the Duc d'Enghien such a phrase was more than an idle threat. It brought the stubborn Ferdinand to his knees at last. That evening he wrote out a simple and straightforward form of abdication—'without any motive, save that I limited my former proposal for resignation by certain proper conditions, your majesty has thought fit to insult me in the presence of my mother and the Emperor. I have been abused in the most humiliating terms: I have been told that unless I make an unconditional resignation I and my companions

---

[1] Dispatch to Murat of May 5.

[2] 'Prince, il faut opter entre la cession et la mort' (Cevallos, p. 60).

shall be treated as criminals guilty of conspiracy. Under such circumstances I make the renunciation which your majesty commands, that the government of Spain may return to the condition in which it was on March 19 last, the day on which your majesty *spontaneously* laid down your crown in my favour[1]' [May 6].

Ferdinand having abdicated, Napoleon at once produced a treaty which King Charles had ratified on the previous day, twenty-four hours before his son gave in. By it the old man 'resigned all his rights to the throne of Spain and the Indies to the Emperor Napoleon, the only person who in the present state of affairs can re-establish order.' He only annexed two conditions: '(1) that there should be no partition of the Spanish monarchy; (2) that the Roman Catholic religion should be the only one recognized in Spain: there should, according to the existing practice, be no toleration for any of the reformed religions, much less for infidels.' If anything is wanting to make the silly old man odious, it is the final touch of bigotry in his abdication. The rest of the document consists of a recital of the pensions and estates in France conferred by the Emperor on his dupe in return for the abdication. It took five days more to extort from Don Ferdinand a formal cession of his ultimate rights, as Prince of the Asturias, to the succession to the throne. It was signed on May 10, and purported to give him in return a palace in France and a large annual revenue. But he was really put under close surveillance at Talleyrand's estate of Valençay, along with his brother Don Carlos, and never allowed to go beyond its bounds. The Emperor's letter of instructions to Talleyrand is worth quoting for its cynical brutality. He wrote to his ex-minister, who was much disgusted with the invidious duty put upon him: 'Let the princes be received without any show, but yet respectably, and try to keep them amused. If you chance to have a theatre at Valençay there would be no harm in importing some actors now and then. You may bring over Mme de Talleyrand [the notorious Mme Grand of 1800], and four or five ladies in attendance on her. If the prince should fall in love with some pretty girl among them, there would be no harm in it, especially if you are quite sure of her. The prince must not be allowed to take any false step, but must be amused and occupied. I ought, for political safety, to put him in Bitche

[1] Toreño, Appendix, i. 466, 467.

or some other fortress-prison : but as he placed himself into my clutches of his own free will, and as everything in Spain is going on as I desire, I have resolved merely to place him in a country house where he can amuse himself under strict surveillance. . . . Your mission is really a very honourable one—to take in three[1] illustrious guests and keep them amused is a task which should suit a Frenchman and a personage of your rank[2].' Napoleon afterwards owned that he was framing what he called 'a practical joke' on Talleyrand, by billeting the Spaniards on him. The Prince of Benevento had wished to make no appearance in the matter, and the Emperor revenged himself by implicating him in it as the jailor of his captives. Talleyrand's anger may be imagined, and estimated by his after conduct.

At Valençay the unfortunate Ferdinand was destined to remain for nearly six years, not amusing himself at all according to Napoleon's ideas of amusement, but employed in a great many church services, a little partridge shooting, and (so his unwilling jailor tells us) the spoiling of much paper, not with the pen but with the scissors ; for he developed a childish passion for clipping out paper patterns and bestowing them on every one that he met. One could pardon him everything if he had not spoilt his attitude as victim and martyr by occasionally sending adulatory letters to the Emperor, and even to his own supplanter, Joseph Bonaparte the new King of Spain.

[1] The *third* prisoner was Ferdinand's uncle, Don Antonio.
[2] This letter, eliminated by the editors of the *Correspondance de Napoléon*, may be found in Lecestre, *Lettres inédites de Napoléon I*, i. p. 207.

SECTION I : CHAPTER VI

THE SECOND OF MAY : OUTBREAK OF THE SPANISH
INSURRECTION

WHEN King Ferdinand had taken his departure to Bayonne, the position of Murat in Madrid became very delicate. He might expect to hear at any moment, since the Emperor's plans were more or less known to him, either that the Spanish king had been made a prisoner, or that he had taken the alarm, escaped from his escort, and fled into the mountains. In either case trouble at Madrid was very probable, though there was no serious military danger to be feared, for of Spanish troops there were only 3,000 in the city, while some 35,000 French were encamped in or about it. But there might be a moment of confusion if the Junta of Regency should take violent measures on hearing of the King's fate, or the populace of Madrid (and this was much more likely) burst into rioting.

From the tenth of April, the day of the King's departure for the north, down to the twenty-ninth there was no serious cause for apprehension. The people were no doubt restless : they could not understand why the French lingered in Madrid instead of marching on Portugal or Gibraltar, according to their expressed intention. Rumours of all kinds, some of which hit off fairly well the true projects of Bonaparte, were current. Murat's conduct was not calculated to reassure observers ; he gave himself the airs of a military governor, rather than those of an officer engaged in conducting an allied army through friendly territory. Some of his acts gave terrible offence, such as that of insisting that the sword of Francis I, taken at Pavia in 1525, the pride for three centuries of the royal armoury, should be given up to him [1]. His

---

[1] Napoleon, disapproving of Murat's action on this point, committed himself to two astounding historical statements. ' Why trouble about the sword,' he wrote ; ' Francis I was a Bourbon [!] and he was taken by the Italians, not the Spaniards' [!!] (*Nap. Corresp.*, 13,724).

call on the Junta for the surrender of the Prince of the Peace,
whom he forwarded under French escort to Bayonne, could not
fail to be unpopular. But the first real signs of danger were not
seen till the twenty-second of April, when Murat, in obedience to
his master, intended to publish the protest of Charles IV against
his abdication. It was to be presented to the Junta in the form of
a letter to its president, Don Antonio. Meanwhile French agents
were set to print it : their Spanish underlings stole and circulated
some of the proofs. Their appearance raised a mob, for the name
of Charles IV could only suggest the reappearance of Godoy. An
angry crowd broke into the printing office, destroyed the presses,
and hunted away the Frenchmen. Murat at once made a great
matter of the affair, and began to threaten the Junta. 'The army
which he commanded could not without dishonouring itself allow
disorders to arise : there must be no more anarchy in Spain. He
was not going to allow the corrupt tools of the English government
to stir up troubles.' The Junta replied with rather more spirit
than might have been expected, asked why an army of 35,000
French troops had now lingered more than a month around the
capital, and expressed an opinion that the riot was but an explosion
of loyalty to Ferdinand. But they undertook to deal severely with
factious persons, and to discourage even harmless assemblies like
that of the twenty-second.

Meanwhile Murat wrote to the Emperor that it was absurd that
he could not yet establish a police of his own in Madrid, that he
could not print what he pleased, and that he had to negotiate with
the Junta when he wished his orders published, instead of being
able to issue them on his own authority[1]. He was answered in
a style which must have surprised him. Napoleon was ashamed, he
said, of a general who, with 50,000 men at his back, asked for
things instead of taking them. His letters to the Junta were
servile ; he should simply assume possession of the reins of power,
and act for himself. If the *canaille* stirred, let it be shot down[2].
Murat could only reply that 'if he had not yet scattered rioters by
a blast of grape, it was only because there were no mobs to shoot :
his imperial majesty's rebuke had stunned him "like a tile falling
on his head" by its unmerited severity[3].'

Within three days of this letter there was to be plenty of

---

[1] Murat to Napoleon, April 22.   [2] Napoleon to Murat, April 26.
[3] Murat to Napoleon, April 30.

grape-shot, enough to satisfy both Emperor and Grand-Duke. They probably had the revolt of Cairo and the 13th Vendémiaire in their mind, and were both under the impression that a good *émeute* pitilessly crushed by artillery was the best basis of a new régime.

On the night of April 29 the first clear and accurate account of what was happening at Bayonne arrived at Madrid. Napoleon had intercepted all the letters which Don Ferdinand had tried to smuggle out of his prison. He read them with grave disapproval, for his guest had not scrupled to use the expression 'the cursed French,' and had hinted at the propriety of resistance. He had not yet been cowed by the threat of a rebel's death. But on the twenty-third one of the Spaniards at Bayonne succeeded in escaping in disguise, crossed the mountains by a lonely track, and reached Pampeluna, whence he posted to Madrid. This was a certain Navarrese magistrate named Ibarnavarro, to whom Ferdinand had given a verbal message to explain Napoleon's plans and conduct to the Junta, and to inform them that he would never give in to this vile mixture of force and fraud. He could not send them any definite instructions, not knowing the exact state of affairs at Madrid, and a premature stroke might imperil the life of himself, his brother, and his companions: let them beware therefore of showing their warlike intentions till preparations had been fully made to shake off the yoke of the oppressor.

This message Ibarnavarro delivered on the night of April 29–30 to the Junta [1], who had summoned in to hear it a number of judges and other magnates of the city. Next morning, of course, the information, in a more or less garbled shape, spread all round Madrid: there were foolish rumours that the Biscayans had already taken arms, and that 30,000 of them were marching on Bayonne to save the King, as also that certain of the coast towns had invited the English to land. On the thirtieth leaflets, both written and printed, were being secretly circulated round the city, setting forth the unhappy condition of the King, and bidding his subjects not to forget Numancia [2]. It is astonishing that riots did

---

[1] Ibarnavarro's story, written down by himself on September 27, 1808, can be found printed in full on pp. 457–9 of the Appendix to Toreño's first volume.

[2] For a specimen see the document on p. 462 of Count Murat's *Murat en Espagne* (Paris, 1897).

not break out at once, considering the growing excitement of the people, and the habitual insolence of the French soldiery. But leaders were wanting, and in especial the Junta of Regency and its imbecile old president made no move whatever, on the pretext, apparently, that any commotion might imperil the lives of Napoleon's prisoners.

It was Murat himself who brought matters to a head next day, by ordering the Junta to put into his hands the remaining members of the royal family, Ferdinand's youngest brother Don Francisco, a boy of sixteen, and his sister the widowed and exiled Queen of Etruria, with her children. Only Don Antonio, the incapable president of the Junta, and the Archbishop of Toledo, the King's second-cousin, were to be left behind: the rest were to be sent to Bayonne. Knowing what had happened to Don Ferdinand and Don Carlos, the people were horrified at the news; but they trusted that the Regency would refuse its leave. To its eternal disgrace that body did nothing: it did not even try to smuggle away the young Don Francisco before Murat should arrest him.

On the morning, therefore, of May 2 the streets were filled with people, and the palace gates in especial were beset by an excited mob. It was soon seen that the news was true, for the Queen of Etruria appeared and started for the north with all her numerous family. She was unpopular for having sided with her mother and Godoy against Don Ferdinand, and was allowed to depart undisturbed. But when the carriage that was to bear off Don Francisco was brought up, and one of Murat's aides-de-camp appeared at the door to take charge of the young prince, the rage of the crowd burst all bounds. The French officer was stoned, and saved with difficulty by a patrol: the coach was torn to pieces. Murat had not been unprepared for something of the kind: the battalion on guard at his palace was at once turned out, and fired a dozen volleys into the unarmed mob, which fled devious, leaving scores of dead and wounded on the ground.

The Grand-Duke thought that the matter was over, but it had but just begun. At the noise of the firing the excited citizens flocked into the streets armed with whatever came to hand, pistols, blunderbusses, fowling-pieces, many only with the long Spanish knife. They fell upon, and slew, a certain number of isolated French soldiers, armed and unarmed, who were off duty and wandering round the town, but they also made a fierce attack

on Murat's guard. Of course they could do little against troops
armed and in order: in the first hour of the fight there were only
about 1,000 men at the Grand-Duke's disposal, but this small force
held its own without much loss, though eight or ten thousand
angry insurgents fell upon them. But within seventy minutes the
French army from the suburban camps came pouring into the city,
brigade after brigade. After this the struggle was little more than
a massacre: many of the insurgents took refuge in houses, and
maintained a fierce but futile resistance for some time; but the
majority were swept away in a few minutes by cavalry charges.
Only at one point did the fight assume a serious shape. Almost
the entire body of the Spanish garrison of Madrid refrained from
taking any part in the rising: without the orders of the Junta the
chiefs refused to move, and the men waited in vain for the orders
of their officers. But at the Artillery Park two captains, Daoiz
and Velarde, threw open the gates to the rioters, allowed them
to seize some hundreds of muskets, and when the first French
column appeared ran out three guns and opened upon it with
grape[1]. Though aided by no more than forty soldiers, and
perhaps 500 civilians, they beat off two assaults, and only
succumbed to a third. Daoiz was bayonetted, Velarde shot dead,
and their men perished with them; but they had poured three
volleys of grape into a street packed with the enemy, and caused
the only serious losses which the French suffered that day.

The whole struggle had occupied not more than four hours:
when it was over Murat issued an 'order of the day,' sentencing
all prisoners taken with arms in their hands, all persons discovered
with arms concealed in their houses, and all distributors of
seditious leaflets, 'the agents of the English government,' to be
shot. It seems that at least a hundred persons were executed under
this edict, many of them innocent bystanders who had taken no
part in the fighting. Next morning Murat withdrew his Draconian
decree, and no further fusilades took place. It is impossible, in the
conflict of authorities, to arrive at any clear estimate of the
numbers slain on each side on May 2[2]. Probably Toreño is not

---

[1] Napier (i. 15) says that Daoiz and Velarde were ' in a state of excitement
from drink,' a disgraceful French calumny. How could he bear to reproduce
such a libel on these unfortunate officers?

[2] The Junta, to soothe the feelings of Madrid, gave out that only 150
Spaniards had fallen. The *Moniteur* said that 2,000 criminals had been cut

far out when he estimates the whole at something over a thousand. Of these four-fifths must have been Spaniards, for the French only lost heavily at the arsenal: the number of isolated soldiers murdered in the streets at the first outbreak of the riot does not seem to have been very large.

Many French authors have called the rising a deliberate and preconcerted conspiracy to massacre the French garrison. On the other hand Spanish writers have asserted that Murat had arranged everything so as to cause a riot, in order that he might have the chance of administering a 'whiff of grape-shot,' after his master's plan. But it is clear that both are making unfounded accusations: if the insurrection had been premeditated, the Spanish soldiery would have been implicated in it, for nothing would have been easier than to stir them up. Yet of the whole 3,000 only forty ran out to help the insurgents. Moreover, the mob would have been found armed at the first commencement of trouble, which it certainly was not. On the other hand, if Murat had been organizing a massacre, he would not have been caught with no more than two squadrons of cavalry and five or six companies of infantry under his hand. These might have been cut to pieces before the troops from outside could come to their help. He had been expecting riots, and was prepared to deal with them, but was surprised by a serious insurrection on a larger scale than he had foreseen, and at a moment when he was not ready.

For a few days after May 2, Murat at Madrid and his master at Bayonne were both living in a sort of fools' paradise, imagining that 'the affairs of Spain were going off wonderfully well,' and that 'the party of Ferdinand had been crushed by the prompt suppression of its conspiracy.' The Grand-Duke had the simplicity or the effrontery to issue a proclamation in which he said 'that every good Spaniard had groaned at the sight of such disorders,' and another in which the insurrection was attributed to 'the machinations of our common enemy, i.e. the British government[1].' On May 4 Don Antonio laid down the presidency of the Junta without a word of regret, and went off to Bayonne, having first borrowed 25,000 francs from Murat. The latter, by virtue of

down or executed! Murat reported a loss of eighty men only, while Napier says that he has excellent French authority and eye-witnesses to the effect that 750 fell.

[1] Proclamations of May 2 and 3: there are originals in the *Vaughan Papers*.

a decree issued by Charles IV, then assumed the presidency of
the Junta of Regency. The rest of the members of that ignoble
body easily sank into his servile instruments, though they had at
last received a secret note smuggled out from Bayonne, in which
Ferdinand (the day before his abdication) told them to regard his
removal into the interior of France as a declaration of war, and to
call the nation to arms. To this they paid no attention, while
they pretended to take the document of resignation, which Bonaparte had forced him to sign, as an authentic and spontaneous
expression of his will. The fact is that twenty years of Godoy
had thoroughly demoralized the bureaucracy and the court of
Spain: if the country's will had not found better exponents than
her ministers and officials, Napoleon might have done what he
pleased with the Peninsula.

At present his sole interest seems to have lain in settling the
details of his brother Joseph's election to the Spanish throne.
Ferdinand's final resignation of all his rights having been signed
on May 10, the field was open for his successor. The Emperor
thought that some sort of deputation to represent the Spanish
nation ought to be got together, in order that his brother might
not seem to receive the crown from his own hands only. Murat
was first set to work to terrorize the Junta of Regency, and the
'Council of Castile,' a body which practically occupied much the
same position as the English Privy Council. At his dictation
the Junta yielded, but with an ill grace, and sent petitions to
Bayonne asking for a new monarch, and suggesting (as desired)
that the person chosen might be Joseph Bonaparte, King of
Naples [May 13]. Murat had just been informed that as all had
gone well with the Emperor's plans he should have his reward: he
might make his choice between the thrones of Naples and of
Portugal. He wisely chose the former, where the rough work of
subjection had already been done by his predecessor.

But resolved to get together something like a representative body
which might vote away the liberty of Spain, Napoleon nominated,
in the Madrid Gazette of May 24, 150 persons who were to go to
Bayonne and there ask him to grant them a king. He named a most
miscellaneous crowd—ministers, bishops, judges, municipal officers of
Madrid, dukes and counts, the heads of the religious orders, the Grand
Inquisitor and some of his colleagues, and six well-known Americans
who were to speak for the colonies. To the eternal disgrace of

the ruling classes of Spain, no less than ninety-one of the nominees were base enough to obey the orders given them, to go to Bayonne, and there to crave as a boon that the weak and incompetent Joseph Bonaparte might be set to govern their unhappy country, under the auspices of his brother the hero and regenerator.   Long before the degrading farce was complete, the whole country was in arms behind them, and they knew themselves for traitors.   The election of King Joseph I was only taken in hand on June 15, while twenty days before the north and south of Spain had risen in arms in the name of the captive Ferdinand VII.

It took a week for the news of the insurrection of May 2 to spread round Spain : in the public mouth it of course assumed the shape of a massacre deliberately planned by Murat.   It was not till some days later that the full details of the events at Bayonne got abroad.   But ever since the surprise of the frontier fortresses in February and March, intelligent men all over the country had been suspecting that some gross act of treachery was likely to be the outcome of the French invasion.   Yet in most of the districts of Spain there was a gap of some days between the arrival of the news of the King's captivity and the first outbreak of popular indignation.   The fact was that the people were waiting for the lawful and constituted authorities to take action, and did not move of themselves till it was certain that no initiative was to be expected from those in high places.   But Spain was a country which had long been governed on despotic lines ; and its official chiefs, whether the nominees of Godoy or of the knot of intriguers who had just won their way to power under Ferdinand, were not the men to lead a war of national independence.   Many were mere adventurers, who had risen to preferment by flattering the late favourite.   Others were typical bureaucrats, whose only concern was to accept as legitimate whatever orders reached them from Madrid : provided those orders were couched in the proper form and written on the right paper, they did not look to see whether the signature at the bottom was that of Godoy or of the Infante Don Antonio, or of Murat.   Others again were courtiers who owed their position to their great names, and not to any personal ability.   It is this fact that accounts for the fortnight or even three weeks of torpor that followed the events of the second and sixth of May.   Murat's orders during that space travelled over the country, and most of the captains-general and other authorities

seemed inclined to obey them.   Yet they were orders which should
have stirred up instant disobedience; the Mediterranean squadron
was to be sent to Toulon, where (if it did not get taken on the way
by the British) it would fall into the hands of Napoleon.   A large
detachment of the depleted regular army was to sail for Buenos
Ayres, with the probable prospect of finding itself ere long on the
hulks at Portsmouth, instead of on the shores of the Rio de la
Plata.   The Swiss regiments in Spanish pay were directed to be
transferred to the French establishment, and to take the oath to
Napoleon.   All this could have no object save that of diminishing
the fighting power of the country.

The first province where the people plucked up courage to act
without their officials, and to declare war on France in spite of
the dreadful odds against them, was the remote and inaccessible
principality of the Asturias, pressed in between the Bay of Biscay
and the Cantabrian hills.   Riots began at its capital, Oviedo, as
early as the first arrival of the news from Madrid on May 9, when
Murat's edicts were torn down in spite of the feeble resistance of
the commander of the garrison and some of the magistrates.   The
Asturias was one of the few provinces of Spain which still preserved
vestiges of its mediaeval representative institutions.   It had a
'Junta General,' a kind of local 'estates,' which chanced to be in
session at the time of the crisis.   Being composed of local magnates and citizens, and not of officials and bureaucrats, this body
was sufficiently in touch with public opinion to feel itself borne on
to action.   After ten days of secret preparation, the city of Oviedo
and the surrounding country-side rose in unison on May 24: the
partisans of the new government were imprisoned, and next day
the estates formally declared war on Napoleon Bonaparte, and
ordered a levy of 18,000 men from the principality to resist invasion.   A great part of the credit for this daring move must be
given to the president of the Junta, the Marquis of Santa Cruz,
who had stirred up his colleagues as early as the thirteenth by
declaring that 'when and wherever one single Spaniard took arms
against Napoleon, he would shoulder a musket and put himself at
that man's side.'   The Asturians had no knowledge that other
provinces would follow their example; there was only one battalion
of regular troops and one of militia under arms in the province;
its financial resources were small.   Its only strength lay in the
rough mountains that had once sheltered King Pelayo from the

OMAN. I   F

Moors. It was therefore an astounding piece of patriotism when the inhabitants of the principality threw down the challenge to the victor of Jena and Austerlitz, confiding in their stern resolution and their good cause. All through the war the Asturias played a very creditable part in the struggle, and never let the light of liberty go out, though often its capital and its port of Gijon fell into French hands.

One of the first and wisest measures taken by the Asturian Junta was an attempt to interest Great Britain in the insurrection. On May 30 they sent to London two emissaries (one of whom was the historian Toreño) on a Jersey privateer, whose captain was persuaded to turn out of his course for the public profit. On June 7 they had reached London and had an interview with Canning, the Foreign Secretary of the Tory government which had lately come into power. Five days later they were assured that the Asturias might draw on England for all it required in the way of arms, munitions, and money. All this was done before it was known in England that any other Spanish province was stirring, for it was not till June 22 that the plenipotentiaries of the other juntas began to appear in London.

The revolt of other provinces followed in very quick succession. Galicia rose on May 30, in spite of its captain-general, Filanghieri, whose resistance to the popular voice cost him his popularity and, not long after, his life. Corunna and Ferrol, the two northern arsenals of Spain, led the way. This addition to the insurgent forces was very important, for the province was full of—troops the garrisons that protected the ports from English descents. There were eighteen battalions of regulars and fourteen of militia— a whole army—concentrated in this remote corner of Spain. Napoleon's plan of removing the Spanish troops from the neighbourhood of Madrid had produced the unintended result of making the outlying provinces very strong for self-defence.

It is more fitting for a Spanish than an English historian to descend into the details of the rising of each province of Spain. The general characteristics of the outburst in each region were much the same : hardly anywhere did the civil or military officials in charge of the district take the lead. Almost invariably they hung back, fearing for their places and profits, and realizing far better than did the insurgents the enormous military power which they were challenging. The leaders of the movement were either

local magnates not actually holding office—like the celebrated
Joseph Palafox at Saragossa—or demagogues of the streets, or
(but less frequently than might have been expected) churchmen.
Napoleon was quite wrong when he called the Spanish rising 'an
insurrection of monks.' The church followed the nation, and not
the nation the church: indeed many of the spiritual hierarchy
were among the most servile instruments of Murat. Among them
was the primate of Spain, the Archbishop of Toledo, who was
actually a scion of the house of Bourbon. There were many
ecclesiastics among the dishonoured ninety-one that went to
Bayonne, if there were others who (like the Bishop of Santander)
put themselves at the head of their flocks when the country took
arms.

It was a great misfortune for Spain that the juntas, which were
everywhere formed when the people rose, had to be composed in
large part of men unacquainted with government and organization.
There were many intelligent patriots among their members, a certain
number of statesmen who had been kept down or disgraced by
Godoy, but also a large proportion of ambitious windbags and
self-seeking intriguers. It was hard to constitute a capable government, on the spur of the moment, in a country which had suffered
twenty years of Godoy's rule.

An unfortunate feature of the rising was that in most of the
provinces, and especially those of the south, it took from the first
a very sanguinary cast. It was natural that the people should
sweep away in their anger every official who tried to keep them
down, or hesitated to commit himself to the struggle with France.
But there was no reason to murder these weaklings or traitors, in
the style of the Jacobins. There was a terrible amount of assassination, public and private, during the first days of the insurrection.
Three captains-general were slain under circumstances of brutal
cruelty—Filanghieri in Galicia, Torre del Fresno in Estremadura,
Solano at Cadiz. The fate of Solano may serve as an example: he
tried to keep the troops from joining the people, and vainly
harangued the mob: pointing to the distant sails of the English
blockading squadron he shouted, 'There are your real enemies!'
But his words had no effect: he was hunted down in a house where
he took refuge, and was being dragged to be hung on the public
gallows, when the hand of a fanatic (or perhaps of a secret friend
who wished to spare him a dishonourable death) dealt him a fatal

stab in the side. Gregorio de la Cuesta, the Governor-General of Old Castile, who was destined to play such a prominent and unhappy part in the history of the next two years, nearly shared Solano's fate. The populace of Valladolid, where he was residing, rose in insurrection like those of the other cities of Spain. They called on their military chief to put himself at their head; but Cuesta, an old soldier of the most unintelligent and brainless sort, hated mob-violence almost more than he hated the French. He held back, not from a desire to serve Bonaparte, but from a dislike to being bullied by civilians. The indignant populace erected a gallows outside his house and came to hang him thereon. It was not, it is said, till the rope was actually round his neck that the obstinate old man gave in. The Castilians promptly released him, and put him at the head of the armed rabble which formed their only force. Remembering the awful slaughter at Cabezon, at Medina de Rio Seco, and at Medellin, which his incapacity and mulish obstinacy was destined to bring about, it is impossible not to express the wish that his consent to take arms had been delayed for a few minutes longer.

All over Spain there took place, during the last days of May and the first week of June, scores of murders of prominent men, of old favourites of Godoy, of colonels who would not allow their regiments to march, of officials who had shown alacrity in obeying the orders of Murat. In the Asturias and at Saragossa alone do the new juntas seem to have succeeded in keeping down assassination. The worst scenes took place at Valencia, where a mad priest, the Canon Baltasar Calvo, led out a mob of ruffians who in two days [June 6–7] murdered 338 persons, the whole colony of French merchants residing in that wealthy town. It is satisfactory to know that when the Junta of Valencia felt itself firmly seated in the saddle of power, it seized and executed this abominable person and his chief lieutenants. In too many parts of Spain the murderers went unpunished: yet remembering the provocation which the nation had received, and comparing the blood shed by mob-violence with that which flowed in Revolutionary France, we must consider the outburst deplorable rather than surprising.

When the insurrection had reached its full development, we find that it centred round five points, in each of which a separate junta had seized on power and begun to levy an army. The most powerful focus was Seville, from which all Andalusia took its directions : indeed the Junta of Seville had assumed the arrogant style of ' supreme Junta of Spain and the Indies,' to which it had no legitimate title. The importance of Andalusia was that it was full of troops, the regular garrisons having been joined by most of the expeditionary corps which had returned from southern Portugal. Moreover it was in possession of a full treasury and a fleet, and had free communication with the English at Gibraltar. On June 15 the Andalusians struck the first military blow that told on Napoleon, by bombarding and capturing the French fleet (the relics of Trafalgar) which lay at their mercy within the harbour of Cadiz.

The second in importance of the centres of resistance was Galicia, which was also fairly well provided with troops, and contained the arsenals of Ferrol and Corunna. The risings in Asturias, and the feebler gatherings of patriots in Leon and Old Castile, prac- tically became branches of the Galician insurrection, though they were directed by their own juntas and tried to work for themselves. It was on the army of Galicia that they relied for support, and without it they would not have been formidable. The boundaries of this area of insurrection were Santander, Valladolid, and Sego- via: further east the troops of Moncey and Bessières, in the direction of Burgos and Aranda, kept the country-side from rising. There were sporadic gatherings of peasants in the Upper Ebro valley and the mountains of Northern Castile, but these were mere un- organized ill-armed bands that half a battalion could disperse. It was the same in the Basque Provinces and Navarre : here too the French lay cantoned so thickly that it was impossible to meddle with them: their points of concentration were Vittoria and the two fortresses of Pampeluna and San Sebastian.

The other horn of the half-moon of revolt, which encircled Madrid, was composed of the insurrections in Murcia and Valencia to the south and Aragon to the north. These regions were much less favourably situated for forming centres of resistance, because they were very weak in organized troops. When the Aragonese elected Joseph Palafox as their captain-general and declared war on France, there were only 2,000 regulars and one battery of artillery in their realm. The levies which they began to raise were nothing more than half-armed peasants, with no adequate body of officers to train and drill them. Valencia and Murcia were a little better off, because the arsenal of Cartagena and its garrison lay within their boundaries, but there were only 9,000 men in all under arms in the two provinces. Clearly they could not hope to deliver such a blow as Galicia or Andalusia might deal.

The last centre of revolt, Catalonia, did not fall into the same strategical system as the other four. It looked for its enemies not at Madrid, but at Barcelona, where Lecchi and Duhesme were firmly established ever since their *coup de main* in February. The Catalans had as their task the cutting off of this body of invaders from its communication with France, and the endeavour to prevent new forces from joining it by crossing the Eastern Pyrenees. The residence of the insurrectionary Junta was at Tarragona, but the most important point in the province for the moment was Gerona, a fortress commanding the main road from France, which Napoleon had not had the foresight to seize at the same moment that he won by treachery Barcelona and Figueras. While the Spaniards could hold it, they had some chance of isolating the army of Duhesme from its supports. In Catalonia, or in the Balearic Isles off its coast, there were in May 1808, about 16,000 men of regular troops, among whom there were only 1,200 soldiers of the cavalry arm. There was no militia, but by old custom the *levée en masse* might always be called out in moments of national danger. These irregulars, *somatenes* as they were called (from *somaten*, the alarm-bell which roused them), turned out in great numbers according to ancient custom : they had been mobilized thirteen years before in the French War of 1793–5 and their warlike traditions were by no means forgotten. All through the Peninsular struggle they made a very creditable figure, considering their want of organization and the difficulty of keeping them together.

The French armies, putting aside Duhesme's isolated force at Barcelona, lay compactly in a great wedge piercing into the heart of Spain. Its point was at Toledo, just south of Madrid : its base was a line drawn from San Sebastian to Pampeluna across the Western Pyrenees. Its backbone lay along the great high road from Vittoria by Burgos to Madrid. The advantageous point of this position was that it completely split Central Spain in two : there was no communication possible between the insurgents of Galicia and those of Aragon. On the other hand the wedge was long and narrow, and exposed to be pierced by a force striking at it either from the north-east or the north-west. The Aragonese rebels were too few to be dangerous ; but the strong Spanish army of Galicia was well placed for a blow at Burgos, and a successful attack in that direction would cut off Madrid from France, and leave the troops in and about the capital, who formed the point of the intrusive wedge, in a very perilous condition. This is the reason why, in the first stage of the war, Napoleon showed great anxiety as to what the army of Galicia might do, while professing comparative equanimity about the proceedings of the other forces of the insurrection.

Having thus sketched the strategic position of affairs in the Peninsula during the first days of June, we must set ourselves to learn the main characteristics of the military geography of Spain, and to estimate the character, organization, and fighting value of the two armies which were just about to engage. Without some knowledge of the conditions of warfare in Spain, a mere catalogue of battles and marches would be absolutely useless.

SECTION II
THE LAND AND THE COMBATANTS

CHAPTER I

MILITARY GEOGRAPHY OF THE PENINSULA : MOUNTAINS, RIVERS, ROADS

Of all the regions of Europe, the Iberian Peninsula possesses the best marked frontier. It is separated from France, its only neighbour, by one broad range of mountains, which defines its boundaries even more clearly than the Alps mark those of Italy. For the Alps are no single chain, but a system of double and triple chains running parallel to each other, and leaving between them debatable lands such as Savoy and the Southern Tyrol. Between Spain and France there is no possibility of any such claims and counter-claims. It is true that Roussillon, where the eastern end of the Pyrenean range runs into the sea, was Spanish down to 1659, but that was a political survival from the Middle Ages, not a natural union : there can be no doubt that geographically Roussillon is a French and not an Iberian land : the main backbone of the boundary chain lies south and not north of it.

The Pyrenees, though in height they cannot vie with the Alps, and though they are not nearly so jagged or scarped as the greater chain, are extremely difficult to cross, all the more so because the hand of man has seldom come to help the hand of nature in making practicable lines of access between France and Spain. In the whole length between the Bay of Biscay and the Mediterranean there are only two short fronts where intercommunication is easy, and these lie at the extreme east and west, where the mountains touch the sea. In the 250 miles which intervene there is hardly one good pass practicable for wheeled traffic or for the march of an army : most are mere mule-paths, rarely used save by smugglers and shepherds. The only one of these minor routes employed in the war was that which leads from Jaca in Aragon to Oloron in

Béarn, and that was not much used: only on one single occasion in 1813 does it appear prominently in history, when Clausel's French division, fleeing before Wellington and pressed up against the foot of the mountains, escaped across it with some difficulty.

The only passes that were systematically employed during the war were those which lie close to the water at each end of the Pyrenean chain. At the eastern end there are three which lead from Roussillon into Catalonia. One hugs the water's edge, and crawls along under the cliffs from Perpignan to Rosas: this was not in 1808 the most important of the three, though it is the one by which the railway passes to-day. Inland there are two other roads over difficult crests—one ten, the other forty miles from the shore— the former from Bellegarde to Figueras, the other from Mont-louis to Puycerda and Vich. The first was the pass most used in the war, being less exposed than the Rosas route to English de-scents from the sea: the coast road could actually be cannonaded by warships at some corners. It was blocked indeed by the fortress of Figueras, but that stronghold was only in Spanish hands for a very short period of the war. The inmost, or Mont-louis-Puycerda road was bad, led into nothing more than a few upland valleys, and was very little employed by the French. It would have been of importance had it led down into the lowlands of Aragon, but after taking a long turn in the hills it harks back towards the Catalan coast, and joins the other two roads near Gerona—a fortress which is so placed as practically to command every possible access into Eastern Spain.

Taking all three of these paths into Catalonia together, they do but form a sort of back door into the Iberian Peninsula. They only communicate with the narrow eastern coast-strip from Bar-celona to Valencia. There is no direct access from them into Castile, the heart of the country, and only a roundabout entrance by Lerida into Aragon. The great mass of the Catalan and Valencian Sierras bars them out from the main bulk of the Spanish realm. Catalonia and Valencia, wealthy and in parts fertile as they are, are but its back premises.

The true front door of the kingdom is formed by the passes at the other, the western, end of the Pyrenees. Here too we have three available routes, but they differ in character from the roads at the edge of the Mediterranean, in that they open up two com-pletely separate lines of advance into Spain, and do not (like the

Catalan defiles) all lead on to the same goal. All three start from Bayonne, the great southern fortress of Gascony. The first keeps for some time close to the seaside, and after crossing the Bidassoa, the boundary river of France and Spain, at Irun, leaves the fortress of San Sebastian a few miles to its right and then charges the main chain of the mountains. It emerges at Vittoria, the most northerly town of importance in the basin of the Ebro. A few miles further south it crosses that stream, and then makes for Burgos and Madrid, over two successive lines of Sierras. It opens up the heart of both Old and New Castile. The other two roads from Bayonne strike inland at once, and do not hug the Biscayan shore like the Irun-Vittoria route. They climb the Pyrenees, one by the pass of Maya, the other, twenty miles further east, by the more famous pass of Roncesvalles, where Charlemagne suffered disaster of old, and left the great paladin, Roland, dead behind him. The Maya and Roncesvalles roads join, after passing the mountains, at the great fortress of Pampeluna, the capital of Navarre. From thence several lines are available for the invader, the two chief of which are the roads into Old Castile by Logroño and into Aragon by Tudela. Pampeluna is quite as valuable as Vittoria as the base for an attack on Central Spain.

The whole Iberian Peninsula has been compared, not inaptly, to an inverted soup-plate: roughly it consists of a high central plateau, surrounded by a flat rim. But no comparison of that kind can be pressed too hard, and we must remember that the rim is variable in width: sometimes, as on the north coast, and in the extreme south-east of the peninsula, it is very narrow, and much cut up by small spurs running down to the sea. But as a rule, and especially in Central Portugal, Andalusia, Murcia, and Valencia, it is broad and fertile. Indeed if we set aside the northern coast—Biscay, Asturias, and Galicia—we may draw a sharp division between the rich and semi-tropical coast plain, and the high, wind-swept, and generally barren central plateau. All the wealth of the land lies in the outer strip: the centre is its most thinly inhabited and worthless part. Madrid, lying in the very midst of the plateau, is therefore not the natural centre of the land in anything save a mathematical sense. It is a new and artificial town of the sixteenth century, pitched upon as an administrative capital by the Hapsburg kings; but in spite of the long residence of the court there, it never grew into a city of the first class. Summing

up its ineligibilities, an acute observer said that Madrid combined
'the soil of the Sahara, the sun of Calcutta, the wind of Edinburgh,
and the cold of the North Pole.' Though in no sense the natural
capital of the country, it has yet a certain military importance as
the centre from which the road-system of Spain radiates. There
is, as a glance at the map will show, no other point from which all
the main avenues of communication with the whole of the provinces
can be controlled. An invader, therefore, who has got possession
of it can make any combined action against himself very difficult.
But he must not flatter himself that the capture of Madrid carries
with it the same effect that the capture of Paris or Berlin or
Vienna entails. The provinces have no such feeling of dependence
on the national capital as is common in other countries. France
with Paris occupied by an enemy is like a body deprived of its
head. But for Andalusians or Catalonians or Galicians the occupation of Madrid had no such paralysing effect. No sentimental
affection for the royal residence—and Madrid was nothing more—
existed. And a government established at Seville or Cadiz, or any
other point, would be just as well (or as ill) obeyed as one that
issued its orders from the sandy banks of the Manzanares.

The main geographical, as well as the main political, characteristics of Spain are determined by its very complicated mountain-
system. It is a land where the rivers count for little, and the hills
for almost everything, in settling military conditions. In most
countries great rivers are connecting cords of national life: their
waters carry the internal traffic of the realm: the main roads lie
along their banks. But in Spain the streams, in spite of their
length and size, are useless. They mostly flow in deep-sunk beds,
far below the level of the surrounding country-side. Their rapid
current is always swirling round rocks, or dashing over sandbanks:
often they flow for mile after mile between cliffs from which it
is impossible to reach the water's edge. In the rainy season they
are dangerous torrents: in the summer all save the very largest
dwindle down into miserable brooks. A river in Spain is always
a sundering obstacle, never a line of communication. Only for a
few scores of miles near their mouths can any one of them be
utilized for navigation: the Douro can be so employed as far as
Freneda on the frontier of Portugal, the Tagus in good seasons
as far as Abrantes, the Guadalquivir to Seville. For the rest of
their long courses they are not available even for the lightest boats.

Spanish rivers, in short, are of importance not as lines of transit, but as obstacles. They form many fine positions for defence, but positions generally rendered dangerous by the fact that a very few days of drought may open many unsuspected fords, where just before there had been deep and impassable water. Rivers as broad as the Tagus below Talavera and the Douro at Toro were occasionally crossed by whole armies in dry weather. It was always hazardous to trust to them as permanent lines of defence.

It is the mountains which really require to be studied in detail from the military point of view. Speaking generally we may describe the Iberian system—as distinct from the Pyrenees—as consisting of one chain running roughly from north to south, so as to separate the old kingdoms of Castile and Aragon, while at right angles to this chain run a number of others, whose general courses are parallel to each other and run from east to west. There is no single name for the mountains which separate Castile and Aragon, nor do they form one continuous range. They are a number of separate systems, often divided from each other by wide gaps, and sometimes broadening out into high tablelands. The central nucleus, from which the rest run out, lies between the provinces of New Castile and Valencia, from Guadalajara in the former to Morella in the latter. Here there is a great ganglion of chaotic sierras, pierced by hardly a single practicable road. Northward, in the direction of Aragon, they sink down into the plain of the Ebro: southward they spread out into the lofty plateau of Murcia, but rise into higher and narrower ranges again as they get near the frontier of Andalusia.

This block of chains and plateaus forms the central watershed of Spain, which throws westward the sources of the Douro, Tagus, Guadiana, and Guadalquivir, and eastward those of the Xucar and Segura. The basins of these streams and their tributaries form three-fourths of the Iberian Peninsula. The rest consists mainly of the great valley of the Ebro: this hardly falls into the system, and is somewhat exceptional. It has been described as serving as a sort of wet-ditch to the main fortification of the peninsula. Starting in the western extension of the Pyrenees, quite close to the Bay of Biscay, it runs diagonally across Spain, more or less parallel to the Pyrenees, and falls into the Mediterranean between Catalonia and Valencia. It is more low-lying than the rest of the main valleys of Spain, is broader, and is not so much cramped and cut up by mountains running down to it at right angles to its course.

Behind the Ebro lie, chain after chain, the parallel sierras which mark off the divisions of the great central plateau of Spain. Arteche compares them to the waves of a great petrified sea, running some higher and some lower, but all washing up into jagged crests, with deep troughs between them.

The first and most northerly of these waves is that which we may call the range of Old Castile, which separates the basin of the Ebro from that of the Douro. At one end it links itself to the Pyrenean chain in the neighbourhood of Santander: at the other it curves round to join the more central sierras in the direction of Soria and Calatayud. It is the lowest of the chains which bound the central plateau of Spain, and is pierced by three practicable roads, of which the most important is that from Vittoria to Burgos.

Between this chain on the east and the Cantabrian mountains on the north lies the great plain of Old Castile and Leon, the heart of the elder Spanish monarchy, in the days when Aragon was still independent and Andalusia remained in the hands of the Moor. It is a fairly productive corn-producing land, studded with ancient cities such as Burgos, Palencia, Valladolid, Toro, Zamora, Salamanca. The *Tierra de Campos* (land of the plains), as it was called, was the granary of Northern Spain, the most civilized part of the kingdom, and the only one where there existed a fairly complete system of roads. For want of the isolated mountain chains which cut up most provinces of the Iberian Peninsula, it was hard to defend and easy to overrun. If the mountains that divide it from the Ebro valley are once passed, there is no way of stopping the invader till he reaches the border of Asturias, Galicia, or New Castile. The whole plain forms the valley of the Upper Douro and its tributaries, the Adaja, Pisuerga, Esla, Tormes, and the rest. It narrows down towards Portugal, as the mountains of Galicia on the one side and Estremadura on the other throw out their spurs to north and south. Hence the Lower Douro valley, after the Portuguese frontier has been passed, is a defile rather than a plain. Before Oporto and the estuary are reached, there are many places where the mountains on either side come right down to the river's edge.

The second chain is much more important, and more strongly

marked: it divides Old from New Castile, the valley of the Douro from that of the Tagus. In its central and western parts it is really a double range, with two narrow valleys between its chief ridges. These valleys are drained by the Zezere and Alagon, two tributaries of the Tagus which flow parallel for many scores of miles to the broad river which they feed. If we call this great system of mountains the chain of New Castile it is only for con-venience' sake: the Spaniards and Portuguese have no common name for them. In the east they are styled the Sierra de Ayllon ; above Madrid they are known as the Guadarrama—a name some-times extended to the whole chain. When they become double, west of Madrid, the northern chain is the Sierra de Gata, the southern the Sierra de Gredos. Finally in Portugal the extension of the Sierra de Gata is called the Sierra da Estrella, the southern parallel ridge the Sierra do Moradal. The whole system forms a very broad, desolate, and lofty belt of hills between the Tagus and Douro, through which the practicable passes are few and difficult. Those requiring notice are (1) the Somosierra Pass, through which runs the great northern road from Burgos to Madrid: its name is well remembered owing to the extraordinary way in which Napoleon succeeded in forcing it (against all the ordinary rules of war) in the winter of 1808. (2) There is a group of three passes, all within twelve miles of each other, across the Guadarrama, through which there debouch on to Madrid the main roads from North-western Spain—those from (*a*) Valladolid and Segovia, (*b*) from Astorga, Tordesillas, and Arevalo, (*c*) from Salamanca by Avila. After this group of passes there is a long space of impracticable hills, till we come to the chief road from north to south, parallel to the Portuguese frontier: it comes down the valley of the Alagon from Salamanca, by Baños and Plasencia, on to the great Roman bridge of Alcantara, the main passage over the Middle Tagus. This is a bad road through a desolate country, but the exigencies of war caused it to be used continually by the French and English armies, whenever they had to transfer them-selves from the valley of the Douro to that of the Tagus. Occasion-ally they employed a still worse route, a little further west, from Ciudad Rodrigo by Perales to Alcantara. When we get within the Portuguese frontier, we find a road parallel to the last, from Almeida by Guarda to Abrantes, also a difficult route, but like it in perpetual use: usually, when the French marched from Salamanca to Alcantara, Wellington moved in a corresponding way from near Almeida to Abrantes. This road runs along the basin of the Zezere, though not down in the trough of the river, but high up the hillsides above it. Spanish and Portuguese roads, as we shall see, generally avoid the river banks and run along the slopes far above them.

The next great chain across the Peninsula is that which separates the barren and sandy valley of the Upper Tagus from the still more desolate and melancholy plateau of La Mancha, the basin of the Guadiana. Of all the regions of Central Spain, this is the most thinly peopled and uninviting. In the whole valley there are only two towns of any size, Ciudad Real, the capital of La Mancha, and Badajoz, the frontier fortress against Portugal. The mountains north of the Guadiana are called first the Sierra de Toledo, then the Sierra de Guadalupe, lastly on the Portuguese frontier the Sierra de San Mamed. Their peculiarity, as opposed to the other cross-ranges of the Peninsula, is that at their eastern end they do not unite directly with the mountains of Valencia, but leave a broad gap of upland, through which the roads from Madrid to Murcia and Madrid to Valencia take their way. When the Sierra de Toledo once begins roads are very few. There are practically only three— (1) Toledo by San Vincente to Merida, a most break-neck route winding among summits for forty miles; (2) Almaraz by Truxillo to Merida, the main path from Tagus to Guadiana, and the most used, though it is difficult and steep; (3) Alcantara by Albuquerque to Badajoz, a bad military road parallel to the Portuguese frontier, continuing the similar route from Salamanca to Alcantara.

Leaving the barren basin of the Guadiana to proceed southward, we find across our path a range of first-rate importance, the southern boundary of the central plateaux of Spain: dropping down from its crest we are no longer among high uplands, but in the broad low-lying semi-tropical plain of Andalusia, the richest region of Spain. The chain between the fertile valley of the Guadalquivir and the barren plateau of La Mancha is known for the greater part of its course as the Sierra Morena, but in its western section it takes the name of Sierra de Constantino. The passes across it require special notice: the most eastern and the most important is that of Despeña-Perros, through which passes the high road from Madrid to Cordova, Seville, and Cadiz. At its southern exit was fought the fight of Baylen, in which the armies of Napoleon received their first great check by the surrender of Dupont and his 20,000 men on July 23, 1808. Higher up the defile lies another historic spot, on which Christian and Moor fought the decisive battle for the mastery of Spain in the early years of the thirteenth century, the well-known fight of Las Navas de Tolosa. The Despeña-Perros has two side-passes close to its left and right: the former is that of San Estevan del Puerto: the latter is known as the 'King's Gate' (Puerto del Rey). All these three defiles present tremendous difficulties to an assailant from the north, yet all were carried in a single rush by the armies of Soult and Sebastiani in 1810. The central pass of the Sierra Morena lies ninety miles to the left, and is of much less importance, as it starts from the most arid corner of La Mancha, and does not connect itself with any of the great roads from the north. It leads down on to Cordova from Hinojosa. Again sixty miles to the west three more passes come down on to Seville, the one by Llerena, the second by Monasterio, the third by Fregenal: they lead to Badajoz and Merida. These are easier routes through a less rugged country: they were habitually used by Soult in 1811 and 1812, when, from his Andalusian base at Seville, he used to go north to besiege or to relieve the all-important fortress of Badajoz.

Last of all the great Spanish chains is that which lies close along the Mediterranean Sea, forming the southern edge of the fertile Andalusian plain. It is the Sierra Nevada, which, though neither the longest nor the broadest of the ranges of the south, contains the loftiest peaks in Spain, Mulhaçen and La Veleta. This chain runs from behind Gibraltar along the shore, till it joins the mountains of Murcia, leaving only a very narrow coast-strip between its foot and the southern sea. Three roads cut it in its western half, which, starting from Granada, Ronda, and Antequera all come down to the shore at, or in the neighbourhood of, the great port of Malaga. The parts of the coast-line that are far from that city are only accessible by following difficult roads that run close to the water's edge.

We have still to deal with two corners of the Iberian Peninsula, which do not fall into any of the great valleys that we have described—Galicia and Northern Portugal in the north-west, and Catalonia in the north-east. The geographical conditions of the former region depend on the Cantabrian Mountains, the western continuation of the Pyrenees. This chain, after running for many miles as a single ridge, forks in the neighbourhood of the town of Leon. One branch keeps on in its original direction, and runs by the coast till it reaches the Atlantic at Cape Finisterre. The other turns south-west and divides Spain from Portugal as far as the sea. The angle between these forking ranges is drained by a considerable river, the Minho. The basins of this stream and its tributary the Sil, form the greater part of the province of Galicia. Their valleys are lofty, much cut up by cross-spurs, and generally barren. The access to them from Central Spain is by two openings. The main one is the high road from Madrid to Corunna by Astorga; it does not follow the course of either the Sil or the Minho, but charges cross-ridge after cross-ridge of the spurs of the Galician hills, till at last it comes down to the water, and forks into two routes leading the one to Corunna, the other to the still more important arsenal of Ferrol. The other gate of Galicia is a little to the south of Astorga, where a pass above the town of Puebla de Sanabria gives access to a steep and winding road parallel to the Portuguese frontier, which finally gets into the valley of the Minho, and turns down to reach the port of Vigo. It will be remembered that Sir John Moore, in his famous retreat, hesitated for some time at Astorga between the Vigo and Corunna roads, and finally chose the latter. His judgement was undoubtedly correct, but the best alternative was bad, for in winter even the Madrid-Corunna road, the main artery of this part of Spain, is distressing enough to an army. It does not follow any well-marked valley, but cuts across four separate ranges, every one of which in January was a nursery of torrents in its lower slopes, and an abode of snow in its upper levels. Besides the roads with which we have already dealt there is a third important line of communication in Galicia, that by the narrow coast-plain of the Atlantic, from Corunna by Santiago to Vigo, and thence into Portugal as far as Oporto. This would be a good road but for the innumerable river-mouths, small and great, which it has to cross: the road passes each stream just where it ceases to be tidal, and at each is fronted at right angles by a defensible position, which, if held by a competent enemy, is difficult to force from the front, and still more difficult to turn by a detour up-stream. Nevertheless it was by this route that Soult successfully invaded Northern Portugal in the spring of 1809. It must be remembered that he was only opposed by bands of peasants not even organized into the loosest form of militia.

The geography of Catalonia, the last Iberian region with which we have to deal, is more simple than that of Galicia. The land is formed by a broad mountain belt running out from the eastern end of the Pyrenees, parallel to the Mediterranean. From this chain the slopes run down and form on the eastern side a coast-plain, generally rather narrow, on the western a series of parallel valleys drained by tributaries of the Segre, the most important affluent of the Ebro. They all unite near Lerida, an important town and a great centre of roads. But two considerable rivers, the Ter and the Llobregat, have small basins of their own in the heart of the central mountain mass, which open down into the coast-plain by defiles, the one blocked by the peak of Montserrat, the other by the town of Gerona. During the greater part of the Peninsular War the French held the larger share of the shoreland, dominating it from the great fortress of Barcelona, which they had seized by treachery ere hostilities began. In 1811 they captured Tarragona also, the second capital of the sea coast. But they never succeeded in holding down all the small upland plains, and the minor passes that lead from one to the other. Hunted out of one the Spanish army took refuge in the next, and, though it dwindled down ultimately to a mass of guerilla bands, was never caught *en masse* and exterminated. There were too many bolt-holes among the network of hills, and the invaders never succeeded in stopping them all, so that down to the end of the war the patriots always maintained a precarious existence inland, descending occasionally to the shore to get ammunition and stores from the English squadrons which haunted the coast. They were supplied and reinforced from the Balearic Isles, which Napoleon could never hope to touch, for his power (like that of the witches of old) vanished when it came to running water. The survival of the Catalan resistance after the French had drawn a complete cordon around the hill-country, holding the whole coast-plain on the one hand, and Lerida and the Segre valley on the other, is one of the incidents of the war most creditable to Spanish constancy.

Having dealt with the physical geography of Spain, it is necessary for us to point out the way in which the natural difficulties of the country had influenced its main lines of communication. Roads always take the 'line of least resistance' in early days, and seek for easy passes, not for short cuts. The idea that 'time is money,' and that instead of going round two sides of a triangle it may be worth while to cut a new path across its base, in spite of all engineering difficulties, was one very unfamiliar to the Spaniard. Nothing shows more clearly the state of mediaeval isolation in which the kingdom still lay in 1808 than the condition of its roads. Wherever the country presented any serious obstacles, little or no attempt had been made to grapple with them since the days of the Romans. The energetic Charles III, alone among the kings of the seventeenth and eighteenth centuries, had done something to improve the system of intercommunication. He had, for example, superseded the old break-neck road from the plains of Leon into Galicia, by building the fine new *chaussée* from Astorga to Villafranca by Manzanal; but among the line of Hapsburg and Bourbon sovereigns Charles was a rare exception. Under the imbecile rule of his son (or rather of Godoy) improvements ceased, and internal communications were as much neglected as any other branch of state management. What roads there were, when the war of 1808 broke out, were in a state of dreadful neglect. The Spaniard was still too prone to go round an intolerable distance rather than attempt a serious piece of engineering work. Let us take, for example, the northern coast of Spain: the Cantabrian range is no doubt a most serious obstacle to intercourse between Castile and Leon, on the one side, and the maritime provinces of Asturias and Biscay on the other. But who would have conceived it possible that in a length of 300 miles of mountain, there should be no more than five roads practicable for wheeled traffic and artillery? Yet this was so: to get down from the central plateau to the coast there are only available these five routes—one from Leon to Oviedo, one from Burgos to Santander, one from Burgos to Bilbao, one from Vittoria to Bilbao, and one from Vittoria to San Sebastian and Irun. There were many other points at which a division travelling in light order without guns or baggage could cross the watershed—as was shown in Blake's flight from Reynosa and Ney's invasion of the Asturias. But for an army travelling with all its *impedimenta* such bypaths were impracticable.

Let us take another part of the Peninsula—its eastern side. The ancient separation between Aragon and Castile is fully reflected by the utter isolation of the two for intercommunication. To get from Madrid to the east coast there are only three roads suitable for wheeled traffic: one goes by the main gap in the hills by Chinchilla to Murcia, another by Requeña to Valencia. The third passes by Calatayud to Saragossa and ultimately to Barcelona. Between it and the Valencia road there is a gap of no less than 120 miles unpierced by any good practicable line of communication[1]. This being so, we begin to understand how it was that the operations on the eastern side of Spain, during the whole of the struggle, were a sort of independent episode that never exercised any great influence on the main theatre of the war, or, on the other hand, was much affected by the progress of the strife in Castile or Portugal. Soult's conquest of Andalusia did not help Suchet to conquer Valencia. On the other hand, when the latter did, in January, 1812, succeed in his attempt to subdue the eastern coast-line, it did not much affect him that Wellington was storming Ciudad Rodrigo and pressing back the French in the west. He was able to hold on to Valencia till the allies, in 1813, got possession of the upper valley of the Ebro and the great road from Madrid to Saragossa and Lerida, after the battle of Vittoria. It was only then that his flank was really turned, and that he was compelled to retreat and to abandon his southern conquests.

Summing up the general characteristics of the road-system of Spain, we note first that the main routes are rather at right angles to the great rivers than parallel to them. The sole exception is to be found in the valley of the Ebro, where the only good cross-road of Northern Spain does follow the river-bank from Logroño and Tudela on to Saragossa and Lerida.

Just because the roads do not cling to the valleys, but strike across them at right angles, they are always crossing watersheds by means of difficult passes. And so there is hardly a route in the whole Peninsula where it is possible to find fifty miles without a good defensive position drawn across the path. Moreover, the continual passes make the question of supplies very difficult: in crossing a plain an army can live, more or less, on the supplies of the country-side; but among mountains and defiles there is no population, and therefore no food to be had. Hence an army on the move must take with it all that it consumes, by means of a heavy wagon train, or an enormous convoy of pack-mules. But only the best roads are suitable for wheeled traffic, and so the lines practicable for a large host are very restricted in number. The student is often tempted to consider the movements of the rival generals very slow. The explanation is simply that to transfer an

[1] The bad cross-roads Cuenca-Teruel and Molina-Teruel hardly count.

army from one river-basin to another was a serious matter. It was necessary to spend weeks in collecting at the base food and transport sufficient to support the whole force till it reached its goal. In 1811 or 1812 the French and English were continually moving up and down the Portuguese frontier parallel to each other, the one from Salamanca to Badajoz, the other from Almeida or Guarda to Elvas. But to prepare for one of these flittings was such a serious matter that by the time that the army was able to move, the enemy had usually got wind of the plan, and was able to follow the movement on his own side of the frontier. There were months of preparation required before a few weeks of active operations, and when the concentration was over and the forces massed, they could only keep together as long as the food held out, and then had to disperse again in order to live. This was what was meant by the old epigram, that 'in Spain large armies starve, and small armies get beaten.'

Half the strategy of the campaigns of 1811–12–13 consisted in one of the combatants secretly collecting stores, concentrating his whole army, and then dashing at some important part of his adversary's line, before the other could mass his forces in a corresponding way. If prompt, the assailant might gain a fortnight, in which he might either try to demolish the enemy in detail before he could concentrate, or else to take from him some important position or town. In 1811 Marmont and Dorsenne played this trick on Wellington, during the short campaign of El Bodon and Aldea da Ponte. They relieved Ciudad Rodrigo, and nearly caught some divisions of the English army before the rest could join. But missing the instant blow, and allowing Wellington time to draw in his outlying troops, they failed and went home. In 1812, on the other hand, the British general successfully played off this device on the French. He first concentrated in the north, and captured Ciudad Rodrigo in eleven days, before Marmont could mass his scattered divisions; then going hastily south he took Badajoz in exactly the same way, storming it after only nineteen days of siege. Soult drew his army together at the news of Wellington's move, but had to bring troops from such distances, and to collect so much food, that he arrived within three marches of Badajoz only to hear that the place had just fallen.

In dealing with the main geographical facts of the war it is fair to recollect that an invasion of Spain from France is one of the

most difficult of undertakings, because the whole river and mountain system of the Peninsula lies *across* the main line of advance
from Bayonne to Cadiz, which the invader must adopt. While the
French conquest must be pushed from north to south, both the
streams and the Sierras of Spain all run at right angles to this
direction, i. e. from east to west. In advancing from the Pyrenees
to Madrid, and again from Madrid to Seville and Cadiz, the
invader has to cross every main river—Ebro, Douro, Tagus,
Guadiana, and Guadalquivir—and to force the passes of every
main range. Moreover, as he advances southward, he has to keep
his flanks safe against disturbance from the two mountainous
regions, Catalonia and Portugal, which lie along the eastern and
western coasts of the Peninsula. Unless the whole breadth of
Spain, from the Atlantic to the Mediterranean, be occupied step
by step as the invader moves on towards the Straits of Gibraltar,
he can always be molested and have his lines of communication
with France threatened. In the end it may be said that Napoleon's whole scheme of conquest was shipwrecked upon the blunder of
attacking Andalusia and Cadiz while Portugal was still unsubdued.
Wellington's constant sallies out of that country upon the French
flank, in Leon and Estremadura, detained such large forces to
protect the valleys of the Central Douro and Tagus that enough
men were never found to finish the conquest of the south and east.
And finally one crushing victory at Salamanca, in the plains of
Leon, so threatened the invader's line of touch with France, that he
had to abandon the whole south of Spain in order to concentrate
an army large enough to force Wellington back from Burgos and
the great northern road.

On the other hand, one tremendous advantage possessed by the
French in the central years of the war must be remembered. It
is manifest that Madrid is the only really important road-centre in
Spain, and that its undisturbed possession by the French in 1809–11
gave them the advantage of being able to operate from a single
point, against enemies who lay in a vast semicircle around, with no
good cross-roads to join them and enable them to work together.
The small 'Army of the Centre,' which was always kept in and
around Madrid, could be used as a reserve for any other of the
French armies, and transferred to join it in a few marches, while
it was infinitely more difficult to unite the various forces lying
on an outer circle at Astorga, Almeida, Abrantes, and Cadiz,

which the Spaniards and the British kept in the field. In short, in estimating the difficulties of the two parties, the advantage of the central position must be weighed against the disadvantage of long and exposed lines of communication.

One of the cardinal blunders of Napoleon's whole scheme for the conquest of the Peninsula was that he persisted in treating it as if it were German or Italian soil, capable of supporting an army on the march. His troops were accustomed to live on the country-side while crossing Central Europe, and therefore made no proper preparations for supplying themselves by other means than plunder. But in Spain there are only a few districts where this can be done : it may be possible to get forward without an enormous train of convoys in Andalusia, the coast plain of Valencia, and certain parts of the rather fertile plateau of Leon, the wheat-bearing *Tierra de Campos*. But over four-fifths of the Peninsula, an army that tries to feed on the country-side will find itself at the point of starvation in a few days, and be forced to disperse in order to live.

Till he had seen Spain with his own eyes Napoleon might perhaps have been excused for ignoring the fact that his ordinary method of ' making war support itself' was not in this case possible. But even after he had marched from Bayonne to Madrid, and then from Madrid to Astorga, in 1808, he persisted in refusing to see facts as they were. We find him on his way back to Paris from the campaign uttering the extraordinary statement that 'Spain is a much better country than he had ever supposed, and that he had no idea what a magnificent present he had made to his brother Joseph till he had seen it [1].' Of his utter failure to grasp the difficulties of the country we may get a fair conception from his orders, given at the same time, to Marshal Soult, who was at that moment occupied in pushing Sir John Moore towards Corunna. He told the Duke of Dalmatia that if he reached Lugo on January 9, and the English got away safely by sea, he was to march on Oporto, where he ought to arrive on the first of February; after seizing that city he was to go on to Lisbon, which he might reach on or about February 10. As a matter of fact Soult saw the English depart, and occupied Corunna on January 19, but his army was so utterly worn out, and his stores so entirely exhausted, that with the best will in the world he could not move again till February 20, only took Oporto on March 29, and had not yet started for Lisbon

[1] He said this to De Pradt (*Révolutions d'Espagne*, p. 224).

when Wellesley suddenly fell on him and drove him out of the country on May 12, 1809. The Emperor, in short, had given Soult orders executable perhaps, according to the distance, in Lombardy or Bavaria, but utterly absurd when applied to a country where roads are few and bad, with a defile or a river crossing the path at every few miles, and where food has to be carefully collected before a move, and taken on with the army by means of enormous convoys. Moreover the month was January, when every brook had become a raging mountain stream, and every highland was covered with snow! With such conceptions of the task before him, it is not wonderful that Napoleon was continually issuing wholly impracticable orders. The one that we have just quoted was sent out from Valladolid : how much worse would the case be when the Emperor persisted in directing affairs from Paris or Vienna, the last news that had reached him from the front being now several weeks old! With all his genius he never thoroughly succeeded in grasping the state of affairs, and to the very last continued to send directions that would have been wise enough in Central Europe, but happened to be inapplicable in the Iberian Peninsula.

It is only fair to Napoleon to add that his Spanish enemies, who ought at least to have known the limitations of their own road-system, and the disabilities of their half-starved armies, used habitually to produce plans of operations far more fantastically impossible than any that he ever drafted. They would arrange far-reaching schemes, for the co-operation of forces based on the most remote corners of the Peninsula, without attempting to work out the 'logistics' of the movement. The invariable result was that such enterprises either ended in disaster, or at the best came to a stop after the first few marches, because some vital point of the calculation had already been proved to have been made on erroneous data.

SECTION II: CHAPTER II

THE SPANISH ARMY IN 1808

WHEN the English student begins to investigate the Peninsular War in detail, he finds that, as regards the Spanish armies and their behaviour, he starts with a strong hostile prejudice. The Duke of Wellington in his dispatches, and still more in his private letters and his table-talk, was always enlarging on the folly and arrogance of the Spanish generals with whom he had to co-operate, and on the untrustworthiness of their troops. Napier, the one military classic whom most Englishmen have read, is still more emphatic and far more impressive, since he writes in a very judicial style, and with the most elaborate apparatus of references and authorities. When the reader begins to work through the infinite number of Peninsular diaries of British officers and men (for there are a very considerable number of writers from among the rank and file) the impression left upon him is much the same. It must be confessed that for the most part they had a very poor opinion of our allies.

Before allowing ourselves to be carried away by the almost unanimous verdict of our own countrymen, it is only fair to examine the state and character of the Spanish army when the war broke out. Only when we know its difficulties can we judge with fairness of its conduct, or decide upon its merits and shortcomings.

The armed force which served under the banners of Charles IV in the spring of 1808 consisted of 131,000 men, of whom 101,000 were regulars and 30,000 embodied militia. The latter had been under arms since 1804, and composed the greater part of the garrisons of the seaports of Spain, all of which had to be protected against possible descents of English expeditions [1].

Of the 101,000 men of the regular army, however, not all were available for the defence of the country. While the war with Russia was still in progress, Bonaparte had requested the Spanish government to furnish him with a strong division for use in the North [March, 1807], and in consequence the Marquis of La Romana

---

[1] See Appendix, containing the state of the Spanish army in 1808.

had been sent to the Baltic with 15,000 men, the picked regiments of the army. There remained therefore only 86,000 regulars within the kingdom. A very cursory glance down the Spanish army-list of 1808 is sufficient to show that this force was far from being in a satisfactory condition for either offensive or defensive operations.

It is well worth while to look at the details of its composition. The infantry consisted of three sorts of troops—the Royal Guard, the line regiments, and the foreign corps in Spanish pay. For Spain, more than any other European state, had kept up the old seventeenth-century fashion of hiring foreign mercenaries on a large scale. Even in the Royal Guard half the infantry were composed of 'Walloon Guards,' a survival from the day when the Netherlands had been part of the broad dominions of the Hapsburg kings. The men of these three battalions were no longer mainly Walloons, for Belgium had been a group of French departments for the last thirteen years. There were Germans and other foreigners of all sorts in the ranks, as well as a large number of native Spaniards. There were also six regiments of Swiss mercenaries—over 10,000 bayonets—and in these the men in the ranks did really come from Switzerland and Germany, though there was a sprinkling among them of strangers from all lands who had 'left their country for their country's good.' There were also one Neapolitan and three Irish regiments. These latter were survivals from the days of the 'Penal Laws,' when young Irishmen left their homes by thousands every year to take service with France or Spain, in the hope of getting some day a shot at the hated redcoats. The regiments bore the names of Hibernia, Irlanda, and Ultonia (i. e. Ulster). They were very much under their proper establishment, for of late years Irish recruits had begun to run short, even after the '98 : they now took service in France and not in Spain. The three Irish corps in 1808 had only 1,900 men under arms, instead of the 5,000 which they should have produced ; and of those the large majority were not real Irish, but waifs of all nationalities. Of late native Spaniards had been drafted in, to keep the regiments from dying out. On the other hand we shall find that not only the foreign regiments but the whole Spanish army was still full of officers of Irish name and blood, the sons and grandsons of the original emigrants of two generations back. An astounding proportion of the officers who rose to some note during the war bore Irish names, and were hereditary soldiers of fortune, who

justified their existence by the unwavering courage which they
always showed, in a time when obstinate perseverance was the main
military virtue. We need only mention Blake, the two O'Donnells,
Lacy, Sarsfield, O'Neill, O'Daly, Mahony, O'Donahue. If none of
them showed much strategical skill, yet their constant readiness to
fight, which no series of defeats could tame, contrasts very well with
the spiritless behaviour of a good many of the Spanish generals.
No officer of Irish blood was ever found among the cowards, and
hardly one among the traitors [1].

The ten foreign corps furnished altogether about 13,000 men
to the Spanish regular army. The rest of the infantry was
composed of thirty-five regiments of troops of the line, of three
battalions each, and twelve single-battalion regiments of light
infantry. They were theoretically territorial, like our own infantry
of to-day, and mostly bore local names derived from the provinces—
Asturias, Toledo, Estremadura, and so forth. All the light infantry
corps belonged to the old kingdoms of Aragon and Navarre, which
were therefore scantily represented in the nomenclature of the
ordinary line regiments. There were altogether 147 battalions of
Spanish infantry, excluding the foreign troops, and if all of these
had been up to the proper establishment of 840 men, the total
would have amounted to 98,000 bayonets. But the state of disorganization was such that as a matter of fact there were only 58,000
under arms. The regiments which Napoleon had requisitioned for
service in the North had been more or less brought up to a war-
footing, and each showed on an average 2,000 men in the ranks.
But many of the corps in the interior of Spain displayed the most
lamentable figures: e. g. the three battalions of the regiment of
Estremadura had only 770 men between them, Cordova 793, and
Navarre 822—showing 250 men to the battalion instead of the
proper 840. Theoretically there should have been no difficulty
in keeping them up to their proper strength, as machinery for
recruiting them had been duly provided. Voluntary enlistment
was the first resource: but when that did not suffice to keep the
ranks full, there was a kind of limited conscription called the
Quinta [2] to fall back upon. This consisted in balloting for men
in the regimental district, under certain rules which allowed an
enormous number of exemptions—e. g. all skilled artisans and all

---

[1] The minister O'Farrill and General Kindelan were the chief exceptions.
[2] So called because it was originally supposed to take the *fifth* man.

middle-class townsfolk were free from the burden—so that the agri-
cultural labourers had to supply practically the whole contingent.
Substitutes were allowed, if by any means the conscript could
afford to pay for them. The conscription therefore should have
kept the regiments up to their proper strength, and if many of
them had only a third of their complement under arms, it was
merely due to the general demoralization of the times. Under
Godoy's administration money was always wanting, more especially
since Napoleon had begun to levy his monthly tribute of 6,000,000
francs from the Spanish monarchy, and the gaps in the ranks
probably represented enforced economy as well as corrupt administration.

The 30,000 embodied militia, which formed the remainder of
the Spanish infantry, had been under arms since 1804, doing
garrison duty; they seem in many respects to have been equal
to the line battalions in efficiency. They bore names derived from
the towns in whose districts they had been raised—Badajoz, Lugo,
Alcazar, and so forth. Their officering was also strictly local,
all ranks being drawn from the leading families of their districts,
and seems to have been quite as efficient as that of the line.
Moreover their ranks were, on the average, much fuller than
those of the regular regiments—only two battalions in the total of
forty-three showed less than 550 bayonets on parade.

It is when we turn to the cavalry that we come to the weakest
part of the Spanish army. There were twelve regiments of heavy
and twelve of light horse, each with a nominal establishment of
700 sabres, which should have given 16,800 men for the whole
force. There were only about 15,000 officers and troopers embodied, but this was a small defect. A more real weakness lay in
the fact that there were only 9,000 horses for the 15,000 men.
It is difficult for even a wealthy government, like our own, to keep
its cavalry properly horsed, and that of Charles IV was naturally
unable to cope with this tiresome military problem. The chargers
were not only too few, but generally of bad quality, especially
those of the heavy cavalry : of those which were to be found in the
regimental stables a very large proportion were not fit for service.
When the five regiments which Napoleon demanded for the expedition to Denmark had been provided with 540 horses each and
sent off, the mounts of the rest of the army were in such a deplorable
state that some corps had not the power to horse one-third of their

troopers: e. g. in June, 1808, the Queen's Regiment, No. 2 of the
heavy cavalry, had 202 horses for 668 men; the 12th Regiment
had 259 horses for 667 men; the 1st Chasseurs—more extraordinary still—only 185 horses for 577 men. It resulted from
this penury of horses that when Napoleon made a second demand
for Spanish cavalry, asking for a division of 2,000 sabres to aid
Junot in invading Portugal, that force had to be made up by
putting together the mounted men of no less than ten regiments,
each contributing two or at the most three squadrons and leaving
the rest of its men dismounted at the dépôt.

Even if the cavalry had all been properly mounted, they would
have been far too few in proportion to the other arms, only 15,000
out of a total force of 130,000—one in eight; whereas in the time
of the Napoleonic wars one in six, or even one in five, was considered
the proper complement. In the Waterloo campaign the French
had the enormous number of 21,000 cavalry to 83,000 infantry—
one to four. What with original paucity, and with want of remounts, the Spaniards took the field in 1808, when the insurrection
began, with a ridiculously small number of horsemen. At Medina
de Rio Seco they had only 750 horsemen to 22,000 foot-soldiers,
at Baylen only 1,200 to 16,000. Later in the war they succeeded
in filling up the ranks of the old cavalry regiments, and in raising
many new ones. But the gain in number was not in the least
accompanied by a gain in efficiency. For the whole six years of
the struggle the mounted arm was the weakest point of their
hosts. Again and again it disgraced itself by allowing itself to be
beaten by half its own numbers, or by absconding early in the
fight and abandoning its infantry. It acquired, and merited, a
detestable reputation, and it is hard to find half a dozen engagements in which it behaved even reasonably well[1]. When Wellington
was made generalissimo of the Spanish armies in 1813 he would
not bring it up to the front at all, and though he took 40,000
Spaniards over the Pyrenees, there was not a horseman among
them. It is hard to account for the thorough worthlessness of these
squadrons, even when we make allowance for all the difficulties
of the time: Spain was notoriously deficient in decent cavalry
officers when the war began. The horses were inferior to the
French, and the equipment bad. From early disasters the troopers

---

[1] The successful and opportune charge of the *regimiento del Rey* at Talavera
was about the only case which ever came under English eyes.

contracted a demoralization which they could never shake off. But granting all this, it is still impossible to explain the consistent misbehaviour of these evasive squadrons. The officers, no doubt, had a harder task in organizing their new levies than those of the infantry and artillery, but it is curious that they should never have succeeded in learning their business even after four or five years of war.

The artillery of the Spanish army, on the other hand, earned on the whole a good reputation. This was not the result of proper preparation. When the struggle began it consisted of thirty-four batteries of field artillery, six of horse, and twenty-one garrison batteries (*compañias fijas*), with a total of 6,500 men. Forty batteries—that is to say 240 guns or somewhat less, for in some cases there seem to have been only four instead of six pieces in the battery—was according to the standard of 1808 a mediocre allowance to an army of 130,000 men, only about two-thirds of what it should have been [1]. But this was not the worst. Deducting four fully-horsed batteries, which had been taken off by Napoleon to Denmark, there remained in Spain four horse and thirty-two field batteries. These were practically unable to move, for they were almost entirely destitute of horses. For the 216 guns and their caissons there were only in hand 400 draught animals ! When the war began, the artillery had to requisition, and more or less train, 3,000 horses or mules before they could move from their barracks ! I do not know any fact that illustrates better the state of Spanish administration under the rule of Godoy. The raising of the great insurrectionary armies in the summer of 1808 ought to have led to an enormous increase to the artillery arm, but the trained men were so few that the greatest difficulty was found in organizing new batteries. Something was done by turning the marine artillery of the fleet into land troops, and there were a few hundreds of the militia who had been trained to work guns. But the officers necessary for the training and officering of new batteries were so scarce, that for many months no fresh forces of the artillery arm could take the field. In the autumn of 1808, at the time of the battles of Espinosa and Tudela, if we carefully add up the

[1] Napoleon had an ideal proportion of five guns per 1,000 men. But, as we shall show in the next chapter, while dealing with the French armies, he never succeeded in reaching anything like this standard in the Peninsula. Yet his opponents were always worse off.

number of guns brought into action by the five armies of Galicia, Estremadura, Aragon, the 'Centre' (i. e. Andalusia and Castile), and Catalonia, we do not find a piece more than the 240 which existed at the outbreak of the war. That is to say, the Spaniards had raised 100,000 new levies of infantry, without any corresponding extension of the artillery arm. During the campaign the conduct of the corps seems on the whole to have been very good, compared with that of the other arms. This was to be expected, as they were old soldiers to a much greater extent than either the infantry or the cavalry. They seem to have attained a fair skill with their weapons, and to have stuck to them very well. We often hear of gunners cut down or bayonetted over their pieces, seldom of a general bolt to the rear. For this very reason the personnel of the batteries suffered terribly : every defeat meant the capture of some dozens of guns, and the cutting up of the men who served them. It was as much as the government could do to keep up a moderate number of batteries, by supplying new guns and amalgamating the remnants of those which had been at the front. Each batch of lost battles in 1808–10 entailed the loss and consequent reconstruction of the artillery. If, in spite of this, we seldom hear complaints as to its conduct, it must be taken as a high compliment to the arm. But as long as Spanish generals persisted in fighting pitched battles, and getting their armies dispersed, a solid proportion of artillery to infantry could never be established. Its average strength may be guessed from the fact that at Albuera the best army that Spain then possessed put in line 16,300 men with only fourteen guns, less than one gun per thousand men—while Napoleon (as we have already noted) believed that five per thousand was the ideal, and often managed in actual fact to have three. In the latter years of the war the pieces were almost always drawn by mules, yoked tandem-fashion, and not ridden by drivers but goaded by men walking at their side—the slowest and most unsatisfactory form of traction that can be imagined. Hence came, in great part, their inability to manœuvre.

Of engineers Spain in 1808 had 169 officers dispersed over the kingdom. The corps had no proper rank and file. But there was a regiment of sappers, 1,000 strong, which was officered from the engineers. There was no army service corps, no military train, no organized commissariat of any kind. When moving about a Spanish army depended either on contractors who undertook to provide horses and wagons driven by civilians, or more frequently on the casual sweeping in by requisition of all the mules, oxen, and carts of the unhappy district in which it was operating. In this respect, as in so many others, Spain was still in the Middle Ages. The fact that there was no permanent arrangement for providing for the food of the army is enough in itself to account for many of its disasters. If, like the British, the Spaniards had possessed money to pay for what they took, things might have worked somewhat better. Or if, like the French, they had possessed an organized military train, and no scruples, they might have contrived to get along at the cost of utterly ruining the country-side. But as things stood, depending on incapable civil commissaries and the unwilling contributions of the local authorities, they were generally on the edge of starvation. Sometimes they got over the edge, and then the army, in spite of the proverbial frugality of the Spanish soldier, simply dispersed. It is fair to the men to say that they generally straggled back to the front sooner or later, when they had succeeded in filling their stomachs, and got incorporated in their own or some other regiment. It is said that by the end of the war there were soldiers who had, in their fashion, served in as many as ten different corps during the six years of the struggle.

Summing up the faults of the Spanish army, its depleted battalions, its small and incompetent cavalry force, its insufficient proportion of artillery, its utter want of commissariat, we find that its main source of weakness was that while the wars of the French Revolution had induced all the other states of Europe to overhaul their military organization and learn something from the methods of the French, Spain was still, so far as its army was concerned, in the middle of the eighteenth century. The national temperament, with its eternal relegation of all troublesome reforms to the morrow, was no doubt largely to blame. But Godoy, the all-powerful favourite who had also been commander-in-chief for the last seven years, must take the main responsibility. If he had chosen, he possessed the power to change everything; and in some ways he had peddled a good deal with details, changing the uniforms, and increasing the number of battalions in each regiment. But to make the army efficient he had done very little: the fact was that the commander-in-chief was quite ignorant of the military needs and tendencies of the day: all his knowledge of the army was gained while carpet-soldiering in the ranks of the royal body-guard. It was natural that the kind of officers who commended themselves to his haughty and ignorant mind should be those who were most ready to do him homage, to wink at his peculations, to condone his jobs, and to refrain from worrying him for the money needed for reforms and repairs. Promotion was wholly arbitrary, and was entirely in the favourite's hands. Those who were prepared to bow down to him prospered: those who showed any backbone or ventured on remonstrances were shelved. After a few years of this system it was natural that all ranks of the army became demoralized, since not merit but the talents of the courtier and the flatterer were the sure road to prosperity. Hence it came to pass that when the insurrection began, the level of military ability, patriotism, and integrity among the higher ranks of the army was very low. There were a few worthy men like Castaños and La Romana in offices of trust, but a much greater proportion of Godoy's protégés. One cannot condone the shocking way in which, during the first days of the war, the populace and the rank and file of the army united to murder so many officers in high place, like Filanghieri, the Captain-General of Galicia, Torre del Fresno, the Captain-General of Estremadura, and Solano, who commanded at Cadiz. But the explanation of the atrocities is simple: the multitude were resenting the results of the long administration of Godoy's creatures, and fell upon such of them as refused to throw in their lot immediately with the insurrection. The murdered men were (rightly or wrongly) suspected either of an intention to submit to Joseph Bonaparte, or of a design to hang back, wait on the times, and make their decision only when it should become obvious which paid better, patriotism or servility. The people had considerable justification in the fact that a very large proportion of Godoy's protégés, especially of those at Madrid, did swear homage to the intruder in order to keep their places and pensions. They were the base of the miserable party of *Afrancesados* which brought so much disgrace on Spain. The misguided cosmopolitan liberals who joined them were much the smaller half of the traitor-faction.

Godoy and his clique, therefore, must take the main responsibility for the state of decay and corruption in which the Spanish army

was found in 1808. What more could be expected when for so
many years an idle, venal, dissolute, ostentatious upstart had
been permitted to control the administration of military affairs,
and to settle all promotions to rank and office? 'Like master
like man' is always a true proverb, and the officers who begged or
bought responsible positions from Godoy naturally followed their
patron's example in spreading jobs and peculation downwards.
The undrilled and half-clothed soldiery, the unhorsed squadrons,
the empty arsenals, the idle and ignorant subalterns, were all,
in the end, the result of Godoy's long domination. But we
do not wish to absolve from its share of blame the purblind
nation which tolerated him for so long. In another country
he would have gone the way of Gaveston or Mortimer long
before.

When this was the state of the Spanish armies, it is no wonder
that the British observer, whether officer or soldier, could never
get over his prejudice against them. It was not merely because
a Spanish army was generally in rags and on the verge of starvation that he despised it. These were accidents of war which
every one had experienced in his own person: a British battalion
was often tattered and hungry. The Spanish government was
notoriously poor, its old regiments had been refilled again and
again with raw conscripts, its new levies had never had a fair start.
Hence came the things which disgusted the average Peninsular
diarist of British origin—the shambling indiscipline, the voluntary
dirt, the unmilitary habits of the Spanish troops. He could not
get over his dislike for men who kept their arms in a filthy, rusty
condition, who travelled not in orderly column of route but like
a flock of sheep straggling along a high road, who obeyed their
officers only when they pleased. And for the officers themselves
the English observer had an even greater contempt: continually
we come across observations to the effect that the faults of the
rank and file might be condoned—after all they were only half-
trained peasants—but that the officers were the source and fount
of evil from their laziness, their arrogance, their ignorance, and
their refusal to learn from experience. Here is a typical passage
from the Earl of Munster's *Reminiscences*:—

'We should not have been dissatisfied with our allies, *malgré*
their appearance and their rags, if we had felt any reason to
confide in them. The men might be "capable of all that men

dare," but the appearance of their officers at once bespoke their
not being fit to lead them in the attempt.   They not only did
not look like soldiers, but even not like gentlemen, and it was
difficult from their mean and abject appearance, particularly
among the infantry, to guess what class of society they could have
been taken from.   Few troops will behave well if those to whom
they should look up are undeserving respect.   Besides their general
inefficiency we found their moral feeling different from what we
expected.   Far from evincing devotion or even common courage
in their country's cause, they were very often guilty, individually
and collectively, of disgraceful cowardice.   We hourly regretted
that the revolution had not occasioned a more complete *bouleverse-*
ment of society, so as to bring forward fresh and vigorous talent
from all classes.   Very few of the regular military showed themselves worthy of command.   Indeed, with the exception of a few
self-made soldiers among the Guerillas, who had risen from among
the farmers and peasantry, it would be hard to point out a
Spanish officer whose opinion on the most trivial military subject was worth being asked.   We saw old besotted generals
whose armies were formed on obsolete principles of the *ancien*
régime of a decrepit government.   To this was added blind
pride and vanity.   No proofs of inferiority could open their
eyes, and they rushed from one error and misfortune to another,
benefiting by no experience, and disdaining to seek aid and
improvement' [pp. 194–5].

A voice from the ranks, Sergeant Surtees of the Rifle Brigade,
gives the same idea in different words.

'Most of the Spanish officers appeared to be utterly unfit
and unable to command their men.   They had all the pride,
arrogance, and self-sufficiency of the best officers in the world,
with the very least of all pretension to have a high opinion
of themselves.   It is true they were not all alike, but the
majority were the most haughty, and at the same time the most
contemptible creatures in the shape of officers that ever I beheld'
[p. 109].

As a matter of fact the class of officers in Spain was filled up in
three different ways.   One-third of them were, by custom, drawn
from the ranks.   In an army raised by conscription from all strata
of society excellent officers can be procured in this way.   But in
one mainly consisting of the least admirable part of the surplus

population, forced by want or hatred of work into enlisting, it was hard to get even good sergeants. And the sergeants made still worse sub-lieutenants, when the colonel was forced to promote some of them. No wonder that the English observer thought that there were 'Spanish officers who did not look like gentlemen.' This class were seldom or never allowed to rise above the grade of captain. The remaining two-thirds of the officers received their commissions from the war office: in the cavalry they were supposed to show proofs of noble descent, but this was not required in the infantry. There was a large sprinkling, however, of men of family, and for them the best places and the higher ranks were generally reserved—a thing feasible because all promotion was arbitrary, neither seniority nor merit being necessarily considered. The rest were drawn from all classes of society: for the last fifteen years any toady of Godoy could beg or buy as many commissions for his protégés as he pleased. But a large, and not the worst, part of the body of officers was composed of the descendants of soldiers of fortune—Irishmen were most numerous, but there were also French and Italians—who had always been seen in great numbers in the Spanish army. They held most of the upper-middle grades in the regiments, for the promoted sergeants were kept down to the rank of captain, while the nobles got rapid promotion and soon rose to be colonels and generals. On the whole we cannot doubt that there was a mass of bad officers in the Spanish army: the ignorant fellows who had risen from the ranks, the too-rapidly promoted scions of the noblesse, and the nominees of Godoy's hangers-on, were none of them very promising material with which to conduct a war *à outrance* for the existence of the realm.

In 1808 there was but one small military college for the training of infantry and cavalry officers. Five existed in 1790, but Godoy cut them down to one at Zamora, and only allowed sixty cadets there at a time, so that five-sixths of the young men who got commissions went straight to their battalions, there to pick up (if they chose) the rudiments of their military education. From want of some common teaching the drill and organization of the regiments were in a condition of chaos. Every colonel did what he chose in the way of manual exercise and manœuvres. A French officer says that in 1807 he saw a Spanish brigade at a review, in which, when the brigadier gave the order 'Ready, present, fire!' the different battalions carried it out in three different times and with wholly distinct details of execution.

Not only was the Spanish army indifferently officered, but even of such officers as it possessed there were not enough. In the old line regiments there should have been seventy to each corps, i.e. 2,450 to the 105 battalions of that arm. But Godoy had allowed the numbers to sink to 1,520. When the insurrection broke out, the vacant places had to be filled, and many regiments received at the same moment twenty or thirty subalterns taken from civil life and completely destitute of military training. Similarly the militia ought to have had 1,800 officers, and only possessed 1,200 when the war began. The vacancies were filled, but with raw and often indifferent material.

Such were the officers with whom the British army had to co-operate. There is no disguising the fact that from the first the allies could not get on together. In the earlier years of the war there were some incidents that happened while the troops of the two nations lay together, which our countrymen could never forgive or forget. We need only mention the midnight panic in Cuesta's army on the eve of Talavera, when 10,000 men ran away without having had a shot fired at them, and the cowardly behaviour of La Peña in 1811, when he refused to aid Graham at the bloody little battle of Barossa.

The strictures of Wellington, Napier, and the rest were un-doubtedly well deserved; and yet it is easy to be too hard on the Spaniards. It chanced that our countrymen did not get a fair opportunity of observing their allies under favourable conditions; of the old regular army that fought at Baylen or Zornoza they never got a glimpse. It had been practically destroyed before we came upon the field. La Romana's starving hordes, and Cuesta's evasive and demoralized battalions were the samples from which the whole Spanish army was judged. In the Talavera campaign, the first in which English and Spanish troops stood side by side, there can be no doubt that the latter (with few exceptions) behaved in their very worst style. They often did much better; but few Englishmen had the chance of watching a defence like that of Saragossa or Gerona. Very few observers from our side saw anything of the heroically obstinate resistance of the Catalonian *miqueletes* and *somatenes*. Chance threw in our way Cuesta and La Peña and Imaz as types of Peninsular generals, and from them the rest were judged. No one supposes that the Spaniards as a nation are destitute of all military qualities. They made good soldiers enough in the past, and may do so in the future : but when, after centuries of intellectual and political torpor, they were called upon to fight for their national existence, they were just emerging from subjection to one of the most worthless adventurers and one of the most idiotic kings whom history has known. Charles IV and Godoy account for an extraordinary amount of the decrepitude of the monarchy and the demoralization of its army.

It is more just to admire the constancy with which a nation so handicapped persisted in the hopeless struggle, than to condemn it for the incapacity of its generals, the ignorance of its officers, the unsteadiness of its raw levies. If Spain had been a first-rate military power, there would have been comparatively little merit in the six years' struggle which she waged against Bonaparte. When we consider her weakness and her disorganization, we find ourselves more inclined to wonder at her persistence than to sneer at her mishaps.

SECTION II: CHAPTER III

THE FRENCH ARMY IN SPAIN

§ 1. THE ARMY OF 1808: ITS CHARACTER AND ORGANIZATION.

IN dealing with the history of the imperial armies in the Peninsula, it is our first duty to point out the enormous difference between the troops who entered Spain in 1807 and 1808, under Dupont, Moncey, and Murat, and the later arrivals who came under Bonaparte's personal guidance when the first disastrous stage of the war was over.

Nothing can show more clearly the contempt which the Emperor entertained, not only for the Spanish government but for the Spanish nation, than the character of the hosts which he first sent forth to occupy the Peninsula. After Tilsit he was the master of half a million of the best troops in the world; but he did not consider the subjugation of Spain and Portugal a sufficiently formidable task to make it necessary to move southward any appreciable fraction of the Grand Army. The victors of Jena and Friedland were left in their cantonments on the Rhine, the Elbe, and the Oder, while a new force, mainly composed of elements of inferior fighting value, was sent across the Pyrenees.

This second host was at Napoleon's disposition mainly owing to the fact that during the late war he had been anticipating the conscription. In the winter of 1806–7 he had called out, a year too soon, the men who were due to serve in 1808. In the late autumn of 1807, while his designs in Spain were already in progress, he had summoned forth the conscription of 1809. He had thus under arms two years' contingents of recruits raised before their proper time. The dépôts were gorged, and, even after the corps which had been depleted in Prussia and Poland had been made up to full strength, there was an enormous surplus of men in hand.

To utilize this mass of conscripts the Emperor found several ways. Of the men raised in the winter of 1806–7 some thousands had been thrown into temporary organizations, called 'legions of reserve,' and used to do garrison duty on the Atlantic coast, in order to guard against possible English descents. There were five of these 'legions' and two 'supplementary legions' in the army sent into Spain : they showed a strength of 16,000 men. None of them had been more than a year under arms, but they were at any rate organized units complete in themselves. They formed the greater part of the infantry in the corps of Dupont.

A shade worse in composition were twenty 'provisional regiments' which the Emperor put together for Spain. Each regimental dépôt in the south of France was told to form four companies from its superabundant mass of conscripts. These bodies, of about 560 men each, were united in fours, and each group was called a 'provisional regiment.' The men of each battalion knew nothing of those of the others, since they were all drawn from separate regiments : there was not a single veteran soldier in the ranks : the officers were almost all either half-pay men called back to service, or young sub-lieutenants who had just received their commissions. These bodies, equally destitute of *esprit de corps* and of instruction, made up nearly 30,000 men of the army of Spain. They constituted nearly the whole of the divisions under Bessières and Moncey, which lay in Northern Spain at the moment of the outbreak of the war.

But there were military units even less trustworthy than the 'provisional regiments' which Napoleon transferred to Spain in the spring of 1808. These were the five or six *régiments de marche*, which were to be found in some of the brigades which crossed the Pyrenees when the state of affairs was already growing dangerous. They were formed of companies, or even smaller bodies, hastily drawn together from such southern dépôts, as were found to be still in possession of superfluous conscripts even after con-tributing to the 'provisional regiments.' They were to be absorbed into the old corps when the pressing need for instant reinforcements for the Peninsula should come to an end. In addition to all these temporary units, Bonaparte was at the same moment making a vast addition to his permanent regular army. Down to the war of 1806-7 the French regiments of infantry had consisted of three battalions for the field and a fourth at the dépôt, which kept drafting its men to the front in order to fill up the gaps in the other three. Napoleon had now resolved to raise the establishment to five battalions per regiment, four for field service, while the newly created fifth became the dépôt battalion. When the Peninsular

War broke out, a good many regiments had already completed their fourth field-battalion, and several of these new corps are to be found in the rolls of the armies which had entered Spain. The multiplication of battalions had been accompanied by a reduction of their individual strength : down to February, 1808, there were nine companies to each unit, and Junot's corps had battalions of a strength of 1,100 or 1,200 bayonets. But those which came later were six-company battalions, with a strength of 840 bayonets when at their full establishment.

All the troops of which we have hitherto spoken were native Frenchmen. But they did not compose by any means the whole of the infantry which the Emperor dispatched into Spain between October, 1807, and May, 1808. According to his usual custom he employed great numbers of auxiliaries from his vassal kingdoms : we note intercalated among the French units seven battalions of Swiss, four of Italians, two each of Neapolitans and Portuguese [1], and one each of Prussians, Westphalians, Hanoverians, and Irish. Altogether there were no less than 14,000 men of foreign infantry dispersed among the troops of Junot, Dupont, Bessières, Moncey, and Duhesme. They were not massed, but scattered broadcast in single battalions, save the Italians and Neapolitans, who formed a complete division under Lecchi in the army of Catalonia.

The cavalry of the army of Spain was quite as heterogeneous and ill compacted as the infantry. Just as 'provisional regiments' of foot were patched up from the southern dépôts of France, so were 'provisional regiments' of cavalry. The best of them were composed of two, three, or four squadrons, each contributed by the dépôt of a different cavalry regiment. The worst were *escadrons de marche*, drawn together in a haphazard fashion from such of the dépôts as had a surplus of conscripts even after they had given a full squadron to the 'provisional regiments.' There were also a number of foreign cavalry regiments, Italians, Neapolitans, lancers of Berg, and Poles. Of veteran regiments of French cavalry there were actually no more than three, about 1,250 men, among the 12,000 horsemen of the army of Spain.

When we sum up the composition of the 116,000 men who lay south of the Pyrenees on the last day of May, 1808, we find that

---

[1] These last were the rear battalions of the unfortunate Portuguese legion which was in march for the Baltic ; they were still on this side of the Pyrenees when the war began, and were hastily utilized against Saragossa.

not a third part of them belonged to the old units of the regular French army.   It may be worth while to give the figures :—

Of veterans we have—

	Infantry.	Cavalry.
(1) A detachment of the Imperial Guard, which was intended to serve as the Emperor's special escort during his irruption into Spain .	3,600	1,750
(2) Twenty-six battalions of infantry of the line and light infantry, being all first, second, or third battalions, and not newly raised fourth battalions	25,800	
(3) Three old regiments of cavalry of the line		1,250
(4) Three newly raised fourth battalions of infantry regiments of the line	1,800	
This gives a total of regularly organized French troops of the standing army of . .	31,200	3,000
(5) Five legions of reserve, and two 'supplementary legions of reserve'	16,000	
(6) Fifteen 'provisional regiments' from the dépôts of Southern France [the remaining five had not crossed the frontier on May 31] . .	31,000	
(7) Six *régiments de marche* of conscripts .	3,200	
(8) Eighteen battalions of Italian, Swiss, German, and other auxiliaries	14,000	
(9) Sixteen 'provisional regiments' of cavalry, and a few detached 'provisional squadrons,' and *escadrons de marche*		9,500
(10) Three regiments of foreign cavalry .		1,000
This makes a total of troops in temporary organization, or of foreign origin, of . .	64,200	10,500

Napoleon, then, intended to conquer Spain with a force of about 110,000 men, of which no more than 34,000 sabres and bayonets belonged to his regular army; the rest were conscripts or foreign auxiliaries.   But we must also note that the small body of veteran troops was not distributed equally in each of the corps, so as to stiffen the preponderating mass of conscripts.   If we put aside the division of Imperial Guards, we find that of the remaining 25,000 infantry of old organization no less than 17,500 belonged to Junot's army of Portugal, which was the only one of the corps that had a solid organization.   Junot had indeed a very fine force, seventeen old line battalions to two battalions of conscripts and

three of foreigners. The rest of the veteran troops were mainly
with Duhesme in Catalonia, who had a good division of 5,000
veterans. In the three corps of Dupont, Moncey, and Bessières on
the other hand old troops were conspicuous by their absence:
among the 19,000 infantry of Dupont's corps, on which (as it
chanced) the first stress of the Spanish war was destined to fall,
there was actually only two battalions (1,700 men) of old troops.
In Moncey's there was not a single veteran unit; in Bessières', only
four battalions. This simple fact goes far to explain why Dupont's
expedition to Andalusia led to the capitulation of Baylen, and
why Moncey's march on Valencia ended in an ignominious retreat.
Countries cannot be conquered with hordes of undrilled conscripts
—not even countries in an advanced stage of political decom-
position, such as the Spain of 1808.

§ 2. THE ARMY OF 1808–14: ITS CHARACTER AND ORGANIZATION.

Baylen, as we shall see, taught Napoleon his lesson, and the
second army which he brought into the Peninsula in the autumn
of 1808, to repair his initial disasters, was very differently constituted from the heterogeneous masses which he had at first judged
to be sufficient for his task. It was composed of his finest old
regiments from the Rhine and Elbe, the flower of the victors of
Jena and Friedland. Even when the despot had half a million good
troops at his disposition, he could not be in force everywhere, and
the transference of 200,000 veterans to Spain left him almost too
weak in Central Europe. In the Essling-Wagram campaign of
1809 he found that he was barely strong enough to conquer the
Austrians, precisely because he had left so many men behind him
in the Peninsula. In the Russian campaign of 1812, vast as were
the forces that he displayed, they were yet not over numerous for
the enterprise, because such an immense proportion of them was
composed of unwilling allies and disaffected subjects. If the masses
of Austrians, Prussians, Neapolitans, Portuguese, Westphalians,
Bavarians, and so forth had been replaced by half their actual
number of old French troops from Spain, the army would have
been far more powerful. Still more was this the case in 1813:
if the whole of the Peninsular army had been available for service

on the Elbe and Oder at the time of Lützen and Bautzen, the effect
on the general history of Europe might have been incalculable.
Truly, therefore, did the Emperor call the Spanish War 'the
running sore' which had sapped his strength ever since its
commencement.

A word as to the tactical organization of the French army in
1808 is required. The infantry regiments of normal formation
consisted, as we have seen, of four field battalions and one dépôt
battalion; the last named never, of course, appeared at the front.
Each field battalion was composed of six companies of 140 men:
its two flank companies, the grenadiers and voltigeurs, were formed
of the pick of the corps[1]: into the grenadiers only tall, into the
voltigeurs only short men were drafted. Thus a battalion should
normally have shown 840 and a regiment 3,360 men in the field.
But it was by no means the universal rule to find the whole four
battalions of a regiment serving together. In the modern armies
of France, Germany, or Russia, a regiment in time of peace lives
concentrated in its recruiting district, and can take the field in a
compact body. This was not the case in Napoleon's ever-wandering
hosts: the chances of war were always isolating single battalions,
which, once dropped in a garrison or sent on an expedition, did not
easily rejoin their fellows. Many, too, of the new fourth battalions
raised in 1807 had never gone forward to Germany to seek the
main body of their regiments. Of the corps which were brought
down to Spain in the late autumn of 1808 there were more with
three battalions than with four concentrated under the regimental
eagle. Some had only two present, a few no more than one[2]. But
the Emperor disliked to have single isolated battalions, and preferred to work them in pairs, if he could not get three or four
together. The object of this was that, if one or two battalions got
much weakened in a campaign, the men could be fused into a
single unit, and the supernumerary officers and sergeants sent back

---

[1] French generals were much addicted to the pernicious practice of massing
the grenadier companies of all the regiments of a division, or an army corps,
in order to make a picked battalion or brigade, to be used as a reserve.
Junot had four such battalions (*grenadiers réunis*) at Vimiero, and Victor
three at Barossa.

[2] To take a later example, of the three *corps d'armée* (II, VI, VIII) with
which Masséna invaded Portugal in 1810, there were only *three* regiments
with four battalions present; while seventeen had three, eight had two, and
ten a single battalion only.

to the dépôt, where they would form a new battalion out of the stock of conscripts. But the fresh organization might very likely be hurried, by some sudden chance of war, to Flushing, or Italy, or the Danube, while the eagle and the main body remained in Spain —or vice versa.

There was therefore, in consequence of the varying strength of the regiments, no regularity or system in the brigading of the French troops in Spain : in one brigade there might be five or six isolated battalions, each belonging to a separate regiment; in another three from one regiment and two from a second ; in a third four from one regiment and one from another. Nor was there any fixed number of battalions in a brigade : it might vary from three (a very unusual minimum) up to nine—an equally rare maximum. Six was perhaps the most frequent number. A division was composed of two, or less frequently of three, brigades, and might have any number from ten up to sixteen or eighteen battalions—i.e. it varied, allowing for casual losses, from 6,000 to 10,000 men. This irregularity was part of Napoleon's system : he laid it down as an axiom that all military units, from a brigade to an army corps, ought to differ in strength among themselves : otherwise the enemy, if he had once discovered how many brigades or divisions were in front of him, could calculate with accuracy the number of troops with which he had to do.

Much confusion is caused, when we deal with Napoleon's army, by the strange system of numeration which he adopted. The infantry, whether called 'line regiments' or 'light infantry regiments,' were drilled and organized in the same way. But the Emperor had some odd vagaries : he often refused to raise again a regiment which had been exterminated, or taken prisoners *en masse*. Hence after a few years of his reign there were some vacant numbers in the list of infantry corps. The regiments, for example, which were garrisoning the colonies at the time of the rupture of the Peace of Amiens, fell one after another into the hands of the English as the war went on. They were never replaced, and left gaps in the army list. On the other hand the Emperor sometimes raised regiments with duplicate numbers, a most tiresome thing for the military historian of the next age. It is impossible to fathom his purpose, unless he was set on confusing his enemies by showing more battalions than the list of existing corps seemed to make possible. Or perhaps he was thinking of the old legions of the

Roman Empire, of which there were always several in existence
bearing the same number, but distinguished by their honorary titles.
Those who wish to read the story of one of these duplicate
regiments may follow in the history of Nodier the tale of the
raising and extermination of Colonel Oudet's celebrated '9th Bis'
of the line [1].

There is another difficulty caused by a second freak of the
Emperor: all regiments ought, as we have said, to have shown four
field battalions. But Bonaparte sometimes added one or even two
more, to corps which stood high in his favour, or whose dépôts
produced on some occasions a very large surplus of conscripts.
Thus we find now and then, in the morning state of a French army
corps, a fifth or even a sixth [2] battalion of some regiment. But as
a rule these units had not a very long existence: their usual fate
was to be sent home, when their numbers ran low from the wear
and tear of war, in order to be incorporated in the normal *cadres*
of their corps.   On the authority of that good soldier and
admirable historian, Foy, we are able to state that on the first
of June, 1808, Napoleon had 417 field battalions, over and above
the dépôts, on his army rolls. If the 113 regiments of the line,
and the thirty-two light infantry regiments had all been in existence and complete, there should have been 580 field battalions.
Clearly then some corps had disappeared and many others had not
more than three battalions ready.   But the units were always
being created, amalgamated, or dissolved, from week to week,
so that it is almost impossible to state the exact force of the
whole French army at any given moment. The most important
change that was made during the year 1808 was the conversion of
those of the provisional regiments which escaped Dupont's disaster
into new permanent corps. By combining them in pairs the
114th–120th of the line and the 33rd léger were created [3]. In
the succeeding five years more and more corps were raised: the

[1] Nodier, *Souvenirs de la Révolution*, ii. 233–5.

[2] In the campaign of 1810 the 26th, 66th, and 82nd regiments in Masséna's
army had 5th and 6th battalions in the field.

[3] This was done on July 7 (see *Nap. Corresp.*, 14,164). Nos. 1 and 2
became the 114th of the line, 3 and 4 the 115th, 5 and 6 the 116th, 7 and 8
the 33rd léger, 9 and 10 the 117th, 11 the 118th, 13 and 14 the 119th,
17 and 18 the 120th. When the 6th, 7th, and 8th were captured at Baylen,
new conscripts had to be brought from France to complete the 116th and
replace the 33rd léger.

annexation of Holland and Northern Germany in 1810-11 ultimately enabled the Emperor to carry the total of his line regiments
up to 156 [1813], and of his light infantry regiments up to thirty-
six [1].

Of the French cavalry we need not speak at such length. When
the Spanish war broke out, Bonaparte was possessed of about
eighty regiments of horsemen, each taking the field with four
squadrons of some 150 to 200 men. There were twelve regiments
of cuirassiers, two of carabineers, thirty of dragoons, twenty-six
of *chasseurs à cheval*, ten of hussars, i. e. fourteen regiments of
heavy, thirty of medium, and thirty-six of light horse. The
cuirassiers were hardly ever seen in Spain—not more than two
or three regiments ever served south of the Pyrenees [2]. On the
other hand the greater part of the dragoons were employed
in the Peninsula—there were in 1809 twenty-five of the thirty
regiments of them in the field against the English and Spaniards.
More than half of the hussars also served in Spain. To the
veteran corps of regulars there were added, at the outset of the
war, as will be remembered, a great number of 'provisional
regiments,' but these gradually disappeared, by being incorporated
in the older *cadres*, or in a few cases by being formed into new
permanent units. There was also a mass of Polish, German, and
Italian cavalry; but these auxiliaries did not bear such a high
proportion to the native French as did the foreign part of the
infantry arm. By far the most distinguished of these corps were
the Polish lancers, whom the English came to know only too well
at Albuera. The Italians were almost exclusively employed on the
east coast of Spain, in the army of Catalonia. The Germans—
mostly from Westphalia, Berg, and Nassau—were scattered about
in single regiments among the cavalry corps of the various armies.
They were always mixed with the French horse, and never appeared
in brigades (much less in divisions) of their own.

The average strength of a French cavalry regiment during the
years 1809-14 was four squadrons of about 150 men each. It
was very seldom that a corps showed over 600 men in the ranks:

[1] See Rousset's excellent *La Grande Armée de* 1813.

[2] The most distinguished of these was the 13th Cuirassiers, a regiment of
new formation, which served throughout the war in Aragon and Catalonia,
and was by far the best of Suchet's mounted corps. For its achievements the
reader may be referred to the interesting *Mémoires* of Colonel de Gonneville.

not unfrequently it sank to 450 [1]. When it grew still further attenuated, it was usual to send back the *cadres* of one or two squadrons, and to complete to full numbers the two or three which kept the field. These figures do not hold good for the raw 'provisional regiments' which Bonaparte used during the first year of the war : they sometimes rose to 700 or even 800 strong, when the dépôts from which they had been drawn chanced to be exceptionally full of recruits [2]. But such large corps are not to be found in the later years of the war. By 1812, when Napoleon, busied in Central Europe, ceased to reinforce his Spanish armies, the average of a cavalry regiment had shrunk to 500 men. In 1813 it was seldom that 400 effective sabres could be mustered by any mounted corps.

As to the scientific arms of the French service, the artillery and engineers, there is no doubt that throughout the war they deserved very well of their master. Artillery cannot be improvised in the manner that is possible with infantry, and the batteries which accompanied Dupont's and Moncey's conscripts into Spain in 1808 were veterans. Without them the raw infantry would have fared even worse than it did, during the first year of the struggle. The proportion of guns which the French employed during the wars of the Empire was generally very large in comparison with the size of their armies—one of the many results of the fact that Bonaparte had originally been an artillery officer. He raised, as was remarked, the number of gunners in the French service to a figure as large as that of the whole regular army of Louis XVI at the moment when the Revolution broke out. But in Spain the difficulties of transport and the badness of the roads seem to have combined to keep down the proportion of guns to something very much less than was customary in the more favourable *terrain* of Italy or Germany. A large part, too, of the pieces were of very light metal—four- and even three-pounders, which were found easier to transport across the mountains than six- or eight-pounders, though much less effective in the field. In many of the campaigns, therefore, of the Peninsular War the French artillery stood in a proportion to the total number

---

[1] In Masséna's army of 1810 the largest cavalry regiment (25th Dragoons) had 650 men. In Suchet's army in the same year there was one exceptionally strong regiment (4th Hussars) with 759 sabres.

[2] The 2nd Provisional Dragoons of Moncey's corps had no less than 872 men in June, 1808.

of men present, which was so low that it barely exceeded that customary among the British, who were notoriously more 'under-gunned' than any other European army save that of Spain.   Junot at Vimiero had twenty-three guns to 13,500 men: Victor at Talavera had eighty guns to about 50,000 men: Masséna in 1810 invaded Portugal with some 70,000 men and 126 guns; at Fuentes d'Oñoro he only showed forty-two guns to 40,000 bayonets and sabres[1]. Soult at Albuera had (apparently) forty guns to 24,000 men: in the autumn campaign of 1813 the same marshal had 125 guns to 107,000 men.   It will be noted that the proportion never rises to two guns per thousand men, and occasionally does not much exceed one gun per thousand[2].   This contrasts remarkably with the 350 guns to 120,000 men which Bonaparte took out for the campaign of Waterloo, or even with the 1,372 guns to 600,000 men of the Russian expedition and 1,056 guns to 450,000 men of the ill-compacted army of 1813.

[1] In this case the low proportion was due to want of horses, not to bad roads.   Even the forty-two guns were only produced when Bessières had lent Masséna many teams.

[2] I take these figures respectively from Thiébault, Fririon, Lapène, Le Clerc, and Rousset.

SECTION II: CHAPTER IV

THE TACTICS OF THE FRENCH AND THEIR ADVERSARIES DURING THE PENINSULAR WAR

An account of the numbers and the organization of an army is of comparatively little interest, unless we understand the principles on which its leaders are accustomed to handle it on the day of battle, and its value as a fighting machine.

Speaking generally, the tactics of the French infantry during the Peninsular War were those which had been developed fifteen years before, during the first struggles of the Revolution. They nearly always attacked with a thick cloud of tirailleurs covering one or two lines of battalions in column. The idea was that the very numerous and powerful skirmishing line would engage the enemy sufficiently to attract all his attention, so that the massed battalions behind arrived at the front of battle almost without sustaining loss. The momentum of the columns ought then to suffice to carry them right through the enemy's lines, which would already have suffered appreciably from the fire of the tirailleurs. This form of attack had won countless victories over Prussian, Austrian, and Russian; and many cases had been known where a hostile position had been carried by the mere impetus of the French columns, without a shot having been fired save by their skirmishers. But this method, which Wellington called 'the old French style,' never succeeded against the English. It had the fatal defect that when the column came up through the tirailleurs and endeavoured to charge, it presented a small front, and only the first two ranks could fire. For the normal French battalion advanced in column of companies, or less frequently of double companies, i. e. with a front of forty or at most of eighty men, and a depth of nine or of eighteen, since the company was always three deep, and there were six companies to a battalion. The rear ranks only served to give the front ranks moral support, and to impress the enemy with a sense of the solidity and inexorable strength of the approaching

mass. Sometimes a whole regiment or brigade formed one dense
column. Now if the enemy, as was always the case with the
British, refused to be impressed, but stood firm in line, held their
ground, and blazed into the head of the mass, the attack was
certain to fail. For 800 men in the two-deep line, which Wellington
loved, could all use their muskets, and thus poured 800 bullets per
volley into a French battalion of the same strength, which only
could return 160. The nine-deep, or eighteen-deep, column was a
target which it was impossible to miss. Hence the front ranks
went down in rows and the whole came to a standstill. If, as was
often the case, the French battalion tried to deploy in front of the
English line, so as to bring more muskets to bear, it seldom or
never succeeded in accomplishing the manœuvre, for each company,
as it straggled out from the mass, got shot down so quickly that
the formation could never be completed. No wonder that Foy in
his private journal felt himself constrained to confess that, for a set
battle with equal numbers on a limited front, the English infantry
was superior. 'I keep this opinion to myself,' he adds, 'and have
never divulged it; for it is necessary that the soldier in the ranks
should not only hate the enemy, but also despise him [1].' Foy kept
his opinion so closely to himself that he did not put it in his
formal history of the Peninsular War: it has only become public
property since his journals were published in 1900.

But the fact that with anything like equal numbers the line
must beat the column was demonstrated over and over again
during the war. It had first been seen at Maida in 1806, but
that obscure Calabrian battle was hardly known, even by name,
save to those who had been present. It was at Talavera, and still
more at Busaco and Albuera, that it became patent to everybody
that the attack in battalion column, even if preceded by a vigorous
swarm of skirmishers, could never succeed against the English. At
the two former fights the French attacked uphill, and laid the
blame of their defeat upon the unfavourable ground. But when
at Albuera three English brigades drove double their own numbers
from the commanding ridge on which Soult had ranged them,
simply by the superiority of their musketry fire, there was no
longer any possibility of disguising the moral. Yet to the end
of the war, down to Waterloo itself, the French stuck to their
old formation: at the great battle in 1815, as Wellington tersely

[1] Diary of Foy, in Girod de l'Ain's *Vie Militaire du Général Foy*, p. 98.

said, 'The French came on once more in the old style, and we beat them in the old style.'

But when Napoleon's armies were opposed to troops who could not stand firm to meet them in a line formation, they generally succeeded. The Spaniards, in their earlier battles, often tried to resist in a line of deployed battalions, but their *morale* was not good enough when the attacking column drew close to them, and they generally gave way at the critical moment and let their assailants break through[1]. The same had often been the case with the Austrians and Prussians, who in their earlier wars with Napoleon used the line formation which Frederick the Great had popularized fifty years before. The great king had accustomed his troops to fight in a three- or four-deep line, with a comparatively small provision of skirmishers to cover their front, for it was by the fire of the whole battalion that his troops were intended to win. The masses of tirailleurs which the French sent forward in front of their columns generally succeeded in engaging the Prussian or Austrian line so closely, that the columns behind them came up without much loss, and then broke the line by their mere momentum and moral effect. Hence in their later wars the German powers copied their enemies, and took to using a very thick skirmishing line backed by battalion columns in the French style.

Wellington never found any reason to do so. His method was to conceal his main line as long as possible by a dip in the ground, a hedge, or a wall, or to keep it behind the crest of the position which it was holding. To face the tirailleurs each battalion sent out its light company, and each brigade had assigned to it several detached companies of riflemen: from 1809 onward some of the 60th Rifles and one or two foreign light corps[2] were broken up and distributed round the various divisions for this special purpose. This gave a line of skirmishers strong enough to hold back the tirailleurs for a long time, probably till the supporting columns

---

[1] The reader who wishes to see a logical explanation of the phenomenon may find it in the remarks of the Spanish Colonel Moscoso (1812) in Arteche, ii. 394. He explains that the skirmishing line of his compatriots was always too thin to keep back the tirailleurs. The latter invariably pushed their way close up to the Spanish main body, and while presenting in their scattered formation no definite mark for volleys, were yet numerous enough to shoot down so many of their opponents as to shake the Spanish formation before the columns in the rear came up.

[2] e. g. *Brunswick-Oels* and the *Chasseurs Britanniques*.

came up to help them. It was only then that the British skirmishing line gave way and retired behind its main body, leaving the
deployed battalions in face of the French column, of which they
never failed to give a satisfactory account. The covering screen of
light troops often suffered terribly; e.g., at Barossa, Brown's 'light
battalion' lost fourteen out of twenty-one officers and more than
half its rank and file [1], while holding off the French advance from
the line which was forming in its rear. But the combat always
went well if the enemy's skirmishers could be kept back, and his
supporting columns forced to come to the front, to engage with the
regiments in two-deep formation which were waiting for them.

Charges with the bayonet are often heard of in narratives—
especially French narratives—of the Peninsular War. But it was
very seldom that the opposing troops actually came into collision
with the white weapon. There were occasions, almost invariably
in fighting in villages or enclosed ground, on which considerable
numbers of men were killed or wounded with the bayonet, but they
were but few. It is certain, however, that the 43rd at Vimiero, the
71st and 88th at Fuentes d'Oñoro, and the 20th at Roncesvalles,
engaged in this fashion [2]; and other cases could be quoted. But as
a rule a 'bayonet charge' in a French historian merely means the
advance of a column up to the enemy's position without firing: it
does not imply actual contact or the crossing of weapons. An
English charge on the other hand was practically an advance in
line with frequent volleys, or independent file-firing. At Albuera,
or Barossa, or Salamanca it was the ball not the bayonet which
did the work; the enemy was shot down, or gave way without any
hand-to-hand conflict.

French cavalry tactics had by 1808 developed into as definite
a system as those of the infantry. Napoleon was fond of massing
his horsemen in very large bodies and launching them at the flank,
or even at the centre, of the army opposed to him. He would
occasionally use as many as 6,000 or 8,000, or (as at Waterloo) even
12,000 men for one of these great strokes. Two or three of his

[1] See Blakeney, *A Boy in the Peninsular War*, edited by Sturges (1899),
pp. 189, 190, for an account of this bloody episode.

[2] The reader who is curious as to details of actual bayonet-fighting may consult Grattan for the 88th, and the anonymous 'T.' S.' of the 71st for Fuentes
d'Oñoro, and Steevens of the 20th for Roncesvalles. The charge of Tovey's
company of the latter corps, on the last-mentioned occasion, much resembled
one of the incidents of Inkerman.

famous battles were won by tremendous cavalry charges—notably Marengo and Dresden, while Eylau was just saved from falling into a disaster by a blow of the same kind. But cavalry must be used at precisely the right moment, must be skilfully led and pushed home without remorse, and even then it may be beaten off by thoroughly cool and unshaken troops. It is only against tired, distracted, or undisciplined battalions that it can count on a reasonable certainty of success. All through the war the Spanish armies supplied the French horsemen with exactly the opportunities that they required: they were always being surprised, or caught in confusion while executing some complicated manœuvre; and as if this was not enough, they were often weak enough in *morale* to allow themselves to be broken even when they had been allowed time to take their ground and form their squares. The battles of Gamonal (1808), Medellin, Alba de Tormes, and Ocaña (1809), the Gebora, and Saguntum (1811) were good examples of the power of masses of horse skilfully handled over a numerous but ill-disciplined infantry.

On the other hand, against the English the French cavalry hardly ever accomplished anything worthy of note. It is only possible to name two occasions on which they made their mark: the first was at Albuera, where, profiting by an opportune cloudburst which darkened the face of day, two regiments of lancers came in upon the flank of a British brigade (Colborne's of the second division), and almost entirely cut it to pieces. The second incident of the kind was at Fuentes d'Oñoro, in the same summer, when Montbrun's cavalry charged with some effect on Houston's division and hustled it back for some two miles, though they never succeeded in breaking its squares.

On the other hand the cases where the French horsemen found themselves utterly unable to deal with the British infantry were very numerous—we need only mention Cacabellos (during Moore's retreat), El Bodon, Salamanca, and several skirmishes during the retreat from Burgos in 1812. After such experiences it was no wonder that Foy, and other old officers of the army of Spain, looked with dismay upon Napoleon's great attempt at Waterloo to break down the long line of British squares between La Haye Sainte and Hougoumont, by the ˆcharges of ten or twelve thousand heavy cavalry massed on a short front of less than a mile [1]. The Emperor

[1] See Foy's diary in Girod de l'Ain, p. 277.

had never seen the British infantry fight, and was entirely ignorant of their resisting power.

Of fights between cavalry and cavalry, where the two sides were present in such equal numbers as to make the struggle a fair test of their relative efficiency, there were but few in the Peninsular War. In the early years of the struggle Wellington was very scantily provided with horsemen, and never could afford to engage in a cavalry battle on a large scale. Later on, when he was more happily situated in this respect, he showed such a marked reluctance to risk great cavalry combats that the old saying that he was 'pre-eminently an infantry general' seems justified. That he could use his horsemen vigorously enough, when he saw his opportunity, he showed at Assaye, long before he had made his name known in Europe. Yet the only one of his great battles in Spain where his dragoons took a prominent part in the victory was Salamanca, where Le Marchant's brigade struck such a smashing blow on the flank of the French army. We have his own authority [1] for the fact that he hesitated to mass great bodies of horse, because he doubted the tactical skill of his officers, and the power of the regiments to manœuvre. 'I considered our cavalry,' he wrote ten years after the war was over, 'so inferior to the French from want of order, that although I considered one squadron a match for two French, I did not like to see four British opposed to four French : and as the numbers increased and order, of course, became more necessary, I was the more unwilling to risk our men without having a superiority in numbers. They could gallop, but could not preserve their order.'

Foy, in his excellent history of the Spanish War, emits an opinion in words curiously similar to those of Wellington, stating that for practical purposes the English troopers were inferior to the French on account of their headlong impetuosity and want of power to manœuvre [2]. When two such authorities agree, there must clearly have been some solid foundation for their verdict. Yet it is hard to quote many combats in their support : there were cases, no doubt, where English regiments threw their chances away by their blind fury in charging, as did the 23rd Light Dragoons at Talavera, the 13th Light Dragoons near Campo Mayor on March 25, 1811, and Slade's brigade at Maguilla on June 11, 1812. Yet with the memory before us of Paget's admirable operations at Sahagun and

[1] Letter to Lord William Russell, July 31, 1826.   [2] Foy, i. 288-90.

Benevente in December, 1808, of Lumley's skilful containing of Latour Maubourg's superior numbers at Albuera, and his brilliant success at Usagre over that same general in 1811, as well as Cotton's considerable cavalry fight at Villa Garcia in 1812, it seems strange to find Wellington disparaging his own troopers. No doubt we must concede that the British horsemen did not show that marked superiority over their rivals of the same arm which Wellington's infantry always asserted. But fairly balancing their faults and their merits, it would seem that there was something wanting in their general no less than in themselves. A lover of the cavalry arm would have got more profit out of the British horse than Wellington ever obtained. It is noticeable that not one of the successful fights cited above took place under the eye or the direction of the Duke.

As to the Spanish cavalry, it was (as we have already had occasion to remark) the weakest point in the national army. In the first actions of the war it appeared on the field in such small numbers that it had no chance against the French. But later on, when the juntas succeeded in raising large masses of horsemen, their scandalous conduct on a score of fields was the despair of Spanish generals. We need only mention Medellin and Ocaña as examples of their misbehaviour. No French cavalry-general ever hesitated to engage with double of his own number of Spanish horse. When vigorously charged they never failed to give way, and when once on the move it was impossible to rally them. It was often found on the night of a battle that the mass of the cavalry was in flight twenty miles ahead of the infantry, which it had basely deserted.

Napoleon, as every student of the art of war knows, had started his career as an officer of artillery, and never forgot the fact. He himself has left on record the statement that of all his tactical secrets the concentration of an overwhelming artillery fire on a given point was the most important. 'When once the combat has grown hot,' he wrote, 'the general who has the skill to unite an imposing mass of artillery, suddenly and without his adversary's knowledge, in front of some point of the hostile position, may be sure of success.' His leading idea was to secure an overwhelming artillery preparation for his infantry attacks: for this reason his typical battle began with the massing of a great number of guns on the points of the enemy's line which he intended ultimately to break down. In this respect he abandoned entirely the vicious tactics that prevailed in the earlier years of the revolutionary war, when the cannon, instead of being concentrated, were distributed about in twos and threes among the infantry battalions. We shall find that his method had been perfectly assimilated by his subordinates: when the ground allowed of it, they were much given to collecting many guns at some salient point of the line, and bringing a concentrated fire to bear on the weak spot in the enemy's position. At Ocaña a battery of this kind had a great share in the credit of the victory; at Albuera it saved Soult's routed troops from complete destruction. The names of artillery generals like Senarmont and Ruty need honourable mention for such achievements. If the French artillery had less effect against the English than against most of Napoleon's foes, it was because of Wellington's admirable custom of hiding his troops till the actual moment of battle. Austrian, Russian, or Prussian generals occupied a hillside by long lines drawn up on the hither slope, of which every man could be counted. Hence they could be thoroughly searched out and battered by the French guns, long before the infantry was let loose. Wellington, on the other hand, loved to show a position apparently but half-defended, with his reserves, or even his main line, carefully hidden behind the crest, or covered by walls and hedges, or concealed in hollows and ravines. Hence the French artillery-preparation was much embarrassed: there were no masses to fire at, and it was impossible to tell how any part of the line was held. By the end of the war the French marshals grew very chary of attacking any position where Wellington showed fight, for they never could tell whether they were opposed by a mere rearguard, or by a whole army skilfully concealed.

The English armies, unlike the French, always took with them a comparatively small proportion of artillery, seldom so much as two guns to the thousand men, as Foy remarks. But what there was was excellent, from its high discipline and the accuracy of its fire. The Duke preferred to work with small and movable units, placed in well-chosen spots, and kept dark till the critical moment, rather than with the enormous lines of guns that Bonaparte believed in. His horse artillery was often pushed to the front in the most daring way, in reliance on its admirable power of manœuvring and its complete steadiness. At Fuentes d'Oñoro, for example, it was made to cover the retreat of the right wing before the masses of French cavalry, in a way that would have

seemed impossible to any one who was not personally acquainted
with Norman Ramsay and his gunners. Hence came the astounding
fact that during the whole war the Duke never in the open field
lost an English gun. Several times cannon were taken and re-
taken ; once or twice guns not belonging to the horse or field
batteries were left behind in a retreat, when transport failed. But
in the whole six years of his command Wellington lost no guns
in battle. Foy gives an unmistakable testimony to the English
artillery in his history, by remarking that in its material it was
undoubtedly superior to the French [1] : the same fact may be verified
from the evidence of our own officers, several of whom have left
their opinion on record, that after having inspected captured
French cannon, limbers, and caissons they much preferred their
own.

This statement, it must be remembered, only applies to the field
and horse artillery. The English siege artillery, all through the
war, was notably inferior to the French. Wellington never
possessed a satisfactory battering train, and the awful cost at
which his sieges were turned into successes is a testimony to the
inadequacy of his resources. The infantry were sent in to win, by
sheer courage and at terrible expense of life, the places that could
not be reduced by the ill-equipped siege artillery. There can
be no doubt that in poliorcetics the enemy was our superior :
but with a very small number of artillery officers trained to siege
work, an insignificant body of Royal Engineers [2], and practically no
provision of trained sappers [3], what was to be expected ? It was
not strange that the French showed themselves our masters in this
respect. But the fault lay with the organization at head quarters,
not with the artillery and engineer officers of the Peninsular army,
who had to learn their trade by experience without having received
any proper training at home.

[1] Foy, i. 296.

[2] It was usual to supplement the meagre supply of engineers by officers
who volunteered from the line.

[3] There were only the ' Royal Military Artificers' in very small numbers.
The rank and file of the engineer corps did not yet exist.

SECTION III
SARAGOSSA AND BAYLEN

CHAPTER I

OPENING OF HOSTILITIES: THE FRENCH INVASIONS OF ANDALUSIA AND VALENCIA

WHILE the provinces of Spain were bursting out, one after another, into open insurrection, Murat at Madrid and Bonaparte at Bayonne were still enjoying the fools' paradise in which they had dwelt since the formal abdication of Ferdinand VII. The former was busy in forcing the Junta of Regency to perform the action which he elegantly styled 'swallowing the pill,' i. e. in compelling it to do homage to Napoleon and humbly crave for the appointment of Joseph Bonaparte as King of Spain. He imagined that his only serious trouble lay in the lamentable emptiness of the treasury at Madrid, and kept announcing smooth things to his master—'The country was tranquil, the state of public opinion in the capital was far happier than could have been hoped: the native soldiery were showing an excellent disposition, the captains-general kept sending in good reports: the new dynasty was likely to be popular, and the only desire expressed by the people was to see their newly designated king arrive promptly in their midst [1].' Letters of this kind continued to flow from the pen of the Duke of Berg till almost the end of the month. Even after details of the insurrection of Aragon and the Asturias began to reach him, he could write on May 31 that a strong flying column would suffice to put everything right. About this time he was seized by a violent fever and took to his bed, just as things were commencing to grow serious. On his convalescence he left for France, after putting everything in charge of Savary, the man who of all Frenchmen most deserved the hatred of Spain. About the middle of June he recrossed the French frontier, and after a few weeks went off to

[1] Murat to Napoleon, May 18.

Naples to take up his new kingship there. Spain was never to see him again : the catastrophe which he had, by his master's orders, brought about, was to be conducted to its end by other hands.

While Murat lay sick at the suburban palace of Chamartin, and while Napoleon was drafting acts and constitutions which the assembly of notables at Bayonne were to accept and publish, the first acts of war between the insurgents and the French army of occupation took place.

We have already had occasion to point out that the main military strength of the insurrection lay in Galicia and Andalusia, the two districts in which large bodies of regular troops had placed themselves at the disposition of the newly organized juntas. In Valencia, Catalonia, and Murcia the movement was much weaker : in Old Castile, Aragon, and the Asturias it had hardly any other forces at its disposal than hordes of half-armed peasants. Clearly then Galicia and Andalusia were the dangerous points for the French, and the former more than the latter, since an army descending from its hills, and falling on the long line of communications between France and Madrid, might cause the gravest inconvenience. If there had been any organized Spanish forces in Aragon, there would have been an equal danger of an attack directed from Saragossa against the eastern flank of the French communications. But while Galicia was possessed of a numerous army of regular troops, Aragon had nothing to show but a mass of hastily assembled peasants, who were not yet fully provided with arms and were only just beginning to be told off into battalions.

Napoleon, at the moment when he began to order his troops to move, was under the impression that he had to deal with a number of isolated riots rather than with a general insurrection of the Spanish nation. His first orders show that he imagined that a few flying columns would be able to scour the disaffected districts and scatter the bands of insurgents without much trouble. Instead of a strategical plan for the conquest of Spain, we find in his directions nothing more than provisions for the launching of a small column against each point where he had been informed that a rising had broken out. He presupposes that the kingdom as a whole is quiet, and that bodies of 3,000 or 4,000 men may march anywhere, without having to provide for the maintenance of their communications with Madrid, or with each other. Only in a friendly country would it have been possible to carry out such orders.

There were at the Emperor's disposition, at the end of May, some 116,000 men beyond the Pyrenees: but the 26,000 troops under Junot in Portugal were so completely cut off from the rest, by the insurrection in Castile and Estremadura, that they had to be left out of consideration. Of the remainder the corps of Dupont and Moncey, 53,000 strong, lay in and about Madrid: Bessières, to whom the preservation of the main line of communications with France fell, had some 25,000 between Burgos and San Sebastian: Duhesme, isolated at Barcelona, and communicating with France by Perpignan and not by Bayonne, had only some 13,000 at his disposal in Catalonia. Up to the first week in June the Emperor thought that the 91,000 men of these four corps would be enough to pacify Spain.

His first design was somewhat as follows: Bessières was to keep a firm hand on the line of communications, but also to detach a division of 4,000 men under Lefebvre-Desnouettes against Saragossa, and a brigade under Merle to pacify Santander and the northern littoral. The Emperor does not at first seem to have realized that, with the army of Galicia hanging on his western flank, Bessières might not be able to spare men for such distant enterprises. He dealt with the corps as if it had nothing to face save the local insurgents of Aragon and Old Castile. From the large body of troops which lay about Madrid, Toledo, and Aranjuez, two strong columns were to be dispatched to strike at the two main centres of the insurrection in Southern Spain. Dupont was to take the first division of his army corps, with two brigades of cavalry and a few other troops, and march on Cordova and Seville. This gave him no more than about 13,000 men for the subjugation of the large and populous province of Andalusia. The other two infantry divisions of his corps remained for the present near Madrid [1].

On the other side of the capital, Marshal Moncey with a somewhat smaller force—one division of infantry from his own army corps and one brigade of cavalry, 9,000 men in all—was to move on Valencia, and to take possession of that city and of the great naval arsenal of Cartagena. His expedition was to be supported by a diversion from the side of Catalonia, for Duhesme (in spite of the small number of his army) was told to send a column along the sea-coast route, by Tarragona and Tortosa, to threaten Valencia

[1] For details of his force see the note on pp. 182–3.

from the north. Moncey's remaining infantry divisions, which were not detailed for the expedition that he was to lead, remained near Madrid, available (like Dupont's second and third divisions) for the reinforcement of Bessières or the strengthening of the two expeditionary columns, as circumstances might decide.

Clearly Dupont and Moncey were both sent forth to undertake impossible tasks. Napoleon had not comprehended that it was not provincial *émeutes* that he had to crush, but the regular resistance of a nation. To send a column of 12,000 men on a march through 300 miles of hostile territory to Cadiz, or a column of 9,000 men on a march of 180 miles to Valencia, presupposes the idea that the expeditions are affairs of police and not strategical operations. Our astonishment grows greater when we consider the character of the troops which Dupont and Moncey commanded. In the army of the former there was *one* veteran French battalion—that of the Marines of the Guard, six of raw recruits of the Legions of Reserve, two of Paris Municipal Guards (strangely distracted from their usual duties), one of the contingent of the Helvetic Confederation, and four of Swiss mercenaries in the Spanish service, who had just been compelled to transfer their allegiance to Napoleon. The cavalry consisted of four 'provisional regiments' of conscripts. It was a military crime of the first order to send 13,000 troops of this quality on an important expedition. Moncey's force was of exactly the same sort—eight battalions of conscripts formed in 'provisional regiments' and two 'provisional regiments' of dragoons, plus a Westphalian battalion, and two Spanish corps, who deserted *en masse* when they were informed that they were to march against Valencia in company with the marshal's French troops. He had not one single company or squadron of men belonging to the old imperial army.

Bessières was much more fortunate, as, among the 25,000 men of whom he could dispose, there were four veteran battalions of the line and two old regiments of cavalry; moreover there were sent ere long to his aid three of the battalions of the Imperial Guard which lay at Madrid, and four hundred sabres of the dragoons, chasseurs, and gendarmes of the same famous corps.

The march of the two expeditionary columns began on May 24, a date at which Murat and his master had but the faintest notion of the wide-spreading revolt which was on foot. Moncey and Dupont were both officers of distinction: the marshal was one of

the oldest and the most respected officers of the imperial army : he
had won the grade of general of division in the days of the Republic,
and did not owe his first start in life to Napoleon. Of all the
marshals he was by several years the senior. He passed as a steady,
capable, and prudent officer of vast experience. Dupont on the
other hand was a young man, who had first won a name by his
brilliant courage at the combat of Dirnstein in the Austrian war
of 1805. Since then he had distinguished himself at Friedland :
he was on the way to rapid promotion, and, if his expedition to
Andalusia had succeeded, might have counted on a duchy and
a marshal's baton as his reward. Napoleon knew him as a brave
and loyal subordinate, but had never before given him an independent command. He could hardly guess that, when left to his own
inspirations, such a brilliant officer would turn out to be dilatory,
wanting in initiative, and wholly destitute of moral courage. It is
impossible to judge with infallible accuracy how a good lieutenant
will behave, when first the load of responsibility is laid upon his
shoulders. On May 24, Dupont quitted Toledo with his 13,000
men : in the broad plains of La Mancha he met with no opposition.
Everywhere the people were sullen, but no open hostility was shown.
Even in the tremendous defiles of the Sierra Morena he found no
enemy, and crossed the great pass of Despeña-Perros without having
to fire a shot. Coming out at its southern end he occupied Andujar,
the town at the main junction of roads in Eastern Andalusia, on
June 5. Here he got clear intelligence that the whole country-
side was up in arms : Seville had risen on May 26, and the rest of
the province had followed its example. There was a large assembly
of armed peasants mustering at Cordova, but the regular troops
had not yet been brought up to the front. General Castaños,
whom the Junta had placed in chief command, was still busily
engaged in concentrating his scattered battalions, forming them
into brigades and divisions, and hastily filling up with recruits the
enormous gaps which existed in the greater part of the corps. The
regulars were being got together at a camp at Carmona, south of
the Guadalquivir, and not far from Seville. The organization of
new battalions, from the large number of volunteers who remained
when the old regiments were completed, took place elsewhere. It
would be weeks, rather than days, before the unorganized mass took
shape as an army, and Dupont might count on a considerable respite
before being attacked. But it was not only with the forces of

Castaños that he had to reckon : at Cordova, Seville, Granada, and
all the other towns of Andalusia, the peasants were flocking in to
be armed and told off into new regiments. There was every probability that in a few days the movement would spread northward
over the Sierra Morena into La Mancha. An insurrection in this
district would sever Dupont's communications with Madrid, for he
had not left behind him any sufficient detachments to guard the
defiles which he had just passed, or to keep open the great post-
road to the capital across the plains of New Castile. When he
started he had been under the impression that it was only local
troubles in Andalusia that he had to suppress.

Dupont was already beginning to find that the insurgents were
in much greater numbers than he had expected when he crossed
the Sierra Morena, but till he had made trial of their strength he
considered that it would be wrong to halt. He had close before
him the great city of Cordova, a most tempting prize, and he
resolved to push on at least so far before taking it upon himself to
halt and ask for reinforcements. His continued movement soon
brought about the first engagement of the war, as at the bridge of
Alcolea he found his advance disputed by a considerable hostile
force [June 7].

The military commandant of the district of Cordova was a certain
Don Pedro de Echávarri, a retired colonel whom the local Junta
had just placed in command of its levies. His force consisted of
10,000 or 12,000 peasants and citizens, who had only received their
arms three days before, and had not yet been completely told off
into regiments and companies. On the 4th of June he had been
sent a small body of old troops—one battalion of light infantry
(Campo Mayor), and one of militia (the 3rd Provincial Grenadiers of
Andalusia)—1,400 men in all, and with them eight guns. To have
abandoned Cordova without a fight would have discouraged the new
levies, and probably have led to Echávarri's own death ; for the
armed mob which he commanded would have torn him to pieces as
a traitor if he had refused to give battle. Accordingly he resolved
to defend the passage of the Guadalquivir at the point where the
high-road from Andujar crossed it, six miles outside Cordova. He
barricaded the bridge and placed his guns and the two old battalions
on the hither side of the river, in a position commanding the defile.
On each flank of them some thousands of the Cordovan insurgents
were drawn up, while the remainder of the levy, including all the

mounted men, were sent across the bridge, and hidden in some hills which overhung the road by which the French were coming. They were ordered to show themselves, and to threaten to fall upon the enemy from the flank, when he should have developed his attack upon the bridge. If Echávarri had been guided by military considerations he would not have dared to offer battle with such a raw and motley force to 12,000 French troops—even if the latter were but the conscripts of Dupont. But political necessity compelled him to make the attempt.

When Dupont found the position of Alcolea occupied, he cannonaded the Spaniards for a time, and then launched his vanguard against the bridge. The leading battalion (it was one of those formed of the Paris Municipal Guards) stormed the barricades with some loss, and began to cross the river. After it the rest of Pannetier's brigade followed, and began to deploy for the attack on the Spanish position. At this moment the Cordovan levies beyond the river showed themselves, and began to threaten a flank attack on Dupont. The latter sent his cavalry against them, and a few charges soon turned back the demonstration, and scattered the raw troops who had made it. Meanwhile Dupont's infantry advanced and overpowered the two regular battalions opposed to them : seeing the line broken, the masses of insurgents on the flanks left the field without any serious fighting. The whole horde gave way and poured back into Cordova and right through the city, whose ruined walls they made no attempt to defend. They had lost very few men, probably no more than 200 in all, while the French had suffered even less, their only casualties being thirty killed and eighty wounded, wellnigh all in the battalion which had forced the barricades at the bridge.

There would be no reason to linger even for a moment over this insignificant skirmish, if it had not been for the deplorable events which followed—events which did more to give a ferocious character to the war than any others, save perhaps the massacre by Calvo at Valencia, which was taking place (as it chanced) on that very same day, June 7.

Dupont, after giving his army a short rest, led it, still ranged in battle array, across the six miles of plain which separated him from Cordova. He expected to find the defeated army of Echávarri rallying itself within the city. But on arriving in front of its gates, he found the walls unoccupied and the suburbs deserted.

The Cordovans had closed their gates, but it was rather for the purpose of gaining time for a formal surrender than with any intention of resisting. Dupont had already opened negotiations for the unbarring of the gates, when a few scattered shots were fired at the French columns from a tower in the wall, or a house abutting on it. Treating this as a good excuse for avoiding the granting of a capitulation, Dupont blew open one of the gates with cannon, and his troops rushed into the empty streets without finding any enemy to defeat. The impudent fiction of Thiers to the effect that the entry of the French was seriously resisted, and that desperate street-fighting took place, is sufficiently disproved by the fact that in the so-called storming of Cordova the French lost altogether two killed and seven wounded.

Nevertheless the city was sacked from cellar to garret. Dupont's undisciplined conscripts broke their ranks and ran amuck through the streets, firing into windows and battering down doors. Wherever there was the least show of resistance they slew off whole households: but they were rather intent on pillage and rape than on murder. Cordova was a wealthy place, its shops were well worth plundering, its churches and monasteries full of silver plate and jewelled reliquaries, its vaults of the strong wines of Andalusia. All the scenes of horror that afterwards occurred at Badajoz or San Sebastian were rehearsed for the first time at Cordova; and the army of Dupont had far less excuse than the English marauders and murderers of 1812 and 1813. The French had taken the city practically without loss and without opposition, and could not plead that they had been maddened by the fall of thousands of their comrades, or that they were drunk with the fury of battle after many hours of desperate fighting at the breaches. Nevertheless, without any excuse of this sort, Dupont's army behaved in a way that would have suited better the hordes of Tilly and Wallenstein. Their commanders could not draw them away from their orgies and outrages till the next day: indeed, it seems that many of the French officers disgraced themselves by joining in the plunder. While the men were filling their haversacks with private property, there were found colonels and even generals who were not ashamed to load carts and coaches with pictures, tapestries, and metal-work from churches and public buildings, and bags of dollars from the treasury, where no less than 10,000,000 reals of specie had been found. Laplanne, whom

Dupont appointed commandant of the place, took 2,000 ducats of blackmail from the Count of Villanueva, on whom he had billeted himself, in return for preserving his mansion from pillage. When the French left Cordova, nine days later, they had with them more than 500 wheeled vehicles seized in the place which were loaded with all sorts of plunder [1].

Dupont had hardly settled down in Cordova, and begun to substitute crushing military contributions for unsystematic pillage, when he found himself cut off from his base. The valley of the Upper Guadalquivir, and the slopes of the Sierra Morena, on both the southern and the northern sides of the passes, rose in arms in the second week of June. The French had left no detachments behind to preserve their communications: between Cordova and Toledo there were only a few posts where stragglers and sick had been collected, some isolated officers busy on surveying or on raising contributions, and some bodies of ten or twenty men escorting couriers or belated trains of wagons bearing food or ammunition to the front. Most of these unfortunate people were cut up by the insurgents, who displayed from the first a most ferocious spirit. The news of the sack of Cordova drove them to the commission of inhuman cruelties; some prisoners were blinded, others tortured to death: Foy says that the brigadier-general Réné, surprised while crossing the Morena, was thrown into a vat of boiling water and scalded to death [2]. The parties which escaped massacre hastily drew back towards Madrid and Toledo, and soon there was not a French soldier within 150 miles of Dupont's isolated division.

That general did not at first realize the unpleasantness of his

---

[1] It is astonishing to find that Napier (i. 114) expressly denies that Cordova was sacked. Foy (iii. 231), the best of the French historians, acknowledges that 'unarmed civilians were shot, churches and houses sacked, and scenes of horror enacted such as had not been seen since the Christian drove out the Moor in 1236.' Captain Baste, the best narrator among French eye-witnesses, speaks of assassination, general pillage, and systematic rape. Cabany, Dupont's laudatory biographer, confesses (p. 89) to drunkenness and deplorable excesses, and allows that Dupont distributed 300,000 francs as a 'gratification' among his general officers. Many of the details given above are derived from the official narrative of the Cordovan municipal authorities printed in the *Madrid Gazette*.

[2] Foy, iii. 233. Cabany (p. 96), on the other hand, says that he was sawn in two between planks. Gille, in his *Mémoires d'un Conscrit de* 1808 (p. 85), gives other distressing details.

position. He had been sufficiently surprised by the opposition offered at Alcolea, and the rumours of the concentration of the army of Castaños, to make him unwilling to advance ¡beyond Cordova. He wrote to Murat asking for reinforcements, and especially for troops to keep open his lines of communication. There were, he said, at least 25,000 regular troops marching against him : the English might disembark reinforcements at Cadiz : the whole province was in a flame : it was impossible to carry out the Grand-Duke of Berg's original orders to push straight on to Seville. But matters were even worse than he thought : in a few days he realized, from the non-arrival of couriers from Madrid, that he was cut off : moreover, his foraging parties, even when they were only a few miles outside Cordova, began to be molested and some-times destroyed.

After waiting nine days, Dupont very wisely resolved to fall back, and to endeavour to reopen communications with his base. On June 16 he evacuated Cordova, much to the regret of his soldiers, who resented the order to abandon such comfortable quarters. On the nineteenth, dragging with him an enormous convoy of plunder, he reached Andujar, the great junction of roads where the routes from the passes of the Morena come down to the valley of the Guadalquivir. It would have been far wiser to go still further back, and to occupy the debouches of the defiles, instead of lingering in the plain of Andalusia. He should have retired to Baylen, the town at the foot of the mountains, or to La Carolina, the fortress in the upland which commands the southern exit of the Despeña Perros. But he was vainly dreaming of resuming the attempt to conquer the whole south of Spain when reinforcements should arrive, and Andujar tempted him, since it was the best point from which he could threaten at once Cordova, Jaen, and Granada, the three chief towns of Eastern Andalusia. Here, therefore, he abode from June 19 to July 18, a wasted month during which the whole situation of affairs in Spain was changed.

Here we must leave Dupont, while we treat of the doings of the other French generals during the month of June. While the invasion of Andalusia was running its course, both Moncey and Bessières had been seriously engaged.

The first named of the two marshals was placed in charge of one-half of the offensive part of Napoleon's plan for the subju-

gation of Spain, while Bessières was mainly responsible for the
defensive part, i. e. for the maintaining of the communications
between Madrid and Bayonne. It is with Moncey's expedition
against Valencia, therefore, that we must first deal. Although
he started a few days later than Dupont, that marshal was (like
his colleague) still dominated by the idea that possessed both
Napoleon and Murat—that the insurrections were purely local,
and that their suppression was a mere measure of police. This
notion accounts for his choice of route : there are two roads from
Madrid to Valencia, a long and fairly easy one which passes
through the gap between the mountains of Murcia and those of
Cuenca, by San Clemente, Chinchilla, and the plain of Almanza,
and a shorter one, full of dangerous defiles and gorges, which cuts
through the heart of the hills by Tarancon, Valverde, and Requeña.
The former crosses the watershed between the valley of the Tagus
and those of the rivers flowing into the Mediterranean Sea at
the easiest point, the latter at one of the most difficult ones. But
Moncey, thinking only of the need to deal promptly with the
Valencian insurgents, chose the shorter and more difficult route.

He left Madrid on June 4 : a week later he was near Cuenca,
in the midst of the mountains. Not a shot had yet been fired
at him, but as he pressed eastward he found the villages more
and more deserted, till at last he had reached a region that seemed
to have become suddenly depopulated. He turned a little out
of his way on the eleventh to occupy the city of Cuenca[1], the
capital of this wild and rugged country, but resumed his advance
on the eighteenth, after receiving from Madrid peremptory orders
to press forward[2]. There lay before him two tremendous defiles,
which must be passed if he was to reach Valencia. The first was
the deep-sunk gorge of the river Cabriel, where the highway
plunges down a cliff, crosses a ravine, and climbs again up a steep
opposing bank. The second, thirty miles further on, was the
Pass of the Cabrillas, the point where the road, on reaching the

[1] Cuenca lies twenty-five miles off the main Madrid-Valencia road, well to
the north of it.
[2] Moncey's delay of a week at Cuenca provoked Savary (now acting for the
invalided Murat) to such an extent, that he sent forward the cavalry-general
Excelmans, nominally to take charge of Moncey's vanguard, really to spur
the cautious marshal on to action. But Excelmans was captured on the way
by peasants, and sent a prisoner to Valencia.

edge of the central plateau of Spain, suddenly sinks down into the low-lying fertile plain of Valencia.

If the Conde de Cervellon, the general whom the Valencian Junta had put in charge of its army, had concentrated on these defiles the 7,000 or 8,000 regular troops who were to be found in the province and in the neighbouring district of Murcia, it is probable that Moncey would never have forced his way through the mountains; for each of the positions, if held in sufficient force, is practically impregnable. But the Spaniards had formed a deeply rooted notion that the invader would come by the easy road over the plains, by San Clemente and Almanza, and not through the mountains of Cuenca. The whole of the troops of Murcia and the greater part of those of Valencia had been directed on Almanza, where there was a good position for opposing an army descending from Castile. Only a small detachment had been sent to watch the northern road, and its commander, Don Pedro Adorno, had stationed at the bridge of the Cabriel no more than one battalion of Swiss mercenaries (No. 1 of Traxler's regiment) and 500 armed peasants with four guns. The position was too extensive to be held by 1,500 men : Moncey found that the river was fordable in several places, and detached a small column to cross at each, while two battalions dashed at the bridge. In spite of the steepness of the ravine the French got over at more than one point, and climbed the opposite slope, whereupon the peasants fled, and half the Swiss battalion was surrounded and captured while it was trying to cover the retreat of the guns [1]. Adorno, who was lying some miles to the rear, at Requeña, when he should have been present in full force at the bridge, ought now to have fallen back to cover Valencia, but in a moment of panic he fled across country to join the army at Almanza [June 21].

This disgraceful flight left the Valencian Junta almost destitute of troops for the defence of the still stronger defile of the Cabrillas, which Moncey had yet to force before he could descend into the plain. The Junta hurried up to it two regiments of recruits—one of which is said to have been first practised in the manual exercise the day before it went into action [2]. These, with 300 old soldiers, the wrecks of the combat at the Cabriel, and three guns, tried

[1] Moncey induced a good many of these mercenaries to take service with him ; but they deserted him when the time of trouble began.

[2] Arteche, *Guerra de la Independencia*, ii. 150.

to hold the pass.   Moncey turned both flanks of this very inadequate defending force, and then broke through its centre.
Many of the Spaniards dispersed, 500 were slain or captured, and
the rest fled down the pass to Valencia.   After riding round the
position, Moncey remarked that it was so strong that with 6,000
steady troops he would undertake to hold it against Napoleon
himself and the Grand Army [June 24].

Two days later, after a rapid march down the defile and across
the fertile Valencian plain, Moncey presented himself before the
gates of its capital, and demanded its surrender.   But he found
that there was still much fighting to be done : a small column
of regulars had arrived in the city, though the main army from
Almanza was still far distant.   With three battalions of old troops
and 7,000 Valencian levies, Don José Caro, a naval officer and
brother of the celebrated Marquis of La Romana, had taken up
a position four miles outside the city at San Onofre.   He had
covered his front with some irrigation canals, and barricaded the
road.   Moncey had to spend the twenty-seventh in beating back
this force into Valencia, not without some sharp fighting.

On the next day he made a general assault upon the city.
Valencia was not a modern fortress : it had merely a wet ditch and
an enceinte of mediaeval walls.   There were several points where it
seemed possible to escalade the defences, and the marshal resolved
to storm the place.   But he had forgotten that he had to reckon
with the auxiliary fortifications which the populace had constructed
during the last three days.   They had built up the gates with
beams and earth, barricaded the streets, mounted cannon on the
walls where it was possible, and established several batteries of
heavy guns to sweep the main approaches from the open country.
The city being situated in a perfectly level plain, and in ground
much cut up by irrigation canals, it had been found possible to
inundate much of the low ground.   As the river Guadalaviar washed
the whole northern side of the walls, Moncey's practicable points
of attack were restricted to certain short spaces on their southern
front.

The marshal first sent a Spanish renegade, a Colonel Solano, to
summon the place.   But the Valencians were exasperated rather
than cowed by their late defeats ; their leaders—especially Padre
Rico, a fighting priest of undoubted courage and capacity—had
worked them up to a high pitch of enthusiasm, and they must

have remembered that, if they submitted, they would have to render an account for Calvo's abominable massacre of the French residents. Accordingly the Junta returned the stirring answer that 'the people of Valencia preferred to die defending itself rather than to open any sort of negotiations.' A mixed multitude of 20,000 men, of whom some 8,000 were troops of one sort and another [1], manned the walls and barricades and waited for the assault.

After riding round the exposed front of the city, Moncey resolved to attack only the south-eastern section. He formed two columns, each of a brigade, of which one assailed the gate of San José near the river, while another marched on the gate of Quarte, further to the south. Considering the weak resistance that he had met at the Cabriel and at the Pass of the Cabrillas, he had formed a sanguine expectation that the Valencians would not make a firm stand, even behind walls and barricades. In this he was wofully deceived : the French had yet to learn that the enemy, though helpless in the open, was capable of the most obstinate resistance when once he had put himself under cover of bricks and earth. The first assault was beaten off with heavy loss, though Moncey's conscripts showed great dash, reached the foot of the defences, and tried to tear down the palisades with their hands. The marshal should have seen at once that he had too large a business in hand for the 8,000 men of whom he could dispose. But he persevered, bringing forward his field artillery to batter the gates and earthworks before a second assault should be made. It was to no purpose, as they were soon silenced by the guns of position which the besieged had prepared for this very purpose. Late in the afternoon Moncey risked a second general attack, embracing the gate of Santa Lucia as well as the other points which he had before assailed. But the stormers were beaten off with even heavier loss than on the first assault, and bodies of the defenders, slipping out by posterns and side-gates, harassed the retreating columns by a terrible flanking fire.

Clearly the game was up : Moncey had lost at least 1,200 men, a sixth of his available infantry force [2]. He was much to blame

---

[1] But only 1,500 were regulars ; the rest were newly incorporated levies.

[2] Foy, generally a very fair calculator of French casualties, gives the marshal's losses at 2,000 men in all, which seems rather a high figure. Napier (i. 95) says that he had 800 wounded to carry, which supposes a total

for pressing the attack when his first movement failed, for as
Napoleon (wise after the event) said in his commentary on the
marshal's operations : 'On ne prend pas par le collet une ville de
quatre-vingt mille âmes.' If the first charge did not carry the
walls, and the garrison stood firm, the French could only get in
by the use of siege artillery, of which they did not possess a single
piece.

Moncey's position was now very dangerous : he knew that the
country was up in arms behind him, and that his communications
with Madrid were completely cut.   He was also aware that
Cervellon's army from Almanza must be marching towards him,
unless it had taken the alternative course of pressing in on his rear,
to occupy the difficult passes by which he had come down into the
Valencian coast-plain.   His conscripts were dreadfully discouraged
by their unexpected reverse : he was hampered by a great convoy
of wounded men, whose transport would cause serious delays.
Nothing had been heard of the diversion which General Chabran,
with troops detached from Duhesme's army in Catalonia, had
been ordered to execute towards the northern side of Valencia. As
a matter of fact that general had not even crossed the Ebro.
Retreat was necessary : of the three possible lines on which it
could be executed, that along the coast road, in the direction where
Chabran was to be expected, was thought of for a moment, but
soon abandoned : it was too long, and the real base of the
marshal's corps was evidently Madrid, and not Barcelona. The
route by Tarancon and the Cabrillas, by which the army had
reached Valencia, was terribly difficult : clearly it would be necessary to force again the defiles which had been cleared on the way
down to the coast.   And it was possible that 9,000 or 10,000
regular troops might now be occupying them.

Accordingly, Moncey resolved to retire by the third road, that
through the plains by Almanza and San Clemente. If, as was
possible, Cervellon's whole army was now blocking it, they must
be fought and driven off : a battle in the plain would be less
dangerous than a battle at the Cabrillas or the bridge of the
Cabriel. Before daylight on June 29, therefore, the marshal moved
off on this road.

loss of 1,100 or 1,200. Thiers' estimate of 300 is as obviously absurd as most
of the other figures given by that historian. No such loss would have stopped
a French army—even an army of conscripts.

Luck now came to his aid: the incapable Spanish commander had made up his mind that the French would retreat by the way that they had come, and had sent forward General Llamas with all the troops of Murcia to seize the defile of the Cabrillas. He himself followed with the rest of the regulars, but halted at Alcira, behind the Xucar. Thus while Moncey was marching to the south, the main body of his enemies was moving northward. Cervellon refused to fight in the absence of Llamas, so nothing was left in the marshal's way save bands of peasants who occupied the fords of the Xucar and the road between Jativa and Almanza: these he easily brushed away in a couple of skirmishes. Nor did a small column detached in pursuit from Valencia dare to meddle seriously with his rearguard. So without even exchanging a shot with the Spanish field-army, which Cervellon had so unwisely scattered and sent off on a false track, Moncey was able to make his way by Jativa, Almanza, and Chinchilla back towards La Mancha [July 2-6].

At San Clemente he met with reinforcements under General Frère, consisting of the third division of Dupont's original corps, some 5,000 strong. This division had been sent to search for him by Savary, who had been filled with fears for his safety when he found that the communications were cut, and that Cuenca and all the hill-country had risen behind the expeditionary force. After vainly searching for Moncey on the northern road, in the direction of Requeña, Frère at last got news that he had taken the southern line of retreat, and successfully joined him on July 8. At San Clemente the marshal intended to halt and to wait for Cervellon's arrival, in the hope of beating him in the open. But a few days later he received news from Madrid, to the effect that Savary wished to draw back the French forces nearer to the capital, and that Frère, at least, must move in to Ocaña or Toledo. Much displeased at finding a junior officer acting as the lieutenant of the Emperor—for Savary was but a lieutenant-general, while he himself was a marshal—Moncey threw up the whole scheme of waiting to fight the Valencian army, and marched back to the immediate neighbourhood of Madrid [July 15].

There can be no doubt that the marshal had extraordinary luck in this short campaign. If he had been opposed by a general less timid and incapable than the Conde de Cervellon, he might have found arrayed against him, at the bridge of the Cabriel, or at the

Cabrillas, a considerable body of regulars—eight or nine thousand men—with a numerous artillery, instead of the insignificant forces which he actually defeated. Again, while he was trying to storm Valencia, Cervellon might have attacked him in the rear with great chance of success ; or the Spaniard might have kept his forces united, and opposed Moncey as he retreated from before Valencia. Instead of doing so he split up his army into detachments, and the greater part of it was sent off far from the central point of his operations, and did not fire a shot. Truly such a general was, as Thucydides remarks concerning the Spartans of old, 'very convenient for his adversaries.' A less considerate enemy would have had a fair chance of bringing Moncey's campaign to the same disastrous end that befell that of Dupont.

SECTION III : CHAPTER II

OPERATIONS IN THE NORTH : THE SIEGE OF SARAGOSSA

HAVING watched the failure of the expeditions by which Napoleon had hoped to complete the conquest of Southern Spain, we must turn our eyes northward, to Madrid and the long line of communications which joined the capital to the French base of operations at Vittoria, Pampeluna, and San Sebastian. At the moment when the Valencian and Andalusian expeditions were sent out from Madrid and Toledo, Murat had still under his hand a large body of troops, the second and third division of Moncey's corps, the second and third of Dupont's, and the 5,000 horse and foot of the Imperial Guard—in all more than 30,000 men. Bessières, if the garrison of the northern fortresses and some newly arrived reinforcements are added to his original force, had more than 25,000. With these the grand-duke and the marshal had to contain the insurrection in Northern Spain, and to beat back the advance of the army of Galicia.

The furthest points to the north and east to which the wave of insurrection had washed up were Logroño and Tudela in the Ebro valley, Santander on the coast of the Bay of Biscay, and Palencia and Valladolid in Old Castile. All these places lay in Bessières' sphere of action, and he promptly took measures to suppress the rising at each point. On June 2 a column sent out from Vittoria reoccupied Logroño, slaying some hundreds of half-armed peasants, and executing some of their leaders who had been taken prisoners. On the same day a stronger force, six battalions and two squadrons under General Merle, marched from Burgos on Santander. Driving before him the insurgents of the Upper Ebro valley, Merle advanced as far as Reynosa, and was about to force the defiles of the Cantabrian Mountains and to descend on to Santander, when he received orders to return and to take part in suppressing the more dangerous rising in the plains of Old Castile. News had arrived that the captain-general, Cuesta, was collecting a force at Valladolid, which threatened to cut the road between Burgos and Madrid. To deal with him Bessières told off Merle, and another small column of four battalions and two regiments of *chasseurs* under his brilliant cavalry-brigadier, Lasalle, one of the best of Napoleon's younger generals. After sacking Torquemada (where some peasants attempted an ineffectual resistance) and ransoming the rich cathedral town of Palencia, Lasalle got in touch with the forces of Cuesta at the bridge of Cabezon, where the main road from Burgos to Valladolid crosses the river Pisuerga. On the eleventh of June Merle joined him: on the twelfth their united forces, 9,000 strong, fell upon the levies of the Captain-general.

Throughout the two years during which he held high command in the field, Gregorio de la Cuesta consistently displayed an arrogance and an incapacity far exceeding that of any other Spanish general. Considering the state of his embryo 'army of Castile,' it was insane for him to think of offering battle. He had but four cannon; his only veteran troops were 300 cavalry, mainly consisting of the squadrons which had accompanied Ferdinand VII as escort on his unhappy journey to Bayonne. His infantry was composed of 4,000 or 5,000 volunteers of the Valladolid district, who had not been more than a fortnight under arms, and had seen little drill and still less musketry practice. It was absolutely wicked to take them into action. But the men, in their ignorance, clamoured for a battle, and Cuesta did not refuse it to them. His dispositions were simply astounding; instead of barricading or destroying the bridge and occupying the further bank, he led his unhappy horde across the river and drew them up in a single line, with the bridge at their backs.

On June 12 Lasalle came rushing down upon the 'army of Castile,' and dashed it into atoms at the first shock. The Spanish cavalry fled (as they generally did throughout the war), the infantry broke, the bridge and the guns were captured. Some hundreds of the unfortunate recruits were sabred, others were drowned in the river. Cuesta fled westwards with the survivors to Medina de Rio Seco, abandoning to its fate Valladolid, which Lasalle occupied without opposition on the same evening. The combat by which this important city was won had cost the French only twelve killed and thirty wounded.

This stroke had completely cleared Bessières' right flank: there could be no more danger from the north-west till the army of Galicia should think proper to descend from its mountains to contest with the French the dominion of the plains of Leon and Old Castile. The marshal could now turn his attention to other fronts of his extensive sphere of command. After the fight of Cabezon Merle's division was sent northward, to conquer the rugged coast-land of the province of Santander. There were frightful defiles between Reynosa and the shore of the Bay of Biscay : the peasants had blocked the road and covered the hillsides with *sungahs*. But the defence was feeble—as might be expected from the fact that the district could only put into the field one battalion of militia [1] and a crowd of recent levies, who had been about three weeks under arms. On June 23 Merle finished clearing the defiles and entered Santander, whose bishop and Junta fled, with the wreck of their armed force, into the Asturias.

Meanwhile the troops under Bessières had been equally active, but with very different results, on the Middle Ebro and in the direction of Aragon. It was known at Burgos and at Bayonne that Saragossa had risen like the rest of the Spanish cities. But it was also known that there was hardly a man of regular troops in the whole kingdom of Aragon : here, as in Old Castile or in Santander, the invaders would have to deal only with raw levies, who would probably disperse after their first defeat. Saragossa itself, the central focus of the rising, was no modern fortress, but a town of 60,000 souls, surrounded by a mediaeval wall more fitted to assist in the levy of *octroi* duties, than in a defence against a regular army. Accordingly the column under Lefebvre Desnouettes, which was directed to start from Pampeluna against the Aragonese insurgents, was one of very moderate size—3,500 infantry, 1,000 horse, and a single battery of field artillery [2]. But it was to be joined a few days later by another brigade [3] and battery, which would bring its total force up to something more than 6,000 men.

The resources of the kingdom of Aragon were large, but the patriots were, when the war broke out, in a condition most unfavourable for strenuous action. The province was one of those which had been denuded of its usual garrison : there only remained part of

[1] 'Provincial of Laredo,' 571 bayonets.

[2] They were a battalion each of the 15th, 47th, and 70th of the line, all old troops, and the 2nd 'Supplementary Regiment of the legions of Reserve,' two battalions strong, with a regiment of Polish lancers and the 5th *escadron de marche*.

[3] The 1st regiment of the Vistula (two batts.) and the 6th *bataillon de marche*.

a cavalry regiment, the 'King's Dragoons,' whose squadrons had been so depleted that it had only 300 men and ninety horses, with a weak battalion of Volunteers of Aragon—some 450 men—and 200 gunners and sappers.   In addition there had straggled into Saragossa about 500 men from various Spanish corps at Madrid, Burgos, and elsewhere, who had deserted their colours when the news of the insurrection reached them.   This was a small *cadre* on which to create a whole army, but the feat was accomplished by the energetic young man who put himself at the head of the rising in the middle valley of the Ebro.   Joseph Palafox, the second son of a noble family of Aragon, had been one of the suite which accompanied Ferdinand VII to Bayonne, and was an indignant spectator of the abominable treachery which there took place.   When the tragedy was over he was fortunate enough to escape to Spain : he retired to his native district, took a prominent part in rousing the Aragonese, and was chosen by them as Captain-general when the weak or incapable Guillelmi was deposed.   He was only twenty-eight years of age, and had no military experience, for he had only served in the peaceful ranks of the king's bodyguard [1].   He had been a courtier rather than a soldier, yet at the critical moment of his life it can-

[1] Palafox has been so often abused that I take the opportunity of quoting the description of him given by Sir Charles Vaughan, one of the three or four Englishmen who saw him at Saragossa in the day of his power, and the only one who has left his impressions on record.   He lived with Palafox for some five weeks in October–November, 1808.   'This distinguished nobleman is about thirty-four years of age [an overstatement by six years] ; his person is of middling stature, his eyes lively and expressive, and his whole deportment that of a perfectly well-bred man.   In private life, so far as my daily intercourse gave me an opportunity of judging, his manners were kind, unaffected, and ingratiating.   From the great readiness with which he dispatched business, and from the letters and public papers which were written by him with apparent great ease in my presence, I was led to form a very favourable opinion of his talents.   There was a quickness in his manner of seizing objects, an impatience until they were accomplished.   He was fond of talking of the events of the siege, and anxious to introduce to us men of every class who had distinguished themselves.   There was a vivacity in his manner and conversation, an activity in his exertions as an officer, that is rarely met in a Spaniard.   It was always a most cheering and interesting thing to ride with him through the streets of Saragossa.   The joy and exultation of the people as he passed evidently sprung from the heart.   To have acquitted himself to their satisfaction was no mean reward, and forms a sufficient answer to all the unworthy attempts (which I have been disgusted to witness) to depreciate his character' (*Vaughan Papers*, from an unpublished journal of 1808).

not be denied that he displayed a courage and energy which justified the high opinions which the Aragonese entertained of him. He kept Saragossa clean from the plague of political assassination, which was so rife in every other corner of Spain. He wisely got his appointment as Captain-general confirmed by the Cortes of Aragon, which he summoned to meet in its ancient form. He found out the most capable leaders of the populace, and always asked their advice before taking any important step. But his main virtue was his untiring activity: considering the procrastination and want of organizing power displayed by most of the Spanish generals, his talent for rapid work seems remarkable. He was only placed in power on May 26, and by June 8 he was already engaged with the French. In this short time he had raised and organized seven regiments of new levies—7,400 men in all. They were stiffened with the deserters from Madrid, and commanded by such retired and half-pay officers as could be got together. There were some scores of cannon in the arsenal of Saragossa, but hardly any gunners, and a very small store of ammunition. Palafox started a powder factory and a manufactory of small arms, turned the workmen of the Canal of Aragon into a corps of sappers, and made a general levy of horses to remount his single regiment of dragoons, and to provide his artillery with draught animals. This was but the commencement of Palafox's activity: ere Saragossa was saved he had raised the whole kingdom, and got more than 30,000 men under arms[1].

Already by the eighth of June he had hurried out a small force to meet Lefebvre Desnouettes at Tudela, the frontier town on the Ebro, which in the Middle Ages had been known as 'the key of Aragon.' This force, which consisted of 2,000 of his new levies, was placed under the command of his own elder brother the Marquis of Lazan, who had escaped from Madrid under the pretext that he would bring pressure to bear upon the Captain-general and induce him to submit to Murat. The marquis, though joined by

[1] Napier is always hard on Spanish officers and administrators, but I think that of the whole class Palafox receives the most undeserved contumely from his pen. He holds him to have been a mere puppet, whose strings were pulled by obscure Saragossan demagogues like the celebrated Tio Jorge. He even doubts his personal courage. Both Spanish and French historians unite in taking the Captain-general quite seriously, and I think they are right. His best testimonial is the harsh and vindictive treatment that he received at Napoleon's hands.

3,000 or 4,000 peasants and citizens of Tudela, was easily routed by the French column, and forced back to Mallen sixteen miles nearer to Saragossa. Lefebvre followed him, after having executed a certain number of the notables of Tudela and sacked the town. Reinforced by more of his brother's new levies, Lazan offered battle again at Mallen, in a bad position, where his men had little protection against the enemy's artillery and the charges of his Polish lancers. He was naturally routed with severe losses. But even then the Aragonese were not broken in spirit : Palafox himself marched out with the remainder of his new levies, some of whom had not been five days under arms. At Alagon, only seventeen miles from the gates of Saragossa, he drew up 6,000 infantry (of whom 500 were regulars) 150 dragoons and four guns, trying to cover himself by the line of the Canal of Aragon and some olive groves. It is hardly necessary to say that his artillery was overpowered by the fourteen pieces of the French, and that his infantry gave back when furiously assailed by the Poles. Palafox charged at the head of his two squadrons of dragoons, but was wounded in the arm and had his horse killed under him. His routed followers carried him back into the city, where the majority took refuge, while the more faint-hearted fled beyond it to Alcaniz and other points in Upper Aragon.

Elated by three easy victories, Lefebvre thought that there was nothing more to do but to enter Saragossa in triumph. He was much deceived: the citizens were standing at bay behind their flimsy defences, having recovered in a single night from the dismay caused by the arrival of the broken bands who had fought at Alagon. The military conditions were not unlike those which Moncey had to face in another region, a fortnight later : Saragossa like Valencia lies in an extensive plain, with its northern side washed by the waters of the Ebro, and its eastern by those of the shallow and fordable Huerba : but its southern and western fronts are exposed to attack from the open. It was surrounded by a brick wall of ten to twelve feet high, interrupted in several places by convents and barracks whose blank back-faces continued the line of the *enceinte* [1]. Inside the wall were the crowded lanes in which dwelt the 60,000 citizens, a tangle of narrow streets save the one broad Coso which intersects the place from east to west. The

---

[1] The chief of these buildings inserted in the wall were the convents of Santa Engracia and the Misericordia, and the cavalry barracks.

houses were mostly solid and lofty structures of brick and stone, with the heavy barred windows and doors usual in Spain. The strength, such as it was, of Saragossa consisted not in its outer shell, but in the closely packed houses, convents, and churches, each of which might serve at need as a small fortress. Many of them were solid enough to resist any form of attack save that of being battered by artillery. When barricades had been thrown across the lanes from side to side, each square of buildings would need to be assaulted and captured piecemeal. But none of the French officers who arrived in front of Saragossa on June 15, 1808, had any conception that the problem about to be presented to them was that of street-fighting carried on from house to house. There had been many sieges since the war of the French Revolution began, but none carried on in this manner. In Italy or Germany no one had ever heard of a city which tried, for want of bastions and curtains, to defend itself by barricades : such places always saved themselves by an obvious and blameless surrender.

But if a siege was coming, there was one position just outside the town which was clearly destined to play a chief part in it. Just across the Huerba lay a broad flat-topped hill, the Monte Torrero, which rose to the height of 180 feet, and overlooked all the south side of the place. It was such a splendid vantage-ground for siege-batteries, that the defenders were bound to hold it, lest it should fall into the power of the French. It should have been crowned by a strong detached fort, or even by an entrenched camp. But Palafox in the short time at his disposal had only been able to throw up a couple of open batteries upon it, and to loophole the extensive magazines and workshops of the Canal of Aragon, which were scattered over the summit of the hill, while the canal itself flowed, as a sort of outer defence, around its further foot.

Saragossa had two other outlying defences : the one was the Aljafferia, an old square castle with four towers at its corners, which had been the abode of Moorish emirs, and of Aragonese kings, but now served as the prison of the Inquisition. It lay a couple of hundred yards outside the western gate (Puerto del Portillo) of the city. It was a solid brick structure, but quite unsuited to resist a serious artillery attack. The second outwork was the suburb of San Lazaro beyond the Ebro : it was connected with Saragossa by a new and handsome bridge, known as the

' Puente de Piedra,' or 'Stone Bridge.'   Cannon were mounted at
its southern end so as to sweep its whole length.

On June 15, Lefebvre-Desnouettes appeared before the city,
driving before him some Spanish outposts which he had met upon
the way.   He resolved at once to carry the place by storm, a task
which, considering the weakness of its walls, did not seem impossible,
and all the more so because the gates stood open, each defended
only by an earthwork containing two or three guns.   The French
general, neglecting the Monte Torrero and its commanding slopes,
attacked only the western front between the gate of Portillo, near
the Ebro, and the gate of Santa Engracia, close to the banks of the
Huerba.   His French brigade assailed the northern and his Polish
regiment the southern half of this long line of walls and buildings.
His two field-batteries were run up into the fighting line, to batter
the earthworks and to reply to the Spanish guns.   The only reserve
which he kept in hand consisted of his brigade of cavalry.

The resistance offered to Lefebvre was of the most irregular
sort : Palafox himself was not present, and his second-in-command,
Bustamante, seems to have done little in the way of issuing orders.
The 6,000 half-trained levies which had fought at Alagon had not
recovered their organization, and were hopelessly mixed in the line
of defence with 4,000 or 5,000 armed citizens of all ages and
classes who had gone to the walls, each parish under the charge of
two or three local leaders, who paid little obedience to the commands of the regular officers.

The Captain-General himself had started out that morning at the
head of 150 dragoons, and 200 infantry, all regulars, by the road
beyond the Ebro.   He had told his subordinates that he was
intending to raise in Upper Aragon a force with which he would
fall on Lefebvre's line of communications, and so compel him to
abandon his attack on the city.   But there is no doubt that he
had really conceived grave doubts as to the possibility of Saragossa
defending itself, and intended to avoid being captured within its
walls.   He wished to have the power of continuing the struggle
outside, in case the French should penetrate into the city.   On the
morning after the fight at Alagon, bruised and wounded, he was
in a pessimistic frame of mind, as his resolve shows.   But there
is no occasion to brand him, as does Napier, with timidity : his
previous and his subsequent conduct preclude such a charge.   It
was merely an error of judgement : the Captain-General should have

stayed behind to defend his capital, and have sent his brother Lazan, or some other officer whom he could trust, to raise the country-side in the rear of the French [1]. His retirement might well have discouraged the Saragossans and led to deplorable results; but as a matter of fact, Lefebvre's attack began so soon after he had ridden out over the bridge, that the news of his departure had not yet got abroad, and the populace were still under the impression that he was among them. It was not till the fighting was over that he was missed.

Lefebvre-Desnouettes before Saragossa was in exactly the same position as Moncey before Valencia, and acted in the same way, pushing forward a rather reckless attack on the city in full confidence that the Spaniards would not stand before an assault pressed home. He had, moreover, the advantages of being able to attack a wider front, of having no ditches and inundations to cramp his operations, and of dealing with walls even weaker than those of Valencia, and defended by artillery of which very few were pieces of heavy calibre.

The first attack was delivered in the most dashing, not to say foolhardy, style. At the gate of Santa Engracia a squadron of Polish lancers, who led the van, charged into and over the small battery which covered the ingress into the city. Their wild rush carried them right into the place, in spite of a dropping fire of musketry directed upon them from every house that they passed. Turning into a broad lane to the left, these headstrong horsemen rode forward, losing men at every step, till they were brought to a stand in the Plaza del Portillo, where the majority were shot down; a very few succeeded in escaping by the way along which they had come. The Polish infantry, which should have followed closely on the heels of the lancers, penetrated no further than the earthwork at the gate, where it got closely engaged with the Spaniards who held the neighbouring convent of Santa Engracia. Exposed in the open street to a heavy fire from behind walls and windows, the leading battalion gave way, and retired into the olive groves and buildings outside the gate.

[1] That Palafox and those about him despaired of the defence is honestly confessed in the Marquis de Lazan's *Campaña del verano de* 1808. He and his brother ' had not believed that an open town defended by untrained peasants could defend itself,' and the news of Lefebvre's first repulse astonished as much as it pleased them.

Meanwhile the French brigade of Lefebvre's division attacked the gates of Portillo and the Carmen and the adjoining cavalry barracks. At the last-named post they scaled the walls, which were particularly low and weak at this point, and got into the city. But at the gates the batteries in the narrow ingress held them back. After a sharp skirmish, a general rush of peasants, soldiers, and citizens, swept out the invaders from the cavalry barracks, and the front of defence was restored. Lefebvre would have done well to pause before renewing his assault: but (like Moncey at Valencia) he was loth to believe that the enemy would face a persistent attempt to break in. He accordingly ordered both the columns to renew their attacks: for some time it seemed likely that he might succeed, for the French forced both the Carmen and the Portillo gates and reoccupied the cavalry barracks, while the Poles burst in for a second time at Santa Engracia. But it proved impossible to make any further advance into the city, where every house was full of musketeers and the narrow lanes were blocked with artillery, which swept them from end to end. When it became clear that the enemy were making no further progress, the Spaniards rallied behind the Bull-Ring on the Portillo front, and in the convent of Santa Engracia on the southern front, and swept out the decimated battalions of Lefebvre by a determined charge [1].

It is not surprising to find that the assailants had suffered very heavily in such a desperate attack on walls and barricades teeming with defenders worked up to a high pitch of patriotic frenzy. Lefebvre lost 700 men, and left behind him at the Portillo gate several guns which had been brought up too close to the place, and could not be dragged off under the dreadful musketry fire from the walls, and the flanking discharges from the neighbouring castle of Aljafferia. The Spaniards, fighting under cover except at the moment of their final charges, had suffered comparatively little: their loss is estimated at not much over 300 men. They might well be proud of their success: they had certainly showed a heroic spirit in fighting so obstinately after three crushing defeats in the open field. That a practically unfortified town should defend itself by street-fighting was a new idea: and that

[1] The Spaniards have called this first attack on Saragossa the action of the Eras del Rey, the name of the meadows outside the Portillo and Carmen gates, in which the French columns massed themselves for the attack.

peasants and citizens (there were not 900 regulars in the place) should not only hold out behind walls, but execute desperate charges *en masse*, would till that day have been regarded as impossible by any soldier of Napoleon. Every thinking man in the French army must have looked with some dismay on the results of the fight, not because of the loss suffered, for that was a mere trifle, but because of the prospect of the desperate national resistance which had evidently to be faced.

Meanwhile, Lefebvre-Desnouettes retired for some thousands of yards from the city, and pitched his camp facing its western front. He sent pressing letters asking for reinforcements both to Madrid and to Bayonne, and attempted no offensive action for ten days. If he sent a formal summons of surrender to the Saragossans, it was to waste time and allow fresh troops to arrive, rather than with any hope that he could intimidate the citizens. He was himself more likely to be attacked during the next few days than to make any forward movement. But he was already beginning to receive reinforcements: on June 21 there arrived two battalions of the 2nd Regiment of the Vistula, and more troops were behind.

Palafox, on the other hand, received much unexpected encouragement from the combat of the sixteenth. On receiving the news of it at Belchite on the following morning, he sent back his brother, the Marquis de Lazan, giving him the command of the city, and bidding him tell the Saragossans that he would endeavour to raise the siege in a very few days. There was already a considerable body of insurgents in arms in South-western Aragon, under the Baron de Versage, who had raised at Calatayud two battalions of new levies [1], and gathered in some fugitives from the Spanish garrison of Madrid. Palafox ordered the baron to join him with every man that he could bring, and their two detachments met at Almunia on June 21, and from thence marched towards Saragossa by the road which leads down the valley of the Xalon by Epila. At the last-named place they were only fifteen miles from Lefebvre-Desnouettes' camp, and were already threatening the French communications with Logroño and Vittoria. But their army was still very small—no more than 550 regular infantry, 1,000 men of Versage's new regiments, 350 cavalry, and a couple of thousand

[1] He called them the 'Regiment of Ferdinand VII,' and the 'Second Regiment of the kingdom of Aragon.'

levies of all kinds, among whom were noted a company of eighty armed Capuchin friars and a body of mounted smugglers.

The French general had now to make up his mind whether he would raise the siege and fall upon Palafox with his whole army, or whether he would dare to divide his scanty resources, and maintain the attack on the city with one part, while he sent a containing force against the Captain-General's bands. He resolved to take the latter course—a most hazardous one considering the fact that he had, even with his last reinforcements, not much more than 6,000 sound men in his camp. He dispatched the Polish Colonel Chlopiski with the first regiment of the Vistula, one French battalion, a squadron of lancers and four guns to hold back Palafox, while with the 3,000 men that remained he executed several demonstrations against outlying parts of the defences of Saragossa, in order to distract the attention of the citizens.

This very risky plan was carried out with complete success. While the Saragossans were warding off imaginary attacks, Chlopiski made a forced march and fell upon Palafox at Epila on the night of June 23–24. The Aragonese army was completely surprised and routed in a confused engagement fought in the dark. Several hundred were cut up, and the town of Epila was sacked: Palafox fell back in disorder towards Calatayud and the mountains, while Chlopiski returned to the siege.

The Captain-General, much disconcerted by this disaster, resolved that he would fight no more battles in the open, but merely reinforce the city with the best of his soldiers and resist behind its walls. So sending back Versage and his levies to the hills, he made an enormous detour with his handful of veteran troops and a few hundred irregulars, and re-entered Saragossa by the northern side, which still remained open. He had great difficulty in holding his followers together, for many (and especially his untrustworthy cavalry) wished to retire on Valencia and to abandon the struggle in Aragon. But by appealing to their patriotism—'he would give every man who insisted on it a passport for Valencia, but those who loved him would follow him'—he finally carried off the whole force, and took somewhat over 1,000 men back to the besieged city [July 1].

During his absence the condition of affairs in Saragossa had been considerably altered. On the one hand the defences had been much improved: the gates had been strongly stockaded, and the

walls had been thickened with earth and sandbags, and furnished
with a continuous *banquette*, which had hitherto been wanting.   On
the other hand the French were beginning to receive reinforcements:
on the twenty-sixth General Verdier arrived with three battalions of
his division (the second of Bessières' corps)[1] and two *bataillons de
marche*, in all some 3,000 or 3,500 men.   From this time forward
small bodies of troops began to reach the besiegers at short intervals,
including two more Polish battalions[2], one battalion of French
regulars, two Portuguese battalions (the last of the unfortunate
division which was on its way across Spain towards the Baltic),
1,000 National Guards of the Hautes Pyrénées and Basses Pyrénées,
hastily sent across the frontier from Bayonne, and three squadrons
of cavalry[3].   What was more important than the mere numbers
was that they brought with them siege-guns, in which Lefebvre
had hitherto been entirely deficient.   These pieces came from the
citadel of Pampeluna, and were part of those resources of which
the French had so treacherously taken possession in the preceding
February.

Verdier on his arrival superseded Lefebvre-Desnouettes, who was
considerably his junior, and took charge of the siege.   His first
act was to develop an attack on the Monte Torrero, the hill
in the suburbs, beyond the Huerba, which dominates, at a distance
of 1,800 yards, the southern front of the city.   The Spaniards
had neither encircled it with continuous lines, nor crowned it with
any closed work.   It was protected only by two small batteries
and some trenches covering the most obvious points of attack.
The garrison was composed of no more than 500 men, half
peasants, half regulars of the Regiment of Estremadura, of which
three weak battalions had arrived from Tarrega on the previous day
(June 27)[4].   Verdier sent three columns, each of one battalion,
against the more accessible parts of the position, and drove out
the small defending force with ease.   His task was made lighter
by a piece of casual luck : on the night before the assault the
main powder-magazine of the Saragossans, situated in the Seminary,

[1] They belonged to the 14th Provisional Regiment, and the accompanying
corps were the 4th and 7th *bataillons de marche*.

[2] 3rd Regiment of the Vistula.

[3] 3rd, 6th, and 9th *escadrons de marche*.

[4] The Regiment of Estremadura was so weak at the outbreak of hostilities
that its three battalions had only 770 men.   It had been hastily brought up to
900 bayonets before entering the city.

was ignited by the carelessness of a workman, and blew up, killing many persons and wrecking the Seminary itself and many houses in its vicinity. A few hours after this disaster had taken place, and while the whole city was busy in extinguishing the conflagration, the French attack was delivered; hence the original garrison got no help from within the walls. But its own conduct was deplorably weak: the colonel in command[1] headed the rush to the rear, a piece of cowardice for which he was imprisoned and (after the siege had been raised) was sent before a court-martial and shot.

On the evening of the twenty-eighth Verdier began to construct heavy breaching batteries on the slopes of the Monte Torrero, commanding all the southern side of the city. Others were thrown up on the south-western front, opposite the points which had been unsuccessfully assaulted twelve days before. On the thirtieth of June the works were armed with thirty siege-guns, four mortars, and twelve howitzers, which opened simultaneously on Saragossa at midnight, and continued to play upon the place for twenty-four hours, setting many houses on fire, and breaching the flimsy ramparts in half a dozen places. The old castle of the Aljafferia was badly injured, and the gates of Portillo and the Carmen knocked out of shape: there were also large gaps in the convent of the Augustinians, and in the Misericordia, whose back wall formed part of the *enceinte*. All the unarmed population was forced to take refuge in the cellars, or the more solidly built parts of the churches, while the fighting-men were trying to construct barricades behind the worst breaches, and to block up with sandbags, beams, and barrels all the lanes that opened upon them.

Palafox entered Saragossa on the morning of July 2, just in time to see Verdier launch his whole available infantry force upon the shattered western and southern fronts of the city. The assault was made under much more favourable conditions than that of June 16, since the strength of the storming columns was more than doubled, and the defences had been terribly mishandled by the bombardment. On the other hand the garrison was in no degree shaken in spirit: the fire of the last twenty-four hours had been much more dangerous to buildings than to men, and the results of the first assault had given the defenders a confidence which they had not felt on the previous occasion. Hence it came

[1] His name was Vincente Falco; he belonged to the artillery.

to pass that of the six columns of assault not one succeeded in making a permanent lodgement within the walls.   Even the isolated castle of Aljafferia and the convent of San José, just outside the Porta Quemada, were finally left in the hands of the besieged, though the latter was for some hours held by the French. The hardest fighting was at the Portillo gate, where the assaulting battalions more than once reached the dilapidated earthwork that covered the ingress to the north-western part of the city.   It was here that there occurred the well-known incident of the ' Maid of Saragossa.'   The gunners at the small battery in the gate had been shot down one after another by the musketry of the assailants, the final survivors falling even before they could discharge the last gun that they had loaded.   The infantry supports were flinching and the French were closing in, when a young woman named Agostina Zaragoza, whose lover (an artillery sergeant) had just fallen, rushed forward, snatched the lighted match from his dying hand, and fired the undischarged twenty-four-pounder into the head of the storming column[1].   The enemy was shaken by a charge of grape delivered at ten paces, the citizens, shamed by Agostina's example, rushed back to reoccupy the battery, and the assault was beaten off.   Palafox states that the incident occurred before his own eyes: he gave the girl a commission as sub-lieutenant of artillery, and a warrant for a life-pension: she was seen a year later by several English witnesses, serving with her battery in Andalusia[2].

[1] Sir Charles Vaughan was introduced to the heroine by Palafox while he was staying in Saragossa in October.   He describes her as ' a handsome young woman of the lower class,' and says that when he met her she was wearing on her sleeve a small shield of honour with the name ' Zaragoza ' inscribed on it.   The fact that the dead sergeant was her lover is given by Palafox in his short narrative of the siege, which ought to be a good authority enough.

[2] Napier, with all his prejudice against the Spaniards, does not venture to absolutely reject the story.   ' Romantic tales of women rallying the troops and leading them forward at the most dangerous period of the siege were current ; their truth may be doubted.   Yet when suddenly environed with horrors, the sensitiveness of women, driving them to a kind of frenzy, might have produced actions above the heroism of men ' (i. 45). W. Jacob, M.P., in his *Travels in the South of Spain in* 1809–10 (p. 123), says that he met Agostina at Seville, wearing a blue artillery tunic, with one epaulette, over a short skirt ; she was present when Lord Wellesley entered Seville, and was welcomed by the Junta.

The fruitless attack of July 2 cost the French 200 killed and 300 wounded. The Saragossan garrison lost somewhat less, in spite of the bombardment, since they had been fighting under cover against enemies who had to expose themselves whenever they got near the wall. Verdier resolved for the future to shun attempts at escalade, and to begin a regular siege. He commenced on the third of July to construct parallels, for a main attack on the southern side of the place, and a secondary attack on the north-western. He also threw a detachment across the Ebro [July 11], to close the hitherto undisturbed access to the city through the suburb of San Lazaro and the stone bridge. The force which could be spared for this object from an army of no more than 12,000 or 13,000 men was not really sufficient to hold the left bank of the Ebro, and merely made ingress and egress difficult without entirely preventing it. On two or three occasions when considerable bodies of Spaniards presented themselves, the French could do no more than skirmish with them and try to cut off the convoys which they were bringing to the city. They could not exclude them, and for the whole remainder of the siege the communications of the Saragossans with the open country were never entirely closed[1].

By July 15, Verdier's trenches were commencing to work up close to the walls, and the next ten days of the month were occupied in desperate struggles for the convents of San José, of the Capuchins and Trinitarians, which lie outside the city near the Carmen and Porta Quemada gates. By the twenty-fourth the French had occupied them, connected them with their approaches, and begun to establish in them breaching batteries. Another, but less powerful, attack was directed against the Portillo gate. The mortars and howitzers bombarded the city continuously from the first to the third. But it was not till the dawn of August 4 that the heavy guns were ready to begin their task of battering down the gates and walls of Saragossa. After five hours of steady firing the Spanish batteries were silenced, and several breaches had been made, mostly in or about the Convent of Santa Engracia, at the southernmost point of the city. The streets behind it had been terribly shattered by the previous bombardment, and many buildings

---

[1] Foy exaggerates considerably when he says that from July 12 onward ' the blockade of Saragossa was complete' (iii. 300). Reinforcements entered on several subsequent occasions.

destroyed, notably the central hospital, from which the Spaniards
had to remove, under a terrible hail of shells, more than 500 sick
and wounded, as well as a number of lunatics and idiots: the
institution had been used as an asylum before the outbreak of
the war.   Many of these unfortunate creatures were destroyed by
the besiegers' fire[1], as were also no small number of the wounded
and of their doctors and nurses.

Palafox and his brother the marquis remained near Santa
Engracia, trying to encourage their followers to repair the barricades behind the breaches, and to loophole and strengthen those
of the houses which still stood firm.   But amid the dreadful and
unceasing storm of projectiles it was hard to keep the men together,
and most of the projected retrenchments were battered down before
they could be finished.   At two o'clock in the afternoon of the
fourth, Verdier let loose his storming columns, composed of four
Polish and nine French battalions[2].   They were directed in three
bodies against three separate breaches, the easternmost in the

---

[1] Cavallero and Toreño put the distressing scenes at the hospital and the
escape of the lunatics during the assault on the 4th, but Arteche seems more
correct in placing them during the bombardment of the preceding day.

[2] I find in the *Vaughan Papers* the following note : ' General Lefebvre-Desnouettes was residing at Cheltenham on parole, having been taken prisoner
at Benavente by Lord Paget.   I went to Cheltenham on May 27, 1809, for
the express purpose of seeing the general.   He told me that he had advanced
at first with no more than 3,000 men, but that after General Verdier joined
him, the French force employed against Saragossa was 15,000 men.   I understood that in the attack of July 2 and the previous fighting they lost 2,000
men, and that their total loss in the whole siege was 4,000, including three
generals wounded.' *Nap. Corresp.* (xvii. 389, 426) calls the whole force
before Saragossa on August 2, 17,300 men.   But there seems to have been
present in all only—

(1) Lefebvre-Desnouettes' column :

Brigade Grandjean	2nd of the Vistula (1st and 2nd batts.)	.	.	1376	
	70th of the line (3rd batt.) .	.	.	.	379	
	4th *bataillon de marche*	.	.	.	581	
	6th ditto	.	.	.	655 = 2991
Brigade Habert	1st of the Vistula (1st and 2nd batts.)	.	.	1243	
	1st supplementary regiment of the Legions of Reserve (1st and 2nd batts.)	.	.	1030	
	47th of the line (3rd batt.) .	.	.	.	420	
	15th ditto (4th batt.) .	.	.	.	411 = 3104
Cavalry	Regiment of Polish Lancers	.	.	.	717	
	5th *escadron de marche*	.	.	.	217 = 934

Convent of Santa Engracia, the second at the gate of the same name, the third more to the left, in the wall near the gate of the Carmen. All three were successful in forcing their way into the city: the defences had been completely shattered, and at one point 300 continuous yards of the outer wall had fallen. The Spaniards clung for some time to the cloisters and church of Santa Engracia, but were at last expelled or exterminated, and 1,000 yards of the *enceinte* with the adjoining buildings were in the hands of the French.

It was at this moment, apparently, that Verdier sent in a *parlementaire* with the laconic note—'Head Quarters, Santa Engracia. Capitulation?' To which Palafox returned the well-known reply—'Head Quarters, Saragossa. War to the knife[1].'

All through the afternoon of the fourth of August, the French slowly pushed their way up the streets which lead northward towards the Coso, the main thoroughfare of Saragossa. They could only get forward by storming each house, and turning each barricade that offered resistance, so that their progress was very slow. While inflicting terrible losses on the Spaniards, they were also suffering very heavily themselves. But they drove a broad

(2) Division of Gomez Freire :

14th Provisional Regiment(1st, 2nd, and 3rd batts.)	1173
7th *bataillon de marche*	334
5th Portuguese infantry	265
Portuguese Cazadores	288 = 2060

(3) Column of Colonel Piré (arrived June 29) :

3rd of the Vistula (1st and 2nd batts.) . .	1332
National Guards *d'élite* (two batts.) . . .	971
3rd, 8th, and 9th *escadrons de marche* . .	275 = 2578

(4) Bazancourt's Brigade (arrived August 1) :

14th of the line (1st and 2nd batts.) . . .	1488
44th ditto (1st and 2nd batts.)	1614
11th *escadron de marche*	205 = 3307

(5) Artillery and train	561 = 561
Total . . .	15,535

These are mainly Belmas's figures. He mentions a battalion of the 16th of the line as present at the great assault. There must be some error here, as that regiment was not in Spain. It is probably a misprint for the 70th of the line, which is not mentioned by him as present, though it certainly was so.

[1] The story sounds theatrical, but is vouched for by good authorities, Vaughan and Palafox himself, who chose the words for the type of the reverse of the medal that was issued to the defenders of Saragossa (see Arteche, ii. 394).

wedge into the city, till finally they reached and crossed the Coso, halfway between the southern wall and the river. In the streets beyond the Coso their impetus seemed to have exhausted itself: many of the men were too tired to press forward any longer; others turned aside to plunder the churches and the better sort of houses[1]. Verdier tried to cut his way to the great bridge, so as to divide the defenders into two separate bodies, and was so far successful that many of the Spaniards began to troop off across the river into the suburb of San Lazaro. But he himself was wounded, his main column lost its way in the narrow side-streets, and the attack died down.

In the late afternoon there was almost a suspension of hostilities, and the firing slackened for a space. But at last the Aragonese, encouraged by the exhaustion of their enemies, began to resume the offensive. The fugitives who had crossed to the northern side of the Ebro were hustled together and driven back by their leaders, while a loaded gun was placed on the bridge to prevent their return. The garrison of the eastern front, which had not been seriously attacked, sent all the reinforcements that it could spare into the centre of the town. At dusk masses of Spaniards debouched from the neighbourhood of the two cathedrals, and began to assail the positions held by the French beyond the line of the Coso. The first charge into the open street is recorded to have been led by a monk [2] and sixteen peasants, every one of whom were killed or wounded; but endless reinforcements poured out of every lane, and the exhausted French began to lose ground. The fighting was of that deadly sort in which the question has to be settled, whether the defenders of the houses in a street can shoot down their assailants, exposed in the roadway, before the latter can burst into each separate dwelling and exterminate its garrison in detail. Often the French held the upper stories long after the Spaniards had seized the ground floor, and the staircases had to be stormed one after the other. It was natural that in such struggles the defenders should receive no quarter. Though the fight raged with many variations of fortune in all the central

---

[1] Napier maintains (i. 45) that the city was saved only because the French fell to pillaging, a contention which seems very unjust to the Saragossans.

[2] Perhaps his name, Fray Ignacio de Santaromana, deserves as much remembrance as that of Agostina. His conduct in a critical moment was just as inspiring and told as much as hers (see Arteche, ii. 406).

parts of the city, there was after a time no doubt that the Aragonese were gaining ground.   The French detachments which
had penetrated furthest into the place were gradually cut off and
exterminated; the main bodies of the columns drew back and
strengthened themselves in two large stone buildings, the convents
of San Francisco and San Diego.   At nightfall they retained only
a wedge-like section of the city, whose apex near San Francisco just
touched the southern side of the Coso, while its base was formed by
the line of wall between the gates of Santa Engracia and the
Carmen.

The French had lost nearly 2,000 men in the struggle : the
engineer Belmas gives the total as 462 killed and 1,505 wounded [1],
more than a fifth of the troops which had actually been engaged
in the assault.   Among the Saragossans, who before the street-
fighting began had been subjected to a severe bombardment for
many hours, the casualties must have been nearly as great.   But
they could spare combatants more easily than their enemies : indeed
they had more men than muskets, and as each defender fell there
was a rush of the unarmed to get possession of his weapon.

During the night of August 4–5 both sides, fatigued though
they were, set to work to cover themselves with barricades and
works constructed with the débris of ruined houses.   In the
morning both French and Spaniards had rough but continuous
lines of defence, those of the latter circling round those of the
former, with nothing but the width of a narrow street between
them.   Wherever there was anything approaching an open space
cannon had been brought up to sweep it.   Where the houses still
stood firm, communications had been made between them by
breaking holes through the party walls.   In the streets the corpses
of both sides lay thick, for under the deadly cross-fire no one dared
venture out to remove them : in a day or two the sanitary conditions would be horrible.

Meanwhile both besiegers and besieged were too exhausted to
undertake any more serious operations, and the fighting sank
to little more than a desultory fusillade between enemies equally

---

[1] Arteche accuses Belmas of giving only 505 wounded, remarking that
Verdier stated the higher number of 900.   But my edition of Belmas (Paris,
1836) distinctly says ' quinze cent cinq blessés ' (ii. 64).   Napier gives no
figures at all : Thiers, understating French losses in his usual style, speaks of
300 dead and 900 wounded.

well protected by their defences.   Such interest as there was in the
operations of August 5-6 lay outside the walls of Saragossa.
On the afternoon of the day of the great assault a column of
Spanish troops from Catalonia—two line battalions and 2,000 or
3,000 new levies and armed peasants—arrived at Villamayor on the
north of the Ebro, only seven miles from the city.   It escorted a
much-desired convoy of ammunition, for the supplies in the city
were running very low.   While the fighting was still raging in the
streets Palafox rode out of the suburb of San Lazaro with 100
dragoons and joined this force.   On the next morning (August 5)
he skirmished with the French troops which lay beyond the Ebro,
and passed into the city one veteran battalion and a few wagons
of munitions.   He then proposed to attack the detached French
brigade (that of Piré) with his whole remaining force on the next
day, in order to clear the northern front, and to send the rest of his
convoy—no less than 200 wagons—into Saragossa.   But on the
same night he received news of the battle of Baylen and the
surrender of Dupont's army.   Moreover, he was informed that a
division of the army of Valencia, under Saint-March, was on the
way to reinforce him.   This induced him to halt for two days, to
see whether the French would not raise the siege without further
fighting.

Verdier had got the same intelligence at the same hour, with
orders to be ready to retreat at a moment's notice, and to avoid
entangling himself in further engagements.   He was preparing to
withdraw, when on the seventh he received supplementary dispatches
from Madrid, with directions to hold on for the present, and to
keep the Saragossans occupied, without, however, compromising
himself too much.   Accordingly he resumed the bombardment,
and began to throw into the city an immense number of shells : for
he saw that when his retreat was definitely ordered, he would not
be able to carry off with him the vast stores of munitions that he
had accumulated in his camp.

Seeing that the French did not move, Palafox attacked the
covering force on the left bank of the Ebro on August 8.   His
enemies were very inferior in numbers and had been told not to
risk anything, considering the delicate state of affairs.   Accordingly the relieving force crossed the river Gallego, pushed back
Piré's 2,000 men in a long skirmishing fight, and ultimately
established themselves on ground just outside the suburb of San

Saragossa

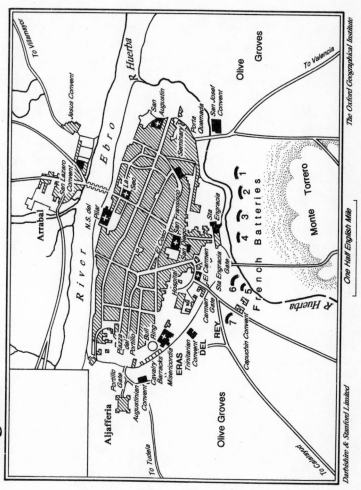

Darbishire & Stanford Limited   One Half English Mile   The Oxford Geographical Institute

Lazaro : the convoy, under cover of the fighting, successfully entered the city over the great bridge. That night Verdier withdrew Piré's brigade across the river, thus leaving the whole northern front of the place free from blockade. Clearly this could only mean that he was about to raise the siege, but for five days more he continued to ravage the central parts of the city with his bombs, and to bicker at the barricades with the Saragossans. But on the thirteenth the Spaniards noted that his camps seemed to be growing empty, and on the fourteenth a series of explosions told them that he was abandoning his siege works. Santa Engracia and the other points held inside the city were all destroyed on that day, and the ammunition which could not be carried off was blown up. The guns which had been pressed forward into the ruined streets were spiked and left behind, as it would have been impossible to extricate them under the Spanish fire. Of those in the outer batteries some were thrown into the canal, others disabled by having their trunnions knocked off, others merely spiked. Altogether no less than fifty-four pieces, all more or less injured, but many susceptible of repair, were left behind to serve as trophies for the Saragossans.

Finally Verdier withdrew by slow marches up the Ebro to Tudela, where he took post on August 17. He had lost in all over 3,500 men in his long-continued struggle with the heroic city. The Aragonese must have suffered at least as much, but the figures are of course impossible to verify. They said that their casualties amounted to no more than 2,000, but this must surely be an understatement, for Palafox says that by August 1 there were of his original 7,000 levies only 3,500 left under arms. Even allowing for heavy diminution by desertion and dispersion, this implies very serious losses in action, and these seven Aragonese battalions formed only a part of the garrison, which counted 13,000 men on August 13. Probably the unembodied citizens and peasants suffered in a still heavier proportion than troops which had received even a small measure of organization. If the whole losses came to 4,500 it would not be surprising—but nothing can be stated with certainty. Yet whatever were their sufferings, the Saragossans had turned over a new page in the history of the art of war. They had defended for two months an unfortified place, by means of extemporized barricades, retrenchments, and earthworks, and had proved their ability to resist even a formidable train of siege artillery. If the news of Dupont's disaster had not arrived in time to save them, they would no doubt have succumbed in the end, as must any besieged place which is not sooner or later relieved from the outside. But meanwhile they had accomplished a rare feat : almost unaided by regular troops, almost destitute of trained artillerymen and engineers, they had held at bay a force which Napoleon at the commencement of the siege would have supposed to be equal to the task of conquering not only Aragon, but the whole eastern side of the Iberian Peninsula.

OPERATIONS IN THE NORTH: BATTLE OF MEDINA DE RIO SECO

WHILE Lefebvre-Desnouettes and Verdier were making their long series of attacks on Saragossa, matters were coming to a head in the north-west of Spain. The army of Galicia had at last descended into the plains, and commenced to threaten the right flank of Bessières and the communications between Burgos and Madrid. This forward movement was due neither to the Galician Junta, nor to the officer whom they had placed in command of their army, but to the obstinate persistence of Cuesta, who had not in the least learnt the lesson of caution from his defeat at Cabezon, and was eager to fight a pitched battle with all the forces that could be collected in Northern Spain.

The resources at hand were not inconsiderable: in Galicia, or on the way thither from Portugal, were no less than thirty-nine battalions of regular infantry—though most of them were very weak: there were also thirteen battalions of embodied militia, some thirty guns, and a handful of cavalry (not more than 150 sabres). The Junta had placed in command, after the murder of the captain-general Filanghieri, a comparatively young general—Joachim Blake, one of those many soldiers of fortune of Irish blood who formed such a notable element in the Spanish army. When the insurrection broke out he had been merely colonel of the regiment named 'the Volunteers of the Crown': he had never had more than three battalions to manage before he found himself placed at the head of the whole Galician army. Though a most unlucky general—half a dozen times he seems to have been the victim of ill fortune, for which he was hardly responsible—Blake was in real merit far above the average of the Spanish commanders. He had neither the slackness nor the arrogance which were the besetting sins of so many of the Peninsular generals: and his dauntless courage was not combined with recklessness or careless over-confidence. He showed from the first very considerable

organizing power: all his efforts were directed to the task of inducing the Junta and the people of Galicia to allow him to draft
the crowds of recruits who flocked to his banner into the old
regiments of the line and the militia, instead of forming them
into new corps. With some trouble he carried his point, and
was able to bring up to their full complement most of the old
battalions: of new units very few [1] were created. When he took
the field it was only the old *cadres* thus brought up to strength
that accompanied him, not raw and unsteady troops of new
organization.

After hastily concentrating and brigading his army at Lugo,
Blake led them to the edge of the mountains which divide Galicia
from the plains of Leon. It was his original intention to stand
at bay on the hills, and force the French to attack him. With
this object he occupied the passes of Manzanal, Fuencebadon, and
Puebla de Sanabria, the only places where roads of importance
penetrate into the Galician uplands [June 23]. His whole field
force, distributed into four divisions and a 'vanguard brigade' of
light troops, amounted to some 25,000 men fit for the field: in
addition, 8,000 or 10,000 new levies were being organized behind
him, but he refused—with great wisdom—to bring them to the
front during his first movements.

On Blake's left flank were other Spanish troops: the Junta of
the Asturias had raised some 15,000 men: but these—unlike the
Galician army—were utterly raw and untrained. Of old troops
there was but one single militia battalion among them. The
Junta had dispersed them in small bodies all along the eastern
and southern side of the province, arraying them to cover not
only the high road from Madrid and Leon to Oviedo, but every
impracticable mule-path that crosses the Cantabrian Mountains.
By this unwise arrangement the Asturian army was weak at every
point: it was impossible to concentrate more than 5,000 men for
the defence of any part of the long and narrow province. The
fact was that the Junta looked solely to the defence of its own
land, and had no conception that the protection of the Asturias
should be treated as only a section of the great problem of the
protection of the whole of Northern Spain.

While the Galicians and the Asturians were taking up this

---

[1] The best known was the *batallon literario*, composed of the students of the
University of Santiago.

purely defensive attitude, they had forgotten to reckon with one factor in their neighbourhood. Right in front of them lay the old Captain-General of Castile, with the wrecks of the army that had been so signally routed at Cabezon. He had retired to Benavente on the Esla, and there had halted, finding that he was not pursued by Lasalle. Here he reorganized his scattered Castilian levies into three battalions, and raised three more in the province of Leon. He had still 300 or 400 regular cavalry, but not a single gun. Quite undismayed by his late defeat, he persisted in wishing to fight in the plain, and began to send urgent messages both to Blake and to the Juntas of Asturias and Galicia, begging them to send down their armies from the hills, and aid him in making a dash at Valladolid, with the object of cutting off Bessières' communications with Madrid, and so disarranging the whole system of Napoleon's plan for the conquest of Spain.

The Asturians, partly from a well-justified disbelief in Cuesta's ability, partly from a selfish desire to retain all their troops for the defence of their own province, refused to stir. They sent the Captain-General a modest reinforcement, two battalions of the newly raised regiment of Covadonga, but refused any more aid. Instead, they suggested that Cuesta should fall back on Leon and the southern slope of the Asturian hills, so as to threaten from thence any advance of the French into the plains of Leon.

But the Galician Junta showed themselves less unyielding. Despite of the remonstrances of Blake, who was set on maintaining the defensive, and holding the passes above Astorga, they consented to allow their army to move down into the plain of Old Castile and to join Cuesta. After some fruitless remonstrances Blake moved forward with the bulk of his host, leaving behind him his second division to hold the passes, while with the other three and his vanguard brigade he marched on Benavente [July 5].

On July 10 the armies of Galicia and Castile met at Villalpando, and a brisk quarrel at once broke out between their commanders. Cuesta was for attacking the French at once: Blake pointed out that for an army with no more than thirty guns and 500 or 600 cavalry to offer battle in the plains was sheer madness. The Irish general had the larger and more effective army, but Cuesta was thirteen years his senior as lieutenant-general, and insisted on assuming command of the combined host in accordance with the normal rules of military precedence. After some fruitless resistance Blake yielded, and the whole Spanish army moved forward on Valladolid: all that Cuesta would grant on the side of caution was that the third Galician division, 5,000 strong, should be left as a reserve at Benavente. Even this was a mistake: if the two generals were to fight at all, they should have put every available man in line, and have endeavoured at all costs to induce the Asturians also to co-operate with them. They might have had in all for the oncoming battle 40,000 men, instead of 22,000, if the outlying troops had been collected.

A blow from the north-west was precisely what Napoleon at Bayonne and Savary at Madrid had been expecting for some weeks. Both of them were perfectly conscious that any check inflicted on Bessières in Old Castile would wreck the whole plan of invasion. So much of the marshal's *corps d'armée* had been distracted towards Saragossa, that it was clearly necessary to reinforce him. From Madrid Savary sent up half of the troops of the Imperial Guard which had hitherto been in the capital— three battalions of fusiliers (first regiment) and three squadrons of cavalry[1]. Napoleon afterwards blamed him severely for not having sent more, saying that from the mass of troops in and about Madrid he might have spared another complete division— that of Gobert, the second division of Moncey's corps. Without its aid the Emperor half-expected that Bessières might be checked, if the Galicians came down in full force[2]. He himself sent up from Bayonne nearly all the troops which were at that moment under his hand, ten veteran battalions just arrived from Germany, forming the division of General Mouton.

The reinforcements being hurried on to Bessières by forced marches, that general found himself on July 9 at the head of a force with which he thought that he might venture to attack Blake and Cuesta. If they had brought with them all their troops, and had called in the Asturians, it is probable that the marshal would have found himself too weak to face them: fortunately for him he had only five-ninths of the army of Galicia

---

[1] Oddly enough, in the Duke of Rovigo's own *Mémoires* the statement is made that these troops arrived too late to fight at Rio Seco, a curious error (ii. 248).

[2] See the dispatch of July 13, to Savary, and that of the same day to King Joseph (*Nap. Corresp.*, 14,191).

and Cuesta's miserable levies in front of him.   His own fighting
force was formed of odd fragments of all the divisions which
formed his *corps d'armée* : large sections of each of them were left
behind to guard his communications with France, and others
were before Saragossa.   Bessières marched from Burgos with the
brigade of the Imperial Guard : at Palencia he picked up Lasalle's
cavalry with half Mouton's newly arrived division of veterans (the
second brigade was left at Vittoria) and a small part of Merle's
division, which had been hastily brought over the mountains
from Santander to join him.   There was also present the larger
half of Verdier's division, of which the rest was now in Aragon
with its commander [1].

On the evening of July 13, Lasalle's light cavalry got in touch
with the outposts of the Spaniards near Medina de Rio Seco,

---

[1] Bessières' army seems to have consisted of the following elements :—

		Infantry.	Cavalry.
(1) One regiment of the Fusiliers of the Imperial Guard (three batts.)		1,900	
Three squadrons of cavalry of the Imperial Guard			300
(2) From Verdier's Division :			
Ducos' Brigade { 13th Provisional Regiment (four batts.) .		2,000	
14th Provisional Regiment (one batt.) [a] .		500	
Sabathier's Brigade { 17th Provisional Regiment (four batts.) } 18th Provisional Regiment (four batts.) [b] }		2,800	
(3) From Merle's Division :			
D'Armagnac's Brigade { 47th of the Line (one batt.) [c] } 3rd Swiss Regiment (one batt.) } . .		1,600	
(4) From Mouton's Division :			
Reynaud's Brigade { 4th Léger (three batts.) . } 15th of the Line (two batts.) [d] } . . .		3,000	
(5) Lasalle's Cavalry Brigade :			
10th Chasseurs } 22nd Chasseurs }			850
		11,800	1,150

We may add 750 men for the five batteries of artillery and the train, and so
get a total strength of 13,700.   Napoleon (*Corresp.*, 14,213) called the force
15,000.

---

[a] The other three batts. of the 14th were with Verdier at Saragossa.   This
odd battalion was in the battle attached to D'Armagnac's brigade.   Merle was
given Ducos' and D'Armagnac's brigades to make up a division.

[b] These battalions were much weakened by detachments.

[c] A very strong battalion : it was 1,200 strong on June 1, and must still have
had 1,000 bayonets.

[d] Both regiments were incomplete, having dropped men at Vittoria and Burgos.

and reported that Blake and Cuesta were present in force. On
the next morning Bessières marched before daybreak from Palencia,
and just as the day was growing hot, discovered the enemy drawn
up on rising ground a little to the east of the small town which
has given its name to the battle. Blake had 15,000 infantry and
150 cavalry with twenty guns [1]; Cuesta 6,000 infantry and 550
cavalry, but not a single cannon. They outnumbered Bessières
by nearly two to one in foot soldiery, but had little more than
half his number of horse, and only two-thirds as many guns.

A more prudent general than Cuesta would have refused to fight
at all with an army containing in its ranks no less than 9,000
recruits, and almost destitute of cavalry. But if fighting was to
be done, a wise man would at any rate have chosen a good position,
where his flanks would be covered from turning movements and
inaccessible to the enemy's very superior force of horsemen. The
old Captain-General cared nothing for such caution: he had merely
drawn up his army on a gentle hillside, somewhat cut up by low
stone walls, but practicable for cavalry at nearly every point. His
flanks had no protection of any kind from the lie of the ground:
behind his back was the town of Medina de Rio Seco, and the dry
bed of the Sequillo river, obstacles which would tend to make
a retreat difficult to conduct in orderly fashion. But a retreat
was the last thing in Cuesta's thoughts.

Bad as was the position selected, the way in which it was
occupied was still more strange. The Captain-General had divided
his host into two halves, the one consisting of the first division of

---

[1] In the *Vaughan Papers* I find a ' Journal of the operations of General
Blake,' by some officer of his staff, unnamed. It gives the force of the
Galician army at Rio Seco as follows :—

	Officers.	Sergeants.	Drummers, &c.	Veteran rank and file.	Recruits.	Total.
Vanguard :						
Gen. Count Maceda	75	81	76	1,678	277 =	2,187
1st Division :						
Gen. Cagigal	186	194	166	4,795	1315 =	6,470
4th Division :						
Marquis Portago	188	185	144	3,208	2281 =	5,818
Head-quarters Guard :						
Volunteers of Navarre	29	30	43	681	— =	754
	478	490	429	10,362	3,873 =	15,229

This total only differs by 26 from that given by Arteche (ii. 654).

Battle of Medina de Rio Seco.

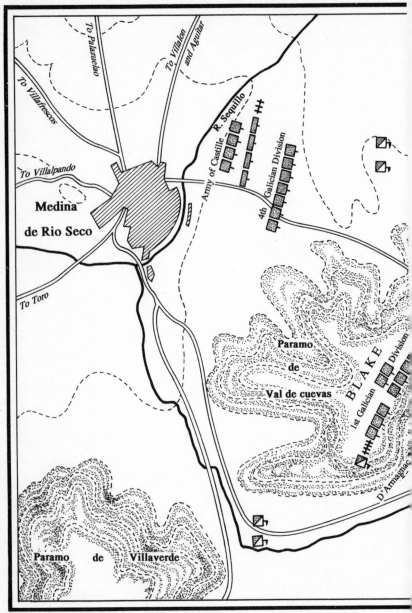

To Palazuelo

To Villalon and Aguilar

To Villafrescos

R. Sequillo

Army of Castille

4th Galician Division

To Villalpando

Medina
de Rio Seco

To Toro

Paramo

de

Val de cuevas

BLAKE

1st Galician Division

D'Armagnac

Paramo   de   Villaverde

Darbishire & Stanford Limited

July 14. 1808

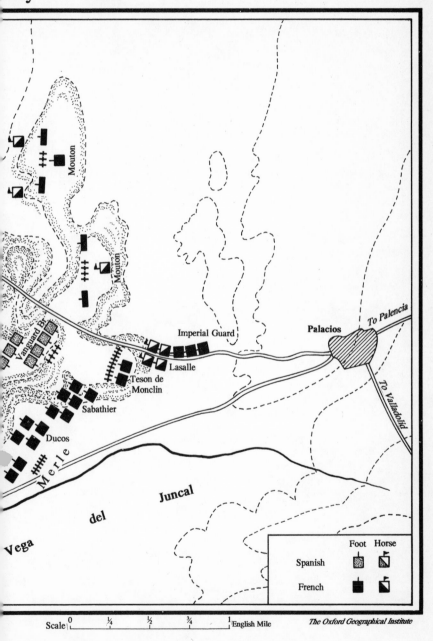

Mouton

Mouton

Imperial Guard

Palacios

To Palencia

To Valladolid

Lasalle

Vanguard B^e

Teson de
Monclin

Sabathier

Ducos

Merle

Juncal

del

Vega

	Foot	Horse
Spanish		
French		

Scale 0   ¼   ½   ¾   1 English Mile   *The Oxford Geographical Institute*

the army of Galicia and of the vanguard brigade, the other of the
fourth Galician division and the raw 'Army of Castile.' Blake
with the first-named force was drawn up in a short, compact
formation, three lines deep, at the south-eastern front of the hill,
the 'Plateau of Valdecuevas,' as it is called. His right looked
down into the plain, his left, in the centre of the plateau, stood
quite 'in the air.' But nearly a mile to his left rear, and quite
out of sight, lay the other half of the army, just too far off to
protect Blake's exposed flank if it should be attacked, and in a very
bad position for defending itself. Why Cuesta ranged his left
wing (or second line, if it may so be called) low down on the
reverse slope of the plateau, and in a place where it could not even
see Blake's corps, it is impossible to conceive. Toreño hazards the
guess that, in his arrogant confidence, he placed Blake where he
would have to bear the stress of the battle, and might probably
lose ground, intending to come up himself with the left wing and
restore the fight when his colleague should be sufficiently humbled.
Such a plan would not have been outside the scope of the old man's
selfish pride.

Bessières, marching up from the east, came in sight of the
Spaniards in the early morning. He at once deployed his whole
army, and advanced in battle array over the plain. In front was
a slight cavalry screen of Lasalle's chasseurs ; next came Mouton's
division, deployed to the right, and Merle's division, with Sabathier's
brigade, to the left of the country-road which leads, over the
plateau, towards Medina de Rio Seco. The Imperial Guard,
horse and foot, and the bulk of Lasalle's cavalry brigade were in
reserve behind the centre. On getting near the enemy's position,
Bessières soon discovered the two halves of the Spanish army and
the broad gap which lay between them. His mind was at once
made up : he proposed to contain Cuesta with a small force, and
to fall upon and envelop Blake with the rest of his army before
the Captain-General of Castile could come to his aid. This excellent plan was carried out to the letter, thanks to the incapacity
of Cuesta.

Not far east of the plateau of Valdecuevas lay an isolated
eminence, the mound of Monclin : on it the marshal drew up the
greater part of his artillery (twenty guns) which began to batter
Blake's front line : the Galician batteries replied, and held their
own though outnumbered by two to one. Then Sabathier's eight

weak battalions deployed and commenced a cautious attack upon Blake's front: this was not to be pressed home for a time. Meanwhile Merle's seven battalions pushed into the fight, continuing Sabathier's line to the south-west and trying to envelop Blake's southern flank. They forced the Galicians to throw back their right wing, and to keep continually extending it, in order to avoid being turned. The Spaniards fought not amiss, and for some hour or more the battle was almost stationary.

Meanwhile, far to the French right, Mouton's five battalions were executing a cautious demonstration against Cuesta's forces, across the northern folds of the plateau. The old general allowed himself to be completely occupied by this trifling show of attack, and made no movement to aid Blake's wing. The gap between him and his colleague was not filled up. Then came the sudden development of Bessières' plan: Sabathier and Merle were told to attack in earnest, and while Blake was deeply engaged with their fifteen battalions, Lasalle rode into the open space on the left of the Galicians, formed up the 22nd *chasseurs à cheval* at right angles to the Spanish line, and charged in furiously upon Blake's flank. The unfortunate troops on whom the blow fell were deployed in line, and utterly unprepared for a cavalry shock from the side. The first battalion which received the attack broke at once and ran in upon the second[1]: in a few minutes Blake's whole left wing fell down like a pack of cards, each corps as it fled sweeping away that next to it. The French infantry, advancing at the same moment, ran in with the bayonet, seized the Spanish guns, and hustled the Galicians westward along the plateau in a mob. Blake's troops were only saved from complete destruction by the steadiness of a Navarrese battalion, which formed square to cover the retreat, and at the cost of one-third of its strength allowed the other corps to get a long start in their flight. They retired due west, and crossed the Sequillo to the south of the town of Rio Seco before they could be rallied.

It was now the turn of Cuesta to suffer. The moment that Blake was disposed of, Bessières marched over the hill towards the

[1] The flank battalion which started the rout was the ' Regiment of Buenos Ayres,' a provisional corps which had been formed out of the prisoners lately returned from England, who had been captured during our unlucky South American expedition, before Whitelock's final fiasco (see the ' Journal of Blake's Operations,' in the *Vaughan Papers*).

other half of the Spanish army : leaving some of Lasalle's cavalry
and Sabathier's brigade to pursue the routed corps, he formed the
whole of his remaining troops in a line, bringing up the reserve of
the Imperial Guard to make its centre, while Mouton formed the
right wing and the two brigades of Merle the left. Cuesta, outnumbered and attacked down hill, would have done wisely to retreat
and to seek for shelter in and behind the town of Rio Seco in his
immediate rear. But he had prepared a new surprise for the
enemy; as they descended upon him they were astonished to see
his front line, the eight battalions which formed the fourth Galician
division, form itself into columns of attack and slowly commence
to climb the hill with the object of attacking their right and
centre. Meanwhile Cuesta's handful of cavalry rode out on the
northern end of the line and fell upon the skirmishers of Mouton's
division, whom it chased back till it was met and driven off by the
three squadrons of the Imperial Guard.

The up-hill charge of the fourth Galician division was a fine but
an utterly useless display of courage. They were attacking nearly
double their own numbers of victorious troops, who outflanked
them on both wings and tore them to pieces with a concentric fire
of artillery to which they could not respond. The regiments at each
end of the line were soon broken up, but in the centre two battalions
of picked grenadiers [1] actually closed with the French, captured
four guns of the Imperial Guard, and forced back the supporting
infantry of the same corps for a short space, till Bessières hurled
upon them the three squadrons of the Guard-Cavalry, which broke
them and swept them down hill again.

Seeing his attack fail, Cuesta bade his last reserve, the raw
Castilian and Leonese levies, retreat behind the river and the town
of Medina de Rio Seco, which they did without much loss, covered
to a certain extent by the two Asturian battalions, the only part
of Cuesta's own force which was seriously engaged.

The 'Army of Castile,' therefore, had no more than 155 casualties,
but the two Galician divisions had suffered heavily. They left
behind them on the field nearly 400 dead, and over 500 wounded,
with some 1,200 prisoners. The ten guns of Blake's wing had all
been captured, and with them several pairs of colours. In addition

---

[1] In accordance with the unwise practice prevailing in most Continental
armies, Blake had massed the grenadier companies of all his line regiments
into two battalions, to act as a select reserve.

more than a thousand of the Galician recruits had dispersed, and could not be rallied. Altogether Blake's army had lost over 3,000 men. The French, as might have been expected, had suffered comparatively little: they had 105 killed and 300 wounded, according to Foy; other historians give even smaller figures.

A vigorous pursuit might have done much further harm to the defeated Spaniards; but Bessières' men had been marching since two in the morning, and fighting all through the midday. They were much fatigued, and their commander did not press the chase far beyond the river. But the town of Rio Seco was sacked from cellar to garret, with much slaying of non-combatants and outrages of all kinds [1], a fact very discreditable to the marshal, who could have stopped the plunder had he chosen.

The defeated generals met, a little to the west of the battle-field, and after a bitter altercation, in which Blake used the plainest words about Cuesta's generalship, parted in wrath. The Galicians retired by the way they had come, and joined the division which had been left behind three days before; they then went back to the passes above Astorga, abandoning a considerable amount of stores at Benavente. Cuesta took the army of Castile to Leon, retiring on the Asturias rather than on Galicia.

Bessières' well-earned victory was creditable to himself and his troops, but the way had been made easy for him by the astounding tactical errors of the Captain-General of Castile. The rank and file of the Spanish army had no reason to be ashamed of their conduct: it was their commander who should have blushed at the reckless way in which he had sacrificed his willing troops. Handled by Cuesta the best army in the world might have been defeated by inferior numbers.

The strategical results of the battle of Rio Seco were great and far-reaching. All danger of the cutting of the communications between Madrid and Bayonne was averted, and Napoleon, his mind set at rest on this point, could now assert that Dupont's position in Andalusia was henceforth the only hazardous point in his great scheme of invasion [2]. It would clearly be a very long time before the army of Galicia would again dare to take the offensive, and meanwhile Madrid was safe, and the attempt to conquer Southern

---

[1] When Stuart and Vaughan passed through Medina in September, they were given many harrowing details by the local authorities.

[2] See his remarks in the document of July 21, *Nap. Corresp.*, 14,223.

Spain could be resumed without any fear of interruption. Bessières, after such a victory, was strong enough not to require any further reinforcements from the central reserve in and about the capital.

The most obvious result of Rio Seco was that King Joseph was now able to proceed on his way to Madrid, and to enter the city in triumph. After receiving the homage of the Spanish notables at Bayonne, and nominating a ministry, he had crossed the frontier on July 9. But he had been obliged to stop short at Burgos, till Bessières should have beaten off the attack of Blake and Cuesta: his presence there had been most inconvenient to the marshal, who had been forced to leave behind for his protection Rey's veteran brigade of Mouton's division, which he would gladly have taken out to the approaching battle.

When the news of Medina de Rio Seco arrived at Burgos, the usurper resumed his march on Madrid, still escorted by Rey's troops. He travelled by short stages, stopping at every town to be complimented by reluctant magistrates and corporations, who dared not refuse their homage. The populace everywhere shut itself up in its houses in silent protest. Joseph's state entry into Madrid on July 20 was the culminating point of the melancholy farce. He passed through the streets with a brilliant staff, between long lines of French bayonets, and amid the blare of military music. But not a Spaniard was to be seen except the handful of courtiers and officials who had accepted the new government. The attempts of the French to produce a demonstration, or even to get the town decorated, had met with passive disobedience. Like Charles of Austria when he entered Madrid in 1710, Joseph Bonaparte might have exclaimed that he could see 'a court, but no people' about him. But he affected not to notice the dismal side of the situation, assumed an exaggerated urbanity, and heaped compliments and preferment on the small section of *Afrancesados* who adhered to him.

The usurper had resolved to give himself as much as possible the air of a Spanish national king. Of all his Neapolitan court he had brought with him only one personage, his favourite Saligny, whom he had made Duke of San Germano. The rest of his household was composed of nobles and officials chosen from among the herd which had bowed before him at Bayonne. There were among them several of the late partisans of King Ferdinand, of whom some had frankly sold themselves to his supplanter, while others (like the Duke of Infantado) were only looking for an opportunity to abscond when it might present itself. The first list of ministers was also full of names that were already well known in the Spanish bureaucracy. Of the cabinet of Ferdinand VII, Cevallos the minister of Foreign Affairs, O'Farrill at the War Office, Piñuela at the ministry of Justice, were base enough to accept the continuation of their powers by the usurper. Urquijo, who took the Secretary-ship of State, was an old victim of Godoy's, who had once before held office under Charles IV. Mazarredo, who was placed at the ministry of Marine, was perhaps the most distinguished officer in the Spanish navy. But Joseph imagined that his greatest stroke of policy was the appointment as minister of the Interior of Gaspar de Jovellanos, the most prominent among the Spanish liberals, whose reputation for wisdom and patriotism had cost him a long imprisonment during the days of the Prince of the Peace. The idea was ingenious, but the plan for strengthening the ministry failed, for Jovellanos utterly refused to take office along with a clique of traitors and in the cabinet of a usurper. Yet even without him, the body of courtiers and officials whom Joseph collected was far more respectable, from their high station and old experience, than might have been expected—a fact very disgraceful to the Spanish bureaucrats.

In less troublous times, and with a more legitimate title to the crown, Joseph Bonaparte might have made a very tolerable king. He was certainly a far more worthy occupant of the throne than any of the miserable Spanish Bourbons: but he was not of the stuff of which successful usurpers are made. He was a weak, well-intentioned man, not destitute of a heart or a conscience: and as he gradually realized all the evils that he had brought on Spain by his ill-regulated ambition, he grew less and less satisfied with his position as his brother's tool. He made long and untiring efforts to conciliate the Spaniards, by an unwavering affability and mildness, combined with a strict attention to public business. Unfortunately all his efforts were counteracted by his brother's harshness, and by the greed and violence of the French generals, over whom he could never gain any control. It is a great testimony in his favour that the Spanish people despised rather than hated him: their more violent animosity was reserved for Napoleon. His nominal subjects agreed to regard him as a humorous character:

they laughed at his long harangues, in which Neapolitan phrases were too often mixed with the sonorous Castilian : they insisted that he was blind of one eye—which did not happen to be the case. They spoke of him as always occupied with the pleasures of the table and with miscellaneous amours—accusations for which there was a very slight foundation of fact. They insisted that he was a coward and a sluggard—titles which he was far from meriting. He was, they said, perpetually hoodwinked, baffled, and bullied, alike by his generals, his ministers, and his mistresses. But they never really hated him—a fact which, considering the manner of his accession, must be held to be very much to his credit.

But the first stay of the 'Intrusive King,' as the Spaniards called him, in his capital, was to be very short. He had only arrived there on July 20: his formal proclamation took place on the twenty-fourth. He had hardly settled down in the royal palace, and commenced a dispute with the effete 'Council of Castile'—which with unexpected obstinacy refused to swear the oath to him and to the constitution of Bayonne—when he was obliged to take to flight. On the twenty-fourth rumours began to be current in Madrid that a great disaster had taken place in Andalusia, and that Dupont's army had been annihilated. On the twenty-eighth the news was confirmed in every particular. On August 1, the King, the court, and the 20,000 French troops which still remained in and about the capital, marched out by the northern road, and took their way towards the Ebro. This retreat was the result of a great council of war, in which the energetic advice of Savary, who wished to fight one more battle in front of the capital, with all the forces that could be concentrated, was overruled by the King and the majority of the generals. 'A council of war never fights,' as has been most truly observed.

SECTION III: CHAPTER IV

DUPONT IN ANDALUSIA: THE CAPITULATION OF BAYLEN

WE left General Dupont at Andujar, on the upper course of the Guadalquivir, whither he had retired on June 19 after evacuating Cordova. Deeply troubled by the interruption of his communications with Madrid, and by the growing strength displayed by the Spanish army in his front, he had resolved that it was necessary to draw back to the foot of the Sierra Morena, and to recover at all costs his touch with the main French army in the capital. He kept sending to Murat (or rather to Savary, who had now superseded the Grand-Duke) persistent demands for new orders and for large reinforcements. Most of his messengers were cut off on the way by the insurgents, but his situation had become known at head quarters, and was engrossing much of Savary's attention—more of it indeed than Napoleon approved. The Emperor wrote on July 13 that the decisive point was for the moment in Castile, and not in Andalusia, and that the best way to strengthen Dupont was to reinforce Bessières [1].

Such had not been Savary's opinion: frightened at the isolation in which Dupont now lay, he sent to his assistance the second division of his corps, 6,000 men under General Vedel, all recruits of the 'legions of reserve,' save one single battalion of Swiss troops. The division was accompanied by Boussard's cavalry, the 6th Provisional Dragoons, some 600 strong. Vedel made his way through La Mancha without difficulty, but on entering the Despeña Perros defiles found his passage disputed by a body of insurgents—2,000 peasants with four antique cannon—who had stockaded themselves in the midst of the pass. A resolute attack scattered them in a few minutes, and on reaching La Carolina on the southern slope of

---

[1] See Foy (iv. 45), and *Nap. Corresp.*, 14,192, where the Emperor goes so far as to say : ' Si le Général Dupont éprouvait un échec, cela ait de peu de conséquence. Il n'aurait d'autre résultat que de lui faire repasser les montagnes' (i. e. the Sierra Morena).

the mountains Vedel got in touch with Dupont, who had hitherto no notice of his approach [June 27].

Instead of leaving the newly arrived division to guard the passes, Dupont called it down to join him in the valley of the Guadalquivir. With the assistance of Vedel's troops he considered himself strong enough to make head against the Spanish army under Castaños, which was commencing to draw near to Andujar. Keeping his original force at that town—a great centre of roads, but a malarious spot whose hospitals were already crowded with 600 sick, —he placed Vedel at Baylen, a place sixteen miles further east, but still in the plain, though the foot-hills of the Sierra Morena begin to rise just behind it. To assert himself and strike terror into the insurgents, Dupont ordered one of Vedel's brigades to make a forced march to Jaen, the capital of a province and a considerable focus of rebellion. This expedition scattered the local levies, took and sacked Jaen, and then returned in safety to Baylen [July 2–3].

Meanwhile Castaños was drawing near: he had now had a month in which to organize his army. Like Blake in Galicia, he had used the recruits of Andalusia to fill up the gaps in the depleted battalions of the regular army. But less fortunate than his colleague in the north, he had not been able to prevent the Juntas of Seville and Granada from creating a number of new volunteer corps, and had been obliged to incorporate them in his field army, where they were a source of weakness rather than of strength. His total force was some 33,000 or 34,000 men, of whom 2,600 were cavalry, for in this arm he was far better provided than was the army of the North. The whole was organized in four divisions, under Generals Reding, Coupigny, Felix Jones (an Irish officer, in spite of his Welsh name), and La Peña. In addition there was a flying brigade of new levies under Colonel Cruz-Murgeon, which was pushed forward along the roots of the mountains, at a considerable distance in front of the main body: it was ordered to harass Dupont's northern flank and to cut his communications with Baylen and La Carolina.

With 16,000 or 17,000 men, including nearly 3,500 cavalry, Dupont ought to have been able to contain Castaños, if not to beat him. The proportion of his forces to those of the enemy was not much less than that which Bessières had possessed at Medina de Rio Seco. But, unfortunately for himself and his master, Dupont was far from possessing the boldness and the skill of the marshal.   By assuming not a vigorous offensive but a timid defensive along a protracted front, he threw away his chances. The line which he had resolved to hold was that of the Upper Guadalquivir, from Andujar to the next passage up the river, the ferry of Mengibar, eight miles from Baylen.   This gave a front of some fifteen miles to hold : but unfortunately even when drawn out to this length the two divisions of Barbou and Vedel did not cover all the possible lines of attack which Castaños might adopt. He might still march past them and cut them off from the defiles of the Morena, by going a little higher up the river and crossing it near Baeza and Ubeda.   Dupont was wrong to take this line of defence at all : unless he was prepared to attack the army of Andalusia in the open, he should have retired to Baylen or to La Carolina, where he would have been able to cover the passes for as long as he might choose, since he could not have had either of his flanks turned.

Meanwhile he was gratified to hear that further reinforcements were being sent to him.   Unreasonably disquieted about Andalusia, as Napoleon thought, Savary proceeded to send a third division to aid Dupont.   This was Gobert's, the second of Moncey's corps : it started from Madrid not quite complete, and left strong detachments at the more important towns along the road through La Mancha.   Though originally seventeen battalions strong, it reached the northern slope of the Sierra Morena with only ten.   Savary had not intended it to go any further : he had told Dupont that it was to be used to cover his retreat, if a retreat became necessary, but not for active operations in Andalusia.   But disregarding these directions Dupont commanded Gobert to cross the Morena and come down to join Vedel : this he did, bringing with him nine 'provisional battalions [1]' and the second provisional regiment of cuirassiers, perhaps 5,000 men in all.   There were now over 20,000 French on the south side of the mountain, a force amply sufficient to deal with Castaños and his 33,000 Andalusians [July 7].   But

---

[1] Of Gobert's division the 5th provisional regiment and the Irish battalion never marched south.   The 6th, 7th, and 8th provisional regiments—twelve battalions—formed the column ; they left one battalion at Madridejos, another at Manzanares.   One more remained in the pass at the Puerto del Rey ; nine and the cuirassiers (700 strong) descended into the plains.   See for details Cabany's *Baylen*, p. 115.

they were still widely scattered. Dupont lay at Andujar with 9,000 or 10,000 sabres and bayonets: Vedel was sixteen miles away at Baylen, with 6,000 men, of whom 2,000 under General Liger-Belair were pushed forward to the ferry of Mengibar. Gobert was at La Carolina, at the foot of the passes, with five battalions about him, and a sixth encamped on the summit of the defile. He had sent forward the remainder of his division (the four battalions of the sixth provisional regiment, and half the second provisional cuirassiers) to join Dupont at Andujar, so that he had not more than 2,800 bayonets and 350 cavalry with him.

Castaños, meanwhile, had brought up his whole army, with the exception of the flying corps of Cruz-Murgeon, to a line close in front of Andujar: the heads of his columns were at Arjona and Arjonilla, only five miles from Dupont. On July 11 the Spanish generals held a council of war at Porcuña, and drew out their plan of operations. Since the enemy seemed to be still quiescent, they resolved to attack him in his chosen position behind the river. Castaños, in person—with the divisions of Jones and La Peña, 12,000 strong—undertook to keep Dupont employed, by delivering an attack on Andujar, which he did not intend to press home unless he got good news from his second and third columns. Meanwhile, six miles up the river, Coupigny with the second division, nearly 8,000 strong, was to attempt to cross the Guadalquivir by the ford of Villa Nueva. Lastly, Reding with the first division, the best and most numerous of the whole army, 10,000 strong, was to seize the ferry of Mengibar and march on Baylen. Here he was to be joined by Coupigny, and the two corps were then to fall upon the rear of Dupont's position at Andujar, while Castaños was besetting it in front. It was their aim to surround and capture the whole of the French division, if its general did not move away before the encircling movement was complete. Meanwhile the flying column of Cruz-Murgeon, about 3,000 strong, was to cross the Guadalquivir below Andujar, throw itself into the mountains in the north, and join hands with Reding and Coupigny behind the back of Dupont.

This plan, though ultimately crowned with success, was perilous in the highest degree. But Castaños had seriously underestimated the total force of Dupont, as well as misconceived his exact position. He was under the impression that the main body of the French, which he did not calculate at more than 12,000 or 14,000 men, was concentrated at Andujar, and that there were nothing more than weak detachments at Mengibar, Baylen, or La Carolina. These, he imagined, could not stand before Reding, and when the latter had once got to the northern bank of the river, he would easily clear the way for Coupigny to cross. But as a matter of fact Vedel had 6,000 men at Mengibar and Baylen, with 3,000 more under Gobert within a short march of him. If the Spanish plan had been punctually carried out, Reding should have suffered a severe check at the hands of these two divisions, while Dupont could easily have dealt with Castaños at Andujar. Coupigny, if he got across at Villa Nueva, while the divisions on each side of him were beaten off, would have been in a very compromised position, and could not have dared to push forward. But in this curious campaign the probable never happened, and everything went in the most unforeseen fashion.

On July 13 the Spanish plan began to be carried out, Reding marching for Mengibar and Coupigny for Villa Nueva. Castaños kept quiet at Arjonilla, till his lieutenants should have reached the points which they were to attack. On the same day Dupont received the news of Moncey's repulse before Valencia, and made up his mind that he must persevere in his defensive attitude, without making any attempt to mass his troops and fall upon the enemy in his front [1]. Just at the moment when his enemies were putting the game into his hands, by dividing themselves into three columns separated from each other by considerable gaps, he relinquished every intention of taking advantage of their fault.

On July 14 Reding appeared in front of the ferry of Mengibar, and pushed back beyond the river the outlying pickets of Liger-Belair's detachment. He made no further attempt to press the French, but Dupont, disquieted about an attack on this point, ordered Gobert to bring down the remains of his division to Baylen, to join Vedel. Next morning the Spaniards began to develop their whole plan: Castaños appeared on a long front opposite Andujar, and made a great demonstration against the position of Dupont, using all his artillery and showing heads of columns at several points. Coupigny came down to the river

---

[1] Dupont considered that Savary's intention was to stop all offensive movements whatever : ' Le général-en-chef me fait entrevoir que nous aurons peut-être à garder notre position jusqu'à ce que Valence et Saragosse soient soumises' (Dupont to Vedel, July 13).

at Villa Nueva, and got engaged with a detachment which was sent out from Andujar to hold the ford. Reding, making a serious attempt to push forward, crossed the Guadalquivir at Mengibar and attacked Liger-Belair. But Vedel came up to the support of his lieutenant, and when the Swiss general found, quite contrary to his expectation, a whole division deployed against him, he ceased to press his advance, and retired once more beyond the river.

Nothing decisive had yet happened : but the next day was to be far more important. The operations opened with two gross faults made by the French: Dupont had been so much impressed with the demonstration made against him by Castaños, that he judged himself hopelessly outnumbered at Andujar, and sent to Vedel for reinforcements. He bade him send a battalion or two, or even a whole brigade, if the force that he had fought at Mengibar seemed weak and unenterprising [1]. This was an error, for Castaños only outnumbered the French at Andujar by two or three thousand men, and was not really to be feared. But Vedel made a worse slip : despising Reding overmuch, he marched on Baylen, not with one brigade, but with his whole division, save the original detachment of two battalions under Liger-Belair which remained to watch Mengibar. Starting at midnight, he reached Andujar at two on the afternoon of the sixteenth, to find that Castaños had done no more than repeat his demonstration of the previous day, and had been easily held back. Cruz-Murgeon's levies, which the Spanish general had pushed over the river below Andujar, had received a sharp repulse when they tried to molest Dupont's flank. Coupigny had made an even feebler show than his chief at the ford of Villa Nueva, and had not passed the Guadalquivir.

But Reding, on the morning of the sixteenth, had woken up to unexpected vigour. He had forded the river near Mengibar, and fallen on Liger-Belair's detachment for the second time. Hard pressed, the French brigadier had sent for succour to Baylen, whither Gobert had moved down when Vedel marched for Andujar. The newly arrived general came quickly to the aid of the com-promised detachment, but he was very weak, for he had left a battalion at La Carolina and sent another with a squadron of cuirassiers to Liñares, to guard against a rumoured movement of the Spaniards along the Upper Guadalquivir. He only brought with him three battalions and 200 cavalry, and this was not

---

[1] Dupont to Vedel, evening of July 15.

enough to contain Reding. The 4,000 men of the two French detachments were outnumbered by more than two to one ; they suffered a thorough defeat, and Gobert was mortally wounded. His brigadier, Dufour, who took over the command, fell back on Baylen, eight miles to the rear. Next morning, though not pressed by Reding, he retired towards La Carolina, to prevent himself being cut off from the passes, for he credited a false rumour that the Spaniards were detaching troops by way of Liñares to seize the Despeña Perros.

Dupont heard of Gobert's defeat on the evening of the sixteenth. It deranged all his plans, for it showed him that the enemy were not massed in front of Andujar, as he supposed, but had a large force far up the river. Two courses were open to him—either to march on Baylen with his whole army in order to attack Reding, and to reopen the communications with La Carolina and the passes, or to fall upon Castaños and the troops in his immediate front. An enterprising officer would probably have taken the latter alternative, and could not have failed of success, for the whole French army in Andalusia save the troops of Belair and Dufour was now concentrated at Andujar, and not less than 15,000 bayonets and 3,000 sabres were available for an attack on Castaños' 12,000 men [1]. Even if Coupigny joined his chief, the French would have almost an equality in numbers and a great superiority in cavalry and guns. There cannot be the slightest doubt that the Spaniards

---

[1] Dupont's available force at this moment consisted of the following troops. The numbers given are their original strength, from which deductions must of course be made :—

Infantry—Barbou's Division :

Chabert's Brigade	4th Legion of Reserve (three batts.)	3,084
	4th Swiss Regiment (one batt.)	709
	Marines of the Guard (one batt.)	532
Pannetier's Brigade	3rd Legion of Reserve (two batts.)	2,057
	Garde de Paris (two batts.)	1,454
Schramm's Brigade	Swiss regiments of Reding and Preux (four batts.) .	2,000

Vedel's Division :

Poinsot's Brigade	5th Legion of Reserve (three batts.)	2,695
	3rd Swiss Regiment	1,174
Cassagnes' Brigade	1st Legion of Reserve (one batt.) [two batts. detached under Liger-Belair]	1,003

From Gobert's Division :

6th Provisional Regiment (four batts.) . . .	1,851

would have suffered a defeat, and then it would have been possible
to expel Reding from Baylen without any danger of interference
from other quarters.

But, in a moment of evil inspiration, Dupont chose to deprive
himself of the advantage of having practically his whole army
concentrated on one spot, and determined to copy the error of the
Spaniards by splitting his force into two equal halves. He resolved
to retain his defensive position in front of Andujar, and to keep
there his original force—Barbou's infantry and Fresia's horse.
But Vedel with his own men, the four battalions from Gobert's
division which were at Andujar, and 600 cavalry, was sent off to
Baylen, where he was directed to rally the beaten troops of Dufour
and Liger-Belair, and then to fall upon Reding and chase him
back beyond the Guadalquivir [1].

On the morning, therefore, of July 17 Vedel set out with
some 6,000 men and marched to Baylen. Arriving there he found
that Dufour had evacuated the place, and had hurried on to
La Carolina, on the false hypothesis that Reding had pushed past
him to seize the passes. As a matter of fact the Spaniard had
done nothing of the kind: after his success at Mengibar, he had
simply retired to his camp by the river, and given his men twenty-
four hours' rest. It was a strange way to employ the day after
a victory—but his quiescence chanced to have the most fortunate

Cavalry—Frésia's Division :

Privé's Brigade	{ 1st Provisional Dragoons	778
	{ 2nd ditto	681
Dupré's Brigade	{ 1st Provisional *Chasseurs à Cheval*	556
	{ 2nd ditto	623
Boussard's Brigade	{ 6th Provisional Dragoons	620
From Rigaud's Brigade :		
	Half the 2nd Provisional Cuirassiers	341
Artillery, &c. (36 guns)		900
		21,058

Allowing a deduction of 3,000 men for sick and previous losses, there remain
15,000 bayonets and 3,000 sabres.

[1] 'Je vous prie, mon cher général, de vous porter le plus rapidement
possible, sur Baylen, pour y faire votre jonction avec le corps qui a combattu
aujourd'hui à Mengibar, et qui s'est replié sur cette ville. . . . J'espère que
demain l'ennemi sera rejeté sur Mengibar, au delà du fleuve, et que les postes
de Guarroman et de la Caroline resteront en sûreté; ils sont d'une grande
importance' (Dupont to Vedel, night of July 16). In these orders lies the
foundation of the disaster.

effect. Vedel, on hearing that Dufour had hastened away to defend
La Carolina and the passes, resolved to follow him. He was so
inexcusably negligent that he did not even send a cavalry reconnaissance towards Mengibar, to find out whether any Spanish force
remained there. Had he done so, he would have found Reding's
whole division enjoying their well-earned siesta! In the direction
of La Carolina and the passes there was no enemy save a small
flanking column of 1,800 raw levies under the Count of Valdecañas,
which lay somewhere near Liñares.

On the night of the seventeenth, Vedel and his men, tired out
by a long march of over twenty miles, slept at Guarroman, halfway between Baylen and La Carolina. Dufour and Liger-Belair
had reached the last-named place and Santa Elena, and had found
no Spaniards near them. On the morning of the eighteenth Vedel
followed them, and united his troops to theirs. He had then
some 10,000 or 11,000 men concentrated in and about La Carolina,
with one single battalion left at Guarroman to keep up his touch
with Dupont. The latter had been entirely deceived by the false
news which Vedel had sent him from Baylen—to the effect that
Reding and his corps had marched for the passes, in order to cut
the French communications with Madrid. Believing the story, he
forwarded to his subordinate an approval of his disastrous movement [1], and bade him 'instantly attack and crush the Spanish force
before him, and after disposing of it return as quickly as possible
to Andujar, to deal with the troops of the enemy in that direction.'
Unfortunately, as we have seen, there was no Spanish corps at all
in front of Vedel; but by the time that he discovered the fact
it was too late for him to rejoin Dupont without a battle [2]. His

[1] 'J'ai reçu votre lettre de Baylen. D'après le mouvement de l'ennemi,
le général Dufour a très-bien fait de regagner de vitesse sur La Caroline et sur
Ste-Hélène, pour occuper la tête des gorges. Je vois avec plaisir que vous
vous hâtez de vous réunir à lui, afin de combattre avec avantage. . . . Si
vous trouvez l'ennemi à La Caroline ou sur tout autre point, tâchez de le
battre, pour venir me rejoindre et repousser ce qui est devant Andujar'
(Dupont to Vedel, night of July 17).

[2] Vedel had now with him the following troops :—

(1) His own whole division [he had rallied the two detached battalions of Liger-Belair].   6,800
(2) Nine battalions of Gobert's division (four from Baylen, three
which had fought at Mengibar under Dufour, two from
Liñares and La Carolina)   4,350

Part of **ANDALUSIA,** between Andujar and the Passes. July 19. 1808.

French
Spanish

To Pass of Despena Perros
Sta Elena
La Carolina
Vedel
Guarroman
Baylen
Linares
Baeza
To Ubeda
R. Almudiel
Guadalquivir R.
R. Guadiel
Coupigny and Reding
Dupont
Ferry
Mengibar
Villanueva
Jaen
La Pena
R. Rumblar
Andujar
Castanos
Arjonilla
Arjona O
To Cordova
To Baena
Porcuna
R. Jandala

Darbishire & Stanford Ld

Scale 0   5   10 English Miles

Battle of BAYLEN July 19, 1808. at the moment of DUPONT'S third attack

To Carolina
La Carolina
Vedel
A
To Linares
Cerro del Ahorcado
S. Cristobal
Cerro de Zumacar Grande
Reding's Div
Div
Baylen
Coupigny's Div
Pannetier
Swiss
Chabert
El Cerrajon
Dupre
French Convoy
R. Rumblar
Prive
To Menjibar
From Andujar
La Peña

Foot   Horse

French

Spanish

A *Approach of Vedel in the afternoon*

Scale 0   ¼   ½   ¾   1   English Mile

troops were tired out with two night marches: there were no
supplies of food to be got anywhere but at La Carolina, and he
decided that he must halt for at least twelve hours before returning
to join Dupont.

Meanwhile, on the morning of the eighteenth, Reding's 9,500
men, of whom 750 were cavalry, had been joined by Coupigny and
the second Andalusian division, which amounted to 7,300 foot
and 500 horse. Advancing from Mengibar to attack Baylen, they
found to their surprise that the place was unoccupied: Vedel's
rearguard had left it on the previous afternoon. Reding intended
to march on Andujar from the rear on the next day, being under
the full belief that Vedel was still with Dupont, and that the
troops which had retired on La Carolina were only the fragments
of Gobert's force. For Castaños and his colleagues had drawn up
their plan of operations on the hypothesis that the enemy were
still concentrated at Andujar.

Reding therefore, with some 17,000 men, encamped in and about
Baylen, intending to start at daybreak on July 19, and to fall
on Dupont from behind, while his chief assailed him in front.
But already before the sun was up, musket-shots from his
pickets to the west announced that the French were approaching
from that direction. It was with the head and not with the rear
of Dupont's column that Castaños' first and second divisions were
to be engaged, for the enemy had evacuated Andujar, and was in
full march for Baylen.

On the night of the seventeenth Dupont had received the news
that Vedel had evacuated Baylen and gone off to the north-east,
so that a gap of thirty miles or more now separated him from his
lieutenant. He had at first been pleased with the move, as we
have seen: but presently he gathered, from the fact that Castaños
did not press him, but only assailed him with a distant and
ineffective cannonade, that the main stress of the campaign was
not at Andujar but elsewhere. The Spanish army was shifting

(3) Cavalry	{ 6th Provisional Dragoons	.	.	.	.	.	620
	{ Half 2nd Provisional Cuirassiers	.	.	.	.	340
Artillery, &c. (18 guns)	.	.	.	.	.	.	.	500
							12,610

Deduct 2,500 for losses in action at Mengibar and sick, and about 10,000
remain.

itself eastward, and he therefore resolved that he must do the same, though he would have to abandon his cherished offensive position, his entrenchments, and such part of his supplies as he could not carry with him.   Having made up his mind to depart, Dupont would have done wisely to start at once : if he had gone off early on the morning of the eighteenth, he would have found Reding and Coupigny not established in position at Baylen, but only just approaching from the south.   Probably he might have brushed by their front, or even have given them a serious check, if he had fallen on them without hesitation.

But two considerations induced the French general to wait for the darkness, and to waste fourteen invaluable hours at Andujar. The first was that he hoped by moving at night to escape the notice of Castaños, who might have attacked him if his retreat was open and undisguised.   The second was that he wished to carry off his heavy baggage train : not only had he between 600 and 800 sick to load on his wagons, but there was an enormous mass of other impedimenta, mainly consisting of the plunder of Cordova.   French and Spanish witnesses unite in stating that the interminable file of 500 vehicles which clogged Dupont's march was to a very great extent laden with stolen goods[1].   And it was the officers rather than the men who were responsible for this mass of slow-moving transport.

It was not therefore till nine in the evening of the eighteenth that the French general thought fit to move.   After barricading and blocking up the bridge of Andujar—he dared not use gun-powder to destroy it for fear of rousing Castaños—he started on his night march.   He had with him thirteen battalions of infantry and four and a half regiments of cavalry, with twenty-four guns, in all about 8,500 foot soldiers and 2,500 horse, allowing for the losses which he had sustained in sick and wounded during the earlier phases of the campaign[2].   His march was arranged as

[1] Against Cabany's defence of Dupont on this point there must be set the impression of almost every French witness from Napoleon downwards.

[2] Of the troops which we have recapitulated on page 182 there still remained with Dupont the whole of Barbou's infantry, four of the five regiments of Frésia's cavalry (the fifth had marched with Vedel), half of the 2nd Provisional Cuirassiers, and the two Swiss regiments of Reding and Preux. The original total of these corps had been 13,274.   There remained about 11,000, for that number can be accounted for after the battle.   The official Spanish dispatch gave 8,242 unwounded prisoners and 2,000 casualties.

follows:—Chabert's infantry brigade led the van: then came the great convoy: behind it were the four Swiss battalions under Colonel Schramm, which had lately been incorporated with the French army. These again were followed by Pannetier's infantry brigade and Dupré's two regiments of *chasseurs à cheval*. The rearguard followed at some distance: it was composed of two and a half regiments of heavy cavalry, placed under the command of General Privé, with the one veteran infantry battalion which the army possessed, the 500 Marines of the Guard, as also six *compagnies d'élite* picked from the 'legions of reserve.' From the fact that Dupont placed his best troops in this quarter, it is evident that he expected to be fighting a rearguard action, with Castaños in pursuit, rather than to come into contact with Spanish troops drawn up across his line of march. He was ignorant that Reding and Coupigny had occupied Baylen on the previous day—a fact which speaks badly for his cavalry: with 2,500 horsemen about him, he ought to have known all that was going on in his neighbourhood. Probably the provisional regiments, which formed his whole mounted force, were incapable of good work in the way of scouting and reconnaissances.

The little town of Baylen is situated in a slight depression of a saddle-backed range of hills which runs southward out from the Sierra Morena. The road which leads through it passes over the lowest point in the watershed, as is but natural: to the north and south of the town the heights are better marked: they project somewhat on each flank, so that the place is situated in a sort of amphitheatre. The hill to the south of Baylen is called the Cerrajon: those to the north the Cerro del Zumacar Chico, and the Cerro del Zumacar Grande. All three are bare and bald, without a shrub or tree: none of them are steep, their lower slopes are quite suitable for cavalry work, and even their rounded summits are not inaccessible to a horseman. The ground to the west of them, over which the French had to advance, is open and level for a mile and a half: then it grows more irregular, and is thickly covered with olive groves and other vegetation, so that a force advancing over it is hidden from the view of a spectator on the hills above Baylen till it comes out into the open. The wooded ground is about two and a half miles broad: its western limit is the ravine of a mountain torrent, the Rumblar (or Herrumblar, as the aspirate-loving Andalusians sometimes call it). The road from Andujar to Baylen crosses this stream by a bridge, the only place where artillery can pass the rocky but not very deep depression.

It is necessary to say a few words about the ground eastward from Baylen, as this too was not unimportant in the later phases of the battle. Here the road passes through a broad defile rather than a plain. It is entirely commanded by the heights on its northern side, where lies the highest ground of the neighbourhood, the Cerro de San Cristobal, crowned by a ruined hermitage. The difference between the approach to Baylen from the west and from the east, is that on the former side the traveller reaches the town through a semicircular amphitheatre of upland, while by the latter he comes up a V-shaped valley cut through the hills.

Reding and Coupigny were somewhat surprised by the bicker of musketry which told them that the French had fallen upon their outposts. But fortunately for them their troops were already getting under arms, and were bivouacking over the lower slopes of the hills in a position which made it possible to extemporize without much difficulty a line of battle, covering the main road and the approaches to Baylen. They hastily occupied the low amphitheatre of hills north and south of the town. Reding deployed to the right of the road, on the heights of the Cerro del Zumacar Chico, Coupigny to its left on the Cerrajon. Their force was of a very composite sort—seventeen battalions of regulars, six of embodied militia, five of new Andalusian levies. The units varied hopelessly in size, some having as few as 350 men, others as many as 1,000. They could also dispose of 1,200 cavalry and sixteen guns. The greater part of the latter were placed in battery on the central and lowest part of the position, north and south of the high road and not far in front of Baylen. The infantry formed a semicircular double line : in front were deployed battalions near the foot of the amphitheatre of hills; in rear, higher up the slope or concealed behind the crest, was a second line in columns of battalions. The cavalry were drawn up still further to the rear. Finally, as a necessary precaution against the possible arrival of Vedel on the scene from La Carolina, Reding placed seven battalions far away to the east, on the other side of Baylen, with cavalry pickets out in front to give timely notice of any signs of the enemy in this quarter. These 3,500 men were quite out of the battle as long as Dupont was the only enemy in sight.

Before it was fully daylight General Chabert and his brigade had thrust back the Spanish outposts. But the strength of the insurgent army was quite unknown to him: the morning dusk still lay in the folds of the hills, and he thought that he might possibly have in front of him nothing but some flying column of insignificant strength. Accordingly, after allowing the whole of his brigade to come up, Chabert formed a small line of attack, brought up his battery along the high road to the middle of the amphitheatre, between the horns of the Spanish position, and made a vigorous push forward. He operated almost entirely to the south of the road, where, opposite Coupigny's division, the hill was lower and the slope gentler than further north.

To dislodge 14,000 men and twenty guns in position with 3,000 men and six guns was of course a military impossibility. But Chabert had the excuse that he did not, and could not, know what he was doing. His attempt was of course doomed to failure: his battery was blown to pieces by the Spanish guns, acting from a concentric position, the moment that it opened. His four battalions, after pushing back Coupigny's skirmishing line for a few hundred yards, were presently checked by the reserves which the Spaniard sent forward. Having come to a stand they soon had to retire, and with heavy loss. The brigade drew back to the cover of the olive groves behind it, leaving two dismounted guns out in the open.

Behind Chabert the enormous convoy was blocking the way as far back as the bridge of the Rumblar. Five hundred wagons with their two or four oxen apiece, took up, when strung along the road, more than two and a half miles. Dupont, who rode up at the sound of the cannon, and now clearly saw the Spanish line drawn up on a front of two miles north and south of the road, realized that this was no skirmish but a pitched battle. His action was governed by the fact that he every moment expected to hear the guns of Castaños thundering behind him, and to find that he was attacked in rear as well as in front. He accordingly resolved to deliver a second assault as quickly as possible, before this evil chance might come upon him. With some difficulty the Swiss battalions, Dupré's brigade of light cavalry, and Privé's dragoons pushed their way past the convoy and got into the open. They were terribly tired, having marched all night and covered fifteen miles of bad road, but their general threw them at once into the fight: Pannetier's brigade and the Marines of the Guard were still far to the rear, at or near the bridge of the Rumblar.

Dupont's second attack was a fearful mistake: he should at all costs have concentrated his whole army for one desperate stroke, for there was no more chance that 6,000 men could break the Spanish line than there had been that Chabert's 3,000 could do so. But without waiting for Pannetier to come up, he delivered his second attack. The four Swiss battalions advanced to the north of the road, Chabert's rallied brigade to the south of it: to the right of the latter were Privé's heavy cavalry, two and a half regiments strong, with whom Dupont intended to deliver his main blow. They charged with admirable vigour and precision, cut up two Spanish battalions which failed to form square in time, and cleared the summit of the Cerrajon. But when, disordered with their first success, they rode up against Coupigny's reserves, they failed to break through. Their own infantry was too far to the rear to help them, and after a gallant struggle to hold their ground, the dragoons and cuirassiers fell back to their old position. When they were already checked, Chabert and Schramm pushed forward to try their fortune: beaten off by the central battery of the Spanish line and its infantry supports, they recoiled to the edge of the olive wood, and there reformed.

The French were now growing disheartened, and Dupont saw disaster impending over him so closely that he seems to have lost his head, and to have retained no other idea save that of hurling every man that he could bring up in fruitless attacks on the Spanish centre. He hurried up from the rear Pannetier's brigade of infantry, leaving at the bridge of the Rumblar only the single battalion of the Marines of the Guard. At eight o'clock the reinforcements had come up, and the attack was renewed. This time the main stress was at the northern end of the line, where Pannetier was thrown forward, with orders to drive Reding's right wing off the Cerro del Zumacar Grande, while the other battalions renewed their assault against the Spanish centre and left. But the exhausted troops on the right of the line, who had been fighting since daybreak, made little impression on Coupigny's front, and Reding's last reserves were brought forward to check and hold off the one fresh brigade of which Dupont could dispose.

The fourth attack had failed. The French general had now but one intact battalion, that of the Marines of the Guard, which had been left with the baggage at the bridge over the Rumblar, to protect the rear against the possible advent of Castaños. As there were still no signs of an attack from that side, Dupont brought up this corps, ranged it across the road in the centre of the line, and drew up behind it all that could be rallied of Chabert's and Pannetier's men. The whole formed a sort of wedge, with which he hoped to break through the Spanish centre by one last effort. The cavalry advanced on the flanks, Privé's brigade to the south, Dupré's to the north of the road. Dupont himself, with all his staff around him, placed himself at the head of the marines, and rode in front of the line, waving his sword and calling to the men that this time they must cut their way through [12.30 P.M.].

All was in vain : the attack was pressed home, the marines pushed up to the very muzzles of the Spanish cannon placed across the high road, and Dupré's chasseurs drove in two battalions in Reding's right centre. But the column could get no further forward : the marines were almost exterminated : Dupré was shot dead : Dupont received a painful (but not dangerous) wound in the hip, and rode to the rear. Then the whole attack collapsed, and the French rolled back in utter disorder to the olive groves which sheltered their rear. The majority of the rank and file of the two Swiss regiments in the centre threw up the butts of their muskets in the air and surrendered—or rather deserted—to the enemy [1].

At this moment, just as the firing died down at the front, a lively fusillade was heard from another quarter. Cruz-Murgeon's light column, from the side of the mountains, had come down upon the Rumblar bridge, and had begun to attack the small baggage-guard [2] which remained with the convoy. All was up. Cruz-Murgeon was the forerunner of La Peña, and Dupont had not a man left to send to protect his rear. The battalions were all broken up, the wearied infantry had cast themselves down in the shade of the olive groves, and could not be induced even to rise to their feet. Most of them were gasping for water, which could not be got, for

---

[1] That the desertion was pretty general is shown by the fact that of 2,000 men of these corps only 308 were recorded as prisoners in the Spanish official returns. If 300 more had been killed and wounded, 1,400 must have deserted. Hardly any officers were among those who went over to the enemy ; Schramm, their commander, was wounded.

[2] Three companies of Pannetier's brigade.

the stream-beds which cross the field were all dried up, and only at the Rumblar could a drink be obtained. Not 2,000 men out of the original 11,000 who had started from Andujar could be got together to oppose a feeble front to Reding and Coupigny. It was only by keeping up a slow artillery fire, from the few pieces that had not been silenced or dismounted, that any show of resistance could be made. When the attack from the rear, which was obviously impending, should be delivered, the whole force must clearly be destroyed.

Wishing at least to get some sort of terms for the men whom he had led into such a desperate position, Dupont at two o'clock sent his aide-de-camp, Captain Villoutreys, one of the Emperor's equerries, to ask for a suspension of hostilities from Reding. He offered to evacuate Andalusia, not only with his own troops but with those of Vedel and Dufour, in return for a free passage to Madrid. This was asking too much, and if the Spanish general had been aware of the desperate state of his adversary, he would not have listened to the proposal for a minute. But he did not know that La Peña was now close in Dupont's rear, while he was fully aware that Vedel, returning too late from the passes, was now drawing near to the field from the north. His men were almost as exhausted as those of Dupont, many had died from sunstroke in the ranks, and he did not refuse to negotiate. He merely replied that he had no power to treat, and that all communications should be made to his chief, who must be somewhere in the direction of Andujar. He would grant a suspension of arms for a few hours, while a French and a Spanish officer should ride off together to seek for Castaños.

Dupont accepted these terms gladly, all the more so because La Peña's division had at last reached the Rumblar bridge, and had announced its approach by four cannon-shots, fired at regular intervals, as a signal to catch Reding's ear. It was with the greatest difficulty that the commander of the fourth Andalusian division could be got to recognize the armistice granted by his colleague ; he saw the French at his mercy, and wanted to fall upon them while they were still in disorder. But after some argument he consented to halt. Captain Villoutreys, accompanied by the Spanish Colonel Copons, rode through his lines to look for Castaños.

The Spanish commander-in-chief had displayed most blameworthy torpidity on this day. He had let Dupont slip away from

Andujar, and did not discover that he was gone till dawn had
arrived. Then, instead of pursuing at full speed with all his forces,
he had sent on La Peña's division, while he lingered behind with
that of Felix Jones, surveying the enemy's empty lines. The fourth
division must have marched late and moved slowly, as it only reached
the Rumblar bridge—twelve miles from Andujar—at about 2 p.m.
It could easily have been there by 8 or 9 a.m., and might have
fallen upon Dupont while he was delivering one of his earlier
attacks on the Baylen position.

At much the same moment that Villoutreys and Copons
reached Castaños at Andujar, at about five o'clock in the afternoon, the second half of the French army at last appeared upon
the scene. General Vedel had discovered on the eighteenth that
he had nothing to fear from the side of the passes. He therefore
called down all Dufour's troops, save two battalions left at Santa
Elena, united the two divisions at La Carolina, and gave orders
for their return to Baylen on the following morning. Leaving
the bivouac at five o'clock Vedel, with some 9,000 or 9,500 men,
marched down the defile for ten miles as far as the village of
Guarroman, which he reached about 9.30 or 10 a.m.[1] The day
was hot, the men were tired, and though the noise of a distant
cannonade could be distinctly heard in the direction of Baylen, the
general told his officers to allow their battalions two hours to cook,
and to rest themselves. By some inexplicable carelessness the two
hours swelled to four, and it was not till 2 p.m. that the column
started out again, to drop down to Baylen. An hour before the
French marched, the cannonade, which had been growling in the
distance all through the mid-day rest, suddenly died down. Vedel
was in nowise disturbed, and is said to have remarked that his
chief had probably made an end of the Spanish corps which had
been blocking the road between them.

After this astonishing display of sloth and slackness, Vedel proceeded along the road for ten miles, till he came in sight of the
rear of the Spanish position at Baylen. His cavalry soon brought
him the news that the troops visible upon the hillsides were
enemies: they consisted of the brigade which Reding had told off

---

[1] There is some dispute as to the exact hours of Vedel's start and halt :
I have adopted, more or less, those given by Cabany. Vedel himself, when
examined by the court-martial, said ' qu'il ne pouvait pas préciser l'heure,'
which is quite in keeping with the rest of his doings.

at the beginning of the day to hold the height of San Cristobal and the Cerro del Ahorcado against a possible attack from the rear.   It was at last clear to Vedel that things had not gone well at Baylen, and that it was his duty to press in upon the Spaniards, and endeavour to cut his way through to his chief.   He had begun to deploy his troops across the defile, with the object of attacking both the flanking hills, when two officers with a white flag rode out towards him.   They announced to him that Dupont had been beaten, and had asked for a suspension of hostilities, which had been granted.   La Peña's troops had stayed their advance, and he was asked to do the same.

Either because he doubted the truth of these statements, or because he thought that his appearance would improve Dupont's position, Vedel refused to halt, and sent back the Spanish officers to tell Reding that he should attack him.   This he did with small delay, falling on the brigade opposed to him with great fury. Boussard's dragoons charged the troops on the lower slopes of the Cerro del Ahorcado, and rode into two battalions who were so much relying on the armistice that they were surprised with their arms still piled, cooking their evening meal.   A thousand men were taken prisoners almost without firing a shot[1].   Cassagnes' infantry attacked the steep height of San Cristobal with less good fortune: his first assault was beaten off, and Vedel was preparing to succour him, when a second white flag came out of Baylen.   It was carried by a Spanish officer, who brought with him De Barbarin, one of Dupont's aides-de-camp.   The general had sent a written communication ordering Vedel to cease firing and remain quiet, as an armistice had been concluded, and it was hoped that Castaños would consent to a convention.   The moment that his answer was received it should be passed on; meanwhile the attack must be stopped and the troops withdrawn.

Vedel obeyed: clearly he could do nothing else, for Dupont was his hierarchical superior, and, as far as he could see, was still a free agent.   Moreover, De Barbarin told him of the very easy terms which the commander-in-chief hoped to get from Castaños.   If they could be secured it would be unnecessary, as well as risky, to continue the attack.   For La Peña might very possibly have anni-

[1] Apparently they were the 1st battalion of the Irlanda regiment, and the militia of Jaen, according to the narrative of Maupoey and Goicoechea (Arteche, ii. 512).

hilated the beaten division before Vedel could force his way to its aid,
since horse and foot were both 'fought out,' and there was neither
strength nor spirit for resistance left among them. Vedel therefore
was justified in his obedience to his superior, and in his withdrawal
to a point two miles up the La Carolina road.

Meanwhile Villoutreys, the emissary of Dupont, had reached the
camp of Castaños at Andujar [1] late in the afternoon, and laid his
chief's proposals before the Spaniard. As might have been expected,
they were declined—Dupont was in the trap, and it would have
been absurd to let him off so easily. No great objection was made
to the retreat of Vedel, but Castaños said that the corps caught
between La Peña and Reding must lay down its arms. Early next
morning (July 20) Villoutreys returned with this reply to the
French camp.

Dupont meanwhile had spent a restless night. He had gone
round the miserable bivouac of his men, to see if they would be in
a condition to fight next morning, in the event of the negotiations
failing. The result was most discouraging: the soldiers were in
dire straits for want of water, they had little to eat, and were so
worn out that they could not be roused even to gather in the
wounded. The brigadiers and colonels reported that they could
hold out no prospect of a rally on the morrow [2]. Only Privé, the
commander of the heavy-cavalry brigade, spoke in favour of
fighting: the others doubted whether even 2,000 men could be got
together for a rush at the Spanish lines. When an aide-de-camp,
whom Vedel had been allowed to send to his chief, asked whether
it would not be possible to make a concerted attack on Reding
next morning, with the object of disengaging the surrounded
division, Dupont told him that it was no use to dream of any such
thing. Vedel must prepare for a prompt retreat, in order to save
himself; no more could be done.

At dawn, nothing having been yet settled, La Peña wrote to
Dupont threatening that if the 1,000 men who had been captured

[1] Or, according to some authorities, met Castaños at the first post-house
out of Andujar, on the Baylen road.
[2] No one confesses the demoralization of the French troops more than Foy.
' Dupont voulait combattre encore. . . . Mais pour exécuter des résolutions
vigoureuses il fallait des soldats à conduire. Or, ces infortunés n'étaient plus
des soldats ; c'était un troupeau dominé par les besoins physiques, sur lequel
les influences morales n'avaient plus de prise. La souffrance avait achevé
d'énerver les courages.'

by Vedel on the previous day were not at once released, he should consider the armistice at an end, and order his division to advance. The request was reasonable, as they had been surprised and taken while relying on the suspension of arms.   Dupont ordered his subordinate to send them back to Reding's camp.   Castaños meanwhile was pressing for a reply to his demand for surrender : he had brought up Felix Jones's division to join La Peña's in the early morning, so that he had over 14,000 men massed on the right bank of the Rumblar and ready to attack [1].   Dupont was well aware of this, and had made up his mind to surrender when he realized the hopeless demoralization of his troops.   Early in the morning he called a council of war ; the officers present, after a short discussion, drew up and signed a document in which they declared that ' the honour of the French arms had been sufficiently vindicated by the battle of the previous day : that in accepting the enemy's terms the commander-in-chief was yielding to evident military necessity : that, surrounded by 40,000 enemies, he was justified in averting by an honourable treaty the destruction of his corps.'   Only the cavalry brigadier Privé, refused to put his name to the paper, on which appear the signatures of three generals of division, of the officers commanding the artillery and engineers, of two brigadiers, and of three commanders of regiments.

After this formality was ended Generals Chabert and Marescot rode out from the French camp and met Castaños.   They had orders to make the best terms they could : in a general way it was recognized that the compromised division could not escape surrender, and that Vedel and Dufour would probably have to evacuate Andalusia and stipulate for a free passage to Madrid.   The Spaniards were not, as it seems, intending to ask for much more. But while they were haggling on such petty points as the forms of surrender, and the exemption of officers' baggage from search, a new factor was introduced into the discussion.   Some irregulars from the Sierra Morena came to Castaños, bringing with them as a prisoner an aide-de-camp of Savary [2].   They had secured his dispatch, which was a peremptory order to Dupont to evacuate Andalusia with all his three divisions, and fall back towards Madrid.   This put a new face on affairs, for Castaños saw that

[1] Namely, 6,600 of La Peña's men, 5,400 of Jones's, and 2,500 or 3,000 of Cruz-Murgeon's flying column.

[2] His name was Captain de Fénelon (Cabany, p. 178).

if he conceded a free retreat to Vedel and Dufour, he would be enabling them to carry out exactly the movement which Savary intended. To do so would clearly be undesirable : he therefore interposed in the negotiations, and declared that the troops of these two generals should not be allowed to quit Andalusia by the road which had been hitherto proposed. They must be sent round by sea to some port of France not immediately contiguous with the Spanish frontier.

Chabert and Marescot, as was natural, declaimed vehemently against this projected change in the capitulation, and declared that it was inadmissible. But they were answered in even more violent terms by the turbulent Conde de Tilly, who attended as representative of the Junta of Seville. He taunted them with their atrocities at the sack of Cordova, and threatened that if the negotiations fell through no quarter should be given to the French army. At last Castaños suggested a compromise: he offered to let Dupont's troops, no less than those of Vedel, return to France by sea, if the claim that the latter should be allowed to retreat on Madrid were withdrawn. This was conceding much, and the French generals accepted the proposal.

Accordingly Castaños and Tilly, representing the Spaniards, and Chabert and Marescot, on behalf of Dupont, signed preliminaries, by which it was agreed that the surrounded divisions should formally lay down their arms and become prisoners of war, while Vedel's men should not be considered to have capitulated, nor make any act of surrender. Both bodies of men should leave Andalusia by sea, and be taken to Rochefort on Spanish vessels. 'The Spanish army,' so ran the curiously worded seventh article of the capitulation, 'guarantees them against all hostile aggression during their passage.' The other clauses contain nothing striking, save some rather liberal permissions to the French officers to take away their baggage—each general was to be allowed two wheeled vehicles, each field officer or staff officer one—without its being examined. This article caught the eye of Napoleon, and has been noted by many subsequent critics, who have maintained that Dupont and his colleagues, gorged with the plunder of Cordova, surrendered before they needed, in order to preserve their booty intact. That they yielded before it was inevitable we do not believe : but far more anxiety than was becoming seems to have been shown regarding the baggage. This anxiety finds

easy explanation if the Spanish official statement, that more than
£40,000 in hard cash, and a great quantity of jewellery and silver
plate was afterwards found in the *fourgons* of the staff and the
superior officers, be accepted as correct[1].

The fifteenth clause of the capitulation had contents of still
more doubtful propriety : it was to the effect that as many pieces
of church plate had been stolen at the sack of Cordova, Dupont
undertook to make a search for them and restore them to the
sanctuaries to which they belonged, if they could be found in
existence.   The confession was so scandalous, that we share
Napoleon's wonder that such a clause could ever have been passed
by the two French negotiators; if they were aware that the charge
of theft was true (as it no doubt was), shame should have prevented
them from putting it on paper : if they thought it false, they were
permitting a gratuitous insult to the French army to be inserted
in the capitulation.

While the negotiations were going on, Dupont sent secret orders
to Vedel to abscond during the night, and to retreat on Madrid
as fast as he was able.   Chabert and Marescot had of course no
knowledge of this, or they would hardly have consented to include
that general's troops in the convention.   In accordance with his
superior's orders, and with the obvious necessities of the case,
Vedel made off on the night of July 20–21, leaving only a screen
of pickets in front of his position, to conceal his departure from
the Spaniards as long as was possible.   On the return of his
plenipotentiaries to his camp on the morning of the twenty-first,
Dupont learnt, to his surprise and discontent, that they had included Vedel's division in their bargain with Castaños.   But as
that officer was now far away—he had reached La Carolina at
daybreak and Santa Elena by noon—the commander-in-chief hoped
that his troops were saved.

The anger of the Spaniards at discovering the evasion of the
second French division may easily be imagined.   Reding, who was
the first to become aware of it, sent down an officer into Dupont's
camp, with the message that if Vedel did not instantly return, he
should regard the convention as broken, and fall upon the surrounded troops : he should give no quarter, as he considered that

---

[1] It will be found in the *Gazeta de Madrid* of October 9, 1808.   It is stated
that 60,000 dollars in silver and 136,000 dollars in gold, besides much plate
and jewellery, were found in the *fourgons* of Dupont and his staff.

treachery had been shown, and that the armistice had been abused. Dupont could not hope to make a stand, and was at the enemy's mercy. He directed his chief of the staff to write an order bidding Vedel to halt, and sent it to him by one of his aides-de-camp, accompanied by a Spanish officer. This did not satisfy Reding, who insisted that Dupont should write an autograph letter of his own in stronger terms. His demand could not be refused, and the two dispatches reached Vedel almost at the same hour, as he was resting his troops at Santa Elena before plunging into the passes.

Vedel, as all his previous conduct had shown, was weak and wanting in initiative. Some of his officers tried to persuade him to push on, and to leave Dupont to make the best terms for himself that he could. Much was to be said in favour of this resolve : he might have argued that since he had never been without the power of retreating, it was wrong of his superior to include him in the capitulation. His duty to the Emperor would be to save his men, whatever might be the consequences to Dupont. The latter, surrounded as he was, could hardly be considered a free agent, and his orders might be disregarded. But such views were far from Vedel's mind : he automatically obeyed his chief's dispatch and halted. Next day he marched his troops back to Baylen, in consequence of a third communication from Dupont.

On July 23 Dupont's troops laid down their arms with full formalities, defiling to the sound of military music before the divisions of La Peña and Jones, who were drawn up by the Rumblar bridge. On the twenty-fourth Vedel's and Dufour's troops, without any such humiliating ceremony, stacked their muskets and cannon on the hillsides east of Baylen and marched for the coast. When the two corps were numbered it was found that 8,242 unwounded men had surrendered with Dupont : nearly 2,000 more, dead or wounded, were left on the battle-field ; seven or eight hundred of the Swiss battalions had deserted and disappeared. With Vedel 9,393 men laid down their arms [1]. Not only did he deliver up his

---

[1] This total of 17,635, given in the Spanish returns, seems absolutely certain. It tallies very well with the original figures of the French divisions, when losses in the campaign are allowed for. I find in the *Vaughan Papers* a contemporary Spanish scrap of unknown provenance, giving somewhat different figures, as follows :—Dupont's corps : unwounded prisoners, 6,000 ; killed and wounded on the field, 3,000 ; Swiss deserters, 1,200 ; sick captured

own column, but he called down the battalion guarding the Despeña Perros pass. Even the troops left beyond the defiles in La Mancha were summoned to surrender by the Spaniards, and some of them did so, though they were not really included in the capitulation, which was by its wording confined to French troops in Andalusia. But the commanders of three battalions allowed themselves to be intimidated by Colonel Cruz-Murgeon, who went to seek them at the head of a few cavalry, and tamely laid down their arms [1].

The Spaniards had won their success at very small cost. Reding's division returned a casualty list of 117 dead and 403 wounded, in which were included the losses of the skirmish of July 16 as well as those of the battle of the nineteenth. Coupigny lost 100 dead and 294 wounded. La Peña's and Cruz-Murgeon's columns, which had barely got into touch with the French when the armistice was granted, cannot have lost more than a score or two of men. The total is no more than 954. There were in addition 998 prisoners captured by Vedel when he attacked from the rear, but these were, of course, restored on the twentieth, in consequence of the orders sent by Dupont, along with two guns and two regimental standards.

Castaños, a man of untarnished honour, had every intention of carrying out the capitulation. The French troops, divided into small columns, were sent down to the coast, or to the small towns of the Lower Guadalquivir under Spanish escorts, which had some difficulty in preserving them from the fury of the peasantry. It was necessary to avoid the large towns like Cordova and Seville, where the passage of the unarmed prisoners would certainly have led to riots and massacres. At Ecija the mob actually succeeded in murdering sixty unfortunate Frenchmen. But when the troops had been conducted to their temporary destinations, it was found that difficulties had arisen. The amount of Spanish shipping available would not have carried 20,000 men. This was a comparatively small hindrance, as the troops could have been sent off in detachments. But it was

in the hospitals, 400 ; making a total of 10,600. Whittingham, the English attaché in Castaños' camp, gives another set :—unwounded prisoners, 5,500 ; killed and wounded, 2,600 ; Swiss deserters, 1,100 ; making 9,200. But both of these are confessedly rough estimates, though made on the spot. As to the other French prisoners, the Vaughan document says that 9,100 surrendered with Vedel, 800 in the passes, and 700 more in La Mancha.

[1] Battalions surrendered at Santa Cruz, and at Manzanares. But the officer in command at Madridejos refused to be cajoled, and retreated on Madrid.

more serious that Lord Collingwood, the commander of the British squadron off Cadiz, refused his permission for the embarkation of the French. He observed that Castaños had promised to send Dupont's army home by water, without considering whether he had the power to do so. The British fleet commanded the sea, and was blockading Rochefort, the port which the capitulation assigned for the landing of the captive army. No representative of Great Britain had signed the convention [1], and she was not bound by it. He must find out, by consulting his government, whether the transference of the troops of Dupont to France was to be allowed.

On hearing of the difficulties raised by Collingwood, Castaños got into communication with Dupont, and drew up six supplementary articles to the convention, in which it was stipulated that if the British Government objected to Rochefort as the port at which the French troops were to be landed, some other place should be selected. If all passage by sea was denied, a way by land should be granted by the Spaniards. This agreement was signed at Seville on August 6, but meanwhile the Junta was being incited to break the convention. Several of its more reckless and fanatical members openly broached the idea that no faith need be kept with those who had invaded Spain under such treacherous pretences. The newspapers were full of tales of French outrages, and protests against the liberation of the spoilers of Cordova and Jaen.

Matters came to a head when Dupont wrote to Morla, the Captain-General of Andalusia, to protest against further delays, and to require that the first division of his army should be allowed to sail at once [August 8]. He received in reply a most shameless and cynical letter [2]. The Captain-General began by declaring that there were no ships available. But he then went on to state that no more had been promised than that the Junta would request the British to allow the French troops to sail. He supposed that it was probable that a blank refusal would be sent to this demand. Why should Britain allow the passage by sea of troops who were destined to be used against her on some other point of the theatre of

---

[1] There had been a British attaché, Captain Whittingham, at Castaños' head quarters. The French negotiators had tried to induce him to approve the terms of capitulation. But he very wisely refused, having no authority to do so.

[2] This will be found printed at length in the Appendix of Papers relating to Baylen.

war ? Morla next insinuated that Dupont himself must have been well aware that the capitulation could not be carried out. ' Your Excellency's object in inserting these conditions was merely to obtain terms which, impossible as they were to execute, might yet give a show of honour to the inevitable surrender. . . . What right have you to require the performance of these impossible conditions on behalf of an army which entered Spain under a pretence of alliance, and then imprisoned our King and princes, sacked his palaces, slew and robbed his subjects, wasted his provinces, and tore away his crown ? '

After a delay of some weeks Lord Collingwood sent in to the Junta the reply of his government. It was far from being of the kind that Morla and his friends had hoped. Canning had answered that no stipulations made at Baylen could bind Great Britain, but that to oblige her allies, and to avoid compromising their honour, she consented to allow the French army to be sent back to France, and to be landed in successive detachments of 4,000 men at some port between Brest and Rochefort (i. e. at Nantes or L'Orient). It is painful to have to add that neither the Junta of Seville nor the Supreme Central Junta, which superseded that body, took any steps to carry out this project. Dupont himself, his generals, and his staff, were sent home to France, but their unfortunate troops were kept for a time in cantonments in Andalusia, then sent on board pontoons in the Bay of Cadiz, where they were subjected to all manner of ill usage and half-starved, and finally dispatched to the desolate rock of Cabrera, in the Balearic Islands, where more than half of them perished of cold, disease, and insufficient nourishment[1]. Vedel's men were imprisoned no less than Dupont's, and the survivors were only released at the conclusion of the general peace of 1814.

So ended the strange and ill-fought campaign of Baylen. It is clear that Dupont's misfortunes were of his own creation. He ought never to have lingered at Andujar till July was far spent, but should either have massed his three divisions and fallen upon Castaños, or have retired to a safe defensive position at Baylen or La Carolina and have waited to be attacked. He might have united something over 20,000 men, and could have defied every

[1] For the horrors of Cabrera, the works of three of the prisoners, Ducor of the Marines of the Guard, and Gille and Wagré of Vedel's division, may be consulted. Their story is deeply distressing.

effort of the 35,000 Spaniards to drive him back over the Sierra Morena. By dividing his army into fractions and persisting in holding Andujar, he brought ruin upon himself. But the precise form in which the ruin came about was due less to Dupont than to Vedel. That officer's blind and irrational march on La Carolina and abandonment of Baylen on July 17–18 gave the Spaniards the chance of interposing between the two halves of the French army. If Vedel had made a proper reconnaissance on the seventeenth, he would have found that Reding had not marched for the passes, but was still lingering at Mengibar. Instead, however, of sweeping the country-side for traces of the enemy, he credited a wild rumour, and hurried off to La Carolina, leaving the fatal gap behind him. All that followed was his fault : not only did he compromise the campaign by his march back to the passes, but when he had discovered his mistake he returned with a slowness that was inexcusable. If he had used ordinary diligence he might yet have saved Dupont on the nineteenth : it was his halt at Guarroman, while the cannon of Baylen were thundering in his ears, that gave the last finishing touch to the disaster. If he had come upon the battle-field at ten in the morning, instead of at five in the afternoon, he could have aided his chief to cut his way through, and even have inflicted a heavy blow on Reding and Coupigny. A careful study of Vedel's actions, from his first passage of the Sierra Morena to his surrender, shows that on every possible occasion he took the wrong course.

But even if we grant that Vedel made every possible mistake, it is nevertheless true that Dupont fought his battle most unskilfully. If he had marched on the morning instead of the night of July 18, he probably might have brushed past the front of Reding and Coupigny without suffering any greater disaster than the loss of his baggage. Even as things actually fell out, it is not certain that he need have been forced to surrender. He had 10,000 men, the two Spanish generals had 17,000, but had been forced to detach some 3,500 bayonets to guard against the possible reappearance of Vedel. If Dupont had refused to waste his men in partial and successive attacks, and had massed them for a vigorous assault on the left wing of the Spaniards, where Coupigny's position on the slopes of the Cerrajon was neither very strong nor very well defined, he might yet have cut his way through, though probably his immense baggage-train would have been lost. It is fair, however, to remember that this chance was only granted him because Castaños, in front of Andujar, was slow to discover his retreat and still slower to pursue him. If that officer had shown real energy, ten thousand men might have been pressing Dupont from the rear before eight o'clock in the morning.

As it was Dupont mismanaged all the details of his attack. He made four assaults with fractions of his army, and on a long front. The leading brigades were completely worn out and demoralized before the reserves were sent into action. The fifth assault, in which every man was at last brought forward, failed because the majority of the troops were already convinced that the day was lost, and were no longer capable of any great exertions. It is absurd to accuse Dupont of cowardice—he exposed his person freely and was wounded—and still more absurd to charge him (as did the Emperor) with treason. He did not surrender till he saw that there was no possible hope of salvation remaining. But there can be no doubt that he showed great incapacity to grasp the situation, lost his head, and threw away all his chances.

As to the Spaniards, it can truly be said that they were extremely fortunate, and that even their mistakes helped them. Castaños framed his plan for surrounding Dupont on the hypothesis that the main French army was concentrated at Andujar. If this had indeed been the case, and Dupont had retained at that place some 15,000 or 17,000 men, the turning movement of Reding and Coupigny would have been hazardous in the extreme. But the French general was obliging enough to divide his force into two equal parts, and his subordinate led away one of the halves on a wild march back to the passes. Again Reding acted in the most strange and unskilful way on July 17; after defeating Liger-Belair and Dufour he ought to have seized Baylen. Instead, he remained torpid in his camp for a day and a half: this mistake led to the far more inexcusable error of Vedel, who failed to see his adversary, and marched off to La Carolina. But Vedel's blindness does not excuse Reding's sloth. On the actual day of battle, on the other hand, Reding behaved very well: he showed considerable tenacity, and his troops deserve great credit. It was no mean achievement for 13,000 or 14,000 [1] Spaniards, their ranks full of raw recruits

---

[1] We must deduct the seven battalions (3,500 or 4,000 men) which had been detached to the rear to watch for Vedel's approach, and were never engaged with Dupont's troops.

and interspersed with battalions levied only five weeks before, to withstand the attack of 10,000 French, even if the latter were badly handled by their general. The Andalusians had good reason to be proud of their victory, though they might have refrained from calling Dupont's Legions of Reserve and provisional regiments the 'invincible troops of Austerlitz and Friedland,' as they were too prone to do. They had at least succeeded in beating in the open field and capturing a whole French army, a thing which no continental nation had accomplished since the wars of the Revolution began.

NOTE

Sir Charles Vaughan, always in search of first-hand information, called on Castaños and had a long conversation with him concerning the Convention. I find among his papers the following notes :—

'Among other particulars of the surrender, General Castaños stated that the French General Marescot had the greatest influence in bringing it about. The great difficulty was to persuade them [Marescot and Chabert] to capitulate for Vedel's army as well as Dupont's. A letter had been intercepted ordering Vedel back to Madrid, and another ordering Dupont to retire. This letter had considerable effect with the French : but the offer of carrying away their baggage and the plunder of the country was no sooner made, than the two generals desired to be permitted to retire and deliberate alone. After a few minutes they accepted the proposal. But General Castaños, to make the article of as little value as possible, got them to insert the clause that the French officers should be allowed to embark all their baggage, &c., *according to the laws of Spain*. He well knew that those laws forbid the exportation of gold and silver. The consequence was that the French lost all their more valuable plunder when embarking at Puerto Santa Maria.'

SECTION IV

THE ENGLISH IN PORTUGAL

CHAPTER I

THE OUTBREAK OF THE PORTUGUESE INSURRECTION

Down to the moment of the general outbreak of the Spanish insurrection Junot's task in Portugal had not been a difficult one. As long as Spain and France were still ostensibly allies, he had at his disposition a very large army. He had entered Portugal in 1807 with 25,000 French troops, and during the spring of 1808 he had received 4,000 men in drafts from Bayonne, which more than filled up the gaps made in his battalions by the dreary march from Ciudad Rodrigo to Abrantes[1]. Of the three Spanish divisions which had been lent to him, Solano's had gone home to Andalusia, but he had still the two others, Caraffa's (7,000 strong) in the valley of the Tagus, and Taranco's at Oporto. The last-named general died during the winter, but his successor, Belesta, still commanded 6,000 men cantoned on the banks of the Douro. The discontent of the Portuguese during the early months of 1808 showed itself by nothing save a few isolated deeds of violence, provoked by particular acts of oppression on the part of Junot's subordinates. How promptly and severely they were chastised has been told in an earlier chapter. There were no signs whatever of a general rising: the means indeed were almost entirely wanting. The regular army had been disbanded or sent off to France. The organization of the militia had been dissolved. The greater part of the leading men of the country had fled to Brazil with the Prince-Regent: the bureaucracy and many of the clergy had shown a discreditable willingness to conciliate Junot by a tame subservience to his orders.

The Duke of Abrantes himself thoroughly enjoyed his Vice-

---

[1] See Thiébault, *Expédition de Portugal,* and Foy, iv. 363.

royalty, and still deluded himself into believing that he might yet prove a popular ruler in Portugal : perhaps he even dreamed of becoming some day one of Bonaparte's vassal-kings. He persisted in the farce of issuing benevolent proclamations, and expressing his affection for the noble Portuguese people, till his master at last grew angry. 'Why,' he wrote by the hand of his minister Clarke, 'do you go on making promises which you have no authority to carry out ? Of course, there is no end more laudable than that of winning the affection and confidence of the inhabitants of Portugal. But do not forget that the safety of the French army is the first thing. Disarm the Portuguese : keep an eye on the disbanded soldiers, lest reckless leaders should get hold of them and make them into the nucleus of rebel bands . . . Lisbon is an inconveniently large place : it is too populous, and its people cannot help being hostile to you. Keep your troops outside it, in cantonments along the sea-front ' : and so forth [1]. Meanwhile financial exactions were heaped on the unfortunate kingdom to contribute to the huge fine which the Emperor had laid upon it : but there was evidently no chance that such a large sum could be raised, however tightly the screw of taxation might be twisted. Junot accepted, as contributions towards the £2,000,000 that he was told to raise, much confiscated English merchandise, church plate, and private property of the royal house, but his extortions did little more than pay for his army and the expenses of government. Portugal indeed was in a dismal state : her ports were blocked and her wines could not be sold to her old customers in England, nor her manufactures to her Brazilian colonists. The working classes in Lisbon were thrown out of employment, and starved, or migrated in bands into the interior. Foy and other good witnesses from the French side speak of the capital as 'looking like a desert, with no vehicles, and hardly a foot-passenger in the streets, save 20,000 persons reduced to beggary and trying vainly to live on alms [2].' The only activity visible was in the arsenal and dockyards, where Junot had 10,000 men at work restoring the neglected material of the artillery, and fitting out that portion of the fleet which had been in too bad order to sail for Brazil in the previous November.

The sudden outbreak of the Spanish insurrection in the last days of May, 1808, made an enormous change in the situation of the

[1] Compare *Nap. Corresp.*, 13,608 and 13,620.   [2] Foy, iv. 273-4.

French army in Portugal. Before Junot had well realized what was happening in the neighbouring kingdom, his communications with Madrid were suddenly cut, and for the future information only reached him with the greatest difficulty, and orders not at all. The last dispatch that came through to him was one from the Emperor which spoke of the beginnings of the rising, and bade him send 4,000 men to Ciudad Rodrigo to hold out a hand to Bessières, and 8,000 to the Guadiana to co-operate in Dupont's projected invasion of Andalusia[1]. These orders were dispatched in the last days of May; before they could be carried out the situation had been profoundly modified.

On June 6 there arrived at Oporto the news of the insurrection of Galicia and the establishment of the Provincial Junta at Corunna. The first thought of the new government in Galicia had been to call home for its own defence the division in northern Portugal. When its summons reached General Belesta, he obeyed without a moment's hesitation. The only French near him were General Quesnel, the Governor of Oporto, his staff, and a troop of thirty dragoons which served as his personal escort. Belesta seized and disarmed both the general and his guard, and forthwith marched for Spain, by Braga and Valenza, with his prisoners. Before leaving he called together the notables of Oporto, bade them hoist the national flag, and incited them to nominate a junta to organize resistance against Junot. But he left not a man behind to aid them, and took off his whole force to join General Blake.

On receiving, on June 9, the news of this untoward event, Junot determined to prevent Caraffa's troops on the Tagus from following the example of their countrymen. Before they had fully realized the situation, or had time to concert measures for a general evasion, he succeeded in disarming them. Caraffa himself was summoned to the quarters of the commander-in-chief, and placed under arrest before he knew that he was suspected. Of his regiments some were ordered to attend a review, others to change garrisons; while unsuspectingly on their way, they found themselves surrounded by French troops and were told to lay down their arms. All were successfully trapped except the second cavalry regiment, the 'Queen's Own,' whose colonel rode off to Oporto with his two squadrons instead of obeying the orders sent him, and fractions of the infantry regiments of Murcia and Valencia who escaped to Badajoz

[1] *Nap. Corresp.*, 14,023 (from Bayonne, May 29).

after an ineffectual pursuit by the French dragoons. But 6,000 out of Caraffa's 7,000 men were caught, disarmed, and placed on pontoons moored under the guns of the Lisbon forts, whose commanders had orders to sink them if they gave any trouble. Here they were destined to remain prisoners for the next ten weeks, till the English arrived to release them after the battle of Vimiero.

The imminent danger that Caraffa's force might openly revolt, and serve as the nucleus for a general rising of the Portuguese, was thus disposed of. But Junot's position was still unpleasant: he had only some 26,500 men with whom to hold down the kingdom : if once the inhabitants took arms, such a force could not supply garrisons for every corner of a country 300 miles long and a hundred broad. Moreover, there was considerable probability that the situation might be complicated by the appearance of an English expeditionary army : Napoleon had warned his lieutenant to keep a careful watch on the side of the sea, even before the Spanish insurrection broke out. All through the spring a British force drawn from Sicily was already hovering about the southern coast of the Peninsula, though hitherto it had only been heard of in the direction of Gibraltar and Cadiz. Another cause of disquietude was the presence in the Tagus of the Russian fleet of Admiral Siniavin: the strange attitude adopted by that officer much perplexed Junot. He acknowledged that his master the Czar was at war with Great Britain, and stated that he was prepared to fight if the British fleet tried to force the entrance of the Tagus. But on the other hand he alleged that Russia had not declared war on Portugal or acknowledged its annexation by the Emperor, and he therefore refused to land his marines and seamen to help in the garrisoning of Lisbon, or to allow them to be used in any way on shore. Meanwhile his crews consumed an inordinate amount of the provisions which were none too plentiful in the Portuguese capital.

Junot's main advantage lay in the extreme military impotence of Portugal. That realm found its one sole centre in Lisbon, where a tenth of the population of the whole kingdom and half of its wealth were concentrated. At Lisbon alone was there an arsenal of any size, or a considerable store of muskets and powder. Without the resources of the capital the nation was absolutely unable to equip anything fit to be called an army. Oporto was a small place in comparison, and no other town in the kingdom had over 20,000 souls. Almeida and Elvas, the two chief fortresses of the realm, were safe in the hands of French garrisons. The provinces might rise, but without lavish help from Spain or England they could not put in the field an army of even 10,000 men, for assemblies of peasants armed with pikes and fowling-pieces are not armies, and of field-artillery there was hardly a piece outside Lisbon, Elvas, and Almeida. Nor was there left any nucleus of trained soldiers around which the nation might rally : the old army was dissolved and its small remnant was on the way to the Baltic. The case of Spain and of Portugal was entirely different when they rose against Napoleon. The former country was in possession of the greater part of its own fortresses, had not been systematically disarmed, and could dispose—in Galicia and Andalusia—of large bodies of veteran troops. Portugal was without an army, an arsenal, a defensible fortress, or a legal organization—civil or military—of any kind.

It is necessary to remember this in order to excuse the utter feebleness of the Portuguese rising in June, 1808. Otherwise it would have seemed strange that a nation of over 2,000,000 souls could not anywhere produce forces sufficient to resist for a single day a column of 3,000 or 4,000 French soldiers.

The insurrection—such as it was—started in the north, where the departure of Belesta and his division had left the two provinces of Tras-os-Montes and Entre-Duero-e-Minho free from any garrison, French or Spanish. Oporto had been bidden to work out its own salvation by Belesta, and on the day of his departure (June 6), a junta of insurrection had been acclaimed. But there followed a curious interval of apathy, lasting for ten days : the natural leaders of the people refused to come forward : here, just as in Spain, the bureaucracy showed itself very timid and unpatriotic. The magistrates sent secret offers of submission to Junot : the military commandant, Oliveira da Costa, hauled down the national flag from the citadel of San João da Foz. The members of the insurrectionary junta absconded from the city or kept quiet[1]. It was only on the news that the neighbouring districts and towns had risen, that the people of Oporto threw themselves frankly into the rebellion. The rough mountain districts which

---

[1] For these incidents, so discreditable to the leading men of Oporto, see Foy, iv. 206, and Toreño, i. 152. Most Peninsular historians consign them to oblivion.

lay to the east of them showed a much more whole-hearted
patriotism: between the ninth and the twelfth of June the whole
of the Tras-os-Montes took arms: one junta at Braganza nominated as commander the aged General Sepulveda, who had been
governor of the district in the days of the Prince-Regent: another,
at Villa Real on the Douro, also put in its claim and chose as its
leader Colonel Silveira, an officer who was destined to see much
service during the war of independence. Though the French were
no further off than Almeida, the rival governors nearly came to
blows, but the final insurrection of Oporto created a new power to
which both consented to bow.

On June 18 the false report that a French column was drawing
near Oporto so roused the multitude in that city that they broke
loose from the control of the authorities, rehoisted the Portuguese
flag, threw into prison Da Costa and many other persons suspected,
rightly or wrongly, of a wish to submit to the enemy, and called
for the establishment of a provisional government. Accordingly
a 'Supreme Junta of the Kingdom' was hastily elected with the
Bishop of Oporto at its head. This was a strange choice, for
the aged prelate, Dom Antonio de Castro, though popular and
patriotic, was neither a statesman nor an administrator, and had
no notion whatever as to the military necessities of the situation.
However, the other local juntas of Northern Portugal united in
recognizing his authority. His colleagues started on the organization of an army with more zeal than discretion; they called out
the militia which Junot had disbanded, and tried to reconstruct
some of the old regular battalions, by getting together the half-pay
officers, and the men who had been dismissed from the colours
in December, 1807. But they also encouraged the assembly of
thousands of peasants armed with pikes and scythes, who consumed
provisions, but were of no military use whatever. In the seven
weeks which elapsed before the coming of the English, the Supreme
Junta had only got together 5,000 men properly equipped and
told off into regular corps [1]. The fact was that they could provide arms for no more, Northern Portugal having always looked to
Lisbon for its supplies. Field artillery was almost wholly wanting
—perhaps a dozen guns in all had been found: of cavalry three

---

[1] They re-embodied the old 2nd, 12th, 21st, and 24th battalions of infantry
of the line, the 6th Cazadores, and the 6th, 11th, and 12th light cavalry, as
well as one or two other old corps whose numbers I cannot identify.

skeleton regiments were beginning to be organized. But of half-armed peasantry, disguised under the name of militia, they had from 12,000 to 15,000 in the field.

The Supreme Junta also concluded a treaty of offensive and defensive alliance with the Galician Spaniards, from whom they hoped to get arms, and perhaps a loan of troops. Moreover they sent two envoys to England to ask for aid, and eagerly welcomed at Oporto Colonel Brown, a British agent with a roving commission, who did his best to assist in organizing the new levies. The command of the whole armed force was given to General Bernardino Freire, a pretentious and incapable person, who turned his very moderate resources to no profitable account whatever.

A few days later than the outbreak of the insurrection in the regions north of the Douro, there was a corresponding movement, but of a weaker kind, in the extreme south. On June 16 the small fishing-town of Olhão in Algarve gave the signal for revolt : on the eighteenth Faro, the capital of the province, followed the example. General Maurin, the Governor of Algarve, was lying ill in his bed ; he was made prisoner along with seventy other French officers and men, and handed over to the captain of an English ship which was hovering off the coast. The whole shore between the Sierra de Caldeirão and the sea took arms, whereupon Colonel Maransin, Maurin's second-in-command, resolved to evacuate the province. He had only 1,200 men, a battalion each of the 26th of the line and the *Légion du Midi*, and had lost his communications with Lisbon, wherefore he drew together his small force and fell back first on Mertola and then on Beja, in the Alemtejo. The insurgents whom he left behind him could do little till they had obtained muskets from Seville and Gibraltar, and made no attempt to follow the retreating column northwards.

Meanwhile Junot, even after he had succeeded in disarming Caraffa's Spanish division, was passing through a most anxious time. In obedience to the Emperor's orders he had sent a brigade under General Avril towards Andalusia, to help Dupont, and another under Loison to Almeida to open communications with Bessières. But these detachments had been made under two false ideas, the one that the troubles in Spain were purely local, the other that Portugal would keep quiet. Avril marched southward with 3,000 men, but, when his vanguard reached San Lucar on the Spanish border, he found Andalusian militia provided with artillery watching him across the Guadiana. He also learnt that a large force was assembling at Badajoz, and that Dupont had got no further than Cordova—more than 150 miles away. After some hesitation he retraced his steps till he halted at Estremoz, facing Badajoz. Loison had much the same experience: starting from Almeida he crossed the border and scared away the small Spanish garrison of Fort Concepcion: but when he drew near Ciudad Rodrigo and learnt that the place was strongly held, that all the kingdom of Leon was in revolt, and that Bessières was still far distant in Old Castile, he drew back to Almeida [June 12–15]. Returning thither he heard of the troubles in Northern Portugal, and resolved to march on Oporto, which was still holding back from open insurrection when the news reached him. He determined to hasten to that important city and to garrison it. Taking two battalions and a few guns, while he left the rest of his brigade at Almeida, he marched on Oporto, crossed the Douro at the ferry of Pezo-de-Ragoa, and began to move on Amarante [June 21]. But the moment that he was over the river, he found himself in the middle of the insurrection: among the mountains the peasantry began to fire from above on his long column, to roll rocks down the slopes at him, and to harass his baggage and rearguard. Seeing that he had only 2,000 men in hand, and that the whole country-side was up, Loison wisely returned to Almeida, which he regained by a circular march through Lamego and Celorico, dispersing several bands of insurgents on the way, for the rebellion had already begun to spread across the Douro into the hills of Northern Beira [July 1].

Lisbon in the meanwhile was on the verge of revolt, but was still contained by the fact that Junot held concentrated in and about it the main body of his army, some 15,000 men. On the Feast of Corpus Christi (June 16) the annual religious procession through the streets nearly led to bloodshed. This was the greatest festival of Lisbon, and had always led to the assembly of enormous crowds: Junot allowed it to be once more celebrated, but lined the streets with soldiers, and placed artillery ready for action in the main squares and avenues. While the function was in progress a senseless panic broke out among the crowd, some shouting that they felt a shock of earthquake (always a terror in Lisbon since the catastrophe of 1755), others that the English were landing, others that the soldiers were about to fire on the people. The frantic mob burst through the military cordon, the procession was broken up, the prelate who bore the Sacrament took refuge in a church, and the tumult grew so wild that the artillery were about to open with grape, thinking that they had to deal with a carefully prepared insurrection. A great and miscellaneous slaughter was only prevented by the coolness of Junot, who threw himself into the throng, prevented the troops from firing, cleared the street, prevailed on the clergy to finish the procession, and dispersed the multitudes with no loss of life save that of a few persons crushed or trampled to death in the panic.

But though this tumult passed off without a disaster, Junot's position was uncomfortable. He had just begun to realize the real proportions of the insurrection in Spain, which had now completely cut him off from communication with his colleagues. He had only the vaguest knowledge of how Dupont and Bessières were faring : and the fact that large Spanish forces were gathering both at Ciudad Rodrigo and at Badajoz inclined him to think that affairs must be going ill in Castile and Andalusia. The long-feared English invasion seemed at last to be growing imminent : General Spencer's division from Sicily and Gibraltar was at sea, and had showed itself first off Ayamonte and the coast of Algarve, then off the Tagus-mouth. Ignorant that Spencer had only 5,000 men, and that he had been brought near Lisbon merely by a false report that the garrison had been cut down to a handful, Junot expected a disembarkation. But Spencer went back to Cadiz when he learnt that there were 15,000 instead of 4,000 men ready to defend the capital.

Meanwhile the populace of Lisbon was stirred up by all manner of wild rumours : it was said that Loison had been surrounded and forced to surrender by the northern insurgents, that the Spanish army of Galicia was marching south, that an English corps had landed at Oporto. All sorts of portents and signs were reported for the benefit of the superstitious. The most preposterous was one which we should refuse to credit if it were not vouched for by Foy, and other respectable French authorities. A hen's egg was found on the high-altar of the patriarchal church, with the inscription *Morran os Franceses* ('Death to the French') indented in its shell. This caused such excitement that Junot thought it worth while to show that a similar phenomenon could be produced on any egg by a skilful application of acids. When his chemists exhibited several branded in an equally convincing way with the words, *Vive l'Empereur!* the enthusiasm of the credulous was somewhat damped [1].

Recognizing that he could expect no further help from the French armies in Spain, and that the insurrection would certainly spread over every parish of Portugal that did not contain a garrison, Junot wisely resolved to concentrate the outlying fractions of his army, which lay exposed and isolated at points far from Lisbon. At a council of war, held on June 25, he laid before his chief officers the alternatives of evacuating Portugal and retiring on Madrid by the way of Badajoz, or of uniting the army in the neighbourhood of Lisbon and making an attempt to hold Central Portugal, while abandoning the extreme north and south. The latter plan was unanimously adopted : in the state of ignorance in which the generals lay as to what was going on at Madrid and elsewhere in Spain, the retreat by Badajoz seemed too hazardous. Moreover, it was certain to provoke Napoleon's wrath if it turned out to have been unnecessary. Accordingly it was resolved to place garrisons in the fortresses of Elvas, Almeida and Peniche, to fortify Setuval on the peninsula opposite Lisbon, and to draw in all the rest of the troops to the vicinity of the capital. Dispatches to this effect were sent to Loison at Almeida, to Avril at Estremoz, to Maransin at Mertola, and to Kellermann, who was watching Badajoz from Elvas [2]. Many of the aides-de-camp who bore these orders were cut off by the insurgents [3], but in the end copies of each dispatch were transmitted to their destinations. In several instances the detached corps had begun to fall back on the Tagus, even before they received the command to do so.

This was the case with Maransin at Mertola, who, finding himself hopelessly isolated with 1,200 men in the centre of the insurrection, had marched on Lisbon via Beja. On June 26 he reached the latter place and found its ancient walls manned by a disorderly mass of citizens, who fired upon him as he drew near. But he stormed the town without much difficulty, cruelly sacked it, and resumed his march on Lisbon unharmed. This was not the first fighting that had occurred in the Alemtejo; four days before

---

[1] Foy, iv. 276 ; Napier, i. 97.

[2] For the twelve resolutions arrived at by the council of war, see the analysis given by Thiébault, one of its members.

[3] Foy says that of twenty messages sent to Loison only one got through.

Avril had had to march from Estremoz to chastise the inhabitants of Villa Viciosa, who had taken arms and besieged the company of the 86th regiment which garrisoned their town. He scattered them with much slaughter, and, after the usual French fashion, plundered the little place from cellar to garret.

On receiving Junot's orders, General Kellermann, who bore the chief command in the Alemtejo, left a battalion and a half [1]— 1,400 men—in Elvas and its outlying fort of La Lippe. With the rest he retired on Lisbon, picking up first the corps of Avril and then that of Maransin, which met him at Evora. He then entered the capital, leaving only one brigade, that of Graindorge, at Setuval to the south of the Tagus [July 3].

Loison in the north did not receive his orders for a full week after they were sent out, owing to the disorderly state of the intervening country. But on July 4 he left Almeida, after making for it a garrison of 1,200 men, by drafting into a provisional battalion all his soldiers who did not seem fit for forced marching. He then moved for seven days through the mountains of Beira to Abrantes, skirmishing with small bands of insurgents all the way. At two or three places they tried to block his path, and the town of Guarda made a serious attempt to defend itself, and was in consequence sacked and partly burnt. Leaving a trail of ruined villages behind him, Loison at last reached Abrantes and got into communication with his chief. He had lost on the way 200 men, mostly stragglers whom the peasantry murdered : but he had inflicted such a cruel lesson on the country-side that his popular nickname (*Maneta*, ' One-Hand ') was held accursed for many years in Portugal.

The withdrawal of the French troops from the outlying provinces gave the insurrection full scope for development. It followed close in the track of the retiring columns, and as each valley was evacuated its inhabitants hoisted the national flag, sent in their vows of allegiance to the Junta at Oporto, and began to organize armed bands. But there was such a dearth of military stores that very few men could be properly equipped with musket and bayonet. Junot had long before called in the arms of the disbanded militia, and destroyed them or forwarded them to Lisbon. In the southern provinces the lack of weapons was even worse than in the valley of the Douro : there was practically no armament except a few hundred muskets hastily borrowed from the Spaniards of Badajoz

[1] The 2nd Swiss, and four companies of the 86th regiment.

and Seville, and a small dépôt of cavalry equipment at Estremoz which Avril had forgotten to carry off. An insurrectionary junta for the Alemtejo was formed at Evora, but its general, Francisco Leite, could only succeed in equipping the mere shadow of an army. In the north things were a little better: the rising spread to Coimbra in the last week of June, and one of its first leaders, the student Bernardo Zagalo, succeeded in capturing the small coast-fortress of Figueira by starving out the scanty French garrison, which had been caught wholly destitute of provisions [June 27]. Bernardino Freire then brought up the 5,000 regular troops, which the Junta of Oporto had succeeded in getting together, as far as the line of the Mondego. But the insurrectionary area spread much further southward, even up to Leyria and Thomar, which lie no more than sixty-five miles from the capital. From these two places, however, the rebels were easily cleared out by a small expedition of 3,000 men under General Margaron [July 5]. Junot's army in the second week of July held nothing outside the narrow quadrangle of which Setuval, Peniche, Abrantes, and Lisbon form the four points. But within that limited space there were now 24,000 good troops, concentrated and ready to strike a blow at the first insurrectionary force that might press in upon them.

But for a fortnight the Portuguese made no further move, and Junot now resolved to attack the insurgents who lay beyond the Tagus in the plains of the Alemtejo. His chief motive seems to have been the wish to reopen his communications with Elvas, and to keep the way clear towards Badajoz, the direction in which he would have to retreat, if ever he made up his mind to evacuate Lisbon and retire on Spain. Accordingly, on July 25, he sent out the energetic Loison at the head of a strong flying column—seven and a half battalions, two regiments of dragoons, and eight guns—over 7,000 men in all [1]. This force was directed to march on Elvas by way

---

[1] The column comprised the following troops:—

Two battalions of Reserve Grenadiers	1,100
12th Léger (3rd batt.)	1,253
15th Léger (3rd batt.)	1,305
58th Line (3rd batt.).	1,428
86th Line, twelve companies of the 1st and 2nd batts.	1,667
1st Hanoverian Legion	804
4th and 5th Provisional Dragoons	1,248

Deducting 1,200 for detached grenadier companies, &c., the whole was well over 7,000. For details, see Thiébault's *Expédition de Portugal*.

of Evora, the capital of the Alemtejo, and the seat of its new Junta.
On July 29 Loison appeared before the walls of that city.   To his
surprise the enemy offered him battle in the open ; General Leite
had brought up such of his newly organized troops as he could
collect—they amounted to no more than a battalion and a half of
infantry and 120 horse ; but to help him there had come up from
Badajoz the Spanish Colonel Moretti with about the same number
of foot, a regiment of regular cavalry (the 'Hussars of Maria Luisa'),
and seven guns [1].   In all the allies had under 3,000 men, but they
were presumptuous enough to form a line of battle outside Evora,
and wait for Loison's attack.   A mixed multitude of peasants and
citizens, more of them armed with pikes than with fowling-pieces,
manned the walls of the town behind them.   Leite and his colleague should have drawn back their regulars to the same position :
they might have been able to do something behind walls, but to
expose them in the open to the assault of more than double of
their own numbers of French troops was absurd.

Loison's first charge broke the weak line of the allied army ; the
Spanish cavalry fled without crossing swords with the French, and
General Leite left the field with equal precipitation.   But the
bulk of the infantry fell back on Evora and aided the peasantry to
defend its ruined mediaeval walls.   They could not hold out, however, for many minutes ; the French forced their way in at four or
five points, made a great slaughter in the streets, and ended the
day by sacking the city with every detail of sacrilege and brutality.
Foy says that 2,000 Spaniards and Portuguese fell ; his colleague
Thiébault gives the incredible figure of 8,000.   Even the smaller
number must include a good many unarmed inhabitants of Evora
massacred during the sack.   The French lost ninety killed and 200
wounded [July 29].

On the third day after the fight Loison marched for Elvas, and
drove away the hordes which were blockading it.   He was then
preparing to push a reconnaissance in force against Badajoz, when
he received from his commander-in-chief orders to return at once
to Lisbon.   The long-expected English invasion of Portugal had
at last begun, for on August 1 Sir Arthur Wellesley was already

---

[1] The figures of the Portuguese historian, Accursio das Neves, reproduced
in Arteche (ii. 35), seem indubitable, as they go into minute accounts of the
regiments and fractions of regiments present.   It seems clear that the allies
had nothing like the 5,000 regular troops of which Foy speaks (iv. 267–8).

disembarking his troops in Mondego Bay. Junot was therefore set on concentrating in order to fight, and Loison's expeditionary force was too important a part of his army to be left out of the battle. Dropping the battalion of the Hanoverian Legion as a garrison at Santarem, Loison brought the rest of his 7,000 men to his commander's aid.

SECTION IV: CHAPTER II

LANDING OF THE BRITISH: COMBAT OF ROLIÇA

FROM the first moment when the Asturian deputies arrived in London, with the news of the insurrection in Northern Spain [June 4], the English Government had been eager to intervene in the Peninsula. The history of the last fifteen years was full of the records of unfortunate expeditions sent out to aid national risings, real or imaginary, against France. They had mostly turned out disastrous failures: it is only necessary to mention the Duke of York's miserable campaign of 1799 in Holland, Stewart's invasion of Calabria in 1806, and Whitelock's disgraceful fiasco at Buenos Ayres in 1807. As a rule the causes of their ill success had been partly incapable leading, partly an exaggerated parsimony in the means employed. Considering the vast power of France, it was futile to throw ashore bodies of five thousand, ten thousand, or even twenty thousand men on the Continent, and to expect them to maintain themselves by the aid of small local insurrections, such as those of the Orange party in Holland or the Calabrian mountaineers. The invasion of Spanish South America, on the hypothesis that its inhabitants were all prepared to revolt against the mother-country—a fiction of General Miranda—had been even more unwise.

The 'policy of filching sugar islands,' as Sheridan wittily called it—of sending out expeditions of moderate size, which only inflicted pin-pricks on non-vital portions of the enemy's dominions—was still in full favour when the Spanish War began. There was hardly a British statesman who rose above such ideas; Pitt and Addington, Fox and Grenville, and the existing Tory government of the Duke of Portland, had all persisted in the same futile plans. At the best such warfare resulted in the picking up of stray colonies, such as Ceylon and Trinidad, the Cape, St. Thomas, or Curaçoa: but in 1808 the more important oversea possessions of France and her allies were still unsubdued. At the worst the policy led to checks and disasters small or great, like Duckworth's failure at

Constantinople, the abortive Egyptian expedition of 1807, or the catastrophe of Buenos Ayres. Castlereagh seems to have been the only leading man who dared to contemplate an interference on a large scale in Continental campaigns. His bold scheme for the landing of 60,000 men in Hanover, during the winter of 1805–6, had been foiled partly by the hesitation of his colleagues, partly by the precipitation with which Francis II made peace after Austerlitz [1].

But the policy of sending small auxiliary forces to the Iberian Peninsula was quite a familiar one. We had maintained a few thousand men under Generals Burgoyne and Townsend for the defence of Portugal against Spain in 1762. And again in 1801 there had been a small British division employed in the farcical war which had ended in the Treaty of Badajoz. In the year after Austerlitz, when it seemed likely that Bonaparte might take active measures against Portugal, the Fox-Grenville ministry had offered the Regent military aid, but had seen it politely refused, for the timid prince was still set on conciliating the Emperor.

With so many precedents before them, it was natural that the Portland cabinet should assent to the demands of the Spanish deputies who appeared in London in June, 1808. The insurrection in the Iberian Peninsula was so unexpected [2] and so fortunate a chance, that it was obviously necessary to turn it to account. Moreover, its attendant circumstances were well calculated to rouse enthusiasm even in the breasts of professional politicians. Here was the first serious sign of that national rising against Bonaparte which had been so often prophesied, but which had been so long in coming. Even the Whigs, who had systematically denounced the sending of aid to the 'effete despotisms of the Continent,' and had long maintained that Napoleon was not so black as he was painted, were disarmed in their criticisms by the character of the Spanish rising. What excuse could be made for the treachery at Bayonne? And how could sympathy be refused to a people which, deprived of its sovereign and betrayed by its bureaucracy, had so gallantly taken arms to defend its national

[1] This fine and not unpromising scheme deserves study (see Alison's *Life of Castlereagh*, i. 199–202).

[2] I cannot quite credit the story that Toreño and Arteche repeat of Pitt's dying prophecy, that 'Napoleon could only be overthrown by a national war, and that such a war would probably begin in Spain.'

existence? The debates in the British Parliament during the middle days of June show clearly that both the Government and the Opposition had grasped the situation, and that for once they were united as to the policy which should be pursued. It is only needful to quote a few sentences from the speeches of Canning as Foreign Secretary, and Sheridan as Leader of the Opposition [June 15].

'Whenever any nation in Europe,' said Canning, 'starts up with a determination to oppose that power which (whether professing insidious peace or declaring open war) is alike the common enemy of all other peoples, that nation, whatever its former relations with us may have been, becomes *ipso facto* the ally of Great Britain. In furnishing the aid which may be required, the Government will be guided by three principles—to direct the united efforts of both countries against the common foe, to direct them in such a way as shall be most beneficial to our common ally, and to direct them to such objects as may be most conducive to British interests. But of these objects the last shall never be allowed to come into competition with the other two. I mention British interests chiefly for the purpose of disclaiming them as any material part of the considerations which influence the British Government. No interest can be so purely British as Spanish success: no conquest so advantageous to England as conquering from France the complete integrity of the Spanish dominions in every quarter of the globe.'

Sheridan repeats the same theme in a slightly different key:—'Hitherto Buonaparte has run a victorious race, because he has contended with princes without dignity, ministers without wisdom, and peoples without patriotism. He has yet to learn what it is to combat a nation who are animated with one spirit against him. Now is the time to stand up boldly and fairly for the deliverance of Europe, and if the ministry will co-operate effectually with the Spanish patriots they shall receive from us cordial support . . . Never was anything so brave, so noble, so generous as the conduct of the Spaniards: never was there a more important crisis than that which their patriotism has occasioned to the state of Europe. Instead of striking at the core of the evil, the Administrations of this country have hitherto gone on nibbling merely at the rind: filching sugar islands, but neglecting all that was dignified and consonant to the real interests of the country. Now is the moment to let the world know that we are resolved to stand up for the salvation of Europe. Let us then co-operate with the Spaniards, but co-operate in an effectual and energetic way. And if we find that they are really heart and soul in the enterprise, let us advance with them, magnanimous and undaunted, for the liberation of mankind . . . Above all, let us mix no little interests of our own in this mighty combat. Let us discard or forget British objects, and conduct the war on the principle of generous support and active co-operation.'

It may perhaps be hypercritical to point out the weak spot in each of these stirring harangues. But Canning protested a little too much—within a few weeks of his speech the British Government was applying to the Junta of Seville to allow them to garrison Cadiz, which was refused (and rightly), for in the proposal British interests peeped out a little too clearly. And Sheridan, speaking from vague and overcoloured reports of the state of affairs in the Peninsula, went too far when he extolled the unmixed generosity and nobility of the conduct of the Spaniards : mingled with their undoubted patriotism there was enough of bigotry and cruelty, of self-seeking and ignorance, to make his harangue ring somewhat false in the ears of future generations. Yet both Canning and Sheridan spoke from the heart, and their declarations mark a very real turning-point in the history of the great struggle with Bonaparte.

Fortunately for Great Britain, and for the nations of the Iberian Peninsula, we were far better prepared for striking a heavy blow on the Continent in 1808 than we had been at any earlier period of the war. There was no longer any need to keep masses of men ready in the south-eastern counties for the defence of England against a French invasion. There were no longer any French forces of appreciable strength garrisoned along the English Channel : indeed Castlereagh had just been planning a raid to burn the almost unprotected French flotilla which still mouldered in the harbour of Boulogne. Our standing army had recently been strengthened and reorganized by a not inconsiderable military reform. The system had just been introduced by which Wellington's host was destined to be recruited during the next six years. Every year two-fifths of the 120,000 embodied militia of the United Kingdom were to be allowed to volunteer into the regular army, while the places of the volunteers were filled up by men raised by ballot from the counties. This sort of limited conscription worked well: in the year 1808 it gave 41,786 men to the line, and these not raw recruits, but already more or less trained to arms by their service in the militia. All through the war this system continued: the Peninsular army, it must always be remembered, drew more than half its reinforcing drafts from the 'old constitutional force.' Hence came the ease with which it assimilated its recruits. Meanwhile the embodied militia never fell short in establishment, as it was automatically replenished by the ballot. The result of these changes, for which Castlereagh deserves the chief credit, was a permanent addition of 25,000 men to the regular force available for service at home or in Europe.

In June, 1808, there chanced to be several considerable bodies of troops which could be promptly utilized for an expedition to Spain. The most important was a corps of some 9,000 men which was being collected in the south of Ireland, to renew the attack on South America which had failed so disastrously in 1807. The news of the Spanish insurrection had, of course, led to the abandonment of the design, and General Miranda, its originator, had been informed that he must look for no further support from England. In addition to this force in Ireland there were a couple of brigades in the south-eastern counties of England, which had been intended to form the nucleus of Castlereagh's projected raid on Boulogne. They had been concentrated at Harwich and Ramsgate respectively, and the transports for them were ready. A still more important contingent, but one that lay further off, and was not so immediately available, was the corps of 10,000 men which Sir John Moore had taken to the Baltic. In June it became known that it was impossible to co-operate with the hairbrained King of Sweden, who was bent on invading Russian Finland, a scheme to which the British Ministry refused its assent. Moore, therefore, after many stormy interviews with Gustavus IV, was preparing to bring his division home. With the aid of Spencer's troops, which had so long been hovering about Cadiz and Gibraltar, and of certain regiments picked out of the English garrisons, it was easily possible to provide 40,000 men for service in Spain and Portugal.

But a number of isolated brigades and battalions suddenly thrown together do not form an army, and though Castlereagh had provided a large force for the projected expedition to the Peninsula, it was destitute of any proper organization. With the expedition that sailed from Cork there was only half a regiment of cavalry, and the brigades from Harwich, Ramsgate, and Gibraltar had not a single horseman with them, so that there were actually 18,000 foot to 390 horse among the contingents that first disembarked to contend with Junot's army. Transport was almost equally neglected: only the troops from Cork had any military train with them, and that they were provided with horses and vehicles was only due to the prescience of their commander, who had at the last moment procured leave from London to enlist for foreign service and take with him two troops of the 'Royal Irish Corps of Wagoners.' 'I declare,' wrote Wellesley, 'that I do not understand the principles on which our military establishments are formed, if, when large corps are sent out to perform important and difficult services, they are not to have with them those means of equipment which they require, such as horses to draw artillery, and drivers attached to the commissariat[1].' Without this wise inspiration, he would have found himself unable to move when he arrived in the Peninsula: as it was, he had to leave behind, when he landed, some of his guns and half his small force of cavalry, because the authorities had chosen to believe that both draft and saddle horses could readily be procured in Portugal. Such little *contretemps* were common in the days when Frederick Duke of York, with the occasional assistance of Mrs. Mary Ann Clark, managed the British army.

But the arrangements as to the command of the expedition were the most ill-managed part of the business. The force at Cork was, as we have already explained, under the orders of Sir Arthur Wellesley, the younger brother of the great viceroy who had so much extended our Indian Empire between 1799 and 1805. He was the junior lieutenant-general in the British army, but had already to his credit a more brilliant series of victories than any other officer then living, including the all-important triumph of Assaye, which had so effectually broken the power of the Mahrattas. In 1808 he was a Member of Parliament and Under-Secretary for Ireland, but Castlereagh (who had the most unbounded belief in his abilities, and had long been using his advice on military questions) had picked him out to command the expedition mustering at Cork. When its destination was changed from America to Spain, the Secretary for War still hoped to keep him in command, but the

[1] Wellesley to Castlereagh, June 29, 1808 (*Well. Suppl. Disp.*, vi. 87).

Duke of York and the War Office were against Wellesley [1]. There were many respectable lieutenant-generals of enormous seniority and powerful connexions who were eager for foreign service. None of them had Wellesley's experience of war on a large scale, or had ever moved 40,000 men on the field: but this counted for little at head quarters. The command in Portugal was made over to two of his seniors. The first was Sir Hew Dalrymple, a man of fifty-eight, whose only campaigning had been with the Duke of York in Flanders thirteen years back. He had been Governor of Gibraltar since 1806, knew something of Spanish politics, and was now in active communication with Castaños. The second in command was to be Sir Harry Burrard [2]: he was an old Guards officer who had served during the American rebellion, and had more recently commanded a division during the Copenhagen expedition without any special distinction. The third was Sir John Moore, and to being superseded by him Wellesley could not reasonably have objected. He was at this moment perhaps the most distinguished officer in the British service: he had done splendid work in the West Indies, Egypt, and the Netherlands. He had reorganized the light infantry tactics of the British army, and had won the enthusiastic admiration of all who had ever served under him for his zeal and intelligent activity. But Moore, like Wellesley, was to be placed under Dalrymple and Burrard, and not trusted with an independent command. At the present moment he was still far away in the Baltic, and was not expected to arrive for some time. Meanwhile Wellesley was allowed to sail in temporary charge of the expeditionary force, and still under the impression that he was to retain its guidance. His

[1] For hints on this subject see the letter of W. Wellesley Pole, a kinsman of Sir Arthur, in *Wellington Supplementary Dispatches* (vi. 171). ' The desire that has been manifested at Head Quarters for active command will render it natural for all that has passed to be seen through a false medium. . . . The object of Head Quarters, if it has any object at all, must be to keep down the officer for whom the army has the greatest enthusiasm, and to prevent him from being called by the voice of the nation to the head of the forces upon active service, rather than to crush old officers of known incapacity and want of following. . . . Dalrymple is a Guardsman ; Burrard is a Guardsman ; their connexions are closely united to Windsor and Whitehall, and for years have not only been in the most confidential situation about Head Quarters, but have imbibed all their military notions from thence ; ' &c.

[2] Born in 1755, he was a favourite of the Duke of York, and had acted as his aide-de-camp. At this moment he held a command in the Home District.

transports weighed anchor on July 12, and it was only on July 15 that the dispatch from Downing Street, informing him that he had been superseded by Dalrymple and Burrard, was drafted. It did not reach him till he had already landed in Portugal.

His political instructions had been forwarded as early as June 30. They were drawn up mainly on the data that the Asturian and Galician deputations had furnished to the ministry[1]. Both the Juntas had been unwise enough to believe that the national rising would suffice to expel the French—whose numbers they much underrated—from Spain. While empowering their envoys to ask for money, arms, and stores, they had ordered them to decline the offer of an auxiliary force. They requested that all available British troops might be directed on Portugal, in order to rouse an insurrection in that country (which was still quiet when they arrived in London), and to prevent the troops of Junot from being employed against the rear of the army of General Blake. In deference to their suggestions the British Government had sent enormous stores of muskets, powder, and equipment to Gihon and Ferrol, but directed Wellesley to confine his activity to Portugal. The Spaniards, with their usual inaccuracy, had estimated the total of Junot's army at no more than 15,000 men. Misled by this absurd undervaluation, Castlereagh informed Wellesley that if he found that his own and Spencer's forces sufficed for the reduction of Portugal, he might 'operate against the Tagus' at once. But if more men were required, an additional 10,000 bayonets would be provided from England, and the expeditionary force might meanwhile ask the leave of the Galician Junta to stop at Vigo— a halt which would have cost many weeks of valuable time. Wellesley himself was to choose a fast-sailing vessel and make for Corunna, where he was to confer with the Junta and pick up the latest information as to the state of affairs in the Peninsula.

In accordance with these instructions Sir Arthur preceded the bulk of his armament on the *Crocodile*, and reached Corunna in the short space of eight days [July 20]. He found the Galicians somewhat depressed by the disaster of Medina de Rio Seco, whose details they misrepresented in the most shameless fashion to their distinguished visitor. Bessières, they said, had lost 7,000 men and six guns, and although he had forced Blake and Cuesta to retreat on Benavente, those generals had still 40,000 troops under arms,

[1] Castlereagh to Wellington (*Well. Disp.*, iv. 8, 9).

and had no need of any auxiliary force. 'The arrival of the
British money yesterday has entirely renewed their spirits,' wrote
Wellesley, 'and neither in them nor in the inhabitants of this town
do I see any symptom of alarm, or doubt of their final success.'
This vainglorious confidence was supported by an infinity of false
news : Lefebvre-Desnouettes was said to have been thrice defeated
near Saragossa, and Dupont and his whole corps had been taken
prisoners on June 22 in an action between Andújar and La
Carolina—a curious prophecy, for it foresaw and placed a month
too early the catastrophe of Baylen [1], which no reasonable man
could have predicted. Almost the only correct information which
was supplied to Wellesley was the news of the revolt of Oporto and
the rest of Northern Portugal. It was clear that there was now
an opening for the British army in that country, and as the
Galicians continued to display their reluctance to receive any
military aid, Sir Arthur went to sea again, joined his fleet of
transports off Cape Finisterre, and bade them make for the mouth
of the Douro. He himself put into Oporto, where he landed and
interviewed the Bishop and the Supreme Junta. He found them
in no very happy frame of mind : they had, as they confessed, only
been able to arm 5,000 infantry and 300 cavalry, who lay under
Bernardino Freire at Coimbra, and 1,500 men more for a garrison
at Oporto. The rest of these levies consisted of 12,000 peasants
with pikes, 'and though the people were ready and desirous to take
arms, unfortunately there were none in the country'—not even
enough to equip the disbanded regulars. The Bishop expressed
himself as much alarmed at the news of the disaster at Medina de
Rio Seco, and his military advisers acknowledged that in consequence of that battle they had given up any hope of aid from
Spain [2]. They asked eagerly for arms, of which the English fleet
carried many thousand stand, and were anxious to see Wellesley's
troops landed. The place which they recommended for putting
the army ashore was Mondego Bay, near Coimbra, where the
mouth of the Mondego River furnishes an indifferent harbour,
guarded by the fort of Figueira. That stronghold, it will be

---

[1] Wellesley to Castlereagh, from Corunna, July 21 (*Well. Disp.*, vi. 23–5).

[2] Napier's statement that Wellesley found the Supreme Junta in an
extravagant and irrational frame of mind is by no means borne out by the
dispatches which he sent off from Oporto on July 25. They rather represent
the Portuguese as in a state of pronounced depression of spirits.

remembered, had been seized by the bold exploit of the student Zagalo; it was now garrisoned by 300 British marines, so that the disembarkation would be safe from disturbance by anything save the heavy Atlantic surf, which always beats against the western coast of Portugal. There was no other port available along the shore save Peniche, which was dangerously close to Lisbon, and guarded by a castle still in French hands. Nearer still to the capital, landing is just possible at Cascaes and a few other places: but there was no regular harbour, and Admiral Cotton agreed with Wellesley in thinking that it would be mad to attempt to throw troops ashore on a dangerous rock-bound coast in the midst of Junot's cantonments. Mondego Bay was therefore appointed as the general place of rendezvous for the fleet, which had now begun to arrive opposite the mouth of the Douro.

As to the Portuguese troops, the Supreme Junta agreed that Bernardino Freire and his 5,000 men should go forward with the British army, while the new levies should blockade Almeida, and guard the frontier along the Douro against any possible advance on the part of Marshal Bessières from Castile. The Junta calcu- lated that, if supplied with arms, they could put into the field from the three northern provinces of Portugal 38,000 foot and 8,000 horse—a liberal estimate, as they had, including their peasant levies, no more than 19,000 collected on July 25. They asked for weapons and clothing for the whole mass, and for a loan of 300,000 Cruzado Novas (about £35,000)—no very large sum con- sidering the grants that were being made to the Spaniards at this time. Wellesley would only promise that he would arm the militia and peasantry who were lying along the Mondego in company with Freire's regulars, 'if he found them worth it[1].' The Bishop undertook to forward from Oporto all the remounts for cavalry and all the draught-mules for commissariat purposes that he could get together. He thought that he could procure 150 of the former and 500 of the latter in six days.

On August 1, 1808, the disembarkation in Mondego Bay began, in the face of a heavy surf which rendered landing very dangerous, especially for the horses, guns, and stores. Many boats were upset and a few lives lost[2]; but the troops and their commander

---

[1] Wellesley to Castlereagh, from Oporto, July 25 (*Well. Disp.*, vi. 31).

[2] For the difficulties of disembarkation see the interesting narrative of Landsheit of the 20th Dragoons, p. 243. He was himself upset in the surf.

were in good spirits, for the news of the surrender of Dupont at Baylen on July 20 had reached them the day before the disembarkation began. Wellesley was convinced that General Spencer would have sailed from Andalusia to join him, the moment that this great victory made the presence of British troops in the south unnecessary. He was right, for Spencer, before receiving any orders to that effect, had embarked his men for Portugal and came into Mondego Bay on August 5, just as the last of the division from Cork had been placed on shore. It was therefore with some 13,000 men that Wellesley began his march on Lisbon[1]. But to his bitter disappointment the young lieutenant-general had just learnt that three commanders had been placed over his head, and that he might soon expect Dalrymple to arrive and assume charge of the army. Castlereagh's dispatch of July 15, containing this unwelcome news, was delivered to Wellesley as he lay in Mondego Bay on the thirtieth, and he had to make all his arrange-

---

[1] The force consisted of :—

	Infantry.	Cavalry.	Artillery.
(1) Division embarked at Cork :			
20th Light Dragoons (only 180 with horses)		394	
Artillery			226
5th Regiment (1st batt.)	990		
9th ,, ,, ...	833		
36th ,, ...	591		
38th ,, (1st batt.)	957		
40th ,, ,, ...	926		
45th ,, ,, ...	670		
60th Rifles (5th batt.)	936		
71st Regiment (1st batt.)	903		
91st ,, ,, ...	917		
95th Rifles (2nd batt., four companies) .	400		
	8,123		
(2) Spencer's troops from Andalusia :			
Artillery			245
6th Regiment (1st batt.)	946		
29th ,, ...	806		
32nd ,, (1st batt.)	874		
50th ,, ,, ...	948		
82nd ,, ,, ...	929		
	4,503	394	471

A total of 12,626 infantry, 394 cavalry, 471 artillery = 13,491; adding forty-five men of the Staff Corps we get 13,536.

ments for disembarkation while suffering under this unexpected slight. Many men would have resigned under such a blow, and Wellesley with his unbounded ambition, his strong sense of his deserts, and his well-marked tendency to take offence [1], must have been boiling over with suppressed indignation. But he felt that to ask to be recalled, because he had been degraded from a commander-in-chief to a mere general of division, would be an unsoldierly act. To Castlereagh he merely wrote that 'whether he was to command the army or to quit it, he would do his best to ensure its success, and would not hurry operations one moment in order to acquire credit before the arrival of his superiors [2].'

Meanwhile there were yet a few days during which he would retain the command, and it was in his power to start the campaign on the right lines, even if he was not to reap the reward of its success. His first eight days on shore (August 2–9), were spent in the organization of the commissariat of his army, which the Home Government had disgracefully neglected. Except the two troops of the Irish Wagon Train, which he had insisted on bringing with him, he had no transport at his disposal, and, as he wrote to Castlereagh, 'the existence of the army depends upon the commissariat, and yet the people who manage it are incapable of managing anything out of a counting-house [3].' All that could be got out of the country he utilized: the Bishop of Oporto had sent him a few horses which enabled him to raise his force of mounted men from 180 to 240 [4], and to give some animals to the artillery [5], to add to those that had come from Ireland [5]. But though he succeeded in equipping his own three batteries, the two which Spencer brought from Andalusia had to be left behind on the Mondego for want of draught-horses [6]: the dismounted men of the 20th Dragoons had also to be dropped. For the commissariat the Bishop of Oporto had sent some mules, which were raised to a total of 500 by purchases in the country-side, while 300 bullock-

[1] To understand what Wellesley must have felt, we have only to read his rather captious letter of 1801 (*Suppl. Disp.*, ii. 362) to his own brother concerning his merits, his promotion, and his career. The man who could so write must have felt the blow in the worst way.

[2] *Well. Disp.*, iv. 43.

[3] Ibid., iv. 59; cf. pp. 168, 169.

[4] Ibid., iv. 168. Cf. the returns for Vimiero of men present, with the 180 horsed men brought from Ireland.

[5] Ibid., iv. 168.   [6] Ibid., iv. 59.

carts were procured for the heavier stores by requisition from the neighbouring villages. It was only on the ninth that things were so far ready that the army could move forward. It was now divided into six small brigades under Generals Hill, Ferguson, Nightingale, Bowes, Catlin Crawfurd, and Fane: the third, fourth, and fifth brigades had only two battalions each, the other four had three [1].

Wellesley had resolved to advance by the coast-road on Lisbon, via Alcobaça, Obidos, and Torres Vedras, and it was along the desolate shore 'up to the knees in sand and suffering dreadfully from thirst [2],' that his men made their first march of twelve miles to Lugar. The distance was moderate, but the troops had been so long cramped on shipboard that some of the regiments had fallen out of condition and left many stragglers.

The reasons which had determined Wellesley to take the coast route, rather than that which leads from the Mondego to Lisbon via Santarem, were, as he afterwards explained, partly a wish to keep in touch with the fleet for the purpose of obtaining supplies —for he found that the country could support him in wine and beef, but not in flour—and partly the fact that he had learnt that new reinforcements from England were likely to appear within a few days. The brigades from Harwich and Ramsgate, under Generals Acland and Anstruther, had sailed on July 19 and might be looked for at any moment. Sir John Moore, with the division from Sweden, was also reported to be on his way to the south, but could not be expected to arrive for some time. Having ascertained that the French force in Portugal was somewhat larger than he originally supposed, Sir Arthur wished to pick up the troops of Acland and Anstruther before giving battle. In this he was even wiser than he knew, for he still estimated Junot's total disposable force at 18,000 men [3], while it was really 26,000. To have attacked

---

[1] The brigading was as follows :—1st Brigade (Hill), 5th, 9th, 38th ; 2nd Brigade (Ferguson), 36th, 40th, 71st ; 3rd Brigade (Nightingale), 29th, 82nd ; 4th Brigade (Bowes), 6th, 32nd ; 5th Brigade (C. Crawfurd), 50th, 91st ; 6th Brigade (Fane), 45th, 5/60th, 2/95th. Before Vimiero the 45th and 50th changed places (see the narrative of Col. Leach of Fane's Brigade). It is worth noting that six of these sixteen battalions, as also the 20th Light Dragoons, had just returned from the disheartening work of the Buenos Ayres expedition. They were the 5th, 36th, 38th, 40th, 45th, and 71st.

[2] *Journal of a Soldier of the 71st Regiment* (Edin. 1828), p. 47.

[3] Wellesley to Burrard, August 8 (*Well. Disp.*, iv. 53).

Lisbon with no more than the 13,000 troops who had originally disembarked at the mouth of the Mondego would have been most hazardous.

Wellesley had at first intended to take on with him the whole of Bernardino Freire's army. He had visited the Portuguese commander at Montemor Velho on the seventh, and had issued to his ally a supply of 5,000 muskets. Freire was anxious to persuade him to give up the coast route, and to throw himself into the interior on the side of Santarem. But the cogent reasons which compelled him to prefer the road which allowed him to keep in touch with the fleet, made him refuse to listen to this plan, and he invited the Portuguese general to transfer himself on to the same line. Freire so far submitted as to move to Leiria, where he met the British army on August 10. But here the two commanders came to hard words and parted. Freire, a self-willed and shifty man, was determined not to act in unison with Wellesley. Whether he wished to preserve his independent command, or whether he feared (as Napier hints) to oppose his raw levies to the French, even when supported by 13,000 British bayonets [1], he now showed himself utterly impracticable. He began by laying hands on all the stores of food in Leiria, though they had been promised to Wellesley. Then he made the absurd and impudent statement that he could only co-operate with his allies if Wellesley would undertake to provide rations for his 6,000 men. This proposal was all the more astounding because he had just been trying to persuade his colleague to move into the inland, by the statement that resources of every kind abounded in Estremadura, and that the whole British army could easily live upon the country-side! Wellesley's men had now been subsisting for ten days on biscuit landed by the fleet, and it was ludicrous that he should be asked to take upon his shoulders the whole burden of feeding the Portuguese in their own country. Accordingly he utterly rejected the proposal, but he insisted that Freire should lend him some cavalry and light troops, and these he promised to maintain. The bulk of the Portuguese, therefore, remained behind at Leiria, their general being left free to take up, if he should choose, his favourite plan of marching on Santarem. But 260 horsemen—the skeletons of three old cavalry regiments—a battalion of Cazadores, and three weak line-regiments were placed at Wellesley's disposition: they

[1] Napier, i. 197.

amounted to about 2,300 men[1], according to the Portuguese official figures, but the British commander repeatedly states that he saw no more than 260 horse and 1,600 infantry[2]; so it is probable that the regiments were somewhat under the estimate given by Freire. They were commanded by Colonel Trant, a British officer in the Portuguese service[3].

Turning once more into the road that skirts the coast, Wellesley marched on the thirteenth from Leiria, and reached Alcobaça on the fourteenth. Here he got his first news of the French: a brigade under Thomières had occupied the village till the previous day, and he learnt that General Delaborde, with a weak division, was somewhere in his front, in the direction of Obidos and Roliça.

Junot had received prompt information of the landing of the British in Mondego Bay; on the very day after it had commenced he was able to send orders to Loison to abandon his post in front of Badajoz and to march at once to join the main army. Meanwhile Delaborde was sent out from Lisbon on August 6 to observe and, if possible, contain Wellesley, till Junot should have concentrated his whole field-army and be ready to fight. He was told to expect Loison from the direction of Thomar and Santarem, and to join him as soon as was possible. For his rather hazardous task he was given no more than five battalions of infantry and a single

[1] According to the figures given by the Portuguese historian of the war, Da Luz Soriano, they stood as follows :—

Cavalry of the 6th, 11th, and 12th Regiments	.	258 sabres.
6th battalion of Cazadores	.	562 bayonets.
12th, 21st, and 24th line battalions . .	.	1,514 ,,

A few troopers of the Lisbon Police Guard, forty-one in all, according to Soriano, deserted Junot and joined the army before Vimiero. Landsheit of the 20th Light Dragoons mentions their arrival, and says that they were put in company with his regiment. This would give 2,375 as the total of the Portuguese whom Trant commanded.

[2] *Well. Disp.* (iv. 78) says 1,400, but in his narrative of Roliça Sir Arthur accounts for 1,600, 1,200 in his right and 400 in his centre column. As a middle figure between Wellesley and Soriano, 2,000 would probably be safe.

[3] Their allies did not think much of their looks. Col. Leslie describes them thus : 'The poor fellows had little or no uniform, but were merely in white jackets, and large broad-brimmed hats turned up at one side, some having feathers and others none, so that they cut rather a grotesque appearance' (p. 40).

regiment of *chasseurs à cheval*, with five guns [1]—not much more than 5,000 men.

Delaborde at first thought of making a stand, and compelling Wellesley to show his force, at Batalha near Alcobaça, where John I had beaten the Spaniards, four and a half centuries ago, at the decisive battle of Aljubarotta. But, after examining the position, he found it so much surrounded by woods, and so destitute of good points of view, that he feared to be enveloped if he committed

---

[1] Delaborde's numbers at the combat of Roliça have been the cause of much controversy. Wellesley in one of his dispatches estimated them at as much as 6,000 men ; the unveracious Thiébault would reduce them as low as 1,900. But it is possible to arrive at something like the real figures.

Delaborde brought out from Lisbon two battalions of the 70th, the 26th *Chasseurs à Cheval*, and five guns. Thomières joined him from Peniche with the 1st Provisional Light Infantry (a battalion each of the 2nd and 4th Léger) and with the 4th Swiss.

The numbers of these corps had been on July 15 :—

70th of the Line (two batts.)	2,358
2nd Léger (one batt.)	1,075
4th ,, ,, ...	1,098
4th Swiss ,, ...	985
26th Chasseurs	263
	5,779

But each of the four French corps had given its grenadier company as a contribution to the ' Reserve Grenadier Battalions' which Junot had organized. The battalions being on the old nine-company establishment (see Foy's large table of the *Armée d'Espagne*, note *d*) we must deduct one-ninth of each, or about 500 men in all. We have also to allow for six companies of the 4th Swiss sent to garrison Peniche ; not for the whole battalion, as Foy says in iv. 306, for there were Swiss in the fight of Roliça (Leslie's *Military Journal*, p. 43), and at Vimiero in the official state of Junot's army we find two companies of this corps with Brennier's brigade. We must deduct, then, three-fourths of them from the force present with Delaborde, i. e. some 740 men. This leaves 4,276 men for the four and a quarter battalions under fire at Roliça. Of course Junot's troops must have had a few men in hospital since July 15, the date of the return which we are using. But they cannot have been many. The 70th had been quiet in its quarters in Lisbon. The other three battalions had been in Loison's Beira expedition, and had lost some men therein, but all before July 11. If we concede 300 sick on August 16, it is ample. We can allow therefore for 4,000 infantry, 250 cavalry, and some 100 gunners present with Delaborde, i. e. his total force must have been about 4,350 men—a number much closer to Wellesley's 6,000 than to Thiébault's 1,900 ; Foy, usually so accurate, is clearly wrong in bringing the figures down to 2,500 (iv. 310).

himself to a fight. Accordingly he drew back to Roliça, leaving only a rearguard at Obidos to observe the approach of the British. At the same time he detached six companies of the 4th Swiss to garrison Peniche, thus reducing his available force to 4,350 men.

Wellesley, meanwhile, knowing himself to be close to the enemy, advanced steadily but with caution. He left behind his tents and other weighty baggage at Leiria, and moved forward with a lightly equipped army to Alcobaça on the fourteenth, to Caldas on the fifteenth. On that day the first shot of the campaign was fired : four companies of the fifth battalion of the 60th and of the second battalion of the 95th Rifles discovered the French outposts at Brilos in front of Obidos, drove them in, and pursuing furiously for three miles, came on the battalion which formed Delaborde's rearguard. This corps turned upon them, checked them with the loss of two [1] officers and twenty-seven men killed and wounded, and only retired when General Spencer led up a brigade to save the riflemen.

Next morning the French were discovered to have fallen back no further than Roliça, where Delaborde had found the position that he had sought in vain at Batalha. The road from Caldas and Obidos towards Torres Vedras and Lisbon passes for some miles over a sandy plain enclosed on either flank by bold hills. The southern limit of the basin is a cross-ridge, which connects the other two : in front of it lies Roliça, on the side-slope of an isolated eminence which overlooks the whole plain : a mile further south the road passes over the cross-ridge by a sort of gorge or defile, on the right hand of which is the village of Columbeira, while to its left rear lies that of Zambugeira. Though Delaborde had drawn up his men on the hill of Roliça down in the plain, it was not this advanced position that he intended to hold, but the higher and steeper line of the cross-ridge, on either side of the defile above Columbeira. Here he had a short front, only three-quarters of a mile in length, scarped by precipitous slopes, and covered by thickets and brushwood, which served to mask the strength (or rather the weakness) of his division.

Discovering Delaborde drawn up on the isolated hill of Roliça, where both his flanks could easily be turned, the British commander resolved to endeavour to envelop and surround him. He waited

[1] The name of Lieutenant Bunbury, of the 2/95th, perhaps deserves remembrance as that of the first British officer killed in the Peninsular War.

on the sixteenth till the rear of the army had come up, and marched at dawn on the seventeenth with his whole force—13,000 British and 2,000 Portuguese, drawn up in a crescent-shaped formation with the centre refused and the wings thrown far forward.   On the right Colonel Trant, with three battalions of Portuguese infantry and fifty horse of the same nation, moved along the foot of the western range of heights, to turn the Roliça position by a wide circular movement.   On the left General Ferguson, with his own brigade, that of Bowes, and six guns, struck over the hills to get round the eastern flank of the French.   In the centre the remainder of the army—four brigades of British infantry, 400 cavalry, half English and half Portuguese, with the battalion of Cazadores and twelve guns, advanced on a broad front in two lines, forming a most magnificent spectacle : 'they came on slowly but in beautiful order, dressing at intervals to correct the gaps caused by the inequalities of ground, and all converging on the hill of Roliça[1].' Hill's brigade formed the right, Fane's the left, Nightingale's the centre, while Catlin Crawfurd's two battalions and the Cazadores acted as the reserve.

Delaborde had warned his men to be ready for a sudden rush to the rear the minute that the enveloping movement should grow dangerous.   Waiting till the last possible moment, when Fane's riflemen were already engaged with his tirailleurs, and Trant and Ferguson were showing on the flanks, he suddenly gave the order for retreat.   His men hurried back, easily eluding the snare, and took post on the wooded heights above Columbeira a mile to the rear.   Wellesley had to rearrange his troops for an attack on the second position, and half the morning had been wasted to no effect. He resolved, however, to repeat his original manœuvre.   Trant and the Portuguese once more made a long sweep to the right : Ferguson's column mounted the foot-hills of the Sierra de Baragueda and commenced a toilsome detour to the left[2].   In the centre two batteries formed up near a windmill on the northern slope of Roliça hill and began to bombard the French position, while Fane's brigade to the left on the main road, and Hill's and Nightingale's to the right deployed for the attack.

Wellesley had not intended to assault the Columbeira heights till the turning movements of Trant and Ferguson should be well

---

[1] Foy, iv. 309.

[2] I cannot find the authority for Napier's statement that Fane joined Ferguson in the second move.   He seems still to have acted in the centre.

developed. But, contrary to his intention, part of his centre pushed forward at once, and when it was engaged the other troops in the front line were sent up to its aid. The face of the hill was scarred by four 'passes' as Wellesley called them, or rather large ravines, up each of which some of the British troops tried to penetrate. On the extreme right the light companies of Hill's brigade, supported by the first battalion of the 5th Regiment from the same brigade, delivered their attack up one gully. The second pass, just beyond the village of Columbeira, was assayed by the 29th from Nightingale's brigade, with the 9th of Hill's in support. The 82nd went towards the centre, while Fane's two rifle battalions and the 45th tried the heights far to the left.

The 29th Regiment, urged on by the rash courage of its colonel, Lake, attacked some time before any other corps was engaged. It pushed up a narrow craggy pass, the bed of a dried-up mountain torrent, where in some places only two or three men abreast could keep their footing: the further that the battalion advanced, the more did the ravine recede into the centre of the enemy, and the 29th was soon being fired on from three sides. The right wing, which led, at last forced its way to the brow of the hill, and was able to deploy in a more or less imperfect way, and to commence its fire. In front of it were the few companies of the 4th Swiss, some of whom tried to surrender, calling out that they were friends, turning up their musket butts, and rushing in to shake hands with the British [1]. But before the 29th could fully recover its formation, it was fiercely charged from the rear: some of the French troops on the lower slopes of the position, finding themselves likely to be cut off, formed in a dense mass and rushed straight through the right wing of Colonel Lake's regiment from behind, breaking it, killing its commander and capturing six officers and some thirty of its rank and file, whom they took back with them in triumph. The 29th reeled down the slope into a wood, where it reformed on its comparatively intact left wing, and then resumed the fight, aided by the 9th, its supporting regiment. About this moment the 5th and Fane's rifles made other attacks on the two ends of the hostile line, but were at first checked. Delaborde and his brigadier,

---

[1] Col. Leslie's narrative, p. 43. The 4th Swiss was a very discontented corps ; individuals of it had begun to desert to the British even before Roliça (Leach, p. 44), and a considerable number of them took service in the 60th Rifles after the Convention of Cintra, refusing to return to France.

Brennier, had only four battalions on the ridge, as they had detached three companies of the 70th far to their right in the direction in which Ferguson was moving. But they held their ground very gallantly, waiting till the British skirmishers had begun to get a lodgement on the brow, and then charging each detachment as it tried to deploy, and forcing it down to the edge of the wood that covered the lower slopes. Three assaults were thus repulsed, but the British troops would not be denied—Wellesley wrote that he had never seen more gallant fighting than that of the 9th and the 29th [1]—and after each reverse formed up again and came on once more. After two hours of desperate struggles they made good their lodgement on the crest at several points: Ferguson's troops (though they had lost their way and wasted much time) began to appear on the extreme left, and Delaborde then saw that it was time for him to go.

He retired by alternate battalions, two in turn holding back the disordered pursuers, while the other two doubled to the rear. His regiment of *chasseurs à cheval* also executed several partial charges against the British skirmishers, and lost its commander mortally wounded: the Portuguese cavalry refused to face them. In this way the French reached the pass behind Zambugeira, a mile to the rear, without any great loss. But in passing through this defile, they were forced to club together by the narrowness of the road, were roughly hustled by their pursuers, and lost three [2] of their guns and a few prisoners. The rest of the force escaped in some disorder to Cazal da Sprega, where Wellesley halted his men, seeing that it was now impossible to catch Delaborde's main body. Two miles to the rear the French were rejoined by the three companies of the 70th Regiment which had been detached to the east. They then retreated to Montechique some fifteen miles from Lisbon, where they at last got news of Loison and Junot.

Delaborde had fought a most admirable rearguard action, holding on to the last moment, and escaping by his prompt manœuvres the very serious risk of being enveloped and captured by the forces of the English, who outnumbered him fourfold. But he had lost 600 men and three guns, while his assailants had only suffered to

[1] *Well. Disp.*, iv. 83, 87.
[2] Foy says only one gun, but Wellesley, who had better opportunities of knowing, says that he took three (*Well. Disp.*, iv. 83).

the extent of 474 killed, wounded, and prisoners[1], nearly half of
whom were in the ranks of the 29th[2]. The French flattered
themselves that they had somewhat shaken the *morale* of Wellesley's
men by their obstinate resistance: but this was far from being the
case. The English had only put five and a half battalions[3] into the
fighting line, and were proud of having turned the enemy out of
such a position as that of Columbeira without engaging more than
4,600 men.

It is doubtful whether Delaborde should have fought at all:
he was holding on in the hope that Loison's division would come
up and join him, but this junction was very problematical, as
nothing had been heard of that general for many days. By
fighting at Columbeira, Delaborde risked complete destruction for
an inadequate end. It was true that if Loison was now close at
hand Wellesley's further advance might cut him off from Lisbon.
But as a matter of fact Loison was still far away. He had reached
Santarem on August 13, with his troops so tired by his long
march from the Alemtejo, that he halted there for two days to
rest them and allow his stragglers to come up. Marching again
on the sixteenth, he was at Cercal, fifteen miles from Roliça to the
east, while Delaborde was fighting. He barely heard the distant
cannonade, and rejoined the rest of the army at Torres Vedras, by
a route through Cadaval and Quinta da Bugagliera, which crossed
his colleague's line of retreat at an acute angle [August 18].

It is true that if Wellesley had been accurately informed of
Loison's position on the seventeenth, he could have so manœuvred
as to place himself directly between that general and Lisbon on the
following day, by seizing the cross-roads at Quinta da Bugagliera.
In that case Loison's division could only have rejoined Junot by
a perilous flank march through Villafranca and Saccavem, or by
crossing the Tagus and moving along its eastern bank to the
heights of Almada opposite the capital. But the English general's
object at this moment was not to cut off Loison, but to pick

[1] Thiébault solemnly states our loss at 2,000 men! *Mémoires,* iv. 186.

[2] That corps lost no less than 190 officers and men, among whom were six
officers taken prisoners.

[3] The 5th, 9th, 29th, 82nd, 5/60th, and four companies of the 2/95th, in
all 4,635 men. They lost respectively 46, 72, 190, 25, 66, and 42 men, or 441
in all ; while the rest of the army (ten British and four Portuguese battalions)
only lost the remaining 38 of the total of 479 casualties suffered on the 17th,
i. e. were not really engaged.

up a considerable reinforcement, of whose approach he had just heard. On the morning of the eighteenth the brigade of General Acland from Harwich had arrived off the Peniche peninsula, and its advent was reported to Wellesley, with the additional news that that of General Anstruther, which had sailed from Ramsgate, was close behind. It was all-important to get these 4,000 men ashore : they could not be landed at Peniche, whose fort was still in French hands, and the only other anchorage near was that of Porto Novo, at the mouth of the little river Maceira, twelve miles south of Roliça. To cover their disembarkation Wellesley marched by the coast-road through Lourinhão, and encamped on the heights of Vimiero. This movement allowed Loison, who moved by the parallel road more inland, to pass the English and reach Torres Vedras.

NOTE TO CHAPTER II

By far the best English account of Roliça is that by Col. Leslie of the 29th, in his *Military Journal*, which was not printed till 1887 (at the Aberdeen University Press). He corrects Napier on several points. I have also found useful details in the letters (unpublished) of Major Gell, of the same regiment, which were placed at my disposition by Mr. P. Lyttelton Gell. Leslie and Gell agree that Colonel Lake led on his regiment too fast, contrary to Wellesley's intentions. The narrative of Colonel Leach of the 2/95th is also valuable. The accounts of Landsheit of the 20th Light Dragoons, of Colonel Wilkie in Maxwell's *Peninsular Sketches* (vol. i), and the anonymous 'T. S.' of the 71st (Constable, Edinburgh, 1828) have some useful points. Foy and Thiébault, the French narrators of the fight, were not eye-witnesses, like the six above-named British writers.

SECTION IV : CHAPTER III

VIMIERO

JUNOT much disliked leaving Lisbon : he greatly enjoyed his viceregal state, and was so convinced that to retain the capital was equivalent to dominating the whole of Portugal [1], that he attached an exaggerated importance to his hold on the place, and was very reluctant to cut down its garrison. But it was clearly necessary to support Delaborde and Loison, and at last he took his departure. As a preliminary precaution he resolved to deal a blow at the Alemtejo insurgents, who, emboldened by Loison's retreat, were creeping nearer to the mouth of the Tagus, and showing themselves opposite Setuval. On August 11, five days after Delaborde had marched off, General Kellermann was sent out with two battalions and a few dragoons to drive off these hovering bands, a task which he executed with ease, giving them a thorough beating at Alcacer do Sal. Having cleared this flank Junot evacuated Setuval and his other outlying posts beyond the Tagus, and only retained garrisons at Forts Bugio and Trafaria, which command the entrance of the river, and on the heights of Almada, which face Lisbon across the 'Mar de Palio.' He put in a state of defence the old citadel which crowns the highest of the seven hills on which the city is built, and established a battalion in each of the suburban villages of Belem and Saccavem, another in Fort San Julian at the mouth of the Tagus, and two at Cascaes, in the batteries which command the only point where a disembarkation from the side of the Atlantic is barely possible. This excess of pre-caution was largely due to the fact that a small English convoy of transports, carrying the 3rd Regiment (the Buffs) from Madeira, had been seen off the mouth of the Tagus. The duke feared that this por-tended an attempt to throw troops ashore in the immediate vicinity of the capital, when he should have gone off to meet Wellesley.

Altogether Junot left seven battalions, not less than 6,500 men, in Lisbon and the neighbouring forts, a much greater number than

---

[1] As Foy well puts it, the idea was that ' le Portugal était dans Lisbonne, et Lisbonne était à elle seule tout le Portugal ' (iv. 283).

was really required, for, as Napoleon afterwards observed, capitals
wait, before declaring themselves, for events outside to cast their
shadows before [1]. Knowing that a decisive blow given to the
English would be the best way to keep the city quiet, the Duke
of Abrantes would have been wise to cut down his garrisons round
Lisbon to 3,000 men, however great the risk, and take every
available man to meet Wellesley [2]. It is probable that his error,

[1] See his curious criticism on Junot, recorded by Thiébault in iv. 268, 269
of his *Mémoires*.

[2] For clearness it may be worth whilè to give the dislocation of Junot's
army on the day of the battle of Vimiero, adding the force of each unit on
July 15, the last available return.

1st Division, Delaborde :—

Brigade Avril :		*Men.*	*Station.*
15th Line (3rd batt.)	.	1,086	At Saccavem and in Lisbon city.
47th ,, (2nd batt.)	.	1,541	In forts south of the Tagus-mouth.
70th ,, (1st and 2nd batts.)		2,358	Field-army. Present at Vimiero.
Brigade Brennier :			
86th Line (1st and 2nd batts.)		2,501	Field-army. Present at Vimiero (except four companies left at Elvas).
4th Swiss (1st batt.)	.	985	Six companies at Peniche. Two present at Vimiero.

2nd Division, Loison :—

Brigade Thomières :			
' 1st Provisional Léger '—			
2nd Léger (3rd batt.)	.	1,075	Field-army. Present at Vimiero.
4th ,, ,,	.	1,098	Field-army. Present at Vimiero.
' 2nd Provisional Léger '—			
12th Léger (3rd batt.)	.	1,253	Field-army. Present at Vimiero.
15th ,, ,,	.	1,305	Field-army. Present at Vimiero.
Brigade Charlot :			
32nd Line ,,	.	1,034	Field-army. Present at Vimiero.
58th ,, ,,	.	1,428	Field-army. Present at Vimiero.
2nd Swiss (2nd batt.)	.	1,103	In garrison at Elvas.

3rd Division, Travot :—

Brigade Graindorge :			
31st Léger (3rd batt.)	.	846 ⎰	Partly on the heights of Almada, partly guarding the Spanish prisoners at Lisbon.
32nd ,, ,,	.	1,099 ⎱	
26th Line ,,	.	517	At Belem.
66th ,, (3rd and 4th batts.)		1,125	At Cascaes.
Brigade Fusier :			
82nd Line (3rd batt.)	.	963	Field-army. Present at Vimiero.
Légion du Midi	. .	842	At Fort San Julian.
1st Hanoverian Legion	.	804	At Santarem.

All the four cavalry regiments of Margaron's division, 1,754 sabres, were present at Vimiero, save one troop of dragoons captured with Quesnel at Oporto.

which no French general would have committed at a later period of the war, was due to that tendency to despise the fighting power of the British which was prevalent on the Continent all through the early years of the century.

Not the least of Junot's troubles was the obstinate torpidity of the Russian admiral, Siniavin, whose 6,000 seamen and marines might have taken over the whole charge of Lisbon, if only their commander had been willing. The Russian had refused to take part in the war as long as only Portuguese were in the field, on the plea that his master had never declared war on the Prince-Regent or recognized the French annexation. But when the British had landed, Junot hoped to move him to action, for there was no doubt that Russia and the United Kingdom were technically at war. The Duke of Abrantes first tried to induce Siniavin to put out from the Tagus, to fall upon scattered British convoys, and to distract the attention of the blockading squadron under Cotton. But the reply that to sally forth into the Atlantic would probably mean destruction in two days by the British fleet was too rational to be overruled. Then Junot proposed that Siniavin should at least take charge of the pontoons containing the captive Spanish division of Caraffa: but this too was denied him, and he had to leave a battalion of Graindorge's brigade to mount guard on the prisoners [1]. The Russians were perfectly useless to Junot, except in so far as their guns helped to over-awe Lisbon, and presented a show of force to deter British vessels from trying to force the passage of the forts at the mouth of the Tagus. The fact was that Siniavin was not so much stupid as disaffected : he belonged to the party in Russia which was opposed to France, and he had perhaps received a hint from home that he was not expected to show too much zeal in supporting the projects of Napoleon.

On the night of August 15, Junot marched out of Lisbon at the head of his reserve, a very small force consisting of a battalion of the 82nd of the line, one of the two regiments of grenadiers, which he had created by concentrating the grenadier companies of the eighteen line battalions in his army [2], the 3rd provisional regiment

---

[1] I cannot make out whether this was the 31st or the 32nd Léger. Foy and Thiébault omit to give the detail.

[2] Junot had created two of these regiments of grenadiers, each of two battalions. The second was at this moment with Loison.

of dragoons, a squadron of volunteer cavalry formed by the French
inhabitants of Lisbon, and his reserve artillery—ten guns under
General Taviel.   He also took with him the reserve ammunition-
train, a large convoy of food, and his military chest containing
a million of francs in specie.   On the morning of the seventeenth
the troops had reached Villafranca, when a false report that the
English were trying to land at Cascaes caused them to retrace
their steps for some miles, and to lose half a day's march.   On
learning that Lisbon and its neighbourhood were quiet, Junot
returned to the front, and growing vexed at the slow march of
the great convoy which the reserve was escorting, pushed on ahead,
and joined Loison at Cercal.   He heard the distant thunder of
the guns at Roliça in the afternoon, but was too far away to help
Delaborde.

On the eighteenth Loison and Junot marched southward to
Torres Vedras, and heard that Delaborde had fallen back so far
that he was ten miles to their rear, at Montechique.   He only
came up to join them next day [August 19], and the reserve with
its heavy convoy, much hampered by bad country roads in the
Monte Junto hills, did not appear till the twentieth.

Junot had been much exercised in mind by the doubt whether
Wellesley would march by the direct road on Lisbon through
Torres Vedras and Montechique, or would continue to hug the
shore by the longer route that passes by Vimiero and Mafra.   Not
knowing of the approach of Acland's and Anstruther's brigades,
he was ignorant of the main fact which governed his adversary's
movements.   But learning on the twentieth that the British were
still keeping to the coast-road, by which they could in one more
march turn his position at Torres Vedras, he determined to rush
upon them with his united forces and give battle.   At the last
moment he resolved to draw a few more men from Lisbon, and
called up a battalion of the 66th of the line, and another composed
of four picked companies selected from the other corps of the
garrison—a trifling reinforcement of 1,000 or 1,200 men, which
arrived just too late for the fight at Vimiero.

The organization of the French army had been so much cut up
by the numerous garrisons which Junot had thought fit to leave
behind him, that although five of his six infantry brigades were
more or less represented in his field-army, not one of them was
complete.   He accordingly recast the whole system, and arranged

his force in two divisions under Delaborde and Loison, and a reserve brigade of Grenadiers under Kellermann. His cavalry on the other hand was intact : every one of the four regiments of Margaron's division was present, and over and above them he had the squadron of French volunteers raised in Lisbon. He had also twenty-three guns : there should have been twenty-six, but Delaborde had lost three at Roliça. The total of men present amounted to 10,300 foot and 2,000 horse, with 700 artillerymen and men of the military train [1], or about 13,000 in all.

[1] Junot's numbers at Vimiero are as much disputed as Delaborde's at Roliça. Among the French accounts the figures vary from 12,500 to 9,200. Foy, usually the most conscientious historian, gives 11,500 ; Thiébault, both in his narrative, published in 1816, and in his private *Mémoires*, descends to 9,200. Wellesley estimated the army that he had fought at 14,000 (*Well. Disp.*, iv. 101).

It will be well to give the corps present, and to examine into their probable strength. Just before the landing of the British they had stood as follows (I have arranged them in their new brigading) :—

(1) Division Delaborde :—

Brigade Brennier :

2nd Léger (3rd batt.)	1,075
4th ,, ,, ...	1,098
70th of the Line (1st and 2nd batts.) . . .	2,358

——— 4,531

Brigade Thomières :

86th of the Line (1st and 2nd batts.) (minus four companies left at Elvas)	1,945
4th Swiss (two companies)	246

——— 2,191

(2) Division Loison :—

Brigade Solignac :

12th Léger (3rd batt.)	1,253
15th ,, ,, ...	1,305
58th of the Line (3rd batt.)	1,428

——— 3,986

Brigade Charlot :

32nd of the Line (3rd batt.)	1,034
82nd ,, ,, ...	963

——— 1,997

——— 12,705

[(3) Reserve of Grenadiers :—

1st Regiment (1st and 2nd batts.) } 2,100
2nd ,, ,, ,,

This corps, being formed of companies drawn from every battalion in Portugal, except the three foreign regiments and the *Légion du Midi*, must not be counted in our first estimate.]

Hearing that Wellesley was stationary in Vimiero since the morning of the nineteenth, Junot determined to attack him at the

Brought forward	.	.	.	12,705

(4) Cavalry Division Margaron :—

1st Provisional Chasseurs	.	.	.	.	263
3rd ,, Dragoons	.	.	.	.	640
4th ,, ,,	.	.	.	.	589
5th ,, ,,	.	.	.	.	659
Squadron of volunteer cavalry	.	.	.	.	100

	2,251
(5) Artillerymen for 23 guns, engineers, train, &c. . . .	700
	15,656

But from this 15,656 large deductions have to be made ; each of the eleven line battalions present had given its grenadier company to contribute to the four battalions of 'Reserve Grenadiers' which Junot had formed. We must therefore deduct from them about 1,350 bayonets. Delaborde had lost 600 men at Roliça. Loison's regiments had been thinned by the dépôt battalion left to garrison Almeida, and by his losses in his campaign on the Douro and in the Alemtejo. Thiébault states that the casualties had amounted to 450 during these operations : the details left at Almeida, including many sick, were 1,000 strong, so we must subtract 1,450 from Loison's total. This is liberal, as some, both of the Almeida force and of the Alemtejo losses, came from regiments not present at Vimiero (e. g. the 1st Hanoverians and the 4th Swiss).

We must make some deduction for the ordinary hospital wastage of the troops which had come out of Lisbon with Delaborde and Junot, seven battalions and two regiments of cavalry. Loison's sick are already partly accounted for by the Almeida details. It would seem that 1,000 would be an ample allowance. When the French evacuated Portugal they had 3,281 men in hospital. Of these, 1,200 were the wounded of Vimiero. Of the remainder, 1,000 may have belonged to the ten and two-thirds battalions present at the battle, the other 1,081 to the eleven and one-third not present.

For the infantry then we allow—

12,705 of original strength, minus 1,350 Grenadiers, 600 lost at Roliça, and 1,450 in garrison at Almeida or lost in the insurrection, and 1,000 sick (4,400 in all)	8,305
Add for four battalions of Reserve Grenadiers . . .	2,100
Total .	10,405
Margaron's cavalry was practically intact : on July 15 it was 2,151 strong (Thiébault); it hardly suffered in the insurrection. If we allow 300 men for casual losses and troopers on detachment or acting as orderlies, it is ample . . .	1,851
We must add the 100 volunteer horse	100
Lastly, for artillerymen of four batteries (23 guns), engineers and train, &c., we allow	700
Total .	13,056

This is not far from Wellesley's estimate of 14,000 men.

earliest possible moment. He was ignorant that his adversary's halt was due to the arrival of Anstruther and Acland, but knowing that more troops were expected from the sea he resolved to fight at once. The reserve and convoy joined him on the morning of the twentieth: the same night he marched under cover of the darkness and traversed the ten miles which separated him from the hostile position: at dawn he was close under it.

But Wellesley meanwhile had received his reinforcements, and was 4,000 men stronger than the Duke of Abrantes supposed. On the nineteenth Anstruther's [1] brigade had accomplished its dangerous disembarkation, through the surf that beats upon the sandy shore north of the mouth of the Maceira. It had been a tedious business, many boats having been upset and some lives lost. On the afternoon of the twentieth the convoy that brought Acland's brigade was got inshore, and the greater part of the men disembarked in the dusk in the actual mouth of the little river, and slept upon the beach. But some of them were still on shipboard on the morning of the twenty-first, and came too late for the battle of that day [2].

While covering this disembarkation Wellesley had taken up an excellent position on the heights of Vimiero, with the sea at his back. The surrounding country was pleasant, good water was forthcoming in abundance, and the neighbouring villages provided a considerable quantity of food. The region is both more fertile and better wooded than most of central Portugal. The only fault

---

[1] Anstruther's Brigade from Ramsgate consisted of—

9th Regiment (2nd batt.)	.	.	.	633
43rd	,,	,,	.	.	.	.	721
52nd	,,	,,	.	.	.	.	654
97th	,,	.	.	.	.	.	695
						2,703

With them the 43rd and 52nd, so famous in many a Peninsular battle-field in the Light Division, made their appearance.

[2] Of Acland's Brigade from Harwich there disembarked—

2nd or Queen's Regiment	.	.	.	731
20th Regiment (seven and a half companies)	401
95th Rifles (1st batt., two companies)	.	200
			1,332

The ship that bore Colonel Ross and two and a half companies of the 20th had drifted so far off the shore that it did not succeed in getting its freight delivered till late on the twenty-first.

Battle of Vimiero.   August 21. 1808

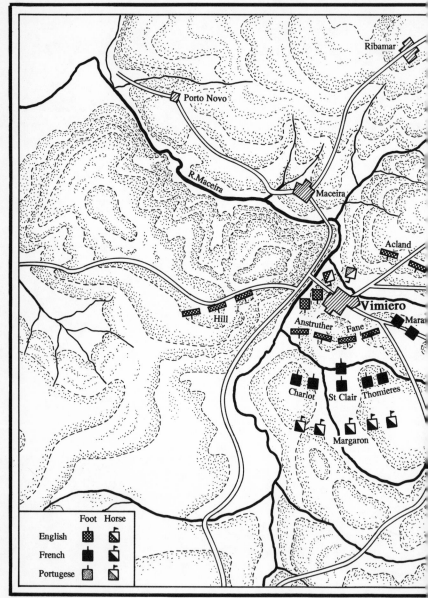

Ribamar

Porto Novo

R.Maceira

Maceira

Acland

Vimiero

Hill

Anstruther   Fane   Mara

Charlot   St Clair   Thomieres

Margaron

	Foot	Horse
English		
French		
Portugese		

Darbishire & Stanford Limited

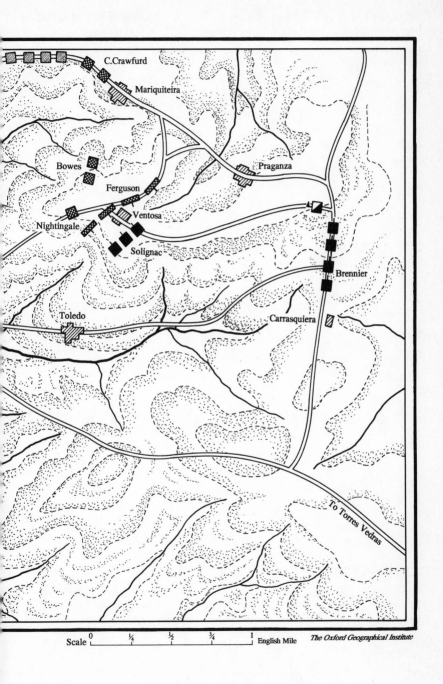

C.Crawfurd

Mariquiteira

Bowes

Praganza

Ferguson

Nightingale

Ventosa

Solignac

Brennier

Toledo

Carrasquiera

To Torres Vedras

Scale 0 ¼ ½ ¾ 1 English Mile   *The Oxford Geographical Institute*

of the position was that it was one from which retreat would have been very difficult. But confident in himself and his men, and somewhat under-estimating the possible maximum of force that Junot could bring against him, Wellesley was thinking of nothing less than of retreat. If he had not been attacked on the twenty-first, he would himself have pushed on towards the enemy next day. He had now 16,778 British troops, besides Trant's 2,000 Portuguese, and thought himself competent to cope with any force that Junot could collect.

The position of Vimiero consists of a well-marked line of heights sweeping from the north to the south-west, and cut through the centre by the narrow valley of the river Maceira, on which the village of Vimiero stands. The southern part of the range, which lies nearest the sea, is especially steep and formidable : the northern part, beyond the Maceira, is lower and broader: along its ridge runs a country road leading northward to Lourinhão. But even here the position is very strong, for a ravine creeps along its eastern foot and acts as a sort of ditch to the broad ridge, or rather plateau, which the British army was holding. Its only accessible side is the north, where it sinks down into a rolling upland beyond the village of Ventosa. In the very centre of the position, well in front of the main ridge, just above the village of Vimiero, lies an isolated hill, well suited to serve as an outwork or first line of defence. It was partly occupied by vineyards and thickets, partly by open fields, and gave admirable cover for its defenders.

This hill Wellesley had chosen as the key of his position: on it were placed the two brigades of Fane and Anstruther, seven battalions in all. The high ridge running from behind it to the sea was held by the brigades of Hill, Bowes, Catlin Crawfurd, Nightingale, and Acland. That of Ferguson lay behind Vimiero, astride of the valley of the Maceira. Trant's four battalions of Portuguese were near Ferguson, on the lower heights north of Vimiero, ready to act as a reserve to Fane and Anstruther. The handful of cavalry, 240 English and 260 Portuguese sabres, were in the low ground on the banks of the Maceira, close under Crawfurd's position. Of the three batteries which Wellesley had been able to bring with him, six guns were on the projecting height with Anstruther, eight were on the high mountain south of Vimiero, and four were with the reserve.

A glance at this order of battle shows that Wellesley expected to be attacked from the south, up the valley of the Maceira, and that he thought that the enemy's plan would be to force his right-centre. Little or no provision is made against the plan which Junot actually adopted, that of assaulting the British left-centre and simultaneously turning their extreme left flank, while leaving the right unmolested. But the whole position was so short—it was less than three miles in length—that there was no difficulty in shifting troops rapidly from one end of it to the other, and, as the event showed, no risk whatever was run.

Wellesley was busy arranging his line of battle, when to his bitter disappointment he received the news that he was superseded, a calamity which he had been expecting to occur at any moment. Sir Harry Burrard had arrived from England at the tail of Acland's convoy, and was now on board the sloop *Brazen* in Maceira Bay. Sir Arthur at once went off in a boat to greet him, and to give him an account of the condition in which affairs stood. Burrard heard him out, and then placed a strong embargo on any further offensive movement. He had learnt that Sir John Moore, with the division from the Baltic, was now off the Portuguese coast, and was resolved not to stir till those troops should have been landed. Being, as it seems, a leisurely sort of man, he resolved to sleep on board his ship for one night more, and to come ashore next morning—a resolve which cost him that chance of commanding a British army in a pitched battle which so many generals have in vain desired. Wellesley went back through the surf charged, for a short fifteen hours more, with the destinies of the army of Portugal[1].

---

[1] It may be well to give Wellesley's army at Vimiero :—

Cavalry, 20th Light Dragoons		240
Artillery, three batteries		226
1st Brigade, Hill :		
5th (1st batt.)	944	
9th ,, ...	761	
38th ,, ...	953	
		2,658
2nd Brigade, Ferguson :		
36th	591	
40th (1st batt.)	923	
71st ,, ...	935	
		2,449
		5,573

The French cavalry had been hovering around Vimiero all through the twentieth, and knowing that Junot was not far off,

Brought forward . . .		5,573
3rd Brigade, Nightingale :		
29th	616	
82nd (1st batt.)	904	
		1,520
4th Brigade, Bowes :		
6th (1st batt.)	943	
32nd ,, ...	870	
		1,813
5th Brigade, C. Crawfurd :		
45th (1st batt.)	915	
91st	917	
		1,832
6th Brigade, Fane :		
50th (1st batt.)	945	
60th (5th batt.)	604	
95th (2nd batt., four companies) .	456	
		2,005
7th Brigade, Anstruther :		
9th (2nd batt.)	633	
43rd ,, ...	721	
52nd ,, ...	654	
97th ,, ...	695	
		2,703
8th Brigade, Acland :		
2nd	731	
20th (seven and a half companies) .	401	
95th (1st batt., two companies) .	200	
		1,332
Total British present		16,778

We have also to add the Portuguese of Trant, 2,000 or 2,100 men, making 18,800 for the whole force.

Napier's estimate on p. 499 of vol. i. of his *Peninsular War,* is unfortunately quite inaccurate ; he has—

(1) Omitted to deduct from each regiment the losses at Roliça, 474 in all.

(2) Counted the 50th Regiment twice. It had been moved from Catlin Crawfurd's to Fane's brigade the day after Roliça, in exchange for the 45th. Napier has inserted it, and counted it, in both places with its 945 men.

(3) Forgotten that Spencer's artillery, 245 men, had been left behind for want of horses.

(4) Omitted (very excusably) to note that two and a half companies of the 20th Regiment were not ashore yet, having drifted away on a disabled transport, so that the regiment is given 135 too strong.

There is therefore a total excess of no less than 1,799 British troops. On the other hand, the Portuguese of Trant are probably understated by some 350 bayonets.

Sir Arthur had taken all precautions against being surprised. General Fane, in charge of the outposts, had pushed pickets of riflemen into the wooded heights that faced the British position on the northern bank of the Maceira[1]: vedettes of the 20th Light Dragoons were thrown out three or four miles to the front, and especially watched the Torres Vedras road. About midnight they began to hear the approach of the enemy; the rumbling of his guns and caissons over the wooden bridge of Villa Facaia travelled for miles through the still night air. In half an hour Wellesley was warned that the French were drawing near, and sent the order round all his brigades to be under arms and in line on their designated position an hour before daybreak[2].

But the enemy was late in appearing: Junot had halted on the near side of the bridge of Villa Facaia, four miles away, to rest his men after their night march and to allow them to cook their breakfast. It was not till nearly nine in the morning that dense clouds of dust rolling along the Torres Vedras road bore witness to the approach of the French. They were indistinctly visible, among woods and rolling upland, as they advanced with a broad front on each side of the village of Villa Facaia—a regiment of cavalry in front, then Loison on the left and Delaborde on the right side of the road, finally Kellermann's grenadiers, the reserve of artillery, and the bulk of Margaron's cavalry. The English were surprised to note that the columns showed as masses of dust colour, not of the customary dark blue. On account of the hot weather they had been provided with white linen frocks, and were wearing their uniform coats folded and buckled over their knapsacks[3].

Wellesley had been expecting to see the great column swerve to its left, and approach him along the valley of the Maceira, by Cunhados and Sobreiro Curvo. But instead of so doing Junot continued his progress northward, till he had completely marched past the English right wing, and only fronted and deployed when he had got on a level with Vimiero. After driving off the small

[1] Leach's *Sketches*, p. 50. He was himself on the line of pickets, 200 strong, which held the wooded height from which Junot afterwards viewed the battle.

[2] Napier says that the news was brought ' by a German officer of dragoons, who showed some consternation.' This statement much offended the news-bearer Landsheit, a sergeant of the 20th Light Dragoons, not an officer. He has left his protest in his interesting autobiography, p. 264.

[3] Col. Leslie's *Military Journal*, p. 52.

pickets of English riflemen who still lay out in the woods a mile in front of Fane's brigade [1], the French began to form a line of battle whose southern end was opposite Wellesley's centre. But at the same time the cavalry advance-guard was noted riding far away to the north, toward Carasquiera and Praganza, and it was clear that infantry were following them. Obviously there was going to be an attempt to turn the English position at its northern end, on the comparatively gentle slopes along the Lourinhão road.

Junot after reconnoitring the British position in a somewhat perfunctory fashion, had resolved to leave alone the formidable heights occupied by the right wing, and to try to storm the low hill in front of Vimiero with his main body, while he turned Wellesley's left with a secondary column. This detachment was composed of the 3rd provisional regiment of dragoons, and Brennier's brigade, the same four battalions which had fought so handsomely at Roliça. But the moment that Wellesley had seen that his right flank was safe, and that his left was about to be attacked, he rapidly changed his line of battle. Ferguson, from behind Vimiero, started to march north. Behind him followed three of the four brigades which had occupied the hills above the sea. Only Hill was still left on the crest to the south-west of Vimiero; Bowes, Nightingale, and Acland—six battalions in all, taking with them six guns—dropped down into the valley of the Maceira, crossed it behind Vimiero, and marched along the Lourinhão road parallel with Brennier's movement on the opposite side of the valley. In rear of these troops, and nearer the sea, Catlin Crawfurd and the Portuguese also moved northward, and took up a position near Ribamar, where they covered the flank of the other corps and were in a good position for preventing any movement of the French on the extreme north-west. Junot caught a glimpse of the extensive transference of troops to the left which his adversary was making, and struck with a sudden fear lest Brennier might be overwhelmed, sent off another brigade—Solignac's of Loison's division—to support him. He would have been much wiser had he kept these three battalions in hand to support his main attack, and merely directed Brennier to demonstrate against the British left without pressing his attack home. His last movement had divided his army into two halves, separated from each other by a gap of nearly two miles: for the main attack he had only kept eight and

[1] Col. Leach's *Sketches*, pp. 50, 51.

a quarter battalions, three regiments of cavalry and seventeen guns, while seven battalions, one regiment of cavalry, and six guns had gone off on the turning movement. How long their flank march was to be he had not calculated, for, not discerning the steepness of the ravine at the foot of the British position, he had not realized that Brennier and Solignac would have to take a vast sweep to the north in order to cross it. As a matter of fact they got completely out of touch with him and, what was worse, with each other. Their diversion did not begin till the main battle was nearly over [1].

Meanwhile the French general deployed the second brigades of his two divisions, Charlot's of Loison's, and Thomières' of Delaborde's, only four and a quarter battalions in all, as a first line for the attack on Vimiero. Kellermann's four battalions of grenadiers in a second line were for the moment held back, as was the cavalry and the reserve artillery. But seven guns went forward with the first line. The French came on in their usual style, a thick line of tirailleurs, supported by battalion columns close in their rear. Fane and Anstruther were very comfortably placed for repelling the attack: the latter had drawn up the 52nd and 97th in line on the slope of the hill, partly hidden by a dip in the ground and largely covered by vines and brushwood: the 9th and 43rd were in open column to the rear, ready to act as a reserve. Fane had got most of the riflemen of the 60th and 95th out in front, at the foot of the hill, in a very thick skirmishing line: only a few companies of them were in reserve along with the 50th (the famous 'dirty half-hundredth') at the head of the slope. In consequence of the order which Junot had adopted, Thomières' two battalions were opposed to Fane, and Charlot's brigade to Anstruther on the southern half of the hill. In each quarter the course of the fight was much the same: the French tirailleurs pushed up the slope among the brushwood and vineyards, slowly driving the riflemen before them. Then, as they drew near the crest, the two English brigadiers suddenly let loose their formed battalions upon the assailants. There was one fierce volley from the six guns on the hill top, and then the 97th charged Charlot's men in front, while the 52nd swerved round and took them in flank. One

---

[1] Thiébault (iv. 188, 189) expresses (and with reason) his wonder that Junot mixed his divisions so hopelessly, and thinks that it would have been more rational to send Delaborde and his second brigade after Brennier, instead of breaking up Loison's division by taking the supporting brigade from it.

smashing discharge at ten paces blew to pieces the heads of the columns of the 32nd and 82nd, which crumpled up in hopeless disorder and rolled down to the foot of the hill, pursued by their assailants. A few moments later Fane dashed the 50th and the reserve companies of his rifles against Thomières' troops, and sent them flying down the slope in equal disorder. They could not be rallied till they had got out of musketry range, and the seven guns which they had brought forward with them were all captured: Delaborde and Charlot were wounded: the commander of the 82nd was killed [1].

Junot's first attack had failed, but his spirit was not yet broken: he called up half his reserve of grenadiers, two battalions under Colonel St. Clair, and sent them against the hill on the same point, while the débris of the two wrecked brigades were rallied and pushed forward in support. Eight guns under Foy (the historian in after-years of the war), were brought out from the artillery reserve and pushed to the front. The second attack, however, failed even more disastrously than the first: the grenadiers, attacking on a narrow front and a single point, were blown to pieces by the converging fire of the 52nd, the 97th, and Fane's two rifle battalions, as well as by the battery on the hill, which having no longer any British skirmishers in front of it had a free field. It was here, as Wellesley's dispatches show, that shrapnell shell, a recent invention of the British colonel of that name, was first used, and with the most effective results. St. Clair's battalions climbed halfway up the hill, but could do no more, and finally gave way, bearing back with them their half-rallied supports. The fight was rolling down the slope into the pinewood at its foot, when Junot made his last desperate stroke. His only infantry reserve was now the 1st Regiment of Grenadiers, two battalions under Colonel Maransin. He resolved to throw them into the fight *pour en finir*, as he said to his chief of the staff, but they 'made a finish of it' in a way very different from his intention. This time the assailants, led by General Kellermann in person, made not for the front of the hill, but for the gap between it and the heights to the north, trying to turn Fane's flank and to penetrate into the village of Vimiero by coasting round the foot of the higher ground. There were at first

---

[1] The best narrative of the fight on Vimiero Hill is that in General Anstruther's 'Journal,' printed in the memoir attached to Wyld's *Atlas*: Leach and Rifleman Harris give many interesting details.

no troops directly opposed to the column, but soon the grenadiers found themselves under fire from both flanks. On the southern side Anstruther took from his reserve the 43rd, which had not yet fired a shot, and threw it into the cemetery of Vimiero, from whence it descended on the left flank of the leading battalion of grenadiers. On the northern side a new force intervened: General Acland on the heights along the Lourinhão road had been acting as the reserve of Wellesley's left wing: he was not needed there, and seeing Kellermann's attack threatening to break in between himself and Anstruther, took action on his own responsibility. Marching a little southward along the ridge, he sent his two companies of the 95th Rifles, and the light companies of his two line-battalions to fall on the right flank of the grenadiers. At the same time he turned upon them the fire of two field-guns which were in reserve near his brigade.

The double flank attack cost Kellermann many men, and brought his column to a standstill, but he held his ground for some time, till the 43rd closed in upon him at the eastern end of Vimiero village. Both French and English were in great disorder, the houses and enclosure-walls having broken up their formation. There was a furious hand-to-hand fight, volleys were interchanged at the distance of five yards, and both sides used the bayonet freely. At last the grenadiers gave way and retired sullenly towards their original position: they had lost many men, but so had the 43rd, who from a weak battalion of 700 men had forty killed and seventy-nine wounded.

All along the line the French were now falling back, and Junot brought up a regiment of dragoons to cover the retreat of the disordered masses. Wellesley now resolved to make use of his handful of cavalry: close behind Vimiero there were drawn up the 240 sabres of the 20th Light Dragoons, with 260 Portuguese horsemen in two squadrons on their flanks [1]. 'Now, Twentieth, now is the time!' cried Wellesley, lifting his cocked hat, and Colonel Taylor wheeled his regiment from behind the sheltering hill and dashed at the retreating Frenchmen. The two Portuguese squadrons started level with him, but after going a few hundred yards and receiving a shot or two, they broke, fell into disorder, and finally galloped to the rear amid the hoots of Anstruther's

---

[1] All this comes from the narrative, which I have already utilized in more than one place, of Sergeant Landsheit of the 20th.

brigade. But the 20th rode at the French dragoons who stood in
their path, burst through them, and then plunged among the flying
infantry, sabring them to right and left and taking many prisoners.
They could not be stayed till they had hewn their way through
the fugitives, to the place where Junot himself sat watching the
rout of his men. The charge had been pushed beyond all reasonable bounds, for the men were mad with excitement and would not
halt. But as they rode up the French hill they were checked by
a stone wall, and at the same time charged by the two reserve
regiments of Margaron's horse. It was a wonder that the headstrong troopers were not annihilated, but the larger part returned
in safety to the English lines, leaving behind them their colonel[1]
and twenty men slain, twenty-four wounded, and eleven prisoners.

We must now turn to the northern part of the battle-field,
where the main stress of the fighting did not begin till the engagement round Vimiero was nearly over. This was the result of the
reckless way in which Junot had sent his flanking brigades to
attack over unexplored ground. When Brennier reached the point
at which he would naturally have wheeled inward to climb the
slopes along the Lourinhão road, he came upon the deep and
rugged valley of Toledo, the steepness of whose slopes he did not
realize till he had almost reached its brink. Having guns with
him, the French brigadier thought the obstacle impassable, and
turned northward again in a long sweep by the village of Carras-
queira, the 3rd Dragoons still heading his march. In this wide
flanking movement he passed quite out of sight of the British.

But Solignac, with the second brigade which Junot had told off for
the northern diversion, was not so cautious. He too came upon the
ravine; but instead of turning it he sought out its least precipitous
point and passed it near its head, underneath the farm of Ventosa.
Having crossed, he deployed his three battalions, brought up his
right shoulder, and ascended the gentle slope. By this movement
he was devoting his brigade to destruction. On the hill above
he could see only the thin line of British skirmishers, but

---

[1] Taylor, like the heroic Blake, and like Graham the victor of Barossa,
was one of Oxford's few fighting men. Every visitor to Christ Church sees
his memorial stone, stating how he had reformed and disciplined the
regiment, when it came home a skeleton from the West Indies in 1805,
and had practically to be raised anew. Since then it had been in the
unfortunate expedition to Buenos Ayres.

hidden behind the crest was the main body of Wellesley's right wing, the seven battalions of Ferguson, Nightingale, and Bowes. They had long watched the approach of the French, and were lying down in battle order. In front were Ferguson's three regiments, the 36th, 40th, and 71st, and one of Nightingale's, the 82nd. A couple of hundred yards to the rear was the second line, the 29th of Nightingale's brigade, and the 6th and 32nd, which formed Bowes' command. Acland and Catlin Crawfurd were a mile away in different directions, but not too far to have been called in if necessary.

When Solignac's men reached the brow of the hill, the four British battalions in the front line rose up and marched to meet them. Their long array completely overlapped at both ends the advancing columns and their screen of light troops [1]. At the distance of one hundred yards all the four regiments directed a converging volley on the French, which almost swept away the tirailleurs and shook terribly the supporting masses. Then they reloaded and advanced in silence on the enemy, who were shouting, firing irregularly, and endeavouring to deploy, with their officers all in front. For troops in such disorder the near approach of the majestic two-deep line of 3,300 bayonets was too much. They wavered and fled northward along the summit of the ridge, carrying with them their commander, Solignac, desperately wounded. The British pursued, halting at intervals to pour a volley into the retreating masses, and picking up on the way many prisoners, and also the three guns which the enemy had laboriously dragged up the hill.

The pursuit was stopped by an unexpected development. General Brennier had heard from afar the heavy musketry fire which told him that his supporting brigade was engaged. He was now on the summit of the heights, having at last accomplished his long flank march. Pushing hastily forward, he came to the edge of a saddle-backed depression in the ridge, and had the spectacle of the fight at his feet. The 36th and 40th were engaged in driving the wrecks of Solignac's men back in a north-westerly direction, while the 71st and 82nd, halted around the captured guns, were resting and reforming their ranks. Without a moment's hesitation, Brennier threw his four battalions upon the two regiments that

[1] There is a good account of this charge in the anonymous 'T. S.' of the 71st, p. 50.

lay beneath him. He had taken them by surprise; attacked diagonally by fresh troops, and charged by the two squadrons of dragoons that accompanied the French, they reeled back in some disorder and abandoned the guns that they had taken. But they rallied in a moment, and returned to the fight aided by the 29th [1], the reserve regiment of Nightingale's brigade. There was heavy firing for a moment, but very soon Brennier's troops broke and fled up the slope which they had just descended. Their flight was covered by the dragoons, who suffered severely in holding off the pursuers, losing many officers, among them the young Arrighi, a kinsman of the Bonaparte family. Brennier was left on the field wounded and a prisoner, and not only did his men lose the guns which they had just recaptured, but they also left behind the three which had accompanied their own column. Their hurried retreat was accelerated by the fire of a half-battery, brought up from the reserve, which played upon them with effect till they had plunged down into the ravine and regained their original position on the opposite heights.

All the fighting here had been done by Ferguson's and Nightingale's five battalions. Bowes' brigade did not fire a shot or lose a man, and Catlin Crawfurd and the Portuguese were only beginning to approach the scene of action when Brennier's column broke up and fled. The main honours of the fight must be given to the 71st and 82nd, who lost respectively 112 and 61 men out of the total of 272 casualties suffered in this part of the action.

Two and a half hours after the battle began the French, both in the north and the south of the field, were retiring in confusion. The British were awaiting eagerly the order for a general advance —especially Ferguson, who, with the 36th and 40th, had got part of Solignac's brigade pinned into an angle of the hills, from which they could not easily escape when attacked. But instead of the order to advance there came a prohibition to move, and the French were allowed to withdraw unmolested. The stream of fugitives from Brennier's and Solignac's fight joined that from the centre; then both shook themselves together and formed up in more or less order on the heights. The reserve artillery under Hulot and Prost (Foy had been wounded) kept up a distant and ineffective fire towards the hill of Vimiero, more to put heart into their own

[1] There are clear accounts of this fighting in Col. Leslie's autobiography, p. 51, as well as in the narrative of ' T. S.' of the 71st.

infantry by the noise of their guns than in any hope of harming the English. Margaron's cavalry showed a front behind them, and the two belated battalions from Lisbon, which arrived about noon, were sent to the front and displayed on the edge of the heights to make some show of force. But the French would not have stood a serious attack : every single unit of their infantry had been deeply engaged and had suffered a thorough defeat. More than half their guns (thirteen out of twenty-three) had been captured. The cavalry was in better case, though two of its regiments had suffered severely, yet it could not by itself have resisted the attack of the victorious British. A vigorous push would have sent the whole mass reeling backward, not on Torres Vedras or Lisbon— for these roads would have been barred to them when Wellesley advanced—but on the rugged path, over the spurs of the Sierra da Baragueda, which leads to Santarem.

But while the French were striving to rally and to form a new front, the leaden hand of Sir Harry Burrard was laid upon the British army. That leisurely person had only landed on the morning of the twenty-first, and the battle was in full progress before he rode up from the beach to Vimiero. He had the grace not to interfere with the movements of troops which Wellesley had already ordered ; but when the victory was won, and his subordinate rode up to him crying, 'Sir Harry, now is your time to advance, the enemy is completely beaten, and we shall be in Lisbon in three days [1],' he refused to listen. The army, he said, had done enough for one day, and he intended to wait for the arrival of Sir John Moore and the division from the Baltic before making any further move. Greatly disconcerted by this stolid opposition, Wellesley launched forth into argument : the French army, as he pointed out, was now so placed that it had lost control of its line of retreat on Torres Vedras and Lisbon. Hill's intact brigade, and those of Fane and Anstruther had but to advance a mile or so, and the French were irretrievably cut off from their base of operations. At the same time the five brigades of the left wing, of which those of Bowes and Crawfurd were absolutely intact, might so hustle and press the retreating enemy that he could never rally. At this moment arrived an aide-de-camp from Ferguson, who begged to be allowed to go on : 'a column of broken troops 1,500 to 2,000 strong had in their confusion got into a hollow, and could be cut off from

---

[1] Evidence of Col. Torrens at the Court of Inquiry (*Proceedings,* p. 127).

their main body by a movement in advance of his brigade [1].' The
enemy had lost all their artillery, were retiring in the utmost
confusion, none of them save the cavalry were regularly formed,
and it was his hope that he might be allowed to continue to
go forward. Burrard still remained obdurate, though Wellesley
pointed out to him that he had nine thousand fresh troops in
hand, that every soldier had a day's food cooked in his haversack,
that the ammunition reserve was ready to move, and that, with
twelve days' provisions in the camp and an ample store of
munitions, he had it in his power to march forward both
rapidly and with complete security [2]. But all these arguments
were of no effect. The slow and cautious Burrard chose to believe
that Junot might still have a large and intact reserve, that his
cavalry was too dangerous to be meddled with, and that the
dispersion of the British brigades (there were more than three
miles between Hill's extreme right and Ferguson's extreme left)
would make a general advance a very dislocated and hazardous
business [3]. He utterly refused to listen to any further discussion,
and, as the French were now in full retreat and disappearing over
the eastern horizon, ordered the troops back to camp. They
returned with colours flying and bands playing, dragging the
captured French guns, and with a considerable column of prisoners
in their midst. But every one, from Generals Spencer and Ferguson
down to the youngest private, was utterly puzzled at the tame and
inconsequent end to such a glorious day.

The losses had been very moderate—four officers and 131 men
killed, thirty-seven officers and 497 men wounded, two officers and
forty-nine men missing. Of the total of 720 no less than 573 were
from the ten battalions of Fane's, Anstruther's, and Ferguson's
brigades. Those of Hill, Bowes, and Catlin Crawfurd did not
return a single casualty. The handful of prisoners were mainly
supplied by the 20th Light Dragoons, and by the two rifle
battalions, whose pickets had been driven in at the commencement
of the fight [4]. The French losses were very different: both Foy

---

[1] Message sent by Ferguson, borne by his aide-de-camp, Captain Mellish
(*Proceedings of the Court of Inquiry*, p. 121).

[2] Evidence before the Court of Inquiry of Wellesley (*Proceedings*, pp. 116,
117), and of Col. Torrens (p. 127).

[3] Burrard's account of his own views before the Court of Inquiry (*Proceedings*, pp. 115, 116, 135).

[4] See table of losses at Vimiero in the Appendix.

and Thiébault acknowledge a total of 1,800, and this may be taken as a minimum: of these some 300 or 400 were unwounded prisoners. Delaborde and three brigadier-generals—Charlot, Brennier, and Solignac—as well as Colonels Foy and Prost of the artillery, were wounded. Two battalion commanders were killed, a third and the disabled Brennier were prisoners. Men and officers were alike disheartened: every single corps present had been engaged: even the squadron of volunteer cavalry had been in action against Taylor's dragoons: more than half the guns had been lost, and the officers who brought back those that remained asked themselves in wonder how they had ever been permitted to get away[1]. But at least they were unmolested in their retreat: using the two battalions that had just come up from Lisbon as his rearguard, Junot retired unharmed, but full of despair, on Torres Vedras. It was not till early on the next morning that the last stragglers of his scattered army drifted in to join the main body.

[1] *Souvenirs Militaires* of Hulot, who commanded one of the two reserve batteries, p. 235: 'J'étais étonné de ne pas voir l'ennemi fondre sur mes pièces,' &c.

SECTION IV: CHAPTER IV

THE CONVENTION OF CINTRA

FOR only one single day did the incubus of Burrard rest upon the British army in Portugal, though that day was one on which he succeeded in changing a decisive victory, which might have laid a whole kingdom at his feet, into an ordinary successful defensive action. He had stopped Wellesley's triumphant march at noon on August 21; early on the morning of the twenty-second Sir Hew Dalrymple appeared in Maceira Bay, disembarked, and took over the command. He naturally began his tenure of control by interviewing his two predecessors, whose divergent views as to the situation and its requirements were laid before him. He was an old man, and unpractised in the field: he had only seen war in the wretched Flanders campaign of 1793–4. His prejudice was in favour of caution, and he was not slow to let it be seen that he regarded Wellesley's actions in the past, and still more his plans for the future, as rash and hazardous. 'On the first interview that I had with Sir Hew Dalrymple,' said Wellesley at the Court of Inquiry in the following winter, 'I had reason to believe that I did not possess his confidence: nay more, that he was prejudiced against any opinions which I should give him [1].' The veteran's ill-concealed hostility was, we cannot doubt, mainly due to an unhappy inspiration of Castlereagh, who had sent him a letter bidding him 'take Sir Arthur Wellesley into his particular confidence, as he had been, for a length of time past, in the closest habits of communication with His Majesty's ministers with respect to the affairs of Spain.' He was also directed 'to make the most prominent use of him which the rules of the service would permit [2].' Such a letter very naturally caused Dalrymple to look upon the young lieutenant-general as a sort of emissary from the Government, sent to overrule his plans and curb his full power of command. He was inclined, consciously or unconsciously, to entertain a strong

[1] Wellesley's evidence at the Court of Inquiry (*Proceedings*, p. 81).
[2] Castlereagh to Dalrymple, July 15 (*Well. Disp.*, iv. 18).

prejudice against anything that Wellesley might recommend: and we cannot doubt that the latter, always stiff and haughty, was at this moment in a state of suppressed fury at the foiling of his plans by Burrard on the preceding day. Probably, in his own cold way, he let his indignation appear, and Dalrymple may have been glad of an excuse for repressing him.

The plan which Wellesley had drawn up for the conduct of the campaign, and which he now urged upon his chief, is detailed in the proceedings of the Court of Inquiry. He had hoped to get Sir John Moore's division, whose arrival was just reported, sent to Santarem, to cut off any attempt of Junot to escape out of the Lisbon peninsula by following the road along the right bank of the Tagus: the Portuguese were to be brought up to assist. Meanwhile the army which had fought at Vimiero was to turn the position of Torres Vedras, on which the enemy had retired, by marching along the sea-coast by the route that leads to Mafra. If Junot let them march past him, he would infallibly lose Lisbon; for they could, by forcing the pace, arrive in the capital as soon as he. If he abandoned Torres Vedras, and fell back on Mafra or Montechique as soon as he saw them moving, he would have to fight a second battle on the twenty-third or twenty-fourth, with an army which had been gravely demoralized by the events of Roliça and Vimiero, and which could not receive much succour from Lisbon: for the populace of that city, when apprised of the defeat of the French, would undoubtedly have burst into insurrection, and would have required for its repression every man of the 5,000 [1] troops who had been left to hold it down. There was a third possibility, that Junot, on hearing that the English were marching past his flank, might have hastened from Torres Vedras to attack their line of march by one of the cross-roads (such as that from Torres Vedras to Puente de Roll), which cut down to the Atlantic coast. But Wellesley had convinced himself that this chance would not occur: he reckoned, very rightly, on the exhaustion of the enemy on the day after such a crushing blow as Vimiero. As a matter of fact, on the morning of the twenty-second, at the moment when the head of the British column, if it had marched, would have been outflanking their position, Junot

---

[1] This figure, of course, does not include the garrisons of the outlying places, but only those immediately in and about the capital, after the 66th and *compagnies d'élite* marched to Torres Vedras.

and those of his generals who were not *hors de combat* were sitting
in council of war at Torres Vedras, with despair in their souls,
and resolving to ask for terms on which to evacuate Portugal.
Kellermann was just about to ride in to the English lines to open
negotiations[1]. The idea of an 'offensive return' by the French
was in the head of the cautious Burrard[2]: but not in that of
Wellesley, who had made up his mind 'that they would act in
Portugal as they did in Egypt: they tried their strength once in
the field, and having failed they would have continued to retreat
till they could have got into safety. I do not believe that any
corps could have fallen on the flank of our march on the twenty-
third.' The only course open to the French, in his opinion, was
to throw over any idea of holding the capital, withdraw its garrison,
and cross the Tagus at Saccavem or Villafranca, or Santarem, by
means of the ships which lay in the river, and the large fleet of barges
which is always to be found in and near Lisbon. Having passed
the Tagus they might cut their way through the insurgents of the
Alemtejo, disperse the Spanish levies about Elvas and Badajoz,
and press north through Estremadura to join Bessières[3]. This
very idea did for a moment flash through the brains of some of
Junot's council of war at Torres Vedras : but there lay on their
minds, like a nightmare, the remembrance of their awful march
through the Estremaduran mountains in the preceding autumn.
If, journeying unopposed from Ciudad Rodrigo to Lisbon, they had
been nearly starved in that wilderness, what would be their fate
if they had to cut their way through an insurrection, with the
English army hanging on their heels ? The most hopeful could
only say that perhaps half the army might struggle through to
Old Castile.

Wellesley's arguments to Dalrymple had no further effect than
to induce that general to make up his mind that the troops should
march not on the twenty-second but on the twenty-third, and not
on Mafra but on Torres Vedras. Sir John Moore's division was to
be brought down at once to Maceira Bay, to join the main army,
and not to be sent (as Wellesley had urged) to Santarem. With

---

[1] Hulot, *Mémoires Militaires,* p. 236.

[2] Questions asked of Wellesley by Burrard at the Court of Inquiry (*Proceedings,* p. 133).

[3] Wellesley to Mr. Stuart, Aug. 25, 1808 (*Well. Disp.,* iv. 105) ; Wellesley's
address at the Court of Inquiry (*Proceedings,* p. 132).

the aid of this reinforcement Dalrymple hoped to be strong enough
to force back Junot into Lisbon.   The resolve meant fatal delay :
Moore did not begin to disembark till August 25, and his last
men did not get ashore till August 30.   On that day only could
Junot have been attacked seriously, and meanwhile he would have
obtained nine days in which to fortify his positions and to place
Lisbon in a thorough state of defence.   The consequences entailed
would have been a long siege, the probable devastation of the
Portuguese capital, and the protraction of operations into November
and December.   Even then there would still have been Elvas and
Almeida to be recaptured [1].

But things were not destined to take this course.   Dalrymple
was busy drafting his orders for the movement of the next day on
Torres Vedras, when an alarm ran through the camp that the
French were at hand, and the whole force flew to arms.   This
rumour was caused by the folly of a Portuguese cavalry officer,
whose vedettes had seen French horsemen in the distance ; he
imagined an army on the move and reported its approach.   What
he had really seen was General Kellermann, with two squadrons
of dragoons as his escort, bearing the white flag, and about to
propose to the British commander-in-chief the evacuation of
Portugal by the French army under a convention.

We have already mentioned the fact that on the early morning
of the twenty-second, Junot had called together at Torres Vedras
a council of war composed of all his surviving generals—Loison,
Kellermann, Delaborde (who attended though suffering from two
severe wounds), Thiébault, the chief of the staff, Taviel, the commander of the artillery, Col. Vincent, the chief engineer, and
Trousset, the chief commissary at Lisbon.   Junot's spirits were
very low : he began by explaining that he had only fought at
Vimiero to save the honour of the French arms, not because he
hoped for victory—a statement which will not bear investigation
in the light of his previous dispatches and letters [2].   The British,
he said, were expecting huge reinforcements from the sea : Freire
was now moving on Obidos, another Portuguese corps on Santarem :
the reports of the state of public opinion in Lisbon were most
alarming.   Under these circumstances, ought the army to try the
fortune of battle a second time ?   And if it must, what plan

---

[1] This is Wellesley's own view (*Well. Disp.*, iv. 121, 184, 185).
[2] Cf. for Junot's address, Foy, iv. 341, and Thiébault.

should be adopted? If it could not, what alternative remained? When such was the spirit of the leader, it was easy to foresee the replies of his subordinates. The army, they soon resolved, had done its best in the most honourable fashion, but it was not ready for another fight. Indeed the stragglers had not yet finished pouring into Torres Vedras, and the wearied rearguard which covered them had only reached the defile in front of the town two hours after midnight [1]. The army, unmolested as it was, did not get into fighting trim again till two days after Vimiero. On the twenty-second it was still in a state of complete disorganization : if Dalrymple had marched on Mafra he would not have found a man in his path.

Having resolved that the army was not ready for another battle, the council of war had three alternatives before it : to fall back to cover Lisbon on the positions of Mafra and Montechique; to evacuate Lisbon, cross the Tagus, and make for Elvas; or to try to negotiate with the British. The decision was soon made in favour of the third: Lisbon, without regular fortifications, and swarming with a discontented populace, would be a mere snare for the army. The retreat via Elvas on Old Castile would mean the slow but certain destruction of the whole corps [2]. For it was now known that Joseph Bonaparte had evacuated Madrid, and that Burgos was probably the nearest point where a French force was to be found. Not one of the officers present had the heart to make a serious proposal for such a retreat. It only remained to try whether Dalrymple was open to receive an offer : if he could be tempted by the prospect of receiving Lisbon with all its magazines and riches intact, he might allow the French army to return under safe conduct to their own land. Kellermann, who could understand English, more or less, and was considered a skilful diplomatist, was charged with the negotiations. He rode out of Torres Vedras between ten and eleven in the morning with his escort, charged with ample powers to treat. As he passed the rearguard in the pass, four miles outside the town, he told the officer in command that he was going to visit the English 'to see if he could get the army out of the mousetrap [3].'

---

[1] Hulot, *Souvenirs Militaires*, pp. 235, 236.

[2] But it is said that Delaborde urged the possibility of this move.

[3] Hulot heard this himself. Kellermann said 'qu'il allait trouver les Anglais, pour voir à nous tirer de la souricière' (p. 236).

By two o'clock Kellermann was conferring with the English commander—he was astonished to find that it was Dalrymple and not Wellesley. The reception that he met was an agreeable surprise to him. Dalrymple showed his pleasure at the broaching of the idea of a convention in the most undisguised fashion. The fact was that he was very glad to avoid the possible dangers of an immediate advance and a second fight. He called in Burrard and Wellesley to the interview, and from his unguarded 'asides' to them, Kellermann soon learnt that Moore had not yet landed, and that till he was ashore Dalrymple did not feel safe. This gave the Frenchman a confidence which he had not at first possessed, and he at once assumed an air of self-reliance which he had been far from showing when he rode out of Torres Vedras. Instead of merely trying to save the army at all costs, he began to haggle about details, and to speak about the possibility of resuming hostilities—the last thing in the world that he really desired[1].

There was no doubt that a convention by which Portugal and all its fortresses could be recovered without the necessity of firing another shot was an eminently desirable thing. Wellesley did not hesitate a moment in advising his superiors to take the offer. Burrard had given away the certainty of recapturing Lisbon yesterday: Dalrymple, by delaying his advance, had on this very morning sacrificed the second chance (a much less brilliant one, it must be confessed) of ending the campaign by a single blow. If Junot's proposals were rejected and hostilities were resumed, there lay before the British army either a siege of Lisbon, which could not fail to ruin the city, or a long stern-chase after the French, if they should resolve to cross the Tagus and march off through the Alemtejo. No doubt it would sound better in the ears of the British public if the surrender or destruction of Junot's army could be reported. But as a matter of practical expediency, the recovery of Lisbon and all its wealth unharmed was worth far more than the capture of a French army at the cost of much time, many lives, and the ruin of the Portuguese capital. The loss of 25,000 soldiers would be nothing to Napoleon, who disposed of more than half a million men: the blow to his pride would be almost as great if he lost Portugal by a convention as if he lost it by a capitulation. As a matter of fact he was much incensed at Junot, and would have dealt hardly with him if Dupont had not

[1] Foy, iv. 344, 345 ; *Well. Disp.*, iv. 108.

drawn off his wrath by failing in an even more disastrous fashion [1].

After hearing what Kellermann had to say, the three English generals withdrew into an inner room, and after a very short discussion agreed to treat. They told their visitor that he might have a forty-eight hours' suspension of hostilities at once, and that they would open negotiations on the general base that Junot and his army should be allowed to evacuate Portugal by sea without any of the forms of capitulation, and be returned to their own country on British ships. The details would take much discussion: meanwhile they invited Kellermann to dine with them and to settle the main lines of the Convention before he returned to his commander. There was a long post-prandial debate, which showed that on two points there was likely to be trouble; one was the way in which Siniavin's Russian fleet in the Tagus was to be treated: the other was how much the French should be allowed to carry away with them from Portugal. Kellermann said that he asked for no more than their 'military baggage and equipments,' but he seemed to have a large idea of what came under these headings [2].

Meanwhile the terms of the suspension of hostilities were successfully drafted; the line of the Zizandre river was to be fixed as that of demarcation between the two hosts. Neither of them was to occupy Torres Vedras: Dalrymple undertook to get the armistice recognized by Freire and the other Portuguese generals in the field. They were not to advance beyond Leiria and Thomar. The garrisons at Elvas, Almeida, Peniche, and elsewhere were to be included in the Convention, unless it should turn out that any of them had surrendered before August 25—which as a matter of fact they had not. The Russian fleet in the Tagus was to be treated as if in a neutral port. This last clause was much objected to by Wellesley, who found also several minor points in the agreement of which he could not approve. But by the directions of

[1] See the curious account of the Emperor's interviews with Legendre and Thiébault, the chiefs of the staff to Dupont and Junot, who appeared before him simultaneously at Valladolid in January, 1809. The imperial thunders played so fiercely on the army of Andalusia that the army of Portugal got off easily (Thiébault, iv. 247-9). But Napoleon said that the English had saved him the pain of crushing an old friend by sending Dalrymple, Burrard, and Wellesley before a court-martial.

[2] Wellesley at the Court of Inquiry (*Well. Disp.*, iv. 189).

Dalrymple he signed the suspension of arms after a protest; his superior had told him that it was 'useless to drive the French to the wall upon points of form [1].'

The subsequent negotiations for a definite convention occupied seven days, from August 23 to 30. On the first-named day Junot evacuated Torres Vedras, according to the stipulations of the agreement made by Kellermann. He retired to the line of hills behind him, establishing Loison's division at Mafra and Delaborde's at Montechique. Dalrymple, on the other hand, moved his head quarters forward to Ramalhal, a position just north of Torres Vedras, and only nine miles from Vimiero. In this respect he profited less than the French from the suspension of hostilities : it is true that he got leisure to disembark Moore's troops, but Junot gained the much more important advantage of a safe retreat to a good position, and of leisure to strengthen himself in it. It must not be supposed, however, that he was in a comfortable situation ; Lisbon was seething with suppressed rebellion. The news of French victories, which had been published to quiet the people, had soon been discovered to be nothing more than an impudent fiction. At any moment an insurrection might have broken out : the garrison and the mob were alike in a state of extreme nervous tension, which took shape on the one side in assassinations, and on the other in wanton firing at every person who approached a sentinel, or refused to stand when challenged by a patrol.

The negotiations for a definitive convention suffered several checks. At one moment it seemed likely that the Portuguese army might give trouble. General Freire arrived at Ramalhal in a state of high wrath, to protest that he ought to have been made a party to the suspension of hostilities. There was, as Napier remarks, more plausibility than real foundation in his objection [2], for his motley army had taken no part whatever in the operations that had brought Junot to his knees. But he could make a distinct point when he asked by what authority Dalrymple had given promises as to his neutrality in the agreement with Kellermann, or laid down lines which he was not to pass. Freire was all the bolder because his levies were now being strengthened by the forces from Oporto which the Bishop had lately raised, while a small Spanish brigade under the Marquis of Valladares, lent by

[1] Wellesley's evidence before the Court of Inquiry (*Proceedings*, p. 83).
[2] Napier, i. 225.

the Galician Junta, had come down as far as Guarda. But he contented himself with protests, without committing any definite act that might have rendered the Convention impossible.

A more dangerous source of possible rupture was the view of the situation taken by Sir Charles Cotton, the admiral in command of the British blockading squadron off the mouth of the Tagus. As Wellesley had foreseen, the naval men were determined to secure the possession of the Russian ships of Siniavin. Cotton refused to entertain the proposal that such a force should be allowed a free departure from Lisbon, as if from a neutral port, and should be given a long start before being pursued. He had held the Russians under blockade for many a weary month, and was not going to abandon his hold upon them. Why should the French evacuation of Portugal place Siniavin in a better position than he had ever occupied before? The admiral declared that he saw no reason why the Russians should be included in the Convention at all. If there was going to be any agreement made with them, he should conduct it himself, treating directly with Siniavin instead of through a French intermediary.

Sir Hew Dalrymple was forced to report to the French commander these objections of the admiral. It seemed possible for a moment that the difficulty would not be got over, and that war must recommence. Wellesley strongly advised his chief to try the game of bluff—to announce to Junot that operations would be resumed at the end of the stipulated forty-eight hours, as Sir Charles Cotton had objected to the terms of the armistice, but that he was prepared to take into consideration any new proposals which might be made to him before the interval of two days expired [1]. Such a firm policy, he thought, would induce the French to yield the point—all the more because Junot and Siniavin were known to be on very bad terms. But Dalrymple would not accept this plan. He merely reported the admiral's proposals to Junot, without any intimation that the resumption of hostilities must result from their rejection. This move placed the power of playing the game of brag in the Frenchman's hands. Seeing that Dalrymple did not seem to desire to break off negotiations, he assumed an indignant tone, and began to talk of his determination not to concede an inch, and of the harm that he could do if he were forced to fight. 'The English might take away the half-drafted convention: he

[1] Evidence of Wellesley before the Court of Inquiry (*Proceedings*, pp. 87–91).

would have none of it.   He would defend Lisbon street by street:
he would burn as much of it as he could not hold, and it should
cost them dear to take from him what remained [1].'   At the same
time he made a final proposal to Siniavin, that he should put
ashore his 6,000 seamen and marines, to take part in the defence
of Lisbon on the land side.   This was only part of the game of
bluff, and intended for the benefit of the English rather than
of Siniavin, for Junot knew perfectly well, from the latter's previous
conduct, that he was bent on playing his own hand, and would not
fire a single shot to help the French.

All Junot's desperate language was, in fact, no more than a device
to squeeze better terms out of Dalrymple.   The actual point on
which the argument grew hot was a mere pretext, for the Russian
admiral utterly refused to assist the French, and intimated that
he should prefer to conclude a separate convention of his own with
Sir Charles Cotton.   Clearly it was not worth while for the Duke
of Abrantes to risk anything on behalf of such a torpid ally.

Accordingly the Convention was reduced to a definitive form
between August 27 and 30.   Colonel George Murray, the quartermaster-general, acted as the British negotiator, while Kellermann
continued to represent Junot.   The details were settled in Lisbon,
where Murray took up his residence, sending back frequent reports
to his superior officer at Ramalhal.   Dalrymple and Cotton
carried their point in that no allusion whatever was made to the
Russians in the document.   Junot found a salve for his injured
pride by remembering that he had slipped a mention of Napoleon
as 'Emperor of the French,' into the text of the suspension of
hostilities [2]: in this he thought that he had won a great success,
for the British Government had hitherto refused to recognize any
such title, and had constantly irritated its adversaries by allud-
ing to the master of the Continent as 'General Bonaparte,' or the
'actual head of the French executive.'

The terms of the Convention need close study [3]: it comprised
twenty-two articles and three supplementary paragraphs of addenda.
The first article provided that the French should surrender Lisbon

---

[1] Foy, iv. 352, and Thiébault.

[2] Article 1 of the armistice mentioned 'his Imperial and Royal Majesty,
Napoleon I,' though this formula did not recur in the Convention, which only
spoke of the 'French Army.'

[3] The full text will be found in the Appendix.

and the Portuguese fortresses in their existing condition, without harming or dismantling them. The second and third granted the army of Junot a safe departure by sea in English vessels: they were not to be considered prisoners of war, might take their arms and baggage, and were to be landed at any port between Rochefort and L'Orient. The fourth, fifth, and sixth articles attempted to define the property which the French might take away—their horses, their guns of French calibre (but not any that they might have found in the Portuguese arsenals), with sixty rounds for each piece, their wagons, their military chest, in short, 'all their equipment, and all that is comprehended under the name of property of the army.' It was found, later on, that these paragraphs had been too loosely worded, and gave much endless occasion for disputes. The next six articles settled the manner in which the departing army was to embark, and the order in which each of the strongholds that it evacuated was to be given up to the British. The thirteenth and fourteenth articles arranged for the appointment of commissaries by each side, to deal with disputed points in the Convention, and added the curious clause that 'where a doubt arose as to the meaning of any article, it should be explained favourably to the French army.'

But the fifteenth, sixteenth, and seventeenth articles were the most objectionable part of the Convention. It was true that they secured that no more taxes or contributions were to be raised by Junot, and that undischarged fines which he had laid on the Portuguese should be regarded as cancelled. But they also provided that French civilians in Portugal might either depart with the army, or, if they preferred it, might be allowed to remain behind unmolested, and have a year in which to dispose of their property. This might perhaps pass: not so, however, the ensuing clause, which provided that Portuguese subjects should not be rendered accountable for their political conduct during the French occupation: all who had taken service with the usurping government were to be placed under the protection of the British, and to suffer no injury in person or property. They were also to be granted liberty to depart with the French army if they chose.

The five remaining articles were unimportant. The eighteenth secured the release of Caraffa and the rest of Junot's Spanish prisoners, and provided that in return the few French officers of the army of Portugal, whom the Spaniards had captured at Oporto and Elvas, should be liberated. The twenty-first permitted Junot to send one of his aides-de-camp directly to France to carry the news of the Convention, so that preparations might be made for the reception of the troops [1].

Three unimportant supplementary articles were added below the signatures of Murray and Kellermann : one stipulated that French civilian prisoners in the hands of the English and Portuguese should be released, another that Junot's army should subsist on its own magazines till it embarked, a third that the British should permit the entry of provisions into Lisbon, now that the Convention had been concluded.

Such was the celebrated agreement which was destined to gain a most unhappy notoriety in England under the name of the 'Convention of Cintra,' a designation which it is hard to understand, for it was first sketched at Torres Vedras, and was discussed and ratified at Lisbon. The only connexion which it had with Cintra was that Dalrymple's dispatch to the British Government, enclosing the document in its latest form, was dated from that pleasant spot in the environs of Lisbon. But it would perhaps be pedantic to give any other name to such a well-known document, than that under which it has been known for the last ninety-three years.

After a careful investigation of the details of this famous agreement, the conclusion at which the impartial student will probably arrive is that while on the military side it was justifiable, it presented grave political faults. In order to recover Lisbon with its arsenals, its forts and its shipping, all intact, Dalrymple might without serious blame have granted even more to the French. By the Convention he saved, not only the wealth of the capital, and the lives of the troops who must have fallen in storming it, but, most important of all, time. If he had but known the value of that commodity, he might have been in Madrid at the head of all his British troops by October 1, or even earlier. 'I do not know what Sir Hew proposes to do,' wrote Wellesley the morning after the Convention was signed, 'but if I were in his situation I would have 20,000 men in Madrid in less than a month from this day [2].' But the importance of time was never realized by the old commander-in-chief: he was superseded long before his army had

---

[1] For the strange way in which Junot utilized this permission for his personal profit, see page 281.

[2] Wellesley to Mr. Stuart, Sept. 1, 1808 (*Well. Disp.*, iv. 121).

even moved up to the Portuguese frontier.   Looking, therefore, at the Convention in the broadest aspect, we hold that its military advantages entirely outweighed those which might have been secured by a prolongation of hostilities.   But this conclusion does not mean that there were not points in the military part of the agreement that might have been modified with advantage.

It is when we turn to the political section of the Convention that we light upon grave faults and mistakes on the part of Dalrymple.   The first and foremost was that he signed the document without previously submitting certain portions of it to the Portuguese government.   In the sixteenth and seventeenth articles the British general took upon himself to grant certain favours both to French civilians resident in Portugal, and to Portuguese subjects who had taken service under Junot, which he had no authority to concede.   These were points which concerned not the British army but the Portuguese civil administration, and should not have been decided without a consultation with our allies, and a permission from them to make terms on their behalf.   The sixteenth article allowed Frenchmen resident in Lisbon to remain there for a year after the Convention, if they did not chose to leave the country with Junot and his troops.   To permit subjects of the hostile power to remain in Lisbon for so long was, of course, most distasteful to the Portuguese government, which was naturally desirous of expelling at once, according to the ordinary customs of war, a body of persons many of whom had made themselves the partners and instruments of Junot's peculations, and who for the next twelve months would serve as spies and purveyors of intelligence to the French Emperor. Nothing more than the leave to quit Lisbon in Junot's wake should have been secured to them, unless the Junta of Regency gave its consent.   The seventeenth article is even more objectionable: a considerable portion of the bureaucracy of Portugal had been weak and criminal enough to acquiesce in the French usurpation, and to make themselves the tools of the Duke of Abrantes.   It was natural that their countrymen should feel deeply indignant with them ; and their lot was likely to be so hard that it was but rational and humane to give them leave to quit the kingdom.   But considering that they had deserved very ill of the state, it was surely wrong for the British general to promise to take them under his special protection, and to guarantee them against injury to their persons or property.   He had no power to grant them an amnesty for their

T 2

past ill-doing; that could be given only by the Portuguese government. When the latter resumed its ordinary functions at Lisbon, it was absurd that it should be prevented, by the Convention, from taking into consideration the cases of such of these unpatriotic persons as it might wish to deal with. When, therefore, Kellermann broached to Dalrymple the sixteenth and seventeenth articles, the latter should have refused to accept them without a reference to the Junta at Oporto. He might have granted both the French and the Portuguese satellites of Junot a free passage out of Portugal, with such of their goods as they could carry, but more than this he could not rationally concede on his own authority.

It was fortunate, therefore, that the practical harm done did not turn out to be very great. Both the aliens and the natives covered by these two clauses were so perfectly aware of their own unpopularity in Lisbon, that they absconded almost *en masse*. The populace of the capital had given them fair warning of what they might expect, for not only were they threatened and insulted in the streets whenever they were out of sight of a French sentry, but unknown hands posted on the walls lists of houses to be sacked and individuals to be hung as soon as Junot's army should have sailed. The watchwords, 'Death to the French' and 'Death to the traitors,' were muttered even under the muzzles of the cannon, which had been trained on all the main streets, to keep down the insurrection for the few days which had to elapse before the embarkation. The invaders, therefore, had to take away with them a very large body of civilian dependants, headed by the Comte de Novion, a French *émigré*, who, after being hospitably entertained in Lisbon for many years, had shown his gratitude by accepting the post of head of Junot's police—a capacity in which he had much odd business to transact.

But besides Articles XVI and XVII of the Convention there were other clauses to which Dalrymple should not have given his assent without consulting the representatives of his allies. Almeida was being blockaded by a mass of Portuguese militia, and Elvas, a few days after the treaty had been signed, was attacked by a Spanish force sent out from Badajoz by Galluzzo, the Captain-General of Estremadura. No British soldier had yet been seen within a hundred miles of either fortress. What was to be done if the generals of the besieging troops refused to abide by an agreement which they had not been asked to sign, and which had not even been laid before their respective governments ere it was definitively ratified? A grave crisis, as we shall find, was created by Dalrymple's neglect to foresee this difficulty. His conduct all through the days of negotiation was very strange; not only did he make no proper attempt to communicate with the Portuguese authorities, but he actually left his own government uninformed of his proceedings for a fortnight. He failed to send them any dispatch to announce the armistice of August 22, and only forwarded that detailing the Convention of August 30 on the fourth day of the succeeding month.

Dalrymple's main reason for leaving the Portuguese out of the negotiations was that the Junta at Oporto had not yet been formally recognized as the legitimate government of Portugal [1]. Wellesley, no doubt, had conferred with the Bishop, given him arms and munitions, procured from him food and draught animals, and asked his advice, but the British ministry had not yet acknowledged the existence of any regular executive in Portugal. This being so, Dalrymple thought himself justified in acting as if there were none in being; and it cannot be denied that thereby he saved himself much present trouble, at the cost of future friction. All, therefore, that he did was to inform the Junta's agent at the British head quarters, one Pinto da Souza, that he was negotiating with Junot for the evacuation of Lisbon, and that he was open to receive any observations which the Junta might make. The same announcement was made to Bernardino Freire, who had ridden over to Ramalhal [2] to complain that he and his army were not mentioned in the armistice of August 22. Both Freire and the Junta were treated as persons whose opinions it was useful to obtain, not as constituted authorities whose consent to the definitive convention was necessary in order to make it binding. Dalrymple tried to cover himself during the subsequent inquiry by maintaining that the Convention was purely military, and concerned the French and English armies alone: but this plea cannot seriously be put forward in face of Articles XV, XVI, and XVII, all of which are concerned with problems of civil government, which would arise after the French army should have embarked. Each

[1] Dalrymple's *Memoir of the Affairs of Portugal*, p. 66.
[2] Dalrymple says that he signed the armistice so soon after landing, and with such an incomplete knowledge of the situation in Portugal, that he did not know that Freire's army was anywhere in his neighbourhood (p. 65).

of these articles clearly required the ratification of some proper Portuguese authority to make it valid.

Both the Bishop of Oporto and General Freire were deeply wounded by the way in which Dalrymple ignored their status— the prelate more justly than the soldier, for he had done his best to assist the British army, while Freire by his captious and impracticable behaviour had been more of a hindrance than a help. The Bishop charged the representative of the Supreme Junta in London to complain to the British Government as to the behaviour of their generals, denouncing not only their neglect to make the Junta a party to the Convention, but also the terms of that document, which were stated to be far too favourable to Junot. Owing to Dalrymple's extraordinary delay in apprising the ministry of the details of the treaty, the Bishop's excited denunciations of the agreement had currency for nearly a fortnight, before any one in England knew what exactly had been granted to Junot, or how far the Junta was justified in its wrath.

SECTION IV: CHAPTER V

THE FRENCH EVACUATE PORTUGAL

THE Convention of Cintra being once signed, the difficulties which were bound to arise from the unwisdom of some of its articles were not long in showing themselves. Indeed the first fortnight of September turned out to be a very critical time.

The Portuguese authorities were furious: Dalrymple found the greatest trouble in preventing the insurgents of the Alemtejo, who had gathered opposite the mouth of the Tagus under the Conde de Castro Marim [1], from attacking the French detachments in the forts on the left bank. Their commander protested against the Convention, and actually appealed to Admiral Cotton to repudiate it: fortunately he was content to confine his opposition to words. But there was much more trouble at Elvas: the Junta of Estremadura did not object to the settlement, and liberated the French prisoners who were in its hands, according to the proposal in the eighteenth article. But Galluzzo, the Captain-General of that province, showed himself much more disobliging. He refused to call off the troops under his lieutenant De Arce, who were beleaguering Elvas, and behaved in the most dictatorial manner within Portuguese territory, raising not only requisitions of food but contributions of money. He even seized, at Campo Mayor, the military chest of the Portuguese general Leite, who commanded the wrecks of the force that had been beaten at Evora by Loison in July [2]. His detestable behaviour had the good effect of throwing the natives of the country on the English side, and Leite welcomed the arrival of troops from Lisbon, which enabled him to protest with effect against the misdoings and plunderings of the Spaniards. De Arce's troops were doing no real good: they only maintained

---

[1] Better known, from his court office, as the *Monteiro Mor*, which answers to our ' Master of the Horse.'

[2] See Leite's indignant letters to Dalrymple in Napier, vol. i. App. xii. De Arce is the real name of the Dearey of whom Napier speaks on p. 245. Cf. Dalrymple's *Memoir*, p. 82.

a distant and futile bombardment of the citadel of La Lippe, in which the garrison of Elvas had taken refuge. The French commandant, Girod de Novillars, laughed their efforts to scorn, and refused to listen to the proposals for a capitulation which they kept pressing upon him. In spite of orders from the Junta of Seville, bidding him abandon the siege and march for Madrid with his army, Galluzzo persisted in his ridiculous proceedings till nearly the end of September. It was only when Dalrymple moved up to the neighbourhood first the 20th Regiment, and then two whole brigades under Sir John Hope, that the Captain-General drew off his men and retired into Spanish territory [September 25]. Then Girod and his garrison, which was mainly composed of the 4th Swiss Regiment, were able to march to Lisbon under British escort and embark for France. They did not sail till October 9, so long had Galluzzo's freaks delayed them.

The garrison of Almeida departed about the same time: they had maintained themselves without difficulty against the Portuguese insurgents, but duly yielded up the place on the arrival of British troops. They were marched down to Oporto under an escort of 200 men, a force so weak that it nearly led to a disaster. For the mob of Oporto, under the pretext that church plate and other public plunder was being carried off by the French, fell upon them as they were embarking and nearly made an end of them. It required all the exertions of the escort, the Bishop of Oporto, and Sir Robert Wilson—who was then on the spot organizing his well-known 'Lusitanian Legion'—to prevent the populace from boarding the transports and slaying the whole of the French battalion. The baggage of the departing troops was seized and plundered, and they barely succeeded in escaping with their lives [1].

Meanwhile, long before the garrisons of Elvas and Almeida had been brought down to the coast, Junot and the main body of his army had departed. The commander-in-chief himself had sailed on September 13, the first division of his army on the fifteenth, the rest between that day and the thirtieth. The last weeks of the French occupation of Lisbon had been most uncomfortable for all parties concerned. The populace was seething with discontent,

---

[1] Foy, iv. 361, 362 ; Napier, i. 246, 247. Napier suppresses the part taken in saving the French by the Bishop and by Wilson, to neither of whom were his feelings friendly. Foy acknowledges the services of both. There is a good account of the whole by Wilson, in his papers at the Record Office.

assassinating isolated soldiers, and threatening a general rising. The French were under arms day and night, with cannon trained down every street and square. Unpopular officers, such as Loison, could not stir from their quarters without a large escort. Sullen at their defeat, and still more angry at having to abandon the heaps of plunder which they had amassed, the French were in a most disobliging mood in their dealings with the Portuguese, and in a less degree with the English. The main source of irritation was the very necessary measures which had to be taken for searching the baggage of the departing army. A commission had been formed, consisting of Kellermann on the one side and General Beresford and Lord Proby on the other, to settle in all disputed cases what was military equipment and legitimate personal property, and what was not. The English commissioners discovered the most astounding hoards of miscellaneous goods among the bags and boxes of the invaders [1]. The conduct of most of the French officers, from the commander-in-chief downwards, was most disgraceful. A few examples may suffice: Junot, by the twenty-first article of the Convention, had been granted leave to send a single officer to France with news for the Emperor. This officer, his aide-de-camp Lagrave, took with him for his general's private profit the most valuable set of books in the Royal Library of Lisbon, fourteen volumes of a manuscript Bible of the fifteenth century, illustrated with miniatures by the best Florentine artists—a gift to King Emanuel from one of the Renaissance popes. Junot's widow afterwards sold it to the French government for 85,000 francs. Lagrave, having started before the commissioners had begun to work, got off with his boxes unsearched. But other interesting items were discovered in the baggage of the Duke of Abrantes—one was £5,000 worth of indigo in fifty-three large chests, another was a quantity of valuable specimens of natural history from the public museum. General Delaborde was found to be in possession of a large collection of sacred pictures which had adorned Lisbon churches. Scattered through the baggage of many officers was a quantity of church plate—apparently part of the property seized

---

[1] Napier, with his customary tenderness for French susceptibilities, has only very general allusions to these disgraceful peculations. My details are mainly from Thiébault (iv. 198–200), who frankly confesses everything, and gives many scandalous particulars. He was, as Napoleon wrote, 'not delicate in money matters.'

to pay the war contributions which Napoleon had imposed on
Portugal: but it had in some mysterious way passed from public
into private possession [1]. In the military chest were gold bars to
the value of 1,000,000 francs which had come from the same
source, but the paymaster-general tried to get them out of the
country without paying the numerous accounts owed by his department to private individuals in Lisbon. They were not discharged
till this individual, one Thonnellier, had been put under arrest, and
threatened with detention after the rest of the army should have
sailed [2]. Another most scandalous proceeding discovered by the
commissioners was that Junot, after the signature of the Convention, had broken open the Deposito Publico, the chest of the
Supreme Court of Lisbon, which contained moneys whose rightful
ownership was in dispute between private litigants. He took from
it coin to the value of £25,000, which was only wrung out of him
with the greatest difficulty. Even after a vast amount had been
recovered, the French sailed with a military chest containing pay
for three months ahead for the whole army, though they had
entered Portugal penniless. For a general picture of their behaviour
it may suffice to quote the report of the British commissioners.
'The conduct of the French has been marked by the most shameful
disregard of honour and probity, publicly evincing their intention
of departing with their booty, and leaving acknowledged debts
unpaid. Finally they only paid what they were obliged to dis-
gorge. . . . Unmindful of every tie of honour or justice, the French
army has taken away a considerable sum in its military chest, still
leaving its debts unpaid to a very large amount [3].'

It was no wonder that the resentment of the Portuguese was so
great that the last French who embarked could only get away
under the protection of British bayonets, and that many of those
who straggled or lingered too long in remote corners of the town
lost their lives. The wild fury of the Lisbon mob surprised the
British officers who were charged with the embarkation [4]: they

[1] Cf. Thiébault, Napier, and some curious details given in the *Annual
Register* for 1808, with Proby and Beresford's Report.

[2] For previous acts and plans of this shameless person see Thiébault, iv.
151–3.

[3] Report of General Beresford and Lord Proby to Sir Hew Dalrymple
after the evacuation.

[4] For the tumults and murders at the embarkation see Col. Leslie's *Military
Journal*, pp. 66–76, and Col. Wilkie's *English in Spain*, p. 16.

knew little of what had been going on in the capital for the last
nine months, and could not understand the mad rage displayed
against the garrison.

But finally the last French bayonet disappeared from the streets
of Lisbon, and the populace, with no object left on which to vent
their fury, turned to illuminations, feasts, and the childish delights
of fireworks. They did not show themselves ungrateful to the
army of liberation; all the British officers who have described
the first weeks after the evacuation of Lisbon, bear witness to the
enthusiasm with which they were received, and the good feeling
displayed by their allies[1]. It was only in the highest Portuguese
quarters that dissatisfaction was rampant: the Bishop of Oporto,
General Freire, and the Monteiro Mor, had all suffered what they
considered an insult, when their consent was not asked to the
Convention of Cintra, and made no secret of their anger against
Dalrymple. But it does not seem that their feelings affected any
large section of the people.

The French army embarked for its native soil still 25,747 strong.
It had entered Portugal in the previous November with a strength
of nearly 25,000, and had received during the spring of 1808 some
4,500 recruits: in the month of May, before hostilities began, its
full force had been 26,594[2]. Of this total 20,090 were under arms
at the moment that the Convention was signed, 3,522 were in
hospital, sick or wounded: 916 were prisoners in the hands of the
English or the Portuguese. There remain, therefore, some 4,500
men to be accounted for: these, however, were not all dead. More
than 500 had deserted and taken service with the British before the
embarkation: they came, almost without exception, from the ranks
of the three foreign battalions which had been serving with Junot,
the 1st Hanoverians and the 2nd and 4th Swiss[3]. As the total
force of these corps had been only 2,548, it is clear that about
one man in five deserted. This was natural in the case of the
Germans, who were old subjects of George III, and most unwilling
recruits to the French army, but the equally well-marked defection

---

[1] See Col. Steevens' *Reminiscences*, pp. 54, 55 ; Col. Wilkie, p. 14 ; Col.
Leslie, pp. 65, 66.

[2] *Well. Suppl. Disp.*, vi. 207 (figures given for May 23), and Thiébault.

[3] Napier, i. 246 ; Foy, iv. 363. We have already had occasion to note
the proclivity of the 2nd Swiss to desert. The 4th Swiss, who had formed
the garrison of Elvas, showed exactly the same tendency.

of the Swiss is very notable. Most of the latter were enlisted for the 5th Battalion of the 60th Rifles, while the Hanoverians joined their countrymen in the ranks of the King's German Legion [1]. The real deficit, then, in Junot's army was about 4,000 men: this represents the total loss of life by the fights of Roliça and Vimiero, by the numerous combats with the Portuguese, by the stragglers cut off during the forced marches of July and August, and by the ordinary mortality in hospital. It must be considered on the whole a very moderate casualty list: Junot's corps, when it re-entered Spain to serve once more under the Emperor, was still 22,000 strong. It would have been even a trifle higher in numbers if a transport carrying two companies of the 86th Regiment had not foundered at sea, with the loss of every man on board.

It is necessary to give some account of the fate of Siniavin's Russian squadron, before dismissing the topic of the evacuation of Portugal. The admiral, as we have already had occasion to state, had steadfastly refused to throw in his lot with Junot and to join in the Convention of Cintra. He preferred to make an agreement of his own with Sir Charles Cotton. It was a simple document of two articles: the first provided that the nine sail of the line and one frigate, which formed the Russian fleet, should be given up, sent to England, and 'held as a deposit' by his Britannic majesty, to be restored within six months of a peace between Great Britain and Russia. The second was to the effect that Siniavin, his officers and crews, should be sent back to Russia on English ships without being in any way considered prisoners of war, or debarred from further service.

Admiral Cotton, it is clear, regarded the ships as important and the crews as worthy of small attention. It was profitable to Great Britain to keep down the number of vessels in the power of Napoleon, though now that the Danish fleet was captured, and the Spanish fleet transferred to the other side of the balance, there could be no longer any immediate danger of the French taking the offensive at sea. The easy terms of release granted to the *personnel* of the Russian squadron suggest that the British admiral had determined to reward its commander for his persistent refusal to help Junot. It almost appears that Cotton looked upon Siniavin

---

[1] A table in the *Parliamentary Papers relative to Spain and Portugal* shows that the Legion received 163 recruits from this source. The 5/60th obtained a much larger number, having still over 200 Swiss with them in 1809.

as a secret friend, and treated him accordingly. Milder terms could hardly have been devised, for the moment that the harbour-forts of Lisbon were surrendered to the British, the Russians must obviously be made prisoners, since they could not get out of the river. It is probable that the two admirals thoroughly understood each other's mind, and that the Russian was undisguisedly pleased at the disaster of his detested French allies.

The most pressing necessity in Portugal, after the French had departed, was the construction of a new national government, for it was clear that the Supreme Junta at Oporto represented in reality only the northern provinces of the realm, and could not be accepted —as its president, the Bishop, suggested—as a permanent and legitimate executive for the whole kingdom. Constitutionally speaking, if one may use such a phrase when dealing with a country like Portugal, the only body which possessed a clear title of au-thority was the Council of Regency, which Prince John had nomi-nated nine months before, on the eve of his departure for Brazil. But this council had long ceased to act ; its members were dis-persed ; several had compromised themselves by submitting to the French and taking office under Junot ; and its composition gave no promise of vigorous action for the future. If a choice must be made between the Junta at Oporto, which was active and patriotic, though perhaps too much given up to self-assertion and intrigue, and the effete old Regency, there could be no doubt that the former possessed more claims to the confidence of the Portuguese nation and its English allies. But it was not necessary to adopt either alternative in full : Wellesley, who had already got a firm grip upon the outlines of Portuguese politics, advised Dalrymple to invite the old Regency, with the exception of those members who had compromised themselves with the French, to reassemble, and to bring pressure upon them to co-opt to the vacant places the Bishop of Oporto and the other prominent members of the Junta. This proposal would have secured legality of form (since the old Regency would theoretically have continued to exist), while intro-ducing new and vigorous elements of undoubted patriotism into the body [1]. But Dalrymple preferred to reinstate, by a procla-mation of his own, those members of the Regency who had never

---

[1] Wellesley to Lord Castlereagh, Sept. 9 (*Well. Disp.*, iv. 137). In spite of Napier's denunciation of the Bishop, Wellesley bears good witness in his favour, e. g. iv. 146.

wavered in their allegiance to Prince John [Sept. 18]. He called
upon all public bodies and officials in the realm to obey this recon-
stituted executive.   Here was an undoubted mistake; it was
wounding to Portuguese pride to see the central governing body
of the kingdom created by the edict of an English general:
Dalrymple should surely have allowed the Regents to apprise the
nation, by a proclamation of their own, that they had resumed their
former functions.   However, they fell in with Wellesley's plans so
far as to co-opt the Bishop of Oporto as a colleague, though
refusing any places to the rest of his Junta. The whole body now
consisted of three original members, the Conde de Castro Marim
(otherwise known as the Monteiro Mor), Francisco Da Cunha, and
Xavier de Noronha, of two persons chosen from a list of possible
substitutes, which the Prince-Regent had left behind, Joam de
Mendonça and General Miguel Forjas Coutinho, and of two
co-opted members, the Bishop and the Conde das Minas, an old
nobleman who had shown a very determined spirit in resisting
Junot during the days of his power.

On the reconstitution of the Regency the Junta of Oporto, with
more self-denial than had been expected, dissolved itself. The
minor juntas in the Algarve, the Alemtejo, and the Tras-os-Montes
followed its example, and Portugal was once more in possession of
a single executive, whose authority was freely recognized throughout the kingdom.   Unfortunately it turned out to be slow, timid,
and divided into cliques which were always at variance with each other.

We have already seen that owing to various causes of delay, of
which Galluzzo's preposterous proceedings at Elvas were the most
prominent, the last French troops did not quit Portugal till September had expired, and that Junot himself and the main body of
his army had only begun to leave on the fifteenth of that month.
It would have been impossible for Dalrymple to advance into
Spain till the French had left Lisbon, however urgently his
presence might have been required.   But it would perhaps have
proved feasible to push forward towards the Spanish frontier a
considerable part of his army, and to make preparations for the
movement of the whole towards Madrid or Salamanca as soon as
the evacuation should be complete.   Dalrymple, however, was as
leisurely as the generals of the old days before the Revolutionary
War. He kept his troops cantoned about Lisbon, only pushing
forward two brigades towards Elvas in order to bring Galluzzo to

reason, and dispatching the 6th Regiment as a garrison to Almeida. He seems to have been quite as much interested in the administration of Portugal as in the further prosecution of the war in Spain. We find him much busied in the reconstruction of the Portuguese government and army, reviewing and rearming the Spanish division of Caraffa before shipping it off to Catalonia [Sept. 22], and spending a great deal of time over the redistribution into brigades and divisions of his army, which had now swelled to something like 35,000 men, by the arrival of Moore's force and certain regiments from Madeira, Gibraltar, and England. He was also engaged in endeavours to organize a proper commissariat for this large body of men, a hard task, for every brigade arrived in the same state of destitution as to means of transport as had those which landed with Wellesley at Mondego Bay on the first of August. But in all his actions there was evident a want of vigour and of purposeful resource, which was very distressing to those of his subordinates who were anxious for a rapid and decisive advance towards the main theatre of war in Spain.

No one felt this more clearly than Wellesley, whose views as to his commander's competence had never changed since that hour on the morning of August 22, when Dalrymple had refused to march on Mafra, and had decided to delay his advance till the advent of Moore. Since then he had offered his advice on several points, and had almost always seen it refused. Dealing with the disputed details of the Convention of Cintra, he had spoken in favour of meeting the French demands with high-handed decision : hence he was vexed by Dalrymple's tendency towards weakness and compromise. One of his special grievances was that he had been ordered to sign the armistice of August 22 as representing the British army, although he had privately protested against its details [1]. His unofficial letters home during the first half of September are full of bitter remarks on the weakness of the policy that had been adopted, and the many faults of the Convention [2]. Seeing that warlike operations appeared

---

[1] Wellesley to the Bishop of Oporto, Sept. 6 : 'I was present during the negotiation of the agreement, and by the desire of the Commander-in-chief I signed it. But I did not negotiate it, nor can I in any manner be considered responsible for its contents' (*Well. Disp.*, iv. 134). Wellesley to Castlereagh, Oct. 6 : 'I do not consider myself responsible in any degree for the terms in which it was framed, or for any of its provisions.'

[2] Wellesley to Mr. Stuart (*Well. Disp.*, iv. 120). To Lord Castlereagh (iv. 118). To the Duke of Richmond (*Suppl. Disp.*, vi. 129).

likely to be postponed for an indefinite time, he at last asked and
obtained leave to return to England, after declining in somewhat
acid terms an offer made to him by Dalrymple that he should go
to Madrid, to concert a plan for combined operations with Castaños
and the other Spanish generals. 'In order to be able to perform
the important part allotted to him,' he 'wrote, 'the person sent
should possess the confidence of those who employ him, and be
acquainted with their plans, the means by which they hope to carry
them into execution, and those by which they intend to enable the
Spanish nation to execute that which will be proposed to them.
I certainly cannot consider myself as possessing these advantages [1].'
Wellesley also refused another and a less tempting offer of a
mission to the Asturias, for the purpose of seeing what facilities
that province would offer as the base of operations for a British
army.   He was not a 'draftsman,' he wrote, or a 'topographical
engineer,' and he could not pretend to describe in writing the
character of such a region.   In short he was set on going home,
and would not turn from his purpose.   But before leaving Portugal
he wrote two remarkable letters.   One was to Sir John Moore, the
third in command of the army, telling him that he regarded him
as the right person to take charge of the British forces in the
Peninsula, and would use every effort with the ministers to get the
post secured to him.   'It is quite impossible that we can go on as
we are now constituted: the commander-in-chief must be changed,
and the country and the army naturally turn their eyes to you as
their commander [2].'   The second and longer was a letter to his
patron Castlereagh, in which he laid down his views as to the
general state of the war in Spain, and the way in which the British
army could be best employed.   It is a wonderful document, as he
foretells in it all the disasters that were about to befall the Spaniards
from their reckless self-confidence.   The only real fighting-force
that they possessed was, he said, the army of Castaños: the rest,
with the possible exception of Blake's Galicians, were 'armies of
peasantry,' which could not be relied upon to meet the French in
the field.   Though they might on some occasions fight with success

---

[1] Wellesley to Dalrymple (*Well. Disp.*, iv. 138).
[2] Wellesley to Moore, Sept. 17, 1808 (*Well. Disp.*, p. 142).   Moore, as
a noted Whig, was imagined not to be a *persona grata* at head quarters ;
Wellesley offers, in the most handsome way, to endeavour to smooth matters
for him.

in their own mountains, ' yet in others a thousand French with
cavalry and artillery will disperse thousands of them.' They would
not, and indeed could not, leave their native provinces, and no
officer could calculate upon them for the carrying out of a great
combined operation. How then could the British army of Portugal
be best employed to aid such allies? The only efficient plan,
Wellesley concludes, would be to place it upon the flank and rear
of any French advance to Madrid, by moving it up to the valley
of the Douro, and basing it upon Asturias and Galicia. Posted in
the kingdom of Leon, with its ports of supply at Gihon, Corunna,
and Ferrol, it should co-operate with Blake, and hang upon the
right flank of the French army which was forming upon the line
of the Ebro. The result would be to prevent the invaders from
moving forward, even perhaps (here Wellesley erred from ignorance
of the enemy's numbers) to oblige them to retire towards their own
frontier. But Bonaparte could, unless occupied by the affairs of
Central Europe, increase his armies in Spain to any extent. The
moment that he heard of an English force in the field, he would
consider its destruction as his first object, and so multiply his
numbers in the Peninsula that the British commander would have
to give back. 'There must be a line of retreat open, and that
retreat must be the sea.' Accordingly, Sir Arthur recommended
that the Asturias should be made the ultimate base, and the
transports and stores sent to its port of Gihon [1].

This letter was different in its general character from the other
reports which Castlereagh was receiving: most of the correspondents of the Secretary for War could write of nothing but
the enthusiastic patriotism of the Spaniards and their enormous
resources: they spoke of the French as a dispirited remnant, ready

---

[1] This letter, written to Castlereagh from Zambujal (*Well. Disp.*, iv. 127–32),
is one of the most conclusive proofs of Wellesley's military genius. He
valued the Spanish armies at their true force. He foresaw that Bonaparte
would make ' the driving of the leopard into the sea ' a point of honour, and
would send corps on corps into Spain in order to secure it. He even noted
that the affairs of Central Europe, ' of which I have no knowledge whatever,'
would be the only possible reason that might prevent the Emperor from
inundating the Peninsula with his legions. He saw that the presence of the
British in Leon would be the one thing that would keep the French from
subduing Central Spain : a disaster in the Douro valley was the nightmare of
the Emperor, as half a dozen of his dispatches show. The first news that
Moore was near Valladolid drew Napoleon from Madrid in wild haste, and
deferred for six months the conquest of the valley of the Guadiana.

to fly, at the first attack, behind the line of the Pyrenees. It is therefore greatly to the credit of Castlereagh that he did not hesitate to pin his faith upon Wellesley's intelligence, and to order the execution of the very plan that he recommended. It was practically carried out in the great campaign of Sir John Moore, after the collapse of the Spanish armies·had justified every word that Sir Arthur had written about them.

Wellesley sailed from Lisbon on September 20, and reached Plymouth on October 4. On his arrival in England he was met with news of a very mixed character. On the one hand he was rejoiced to hear that both Dalrymple and Burrard had been recalled, and that Sir John Moore had been placed in command of the British forces in the Peninsula. He wrote at once to the latter, to say that there could be no greater satisfaction than to serve under his orders, and that he would return at once to Spain to join him : 'he would forward with zeal every wish' of his new commander [1]. It was also most gratifying to Wellesley to know that the dispatch of September 25, by which Moore was given the command of the army of Portugal, directed him to move into Northern Spain and base himself upon the Asturias and Galicia, the very plan which formed the main thesis of the document that we have been discussing. There can be no doubt that Castlereagh had recognized the strategical and political verities that were embodied in Wellesley's letter, and had resolved to adopt the line therein recommended.

[1] Wellesley to Moore, Oct. 8 (*Well. Suppl. Disp.*, vi. 150, 151).

SECTION IV : CHAPTER VI

THE COURT OF INQUIRY

THERE was another and a less pleasant surprise in store for
Wellesley when he landed at Plymouth. He learnt that if he
himself disliked the armistice of August 22, and the Convention
of Cintra, the British public had gone far beyond him, and was in
a state of frantic rage concerning them. To his anger and amaze-
ment he also learnt that he himself was considered no less responsible
for the two agreements than were Dalrymple and Burrard. The
fact that the former had told him to set his signature opposite to
that of Kellermann on the document signed at Vimiero, had misled
the world into regarding him as the negotiator and framer of the
armistice. 'Every whisperer who disliked the name of Wellesley[1]'
—and Sir Arthur's brother, the Governor-General, had made it very
unpopular in certain quarters—was busy propagating the story that
of the three generals who had lately commanded in Portugal, each
one was as slack and supine as the others.

The wave of indignation which swept across England on the
receipt of the news of the Convention of Cintra is, at this distance
of time, a little hard to understand. Successes had not been so
plentiful on the Continent during the last fifteen years, that an
agreement which gave back its liberty to a whole kingdom need
have been criticized with vindictive minuteness. But the news of
Baylen had set the public mind on the look-out for further triumphs,
and when the dispatches which gave an account of Roliça and of
Vimiero had come to hand, there had been a confident expectation
that the next news received would be that Junot's army had been
scattered or captured, and that Lisbon had been set free. Then
came a gap of thirteen days, caused by Dalrymple's strange fit of
silence. The only intelligence that reached London in this interval
was the Bishop of Oporto's letter of protest against the armistice,
in which, without giving any definite details about that agreement,

[1] The Duke of Richmond to Wellesley, Oct. 12, 1808 (*Well. Suppl. Disp.*,
vi. 633).

he denounced it as insulting to Portugal and unworthy of England.
The public was prepared, therefore, to hear that something timid
and base had been done, when Dalrymple's dispatch of September 3,
enclosing the Convention of Cintra, came to hand.   It was easy to
set forth the terms of that treaty in an odious light.   Junot, it was
said, had been beaten in the field, he was completely isolated from
all the other French armies, and his surrender must have followed
in a few days, if the British generals had only chosen to press their
advantage.   Instead of this, they preferred to let him return to
France with the whole of his troops, and with most of his plunder.
He was not even compelled to release a corresponding number of
British prisoners in return for the freedom secured to his army.
In fact, his position was much better after than before his defeat
at Vimiero, for the Convention granted him a quiet and safe return
home with his force intact, while, even if he had won some success
in battle, the best that he would have been able to secure himself
would have been a retreat on Northern Spain, through the midst
of great dangers.   Excitable politicians and journalists used the
most exaggerated language, and compared the Convention with
that of Kloster Seven, and the conduct of the generals who had
not pressed the campaign to its logical end with Admiral Byng's
shirking before Minorca.   Caricatures were issued showing
Dalrymple, Burrard, and Wellesley sporting the white feather,
or hanging from three gibbets as traitors[1].   Nor was Admiral
Cotton spared: he was denounced in bitter terms for taking the
Russian ships as 'deposits,' when he should have towed them into
Spithead as prizes: moreover the repatriation of the Russian crews
was asserted to be a deadly blow at our unfortunate ally the King
of Sweden.

The rage against the Convention was not confined to any one
class or faction in the state.   If some Whigs tried to turn it into
the shape of an attack on the government, there were plenty of
Tories who joined in the cry, begging their leaders in the ministry
to dismiss and punish the three unpopular generals.   A number
of public meetings were held with the object of forcing the hands
of the Duke of Portland and his colleagues, but the most prominent
part in the agitation was taken by the Corporation of London.

---

[1] Toreño, then acting as agent for the Asturian Junta in London, has
much interesting information on this point.   He saw the gibbet caricature
and papers published with black edges (i. 251).

Recalling the old days of Wilkes and Beckford, they resolved that the Lord Mayor, with a deputation of Sheriffs, Aldermen, and Common-Councillors, should present a petition to the King begging him to order 'an inquiry into this dishonourable and unprecedented transaction, for the discovery and punishment of those by whose misconduct and incapacity the cause of the kingdom and its allies has been so shamelessly sacrificed.'

Accordingly such a petition was laid before the King on October 12. Its terms are worth a moment's attention, as they show very clearly the points on which popular indignation had been concentrated. 'The treaty,' it states, 'is humiliating and degrading, because after a signal victory, by which the enemy appears to have been cut off from all means of succour or escape, we had the sad mortification of seeing the laurels so nobly acquired torn from the brows of our brave soldiers, and terms granted to the enemy disgraceful to the British name. . . . By this ignominious Convention British ships are to convey to France the French army and its plunder, where they will be at liberty immediately to recommence their active operations against us and our allies. And the full recognition of the title and dignity of Emperor of France [1], while all mention of the Government of Portugal is omitted, must be considered as highly disrespectful to the authorities of that country.' There was another clause denouncing the sending back of the Russian sailors, but not so much stress was laid on this point. Finally the King is asked 'in justice to the outraged feelings of a brave, injured, and indignant people, whose blood and treasure have been thus expended,' to cause the guilty persons to be punished.

King George III replied to these flowers of oratory by a short speech which displays admirably that power of getting an occasional lucid glimpse of the obvious in which he was by no means deficient. He was fully sensible, he said, of the loyalty and good intentions of the City of London, but he wished the deputation to remember that to pronounce judgement without previous trial and investigation was hardly consonant with the principles of British justice. He was always ready to institute an inquiry when the honour of the British arms was in question: and the interposition of the

---

[1] The petitioners ought in fairness to have stated that this was only made in the document setting forth the armistice, and not in the definitive Convention.

City of London was not necessary to induce him to set one on foot in this case, when the hopes and expectations of the nation had been so much disappointed.

It was not, however, till seventeen days later that his majesty's formal orders for the summoning of a Court of Inquiry 'to investigate into the late Armistice and Convention concluded in Portugal, and all the circumstances connected therewith,' were communicated to the Commander-in-Chief. Dalrymple and Burrard, both of whom had now returned to England, were directed to hold themselves in readiness to present themselves before the court, and Wellesley, for the same reason, was directed to abandon his project of going back to the Peninsula in order to serve under Sir John Moore.

The members of the celebrated Court of Inquiry, which commenced its sittings on November 14, 1808, were seven in number, all general officers of great respectability and advanced years, men more likely, for the most part, to sympathize with caution than with daring. The president was Sir David Dundas, the author of a celebrated drill-book which had long been the terror of young officers : the other members were Lord Moira, Lord Heathfield [1], the Earl of Pembroke, and Generals Craig, Sir G. Nugent, and Nicholls. Not one of them has left behind a name to be remembered, save indeed Lord Moira, who, as Lord Rawdon in the old American War, had won the victory of Hobkirk's Hill, and who was destined to be the next Viceroy of India and to make the name of Hastings famous for a second time in the East.

The court began its sittings on November 14, and did not terminate them till December 22. In the great hall of Chelsea Hospital, where its proceedings were held, there was much warm debate. As the details of the Campaign of Portugal were gradually worked out, not only by the cross-examination of Dalrymple, Burrard, and Wellesley, but by that of many of the other officers of rank who had been in Portugal—Spencer, Acland, Ferguson, Lord Burghersh, and others—the points on which the verdict of the court must turn gradually became clear. They were six in number :—Had Burrard been justified in preventing Wellesley from pursuing the French at the end of the battle of Vimiero ? Had Dalrymple erred in refusing to take Wellesley's advice to march

---

[1] Not, of course, the Eliot who had defended Gibraltar so well in 1780–3, but his son, the second Lord Heathfield.

on Mafra the next morning ? Should Kellermann's offer of an
armistice have been accepted on the twenty-second, and, if so, were
the terms granted him too favourable ?   Lastly, was the Convention
of Cintra itself justifiable under the existing circumstances, and
were all its articles reasonable and proper ?   Much evidence was
produced for and against each view on every one of these topics.
On the first two Wellesley practically impeached Burrard and
Dalrymple for unwarrantable slackness and timidity. He was so
much in love with his own bold plans that his superior's caution
appeared to him contemptible. He stood up to them and cross-
questioned them with an acidity and a complete want of deference
that seemed very reprehensible to military men steeped in the old
traditions of unquestioning deference to one's senior officers. Sir
Walter Scott, who followed the inquiry with great interest, called
him ' a haughty devil,' but expressed his admiration for him at the
same moment [1]. It is curious to find that Wellesley showed less
anger with Burrard, whose caution on the afternoon of the twenty-
first really wrecked his plan of campaign, than with Dalrymple.
The latter had snubbed him on his first arrival, had persistently
refused him his confidence, and would not state clearly to the court
that the armistice, though it bore Wellesley's name, had not been
drawn up or approved in detail by him. Of the numerous minor
witnesses who were examined, all who had served at Roliça and
Vimiero spoke on Wellesley's side : Spencer and Ferguson were
especially strong in their statements. The fact was that they were
intensely proud of their two fights, and looked upon Burrard as
the man who had prevented them from entering Lisbon in triumph
after capturing Junot and his whole host. So strong was this
feeling that the brigadiers and field-officers of the eight brigades
that fought at Vimiero had presented Wellesley with a handsome
testimonial—a service of plate worth £1,000—as a sort of mark of
confidence in him, and of protest against those who had stayed his
hand.

On the other hand, Burrard and Dalrymple urged all the justifications of caution. Each had arrived at a crisis, the details of
which could not be properly known to him from sheer want of
time to master them. Each acknowledged that Wellesley had
vehemently pressed him to strike boldly and promptly, but thought
that he had not been justified in doing so till he had made out for

[1] Lockhart's *Life of Sir Walter Scott*, ii. 226.

himself the exact situation of affairs. Burrard pleaded that Junot might have possessed reserves unknown to him, which might have changed the fortune of the fight if a headlong pursuit had been ordered. Wellesley had told him that none such existed (and this turned out to have been the fact), but he himself had not seen any clear proof of it at the time [1]. Dalrymple went even further, and stated that he had considered the whole conduct of the campaign, from the landing in Mondego Bay till the battle of Vimiero, terribly rash [2]. If he had permitted the army to march on Mafra on the twenty-second, the French from Torres Vedras might have taken him in the flank as he passed through a very difficult country, and the most disastrous results might have ensued. He was positive that nothing hazardous ought to have been attempted, and that it was necessary to wait for Sir John Moore's division before pressing the French to extremity.

With regard to the armistice and the Convention, all the three generals, when defending themselves, agreed that they were wise and justifiable. To clear the French out of Portugal without further fighting, and to recover Lisbon and all its resources intact, were ends so important that it was well worth while to sacrifice even the practical certainty of capturing all Junot's army, after a resistance that might have been long and desperate. But as to the wisdom of certain clauses and articles, both in the document of August 22 and that of August 30, there was considerable difference of opinion. Wellesley proved that he had opposed many details of each agreement, and that he was in no way responsible for the final shape taken by them. He only assented to the general proposition that it was right to let the French army depart under a convention, rather than to force it to a capitulation. He considered that Dalrymple had yielded far too much, from his unwillingness to 'drive Junot into a corner.'

On December 22 the Court of Inquiry issued its report. It was a very cautious and a rather inconclusive document. But its main point was that nothing had been done in Portugal which called for the punishment of any of the parties concerned: 'On a consideration of all the circumstances, we most humbly submit our opinion that no further military proceeding is necessary,' i. e. there was no ground for a court-martial on any one of the three British generals. As to

[1] Burrard before the Court of Inquiry (*Proceedings*, pp. 115, 116, 135).

[2] Dalrymple before the Court of Inquiry (*Well. Disp.*, iv. 178, 180, 181).

Burrard's refusal to pursue the French on the afternoon of Vimiero, there were 'fair military grounds' for his decision: the court omitted to say whether the decision itself was right or wrong. 'It could not pronounce with confidence whether or not a pursuit could have been efficacious.' As to the halt on the following day, for which Dalrymple no less than Burrard was responsible, 'under the extraordinary circumstances that two new commanding generals arrived from the ocean and joined the army within the space of twenty-four hours, it is not surprising that the army was not carried forward until the second day after the action, from the necessity of the generals becoming acquainted with the actual state of things, and of their army, and proceeding accordingly.' Finally, as to the Convention, 'howsoever some of us may differ in our sentiments respecting its fitness in the relative situation of the two armies, it is our unanimous declaration that unquestionable zeal and firmness appear to have been exhibited throughout both by Sir Hew Dalrymple, Sir Harry Burrard, and Sir Arthur Wellesley.' There was a special compliment inserted for Wellesley's benefit, to the effect that his whole action, from the landing in Mondego Bay down to the battle of Vimiero, was 'highly honourable and successful, and such as might have been expected from a distinguished officer.'

Such a report amounted to a plain acquittal of all the three generals, but it left so much unsaid that the Government directed the Commander-in-Chief to require from the members of the court their decision as to whether the armistice of the twenty-second and the Convention of the thirtieth were advisable, and, if they were advisable, whether their terms were proper, and honourable. On the twenty-seventh the court returned its answer: there was, this time, no unanimous report, but a series of written opinions, for the members of the body differed from each other on many points. As to the armistice, six members replied that they approved of it, one, but he the most distinguished of the seven—Lord Moira— said that he did not. On the question as to the definitive Convention there was more difference of opinion: Dundas, Lord Heathfield, Craig, and Nugent thought it fair and reasonable; Lord Moira, the Earl of Pembroke, and Nicholls considered it as unjustifiable, considering the relative situations of the two armies. The two last-named officers added short explanatory notes to their opinions, while Lord Moira subjoined to his a long and elaborate argument, a document which does not seem in the least to deserve the slighting reference made to it by Napier [1]. It is very sensible in its general drift.   Lord Moira contended that while on August 22 there was no reason why an armistice should not have been concluded, yet the paper drawn up by Kellermann contained clauses that limited unduly the demands which the British commander might make in the subsequent Convention.   Dalrymple ought, before conceding them, to have reflected that Junot's anxious and hurried offer of terms betokened demoralization.   If the French had been pressed, and a confident and haughty answer returned to their envoy, Junot would have accepted any conditions that might be imposed upon him.   His army was in such a state of disorder and dismay that it was most unlikely that he would have tried either to burn Lisbon or to retreat across the Alemtejo.   Moreover, the contention that the deliverance of Portugal was the one object of the expedition, and that it was duly secured by the Convention, was a mistake. Lord Moira wished to point out that our armies were sent forth, not only to emancipate Portugal, but also to destroy the forces and lower the prestige of France by every means in their power. By forcing Junot to a capitulation, or by making the terms of the Convention more stringent, a much greater blow might have been dealt to Bonaparte's reputation.   As an instance of what might have been done, he suggested that some remote and inconvenient landing-place—Belle Isle for example—might have been imposed upon the French troops, or they might have been compelled to engage not to serve for some specified time against England and her allies.

The Court of Inquiry had thus delivered its last opinion.   But the matter of the Convention was not even yet at an end.   The ministry resolved to inflict a rebuke on Dalrymple, not for his military action, on which they completely accepted the verdict of the seven generals, but for his political action in allowing the Articles XV, XVI, and XVII to be inserted in the Convention. These, it will be remembered, were the clauses which conceded certain privileges to the French inhabitants of Lisbon, and to the Portuguese who had compromised themselves by taking service under Junot.   The Duke of York, as commander-in-chief, was

---

[1] He calls it ' a laboured criticism, which nevertheless left the pith of the question entirely untouched ' (Napier, i. 249).   I have printed Lord Moira's plea in an Appendix, to show that it is well-reasoned and practical.

ordered to convey to Dalrymple 'His Majesty's disapprobation of those articles in the Convention in which stipulations were made affecting the interests and feelings of the Spanish and Portuguese nations[1].' It was to be impressed upon Sir Hew that it was most improper and dangerous to admit into a military convention articles of such a description, which (especially when carelessly and incautiously framed) might lead to the most injurious consequences. Furthermore, Dalrymple was to be gravely censured for his extraordinary delay in not sending the news of the armistice of the twenty-second till September 3, whereby 'great public inconvenience' had been caused.

It cannot be denied that these rebukes were well deserved: we have already pointed out that the three articles to which allusion is made were the only part of the Convention for which no defence is possible. It is equally clear that it was the thirteen days' gap in the information sent home which gave time for the rise and development of the unreasoning popular agitation against the whole agreement made with Junot.

As to the verdict of the court, it does substantial justice to the case. There existed 'fair military reasons' for all that Burrard and Dalrymple had done, or left undone. In a similar way 'fair military reasons' can be alleged for most of the main slips and errors committed during any campaign in the Napoleonic War—for Dupont's stay at Andujar, or for Murray's retreat from Tarragona, or for Grouchy's operations on June 17 and 18, 1815. It would be unjust to punish old and respectable generals for mere errors of judgement, and inability to rise to the height of the situation. Burrard and Dalrymple had sacrificed the most brilliant possibilities by their torpid caution, after refusing to listen to Wellesley's cogent arguments for bold action. But their conduct had resulted neither from cowardice nor from deliberate perversity. The blame must rest quite as much on the government, which had entrusted the expedition to elderly men unaccustomed to command in the field, as on those men themselves. And as to the details of the armistice and Convention, we may well accept Wellesley's verdict, that the gain secured by the rescue of Lisbon with all its wealth intact, and by the prompt termination of the campaign, fully justified the resolve not to drive Junot to extremity.

But there was an unexpressed corollary to the verdict of the

[1] *The King's Opinion on the Convention of Cintra*, paragraphs 4, 5, and 6.

court which the ministry fully realized, and upon which they acted.   Burrard and Dalrymple, with their 'fair military reasons,' must never again appear in the field.   It was not by such men that Bonaparte would be foiled and Spain emancipated, and so they were relegated to home service and quiet retirement for the rest of their lives.   Wellesley, on the other hand, was marked out as a man of energy, resource, and determination, eminently fit to be employed again.   Within four months of the termination of the proceedings of the Court of Inquiry he was once more in command of the British army in the Peninsula[1].

[1] The proceedings terminated Dec. 27, 1808.   Wellesley took up the command at Lisbon on April 25, 1809.

SECTION V

THE STRUGGLE IN CATALONIA

CHAPTER I

DUHESME'S OPERATIONS: FIRST SIEGE OF GERONA
(JUNE–JULY, 1808)

THERE is still one corner of the Iberian Peninsula whose history, during the eventful summer months of 1808, we have not yet chronicled. The rugged and warlike province of Catalonia had already begun that heroic struggle against its French garrison which was to endure throughout the whole of the war. Far more than any other section of the Spanish nation do the Catalans deserve credit for their unswerving patriotism. Nowhere else was the war maintained with such resolution. When the struggle commenced the French were already masters by treachery of the chief fortresses of the land: the force of Spanish regular troops which lay within its borders was insignificant: there was no recognized leader, no general of repute, to head the rising of the province. Yet the attack on the invaders was delivered with a fierceness and a persistent energy that was paralleled in no other quarter of the Peninsula. For six years marshal after marshal ravaged the Catalan valleys, sacked the towns, scattered the provincial levies. But not for one moment did the resistance slacken; the invaders could never control a foot of ground beyond the narrow space that was swept by the cannon of their strongholds. The spirit of the race was as unbroken in 1813 as in 1808, and their untiring bands still held out in the hills, ready to strike at the enemy when the least chance was offered. Other provinces had equal or greater advantages than Catalonia for protracted resistance: Biscay, the Asturias, and Galicia were as rugged, Andalusia far more populous, Valencia more fertile and wealthy. But in none of these was the struggle carried on with such a combination of energy and persistence as in the Catalan hills. Perhaps the greatest testimony that can be quoted in behalf of the people of that devoted province is that Napier, bitter critic as he was of all things Spanish, is forced to say a good word for it. 'The Catalans,' he writes, 'were vain and superstitious; but their courage was higher, their patriotism purer, and their efforts more sustained than those of the rest. The *somatenes* were bold and active in battle, the population of the towns firm, and the juntas apparently disinterested [1].' No one but a careful student of Napier will realize what a handsome testimonial is contained in the somewhat grudging language of this paragraph. What the real credit due to the Catalans was, it will now be our duty to display.

It will be remembered that in the month of February the French general Duhesme had obtained possession of the citadel and forts of Barcelona by a particularly impudent and shameless stratagem [2]. Since that time he had been lying in the city that he had seized, with his whole force concentrated under his hand. Of the 7,000 French and 5,000 Italian troops which composed his corps, all were with him save a single battalion of detachments which had been left behind to garrison Figueras, the fortress close to the French frontier, which commands the most important of the three roads by which the principality of Catalonia can be entered.

Duhesme believed himself to be entirely secure, for of Spanish regular troops there were barely 6,000 in all scattered through the province [3], and a third of these were Swiss mercenaries, who, according to the orders of Bonaparte, were to be taken at once into the French service. That there was any serious danger to be feared from the *miqueletes* of the mountains never entered into the heads of the Emperor or his lieutenant. Nor does it seem to have occurred to them that any insurrection which broke out in Cata-

---

[1] Napier, *History of the Peninsular War*, i. 90.

[2] See pp. 36, 37 of this book.

[3] They were the following:—

Regiment of Estremadura . . .	840 strong	at Tarrega (near Lerida).
Regiment of Ultonia	421 ,,	Gerona.
Two battalions of Wimpfen's Swiss Regiment	2,149 ,,	Tarragona.
Two battalions of Spanish and Walloon Guards	1,700 ,,	Barcelona.
Cavalry Regiment of Borbon . . .	658 ,,	,,
Artillery	300 ,,	in various forts on coast.

6,068

lonia might be immediately supported from the Balearic Isles, where a heavy garrison was always kept, in order to guard against any descent of the British to recover their old stronghold of Port Mahon[1]. If Napoleon had realized in May that the Spanish rising was about to sweep over the whole Peninsula, he would not have dared to leave Duhesme with such a small force. But persisting in his original blunder of believing that the troubles which had broken out were merely local and sporadic, he was about to order Duhesme to make large detachments from a corps that was already dangerously weak.

The geography of Catalonia, as we have had occasion to relate in an earlier chapter, is rather complicated. Not only is the principality cut off by its mountains from the rest of Spain—it faces towards the sea, while its neighbour Aragon faces towards the Ebro—but it is divided by its numerous cross-ranges into a number of isolated valleys, between which communication is very difficult. Its coast-plain along the Mediterranean is generally narrow, and often cut across by spurs which run down from the mountains of the inland till they strike the sea. Except on the eastern side of the principality, where it touches Aragon in the direction of Lerida, there is no broad expanse of level ground within its borders: much the greater part of its surface is upland and mountain.

Catalonia may be divided into four regions : the first is the district at the foot of the Eastern Pyrenees, drained by the Fluvia and the Ter. This narrow corner is called the Ampurdam ; it contains all the frontier-fortresses which protect the province on the side of France. Rosas commands the pass along the sea-shore, Figueras the main road from Perpignan, which runs some twenty miles further inland. A little further south both these roads

---

[1] The Spanish garrisons in the Balearic Isles consisted of the following troops :—

Regiment of Granada (three batts.)	1,183	at Port Mahon.
Regiment of Soria (three batts.)	1,381	,,
Regiment of Borbon (three batts.)	1,570	at Palma.
Swiss Regiment of Beschard (two batts.)	2,121	,,
Light Infantry of Barcelona, No. 2	1,341	at Port Mahon.
,, ,, Aragon, No. 2	1,267	at Palma.
Militia Battalion of Majorca	604	,,
6th Hussars (*Husares Españoles*)	680	,,
Artillery	500	,, and Port Mahon.
	10,647	

meet, and are blocked by the strong city of Gerona, the capital of all this region and its most important strategical point. South of Gerona a cross-range divides the Ampurdam from the coast-plain of Central Catalonia; the defile through this range is covered by the small fortified town of Hostalrich, but there is an alternative route from Gerona to Barcelona along the coast by Blanes and Arens de Mar. (2) The river-basin of Central Catalonia is that of the Llobregat, near whose estuary Barcelona stands. Its lower course lies through the level ground along the coast, but its upper waters and those of its tributaries drain a series of highland valleys, difficult of access and divided from each other by considerable chains of hills. All these valleys unite at the foot of the crag of Montserrat, which, crowned by its monastery, overlooks the plain, and stands sentinel over the approach to the upland. In the mountains behind Montserrat was the main stronghold of the Catalan insurrection, whose rallying-places were the high-lying towns of Manresa, Cardona, Berga, and Solsona. Only three practicable roads enter the valleys of the Upper Llobregat, one communicates by the line of Manresa and Vich with the Ampurdam; a second goes from Manresa via Cervera to Lerida, and ultimately to the plains of Aragon; the third is the high-road from Barcelona to Manresa, the main line of approach from the shore to the upland. But there is another route of high importance in this section of Catalonia, that which, starting from Barcelona, avoids the upper valleys, strikes inland by Igualada, crosses the main watershed between the coast and the Ebro valley below Cervera, and at that place joins the other road from Manresa and the Upper Llobregat, and continues on its way to Lerida and the plains of Aragon. This, passing the mountains at the point of least resistance, forms the great trunk-road from Barcelona to Madrid.

The third region of the principality is the coastland of Tarragona, a district cut off from the coastland of Barcelona by a well-marked cross-ridge, which runs down from the mountains to the sea, and reaches the latter near the mouth of the Llobregat. The communication between the two maritime districts is by two roads, one passing the cross-ridge by the defile of Ordal, the other hugging the beach and finding its way between the hills and the water's edge by Villanueva de Sitjas. The coastland of Tarragona is not drained by a single river of considerable volume, like the

Catalonia

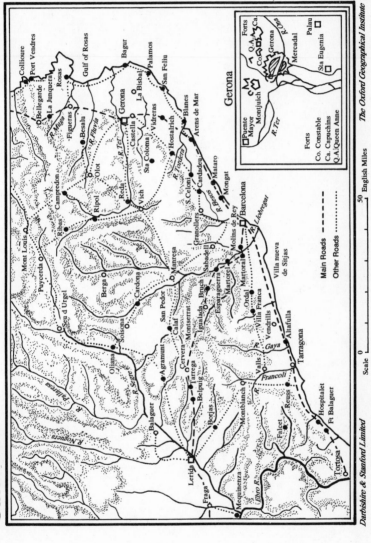

Darbishire & Stanford Limited   The Oxford Geographical Institute

Main Roads – – – –
Other Roads ....

Scale

0   50   English Miles

Gerona

Forts
Co. Constable
Ca. Capuchins
Q.A. Queen Anne

Llobregat, but by a number of small streams such as the Francoli
and the Gaya, running parallel to each other and at right angles
to the coast.   Each is separated from the next by a line of hills of
moderate height.   The southern limit of this region is the Ebro,
whose lower course is protected by the strong fortress of Tortosa.
Its main line of internal communication is the great coast-route
from Barcelona to Tarragona, and from Tarragona to the mouth of
the Ebro.   Its touch with Aragon and Central Spain is maintained
by a good road from Tarragona by Montblanch to Lerida.

The fourth and last region of Catalonia is the inland, which
looks not towards the Mediterranean but to the Ebro and Aragon.
It is drained by the Segre, an important stream, which after being
joined by its tributaries, the Noguera and the Pallaresa, falls into
the Ebro not far to the south of Lerida.   The tracts around that
town are flat and fertile, part of the main valley of the Ebro.   But
the head-waters of the Segre and its affluents flow through narrow
and difficult mountain valleys, starting in the highest and wildest
region of the Pyrenees.   They are very inaccessible, and served by
no roads suitable for the use of an army.   Hence, like the upper
valley of the Llobregat, they served as places of refuge for the
Catalan insurgents when Lerida and the flat country had been lost.
The only place of importance in these highlands is the remote
town of Seu d' Urgel [1], a mediaeval fortress near the sources of the
Segre, approached by mule-paths only, and quite lost in the hills.

Catalonia, then, is pre-eminently a mountain land, and one
presenting special difficulties to an invader, because it has no
central system of roads or valleys, but is divided into so many
heterogeneous parts.   Though not fertile, it was yet rich, and
fairly well peopled when compared with other regions of Spain [2].
Its wealth came not from agriculture but from commerce and
manufactures.   Barcelona, a city of 180,000 souls, was the greatest
Mediterranean port of Spain: on each side of it, along the coast,
are dozens of large fishing-villages and small harbour-towns, drawing their living from the sea.   Of the places which lay farther back
from the water there were many which made an ample profit from

[1] Urgel is more accessible from France than from Spain.   The easiest path
to it is that which, starting from Mont-Louis, crosses the Spanish frontier at
Puycerda, and follows the head-water of the Segre to the foot of the hill on
which the Seu stands.

[2] The population of the Principality in 1803 was 858,000 souls.

their manufactures, for Catalonia was, and still remains, the work-shop of Spain. It is the only province of the kingdom where the inhabitants have developed industries on a large scale: its textile products were especially successful, and supplied the whole Peninsula.

More than any other part of Spain, Catalonia had suffered from the war with England and the Continental System. The closure of its ports had told cruelly upon its merchants and manufacturers, who were fully aware that their sufferings were the logical consequence of the French alliance. They had, moreover, a historic grudge against France: after encouraging them to revolt in the seventeenth century, the Bourbons had then abandoned them to the mercies of the King of the Castilians. In the great war of the Spanish Succession, Catalonia had taken sides against France and Don Philip, and had proclaimed Charles of Austria its king—not because it loved him, but because it hated the French claimant. Even after the Peace of Utrecht the Catalans had refused to lay down their arms, and had made a last desperate struggle for provincial independence. It was in these wars that their *miqueletes* [1] had first made their name famous by their stubborn fighting. These bands were a levy *en masse* of the population of military age, armed and paid by their parishes, not by the central government, which could be called out whenever the principality was threatened with invasion. From their liability to turn out whenever the alarm-bell (*somaten*) was rung, they were also known as *somatenes*. The system of the *Quinta* and the militia ballot, which prevailed in the provinces under the crown of Castile, had never been applied to the Catalans, who gloried in the survival of their ancient military customs. The *somatenes* had been called out in the French war of 1793–5, and had done good service in it, distinguishing themselves far more than the troops of the line which fought on the frontier of the Eastern Pyrenees. The memories of that struggle were still fresh among them, and many of the leaders who had won a name in it were still fit for service. In Catalonia then, more than in any other corner of Spain, there were all the materials at hand for a vigorous popular insurrection, even though the body of regular troops in the principality

[1] So called from Miquelot de Prats, the Catalan *condottiere* who served under Caesar Borgia. From him the light infantry, once called *almogavares*, got the name of *miqueletes*.

was insignificant. The Catalans rose to defend their provincial independence, and to recover their capital, which had been seized so shamelessly by the trickery of Duhesme. They did not concern themselves much with what was going on in Aragon and Valencia, or even in Madrid. Their fight with the invader forms an episode complete in itself, a sort of underplot in the great drama of the Peninsular War, which only touches the main struggle at infrequent intervals. It was not affected by the campaigns of Castile, still less had it any noticeable influence on them. It would be equally possible to write the history of the war in Catalonia as a separate treatise, or to compile a general history of the war in which Catalonia was barely mentioned.

When the echoes of the cannon of the second of May went rolling round Spain, they stirred up Catalonia no less than the other provinces which lie at a distance from the capital. The phenomena which appeared in the South and the West were repeated here, in much the same sequence, and at much the same dates, as elsewhere. But the rising of the Catalans was greatly handicapped by the fact that their populous and wealthy capital was occupied by 12,000 French troops. Barcelona could not set the example to the smaller places, and for some time the outburst was spasmodic and local. The chief focus of rebellion was Lerida, where an insurrectionary Junta was formed on May 29. At Tortosa the populace rose a few days later, and murdered the military governor, Santiago de Guzman, because he had been slow and reluctant to place himself at their head. On June 2 Manresa, in the upper valley of the Llobregat, followed their example, and from it the flame of insurrection spread all over the central upland. In Barcelona itself there were secret meetings, and suspicious gatherings in the streets, on which Duhesme had to keep a watchful eye. But the main preoccupation of the French general was that there were still several thousand Spanish troops in the town, who might easily lead the populace in an *émeute*. He had got rid of one regiment, that of Estremadura, in May: he gave it orders to march to Lerida, where the magistrates and people refused to receive it within their walls, dreading that it might not be ready to join in their projected rising. This was a vain fear, for the corps readily took its part in the insurrection, and marched to join Palafox at Saragossa. But there still remained in Barcelona a battalion each of the Spanish and the Walloon Guards, and the cavalry regiment

of Borbon, some 2,500 men in all. To Duhesme's intense satisfaction, these troops, instead of keeping together and attacking
the French garrison when the news of the revolt reached them,
began to desert in small parties. Far from attempting to compel
them to stay by their colours, Duhesme winked at their evasion,
and took no notice of their proceedings, even when a whole squadron
of the Borbon Regiment rode off with trumpets sounding and its
officers at its head. Within a few days the greater part of the
Spanish troops had vanished, and when Duhesme was directed by
his master to disarm them, there were very few left for him to deal
with. These scattered remnants of the Guard Regiments drifted
in small bands all over Catalonia, some were found at Gerona, others
at Tarragona, others at Rosas. Nearly 400 went to Aragon and
fought under Palafox at Epila : another considerable body joined
the Valencian insurgents [1]. But these two strong veteran battalions
never were united again, or made to serve as a nucleus for the
Catalan levies [2].

Saved from the peril of a rising of the Spanish regiments in
Barcelona, Duhesme had still the insurrection of the province on
his hands. But he was not left free to deal with it according to
his own inspirations. By the last dispatch from Napoleon which
reached him before the communications with Madrid and Bayonne
were cut, a plan of campaign was dictated to him. The Emperor
ordered him to chastise the insurgents of Lerida and Manresa,
without ceasing to keep a strong grip on Barcelona, and on the
line of touch with France through Figueras. But, as if this was
not enough to occupy his small army of 12,000 or 13,000 men,
he was to provide two strong detachments, one of which was to
co-operate with Moncey in Valencia, and the other with Lefebvre-
Desnouettes in Aragon. A glance at the Emperor's instructions
is enough to show how entirely he had misconceived the situation,
and how thoroughly he had failed to realize that all Spain was up
in arms. The first detachment, 4,000 strong, was to march on
Lerida, and to enter Aragon along the line of the Ebro. It was then

---

[1] There were 400 Spanish Guards at the fight on the Cabrillas, who must
have come from the battalion at Barcelona.

[2] I cannot make out the movements of the cavalry regiment of Borbon; it
was certainly at Barcelona, 600 strong, in May. But in July it had got
down to Andalusia, and was marching with a strength of 401 in the army of
Castaños.

to move on Saragossa to join Lefebvre. The second detachment, also 4,000 strong, was to move on Valencia via Tortosa, join Marshal Moncey, and finally occupy the great naval arsenal of Cartagena. With the 5,000 men that remained Duhesme was to hold down Barcelona and Central Catalonia, while keeping open the line of communications with Figueras and Perpignan.

Either Duhesme was as blind to the real state of affairs as his master, or he considered that unquestioning obedience was his first duty. He told off the two columns as directed, only cutting down their strength a little, so as not wholly to ungarnish Barcelona. For the Valencian expedition he told off General Chabran, with the best brigade in his army, three veteran French battalions of the 7th and 16th of the line[1]. With this force he sent his single brigade of French cavalry, two regiments under General Bessières (the brother of the Duke of Istria). The whole amounted to 2,500 foot and 600 horse. For the attack on Lerida, he had to send out troops of more doubtful value—all foreigners, for there were no more French to be spared. General Schwartz was given one Swiss, two Neapolitan, and one Italian battalion[2], with no more than a single squadron of cavalry, for his march was to lie over a very

---

[1] This force was Goulas's Brigade of Chabran's Division, viz. :—

7th of the Line (1st and 2nd batts.) . .	1,785	
16th „ (3rd batt.) . . .	789	
		2,574

and Bessières' Cavalry :

3rd Provisional Cuirassiers (minus one squadron)	205	
3rd Provisional Chasseurs . . .	416	
	621	
with eight guns.		3,195

[2] Schwartz's force was :—

2nd Swiss (3rd batt.)	580	
1st Neapolitans (1st and 2nd batts.) . .	1,944	
1st Italian *Velites* (1st batt.) . . .	519	
	3,043	
One squadron of the 3rd Provisional Cuirassiers .	204	
		3,247

with four guns.

[That the detached squadron were cuirassiers is proved by Arteche, ii. 86. The French authorities do not give the regiment.]

Foy makes the odd mistake of saying ' trois bataillons du deuxième Suisse,' instead of ' le troisième bataillon du deuxième Suisse.' There was only one battalion of this regiment with Duhesme.

mountainous country. His whole force was 3,200 strong. To the general directions given by Napoleon, Duhesme added some supplementary orders of his own. Chabran was to pass by Tarragona, leave a battalion in its citadel, and take as a compensation the two battalions of Wimpfen's Swiss Regiment, which was to be incorporated in the French army. It was expected that he would get into touch with Marshal Moncey when he should reach Castellon de la Plana. Schwartz, on the other hand, was told to march by the mountain road leading to Manresa, in order to punish the inhabitants of that town for their rebellion. He was to fine them 750,000 francs, and to destroy a powder-mill which they possessed. He was then to march on Lerida, from which he was to evict the insurrectionary Junta : the city was to pay a heavy war-contribution, and to receive a garrison of 500 men. With the rest of his brigade Schwartz was to join the French forces before Saragossa, not later than June 19.

Schwartz started from Barcelona on June 4 : a tempest forced him to wait for a day at Martorel, in the coast-plain, but on the sixth he reached the pass of Bruch, at whose foot the roads from Igualada and from Manresa join. Here he met with opposition : the news of his approach had spread all up the valley of the Llobregat, and the *somatenes* of the upland towns were hurrying forward to hold the defile by which the high-road from Barcelona climbs into the upper country. At the moment when the invaders, marching in the most careless fashion, were making their way up the hill, only the levy of Manresa was in position. They were a mere handful, 300 or 400 at most, and many were destitute of muskets. But from the cover of a pine-wood they boldly opened fire upon the head of Schwartz's column. Surprised to find himself attacked, the French general deployed a battalion and drove the *somatenes* out of their position : they retired in great disorder up the hill towards Manresa. Schwartz followed them with caution, under the idea that they must be the vanguard of a larger force, and that there were probably regular troops in support, further along the defile. In this he was wrong, but the retreating Manresans received reinforcements a few miles behind the place of the first skirmish. They were joined by the levies of San Pedor and other villages of the Upper Llobregat, marching forward to the sound of the single drum that was to be found in the upland. The peasants ensconced themselves in the rocks and bushes on either side of the road, and again offered battle. Schwartz took their opposition much too seriously, extended a long front of tirailleurs against them, but did not push his attack home. Soon other bands of *somatenes* from the direction of Igualada began to gather round his left flank, and it seemed to him that he would soon be surrounded and cut off from his line of communications with Barcelona. His regiments were raw and not of the best quality : the Neapolitans who composed more than half his force passed, and with reason, as the worst troops in Europe. He himself was a cavalry officer who had never held independent command before, and was wholly unversed in mountain warfare. Reflecting that the afternoon was far spent, that he was still twelve miles from Manresa, and that the whole country-side was on the move against him, he resolved to abandon his expedition. Instead of hurling his four battalions upon the *somatenes*, who must have been scattered to the winds if attacked by such superior numbers, he drew back, formed his men in a great square, with the cavalry and guns in the middle, and began a retreat across the more open parts of the defile. The Spaniards followed, pressing in the screen of tirailleurs by which the square was covered, and taking easy shots into the solid mass behind them. After six miles of marching under fire, Schwartz's Swiss and Italians were growing somewhat demoralized, for nothing could be more harassing to raw and unwilling troops than such a retreat. At last they found their way blocked by the village of Esparraguera, where the inhabitants barricaded the streets and opened a hot fire upon the front face of the square. Seeing his men hesitate and break their ranks, Schwartz hastily bade them scatter right and left and pass round the village without attempting to storm it. This device succeeded, but when the two halves of the column reunited beyond Esparraguera, they were in such disorder that there was no means of stopping them. The whole streamed into Martorel in a confused mass at nightfall, after a retreat whose incidents remind the military reader, in every detail, of the rout of the British troops in the march to Lexington, on the first day of the old American War of 1775.

When he reached the plains Schwartz was able to retire unharmed to Barcelona, having saved three of his four guns [1] and lost no very

---

[1] One gun was lost after leaving Esparraguera by the fall of a rickety bridge over the Abrera (Arteche, ii. 93, 94). Foy and other French narrators do not mention this loss.

large proportion of his men. But he had suffered the disgrace of being worsted by inferior numbers of undisciplined peasantry, and brought his troops back in a state of demoralization, which was very discouraging to the rest of the garrison of the Catalonian capital. Duhesme, instead of taking him to task, fully approved of his retreat, on the ground that if he had pushed on for Manresa and Lerida he would probably have lost his whole brigade. Realizing at last the true strength of the insurrection, and learning that the *somaten* was sounding in every village, and that the peasantry were flocking together in thousands, Duhesme determined to concentrate his whole force, and sent orders to Chabran to abandon his Valencian expedition and return at once to Barcelona. He was probably quite right in his resolve, though Chabran's retreat was the determining fact that ruined Moncey's campaign in the province south of the Ebro. The Emperor had sketched out the whole plan of operations on false premises, and when the new military situation had developed itself, it would have been absurd for his lieutenants to carry out his original orders in blind and servile obedience.

Chabran's column had reached Tarragona when it received Duhesme's letters of recall. It had started on June 4, and found the coastland still quiet, the insurrection not having yet spread downwards from the hills. On arriving at Tarragona Chabran took possession of the citadel, and issued orders to the two battalions of Wimpfen's Swiss Regiment, which formed the garrison of the place, to prepare to march with him against Valencia. The Swiss officers showed no alacrity in falling in with this plan. They were not animated by the patriotic fury which had carried away the rest of the Spanish regular troops into the insurgent camp. On the other hand they felt no enthusiasm at the idea of joining the French in an attack on their late employers. They were deferring obedience to the orders of the French general on various futile pleas, when the news of Schwartz's defeat at Bruch reached Tarragona. Directed to return in haste and to rejoin Duhesme, General Chabran marched off on June 9, leaving Wimpfen's mercenaries behind : they would not follow him, and declared in favour of the insurgent Junta at Lerida the moment that his back was turned. The retreating French column had to brush aside several considerable bands of *somatenes*, which tried to arrest its progress, for the coastland had taken arms after the combat of Bruch, and its levies hoped to treat Chabran as their compatriots of the upland had treated Schwartz. But the three veteran French battalions were of tougher material than the Neapolitans and Italians who had been routed on the sixth, and successfully cut their way back to Barcelona. They were aided by the unwisdom of the insurgents, who, instead of trying to defend the difficult defile of Ordal, came down into the plain. When they attacked Chabran at Vendrell and Arbos, they were charged by his cavalry and scattered to the winds with heavy loss. The French, when the actions were over, sacked with every circumstance of brutality all the villages which lay along their path [1]. On June 11 they got into touch with Duhesme's outposts, and on the twelfth re-entered Barcelona.

The whole of the ' Army of the Eastern Pyrenees ' was now re-united under its commander's hand, and Duhesme thought himself strong enough to punish the peasantry of the Upper Llobregat for their victory at Bruch.   On the fourteenth Chabran, with his own brigade and the Swiss and Italians of Schwartz, marched from Martorel to assault once more the pass which the uplanders had defended so well eight days before.   But the woods and rocks of Bruch were now manned by many thousands of *somatenes*: all Central Catalonia had sent its levies thither, and they were supported by 400 regulars from Lerida and four pieces of artillery. After feeling the position, and directing against it at least one serious attack, Chabran drew back and refused to press on the action—apparently influenced by the manifest reluctance of Schwartz's troops to advance, no less than by the strength of the ground.   After losing nearly 400 men he retired to the plain and marched back to Barcelona [June 15].

Duhesme had a more pressing business in hand than the chastisement of the mountaineers of the Upper Llobregat. He had now learnt, by the fact that couriers from France had ceased to arrive, that his communications with Figueras and Upper Catalonia had been cut, and it was absolutely necessary that they should be reopened. This was to prove a harder task than he imagined: the *somatenes* were now up in every valley as far as the French frontier; they had driven into the citadel of Figueras the weak battalion of detachments that had been left to hold that

---

[1] For details see Arteche, ii. 98, 99, and Foy, iv. 150, who adds that Arbos ' fut pillé et réduit en cendres, *conformément aux usages de la guerre* ' (!)

town, and some of the bolder spirits were feeling their way through the Pyrenean recesses to commence raids on Roussillon. Such alarm was felt at Perpignan that the general commanding the district had begun to call out the national guards, for he had no regulars at his disposal save a few hundred men of details and detachments, who were waiting to go forward to join their regiments in Duhesme's corps. But all this was unknown at Barcelona, and it was with very little conception of the difficulties before him that Duhesme resolved to march on Gerona and reopen the main road to France. He told off for this service one half of the infantry battalions which composed his army—the Italian division of Lecchi, consisting of the brigades of Schwartz and of Milosewitz, the latter of which had hitherto remained in garrison at Barcelona, and had not taken part in the futile attacks on the defile of Bruch. He also took with him nearly the whole of his cavalry, four French and three Italian squadrons of cuirassiers and chasseurs, and a battery of eight guns. This gave him a formidable force of 5,900 men [1], about half of the total strength of his corps when the losses suffered at Bruch and elsewhere are deducted.

Duhesme had resolved to march on Gerona by the comparatively easy road along the sea-coast, rather than by the alternative route which passes further inland by the valley of the Besos and the town of Hostalrich. Even in the lowland, however, he found the *somatenes* prepared to oppose him. At the castle of Mongat,

---

[1] Brigade of Milosewitz :

2nd Italian Line (2nd batt.) . . .	740	
4th ,, (3rd batt.) . . .	587	
5th ,, (2nd batt.) . . .	806	
		2,133

Brigade of Schwartz :

1st Neapolitans (1st and 2nd batts.). .	1,944	
1st Italian *Velites* (1st batt.) . . .	519	
(Minus 300 men lost in the actions at Bruch on June 6 and 14)		
		2,163

Cavalry :

3rd Provisional Cuirassiers . . .	409	
3rd ,, Chasseurs . . .	416	
Italian *Chasseurs à Cheval* . . .	504	
2nd Neapolitan ,, . . .	388	
(Minus one squadron left at Barcelona, say 200)		
		1,517
Artillerymen for eight guns	150	
		5,963

only six miles outside Barcelona, he met the first swarm 8,000 or
9,000 strong. They had procured a few guns, which they had
mounted so as to sweep the road, and lay in disorderly masses
along the crest of a rising ground. Duhesme, amusing them in
front by a false attack, sent a strong column to turn their right
flank: seeing themselves likely to be enveloped, the peasants fled
after a short skirmish, in which they suffered considerable loss.
Pushing onward, Duhesme arrived that same afternoon at the
large open town of Mataro, a place of 20,000 souls given over to
the manufacture of glass and cotton goods. The populace had
hastily barricaded the outlets of the streets with carts and piles
of furniture, and discharged two or three cannon against the
approaching enemy. But Milosewitz's Italian brigade easily burst
through the feeble defences and took Mataro by storm. Its
attempt at resistance was considered by Duhesme to justify its
sack, and he granted the plunder of the town to his men, who
only moved on the next day after having thoroughly robbed every
dwelling of its portable goods and murdered a considerable number
of the inhabitants. The French army of Catalonia was the most
motley and undisciplined force of all the imperial hosts in Spain,
and for that reason it was by far the most cruel and brutal in its
behaviour to the natives, who had not as yet justified any such
treatment by their manner of conducting the war. Any ferocity
which they showed from this time onward was a well-deserved
revenge for what they had suffered.

Leaving Mataro on the eighteenth, Duhesme arrived before
Gerona on the twentieth, after burning most of the villages on
the road, in revenge for the constant molestation which he suffered
from the *somatenes*. He found the city placed in a state of
defence, so far as was possible in the case of an old-fashioned
fortress called upon to stand a siege at ten days' notice. There
was a small regular garrison, the Irish regiment of Ultonia, under
its two lieutenant-colonels, O'Donovan and O'Daly: but this corps
only counted 350 bayonets. In addition there were a few trained
artillerymen, and the armed citizens of the town, not more than
2,000 in all, for Gerona had but 14,000 inhabitants. The place
lies on either side of the small stream of the Oña, just above its
confluence with the river Ter. On the south bank is the main
part of the town, straggling up the side of a steep hill, which is
crowned at its eastern end by an ancient citadel, known (like those

of several other Catalonian towns) by the name of Monjuich.
Further westward, along the crest of this hill, lie three other forts,
those of the Constable, Queen Anne, and the Capuchins. These, like
the citadel, are detached works, not connected by any line of wall
but only by a ditch. The town, which is completely commanded
by the four forts, has no protection on the south side of the Oña
but a mediaeval wall, destitute of a ditch and not more than
twenty feet high. But on the other side of the river, the northern
suburb, known as the Mercadal, having no line of outlying heights
to protect it, had been fortified in the style of Vauban with a
regular front of five bastions, though, like the fortifications of the
city, it was without a ditch.

Duhesme had no battering-train, and his force of 5,900 men
was insufficient to invest the whole circumference of the city of
Gerona and its forts. But, like Moncey before Valencia, he was
resolved to make an attempt to storm the city by escalade, or by
battering in its gates. He left alone the citadel and the line of
works on the hill, only sending a single battalion to demonstrate
against the fort of the Capuchins. His real attack was directed
against the sole point where the old *enceinte* of the city is not
fully protected by the forts, the gate of the Carmen, on the very
brink of the Oña. In no very honourable spirit, he sent in one
of his aides-de-camp, with a white flag, to demand the surrender
of Gerona, and while that officer was conferring with the governor
and the local Junta, suddenly launched his column of assault
against the gate, hoping to catch the Spaniards off their guard.
The attack was a failure: the heavy guns from the forts above
silenced the French field-artillery which tried to batter in the
gate. Then Duhesme sent forward a storming party, with artillerymen at its head bearing petards with which to blow open the
entrance: but the heavy musketry-fire from the walls laid low
the head of the column, and the rest swerved, and fell back to
get under cover. A feeble demonstration beyond the Oña against
the bastions of Santa Clara and San Francisco had not even the
desired effect of distracting the attention of the defenders of the
Carmen Gate.

Seeing his attack foiled, Duhesme sent in at dusk a second flag
of truce, inviting the Junta of Gerona to send out deputies to
confer with him on certain points which he was desirous of submitting to them. The Catalans were simple enough to comply

with his offer: they would have been wiser to avoid all negotiations with such an enemy. For this parley was only intended to cover a second assault. Seeing that he could not hope to batter his way into the place by means of his light field-artillery, Duhesme was preparing a great escalade under cover of the night. The point which he chose for it was the bastion of Santa Clara, on the centre of the low front of the Mercadal, beyond the Oña. He collected a quantity of ladders from the neighbouring villages, and told off for the assault the three battalions of the brigade of Schwartz.

At ten o'clock[1] the Italians crept up beneath the ramparts, where the citizens on guard do not seem to have kept a good look out, and delivered their attack. But these raw troops, moving in the darkness, made many mistakes: the chief one was that many of the ladder-party went astray among the water-courses and field-walls, so that the provision of ladders proved insufficient. The garrison of the bastion, however, had been taken completely by surprise, and allowed the head of the column to escalade the twenty-foot wall with no more hindrance than a few musket-shots. The Neapolitan Colonel Ambrosio and the leading files had actually mounted, and driven back the citizens to the gorge of the bastion, when there arrived reinforcements, a company of the Regiment of Ultonia, which charged with the bayonet, drove the Italians back, and hurled them over the rampart. An Irish lieutenant, Thomas Magrath, and a Carmelite friar seized and overturned the ladders, at the cost of the life of the former. When the garrison began firing down into the mass of assailants crowded at the foot of the wall, and the neighbouring bastion commenced to discharge a flanking fire of artillery, the Italians broke and fled. A second attempt at an escalade, made two hours later at another bastion, failed even more lamentably, for the garrison were on the alert and detected the assailants before they drew near the walls.

Convinced that he was too weak to take Gerona without siege-artillery, Duhesme broke up his camp and fled under cover of the night, marking his retreat by a third insincere attempt to open

---

[1] Napier says that the assault was delivered at seven in the evening, before dark (i. 79); but all the Spanish accounts speak of it as having taken place long after dark, though before midnight (cf. Arteche, Toreño, and Minali, quoted by the former); so does Foy (iv. 158), who fixes the hour as 'between nine and ten.'

negotiations with the garrison. He hastily made off by the same road by which he had come, and returned to Barcelona by forced marches, dropping on the way one of his Italian brigades at Mataro [June 24]. In the whole expedition he had lost 700 men [1].

So ended the first attempt on Gerona, to the great credit of its gallant defenders, and more especially to that of the weak Irish regiment which had borne the brunt of the fighting. Duhesme's whole campaign bore a singular resemblance to that which Moncey was making at the same moment in Valencia, and, like it, was wrecked on the initial blunder of supposing that Spanish towns, defended by a population in a high state of patriotic enthusiasm, could be carried by escalade without any proper preparation by artillery. French generals soon got to know their adversaries better : the same levies that could be easily scattered in the open field were formidable under cover of stone walls.

On returning to Barcelona, Duhesme found that the insurgents of Central Catalonia had drawn close to the capital in his absence. Eight or ten thousand *somatenes* had come down to the line of the Llobregat, had broken its bridges, had entrenched themselves opposite its fords, and were preparing to blockade Barcelona. They had brought up a considerable number of guns taken from the batteries on the coast, which had so long kept watch upon the English. But of regular troops there were only a few present— a mixed body of 400 men from Lerida, and some small remnants of the old Spanish garrison of Barcelona. The command seems to have been held by Juan Baget, a lawyer of Lerida, who had been named colonel of *miqueletes* by the Junta of his native town. Duhesme was determined not to be deprived of his hold on the coast-plain by this tumultuary army. On the thirtieth he sallied out from Barcelona with Goulas's French brigade and three of Lecchi's Italian battalions, accompanied by the cuirassiers of Bessières. Though the line of the Llobregat is marked by steep banks, and though a considerable number of guns were mounted behind it, the position was too long and too much exposed to be capable of defence by undisciplined bands of mountaineers. While the Italians menaced its front, Goulas and Bessières forded the river and turned the flank of the Catalans. Chased out from the villages

---

[1] Yet he had the hardihood to write to the Emperor that ' after some slight skirmishing, he did not think it worth while to make a serious attack on Gerona' (*Nap. Corresp.*, xvii. 347).

of San Boy and Molins de Rey by a sweeping charge, they were pursued across the plain, stripped of all their artillery, and forced to take refuge in their old positions along the edge of the mountains of Montserrat, after losing a considerable number of men.

Less successful was another stroke against the insurgents which Duhesme endeavoured to deal five days later. General Chabran, with the Italian brigade that had been left at Mataro, a regiment of French cavalry and a field-battery, moved out to clear the hills above the coast, and to sweep the valley of the Besos. He had before him the *somatenes* of the regions about Vich, Hostalrich, and Santa Coloma, under Francisco Milans, a half-pay lieutenant-colonel, who had been placed at their head by the local Junta. Chabran forced his way for some distance inland till he reached Granollers, always harassed but never seriously attacked by the insurgents. Milans, who showed all through his career a real genius for guerilla warfare, had ordered his levies never to stand when pressed, but to hang about the enemy's line of march, cut off his pickets and scouting parties, and fall upon the baggage-train which trailed at the rear of his column. These tactics were perfectly successful: having reached Granollers after a most toilsome march, Chabran refused to push further among the mountains, turned back, and retreated to Mataro, accompanied home by the *somatenes*, who pursued him to the very outskirts of the town, and cut off his stragglers and many of his baggage animals [July 4].

The moment that the Catalan insurrection grew serious, Duhesme had sent repeated appeals for help to the Emperor: the land route to Perpignan being cut, he had to use small vessels which put out to sea at night, risked capture by the English ships lying off the coast, and when fortunate reached the harbours of Collioure or Port-Vendres, just beyond the Pyrenees. Napoleon looked upon the Catalonian war as a very small matter, but he was fully resolved that Duhesme must be succoured. Accordingly he determined to concentrate a division at Perpignan, but he refused to allot to it any of his veteran French troops. He swept together from the Southern Alps and Piedmont a most heterogeneous body of 7,000 or 8,000 men, even worse in quality than the motley army which he had entrusted to Duhesme. The command was entrusted to a capable officer, General Reille, one of the Emperor's aides-de-camp, who was told to advance and relieve Figueras, after which he was to stretch out his hand to Duhesme, who would push northward to meet him. His improvised army consisted of two battalions of recruits just levied in the lately annexed duchy of Tuscany, and constituting the nucleus of a new regiment with the number 113, of a battalion of national guards, some mobilized gendarmerie, a battalion of the 'Legion of Reserve of the Alps' from Grenoble, five 'battalions of detachments,' and the single battalion which formed the contingent of the little republic of the Valais[1]. The cavalry comprised two squadrons of Tuscan dragoons, and two *escadrons de marche* of French cuirassiers and chasseurs. There seem to have been no more than two batteries of artillery allotted to the force[2]. Reille was informed that other troops from Italy would ultimately arrive at Perpignan, but that they were not to be expected till the end of July or the beginning of August. For the relief of Figueras and the opening up of communications with Duhesme he must depend on his own forces.

Travelling with commendable rapidity, Reille arrived at Perpignan on July 3. Of all the detachments that were marching to join him he found that nothing had yet reached the frontier but the local national guards and gendarmerie, the two Tuscan

---

[1] The Valais was a republic from 1802 till 1810, when it was annexed to the Empire, as the 'department of the Simplon.'

[2] From *Nap. Corresp.*, 14,092, 14,150, 14,151, and 14,168, we get the composition of this force. They account for the following :

Two batts. of the 113th (Tuscans)	1,300
National Guards of the Pyrénées Orientales . . .	560
1st Provisional Battalion of Perpignan (companies from the dépôts of the 1st, 5th, 24th, 62nd of the Line, and 16th and 22nd Léger)	840
2nd Provisional Battalion, similarly formed from the 23rd, 60th, 79th, 81st of the Line, and the 8th and 18th Léger	840
A mixed battalion of the 16th and 32nd French and 2nd Swiss	1,100
Another from the 7th and 93rd of the Line	840
Another from the 2nd, 56th, and 37th of the Line . .	840
One battalion of the '5th Legion of Reserve' from Grenoble	500
Battalion of the Valais	800
Two squadrons of Tuscan Dragoons	250
Two *escadrons de marche* (French)	300
Two batteries of artillery	200
	8,370

There were also nine companies of gendarmerie and 'departmental reserves.'

battalions, a company of the 2nd Swiss Regiment, and artillerymen
enough to serve a couple of guns. With no more than the Tuscans
and the Swiss, less than 1,600 men in all, he marched on Figueras
on July 5, dispersing on the way some bands of *somatenes*, who tried
to oppose him at the passage of the Muga. He threw a convoy
into the place and strengthened its garrison, but could do no more,
for all the country beyond Figueras was up in arms, and his raw
Italian recruits could hardly be kept to their colours. Indeed he
was forced to make them march in solid columns whenever he
moved them, for when ordered to deploy they always fell into
disorder, and tried to make off to the rear[1].

But by July 11 Reille had begun to receive many of the drafts
and detachments which the Emperor was pouring into Perpignan,
and having now three or four thousand men disposable, he resolved
to strike a blow at Rosas, the small seaport town which blocks the
coast-road from Perpignan to Barcelona. Marching through the
plains of the Ampurdam he reached his objective, an insignificant
place with a dilapidated outer entrenchment and a citadel of some
small strength. It was defended by no more than 400 *miqueletes*,
and had but five guns on its land-front. But the little garrison
showed a bold face, and when Reille proceeded to invest Rosas he
found himself attacked from the rear by four or five thousand
somatenes levied by Don Juan Claros, a retired infantry captain
who had called to arms the peasantry of the coast. They beset
the besiegers so fiercely that Reille resolved to abandon the investment, a determination which was assisted by the sight of a British
line-of-battle ship[2] landing marines to strengthen the garrison.
Accordingly he cut his way back to Figueras on the twelfth,
harassed all the way by the bands of Claros, who killed or took
no less than 200 of his men[3]. Rosas was to defy capture for some
months more, for Reille's next effort was, by his master's direction,
devoted to a more important object—the clearing of the great road
from Perpignan to Barcelona, and the opening up of communications
with Duhesme.

---

[1] Foy, iv. 165, 166.　　[2] The *Montague*, of 74 guns, Captain R. W. Otway.
　　　　　　　　　　[3] Foy, iv. 169.

SECTION V: CHAPTER II

For the first six weeks of the war in Catalonia Duhesme and Reille had been opposed only by the gallant *somatenes*. Of the handful of regular troops who had been stationed in the principality when the insurrection broke out, the greater part had drifted off to the siege of Saragossa, or to the struggle in the south. Only the Irish regiment at Gerona, and certain fragments of the disbanded battalions of the Guards from Barcelona had aided the peasantry in resisting the invader. The success of the Catalans, in hemming in Duhesme and checking Reille's advance, is all the more notable when we reflect that their levies had not been guided by any central organization, nor placed under the command of any single general. The Junta at Lerida had done little more than issue proclamations and serve out to the *somatenes* the moderate amount of munitions of war that was at its disposition. It had indeed drawn out a scheme for the raising of a provincial army—forty *tercios* of *miqueletes*, each 1,000 strong, were to be levied and kept permanently in the field. But this scheme existed only on paper, and there were no means of officering or arming such a mass of men. Even as late as August 1, there were only 6,000 of them embodied in organized corps: the mass of the men of military age were still at their own firesides, prepared to turn out at the sound of the *somaten*, whenever a French column appeared in their neighbourhood, but not ready to keep the field for more than a few days, or to transfer their service to the more distant regions of the principality. The direction of these irregular bands was still in the hands of local leaders like Claros, Milans, and Baget, who aided each other in a sufficiently loyal fashion when they had the chance, but did not obey any single commander-in-chief, or act on any settled military plan. Their successes had been due to their own untutored intelligence and courage, not to the carrying out of any regular policy.

This period of patriotic anarchy was now drawing to an end;

regular troops were beginning to appear on the scene in considerable numbers, and the direction of the military resources of Catalonia was about to be confided to their generals. The change was not all for the better : during the whole struggle the Spaniards showed themselves admirable insurgents but indifferent soldiers. After one more short but brilliant period of success, the balance of fortune was about to turn against the Catalans, and a long series of disasters was to try, but never to subdue, their indomitable and persevering courage.

We have already shown that the only body of regular troops available for the succour of Catalonia was the corps of 10,000 men which lay in the Balearic Islands. That these thirteen battalions of veterans had not yet been thrown ashore in the principality was mainly due to the over-caution of the aged General Vives, the Captain-General at Palma, to whom the charge of the garrisons of Majorca and Minorca was committed [1]. He had a deeply rooted idea that if he left Port Mahon unguarded, the English would find some excuse for once more making themselves masters of that ancient stronghold, where the Union Jack had waved for the greater part of the eighteenth century. Even the transparent honesty of Lord Collingwood, the veteran admiral of the Mediterranean fleet, could not reassure him. It was only when strong pressure was applied to him by his second in command, the Marquis del Palacio, governor of Minorca, and when he had received the most explicit pledges from Collingwood concerning the disinterested views of Great Britain, that he consented to disgarnish Port Mahon. His mind was only finally made up, when the Aragonese and Catalan battalions of his army burst out into open mutiny, threatening to seize shipping and transport themselves to the mainland without his leave, if any further delay was made [June 30]. A fortnight later Vives permitted Del Palacio, with the greater part of the Balearic garrisons, to set sail for the seat of war. The Aragonese regiment landed near Tortosa, and marched for Saragossa : but the bulk of the expeditionary force, nearly 5,000 strong, was put ashore in Catalonia between July 19 and 23.

Meanwhile affairs in the principality had taken a new turn.

[1] Neither Toreño nor Arteche mentions the trouble caused by this tiresome old man, to whom the delay in succouring Catalonia was due. For the negotiations with him see Lord Collingwood's correspondence (*Life*, ii. 291, 292), and Foy (iv. 181).

Duhesme had remained quiet for six days after Chabran's check at Granollers, though his position at Barcelona grew daily more uncomfortable, owing to the constant activity of the *somatenes*. But when he learnt that Reille's vanguard had reached Figueras, and that he might expect ere long to be aided by a whole division of fresh troops from the north, he resolved to renew his attack on Gerona, the fortress which so completely blocked his communications with France. Sending messages by sea to bid his colleague meet him under the walls of that place, he sallied out from Barcelona, on July 10, with the larger half of his army. This time he took with him the French brigades of Goulas and Nicolas only, leaving Barcelona to the care of Lecchi and the foreign troops. He felt that the situation was too grave for him to trust the fate of Catalonia to the steadiness of Lombard or Neapolitan regiments. So leaving four Italian and one Swiss battalion, 3,500 men in all, in the Barcelona forts, he marched for Gerona with seven French battalions, a regiment of Italian cavalry, and twenty-two guns, of which ten were heavy siege-artillery. At Mataro he picked up Chabran, who had been resting there since his check at Granollers on July 4, and incorporated with his expedition the Italian battalions which that officer had with him, as well as a regiment of French cavalry. This gave him a total force of some 7,000 men [1]; yet his march was slow and difficult. Milans with the *somatenes* of the upland was always hanging upon his left flank, and Lord Cochrane with two British frigates followed him along the coast, bombarding his columns whenever the road came within cannon-shot of the sea. At Arens de Mar Duhesme halted for no less than five days, either from sheer indecision as to the advisability of proceeding with his project, or because he was

---

[1] The numbers of these corps before the fighting commenced in June had been :

Goulas's Brigade (three batts.)	.	.	.	.	2,574
Nicolas's Brigade (four batts.)	.	.	.	.	2,891
Two Italian battalions	.	.	.	.	1,300
3rd Provisional Cuirassiers .	.	.	.	.	409
2nd Neapolitan Chasseurs .	.	.	.	.	388
Artillery .	.	.	.	.	.	250

7,812

But as the Italians, Goulas, and the cuirassiers had all been engaged several times, and had suffered serious losses, we must deduct 800 men at least, in order to get the figures of July 17. Foy gives only 6,000.

waiting for definite news of Reille. At last he made up his mind :
two routes meet at Arens, the main *chaussée* from Barcelona to
Gerona via Tordera, and a cross-road which seeks the same end
by a detour through the small hill-fortress of Hostalrich. The
three battalions of Goulas's brigade were sent by this latter path,
with orders to endeavour to seize the place if they could. The
main column, with the battering-train, followed the high-road.
Goulas found Hostalrich too strong for him : it was garrisoned
by 500 *miqueletes* under Manuel O'Sullivan, a captain of the
Regiment of Ultonia, who gallantly held their own against an
attempt at escalade. The French brigadier thereupon abandoned
the attack, crossed the mountains, and joined his chief before
Gerona on July 22. Duhesme meanwhile had been harassed for
three days by the *somatenes* of Milans, and, though he always
drove them off in the end, had lost much of his baggage, and an
appreciable number of men, before he reached the banks of the
Ter. On the day after he was rejoined by Goulas he forced the
passage of that river and took post before Gerona. On the next
morning [July 24] he was rejoiced to meet with the vanguard
of Reille's division descending from the north. That general had
started from Figueras two days before, with all the fractions of his
motley force that had reached the front, two Tuscan battalions,
the Swiss from the Valais, three French *bataillons de marche*,
the two 'Provisional Battalions of Perpignan,' and some other
improvised units, with a total strength of some 6,500 men. He
established his head quarters at Puente Mayor to the north of the
city, on the right bank of the Ter, while Duhesme placed his at
Santa Eugenia on the left bank. There were good and easy
communications between them by means of two fords, and the
bridge of Salt, a little further from Gerona, was also available.

Thirteen thousand men seemed enough to make an end of an old-
fashioned fortress like Gerona, held by a garrison which down to
the first day of the siege counted no more than 400 regular troops
—that same Irish regiment of Ultonia which had stood out against
Duhesme's first attack in June. It was fortunate for the defenders
that at the very moment of the arrival of the French they received
a powerful reinforcement. The light infantry regiment named the
2nd Volunteers of Barcelona, 1,300 strong, entered the city on the
night of July 22 [1], slipping between the heads of Duhesme's and

----
[1] Not on the twenty-fifth, as Napier says (i. 83), following apparently the

Reille's columns. This corps had formed part of the garrison of Minorca: instead of being landed at Tarragona with the rest of Del Palacio's troops, it was dropped at San Feliu, the nearest port on the coast to Gerona, and had just time to reach that place before its investment was completed.

Duhesme had resolved to avoid for the future the fruitless attempts at escalade, which had cost him so many men during his first siege of Gerona, and to proceed by the regular rules of poliorcetics. He had with him a battering-train more than sufficient to wreck the ancient walls of the city: accordingly he opened a secondary attack on the lower town on the left of the Oña, but turned the greater part of his attention to the citadel of Monjuich. If this work, which from its lofty hill commands the whole city, were once mastered, the place could not hold out for a day longer. By this arrangement the charge of the main attack fell to Reille, and Duhesme himself undertook only the demonstration against the Mercadal. The French began by establishing themselves on the lower slopes of the tableland of which Monjuich occupies the culminating point. They found shelter in three ruined towers which the garrison was too weak to occupy, and raised near them three batteries with six heavy guns and two howitzers, which battered the citadel, and also played upon certain parts of the town wall near the gate of San Pedro. The batteries in Duhesme's section of the siege-lines consisted only of mortars and howitzers, which shelled and several times set fire to the Mercadal, but could make no attempt to open breaches in its walls.

The siege-approaches of the French before Gerona were conducted with an astonishing slowness: it was not till sixteen days after they had established themselves on the slopes round Monjuich, that they began to batter it in a serious fashion [Aug. 12]. This delay was partly due to the steepness of the ground up which the guns had to be dragged, partly to the necessity for sending to Figueras for extra artillery material, which could only be brought slowly and under heavy escort to the banks of the Ter. But Duhesme's slackness, and the want of skill displayed by his engineer officers, were responsible for the greater portion of the delay. Moreover the investment of Gerona was so badly managed, that not only did the garrison keep up a regular communication

dates given by Cabanes. I have followed Arteche here, as his search into times and seasons seems more careful than that of any other authority.

at night with the chiefs of the *somatenes* who lay out on the hills
to the west, but convoys repeatedly left and entered the town in
the dark, without meeting a single French picket or patrol.

This delay of a fortnight in pressing the attack on Gerona led
to two important results. The first was that the news of the
capitulation of Baylen reached both camps, producing grave discouragement in the one, and a disposition for bold action in the
other. The second was that Del Palacio and the troops from
Minorca had time granted to them to prepare for interference in
the siege. The marquis had landed at Tarragona on July 23,
with all his division, save the regiment sent to St. Feliu and the
Aragonese battalion which had been directed on Tortosa. Immediately on his arrival the insurrectionary Junta of Catalonia
transferred itself from Lerida to Tarragona and elected Del Palacio
Captain-General of the principality. Thus a real central authority
was established in the province, and a single military direction
could at last be given to its armies. The new Captain-General
was well-intentioned and full of patriotism, but no great strategist [1].
His plan was to press Barcelona with the bulk of his regular forces,
so that Lecchi might be compelled to call for instant help from
Duhesme, while a small column under the Conde de Caldagues was
to march on Gerona, not so much with the hope of raising the
siege, as to aid the *somatenes* of the Ampurdam in harassing
the investing force and throwing succours into the city [2].

Accordingly the main body of Del Palacio's army, the regiments
of Soria, Granada, and Borbon, with Wimpfen's two Swiss battalions from Tarragona, marched on the Llobregat, drove in
Lecchi's outposts, and confined him to the immediate environs
of Barcelona. The *somatenes* came to give help in thousands,
and a cordon of investment was established at a very short distance
from the great city. On the sea-side Lord Cochrane, with the
Impérieuse and *Cambrian* frigates, kept up a strict blockade, so
that Lecchi, with his insufficient and not too trustworthy garrison
of 3,500 Swiss and Italian troops, was in a most uncomfortable
position. If it had not been that Barcelona was completely commanded by the impregnable citadel of Monjuich, he could not

---

[1] Collingwood (*Correspondence*, ii. 271) calls him 'a fat unwieldy marquess,
who, if his principles are good, has a very limited ability.'

[2] For Del Palacio's intentions see his orders to Caldagues, quoted by
Arteche (ii. 622).

have maintained his hold on the large and turbulent city. His last outpost was destroyed on July 31 : this was the strong castle of Mongat, six miles out on the coast-road from Barcelona to Mataro. It was held by a company of Neapolitans, 150 men with seven guns. Attacked on the land-side by 800 *miqueletes* under Francisco Barcelo, and from the sea by the broadside of the *Impérieuse*, the Italian officer in command surrendered to Lord Cochrane, in order to save his men from massacre by the Catalans. Cochrane then blew up the castle, and destroyed the narrow coast-road on each side of it by cuttings and explosions [1], so that there was no longer any practicable route for guns, horses, or wagons along the shore. Thus hemmed in, Lecchi began to send to Duhesme, by various secret channels, appeals for instant aid, and reports painting his situation in gloomy but not much exaggerated colours. He asserted that the *somatenes* were pushing their incursions to within 600 yards of his advanced posts, and that there were now 30,000 Catalans in arms around him. If he had said 10,000 he would have been within the limits of fact.

On August 6 the Captain-General, after carefully arranging his troops in the positions round Barcelona, sent off Caldagues to harass Duhesme in the north. This enterprising brigadier-general was given no more than four companies of regulars, three guns, and 2,000 *miqueletes* from the Lerida district under their colonel, Juan Baget. Marching by the mountain road that goes by Hostalrich, and picking up many recruits on the way, he established himself on the fourteenth at Castella, in the hills that lie between Gerona and the sea. Here he was met by all the *somatenes* of Northern Catalonia, under their daring leaders, Milans and Claros.

The investment of Gerona was so badly managed, that when the news of Caldagues' approach was received, two colonels (O'Donovan of the Ultonia Regiment and La Valeta of the Barcelona Volunteers) were able to penetrate the French lines and to confer with the commander of the army of succour. These two officers were really conducting the defence, for the titular governor, Bolivar, seems to have been a nonentity [2], who exercised no influence on the course

---

[1] For a good narrative of these operations see Lord Cochrane's autobiography, i. 262–5.

[2] It is very odd, as Arteche remarks (ii. 611), that none of the contemporary Spanish narratives mention the name of Bolivar. They only speak of La Valeta and O'Donovan as heading the defence.

of events. At a council of war which they attended, it was resolved
to try a stroke which was far bolder than anything that the
Captain-General had contemplated when he sent Caldagues northward. The relieving force was to attack from the rear Reille's
troops on the heights before Monjuich, while at the same time
every man that could be spared from the garrison was to be flung
on the breaching batteries from the front. Duhesme's army in the
plain beyond the Oña was to be left alone: it was hoped that
the whole business would be over before he could arrive at the spot
where the fate of battle was to be decided. There were somewhat
over 8,000 men disposable for the attack : 1,000 regulars and four
hundred *miqueletes* were to sally out of Gerona : Caldagues could
bring up 7,000 more, all raw levies except the four companies of old
troops that he had brought from Tarragona. He had also five field-
guns. As Duhesme and Reille had 13,000 men, of whom 1,200
were cavalry, it was a daring experiment to attack them, even though
their forces were distributed along an extensive line of investment.

A bold and confident general, placed in Duhesme's position, would
not have waited to be attacked in his trenches. The moment that
he heard of the approach of Caldagues, he would have drawn off
half his battalions from the siege, and have gone out to meet the
relieving army, before it could get within striking distance of
Gerona. But Duhesme was not in the mood for adventurous
strokes : he was chilled in his ardour by the news of the disaster
of Baylen : he was worried by Lecchi's gloomy reports ; and he
had been pondering for some days whether it would not be well to
raise the siege and march off to save Barcelona. But the ravages
which his bombardment was producing in the beleaguered city, and
the fact that a breach was beginning to be visible in the walls of
Monjuich, induced him to remain before the place, hoping that
it might fall within the next few days. If this was his determination, he should at least have made preparations to receive Caldagues :
but no attempt whatever appears to have been made to resist an
attack from without.

On the morning of August 16, the Spaniards struck their blow.
Between nine and ten o'clock in the morning, the 1,400 men of the
garrison deployed from behind the cover of the citadel, and charged
down upon the trenches and batteries of the besiegers [1]. They

---

[1] The Barcelona Volunteers under La Valeta led ; the Ultonia, under
Major Henry O'Donnell, supported.

completely swept away the battalion of the 5th Legion of Reserve, which was furnishing the guard of the trenches, captured the siege-guns, and set fire to the fascines of the batteries. Then pushing on, they drove off the Swiss battalion of the Valais, and the two Tuscan battalions of the 113th Regiment, pressing them down hill towards Reille's head quarters at Puente Mayor. The French general rallied them upon the 1st *Régiment de Marche*, which formed his reserve at this point of the line, and mounting the slope retook some of the works which had been lost. But at this moment Caldagues' whole army appeared upon the heights, pressing forward in four columns with great confidence. The sight of these multitudes checked Reille, who hastily drew back, evacuated Puente Mayor and withdrew to the other bank of the Ter. Duhesme, on his side, abandoned all his outlying positions and concentrated his whole force in front of the village of Santa Eugenia.

The Catalans were wise enough not to descend into the plain, where Duhesme's cavalry and guns would have had a free hand. Caldagues refrained from passing the Ter, and merely drew up his army on the slopes above Puente Mayor, ready to receive battle. But the expected attack never came ; Duhesme held back all the afternoon, and then fled away under cover of the darkness. His losses in the fighting on the hills had not been heavy—seventy-five killed and 196 wounded—but his spirit was broken. He would not risk an assault on such a strong position with his motley and somewhat demoralized army. For a moment he thought of leading his whole force back to Reille's base at Figueras : but the reflection that in this case Lecchi would probably be destroyed, and he himself be made responsible for the loss of Barcelona by the Emperor, deterred him from such a cowardly move. Bidding Reille take the northern road and keep open the communications with France, he drew off the rest of his army to the south to rejoin his Italian comrades. The move was made with some panic and precipitation : the remaining siege-guns were buried in a perfunctory fashion, and some stores destroyed. Then Duhesme marched away over the mountains, pursued by the *somatenes* of Milans ; while Reille retired across the plains of the Ampurdam, and had a fairly easy journey to Figueras. Claros, who tried to harass his retreat, never dared to close in upon him in the open country, fearing his cavalry and guns. Far more toilsome was the lot of Duhesme's column, which had to march for twenty miles through very broken ground, chased

by the levies of Milans, to whom the whole district was familiar.
When he reached the sea at Malgrat he found that his troubles
were only growing worse. The *somatenes* hung on his right flank,
while Lord Cochrane's frigate the *Impérieuse* followed him on the
left hand, giving him a broadside whenever his march lay within
cannon-shot of the beach. Moreover, the peasants had been cutting
and blasting away the road under Cochrane's direction; and at
each point where one of these obstructions had been made, it was
necessary to drag the guns and wagons of the column across almost
impassable hill-sides [1]. Finding that he was making no appreciable
progress, and that his men were growing utterly demoralized, Duhesme at last took a desperate step. He blew up his ammunition,
burnt his baggage, cast his field-guns into the sea, and fled away
by hill-tracks parallel with the shore. After long skirmishing with
the *somatenes* he reached Mongat, where Lecchi came out to his aid
with 1000 men and a battery—all that could be spared from the
depleted garrison of Barcelona. There the Catalans stayed their
pursuit, and Duhesme's harassed battalions poured back into the
city, sick of mountain warfare, half-starved, and carrying with them
nothing but what they brought in on their backs [August 20]. As
a fighting force for offensive operations they were useless for some
weeks, and all that their general could do was to hold for foraging
purposes as much of the open ground about Barcelona as he could
manage to retain. Nothing more could be essayed till Napoleon
should vouchsafe to send heavy reinforcements to Catalonia, for the
purpose of reopening the severed communications with France.

Two obvious criticisms on these operations in the month of
August must be made. The first is that Del Palacio might probably
have destroyed Duhesme's whole army, if, instead of sending out
his lieutenant Caldagues with a handful of regulars and 2,000
miqueletes, he had marched on Gerona with his entire force, the
5,000 old troops from Port Mahon and the whole of the local levies
of Central Catalonia. Lecchi was so weak in Barcelona that a few
thousand *somatenes* could have kept him in check, for he dared not
ungarnish the city. If the Captain-General had thrown every man
into the struggle at Gerona, it seems certain that Duhesme must
either have been annihilated or have fled away with Reille to
Figueras, abandoning Barcelona to its inevitable fate.

The second comment is equally obvious: Duhesme's generalship

[1] See Cochrane's autobiography, i. 266.

was even worse than that of Del Palacio. Since the Spaniards came against him not with the whole army of Catalonia, but with a mere detachment of 7,000 *somatenes*, he should have formed a covering force of 5,000 men, and have fallen upon them while they were still at some distance from Gerona. Instead of doing this, he allowed them to encamp for three days unmolested at Castella, a village no more than five miles distant from Reille's outposts. There they concerted their operations with the garrison, and fell upon the investing force at the moment that suited them best. It is the extraordinary apathy or neglect displayed by Duhesme that justifies Caldagues' bold stroke at the French lines. Finding the enemy so torpid, he might well venture an assault upon them, without incurring the charge of rashness of which Napier finds him guilty [1]. In other circumstances it would have been mad for the Spaniard, who had no more than 7,000 *somatenes*, to attack a French army 13,000 strong. But seeing Duhesme so utterly negligent—and his army strung out on a long front of investment, without any covering force—Caldagues was quite justified in making the experiment which turned out so successfully. Duhesme tried to extenuate his fault, by giving out that he had been about to abandon the siege even before he was attacked, and that he had orders from Bayonne authorizing such a step. But we may be permitted to join his successor St. Cyr in doubting both the original intention and the imperial authorization [2]. There is at least no trace of it in the correspondence of Napoleon, who as late as August 23, seven days after the fight outside Gerona, was under the impression that Reille's division alone might suffice to capture the city, though he was prepared if necessary to support him with other troops. On the seventeenth of the same month, the day on which Duhesme began his disastrous retreat on Barcelona, Napoleon had already made up his mind to supersede him, and had directed St. Cyr, with two fresh divisions, to take post at Perpignan. But in the orders given to the new commander in Catalonia there is no sign that the Emperor had acquiesced in the raising of the siege of Gerona, though it may perhaps be deduced from a later dispatch that he had not disapproved of the strengthening of Lecchi's garrison at Barcelona by the withdrawal of Chabran's division from the leaguer [3].

[1] Napier, i. 89.   [2] St. Cyr, *Journal de l'Armée de Catalogne*, 1808-9, p. 15.
[3] The notices of the army of Catalonia and its intended operations are not

Meanwhile Napoleon had recognized that even with Reille's reinforcements, Catalonia was not adequately garrisoned, and on August 10 had directed 18,000 fresh troops upon the principality. These, moreover, were not the mere sweepings of his dépôts, like Reille's men, but consisted of two strong divisions of old troops; Souham's was composed of ten French battalions from Lombardy, Pino's of 10,000 men of the best corps of the army of the kingdom of Italy [1]. A little later the Emperor resolved to send one division more, Germans this time, to Catalonia. Instead of the 13,000 men whom he had originally thought sufficient for the subjugation of the province, he had now set aside more than 40,000 for the task, and this did not prove to be one man too many. No better testimonial could be given to the gallant *somatenes*, than that they had forced the enemy to detach so large a force against them. Nor could any better proof be given of the Emperor's fundamental misconception of the Spanish problem in May and June, than the fact that he had so long been under the impression that Duhesme's original divisions would be enough to subdue the rugged and warlike Catalan principality.

Before Souham, Pino, and the rest could arrive on the scene, many weeks must elapse, and meanwhile we must turn back to the main course of the war in Central Spain, where the condition of affairs had been profoundly modified by the results of the Capitulation of Baylen.

very numerous in Napoleon's dispatches. Foy accepts Duhesme's story that he had intended all along to raise the siege after receiving from Bayonne an order to suspend active operations (iv. 177). But it seems difficult to read this into the Emperor's dispatches; Napoleon received the news of Baylen on Aug. 3, but did not begin pushing large reinforcements on to Catalonia till Aug. 10 (*Nap. Corresp.*, 14,249), nor supersede Duhesme by St. Cyr till Aug. 17 (*Nap. Corresp.*, 14,256). On Aug. 23 he concludes that Duhesme would be best placed at Barcelona, but that Reille must take Gerona with his division, which may be reinforced by that of Chabot, newly arrived at Perpignan, or even by more troops due from Italy in a few weeks. The expectation which he expresses, that Reille alone might very possibly be strong enough to capture the place, is enough to show that he did not intend to raise the siege, but (at most) to order Duhesme to strengthen Lecchi with men drawn off from the leaguer—which is a very different thing from that general's statement of the case.

[1] The Emperor writes to Eugène Beauharnais that the 10,000 Italians, horse, foot, and artillery, must be 'un extrait de l'armée italienne dans le cas de se faire honneur,' the best that could be got (*Dispatch* 14,249, Aug. 10).

SECTION VI

THE CONSEQUENCES OF BAYLEN

CHAPTER I

THE FRENCH RETREAT TO THE EBRO

WHILE dealing with the operations of the French armies in the various provinces of Spain, we have observed that at every point the arrival of the news of Dupont's disaster at Baylen produced notable results. It was this unexpected intelligence that drove the intrusive king out of Madrid within a week of his arrival, and ere the ceremonial of his proclamation had been completed. It brought back Bessières from the Esla to the Arlanzon, and raised the siege of Saragossa. Knowing of it Junot summoned his council of war at Torres Vedras with a sinking heart, and Duhesme lacked the confidence to try the ordeal of battle before Gerona. Beyond the Pyrenees its influence was no less marked. Napoleon had imagined that the victory of Rio Seco had practically decided the fate of the Peninsula, and at the moment of Baylen was turning his attention to Austria rather than to Spain. On July 25, five days after Dupont had laid down his arms, he was meditating the reinforcement of his army in Germany, and drafting orders that directed the garrisons of northern France on Mainz and Strasburg [1]. To a mind thus preoccupied the news of the disaster in Andalusia came like a thunderclap. So far was the Spanish trouble from an end, that it was assuming an aspect of primary

---

[1] Napoleon to Jerome, King of Westphalia, July 25 (*Nap. Corresp.*, 14,230): 'L'Autriche arme : elle nie ses armements, elle arme donc contre nous. . . . Puisque l'Autriche arme, il faut donc armer. Aussi j'ordonne que la Grande Armée soit renforcée. Mes troupes se réunissent à Strasbourg, Mayence, Wesel,' &c. Compare this with the great harangue made to Metternich on August 15 (*Nap. Corresp.*, 14,254) and with *Nap. Corresp.*, 14,248, which discusses the co-operation of Russia in a war with Austria.

importance. If Austria was really intending mischief, it was clear
that the Emperor would have two great continental wars on his
hands at the same moment—a misfortune that had never yet
befallen him. It was already beginning to be borne in upon him
that the treachery at Bayonne had been a blunder as well as
a crime. Hence came the wild rage that bursts out in the letters
written upon the days following that on which the news of Baylen
reached him at Bordeaux. 'Has there ever, since the world
began,' wrote Bonaparte to Clarke, his minister of war, 'been such
a stupid, cowardly, idiotic business as this? Behold Mack and
Hohenlohe justified! Dupont's own dispatch shows that all that
has occurred is the result of his own inconceivable folly. . . . The
loss of 20,000 picked men, who have disappeared without even
inflicting any considerable loss on the enemy, will necessarily have
the worst moral influence on the Spanish nation. . . . Its effect on
European politics will prevent me from going to Spain myself. . . .
I wish to know at once what tribunal ought to try these generals,
and what penalty the law can inflict on them for such a crime [1].'
A similar strain runs through his first letter to his brother Joseph
after the receipt of the news—' Dupont has soiled our banners.
What folly and what baseness! The English will lay hands on
his army [2]. Such events make it necessary for me to go to Paris,
for Germany, Poland, Italy, and all, are tied up in the same
knot. It pains me grievously that I cannot be with you, in
the midst of my soldiers [3].' In other letters the capitulation is
'a terrible catastrophe,' 'a horrible affair, for the cowards capitulated to save their baggage,' and (of course) 'a machination paid
for with English gold [4]. These imbeciles are to suffer on the
scaffold the penalty of this great national crime [5].' The Emperor

[1] Napoleon to Clarke, Aug. 3 (*Nap. Corresp.*, 14,242).

[2] i. e. Napoleon is aware that they will never allow the army to be taken
home by sea, as the capitulation provided.

[3] Napoleon to Joseph, Aug. 3 (*Nap. Corresp.*, 14,243) : ' L'Allemagne,
l'Italie, la Pologne etc., tout se lie,' is the Emperor's phrase.

[4] *Nap. Corresp.*, 14,244, 14,272, 14,283.

[5] A few words as to Dupont's fate may be added. His experiences during
the next four years throw a curious light on the administration of military
justice under the Empire. He, together with Vedel, Chabert, Marescot,
Legendre, and the aide-de-camp Villoutreys, were arrested on returning to
France, and thrown into prison. They were told to prepare for a trial before
the Supreme High Court (*Haute Cour Impériale*), and a long series of inter-

did well to be angry, for the shock of Baylen was indeed felt to
every end of Europe.   But he should have blamed his own Macchia-
vellian brain, that conceived the plot of Bayonne, and his own
overweening confidence, that launched Dupont with 20,000 half-
trained conscripts (not, as he wrote to Clarke, with *vingt mille
hommes d'élite et choisis*) on the hazardous Andalusian enterprise.

Meanwhile he had to face the situation : within a few hours of
the moment when Villoutreys placed Dupont's dispatch in his
hands, he had so far got over the first spasms of his wrath that he
was able to dictate a general plan for the reconcentration of his
armies [1].   We have compared the French forces in Spain to a
broad wedge, of which the point, directed against the heart of the
insurrection, was formed by the three divisions of Dupont's corps.
This point had now been broken off; but the Emperor, still
clinging to the idea of the wedge, wished to preserve Madrid and
to form in and about it a new army fit for offensive operations.
With this force he would strike at the insurgents of Andalusia and
Valencia when they marched on the capital, while Bessières in the

rogatories was administered to them.   A military commission drew up a preliminary report on the case: on reading it the Emperor saw that Dupont had a
fair defence to make on all the charges brought against him, with the exception
of that of military incapacity.   He countermanded the order for a trial, and the
prisoners (after nine months of confinement) were released, but left under
police surveillance.   After Dupont had spent two years and a half of peace
in the country-house of a relative, he was suddenly arrested at midnight on
Feb. 12, 1812, and given a secret trial, not before a court of justice or a court-
martial, but before a special military commission.   He was allowed neither
counsel nor documents, and forced to defend himself at forty-eight hours'
notice.   The judges declared him guilty of having signed a capitulation containing ' des conditions honteuses et avilissantes,' but not of having surrendered without necessity, or of having shown cowardice or treason.   Since the
capitulation had been ' contrary to the political interests of the Empire, and
had compromised the safety of the State,' while yet ' there would be grave
inconvenience in giving the accused a public trial,' the court advised the
Emperor to deprive Dupont of rank, title, and pension, and to relegate him
to the country.   The other accused officers might suffer the same penalties.
Refusing to consider this a sufficient punishment, Napoleon shut up Dupont
in the lonely fort of Joux, in the Jura, where he remained a prisoner till the
fall of the Empire.   Vedel and Legendre were pardoned, and afterwards
served in Italy.   Chabert and Villoutreys were put on half-pay.

[1] The 'Note sur la situation actuelle de l'Espagne,' which forms No. 14,241
of the *Correspondance*.   It is dated at Bordeaux, Aug. 2, the very day on which
Villoutreys brought the news of the capitulation.

valley of the Douro, and Verdier in the valley of the Ebro were still to preserve a forward position, and shield the army of the centre from the flank attacks of the Galicians and the Aragonese. The troops left around Madrid at the moment of the disaster of Baylen were parts of the three divisions of Moncey's corps [1], one of Dupont's, and the brigade which had escorted Joseph Napoleon from Burgos, together with 3,000 horse—a total of about 23,000 men. Bonaparte judged that this was not enough to resist the combined attack of Castaños and of the Valencians and Murcians of Saint March and Llamas. Accordingly he intended that Bessières should lend the King two brigades of infantry— a deduction from his force which would compel him to fall back from Leon into Old Castile [2]—and that Verdier should spare a brigade from the army in front of Saragossa [3], though it was none too strong for the task before it. Six battalions from the reserve at Bayonne were to make a forced march to Madrid to join the King. Thus reinforced up to 35,000 men, the corps at Madrid would be able, as the Emperor supposed, to make head against any combination of Spanish troops that could possibly be brought against it.

But all these arrangements were futile. Bonaparte at Bordeaux was separated from his brother at the Retiro by so many miles that his orders were grown stale before they reached their destination. His scheme was made out on August 2, but on the preceding day King Joseph and his whole army had evacuated Madrid. The terror of Baylen was upon them, and they were expecting every moment to find themselves attacked by Castaños, who was as a matter of fact celebrating triumphal feasts at Seville. With a

---

[1] Viz. Musnier's division of Moncey's corps . . . 6,500 men
Frere's division of Dupont's corps . . . . 4,400 „
Bujet's brigade of Morlot's division of Moncey's corps . 3,700 „
Remains (5 batts.) of Gobert's division of Moncey's corps 2,500 „
Rey's brigade of infantry (Joseph's escort) . . 2,000 „
Infantry and Cavalry of the Imperial Guard .' . . 2,500 „
Cavalry of the Line . . . . 1,700 „

23,300 „

[2] Lefebvre's brigade, which belonged to Morlot's division of Moncey's corps —it had been lent to Bessières for the moment—and Reynaud's brigade, i. e. 5,300 foot, also two cavalry regiments, making 6,000 in all.

[3] Bazancourt's brigade of two veteran regiments (14th and 44th of the line), the last that had arrived at Saragossa.

haste that turned out to be altogether unnecessary, Moncey's corps, escorting the King, his court, and his long train of Spanish refugees, crossed the Somosierra and did not halt till they reached Aranda de Duero, in the plains of Old Castile. Napoleon was forced to make other plans in view of this retreat, whose moral consequences were hardly inferior in importance to those of Dupont's capitulation. For both the Spanish nation and the courts of Europe looked upon the evacuation of Madrid as marking the complete downfall of Napoleon's policy, and portending a speedy retirement of the invaders behind the Pyrenees. It is certain that if the spirit of Joseph and his advisers had been unbroken, they might have clung to the capital till the reinforcements which the Emperor was hurrying to their aid had arrived. It is probable that the 35,000 men, of whom Savary and Moncey could then have disposed, might have held Castaños in check till the army from the Rhine had time to come up. Yet there is every excuse for the behaviour of the French commanders, for they could not possibly have known that the Spaniards would move with such astonishing slowness, or that they would refrain from hurling every available man on Madrid. And as a matter of fact the evacuation of the capital turned out in the end to be advantageous to Napoleon, for it inspired his adversaries with a foolish self-confidence which proved their ruin. If they had been forced to fight hard in New Castile, they would have been obliged to throw much more energy into the struggle, and could not have slackened their efforts under the false impression that the French were absconding in dismay to Bayonne.

When Bonaparte learnt that his brother had fled from Madrid and crossed the passes into Old Castile, he was forced to draw out a wholly different scheme from that which he had sketched on August 2. The King, he wrote, with Moncey's corps, must take post at Aranda, where the Douro is crossed by the high-road from France to Madrid. His army should be strengthened to a force of 30,000 men : meanwhile Bessières and Verdier must protect his flanks. The former with 15,000 men should take Valladolid as his head quarters and guard against any attempt of Blake to resume the offensive. As to Verdier, since he had been instructed to abandon the siege of Saragossa—a grave blunder—he must be drawn back as far as Tudela on the Middle Ebro. From that point he would easily be able to 'contain' the tumultuary army of Palafox. If the Spaniards showed signs of pressing in on any part of the front, the King, Verdier, or Bessières—as the case might demand—must not hang back, but endeavour to shatter the vanguard of any advancing force by a bold stroke. At all costs the war must not be waged in a timid style—in short, to adopt a well-known military axiom, 'the best defensive would be a vigorous local offensive[1].' Meanwhile it should be known that enormous reinforcements were in march from the Rhine and the Elbe. This was indubitably correct, for on August 5 the 1st and 6th Corps of the 'Grand Army,' and two divisions of heavy cavalry, had been sent their orders to break up from their garrisons and set out for Spain[2]. The Viceroy of Italy and the Princes of the Confederation of the Rhine had also been directed to send large contingents to the Peninsula: the troops from Italy were to move on Perpignan and strengthen the army of Catalonia; those from the German states were to march on Bayonne and join the main army[3]. Somewhat later the Emperor directed still further masses of men to be drawn off from Germany, namely Marshal Mortier with the 5th Corps and two more divisions of dragoons[4], while the whole of the Imperial Guard came down from Paris on the same errand[5]. There were still nearly 100,000 of the old army left in Spain[6], and the reinforcements would amount to 130,000 more, a force which when united would far surpass both in numbers and in quality any army that the Spaniards would be able to get together in the course of the next two months.

It was from Rochefort and on August 5 that Napoleon sent off his orders to his brother to stay his retreat at Aranda de Duero, and to keep Bessières at Valladolid and Verdier at Tudela. Once more the distances of space and time were too much for him. Before the dispatch from Rochefort came to hand, Joseph and Savary had already abandoned Aranda: they left it on the sixth and by the ninth were at Burgos. At that city they were met by Bessières, who according to the King's orders had fallen back from

---

[1] Note on the situation of Spain, Aug. 5 (*Nap. Corresp.*, 14,245).

[2] Napoleon to Clarke, Aug. 5 (*Nap. Corresp.*, 14,244).

[3] Napoleon to Eugène, Aug. 10 (*Nap. Corresp.*, 14,249), and to Clarke (*Nap. Corresp.*, 14,256).

[4] Napoleon to Clarke, Aug. 17 (*Nap. Corresp.*, 14,256).

[5] Except of course the brigade of fusiliers and the three cavalry regiments which were already in Spain.

[6] Or 98,000 to be exact, unless Reille's force in Roussillon be added.

the Esla to the Arlanzon. Napoleon's elaborate scheme for the maintenance of the line of the Douro had thus fallen through, as completely as his earlier plan for the defence of Madrid. Seeing that his orders were clearly out of date, Moncey and Bessières [1] agreed that they might be disregarded. The next line suitable for an army acting on the defensive was that of the Ebro, and to the banks of that river the dispirited army of France now withdrew.

The head quarters were established at Miranda: the troops of Bessières and Moncey were massed at that place and at Logroño, with a strong detachment across the Ebro at Pancorbo, and some cavalry lying out as far as Burgos: Verdier's army, after finally raising the siege of Saragossa, fell back on Milagro, the point where the Aragon falls into the Ebro. Thus some 70,000 men were concentrated on a comparatively short and compact front, covering the two great roads which lead to France by Vittoria and by Pampeluna. Against any frontal attack from the direction of Madrid the position was very strong. But a glance at the map shows that the flanks were not properly protected: there was nothing to prevent Blake from turning the extreme right by an advance into Biscay, or to prevent Palafox from turning the extreme left by a march on Pampeluna via Tafalla or Sanguesa. If either of these moves were made by a powerful force, the army on the Ebro would be compelled either to abandon its positions in order to go in pursuit, or else to leave them occupied by a detachment insufficient to resist a serious attack along the line of the high-road from Madrid. Both those operations were ulti-mately taken in hand by the Spaniards, but it was at too late an hour, when the reinforcements from Germany had begun to arrive, and when ample means were at the disposal of the French generals for repulsing flank attacks, without drawing off men from the line of the Ebro. The astounding slowness of the Spaniards, and the lamentable want of union between the commanders of the various provincial armies, ruined any chance that there might have been of success. The troops of King Joseph were safely installed in their defensive positions by August 15. On that day the leading columns of the Spanish army had only just arrived at Madrid. It was not till a month later that the number of troops brought forward to the line of the Ebro approached the total strength of the host of the intrusive King. The offensive operations of Blake

[1] Savary had left the army on Aug. 4, and returned to France.

and Palafox did not commence till the second half of September, when the columns of the 'Grand Army' were already drawing near to the Pyrenees, and all possible chance of success had long gone by. They were not developed till October, when the counter-stroke of the French was fully prepared. From August 15 down to the day of the battle of Zornoza (October 31) there are two months and a half of wasted time, during which the Spaniards did nothing more than stir up an ineffectual rising in Biscay and gradually push to the front scattered corps whose total did not amount to much more than 100,000 men. The troops of Bonaparte on the other hand— now under the orders of Jourdan, who arrived at Miranda on August 25 [1]—had little to do but to ward off the feeble attempts to cut their communications in Biscay, and to incorporate, brigade by brigade, the numerous reinforcements which kept marching in from Bayonne. For even ere the three veteran corps from Germany came to hand, there was a continuous stream of troops pouring across the Pyrenees. Most important, perhaps, of all the arrivals was that of Marshal Ney, the toughest and most resolute of all the Emperor's fighting-men, who brought with him a spirit of enterprise and confidence which had long been wanting in the army of Spain [2].

[1] See his *Mémoires* (pp. 66, 67) for the situation at this date.
[2] He arrived at Irun on Aug. 30 (*Madrid Gazette*, Sept. 17th, 1808).

SECTION VI: CHAPTER II

CREATION OF THE 'JUNTA GENERAL'

On August 1, Madrid had seen the last of the French: yet it was not till the thirteenth that the Spanish troops appeared before the gates of the capital. Even then it was not the victorious army of Andalusia which presented itself, but only the Valencian corps of Llamas, a mere division of 8,000 men, which would not have dared to push forward, had it not known that Joseph Bonaparte and all his train were now far on their way towards the Ebro. During the thirteen days which elapsed between his departure and the arrival of the Valencians there was a curious interregnum in Madrid. It took some time to convince the populace and the local authorities that the hated invaders were really gone, and that they were once more their own masters. Nothing reflects the state of public opinion better than the *Madrid Gazette*: down to August 1, it shows the hand of a French editor; 'His Majesty' means King Joseph, and all the foreign intelligence is coloured with French views. On August 2, the foreign influence begins to disappear, and we note a very cautious and tentative proclamation by the old 'Council of Castile.' That effete body, shorn by the French of most of its prominent members, had repeatedly yielded to the orders of Murat and Savary: it had carried out many decrees of the new executive, yet it had never actually recognized the legality of King Joseph's accession. Indeed at the last moment it had striven, by feeble methods of evasion and delay, to avoid committing itself to this final step. But we may guess that, had there been no Baylen, the Council would finally have made up its mind to 'swallow the pill'—if we may use once more Murat's characteristic phrase. However, the flight of Joseph had saved it from being forced to range itself on the side of the traitors, and its members were able to stay behind in Madrid without fearing for their necks. In their first manifesto there is not a word that could have offended Savary, if he had returned the next day. It preaches the necessity of calm, order, and quiet: no one must stir up mobs, compromise the public safety, or vex his respectable neighbours [1]. The rest of the paper on this and the two following days is filled up with essays on geography and political economy, lists of servants seeking places, and colourless foreign news many weeks old. Such piteous stuff was not likely to keep the people quiet : on August 4 a mob assembled, broke open the house of Don Luis Viguri (one of Godoy's old confidants), murdered him, and dragged his body through the streets. Fearing that they too might be considered *Afrancesados* the Council published a second proclamation of the most abject kind. The ' melancholy instance of insubordination ' of the previous day causes them ' intolerable sorrow ' and is ' unlikely to tend to public felicity.' The loyal and generous citizens ought to wait for the working of the law and its ministers, and not to take the execution of justice into their own hands. The clergy, the local officials, every employer of labour, every father of a family, are begged to help to maintain peace and order. Then comes a page of notices of new books, and a short paper on the ethics of emigration ! Of Ferdinand VII or Joseph I, of politics domestic or foreign, there is not a word. Two days later the Council at last makes up its mind, and, after a week of most uncomfortable sitting on the fence, suddenly bursts out into an 'Address to the honourable and generous people of the capital of Spain,' in the highest strain of patriotism : ' Our loved King is in chains, but his loyal subjects have risen in his name. Our gallant armies have achieved triumphs over " the invincibles of Marengo, Austerlitz, and Jena." All Europe stands surprised at their rapid victories. These fellow citizens of ours, crowned with the laurels of success, will soon be with us. Meanwhile the Council must beg the patriotic citizens of Madrid to abstain from riot and murder, and to turn their energies into more useful channels. Let them prostrate themselves before the altar in grateful thanks to God, and make preparations to receive and embrace the oncoming bands of liberators.' Domestic intelligence becomes for the future a list of French atrocities, and of (sometimes apocryphal) victories in the remoter corners of Spain [2]. Foreign intelligence is served up with an English rather

---

[1] Proclamation of the Council, dated Aug. 1, published Aug. 2 in the *Gazette*. There is an original copy of the broadsheet in the *Vaughan Papers*.

[2] On Aug. 9 the reader is invited to believe that Roussillon has risen against Napoleon, and that the peasantry have stormed its frontier-fortress of Bellegarde.

than a French flavour. The arsenal of 'Volovich[1]' is shipping
scores of cannon and thousands of muskets for the use of the
brave Spaniards, the treasures of Great Britain are to be poured
into the hands of the insurrectionary Juntas, and so forth. All
this comes a little late: the good intentions of the Council
would have been more clear if they had been expressed on
August 2 instead of August 7, when the French were still at
Buitrago, rather than when they were far away beyond Aranda
de Duero[2].

It is really astonishing to find that the Council made a bid for
power, and attempted to assume the pose of a senate of warm-
hearted patriots, after all its base servility to Murat and Savary
during the last six months. Its president, Don Arias Mon y Velarde,
actually had the audacity to write a circular-note to the various
provincial Juntas of Spain, proposing that, as a single central
government must obviously be established, they should send representatives to Madrid to concert with the Council on means of
defence, and lend it the aid of their influence and authority.
That such a discredited body should attempt to assume a kind
of presidential authority over the local Juntas who had raised and
directed the insurrection was absurd. The replies which were
returned were of the most uncompromising kind: the Galician
Junta taunted the Council with having been 'the most active
instrument of the Usurper.' Palafox, speaking for Aragon,
wrote that it 'was a corporation which had not done its duty.'
The active and ambitious Junta of Seville wished to accuse
the Council before the face of the Spanish people 'of having
subverted the fundamental laws of the realm, of having given
the enemy every facility for seizing the domination of Spain, of
having lost all legal authority and become null and void, and
of being suspected of deliberate treason of the most atrocious sort
possible.' The Valencians voted that 'no public body of any kind
ought to enter into correspondence with the Council of Castile, or

[1] i. e. Woolwich.

[2] It is hard to agree with Napier's verdict that ' The Council was not
wanting to itself ; the individuals comprising it did not hesitate to seize the
reins of power when the French had departed, and the prudence with which
they preserved tranquillity in the capital, and prevented all reaction, proves
that they were not without merit, and forms a striking contrast to the conduct of the provincial Juntas, under whose savage sway every kind of excess
was committed and even encouraged ' (Napier, i. 299).

come to any understanding with it [1].' All these rebuffs to the Council were well deserved, and it is clear that the provincial Juntas were entirely justified in their action. But it is to be feared that there lay at the bottom of their hearts not merely honest indignation at the impudent proposal that had been laid before them, but a not unnatural desire to cling as long as possible to their existing power and authority. In many of the provinces there was shown a most unworthy and unwise reluctance to proceed at once to the construction of a single governing body for Spain, even when the proposal was put forward not by a discredited corporation like the Council, but by men of undoubted patriotism.

The credit of starting a serious agitation for the erection of a 'Supreme Junta' must be given to the Murcians, whose councils were guided by the old statesman Florida Blanca, a survivor from the days of Charles III. As far back as June 22 they had issued a proclamation setting forth the evils of provincial particularism, and advocating the establishment of a central government. None of the other Juntas ventured openly to oppose this laudable design, and some of them did their best to further it. But there were others who clung to power, and were determined to surrender it at as late a date as they could manage. The Junta of Seville was far the worst: that body—as we have had occasion to mention in another place—was largely in the hands of intriguers, and had put forth unjustifiable claims to domination in the whole southern part of the realm, even usurping the title of 'Supreme Junta of Spain and the Indies [2].' In their desire for self-aggrandizement they took most unjustifiable steps: they suppressed Florida Blanca's Murcian proclamation, lest it might stir up an agitation in Andalusia in behalf of the establishment of a central government [3]. But this was a comparatively venial sin: their worst act was to stay the march of Castaños on Madrid after Baylen. The pretext used was that they wished to welcome the victorious general and his army with triumphal entries and feasts of rejoicing—things entirely out of place, so long as the French were still holding the capital of the realm. To his own entire dissatisfaction Castaños was dragged back to Seville, there to display the captured guns and flags of the French, and to be received with salvos fired by patriotic

---

[1] All these quotations come from the documents inserted by Torefio in his fifth book (i. 262).

[2] See page 69.   [3] Lord Collingwood's *Correspondence*, ii. 98.

ladies who had learnt the drill of the artilleryman [1]. But he soon
found to his disgust that the Junta was really aiming at the
employment of his troops not for national purposes but for their
own aggrandizement. They wished to speak with 40,000 men at
their back, and were most reluctant to let the army pass the
Sierra Morena, lest it should get out of their control. Their most
iniquitous design was to overawe by armed force their neighbours,
the Junta of Granada, who refused to recognize them as a central
authority for Andalusia, and had given their assent to the Murcian
proposal for the prompt formation of a national government.
They were actually issuing orders for a division to march against
the Granadans, when Castaños—though a man of mild and con-
ciliatory manners—burst out in wrath at the council board.
Springing up from his chair and smiting the table a resounding
blow, he exclaimed, ' Who is the man that dares bid the troops
march without my leave ? Away with all provincial differences :
I am the general of the Spanish nation, I am in command of an
honourable army, and we are not going to allow any one to stir
up civil war [2].' Conscious that the regiments would follow the
victor of Baylen, and refuse obedience to mere civilians, the Junta
dropped their suicidal project. But they turned all their energy
into devising pretexts for delaying the march of the army on
Madrid. Their selfishness was undisguised : when Castaños begged
for leave to march on the capital without further delay [3], the
Conde de Tilly (the most intriguing spirit among all the politicians
of Seville) responded with the simple question, ' And what then
will become of *us* ? ' He then moved that the Junta of Andalusia
should concern itself with Andalusia and Portugal alone, and not
interfere in what went on beyond the Sierra Morena. This
proposal was a little too strong even for the narrow-minded
particularists of the Junta : but though they let Castaños go, they
contrived excuses for delaying the march of the greater part of his
army. He did not get to Madrid till August 23, more than
a month after Baylen, and then brought with him only the single
division of La Peña, about 7,000 strong. The other three

---

[1] Arteche, ii. 124.   [2] Toreño, i. 264.

[3] This story is told by Lord Collingwood, in an official dispatch to Castlereagh, dated July 29. He states that he *knows* that the colloquy took place,
and clearly had the information from Castaños himself (*Collingwood Correspondence*, ii. 199).

divisions, those of Reding, Jones, and Coupigny, did not cross the Sierra Morena for many weeks after, and some of the troops had not even left Andalusia at the moment when the French resumed offensive operations in October. On various specious pretences the Junta detained many regiments at Seville and Cadiz, giving out that they were to form the nucleus of a new 'army of reserve,' which was still a mere skeleton three months after Baylen had been fought. If we compare the Andalusian army-list of November with that of July, we find that only seven new battalions[1] had joined the army of Castaños in time to fight on the Ebro. It is true that a new division had been also raised in Granada, and sent to Catalonia under General Reding, but this was due to the energy of the Junta of that small kingdom, which was far more active than that of Seville. Andalusia had 40,000 men under arms in July, and no more than 50,000 at the beginning of November, though the Junta had promised to have at least thirty reserve battalions ready before the end of the autumn, and had received from England enormous stores of muskets and clothing for their equipment.

In the northern parts of Spain there was almost as much confusion, particularism, and selfishness as in the south. The main sources of trouble were the rivalry of the Juntas of Asturias and Galicia, and the extravagant claims of the aged and imbecile Cuesta, in virtue of his position as Captain-General of Castile. It will be remembered that in June insurrectionary Juntas had been established at Leon and Valladolid, the former purporting to represent the kingdom of Leon, the latter the kingdom of Old Castile. Each had been under the thumb of Cuesta, who looked upon them as nothing more than committees established under his authority for the civil government of the provinces of the Douro. But the disaster of Medina de Rio Seco destroyed both the power and the credit of the Captain-General. Flying before the French, the Juntas took refuge in Galicia, where they settled down at Ponferrada for a few days, and then moved to Lugo, whither the Junta of Galicia came out to meet them. The three bodies, joining in common session, chose as their president Don Antonio Valdes, the Bailiff of the Knights of Malta, who was one of the representatives of Castile. They claimed to be recognized as the supreme civil

---

[1] Tiradores de España, Provincial de Cadiz, Carmona, Baylen, Navas de Tolosa, 3rd and 5th Volunteers of Seville.

government of Northern Spain, but their position was weakened by two mischances. The Asturian Junta refused to have anything to do with them, and persisted in remaining sovereign within the borders of its own principality. Even more vexatious was the conduct of Cuesta : though he was wandering in the mountains with only three or four thousand raw levies—the wrecks of Rio Seco—he refused to recognize any authority in the three federated Juntas, and pretended to revoke by his proclamation any powers vested in those of Castile and Leon. The fact was that he knew that they would lend support to his military rival Blake, and not to himself. He feigned to regard the Captains-General and the old *Audiencias*, or provincial tribunals, as the sole legitimate powers left in the kingdom, and to consider the Juntas as irregular assemblies destitute of any valid authority. In what a scandalous form he translated his theories into action, we shall soon see. Meanwhile he refused to co-operate with the troops of Galicia, and made no attempt to follow the retreating French. All his efforts were directed to increasing the numbers of the mass of raw levies which he called the ' Army of Castile.' But from the whole of the provinces over which he claimed authority he had only succeeded in scraping together 12,000 men by the middle of September, though as far as population went they represented nearly a sixth of the people of Spain.

The want of any central executive for directing the armies of the patriots had the most disastrous results. By September 1 Castaños and Llamas had not more than 20,000 men at Madrid. Galluzzo's army of Estremadura, which ought to have joined them long before, was still employed in its futile siege of Elvas. Cuesta was hanging back in Castile, as jealous of Castaños as he had been of Blake. The only armies which were in touch with the French were Palafox's troops on the Ebro and the Valencian division of Saint March, which the Junta of Valencia (showing more patriotism than most of their colleagues) had pushed up to Saragossa to aid the Aragonese. Blake, with the powerful army of Galicia, had descended to Astorga when Bessières retreated to Burgos. But from Astorga he advanced most cautiously, always clinging to the southern slope of the Cantabrian hills, in order to avoid the plains, where the cavalry of the French would have a free hand. It was not till September 10 that he had concentrated his main body at Reynosa, near the sources of the Ebro, where he was at last near enough to the front to be able to commence operations.

The whole month of August, it is not too much to say, was lost
for military purposes because Spain had not succeeded in furnishing
itself with a central government or a commander-in-chief.   It had
been wasted in constitutional debates of the most futile kind.   To
every one, except to certain of the more selfish members of the
Juntas, it was clear that a way must be found out of the existing
anarchy.   Three courses seemed possible : one was to appoint a
Regent, or a small Council of Regency, and to entrust to him (or
to them) the conduct of affairs.   The second was to summon the
Cortes, the old national parliament of Spain.   The third was to
establish a new sort of central government, by inducing each of
the existing Juntas to send deputies, with full powers of representation, to sit together as a 'Supreme Central Junta' for the whole
realm.   The project of appointing a Regent had at first many
advocates : it occurred to both Castaños and Palafox, and each
(as it chanced) pitched upon the same individual as most worthy
of the post [1].   This was the Archduke Charles of Austria, the sole
general in Europe who had won a military reputation of the first
class while contending with the French.   He would have been an
excellent choice—if only he could have been secured.   But it did
not take much reflection to see that if Austria allowed her greatest
captain to accept such a post, she would involve herself in instant
war with Bonaparte, and if such a war broke out the Archduke
would be wanted on the Danube rather than upon the Ebro.
There was no other name likely to command general confidence.
Some spoke of the Cardinal Archbishop of Toledo [2], the last prince
of the Spanish royal house who remained in the realm.   But he
was an insignificant and incapable person, and much discredited
by his dallyings with Murat in the days before the insurrection
had begun.   Clearly he would be no more than a puppet, worked
by some astute person behind the viceregal throne.   Other names
suggested were those of the young Dom Pedro of Portugal (son
of the Prince-Regent John), and of Prince Leopold, the son of
Ferdinand IV of Sicily.   The former was a grandson, the latter a
nephew of Charles IV.   Both therefore were near to the throne,
but both were foreigners, young, untried in matters of state, and
utterly unknown to the Spaniards.   Dom Pedro's claims were not

[1] See Arteche, iii. 118.
[2] First cousin to Charles IV, being the son of the Infante Luis, and brother
of Godoy's unfortunate wife.

strongly pushed, but the Sicilian court made a strenuous attempt
to forward those of Prince Leopold.   Their ambassador in London
tried to enlist the support of the English Government for him :
but Canning and Castlereagh were anxious to avoid any appearance of dictating orders to Spain, and firmly refused to countenance
the project.   Before their reply came to hand, King Ferdinand (or
rather that old intriguer, his spouse, and her son-in-law the Duke
of Orleans) sent the prince to Gibraltar, on a man-of-war which
they had obtained from Mr. Drummond, the British minister at
Palermo.   By lending his aid to the plan this unwise diplomat almost
succeeded in compromising his government.   But most fortunately
our representatives in Spain nipped in the bud this intrigue, which
could not have failed to embroil them with the Juntas, none of whom
had the least love for the Sicilian house.   When the *Thunderer*
arrived at Gibraltar [August 9] Sir Hew Dalrymple—then just on
the eve of starting for Portugal—refused to allow the prince to
land, or to distribute the proclamations which he had prepared.
These were the work of Leopold's brother-in-law, Louis Philippe
of Orleans, who had accompanied him from Palermo with the design of fishing in troubled waters, a craft of which he was to show
himself in later days a past master.   If Leopold should become
regent, Orleans intended to be the ' power behind the throne.'
Dalrymple detained the two princes at Gibraltar, and when he was
gone Lord Collingwood[1] took the same attitude of hostile neutrality.
Tired of detention, Louis Philippe after a few days sailed for London,
in the vain hope of melting the hearts of the British Cabinet.   The
Sicilian prince lingered some time, protesting against the fashion
in which he was treated, and holding secret colloquies with deputations which came to him from many quarters in which the Junta
of Seville was detested.   But there was no real party in his favour.
What benefit could come to Spain from the election of a youth of
nineteen, whose very name was unknown to the people, and who
could help them neither with men nor with money, neither with
the statesmanship that comes from experience, nor with the military
capacity that must be developed on the battle-field ?   After remaining long enough in Spanish waters to lose all his illusions, Prince

---

[1] Napier is wrong in hinting that Canning lent himself to the Sicilian
scheme (i. 177, 178) in order to disoblige Castlereagh.   Collingwood's dispatches show that he opposed it, as much as did Dalrymple, and thereby won
approval from his government (*Collingwood Correspondence*, ii. 216, 217).

Leopold returned to his mother in Sicily [1]. There had never been any foundation for a persistent rumour that he was to be made co-regent along with the Cardinal Archbishop of Toledo and the Conde de Montijo. Not even the least intelligent members of the Juntas would have consented to hand over the rule of Spain to this strange triumvirate—an imbecile, a boy, and a turbulent intriguer. There was about as much chance that another vain project might be carried out—an invitation to General Dumouriez to take command of all the Spanish armies. Yet this plan too was seriously brought forward : the Frenchman would not have been unwilling, but the Spanish officers, flushed with their recent successes, were not the kind of people to welcome a foreign leader, and one whose last military exploit had been to desert his own army and go over to the enemy.

Much more specious, at first sight, than any project for the establishment of a regency, was the proposal mooted in many quarters for the summoning of the Cortes—whose name recalled so many ancient memories, and was connected with the days of constitutional freedom in the Middle Ages. But not only had the Cortes been obscured by the long spell of autocracy under the Hapsburg and Bourbon kings, but it was by its very constitution unsuited to represent a nation seeking for a new and vigorous executive. It was full of mediaeval anomalies: for example the Asturias had never been represented in it, but had possessed (like Wales in the fourteenth and fifteenth centuries) separate governmental machinery of its own. This might have been altered without much difficulty, but it was more fatal that the distribution of seats in the lower estates represented an archaic survival. Many decayed towns in Castile sent members to the Cortes, while on the other hand the warlike and populous province of Galicia had only one single vote. To rearrange the representation on a rational basis would take so long, and cause so much provincial jealousy, that it was recognized as practically impossible.

There remained therefore only the third plan for creating a supreme government in Spain—that which proposed that the various existing Juntas should each send deputies to some convenient spot, and that the union of these representatives should constitute a central authority for the whole realm. This scheme was not so clearly constitutional as the summoning of the Cortes

---

[1] He sailed on Nov. 4 (*Madrid Gazette*).

would have been, nor did it provide for real unity of direction in
so complete a way as would have been secured by the appointment
of a single Regent.   But it had the practical advantage of conciliating the various provincial Juntas: though they sacrificed
their local sovereignty, they obtained at least the power of
nominating their own masters.   In each of them the more active
and ambitious members hoped that they might secure for themselves the places of delegates to the new supreme assembly.
Accordingly the Juntas were induced, one after another, to consent
to the scheme.   Public opinion ran so strongly in favour of unity,
and the existing administrative chaos was so clearly undesirable,
that it was impossible to protest against the creation of a Supreme
Central Junta.   Some of the provinces—notably Murcia, Valencia,
and Granada—showed a patriotic spirit of self-abnegation and
favoured the project from the first.   Even Galicia and Seville,
where the spirit of particularism was strongest, dared not openly
resist the movement.   There were malcontents who suggested that
a federal constitution was preferable to a centralized one, and
that it would suffice for the provinces to bind themselves together
by treaties of alliance, instead of handing themselves over to a
newly created executive.   But even in Aragon, where federal union
with Castile seemed more attractive to many than complete in-
corporation, the obvious necessity for common military action
determined the situation[1].   Every province of Spain at last adhered
to the project for constructing a Supreme Central Junta.   Even the
narrow-minded politicians at Seville had to assume an attitude of
hearty consent.   But their reluctance peeped out in the suggestion
which they made that the Junta should meet, not at Madrid, but
at Ciudad Real or Almagro in La Mancha, places convenient to
themselves, but obscure and remote in the eyes of inhabitants of
Asturias or Galicia.   Their aversion to Madrid was partly caused
by its remoteness from their own borders, but much more by
jealousy of the Council of Castile, which still hung together and
exercised local authority in the capital.   Other Juntas showed
their aversion for the Council in the same way, and ultimately
the place selected for the gathering of the new government was the
royal residence of Aranjuez, which stands to Madrid much as do
Versailles or Windsor to Paris and London.   This choice was an

[1] Note the federalist views of the Aragonese Miguel Principe, quoted by
Arteche (ii. 121).

obvious mistake: the central government of a country loses in dignity when it does not reside in the national capital. It seems to distrust its own power or its legality, when it exiles itself from its proper abode. At the best it casts a slur on the inhabitants of the capital by refusing to trust itself among them. Madrid, it is true, is not to Spain what Paris is to France, or London to England: it is a comparatively modern place, pitched upon by Philip II as the seat of his court, but destitute of ancient memories. Nevertheless, it was at least infinitely superior to Aranjuez as a meeting-place. On geographical or strategical grounds they are so close that no advantage accrues to one that does not belong to the other. But for political reasons the capital was distinctly preferable to the almost suburban palace [1]. If the existence of the Council of Castile so much disturbed the Junta, it would have been quite possible to dissolve that discredited body. No one would have made any serious effort in its favour, even in the city of its abode.

[1] Both Florida Blanca and Jovellanos were in favour of making Madrid the meeting-place. The Andalusians defeated them.

THE 'JUNTA GENERAL' IN SESSION

THE provincial Juntas, when once they had consented to sacrifice their local sovereignty, made no great delay in forwarding their representatives to the chosen meeting-place at Aranjuez. The number of deputies whom they sent to the Supreme Central Junta was thirty-five, seventeen provincial Juntas each contributing two, and the Canary Islands one. The Biscayan provinces, still wholly in the possession of the French, had no local body to speak for them, and could not therefore choose deputies. The number thus arrived at was not a very convenient one: thirty-five is too few for a parliament, and too many for an executive government. Moreover proportional representation was not secured; Navarre and the Balearic Islands were given too much weight by having two members each. Andalusia, having eight deputies for its four Juntas of Seville, Jaen, Granada, and Cordova, was over-represented when compared with Galicia, Aragon, and Catalonia, which had each no more than two. The quality of the delegates was very various: among the most notable were the ex-ministers Florida Blanca and Jovellanos, who represented respectively the better sides of the Conservative and the Liberal parties of Spain—if we may use such terms. The former, trained in the school of 'benevolent despotism' under Charles III, was a good specimen of the eighteenth-century statesman of the old sort—polite, experienced, energetic, a ripe scholar, and an able diplomat. But he was eighty years old and failing in health, and his return to active politics killed him in a few months. Jovellanos, a somewhat younger man [1], belonged in spirit to the end rather than the middle of the eighteenth century, and was imbued with the ideas of liberty and constitutional government which were afloat all over Europe in the early days of the French Revolution. He represented modern liberalism in the shape which it took in Spain. For this reason he had suffered

---

[1] He was born in 1743.

many things at the hands of Godoy, and emerged from a long period of imprisonment and obscurity to take his place in the councils of the nation. Unhappily he was to find that his ideas were still those of a minority, and that bureaucracy and obscurantism were deeply rooted in Spain.

Of the other members [1] of the Supreme Junta, the Bailiff Valdez and Francisco Palafox, fresh from his brother's triumphs at Saragossa, were perhaps the best known. Among the rest we note a considerable number of clergy—two archbishops, a prior, and three canons—but not more than might have been expected in a country where the Church was so powerful. Military men were not so strongly represented, being only five in number, and three of these were militia colonels. The rest were mainly local notables—grandees, marquises, and counts predominated over mere commoners. Some of them were blind particularists, and a few—like the disreputable Conde de Tilly—were intriguers with doubtful antecedents. The whole body represented Spain well enough, but Spain with her weaknesses as well as her strong points. It was not a very promising instrument with which to achieve the liberation of the Peninsula, or to resist the greatest general in Europe. Considered as a government of national defence, it had far too little military knowledge: a haphazard assembly of priests, politicians, and grandees is not adapted for the conduct of a war of independence. Hence came the incredible blindness which led it to refuse to appoint a single commander-in-chief, and the obstinacy with which it buried itself in constitutional debates of the most futile sort when Napoleon was thundering at the gates of Spain.

The meeting of the Supreme Junta was fixed for September 25, but long ere that date came round the military situation was assuming new developments. The first modification in the state of affairs was caused by the abortive attempt of the Basque provinces to free themselves. The news of Baylen had caused as great a stir in the northern mountains as in the south or the east of Spain. But Biscay, Guipuzcoa, and Alava had considerable French garrisons, and the retreat of Joseph Bonaparte to the Ebro only increased the number of enemies in their immediate neighbourhood. It would have been no less patriotic than prudent for these provinces to delay their insurrection till it had some chance of proving useful

[1] For a complete list of the names and professions of the members of the Junta, see the Appendix.

to the general scheme of operations for the expulsion of the French from Spain. If they could have waited till Blake and Castaños had reached the Ebro, and then have taken arms, they might have raised a most dangerous distraction in the rear of the French, and have prevented them from turning all their forces against the regular armies. But it was mad to rise when Blake was still at Astorga, and Castaños had not yet reached Madrid. It could not have been expected that the local patriots should understand this: but grave blame falls on those who ought to have known better. The Duke of Infantado, who was acting under Blake, and Colonel Doyle, the English representative at that general's head quarters, did their best to precipitate the outbreak in Biscay. They promised the Biscayan leaders that a division from Asturias should come to their aid, and that English arms and ammunition should be poured into their harbours[1]. At the first word of encouragement all Biscay took arms [August 6]: a great mass of insurgents collected at Bilbao, and smaller bands appeared along the line of the mountains, even as far as Valcarlos on the very frontier of France. But no external aid came to them: the Asturians—averse to every proposal that came from Galicia—did not move outside their own provincial boundary, and no other Spanish army was within striking distance. Bessières was able, at his leisure, to detach General Merlin with 3,000 men to fall on Bilbao. This brigade proved enough to deal with the main body of the Biscayan insurgents, who after a creditable fight were dispersed with heavy loss—1,200 killed, according to the French commander's dispatch [August 16]. Bilbao was taken and sacked, and English vessels bringing—now that it was too late—5,000 stand of arms for the insurgents, narrowly escaped capture in its harbour. All along the line of the Basque hills there was hanging and shooting of the leaders of the abortive rising[2]. The only result of this ill-advised move was that Bessières was warned of the danger in his rear, and kept a vigilant eye for the future on the coastland. The Biscayans, as was natural, were much discouraged at the way in which they had been left in the lurch by their fellow countrymen, and at the inefficacy of their own unaided efforts. They were loth to rise a second time.

It was not till twenty days had passed since the fall of Bilbao

[1] See the letters of Doyle quoted in Napier, i. 287.
[2] Joseph Bonaparte to Napoleon, Sept. 5, 1808.

that the first attempts at combined action were made by the
Spanish generals. On September 5 there met at Madrid a council
of war, composed of Castaños, Cuesta, the Valencian General
Llamas, and the representatives of Blake and Palafox—the Duke
of Infantado and Calvo de Rozas, intendant-general of the army
of Aragon. These officers met with much suppressed jealousy and
suspicion of each other. The Duke had his eye on Cuesta, in accordance with the instructions of Blake. Castaños and Cuesta were
at daggers drawn, for the old Captain-General had just proposed
a *coup d'état* against the Junta to the Andalusian, and had been
repulsed with scorn[1]. The representative of the army of Aragon
had been charged to see that no one was put above the head
of Palafox. When the meeting opened, Cuesta proposed that it
should appoint a single general to direct all the forces of Spain.
The others demurred: Cuesta was much their senior in the army-
list, and they imagined—probably with truth—that he would
claim the post of commander-in-chief for himself, in spite of the
memories of Cabezon and Rio Seco. They refused to listen to
his arguments, though it was certain that unity of command was
in every way desirable. Nor was any disposition shown to raise
Castaños to supreme authority, though this was the obvious step
to take, as he was the only general of Spain who had won a great
battle in the open field. But personal and provincial jealousy
stood in the way, and Castaños himself, though not without
ambition, was destitute of the arts of cajolery, and made no
attempt to push his own candidature for the post of commander-
in-chief. Perhaps he hoped that the Supreme Junta would do him
justice ere long, and refrained for that reason from self-assertion
before his colleagues. Nothing, therefore, was settled on September 5, save a plan for common operations against the French

---

[1] I find the story of Cuesta's projected *coup d'état* (in Toreño, i. 267), which
was supposed to rest on the authority of Castaños alone, completely corroborated in Sir Charles Vaughan's private diary. On Sept. 15 Vaughan, while
passing through Segovia, met Cuesta, who told him ' that two measures were
absolutely necessary : (1) the abolition of the provincial Juntas, and the
restoration of the ancient authority of the Captains-General and *Real Audi-
encia* ; (2) *The exercise of military force* over the Junta at Ocaña (i. e. the
supreme ' Central Junta') sufficient to compel them to elect an executive
council of three or five persons to be placed at the head of different departments, and to be responsible to the nation at large.' This is precisely what
Cuesta proposed to Castaños.

on the Ebro. Like all schemes that are formed from a compromise
between the views of several men, this was not a very brilliant
strategical effort: instead of providing for a bold stroke with the
whole Spanish army, at some point on the long line between Burgos
and Milagro, it merely brought the insurgent forces in half-a-dozen
separate columns face to face with the enemy. Blake, with his own
army and the Asturians, was to be asked to concentrate near Reynosa,
at the sources of the Ebro, and to endeavour to turn Bessières'
flank and penetrate into Biscay [1]. He would have 30,000 men, or
more, but not a single complete regiment of cavalry. Next to
him Cuesta was to operate against the front of Bessières' corps,
with his ' Army of Castile,' eight or nine thousand raw levies backed
by about 1,000 horse. He undertook to make Burgo de Osma
his point of starting. More to the east, Castaños was to gather
at Soria the four divisions of the army of Andalusia, but at present
he had only that of La Peña in hand: the Junta of Seville was
detaining the rest. Still more to the right, Llamas with his 8,000
Valencians and Murcians was to march on Tudela. Lastly Palafox,
with the army of Aragon and the Valencian division of Saint March,
was to keep north of the Ebro, and turn the left flank of Moncey's
corps by way of Sanguesa: he could bring about 25,000 men into
line, but there were not more than five or six regular battalions
among them; the rest were recent levies. When the army of
Estremadura should come up (it was still about Elvas and Badajoz),
it was to join Castaños; and it was hoped that the English forces
from Portugal might also be directed on the same point.

But meanwhile only 75,000 men were available in the first line;
and this force, spread along the whole front from Reynosa to
Sanguesa, and acting on wide external lines, was not likely to make
much impression on the French. The numbers of the invaders
were considerably greater than those of the patriot-armies. Jourdan
had 70,000 men by September 1, and was being reinforced every
day by fresh battalions, though the three corps from Germany
were still far off. Before the Spaniards could move he appreciably
outnumbered them, and he had the inestimable advantage of
holding a comparatively short front, and of being able to concentrate on any point with far greater rapidity than was possible
to his adversaries. Even had they thrown all their forces on one
single point, the French, always using the ' interior lines,' could have

[1] So Toreño.   Arteche says that he was to concentrate at Aranda.

got together in a very short time. The only weak point, indeed, in the French position was that Bessières' vanguard at Burgos was too far forward, and in some peril of being enveloped between Blake and Cuesta. But this detachment, as we shall see, was ere long drawn back to the Ebro.

Before the campaign began the Spaniards obtained one notable advantage—the removal of Cuesta from command, owing to his own incredible arrogance and folly. It will be remembered that he regarded the Juntas of Leon and Castile as recalcitrant subordinates of his own, and had declared all their acts null and void. When they proceeded, like the other Juntas, to elect representatives for the meeting at Aranjuez, he waited till the deputies of Leon were passing near his camp, and then suddenly descended upon them. Don Antonio Valdez, the Bailiff of the Maltese Knights, and the Vizconde de Quintanilla, were arrested by his troopers and shut up in the castle of Segovia. He announced that they should be tried by court-martial, for failing in obedience to their Captain-General. This astonishing act of presumption drew down on him the wrath of the Supreme Junta, which was naturally eager to protect its members from the interference of the military arm. Almost its first act on assembling was to order him to appear at Aranjuez and to suspend him from command. Cuesta would have liked to resist, but knowing that his own army was weak and that Blake and Castaños were his bitter enemies, he had to yield. He came to Aranjuez, and was superseded by General Eguia. Valdez and Quintanilla were immediately released, and took their seats in the Supreme Junta.

The sessions of that body had begun on September 25. Twenty-four members out of the designated thirty-five had assembled on that day, and after a solemn religious ceremony had re-proclaimed Ferdinand VII, and elected Florida Blanca as their President. They then proceeded to nominate a Cabinet, chosen entirely from outside their own body. Don Pedro Cevallos was to be Minister of Foreign Affairs: he had served Ferdinand VII in that capacity, but had smirched his reputation by his submission to Bonaparte after the treachery at Bayonne. However, his ingenious justification[1]

---

[1] His very elaborate vindication of himself can be read in his pamphlet of September, 1808, which was translated into English in the same winter, and reprinted in London. It contains a good account of the Bayonne business, and many valuable state papers.

of his conduct, and his early desertion of King Joseph, were allowed
to serve as an adequate defence.   Don Antonio Escaño was
Minister of Marine, Don Benito Hermida Minister of Justice, Don
Francisco de Saavedra Minister of the Interior.   The most important place of all, that of Minister of War, was given to an
utterly unknown person, General Antonio Cornel, instead of to
any of the officers who had distinguished themselves during the
recent campaigns.   He was to be aided by a supreme council of
war, consisting of six members of the Junta, three of whom were
civilians without any military knowledge whatever.   No intention
of appointing a commander-in-chief was shown, and the Minister
of War corresponded directly with all the generals in charge of the
provincial armies.   Nothing could have been more ill judged; from
the want of a single hand at the helm all the oncoming operations
were doomed to inevitable failure.   The supreme direction was
nominally entrusted to the obscure war-minister and his councillors,
really it lay with the generals in the field, who obeyed orders from
head quarters only just as much as they chose.   Each played his
own game, and the result was disaster.

A glance at the subjects which were discussed by the members of
the Junta, during its first weeks of session, suffices to show the short-
sightedness of their policy, and their utter inability to grasp the
situation.   They should have remembered that they were a government of national defence, whose main duty was the expulsion of
the French from the soil of Spain.   But military subjects furnished
the smallest portion of their subjects of debate.   They published
indeed a manifesto to the effect that they intended to levy an
army of 500,000 foot, and 50,000 horse—a much greater force
than Spain in her most flourishing days could have raised or
maintained.   But this paper army was never seen in the field:
less than a third of the number were under arms at the moment
in December when the Junta had to fly from Aranjuez, before the
advancing legions of Napoleon.   Nor was it likely that a great
army could be raised, equipped, and disciplined, while the central
government was devoting the greater part of its attention to
futilities.   The most cruel comment on its work lies in the fact
that its troops were ill furnished, badly armed, and half starved,
at the moment when the provinces were doing their best to provide
equipment, and every port in Spain was gorged with cannon,
muskets, munitions, and stores sent from England—a great part

of them destined to fall into the hands of the French. Partly from want of experience, but still more from want of energy, the Junta failed to use the national enthusiasm and the considerable resources placed at its disposal.

When we look at the main topics of its debates we begin to understand its failures. A good deal of time was spent in voting honorary distinctions to its own members. The President was to be addressed as 'his highness,' the Junta as a corporation was 'its majesty,' if we may use the ludicrous phrase. Each member became 'his excellency' and received the liberal salary of 120,000 reals (£1,200), besides the right of wearing on his breast a gold plaque with an embossed representation of the eastern and western hemispheres. There was a good deal of dispensing of places and patronage in the army and the civil service among relatives and dependencies of 'their excellencies,' but not more perhaps than happens in other countries in war-time when a new government comes in. At least the changes led to the getting rid of a good many of Godoy's old bureaucrats. The real fault of the Junta lay in its readiness to fall into factions, and fight over constitutional questions that should have been relegated to times of peace. Among the thirty-five members of the Junta a clear majority were, like their president, Florida Blanca, Spaniards of the old school, whose ideas of government were those of the autocratic sort that had prevailed under Alberoni and Charles III. They looked upon all innovations as tinged with the poison of the French Revolution and savouring of Jacobinism and infidelity. On the other hand there was a powerful minority, headed by Jovellanos and including Martin de Garay, the secretary of the Junta, the Marquis of Campo Sagrado, Valdes, Calvo de Rozas, and others, who held more modern views and hoped that the main result of the war would be to make Spain a constitutional monarchy of the English type. How far this dream was from realization was shown by the fact that among the first measures passed through the Supreme Junta were ordinances allowing the Jesuits (expelled long since by Charles III) to return to Spain, recreating the office of Inquisitor-General, and suspending the liberty of the press. Such measures filled the liberal section in the Junta with despair, by showing the narrow and reactionary views of the majority. But the greater part of the time spent in session by 'its majesty' was wasted on purely constitutional questions.

Firstly there was a long polemic with the Council of Castile, whose hatred for the Junta took the form of starting doubts as to the legality of its constitution[1]. It suggested that all constitutional precedents were against a body so numerous as thirty-five persons taking charge of the governance of the realm. Former councils of regency had been composed of three or five members only, and there was no legal authority for breaking the rule. The Council suggested that the only way out of the difficulty would be to call the Cortes, and that assembly would at once supersede the authority of the Supreme Junta. Instead of arguing with the Council of Castile, the new government would have done well to arrest or disperse that effete and disloyal body; but it chose instead to indulge in a war of manifestos and proclamations which led to nothing. To find the supreme government consenting to argue about its own legality was not reassuring to the nation. Moreover, Jovellanos and his followers spent much time in impressing on their colleagues that it was their duty to appoint a regency, and to cut down their own unwieldy numbers, as well as to provide machinery for the summoning of the Cortes at some not too distant date. To be reminded that they were no permanent corporation, but a temporary committee dressed in a little brief authority, was most unpleasant to the majority. They discussed from every point of view the question of the regency and the Cortes, but would not yield up their own supremacy. Indeed they proposed to begin legislation on a very wide basis for the reform of the constitution—business which should rather have been left to the Cortes, and which was particularly inappropriate to the moment when Napoleon was crossing the Pyrenees. The great manifesto of the Junta [October 26] sets forth its intentions very clearly. 'The knowledge and illustration of our ancient and constitutional laws; the changes which altered circumstances render necessary in their re-establishment; the reforms necessary in civil, criminal, and commercial codes; projects for improving public education; a system of regulated economy for the collection and distribution of the public revenue . . . are the subjects for the investigation of wise and thoughtful men. The Junta will form different committees, each entrusted with a particular department, to whom all writings on matters of government and administration may be addressed. The exertions of each contributing to give

[1] For these documents see the *Madrid Gazette* of Oct. 4.

a just direction to the public mind, the government will be enabled to establish the internal happiness of Spain[1].' From another official document we learn that 'among the most grave and urgent objects of the attention of the Central Junta will be the encouragement of agriculture, the arts, commerce, and navigation[2].'

Clearly nothing could be more inappropriate and absurd than that this government of national defence should turn its attention to subjects such as the reform of national education, or the encouragement of the arts. It is equally certain that if it should propose to 'consider the changes necessary in our ancient laws,' it would be going beyond its competence; for such business belonged only to a permanent and properly constituted national assembly, such as the Cortes. This was not the time for constitutional debates, nor was the Central Junta the body that should have started them. All their energies should have been devoted to the war. But misled as to the situation by the long quiescence of the French army on the Ebro, they turned their minds to every topic that should have been avoided, and neglected the single one that should always have been before their eyes. It was in vain that Calvo de Rozas, the Aragonese deputy, and a few more, tried to keep their colleagues to the point. The majority fell to debating on the subjects on which the despotic and the liberal theories of government clash, and spent themselves on discussions that were as heated as they were futile. Meanwhile the time that should have been turned to account was slipping away, and the army was not being reinforced. A glance at the field-states of the Spanish troops, comparing those of August 1 with those of November 1, sufficiently proves this. The provinces which had been recovered by the retreat of the French to the Ebro were not doing their duty. The wide and populous regions of Old Castile and Leon had sent 4,600 men to Rio Seco in July: in October they had less than 12,000 under arms[3]. From New Castile there seem to have

---

[1] Manifesto of the Junta to the Spanish people, Oct. 26.

[2] *Madrid Gazette* of Oct. 18, p. 1,301.

[3] Napier is not quite correct in saying (i. 293) that 'Leon never raised a single soldier for the cause.' It had three battalions of volunteers (2,400 men) at Rio Seco, and raised four more at Leon, Zamora, Ledesma, and Benavente in September (*Madrid Gazette*, Sept. 28). But this was a poor contribution for a kingdom of four provinces and 620,000 souls.

been raised nothing more than four battalions of Madrid Volunteers, a weak cavalry regiment, and two battalions of *Cazadores de Cuenca* and *Tiradores de Castilla* : at any rate no troops but these are to be found recorded in the lists of the armies that fought in October, November, and December, 1808. Even allowing that New Castile may have supplied recruits to its own corps of embodied militia serving with the Andalusian army [1], it is clear that, with a population of 1,200,000 souls, it ought to have done much more in raising new regiments. And this was the district in whose very midst the Junta was sitting! What little was done in Madrid seems to have been mainly the result of private enterprise: the *Gazette* for October is full of voluntary donations of horses, saddlery, and money, for the equipment of a corps of dragoons for the army of Old Castile, and of similar gifts received by Calvo de Rozas for the army of Aragon. But there are no signs of requisitions by the government for the purpose of raising an army of New Castile, which could certainly have been done. The kingdom with its five provinces ought to have given 40,000 men instead of 4,000 : for Asturias, with only 370,000 souls, had raised 13,000 : Aragon with 650,000 had placed no less than 32,000 levies in the field : and Estremadura with 420,000 had sent to the front 12,000 men by October, while keeping 10,000 more of undrilled recruits in its dépôts [2]. New Castile, as we have already had occasion to remark, had 1,200,000 inhabitants, and yet had only added to its original five battalions of militia six more of volunteers, and a single regiment of horse, at the moment when Napoleon's armies came flooding across the Ebro. The Central Junta's authority in Andalusia or Galicia was much limited by the survival of the ambitious local Juntas. But in Leon and the two Castiles there was, when once Cuesta had been got out of the way, no rival power

---

[1] I see no proof that even this was done. There were only five of them, the *Provinciales* of Cuenca, Toledo, Ciudad Real, Alcazar de Don Juan, and Siguenza. Toledo and Alcazar had 579 and 595 under arms at the time of Baylen, and only 500 each, apparently, in Nov. 1808. See Arteche, iii. 496.

[2] For the Asturians see the table in Arteche (ii. 651): they were still 10,000 strong after having shared in Blake's disastrous campaign. For the Estremadurans compare the list of regiments raised in the *Madrid Gazette* of Oct. 21, giving a total of 23,600 men, with the actual morning state of the Estremaduran troops at Madrid on their way to Burgos, 12,846 in all, given in Arteche (iii. 477).

in the field. No one was to blame but the central government, if the full resources of those regions were not utilized in September, October, and November. The English representatives at Madrid saw all this, and did their best to stir up the Junta. But it was not likely that mere foreigners would succeed, where Castaños and the other more energetic Spanish officers had failed. Already in October the situation appeared most unpromising: 'We have made repeated representations,' wrote Mr. Stuart, the British minister, 'and I have given in paper after paper, to obtain something like promptitude and vigour: but though loaded with fair promises in the commencement, we scarcely quit the members of the Junta before their attention is absorbed in petty pursuits and in wrangling, which impedes even the simplest arrangements necessary for the interior government of the country. . . . In short, we are doing what we can, not what we wish: and I assure you we have infamous tools to work with [1].' Exactly the same impression is produced by a study of the dispatches of Lord William Bentinck, our military representative at Madrid, and of the diary of Sir Charles Vaughan, who carefully attended and followed the debates of the Central Junta at Aranjuez. It was clear to any dispassionate observer that time was being wasted, and that the best was not being done with the available material.

This was all the more inexcusable because the nation was thoroughly in earnest, and prepared to make any sacrifices. The voluntary contributions made both by provinces and by individuals were astounding when the poverty of Spain is taken into consideration [2]. It was the energy and will to use them on the part of the leaders that was wanting. Moreover, England was pouring in supplies of all sorts: before November 16 she had sent at least 122,000 muskets and other military equipment of all kinds to the value of several hundred thousand pounds. Before the same date she had forwarded 4,725,000 dollars in hard cash [3], and Mr. Frere, the newly appointed minister, brought another million to Corunna.

[1] Stuart to Moore, from Madrid, Oct. 18, 1808.

[2] For details see the tables in Arguelles, and the grants recorded in the *Madrid Gazette* for September, October, and November.

[3] I take these figures as to what had been actually received from Vaughan, who was at Madrid, in constant communication with Stuart and Bentinck. They represent what had been paid over and acknowledged, not what had been promised or provided, and may be taken as accurate.

Instead of utilizing every possible resource the government went on debating about things unessential, as if the war had been ended at Baylen.   It would neither conduct the new campaign itself, nor appoint a single commander-in-chief to conduct it in its behalf. With absolute truth Colonel Graham wrote from the head quarters of the Army of the Centre that ' the miserable system established by the Junta was at the bottom of all misfortunes.   I pitied poor Castaños and poor Spain, and came away disgusted to the greatest degree [1].'

[1] Graham to Moore, from Tudela, Nov. 9, 1808.

SECTION VI: CHAPTER IV

AN EPISODE IN THE BALTIC

It will be remembered that one of Napoleon's preliminary measures, in his long campaign against the freedom of Spain, had been the removal of the flower of her army to the shores of the Baltic. In the spring of 1807 the Marquis of La Romana, with fourteen battalions of infantry and five regiments of cavalry, all completed to war strength, had marched for Hamburg. After wintering in the Hanseatic towns, Mecklenburg, and Swedish Pomerania, this corps had been moved up early in 1808 into Denmark[1]. It is clear that there was no military object in placing it there. The Danish fleet was gone, carried off by Lord Cathcart's expedition in the previous September, and there was no probability that the English would return for a second visit, when they had completely executed their plan for destroying the naval resources of Denmark. France and Sweden, it is true, were still at war, but King Gustavus was so much occupied by the defensive struggle against the Russians in Finland, that it was unlikely that he would detach troops for an objectless expedition against the Danes. On the other hand the Anglo-Swedish fleet was so completely dominant in the Baltic and the Sound, that there was no possibility of launching an expedition from Denmark against Southern Sweden. Even between the various islands at the mouth of the Baltic, where the water-distances are very short, troops could only be moved at night, and with infinite precautions against being surprised on the passage by English frigates. Gothenburg and the other harbours of South-western Sweden served as convenient ports of call to the British squadron told off for the observation of the Cattegat, the two Belts, and the Sound. Nothing could be done against Sweden, unless indeed a frost of

---

[1] The Spanish troops, though the best of the whole army, do not seem to have much impressed the German observer with their discipline. See the Mecklenburger Von Suckow's observations on what he saw of them in his *From Jena to Moscow*, p. 92.

exceptional severity might close the waterway between Zealand and Scania. Even then an attempt to make a dash at Helsingborg or Malmö would involve so many difficulties and dangers that few generals would have cared to risk it.

La Romana's corps formed part of an army under Marshal Bernadotte, whose sphere of command extended all over the south-western shores of the Baltic, and whose head quarters were sometimes at Schleswig and sometimes at Lübeck or Stralsund. He had considerable French and Dutch contingents, but the bulk of his force consisted of 30,000 Danes. In preparation for Napoleon's scheme against the Spanish Bourbons, La Romana's forces had been carefully scattered between Jutland and the Danish Isles, so that there was no large central body concentrated under the Marquis's own hand. The garrisons of the Spanish regiments were interspersed between those of Danish troops, so that it would be difficult to get them together. In March, 1808, when the Emperor had at last shown his hand by the treacherous seizure of Pampeluna, Barcelona, and Figueras, the troops of La Romana were cantoned as follows. Six battalions were in the island of Zealand, mainly in and about the old royal residence of Roeskilde [1]. Four battalions and two cavalry regiments were in Fünen, the central island of the Danish group, and with them La Romana himself, whose head quarters were at Nyborg [2]. One battalion lay in the island of Langeland, close to the south coast of Fünen [3]. In the mainland of Jutland were three cavalry regiments and three battalions of infantry [4], quartered in the little towns at the southern end of the Cattegat—Fredericia, Aarhuus, and Randers. In Zealand the 4,000 Spaniards were under the eyes of the main Danish army of observation against Sweden. In Fünen La Romana's 4,500 horse and foot were cantoned in small detachments, while a solid body of 3,000 Danes garrisoned Odense in the centre of the island, separating the Spanish regiments one from another. In Langeland, along with the Catalonian light battalion, were a company of French grenadiers and about 800 Danes. The troops in Jutland were mixed up with a brigade of Dutch light

[1] Infantry regiments of Guadalajara and Asturias, of three battalions each.

[2] Infantry regiment of Princesa (three battalions), light battalion of Barcelona, and cavalry regiments of Almanza and Villaviciosa.

[3] Light battalion of ' Volunteers of Catalonia.'

[4] Infantry regiment of Zamora, cavalry regiments Del Rey, Algarve, Infante.

cavalry and some Danish infantry. Napoleon's own provident eye
had been roving round Denmark, and he had himself given the
orders for the dislocation of the Spanish corps in the fashion that
seemed best calculated to make any common action impossible. To
keep them in good temper he had recently raised the pay of the
officers, and announced his intention of decorating La Romana
with the Grand Cross of the Legion of Honour. Bernadotte, by
his desire, displayed the greatest confidence in his auxiliaries, and
took a troop of the cavalry regiment Del Rey as his personal escort
while moving about in Denmark [1].

In spite of all this, the Marquis and his officers began to grow
uneasy in April, 1808, for the stream of dispatches and letters from
Spain, which had been reaching them very regularly during the
winter, began to dry up in the spring. When the first communication from the new ministry of Ferdinand VII reached La Romana
he found that it contained a complaint that the home government
had received no reports from the expeditionary force since January,
and that fifteen separate dispatches sent to him from Madrid had
failed to get any answer. The fact was that Napoleon had been
systematically intercepting every document which the war minister
at one end of the line, and the Marquis at the other, had been
committing to the French post [2]. The last dispatch had only
come to hand because such an important announcement as that
of the accession of King Ferdinand had been sent by the hands of
a Spanish officer, whom Bonaparte or Fouché had not thought
proper to arrest, though they had intercepted so much official correspondence. The Emperor himself had sent orders to Bernadotte
that the news of the revolution at Aranjuez should be kept as long
as possible from the Marquis and his troops [3] : and so it came to
pass that only a very few days after the events of March 19 became
known in Denmark, there followed the deplorable intelligence of
the treachery of Bayonne and of the Madrid insurrection of May 2.
These tidings produced the same feelings in Nyborg and Fredericia
that they had caused at Seville or Corunna. But on the shores of
the Baltic, further north than any Spanish troops had ever been
before, the expeditionary corps felt itself helpless and surrounded
by enemies. Yet as Joseph O'Donnell, then one of La Romana's

---

[1] Arteche, iii. 151.   [2] Bourrienne, *Mémoires*, viii. 20.
[3] Napoleon to Berthier, March 29, 1808 (*Nap. Corresp.*, 13,699).

staff, observed: 'The more they tried to persuade us that Spain was tranquil, and had settled down to enjoy an age of felicity under Napoleon, the more clearly did we foresee the scenes of blood, strife, and disaster which were to follow these incredible events[1].'

On June 24 there reached Nyborg the intelligence which showed the whole of Napoleon's schemes completed: it was announced to La Romana that Joseph Bonaparte had been proclaimed King of Spain, and he was ordered to transmit the news to his troops, and to inform them in General Orders that they were now serving a new master. The only commentary on this astonishing information which the Spanish officers could procure consisted of the nauseous banalities of the *Moniteur* concerning the 'regeneration of Spain.'

A very few days later the first ray of hope shone upon the humbled and disheartened general. One of the earliest ideas of the British Government, on hearing of the Spanish insurrection, had been to open communications with the troops in Denmark. Castaños, in his first interview with the Governor of Gibraltar, had expressed his opinion that they would strike a blow for liberty if only they were given the chance. The fleet of Sir Richard Keates so completely commanded the Baltic that it would be possible to rescue the Spanish expeditionary force, if only it were willing and able to cut its way to the coast. But it was necessary to find out whether the Marquis was ready to risk his neck in such an enterprise, and whether he could depend on the loyalty of his troops.

To settle this all-important question some agent must be found who would undertake to penetrate to La Romana's head quarters, a task of the most uninviting kind, for it was quite uncertain whether the Spaniard would eagerly join in the plan, or whether he would make up his mind to espouse the cause of Napoleon, and hand over his visitor to the French police. To find a man who knew the Continent well enough to move about without detection, and who would take the risk of placing himself at La Romana's mercy, in case his offers were refused, did not seem easy. But the right person was pitched upon by Sir Arthur Wellesley just before he sailed for Portugal. He recommended to Canning a Roman Catholic priest of the name of James Robertson. This enterprising ecclesiastic was a Scot who had spent most of his life in a monastery at Ratisbon, but had lately come to England and was acting as

[1] See his words quoted in Arteche, iii. 154.

tutor in the house of an English Catholic peer.   He had some time before offered himself to Wellesley as a man who knew Germany well, and was prepared to run risks in making himself useful to the Government [1].

Under the belief that the Spaniards were still quartered in the Hanse towns and Holstein, Canning sent for Robertson and asked him whether he would undertake this dangerous mission to Northern Germany.   The priest accepted the offer, and was dispatched to Heligoland, where Mr. Mackenzie, the British agent in this lately seized island, found him a place on board a smuggling vessel bound for the mouth of the Weser.   He was safely landed near Bremer-hafen and made his way to Hamburg, only to find that the Spaniards had been moved northward into the Danish isles.   This made the mission more dangerous, as Robertson knew neither the country nor the language.   But he disguised himself as a German com-mercial traveller, and laid in a stock of chocolate and cigars—things which were very rare in the North, as along with other colonial produce they were proscribed by the Continental System, and could only be got from smugglers.   It was known that the Spanish officers felt deeply their privation of the two luxuries most dear to their frugal race, so that it seemed very natural that a dealer in such goods should attempt to find a market among them.

Getting to Nyborg without much difficulty, the priest took his fate in his hands, and introduced himself to La Romana with a box of cigars under one arm and a dozen packets of chocolate under the other.   When they were alone, he threw himself on the Marquis's confidence, owning that he was a priest and a British subject, not a German or a commercial traveller.   The Spaniard was at first suspicious and silent, thinking that he had to deal with an *agent provocateur* of the French Government, who was trying to make him show his hand.   Robertson had no written vouchers for his mission—they would have been too dangerous—but had been given some verbal credentials by Canning, which soon convinced La Romana of his good faith.   The Marquis then owned that he was disgusted with his position, and felt sure that Napoleon had plotted the ruin of Spain, though what exactly had happened at Bayonne he had not yet been able to ascertain.   Robertson next laid before him Canning's offer—that if the expeditionary

[1] See his interesting little book, *A Secret Mission to the Danish Isles in 1808*, published at Edinburgh in 1863 by his relative Alexander Fraser.

force could be concentrated and got to the coast, the Baltic fleet should pick it up, and see that it was landed at Minorca, Gibraltar, the Canaries, in South America, or at any point in Spain that the Marquis might select.

La Romana asked for a night to talk the matter over with his staff, and next day gave his full consent to the plan, bidding the priest pass the word on to Sir Richard Keates, and discover the earliest day on which transports could be got ready to carry off his men. Robertson tried to communicate with a British frigate which was hovering off the coast of Fünen, but was arrested by Danish militiamen while signalling to the ship from a lonely point on the beach. His purpose was almost discovered, and he only escaped by a series of ingenious lies to the militia colonel before whom he was taken by his captors. Moving further south, he again tried to get in touch with Sir Richard Keates, and this time succeeded. The news was passed to London, and transports were prepared for the deliverance of the Spaniards. Canning also sent to Fünen an agent of the Asturian Junta, who would be able to give his countrymen full news of the insurrection that had taken place in June.

Meanwhile La Romana had sounded his subordinates, and found them all eager to join in the plan of evasion, save Kindelan, the brigadier-general commanding the troops in Jutland, who showed such unpatriotic views that the officer sent to confer with him dropped the topic without revealing his commission. The plan which the Marquis had formed was rather ingenious: Bernadotte was about to go round the garrisons in his command on a tour of inspection. It was agreed that under the pretext of holding a grand field-day for his benefit, all the scattered Spanish troops in Fünen should be concentrated at Nyborg. The regiments in Zealand and Jutland were to join them, when the arrival of the British fleet should be reported, by seizing the Danish small craft in the harbours nearest to them, and crossing over the two Belts to join their commander.

An unfortunate *contretemps*, however, interfered to prevent the full execution of the scheme. Orders came from Paris that all the Spanish troops were to swear allegiance to Joseph Bonaparte, each corps parading at its head quarters for the purpose on July 30 or 31. This news caused grave disorders among the subordinate officers and the men, who were of course in complete

ignorance of the plan for evasion.   La Romana and his councillors
held that the ceremony had better be gone through—to swear
under compulsion was not perjury, and to refuse would draw down
on the Spanish corps overwhelming numbers of Danes and French,
so that the whole scheme for escape would miscarry.   Accordingly
the troops in Jutland and Fünen went through the ceremony in
a more or less farcical way—in some cases the men are said to have
substituted the name Ferdinand for the name Joseph in their
oath, while the officers took no notice of this rather startling
variation.

But in Zealand things went otherwise : the two infantry regiments
of Guadalajara and Asturias, when paraded and told to take the
oath, burst out into mutiny, drove off those of their own officers
who tried to restrain them, killed the aide-de-camp of the French
General Fririon, who was presiding at the ceremony, and threatened
to march on Copenhagen.   Next day they were surrounded by
masses of Danish troops, forced to surrender, disarmed, and put
in confinement in small bodies at various points in the island
[August 1].

This startling news revealed to Bernadotte the true state of
feeling in the Spanish army, and he wrote to La Romana to
announce that he was about to visit the Danish Isles in order
to inquire into the matter.   Fortunately there came at the same
moment news from England that the time for escape was at hand.
On August 4, only three days after the mutiny at Roeskilde, the
brigantine *Mosquito*, having on board Rafael Lobo (the emissary
of the Asturian deputies), reached the Baltic, and communicated
by night with some of the Spanish officers on the island of
Langeland.   The British fleet had sailed, and the time for
action had arrived.

Accordingly La Romana gave the word to the officers in each
garrison to whom the secret had been entrusted.   On August 7,
the troops in Fünen concentrated, and seized the port of Nyborg :
the Danes were completely taken by surprise, and no resistance
was made save by a gallant and obstinate naval officer commanding
a brig in the harbour.   He fired on the Spaniards, and would not
yield till an English frigate and five gunboats ran into the port
and battered his vessel to pieces.

On August 8 the troops in Jutland struck their blow : the
infantry regiment of Zamora at Fredericia seized a number of

fishing-vessels, and ferried itself over into Fünen with no difficulty. General Kindelan, the only traitor in the camp, had been kept from all knowledge of what was to happen: when he saw his troops on the move, and received an explanatory note from La Romana putting him in possession of the state of affairs, he feigned compliance in the plan, but disguised himself and fled to the nearest French cantonment, where he gave enemy a full account of the startling news.   The cavalry regiments Infante and Del Rey had the same luck as their comrades of Zamora: they seized boats at Aarhuus, and, abandoning their horses, got across unopposed to Fünen.   Their comrades of the regiment of Algarve were less lucky: they were delayed for some time by the indecision of their aged and imbecile colonel: when Costa, their senior captain, took command and marched them from Horsens towards the port of Fredericia, it was now too late.   A brigade of Dutch Hussars, warned by Kindelan, beset them on the way and took them all prisoners.   Costa, seeing that the responsibility would fall on his head, blew out his brains at the moment of surrender.

Romana had concentrated in Fünen nearly 8,000 men, and was so strong that the Danish general at Odense, in the centre of the island, dared not meddle with him.   On August 9, 10, and 11 he passed his troops over to the smaller island of Langeland, where the regiment of Catalonia had already disarmed the Danish garrison and seized the batteries.   Here he was safe, for Langeland was far out to sea, and he was now protected from the Danes by the English warships which were beginning to gather on the spot. A few isolated men from Zealand, about 150 in all, succeeded in joining the main body, having escaped from their guards and seized fishing-boats: but these were all that got away from the regiments of Asturias and Guadalajara, the mutineers of July 31.

For ten days Langeland was crammed with 9,000 Spanish troops, waiting anxiously for the expected British squadron.   On the twenty-first, however, Admiral Keates appeared, with three sail of the line and several smaller craft.   On these and on small Danish vessels the whole army was hastily embarked: they reached Gothenburg in Sweden on August 27, and found there thirty-seven large transports sent from England for their accommodation. After a long voyage they reached the Spanish coast in safety, and the whole expeditionary corps of the North, now 9,000 strong, was concentrated at Santander by October 11.   The infantry was sent to take part in the second campaign of General Blake. The dismounted cavalry were ordered to move to Estremadura, and there to provide themselves with horses. La Romana himself was called to Madrid to interview the Junta, so that his troops went to the front under the charge of his second in command, the Count of San Roman, to take part in the bloody fight of Espinosa.

SECTION VII

NAPOLEON'S INVASION OF SPAIN

CHAPTER I

FRENCH AND SPANISH PREPARATIONS

WHILE the Supreme Junta was expending its energy on discussing the relative merits of benevolent despotism and representative government, and while Castaños fretted and fumed for the moving up of reinforcements that never arrived, the French Emperor was getting ready to strike. It took many weeks for the veteran divisions from Glogau and Erfurt, from Bayreuth and Berlin, to traverse the whole breadth of the French Empire and reach the Pyrenees. While they were trailing across the Rhineland and the plains of France, well fêted and fed at every important town [1], their master employed the time of waiting in strengthening his political hold on Central Europe. We have seen that he was seriously alarmed at the possibility of an Austrian war, and alluded to it in his confidential letters to his kinsfolk. But the court of Vienna was slow to stir, and as August and September slipped by without any definite move on the Danube, Bonaparte began to hope that he was to be spared the dangerous problem of waging two European wars at the same time. Meanwhile he assumed an arrogant and blustering tone with the Austrian Government, warning them that though he was withdrawing 100,000 men from Germany, he should replace them with new levies, and was still strong enough to hold his own [2]. Metternich gave prudent and

---

[1] For the banquets given (under imperial orders) by the cities, see *Nap. Corresp.*, 14,291, 14,331. Clearly Napoleon I understood the 'policy of champagne and sausages' as well as his nephew.

[2] Considering the delicate nature of the political situation, Napoleon's language to the Austrians was most rude and provocative. See the long interview with Metternich [Aug. 15] reported by Champagny in his dispatch (*Nap. Corresp.*, 14,254): 'Vous avez levé 400,000 hommes : je vais en lever

evasive answers, and no immediate signs of a rupture could be discerned. But to make matters sure, the Emperor hastened to invite his ally the Emperor Alexander of Russia to meet him at Erfurt. The ostensible object of the conference was to make a final effort to induce the British Government to accept terms of peace. Its real meaning was that Bonaparte wished to reassure himself concerning the Czar's intentions, and to see whether he could rely upon the support of Russia in the event of a new Austrian war. There is no need to go into the details of the meeting (September 27 to October 14), of the gathering of four vassal kings and a score of minor princes of the Confederation of the Rhine to do homage to their master, of the feasts and plays and reviews. Suffice it to say that Napoleon got what he wanted, a definite promise from the Czar of an offensive and defensive alliance against all enemies whatsoever: a special mention of Austria was made in the tenth clause of the new treaty[1]. In return Alexander obtained leave to carry out his designs against Finland and the Danubian principalities: his ally was only too glad to see him involved in any enterprise that would distract his attention from Central Europe. The Emperor Francis II hastened to disarm the suspicions of Napoleon by sending to Erfurt an envoy[2] charged with all manner of pacific declarations: they were accepted, but the acceptance was accompanied by a message of scarcely concealed threats[3], which must have touched the court of Vienna to the quick. Strong in his Russian alliance, Bonaparte chose rather to bully than to cajole the prince who, by the strangest of chances, was destined within eighteen months to become his father-in-law. The quiet reception given to his hectoring dispatches showed that, for the present at least, nothing need be feared from the side of Austria. The Emperor's whole attention could be turned towards Spain. After telling off a few more regiments for service beyond

---

200,000. La Confédération du Rhin, qui avait renvoyé ses troupes, va les réunir et faire des levées. Je rétablirai les places de Silésie, au lieu d'évacuer cette province et les états Prussiens, comme je me le proposais. L'Europe sera sur pied, et le plus léger incident amènera le commencement des hostilités,' &c.

[1] 'Dans le cas où l'Autriche se mettrait en guerre contre la France, l'Empereur de Russie s'engage à se déclarer contre l'Autriche, et à faire cause commune avec la France' (Article X, clause 2, of the Secret Treaty).

[2] Baron Vincent.

[3] See the dispatch (*Nap. Corresp.*, 14,380).

the Pyrenees, and giving leave to the princes of the Confederation of the Rhine to demobilize their armies, he left Erfurt [October 14] and came rushing back across Germany and France to Paris ; he stayed there ten days and then started for Bayonne, where he arrived on the twentieth day after the termination of the conference [November 3].

Meanwhile the ostensible purpose of that meeting had been carried out, by the forwarding to the King of England of a joint note in which France and Russia offered him peace on the basis of *Uti Possidetis*. It was a vague and grandiloquent document, obviously intended for the eye of the public rather than for that of the old King. The two Emperors expatiated on the horrors of war and on the vast changes made of late in the map of Europe. Unless peace were made 'there might be greater changes still, and all to the disadvantage of the English nation.' The Continental System was working untold misery, and the cessation of hostilities would be equally advantageous to Great Britain and to her enemies. King George should 'listen to the voice of humanity,' and assure the happiness of Europe by consenting to a general pacification.

Though well aware of the hollowness of these protestations, which were only intended to throw on England the odium of continuing the war, the British Cabinet took them into serious consideration. The replies to the two powers were carefully kept separate, and were written, not in the name of the King (for the personal appeal to him was merely a theatrical device), but in that of the ministry. To Russia a very polite answer was returned, but the question on which the possibility of peace rested was brought straight to the front. Would France acknowledge the existing government of Spain as a power with which she was pre-pared to treat ? Canning, who drafted the dispatch, was perfectly well aware that nothing was further from the Emperor's thoughts, and could not keep himself from adding an ironical clause, to the effect that Napoleon had so often spoken of late of his regard for the dignity and welfare of the Spanish people, that it could not be doubted that he would consent. The late transactions at Bayonne, ' whose principles were as unjust as their example was dangerous to all legitimate sovereigns,' must clearly have been carried through without his concurrence or approbation.

The reply to France was still more uncompromising. ' The

King,' it said, 'was desirous for peace on honourable terms. The miserable condition of the Continent, to which allusion had been made, was not due to his policy: a system devised for the destruction of British commerce had recoiled on its authors and their instruments.' But the distress even of his enemies was no source of pleasure to the King, and he would treat at once, if the representatives of Sweden, Portugal, Sicily, and Spain were admitted to take part in the negotiations. It was to be specially stipulated that the 'Central Junta of Government' at Madrid was to be a party to any treaty of peace.

The two British notes brought the replies from St. Petersburg and Paris that Canning expected. Count Romanzoff, writing for the Czar, could only state that his master had acknowledged Joseph Bonaparte as King of Spain, and could not recognize the existence of any other legal authority in that kingdom. But if this point (the only really important one) could be got over, the Russian Government was ready to treat on a basis of *Uti Possidetis*, or any other just and honourable terms. The French reply was, as was natural, couched in very different language. Napoleon had been irritated by Canning's sarcastic allusions to the failure of the Continental System: he thought the tone of the British note most improper and insulting—'it comes from the same pen which the English ministry employs to fabricate the swarm of libels with which it inundates the Continent. Such language is despicable, and unworthy of the imperial attention [1].'

Considering the offensive and bullying tone which Bonaparte was wont to use to other powers—his note written to Austria a few days before was a fair example of it—he had little reason to be indignant at the epigrams of the English minister. Yet the latter might perhaps have done well to keep his pen under control, and to forget that he was not writing for the *Anti-Jacobin*, but composing an official document. Even though Napoleon's offer was hollow and insincere, it should have been met with dry courtesy rather than with humorous irony.

Of course Bonaparte refused to treat the Spaniards as a free and equal belligerent power. He had declared his brother King of Spain, and had now reached that pitch of blind autolatry in which he regarded his own fiat as the sole source of legality. In common honour England could not abandon the insurgents; for

[1] Napoleon to Champagny (*Nap. Corresp.*, 14,643).

the Emperor to allow his brother's claim to be ignored was equally impossible.   In his present state of mind he would have regarded such a concession to the enemy as an acknowledgement of disgraceful defeat.   It was obvious that the war must go on, and when the Emperor suggested that England might treat with him without stipulating for the admission of the Junta as a party to the negotiations[1], he must have been perfectly well aware that he was proposing a dishonourable move which the ministry of Portland could not possibly make.   His suggestions as to a separate treaty with England on the basis of *Uti Possidetis* were futile : he intended that they should be declined, and declined they were.   But he had succeeded in his end of posing before the French nation and the European powers as a lover of peace, foiled in his devices by the unbending arrogance of Great Britain.   This was all that he had desired, and so far his machinations attained their object [2].

Long before the English replies had been sent off to Champagny and Romanzoff, the much-delayed campaign on the Ebro had commenced.   All through the months of August and September the French had behaved as if their adversaries were acting on proper military principles, and might be expected to throw their whole force on the true objective point.   Jourdan and his colleagues had no reason to foresee that the Spanish Government would launch out into the hideous series of blunders which, as a matter of fact, were committed.   That no commander-in-chief would be appointed, that the victorious troops of Baylen would be held back for weeks in Andalusia, that no strenuous effort would be made to raise new

---

[1] Napoleon to Champagny (*Nap. Corresp.*, 14,643).

[2] It is strange to find that Napier was convinced that Napoleon had a real desire for peace, and hoped to secure it by the proposals of October, 1808. He writes (i. 210): ' The English ministers asserted that the whole proceeding was an artifice to sow distrust among his enemies.   Yet what enemies were they among whom he could create this uneasy feeling ?   Sweden, Sicily, Portugal !   the notion as applied to them was absurd ; it is more probable that he was sincere.   He said so at St. Helena, and the circumstances of the period warrant a belief in that assertion.'   But Napier has failed to see that the design was not to ' sow distrust among his enemies.'   The whole business was intended to influence French public opinion, and in a secondary way the public opinion of all Europe.   Bonaparte wished to pose as a friend of peace, and to bestow on England the unenviable rôle of the selfish fomenter of wars. With many simple folk in France and elsewhere he succeeded, but no Englishman, save one blinded by a dislike for everything Tory, could have been deceived.

armies in Leon and the two Castiles, were chances that seemed so improbable that King Joseph and his advisers did not take them into consideration.   They expected that the Spaniards would mass the armies of Andalusia, Estremadura, Castile, and Aragon, and endeavour to turn their left flank on the side of Sanguesa and Pampeluna, or that (the other rational course) they would send the Asturians, the Andalusians, and the Castilians to join Blake, and debouch down the line of the Upper Ebro, from Reynosa on to Vittoria and Miranda.   In the first case 70,000, and in the latter case 80,000 men would be flung against one flank of the French position, and it would be necessary to concentrate in hot haste in order to hold them back.   But, as a matter of fact, the Spanish forces did not even come up to the front for many weeks, and when they did appear it was, as we have seen, not in the form of one great army concentrated for a stroke on a single point, but as a number of weak and isolated columns, each threatening a different part of the long line that lay along the Ebro from Miranda to Milagro.   When feeble demonstrations were made against so many separate sections of his front, Jourdan supposed that they were skilful feints, intended to cover some serious attack on a weak spot, and acted accordingly, holding back till the enemy should develop his real plan, and refusing to commit himself meanwhile to offensive operations on a serious scale.   It must be confessed that the chaotic and inconsequent movements of the Spaniards bore, to the eye of the observer from the outside, something like the appearance of a deep plan.   On August 27 the Conde de Montijo, with a column of the Aragonese army, felt his way up the Ebro as far as the bridge of Alfaro, nearly opposite the extreme left flank of the French at Milagro.   When attacked by Lefebvre-Desnouettes at the head of a few cavalry and a horse-battery, the Spanish general refused to stand, and retreated on Tudela.   Marshal Moncey then pressed him with an infantry division, but Montijo again gave back.   The French thought that this move must be a mere diversion, intended to attract their attention to the side of Aragon, for Montijo had acted with such extreme feebleness that it was unnatural to suppose that he was making anything but a feint.   They were quite wrong however: Palafox had told the count to push as far up the Ebro as he could, without any thought of favouring operations by Blake or Castaños, the former of whom was at this moment not far in front of Astorga, while the latter was still at Madrid.   Montijo had given way simply because his troops were raw levies, and because there were no supports behind him nearer than Saragossa. It was to no effect, therefore, that King Joseph, after the fighting in front of Alfaro and Tudela, moved his reserves up the river to Miranda, thinking that the real attack must be coming from that side. There was no real attack intended, for the enemy had not as yet brought any considerable force up to the front.

It was not till nearly three weeks later that the Spaniards made another offensive move. This time Blake was the assailant. On September 10 he had at last concentrated the greater part of his army at Reynosa—the centre of roads at the source of the Ebro, of which we have already had to speak on several occasions. He had with him four divisions of the army of Galicia, as well as a 'vanguard brigade' and a 'reserve brigade' of picked troops from the same quarter. Close behind him were 8,000 Asturians under General Acevedo. The whole came to 32,000 men, but there were no more than 400 cavalry with the corps—a fact which made Blake very anxious to keep to the mountains and to avoid the plains of Old Castile[1]. He had left behind him in Galicia and about Astorga more than 10,000 men of new levies, not yet fit to take the field. There were also some 9,000 Asturians in similar case, held back within the limits of their own principality[2].

In the elaborate plan of operations which had been sketched out at Madrid on September 5, it will be remembered that Blake's army was intended to co-operate with those of Castaños and of Eguia. But he paid no attention whatever to the promises which his representative, Infantado, had made in his name, and executed an entirely different movement: there was no commander-in-chief to compel him to act in unison with his colleagues. The Castilian and Estremaduran armies were not ready, and Castaños had as yet only a feeble vanguard facing the enemy on the Central Ebro, his rear divisions being still far back, on the road from Andalusia. Blake neither asked for nor received any assistance whatever from his colleagues, and set out in the most light-hearted way to attack 70,000 French with his 32,000 Galicians and Asturians.

His plan was to threaten Burgos with a small portion of his

---

[1] For the organization and state of Blake's force, see the Appendix.

[2] The Asturias had raised nineteen new battalions: of these eight went forward with Blake, and eleven remained behind.

army, while with the main body he marched on Bilbao, in order to
rouse Biscay to a second revolt, and to turn the right flank of the
French along the sea-shore. Accordingly he sent his 'vanguard'
and 'reserve' brigades towards Burgos, by the road that passes by
Oña and Briviesca, while with four complete divisions he moved on
Bilbao. On the twentieth his leading column turned out of that
town General Monthion, who was in garrison there with a weak
brigade of details and detachments.

Here at last, as it seemed to Joseph Bonaparte and to Jourdan,
was the long-expected main attack of the Spaniards. Accordingly
they concentrated to their right, with the object of meeting it.
Bessières evacuated Burgos and drew back to the line of the Upper
Ebro. He there replaced the King's reserve, and the incomplete
corps that was forming at Miranda and Vittoria under the command of Marshal Ney: thus these troops became available for
operations in Biscay. Ney, with two small infantry divisions,
marched on Bilbao by way of Durango: Joseph, with the reserve,
followed him. But when the Marshal reached the Biscayan
capital, the division of Blake's army [1], which had occupied it for
the last six days, retired and took up a defensive attitude in the
hills above Valmaceda, twenty miles to the west. Here it was
joined by a second division of the Galician army [2], and stood fast
in a very difficult country abounding in strong positions. Ney
therefore held back, unwilling to attack a force that might be
30,000 strong (for all that he knew) with the 10,000 men that he
had brought. Clearly he must wait for King Joseph and the
reserve, in case he should find that Blake's whole army was in front
of him.

But the King and his corps failed to appear: Bessières had sent
to inform him that Blake, far from having moved his whole army
on to Bilbao, had still got the bulk of it in positions from which
he could march down the Ebro and attack Miranda and Vittoria.
This was to a certain extent true, for the first and second divisions
of the Galician army were now at Villarcayo, on the southern side
of the Cantabrian hills, a spot from which they could march either
northward to Bilbao or eastward to Miranda. Moreover, Blake's
'reserve' and 'vanguard' brigades were still about Frias and Oña,
whither they had been pushed before the French evacuated Burgos.

[1] The 4th Galician Division under the Marquis of Portago.
[2] The 3rd Galician Division under General Riquelme.

Bessières, therefore, had much to say in favour of his view, that the point of danger was in the Ebro valley and not in Biscay. King Joseph, convinced by his arguments, left Ney unreinforced, and took post with the 6,000 men of the central reserve at Vittoria. His conclusion that Bilbao was not the true objective of the Spaniards was soon confirmed by other movements of the enemy. The feeble columns of Castaños were at last showing on the Central Ebro, and Palafox was on the move on the side of Aragon.

Under the idea that all Blake's Biscayan expedition had been no more than a feint and a diversion, and that the real blow would be struck on the Ebro, Jourdan and the King now directed Ney to come back from Bilbao and to take up his old positions. The Marshal obeyed: leaving General Merlin with 3,000 men in the Biscayan capital, he returned with 7,000 bayonets to La Guardia, on the borders of Alava and Navarre. His old head quarters at Logroño, beyond the Ebro, had been occupied by the head of one of Castaños's columns. He did not attack this force, but merely encamped opposite it, on the northern bank of the river [October 5][1].

It is now time to review the position and forces of the Spanish armies, which were at last up in the fighting line. Blake's 32,000 Asturians[2] and Galicians were divided into two masses, at Valmaceda and Villarcayo, on the two sides of the Cantabrian hills. They were within three marches of each other, and the whole could be turned either against Biscay or against Vittoria, as the opportunity might demand. But between Blake and the central divisions of the Spanish army there was a vast gap. This, at a later period of the campaign, was filled up by bringing forward the 12,000 men of the Estremaduran army to Burgos: but this force, insufficient as it was for the purpose, had not reached the front: in the middle of October it had not even arrived at Madrid[3]. There seems to have been at Burgos nothing more than a detached battalion or two, which had occupied the place when Bessières drew back towards the Ebro[4]. Of all the Spanish forces, the nearest organ-

---

[1] All these moves are best described in Marshal Jourdan's *Mémoires* (edited by Grouchy; Paris, 1899), pp. 71–5.

[2] Acevedo's 8,000 Asturians joined Blake at Villarcayo on Oct. 11 (see his dispatch in *Madrid Gazette*, Oct. 25).

[3] I gather from *Madrid Gazette* (Oct. 21, p. 1,333) that it was still organizing in and about Badajoz on Oct. 6, and did not begin to march till later.

[4] Volunteers of Benavente from the army of Castile, and Tuy Militia of Blake's army.

Part of Northern Spain

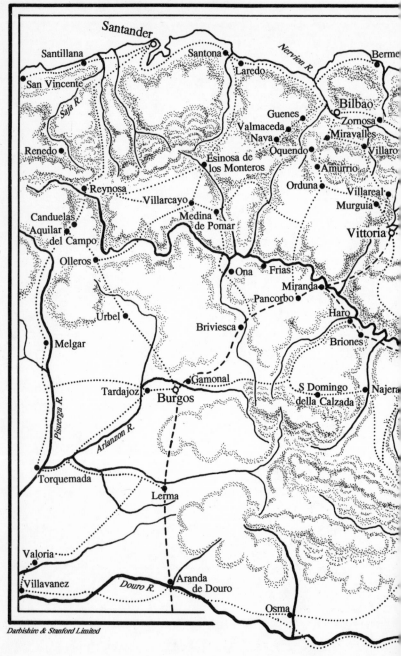

Darbishire & Stanford Limited

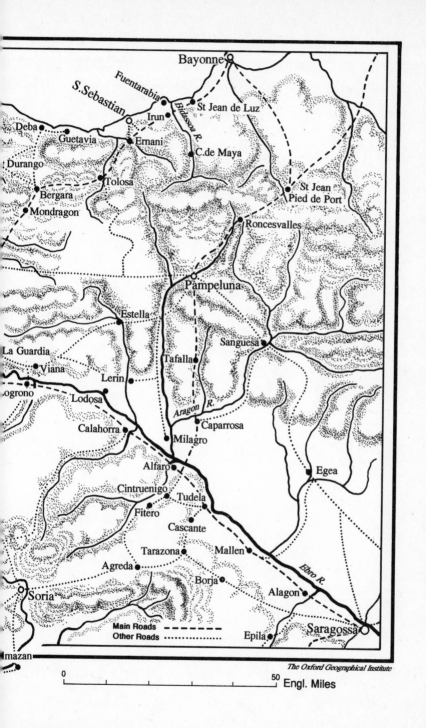

Bayonne

Fuentarabia

S. Sebastian

Deba

Guetavia

Durango

Bergara

Mondragon

Irun

Ernani

Tolosa

St Jean de Luz

C. de Maya

St Jean
Pied de Port

Roncesvalles

Pampeluna

Estella

Sanguesa

La Guardia

Viana

Tafalla

Lerin

Aragon R.

Logrono

Lodosa

Caparrosa

Calahorra

Milagro

Alfaro

Egea

Cintruenigo

Tudela

Fitero

Cascante

Tarazona

Mallen

Agreda

Borja

Ebro R.

Soria

Alagon

Saragossa

Amazan

Epila

Main Roads
Other Roads

The Oxford Geographical Institute

0   50
                                     Engl. Miles

Bidassoa R.

ized corps on Blake's right consisted of the main body of this same army of Castile. This division, for it was no more, consisted of about 10,000 or 11,000 men : it contained a few regular corps (Regiment of Cantabria, a battalion of Grenadiers, the Leon Militia) which had been lent to it by the army of Andalusia, and twelve raw Leonese and Castilian battalions, of the new levy which Cuesta had raised. There were also some 800 cavalry with it. The commander was now Pignatelli, for Eguia (who had originally been told off to the post) had fallen sick. This small and inefficient force was at Logroño on the Central Ebro, having taken possession of that place when it was evacuated by Marshal Ney in the last week of September. A little further down the river lay the 2nd Division of the army of Andalusia, which, under the orders of Coupigny, had taken a creditable part in the battle of Baylen. Released by the Junta of Seville in September, it had at last gone forward and joined Castaños. But it was somewhat changed in composition, for three of its original fourteen battalions had been withdrawn [1] and sent to Catalonia, while three new Andalusian corps had replaced them. Its commander was now General Grimarest, Coupigny having been told off to another sphere of duty. The division numbered about 6,000 bayonets, with 400 or 500 cavalry, and a single battery. It occupied Lodosa, on the north bank of the Ebro, some twelve miles down-stream from Logroño. Quite close to its right there lay at Calahorra the 4th Division of the army of Andalusia, under La Peña—a somewhat stronger force—about 7,500 foot, with 400 horse and two batteries. The only remaining division of Castaños' 'Army of the Centre' consisted of the Murcian and Valencian corps under Llamas. This had entered Madrid 8,000 strong on August 13, but one of its regiments had been left behind at Aranjuez to guard the Junta. It now consisted of no more than 7,000 men, and lay at Tudela, in close touch with La Peña's Andalusians. The total, therefore, of Castaños' army in the second half of October did not amount to more than 31,000 foot and 3,000 horse. The 1st and 3rd divisions of the Andalusian army, long detained beyond the Moreña by the Junta of Seville, were but just commencing to arrive at Madrid :

---

[1] These three Granadan battalions had been sent, along with the rest of the levies of that kingdom, to form part of the division which Reding was leading to Catalonia. They had been replaced by the new Andalusian battalions of Baylen, Navas de Tolosa, and 5th of Seville.

of their 15,000 men less than half reached the front in November, in time to take their share in the rout of Tudela. Even these were not yet at Castaños' disposition in October [1].

The right wing of the Spanish army of the Ebro consisted of the raw and half-organized masses composing the army of Aragon. Palafox had succeeded in getting together a great body of men from that loyal province, but he had not been able to form them into a force fit to take the field. Owing to the way in which Aragon had been stripped of regular troops before the commencement of the war, there was no solid body round which the new levies could be organized, and no supply of trained officers to drill or discipline the thousands of eager recruits. It would seem that in all no less than 32,000 were raised, but no force in any degree approaching these numbers took the field. Every village and every mountain valley had contributed its *partida* or its company, but with the best of wills Palafox had not yet succeeded in incorporating all these small and scattered units into regiments and brigades. Many of them had not even been armed : very few had been properly clothed and equipped. Nevertheless no fewer than thirty-nine battalions in a state of greater or less organization were in existence by the end of October. They varied in strength to the most extraordinary degree : many were no more than 300 strong [2], one or two were enormous and ran up to 1,300 or 1,400 bayonets. Of the whole thirty-nine battalions only three belonged to the old regular army, and these corps—whose total numbers only reached 2,350 men—had been largely diluted with raw recruits [3]. Of the remainder some belonged to the *tercios* who had taken arms in June, and had served through the first siege of Saragossa, but a large number had only been raised after Verdier had retired from before the city in August. It would seem that

[1] Castaños himself, in his exculpatory memoir, will not allow that he ever had more than 26,000 men, even including the belated troops of the 1st and 3rd Andalusian divisions which came up in November.

[2] See the tables in Arteche, iii. 479, 480. The Regiment of Calatayud was only 310 strong, that of Doyle 306, and that of Navarre 302 ; on the other hand the 2nd Volunteers of Aragon had 1,302, the 1st Volunteers of Huesca 1,319, and the overgrown ' Aragonese Fusiliers ' no less than 1,836.

[3] 3rd Spanish Guards 609, Estremadura 600, 1st Volunteers of Aragon 1,141. These figures are from a return of Nov. 1, sent to England by Colonel Doyle, then in high favour with Palafox. It may be found in the Record Office.

the total of Palafox's Aragonese, who went to the front for the campaign of October and November, was about 12,000 men.   The rest were left behind at Saragossa, being not yet organized or equipped for field service.

But Palafox had also in his army troops which did not belong to his native kingdom.   These were the Murcians and Valencians of Saint March and O'Neille, who after taking part in the campaign against Moncey, had not marched with Llamas to Madrid, but had turned off to aid in raising the siege of Saragossa.   Saint March had brought with him fourteen battalions and a cavalry regiment, O'Neille had with him three more infantry corps.   The total of their force reached 11,200 bayonets and 620 sabres. Adding these to the best of his own Aragonese levies, Palafox sent out 23,000 men : of these only about 800 were cavalry [1]. A force such as this, backed by the mass of unorganized levies at Saragossa, was barely sufficient to maintain a defensive position on the frontiers of Aragon.   But the Junta, with great unwisdom, came to the conclusion that Palafox was strong enough not only to hold his own against the French in his immediate front, but to spare some troops to reinforce the army of Catalonia.   By their orders he told off six battalions—some 4,000 men—who were placed under the command of his brother, the Marquis of Lazan, and dispatched to Lerida with the object of aiding the Captain-General of Catalonia to besiege Duhesme in Barcelona.

Nor was this the only force that was drawn off from the main theatre of the war in order to take part in helping the Catalans, who had hitherto proved quite strong enough to help themselves. The Junta directed Reding, the victor of Baylen, to take command

[1] The Valencian and Murcian contributions to the army of Aragon consisted of the following troops :—One old line regiment of three battalions (Volunteers of Castile), the militia battalion of Soria, and of new levies the 1st and 2nd Volunteers of Murcia, the 2nd Volunteers of Valencia, the regiments of Turia (three battalions), Alicante (three battalions), Segorbe (two battalions), Borbon, Chelva, and Cazadores de Fernando VII, the Dragoons of Numancia (an old corps), and two squadrons of new Valencian cavalry.   I get these names partly from the return of Nov. 1 in the Record Office at London, partly from Saint March's return of his killed and wounded at Tudela.   Some more Murcian corps started to join Palafox, but were not in time for Tudela, though they took part in the second defence of Saragossa : viz. 3rd and 5th Volunteers of Murcia, the regiment of Florida Blanca, and 1st and 2nd Tiradores of Murcia. Their start from Murcia on Oct. 13 is noted in the *Madrid Gazette* of 1808 (p. 1,336).

of all the Granadan troops in the army of Andalusia, and lead
them to Tortosa with the object of joining Lazan. With Reding
there marched nearly 15,000 men[1]: to raise this force all the
regiments belonging to the kingdom of Granada had been drafted
out from the 1st and 2nd Divisions of Castaños' army, which were
thus mutilated before they reached the Ebro. To those comparatively veteran troops were added eight new battalions of raw
levies—the regiments of Baza, Almeria, Loxa, and Santa Fé.
Starting on their long march from Granada on October 8, the
head of Reding's column had only reached Murcia on October 22,
and was thus hopelessly distant from any point where it could have
been useful when the campaign began[2]. Nor was this the last
detachment which the Junta directed on Catalonia: it sent thither
part of the prisoners from Lisbon, whom the Convention of Cintra
had delivered—3,500 of the men who had once formed the division
of Caraffa. Laguna, who now held the command, landed from
English transports at La Rapita near Tortosa on October 25,
and marched from thence on Tarragona[3].

It is safe to say that of these 23,000 men transferred to Catalonia
from Aragon, Granada, and Portugal, every man ought to have
been pushed forward to help Castaños on the Ebro, and not
distracted to the side-issue at Barcelona. It was mad to send
them thither when the main force facing Jourdan and King Joseph
did not yet amount to 75,000 men. Catalonia, with such small aid
as the Balearic Islands could give, was strong enough to defend
herself against the motley hordes of Duhesme and Reille.

At the moment when the feeble offensive of Castaños and Palafox
began, on the line of the Ebro, the French had some 65,000 men
ranged opposite them[4], while a reserve of 10,000 was formed at

[1] Just 14,970, according to the details given in the *Madrid Gazette* for
Oct. 12 (p. 1,379). See my Appendix on the Spanish forces in Oct.—Nov.

[2] *Madrid Gazette*, Oct. 28 (p. 1,381).

[3] Ibid., Nov. 1 (p. 1,407).

[4] The figures given by Jourdan in his *Mémoires* seem quite accurate, and are
borne out by all the details in *Nap. Corresp.*; they are :—

Corps of Bessières [2nd Corps] . . .	17,597
Corps of Moncey [3rd Corps]	20,747
Corps of Ney [6th Corps], incomplete . .	8,957
The King's general reserve	6,088
Garrisons of Navarre and Biscay . . .	11,559
	64,948

Bayonne, and the leading columns of the 'Grand Army' from Germany were only ten or twelve marches away. Napoleon had, by a decree issued on September 7, recast the form of his army of Spain. It was in the future to consist of seven army corps. The 1st, 4th, and 5th were to be composed of old divisions from the Rhine and the Elbe. Of the forces already on the spot Bessières' troops were to form the 2nd Corps, Moncey's the 3rd, the still incomplete divisions under Ney the 6th. The army of Catalonia, where St. Cyr was superseding Reille, formed the 7th Corps [1]. Junot's army from Portugal, when it once more appeared upon the scene, made the 8th, but in September Napoleon did not yet know of its fate, and it only received its number and its place in the host at a much later date. Many alterations of detail were made in the brigades and divisions that formed the new 2nd and 3rd Corps. All the *bataillons de marche* were abolished, and their men drafted into the old regiments. The fifteen 'provisional regiments,' which had composed the whole of Moncey's and a considerable part of Bessières' strength, were taken into the regular establishment of the army, and renumbered as the 114th– 120th of the Line and the 33rd Léger, two provisional regiments being told off to form each of the new bodies [2]. There was a certain amount of shifting of units, but in the main the brigades and divisions of these two corps remained intact.

On or about October 8–10 Bessières lay at Miranda and Murguia, guarding against any possible descent of Blake from Villarcayo upon the Upper Ebro. Ney was at La Guardia, facing Pignatelli's Castilians, who occupied his old head quarters at Logroño. Moncey had thrown back his left to guard against a possible descent of Palafox upon Navarre, and was behind the line of the river Aragon, with his right at Estella, his centre at Falces and Tafalla, and his left facing Sanguesa, where it was opposed by the advanced division of the army of Palafox under O'Neille. For the Captain-General of Aragon, pleased with a plan proposed to him by Colonel Doyle, the English military attaché in his camp, had resolved to make a long turning movement under the roots of the Pyrenees, exactly parallel to that which Blake was executing at the other end of the line. With this object he sent out from Saragossa, on September 29,

---

[1] It was originally to be called the 5th, but this title was taken from it, in order that Mortier's corps might keep its old number.

[2] For their distribution see p. 110.

O'Neille with a division of Aragonese strengthened by a few Murcian and Valencian battalions, and numbering some 9,000 bayonets. This detachment, marching in a leisurely way, reached Sanguesa on the Upper Aragon, but there stopped short, on getting information that Moncey's corps lay before it in some strength. Palafox then sent up in support a second division, Saint March's Murcians and Valencians, who advanced to Egea and there halted. There was considerable bickering all through the second half of October on this line, but Sanguesa remained in the hands of the Spaniards, Moncey being too much distracted by the movements of Castaños in the direction of Tudela to dare to concentrate his whole force for a blow at Saint March and O'Neille. The latter, on the other hand, had realized that if they pressed further forward towards Pampeluna, as their commander-in-chief had originally intended, they would leave Moncey so much in their rear that he could cut them off both from Saragossa and from the Army of the Centre. Here then matters had come to a deadlock ; but the position was all in favour of the French, who lay compactly in the centre, while O'Neille and Saint March were separated from Castaños by a gap of sixty miles, and Blake on the other wing was about seventy (as the crow flies) from the army of Castile.

THE PRELIMINARY FIGHTING: ARRIVAL OF NAPOLEON

By the middle of October the French and Spanish armies were in presence of each other along the whole line of the Ebro, and it seemed certain that one or other of them must at last take the offensive. Both were still in expectation of reinforcements, but those which the Spaniards could expect to receive within the next few weeks were comparatively unimportant, while their adversaries knew that more than 100,000 men from Germany were due at Bayonne in the last days of October. Clearly it was for Castaños and his colleagues to make a move now or never. The wasted months of August and September could not be recalled, but there was still time to attack Bessières, Ney, and Moncey, before the arrival of the Emperor and the three veteran corps from the Elbe.

Matters lay thus when the Spanish generals resolved on a perfectly new and wildly impracticable scheme. Castaños had come to the conclusion—a thoroughly sound one—that his 34,000 men were too few to make a frontal attack on the French on the line between Miranda and Calahorra. He left Madrid on October 13, deeply chagrined to find that the Central Junta had no intention of making him commander-in-chief. Instead of being able to issue orders to the other generals, he must meet them on equal terms and endeavour to cajole them into adopting a common plan of operations. Accordingly he rode to Saragossa to visit Palafox, and after long and not very friendly converse drew out a new plan. The Army of the Centre was to shift itself down the Ebro, leaving the troops of Pignatelli (the 'Army of Castile') and of Grimarest (the 2nd Andalusian division) to 'contain' Ney and Bessières. The rest were to concentrate at Tudela, where they were to be joined by as many battalions of the Aragonese levies at Saragossa as could take the field. With some 25,000 or 30,000 men at the highest estimate, Castaños and Palafox were to fall upon Moncey's flank at the bridge of Caparrosa. Meanwhile O'Neille and Saint March, with the advanced divisions of the army of Aragon, were to break up from Sanguesa, march round Pampeluna by the foot-hills of the Pyrenees, and place themselves across the road to France. Moncey was thus to be surrounded, and a second Baylen was to ensue! Indeed, if Blake could be persuaded to push forward once more to Bilbao, and thence into Guipuzcoa, the whole army of King Joseph (as it was hoped) might be cut off and made prisoners. Eighty thousand men, according to this strange scheme, starting from bases 200 miles apart, were to surround 65,000 French in a most difficult mountain country. Meanwhile the enormous gap between Blake's right and Castaños' left was to remain wholly un-guarded, for the army of Estremadura was still in the far distance ; while nothing was to be left opposite Bessières and Ney save Pignatelli's disorderly 'Army of Castile,' and Grimarest's 6,000 Andalusians.

But before the scheme for the cutting off of Moncey had even begun to be carried out, Castaños and Palafox had a rude awakening. They were themselves attacked by the army which they were so confidently proposing to surround. King Joseph, emboldened by the long delay of his adversaries in advancing, had several times discussed with Jourdan, Bessières, and Ney schemes for taking the offensive. Indeed he had sketched out in September no less than five separate plans for bringing the enemy to an action, and it is probable that he might have tried one of them if he had been allowed a free hand[1]. Napoleon, however, having determined to come to Spain in person, put an embargo on any comprehensive scheme for an advance on Madrid, and restricted his brother to minor operations.

But there was nothing in the Emperor's instructions which forbade a blow on a small scale, if the Spaniards should grow too daring. There was now a good excuse for such a move, for both Pignatelli and Grimarest had been trespassing beyond the Ebro. They seem to have moved forward quite contrary to the intentions of Castaños, who at this moment was proposing to refuse battle with his left and centre, and to draw the bulk of his army south-ward to Tudela. But his two divisional generals pushed so far forward, that they at last drew upon themselves most undesired

---

[1] The paper containing them was captured in Joseph's carriage at Vittoria five years later. It will be found printed in full in Napier (Appendix to vol. i, pp. 453, 454).

attentions from the French marshals. Pignatelli had thrown troops across the Ebro to Viana: Grimarest had pushed detachments still further forward into Navarre, to Mendavia, Sesma, and Lerin. Joseph and Jourdan resolved to drive back these outlying posts, and to find out what was behind them. About 25,000 men were put in movement against the 16,000 Spaniards who had so rashly crossed the river. Moncey marched against Grimarest [Oct. 25–6] with two divisions: Ney with a similar force fell upon Pignatelli, while Bessières sent a division down the southern bank of the Ebro by Haro and Briones, to threaten the line of retreat of the army of Castile across the bridge of Logroño.

Against such forces the Spaniards could do nothing: on the twenty-fifth Ney marched on Viana, and drove in Pignatelli's advanced guard. On the following day he opened a fierce cannonade upon Logroño from across the river, while at the same time Bonnet's division, sent by Bessières, marched upon the town from the hither side of the Ebro. Pignatelli was a craven, and his Castilian levies proved to be the worst of all the material which the Spaniards had brought to the front. General and army vanished in the night, without even stopping to blow up the great bridge, though they had mined it and laid the train in due form. Ney's officers crossing at dawn found all prepared, except the sappers who should have applied the match[1]! Neither Ney nor Bonnet got in touch with the flying horde: but in sheer panic Pignatelli abandoned his guns by the roadside, and did not stop till he had joined Castaños at Cintruenigo, near Tudela. His hurried retreat was wholly unnecessary, for the French did not move beyond Logroño, and Castaños was able to send out next morning a brigade which picked up the deserted guns and brought them in without molestation. Rightly indignant, the Commander-in-chief removed Pignatelli from his post, and distributed his demoralized battalions among the divisions of Grimarest, La Peña, and Llamas[2], leaving in separate existence only a single brigade of six battalions under Cartaojal, which mainly consisted of the few regular battalions that had been lent to Pignatelli to

---

[1] For an account of this curious affair see the *Mémoires* of General Boulart, then an artillery officer under Ney, who discovered the flight of the Castilians and the abandoned mine below the bridge (pp. 202, 203). Oddly enough he gives the wrong date for the incident, Oct. 30 instead of Oct. 27.

[2] I cannot find any details as to their redistribution.

stiffen his raw levies.   Thus the 'Army of Castile' ceased to exist [1].

On the same day that the Castilians were routed by Ney, the 2nd Andalusian division was severely handled by Moncey.   When that Marshal advanced against Lerin and Sesma with the divisions of Morlot and Maurice Mathieu, Grimarest withdrew beyond the Ebro, abandoning by some oversight his vanguard.   This force, commanded by a resolute officer, Colonel Cruz-Murgeon, was enveloped at Lerin by the division of Morlot [2].   The colonel shut himself up in the mediaeval castle of that town, and defended himself for two days, in hopes that he might be succoured.   But his chief had fled beyond the river, and could not be induced to return by any appeals.   On October 27 Cruz-Murgeon had to surrender, after two-thirds of his troops had been killed or wounded. Their obstinate defence was the more creditable because they were all new levies, consisting of a single Andalusian battalion (*Tiradores de Cadiz*) and a few Catalan volunteers.   Marshal Moncey then occupied Lodosa and its bridge, but made no attempt to follow Grimarest, who was able to rejoin his chief without further loss.

Castaños was greatly disturbed by the vigorous offensive movement of Ney and Moncey.   Seeing the French so strong and so confident, he was struck with sudden qualms as to the advisability of the movement on Caparrosa and Pampeluna, which he and Palafox had agreed to carry out.   He proposed to his colleague that they should drop their plan for surrounding Moncey, and attempt no more than an attack on his flanks at Caparrosa and Sanguesa. Meanwhile he concentrated the greater part of his army at Calahorra and Tudela [Oct. 29].   The initiative had passed to the French, and if Ney and Moncey did not seize the opportunity for an advance against the Army of the Centre, it was merely because they knew that Napoleon was now close at hand—he reached Bayonne four days later—and would not wish them to attempt anything decisive without his orders.

Meanwhile there arrived from Madrid a deputation from the Supreme Junta, consisting of Francisco Palafox (the younger

---

[1] See Colonel Graham's *Diary*, p. 275 (Oct. 30).   He reached Castaños' camp on that day.

[2] Jourdan in his *Mémoires* (p. 77) says that it was Morlot who acted against Lerin, and I follow him rather than those who state that it was Maurice Mathieu.

brother of the Captain-General), of Coupigny, Reding's colleague at the victory of Baylen, and the intriguing Conde de Montijo. The Junta were indignant that Castaños had not made bricks without straw. Though they had not given him any appreciable reinforcements, they had expected him to attack the French and win a great victory beyond the Ebro. Conscious that the deputies came to him in no friendly spirit, Castaños nevertheless received them with all respect, and laid before them the difficulties of his situation. Joseph Palafox came up from Saragossa to join the conference, and after a long and stormy meeting—this was the conference which so disgusted Colonel Graham [1]—it was decided to resume offensive operations [November 5]. The idea was a mad one, for six days before the council of war was held two French army corps, those of Victor and Lefebvre, had crossed the Bidassoa and entered Spain. There were now 110,000 instead of 65,000 enemies in front of the Spanish armies. Moreover, and this was still more important, Napoleon himself had reached Bayonne on November 3.

Nevertheless it was resolved once more to push forward and fall upon Moncey. Castaños was to leave one division at Calahorra, and to bring the rest of his army over the Ebro to attack the bridge of Caparrosa: O'Neille and Saint March were to come down from Sanguesa to co-operate with him: Joseph Palafox was to bring up the Aragonese reserves from Saragossa. The only sign of prudence that appeared was that the council of war agreed not to commence the attack on Moncey till they had learnt how Blake and the army of Galicia were faring in Biscay. For that general had, as they knew, commenced some days before his second advance on Bilbao. Since the armies on the Central Ebro hung back, it was in the distant region on the coast that the first important collision between the Spaniards and the French reinforcements from Germany was to take place. For a fortnight more there was comparative quiet in front of Tudela and Caparrosa. Meanwhile Castaños, prostrated by an attack of the gout [2], took to his bed, and the Army of the Centre was abandoned for a few days to the tender mercies of the deputation from Madrid.

There is a strange contrast when we turn from the study of the

[1] Cf. p. 366 and Graham's *Diary*, p. 276.

[2] According to Toreño; but Graham, who was present in the camp, calls it rheumatism.

rash and inconsiderate plans of the Spanish generals to mark the movements of Napoleon. The Emperor had left Erfurt on October 14: on the nineteenth he had reached Paris, where he stayed for ten days, busied not only with the 'logistics' of moving the columns of the 'Grand Army' across France, but with all manner of administrative work. He had also to arrange the details of the conscription: though he had raised in 1807 the enormous mass of new levies of which we had to speak in an earlier chapter, he now asked for 140,000 men more[1]. Of these, 80,000 were to be drawn from the classes of 1806-9, which had already contributed so heavily to the army. The balance was to be taken from the class of 1810, whose members were still fifteen months below the legal age. From these multitudes of young soldiers every regiment of the army of Spain was to be brought up to full strength, but the majority were destined to reinforce the depleted armies of Germany and Italy, which had been thinned of veterans for the Peninsular War.

On October 25 Bonaparte presided at the opening of the Legislative Assembly, and made a characteristic harangue to its members. He painted the situation of the Empire in the most roseate colours. 'The sight of this great French family, once torn apart by differences of opinion and domestic hatreds, but now so tranquil, prosperous, and united, had sensibly touched his soul. To be happy himself he only required the assurance that France also was happy. Law, finance, the Church, every branch of the state, seemed in the most flourishing condition. The Empire was strong in its alliances with Russia, the Confederation of the Rhine, Denmark, Switzerland, and Naples. Great Britain, it was true, had landed some troops in the Peninsula, and stirred up insurrections there. But this was a blessing in disguise. The Providence which had so constantly protected the arms of France, had deigned to strike the English ministry with blindness, and to induce them to present an army on the Continent where it was doomed to inevitable destruction. In a few days the Emperor would place himself at the head of his troops, and, with the aid of God, would crown in Madrid the true King of Spain, and plant his eagles on the forts of Lisbon[2].'

[1] See *Nap. Corresp.*, 14,312 (xvii. 505, 506), and compare with 14,601 (xviii. 141, 142).

[2] *Discours prononcé le 25 oct. (Nap. Corresp.*, xviii. 20, 21).

Four days later Bonaparte quitted Paris, and passing hastily through Orleans and Bordeaux reached Bayonne at three o'clock in the morning of November 3. The corps of Victor and Lefebvre, with two divisions of dragoons, were several days ahead of him, and had already crossed the Bidassoa. The Imperial Guard and the divisions destined for Ney [1], as well as a great mass of cavalry, were just converging on the frontier. Mortier's corps was not very far off: Junot's army from Portugal had already landed at Quiberon and Rochefort, and was being directed on Bordeaux. All the machinery for the great blow was now ready.

Napoleon profoundly despised the Spanish army and the Spanish generals. His correspondence is full of contemptuous allusions to them: 'ever since he served at Toulon he knew them for the worst troops in Europe.' 'Nothing could be so bad as the Spaniards—they are mere rabble—6,000 French can beat 20,000 of them.' 'The whole Spanish army could not turn 15,000 good troops out of a position that had been properly occupied [2].' Nevertheless he had determined to run no risks: the second Peninsular campaign must not end like the first, in a fiasco and a humiliating retreat. It was for this reason that the Emperor had massed more than 250,000 good troops against the tumultuary levies of the Junta—a force which, in his private opinion, was far more than enough to sweep the whole of his adversaries into the sea before the year 1808 should have run out. Any expedition in which he himself took part must, for the sake of his prestige, be conducted from beginning to end in a series of spectacular triumphs. It was better to use a larger army than was absolutely necessary, in order to make his blows sufficiently heavy, and to get the Spanish business over as rapidly as possible. If the whole Peninsula were overrun in a few months, and resistance had been completely beaten down ere the winter was over, there would be no chance of that intervention on the part of Austria which was the only danger on the political horizon [3].

---

[1] Those of Marchand and Bisson, forming the old 6th Corps, with which he fought at Jena and Friedland.

[2] Napoleon to Joseph Bonaparte, to Caulaincourt, to Eugène Beauharnais (vols. xvii, xviii of *Nap. Corresp.*).

[3] The clearest proof which I find in the *Napoleon Correspondence* of the Emperor's intention to sweep over the whole Peninsula, with a single rush, is that already in November he was assembling at Bayonne naval officers who

Napoleon, therefore, drew out his plans not merely for a triumphant advance on Madrid, but for the complete annihilation of the Spanish armies on the Ebro and in Biscay. From a careful study of the dispatches of his lieutenants, he had realized the existence of the great gap in the direction of Burgos between the armies of Blake and of Castaños. His plan of campaign, stated shortly, was to burst in through this gap, so as to separate the Spanish armies on his left and right, and then to wheel troops outwards in both directions so as to surround and annihilate them. Both Blake and Palafox were, at this moment, playing the game that he most desired. The further that the former pressed onward into Biscay, the nearer that the latter drew to the roots of the Pyrenees, the more did they expose themselves to being encompassed by great masses of troops breaking out from Burgos and Logroño to fall upon their flank and rear. When the Emperor drew up his scheme he knew that Blake was in front of Zornoza, and that the bulk of the army of Aragon was at Sanguesa. Meanwhile the French advanced divisions were in possession of Miranda, Logroño, and Lodosa, the three chief passages over the Upper Ebro. A glance at the map is sufficient to show that the moment that the Emperor and his reserves reached Vittoria the Spanish armies were in the most perilous position. It would suffice to order a march on Burgos on the one hand and on Tudela on the other, and then the troops of Aragon and Galicia would not merely be cut off from any possible retreat on Madrid, but run grave danger of annihilation. A further advance of the French would probably thrust the one against the Pyrenees, and roll the other into the Bay of Biscay.

For this reason it was the Emperor's wish that his lieutenants should refrain from attacking Blake and Palafox till he himself was ready to march on Burgos. For any premature advance against the Spaniards might force them to retreat from their dangerous advanced positions, and fall back the one on Reynosa the other on Saragossa, where they would be much less exposed.

The distribution of the 'Grand Army' was to be as follows. Lefebvre with the 4th Corps was to present himself in front of

were to take charge of the port of Lisbon, and to reorganize the Portuguese fleet. This was a little premature! (See Napoleon to Decrès, Minister of Marine, *Nap. Corresp.*, 14,514, vol. xviii.)

Blake between Durango and Zornoza, and to hold him fast without pressing him. Moncey with the 3rd Corps, in a similar way, was to 'contain' Palafox and Castaños from his posts at Lodosa, Caparrosa, and Tafalla. Meanwhile Victor, with the newly arrived 1st Corps, was to endeavour to get into Blake's rear, by the road Vittoria—Murguia—Orduña. The main body of the army, consisting of the troops of Bessières and Ney, King Joseph's reserve, the Imperial Guard, and four divisions of cavalry, was to march on Burgos. Napoleon knew that there was no large body of Spaniards in that place : he expected to find there Pignatelli's ' Army of Castile,' but this force (as we have seen) had ceased to exist, having been drafted with ignominy into the ranks of the army of Andalusia [1]. As a matter of fact Burgos was now occupied by a new force from the second line—the long-expected army of Estremadura, some 12,000 strong, which had at last come up from Madrid and taken its place at the front. But Napoleon's reasoning still held good : any Spanish army that might chance to be at Burgos must be overwhelmed by the enormous mass of troops that was about to be hurled upon it. The moment that it was disposed of, Ney with the 6th Corps was to wheel to the east, and march by Aranda and Soria, so as to place himself between Castaños and Palafox and Madrid. Then he would turn their flank at Tarazona and Tudela, and—in conjunction with Moncey—drive them northward against the Pyrenees. In a similar way, upon the other flank, the 2nd Corps was to wheel to the north-west and march from Burgos on Reynosa, there to intercept Blake, if he had not already been cut off by Victor's shorter turning movement. Meanwhile the Emperor with the rest of his army, followed by the new reserves (Mortier's corps and other troops) which were due from France, would march straight from Burgos on Madrid, force the defiles of the Somosievra and Guadarrama, and seize the Spanish capital. He was well aware that there would be no serious hostile force in front of him, since the armies of Blake, Palafox, and Castaños were all provided for. He does not seem to have known of the army of Estremadura, or to have had any idea that the English forces from

---

[1] Napoleon to Bessières, Nov. 6 : ' J'ai vu vos dépêches du 5 novembre sur l'existence d'un corps de 24,000 hommes à Burgos. Si cela est, ce ne peut être que 12,000 hommes de l'armée de Castille qui ont évacué Logroño, et qui ne sont pas en cas de faire tête à 3,000 ou 4,000 de vos gens ' (*Nap. Corresp.*, 14,443, xviii. 38).

Portugal might conceivably be on their way to cover Madrid. There is no mention of Sir John Moore and his host in the imperial dispatches till December 5.

All being ready, Bonaparte rode out of Bayonne on November 4, having stayed there only thirty-six hours. Before leaving he had received one vexatious piece of news : Lefebvre, in direct disobedience to his orders, had attacked Blake on October 31, and forced him back beyond Bilbao. This made the plan for the cutting off of the army of Galicia a little more difficult, since the Spaniards were now forty miles further back, and not nearly so much exposed as they had been hitherto. But it was still not impossible that Victor might succeed in circumventing them, and forcing them into the Bay of Biscay.

It is impossible to withhold our admiration from the Emperor's simple yet all-embracing plan of operations. It is true that the campaign was made more easy by the fact that he was dealing with raw and undisciplined armies and inexpert generals. It is also clear that he rightly reckoned on having two men in the field against every one whom the Spaniards could produce. But the excellence of a scheme is not to be judged merely by the difficulties in its way ; and military genius can be displayed in dealing with an easy as well as with a dangerous problem. Half a dozen other plans for conducting the invasion of Spain might have been drawn up, but it is impossible to see that any better one could have been constructed. In its main lines it was carried out with complete success : the armies of the Junta were scattered to the winds, and Madrid fell almost without a blow.

It was only when the capital had been occupied, and the troops of Blake and Belvedere, of Castaños and Palafox were flying devious over half the provinces of Spain, that the difficulties of the Peninsular War began to develop themselves. Napoleon had never before had any experience of the character of guerilla warfare, or the kind of resistance that can be offered by a proud and revengeful nation which has made up its mind never to submit to the conqueror. In his complete ignorance of Spain and the Spaniards, he imagined that he had a very simple campaign to conduct. The subjugation of the Peninsula was to him an ordinary military problem, like the invasion of Lombardy or of Prussia, and he went forth in cheerful confidence to 'plant the eagles of France on the forts of Lisbon,' and to 'drive the Britannic leopard from the soil of the Peninsula, which it defiles by its presence.' But the last chapter of this story was to be told not at Lisbon but at Toulouse : and 'the Beneficent Providence which had deigned to strike the British ministry with such blindness that they had been induced to send an army to the Continent [1],' had other designs than Bonaparte supposed.

[1] See page 396.

SECTION VII: CHAPTER III

THE MISFORTUNES OF JOACHIM BLAKE: ZORNOZA AND ESPINOSA DE LOS MONTEROS

THE campaign of November 1808 was fought out upon three separate theatres of war, though every movement of the French armies which engaged in it formed part of a single plan, and was properly linked to the operations which were progressing upon other sections of the front. The working out of Napoleon's great scheme, therefore, must be dealt with under three heads—the destruction of Blake's 'Army of the Left' in the north-west; the rout of the armies of Andalusia and Aragon upon the banks of the Ebro; and the central advance of the Emperor upon Burgos and Madrid, which completed the plan.

We must first deal with the misfortunes of Blake and his Galician host, both on chronological grounds—it was he who first felt the weight of the French arms—and also because Napoleon rightly attached more importance to the destruction of this, the most formidable of the Spanish armies, than to the other operations which he was carrying out at the same moment.

It will be remembered that after his first abortive expedition against Bilbao, and his retreat before Ney [October 5], Blake had fallen back to Valmaceda. Finding that he was not pursued, he drew up to that point the divisions which he had hitherto kept in the upper valley of the Ebro, and prepared to advance again, this time with his whole army massed for a bold stroke. On October 11 he again marched into Biscay, and drove out of Bilbao the division of General Merlin, which Ney had left behind him to hold the line of the Nervion. On the twelfth this small force fell back on Zornoza and Durango, and halted at the latter place, after having been reinforced from King Joseph's reserve at Vittoria. Verdier headed the succours, which consisted of three battalions of the Imperial Guard, two battalions of the 118th Regiment, two battalions of Joseph's own Royal Guards, and the 36th Regiment, which had just come up from France. When strengthened by these 7,000 men, Merlin considered himself able to make a stand, and took up a strong position in front of Durango, the important point at which the roads from Bayonne and from Vittoria to Bilbao meet.

When committing himself to his second expedition into Biscay, Blake was not wholly unaware of the dangers of the step, though he failed to realize them at their full value, since (in common with the other Spanish generals) he greatly underrated the strength of the French army on the Ebro. He intended to carry out his original plan of cutting off Bessières and King Joseph from their retreat on Bayonne, by forcing the position of Durango, and seizing the high-road at Bergara; but he was aware that an advance to that point had its dangers. As long as his divisions had lain in or about Villarcayo and Valmaceda, he had a perfectly clear line of retreat westward in the event of a disaster. But the moment that he pushed forward beyond Bilbao, he could be attacked in flank and rear by any troops whom the King might send up from the valley of the Ebro, by the two mountain-roads which run from Vittoria to the Biscayan capital. One of these is the main route from Vittoria to Bilbao via Murguia and Orduña. The other is a more obscure and difficult path, which leads across the rough watershed from Vittoria by Villareal and Villaro to Bilbao. Aware of the fact that he might be assailed by either of these two passes, Blake told off a strong covering force to hold them. Half of Acevedo's Asturian division, 4,000 strong, was placed at Orduña : the other half, with the whole of Martinengo's 2nd Division of Galicia, 8,500 bayonets in all, took its post in the direction of Villaro. These detachments were eminently justifiable, but they had the unfortunate result of enfeebling the main force that remained available for the stroke at the French in front of Durango. For that operation Blake could only count on his 1st, 3rd, and 4th Divisions, as well as the ' Vanguard ' and ' Reserve ' Brigades —a total of 18,000 men[1].

[1] Viz. Vanguard Brigade, General Mendizabel . . 2,884

1st Division, General Figueroa 4,018

3rd Division, General Riquelme 4,789

4th Division, General Carbajal 3,531

Reserve Brigade, General Mahy . . . 3,025

Total . . . 18,247

The detached corps being—

2nd Division, General Martinengo . . . 5,066

Asturian Division, General Acevedo . . . 7,633

Blake had seized Bilbao on October 11 : it is astonishing there-fore to find that he made no forward movement till the twenty-fourth.   By this sluggishness he sacrificed his chance of crushing Merlin before he could be reinforced, and—what was far worse—allowed the leading columns of the ' Grand Army ' to reach Irun. If he had pressed forward on the twelfth or thirteenth, they would still have been many marches away, trailing across Guyenne and Gascony.   Having once put his hand to such a dangerous manœuvre as that of pushing between the French flank and the northern sea, Blake was most unwise to leave the enemy time to divine his object and to concentrate against him.   A rapid stroke at Durango and Bergara, so as to cut the great high-road to France in the rear of Bessières, was his only chance.   Such an attempt would probably have landed him in ultimate disaster, for the enemy (even before the ' Grand Army ' arrived) were far more numerous than he supposed.   He had valued them at 40,000 men, while they were really 64,000 strong.   But having framed the plan, he should at least have made a strenuous attempt to carry it out.   It is possible to explain but not to excuse his delay : his army was not equipped for a winter campaign, and the snow was beginning to lie on the upper slopes of the Cantabrian hills and the Pyrenees.   While he was vainly trying to obtain great-coats and shoes for his somewhat tattered army, from the Central Junta or the English, and while he was accumulating stores in Bilbao, the days slipped by with fatal rapidity.

It was not till October 24 that he at last moved forward from Bilbao, and committed himself to the now hopeless task of clearing the way to Durango and Bergara.   On that day his advanced guard drove Merlin's outlying posts from their positions, and came face to face with the French main body, drawn out on the hillsides of Baquijano, a few miles in front of Durango.   The enemy expected him to attack next day, but he had just received confused notices from the peasantry to the effect that enormous reinforce-ments had reached Irun and San Sebastian, and were within sup-porting distance of the comparatively small force with which he had hitherto been dealing.   This information threw him back into the condition of doubt and hesitation from which he had for a moment emerged, and he proceeded to halt for another full week in front of the Durango position.   Yet it was clear that there were only two rational alternatives before him : one was to attack Merlin and

Verdier before they could draw succour from the newly arrived
corps. The other was to fall back at once to a position in which
he could not be enveloped and outflanked, i.e. to retire behind
Bilbao, holding that town with nothing more than a small detachment which could easily get away if attacked. But Blake did
nothing, and waited in the supremely dangerous post of Zornoza,
in front of Durango, till the enemy fell upon him at his leisure.

The troops whose arrival at Irun had been reported consisted of
the two leading divisions of the 4th Corps, that of Lefebvre,
and of the whole of the 1st Corps, that of Victor. The former,
arriving as early as October 18, only seven days after Blake
captured Bilbao, marched westward, and replaced Merlin and
Verdier in the Durango position. The troops of these two generals
were directed by King Joseph to rejoin their proper commanders
when relieved, so Verdier led the Guards back to the central
reserve, while Merlin reported himself to Ney, at La Guardia. To
compensate Lefebvre for their departure, and for the non-arrival
of his third division, that of Valence, which still lay far to the rear,
Villatte's division of the 1st Corps was sent to Durango. Marshal
Victor himself, with his other two divisions, took the road to
Vittoria, and from thence, at the King's orders, transferred himself
to Murguia, on the cross-road over the mountains to Bilbao. Here
he was in a position to strike at Blake's rear, after driving off the
4,000 men of Acevedo's Asturian division, who (as it will be
remembered) had been told off by the Spanish General to cover
this road [1].

King Joseph, inclining for once to a bold stroke, wished to push
Victor across the hills on to Bilbao, while Lefebvre should advance
along the high-road and drive Blake into the trap. Bessières at
the same moment might move a division by Orduña and Oquendo,
and place himself at Valmaceda, which Blake would have to pass
if he escaped from Victor at Bilbao. This plan was eminently
sound, for there was no doubt that the two marshals, who had at
their disposal some 35,000 men, could easily have brushed out of
their way the two divisions under Acevedo and Martinengo which
Blake had left behind him in the passes. Nothing could have
prevented them from seizing Bilbao and Valmaceda, and the
Spanish army would have been surrounded and captured. At

---

[1] There is a clear and precise account of all these moves in the *Mémoires* of
Jourdan, who was still acting as Joseph's chief of the staff (pp. 79–81).

the best some part of it might have escaped along the coast-road to Santander, if its commander detected ere it was too late the full danger of his position.

This scheme, however, was not carried out: Bessières, Victor, and Ney showed themselves opposed to it: Napoleon had announced that he intended ere long to appear in person, and that he did not wish to have matters hurried before his arrival. His obsequious lieutenants refused to concur in any great general movement which might not win his approval. Victor, in particular, urged that he had been ordered to have the whole of the 1st Corps concentrated at Vittoria, and that if he marched northward into Biscay he would be violating his master's express command[1]. Joseph and Jourdan, therefore, resolved to defer the execution of their plan for the annihilation of Blake, and sent orders to Lefebvre to maintain his defensive position at Durango, and make no forward movement. In so doing they were acting exactly as the Emperor desired.

They had forgotten, however, to reckon with the personal ambition of the old Duke of Dantzig. Lefebvre, in spite of his many campaigns, had never before had the chance of fighting on his own account a pitched battle of the first class. The Spanish army had been lying before him for a week doing nothing, its commander being evidently afraid to attack. Its force was not very great—indeed it was outnumbered by that of the Marshal whose three divisions counted not less than 21,000 bayonets[2]. Noting with the eye of an old soldier Blake's indecision and obvious timidity, he could not resist the temptation of falling upon him. Notwithstanding the King's orders, he resolved to strike, covering his disobedience by a futile excuse to the effect that he had observed preparations for taking the offensive on the part of the enemy, and that his outposts had been attacked.

[1] Jourdan's *Mémoires*, p. 79.

[2] He had Sebastiani's Division, 28th (three batts.), 32nd, 58th
(two batts. each), and 75th of the Line (three batts.)   5,808
   Leval's Division, seven German and two Dutch batta-
   lions   8,347
   Villatte's Division, 27th, 63rd, 94th, and 95th of the
   Line (each of three batts.)   7,169
                              Total . . .   21,324

Arteche gives twelve German battalions (iii. 491); but the Frankfort Regiment had only one battalion, those of Nassau, Baden, and Darmstadt two each. The figures are those of the return of Oct. 10.

Blake's army lay before him, posted in three lines, with the village of Zornoza to its rear.   In front, on a range of comparatively low hills, was the 'Vanguard Brigade,' drawn up across the road with the 1st Division of Galicia to its left on somewhat higher ground.   They were supported by the 3rd and 4th Divisions, while the 'Reserve Brigade' occupied the houses of Zornoza to the rear of all.   There were only six guns with the army, as Blake had sent the rest of his artillery to the rear, when advancing into the mountains : this single battery lay with the Vanguard on the lower heights.   The whole amounted to 19,000 men, a slight reinforcement having just come to hand by the arrival of the 1st Catalonian Light Infantry [1], the advanced guard of La Romana's army from the Baltic.   That general, having landed at Santander on October 11, had reorganized his force as the '5th Division of the army of Galicia' and sent it forward under his senior brigadier, the Conde de San Roman.   But only the single Catalonian battalion had passed Bilbao at the moment when Lefebvre delivered his attack.

The plan of the Marshal's advance was quite simple.   The division of Villatte drove in the front line of the Spanish right, and then spread itself out on a long front threatening to turn Blake's flank. That of Sebastiani, formed in a single dense column, marched along the high-road at the bottom of the valley to pierce the Spanish centre ; meanwhile Leval's Germans attacked the left wing of the enemy, the 1st Division of the army of Galicia [2].   A dense fog, a common phenomenon in the Pyrenees in the late autumn, hid the advance of the French, so that they were close upon the front line of Blake's army before they were observed.   The first line was easily driven in, but the whole army rallied on the heights of San Martin and stood at bay.   Lefebvre cannonaded them for some time, without meeting with any reply, for Blake had hurried off his single battery to the rear when his first line gave way. Then the Marshal sent in the ten battalions of the division of Sebastiani, who completely cut through the Spanish centre, and left the two wings in isolated and dangerous positions.   Without waiting for further developments, Blake gave way and ordered a retreat on Bilbao and Valmaceda.   His intact wing-divisions

---

[1] It counted 1,066 bayonets when entering on the campaign, and was attached to the Vanguard.

[2] Captain Carroll, an eye-witness, gives a good account of this action in his report to General Leith, dated from Valmaceda on Nov. 2.

covered the retreat, and though badly beaten he got away with very small loss, no more than 300 killed and wounded, and about the same number of prisoners. The French casualties were insignificant, not amounting in all to more than 200 men. The whole combat, indeed, though 40,000 men were on the field, was very short and not at all costly. The fact was that Blake had been surprised, and had given way at the first push, without making a serious attempt to defend himself. His sending away the guns, at the very commencement of the action, makes it sufficiently clear that he did not hope for ultimate success, and was already contemplating a retreat on Bilbao. His army, if properly handled, could have made a much more creditable fight; in fact it was tactically beaten rather than defeated by force of arms. It made its retreat in very fair order, and was irritated rather than cowed by the check which it had received. English eye-witnesses vouch for the steadiness and good spirit shown by the troops[1].

Immediately after giving orders for a general retreat behind the river Nervion, Blake had sent dispatches to the two divisions of Acevedo and Martinengo, which were covering his flank against a possible turning movement from the valley of the Ebro. They were told to save themselves, by falling back at once to Bilbao and joining the main army in its retreat. The part of the Asturian division which lay at Orduña succeeded in carrying out this order. But the remainder of Acevedo's men and the whole of those of Martinengo— some 8,000 bayonets in all—were at Villaro, a point higher up in the mountains, on a much more difficult road, and closer to the French. They received Blake's dispatch too late, and on pushing down the northern side of the pass which they had been holding, they learnt at Miravalles, only ten miles from Bilbao, that the latter town was in the hands of the French. Blake had evacuated it on the early morning of November 1, and Lefebvre had occupied it on the same night. Urging his pursuit some way beyond Bilbao in the hope of overtaking Blake, the duke pushed as far as Valmaceda: but even here the Galician army would make no stand, but fell back still further westward to Nava. Seeing that he could not reach his adversary, Lefebvre left the division of Villatte at Valmaceda to observe Blake, and returned with those of Sebastiani and Leval to Bilbao, to feed and rest his men in the town, after four days of marching in the mountains with very insufficient supplies. This

---

[1] Report of Captain Carroll in papers of 1809 in the Record Office.

was a very dangerous step, for Blake had been outmanœuvred rather than beaten, and was still far too strong to be contained by a mere 7,000 men.

When therefore Acevedo and his column drew near to Bilbao, they learnt that 13,000 French troops blocked their road towards Blake [Nov. 3]. They drew back a little up the pass, keeping very quiet, and very fortunately failed to attract the attention of Lefebvre, who thought at the most that there were some bands of stragglers in the mountains on his left.

But their situation was still most uncomfortable, for their rear-guard began to report that French troops were pushing up from Vittoria and entering the southern end of the defile in which they were blocked. King Joseph had been much vexed to hear of Lefebvre's disobedience to his orders at Zornoza, but, wishing to draw what profit he could from the victory, sent Victor up the Murguia—Orduña road, with orders to cut in upon the line of Blake's retreat. This the Duke of Belluno failed to accomplish, on account of the rapidity with which the Spanish army had retired. But reaching Amurrio, a few miles beyond Orduña, he came upon the flank of Acevedo's column, whose head was blocked at Miravalles, ten miles further north, by the presence of Lefebvre at Bilbao. If either marshal had realized the situation, the 8,000 Spaniards, caught in a defile without lateral issues, must have surrendered *en masse*. But Victor had only one division with him, the other was far behind : and imagining that he had chanced upon the whole of Blake's army he came to a dead stop, while Lefebvre, not yet aware of Victor's approach, did not move at all. Acevedo wisely kept quiet, and tried to slip across Victor's front towards Orantia and the river Salcedon : meanwhile the news of his situation reached Blake.

That general was never wanting in personal courage, and had been deeply distressed to hear that his flanking detachment had been cut off. Realizing Acevedo's danger he resolved to make a sudden 'offensive return' against Lefebvre, and to endeavour to clear for a moment the road from Miravalles to Valmaceda, by which his subordinate could escape. On the night of November 4 he concentrated his whole army, which had now been raised to 24,000 men by the arrival of the main body of La Romana's division from Santander. At dawn on the fifth he fell upon the enemy in his front, by the two roads on each side of the river Salcedon, sending one division[1] and the 'Vanguard Brigade' to attack Valmaceda, and two[2] and the 'Reserve Brigade' by Orantia along the southern bank of the stream.   Villatte had been holding both these paths; but on seeing the heavy forces deployed against him, he withdrew from Orantia and concentrated at Valmaceda.   This left the path clear for Acevedo, who escaped along the hillsides without being molested by Victor's advanced guard, and got into communication with his chief.   The inactivity of Victor is inexplicable: when he saw the Asturian division pushing hastily across his front, he should have attacked it at all costs; but though he heard plainly the cannonade of Villatte's fight with Blake at Valmaceda, he held back, and finally retired on Orduña when Acevedo had got out of sight[3]. His only excuse was that he had heard the distant roar of battle die down, and concluded therefore that Villatte (who as he supposed might be supported by the whole of Lefebvre's corps) must have been victorious.

As a matter of fact the isolated French division had almost suffered the fate that should have befallen the Asturians.   Driven out of Valmaceda by Blake, it was falling back on Guenes when it came across Acevedo's men marching on the opposite side of the Salcedon to join their comrades.   Thereupon the Asturian general threw some of his men[4] across the stream to intercept the retiring column.   Villatte formed his troops in a solid mass and broke through, but left behind him one gun (an eight-pounder), many of his baggage-wagons, and 300 prisoners.   That he escaped at all is a fine testimony to his resolution and his capable handling of his troops, for he had been most wantonly exposed to destruction by Victor's timidity and Lefebvre's carelessness [November 5].

---

[1] The 4th Division.

[2] The 1st and 3rd Divisions.   See the dispatches of Captain Carroll from Valmaceda, dated Nov. 5, in the Record Office.

[3] Napoleon, furious at the escape of the Asturians, administered a fiery rebuke to the Marshal.   'He had left one of his own divisions, exposed by Lefebvre's imprudence, to run the risk of annihilation.   He had never gone to the front himself to look at Acevedo, but had allowed the reconnoitring to be done by an incapable subordinate.   His guess that Villatte had been victorious and did not need help was absurd; why should the dying down of the fire mean that the French were successful rather than beaten?   The first principles of the art of war prescribe that a general should march toward the cannon, when he knows that his colleagues are engaged' (*Nap. Corresp.*, 14,445).

[4] One battalion of Segovia and two of volunteers of Galicia.

On hearing of Villatte's desperate situation, the Duke of Dantzig had realized the consequences of his unjustifiable retreat to Bilbao, and marched up in hot haste with the divisions of Sebastiani and Leval. He was relieved to find that Villatte had extricated himself, and resolved to punish Blake for his unexpected offensive move. But he was unable to do his adversary much harm : the Galician general had only advanced in order to save Acevedo, and did not intend to engage in any serious fighting. When Lefebvre moved forward he found that the Spaniards would not stand. Blake had pushed out two flanking divisions to turn the position at Guenes, on to which Villatte had fallen back, and had his main body placed in front of it. But when Lefebvre advanced, the whole Galician army fell back, only fighting two rearguard actions on November 7, in which they suffered small loss. On the next day there was a more serious engagement of the same sort at Valmaceda, to which the Galicians had withdrawn on the previous night. The troops with which Blake covered his retreat were hustled out of the town with the loss of 150 killed and wounded, and 600 missing [1]. In his dispatches the Spanish general explains that he retreated not because he could not have made a better resistance, but because he had used up all his provisions, and was prevented by the bad weather and the state of the roads from drawing further supplies from Santander and Reynosa, the two nearest points at which they could be procured. For Western Biscay had been eaten bare by the large forces that had been crossing and recrossing it during the last two months, and was absolutely incapable of feeding the army for a single day. The men too were in a wretched condition, not only from hunger [2] but from bad equipment : hardly any of them had received great-coats, their shoes were worn out, and sickness was very prevalent. An appreciable number of the raw Galician and Asturian levies deserted during the miserable retreat from Guenes and Valmaceda to Espinosa de los Monteros, the next point on the Bilbao-Reynosa road at which Blake stood at bay. When he reached that place he was short of some 6,000 men, less

---

[1] This engagement, unmentioned by Napier, Thiers, and most other historians, will be found in detail in Carroll's dispatch and Arteche (iii. 273, 274).

[2] Indeed they were only saved from starvation by receiving at Espinosa 250 mules laden with biscuit, from English ships at Santander, which General Leith had pushed across the mountains. Blake in a letter of Nov. 9 to Leith (Record Office) acknowledges that this kept his men alive.

from losses in battle than from wholesale straggling. Moreover he was for the moment deprived of the aid of the greater part of one of his divisions. This was the 4th Galician division, that of General Carbajal : it had formed the extreme left of the army, and had lain nearest to the sea during the fighting about Guenes and Valmaceda. Cut off from the main body, a large portion of it had retreated by the coast-road towards Santander, and only a fraction of it had rejoined the commander-in-chief [1]. The total of Blake's forces would have been nearly 40,000 [2], if his army had been still at the strength with which each corps started on the campaign. But for its decisive battle he had no more than 23,000 in hand.

Beyond Valmaceda he had been pursued no longer by Lefebvre, but by Victor. The latter, soundly rebuked by the Emperor for his inactivity on November 5, had advanced again from Orduña, had picked up the division of Villatte—which properly belonged to his corps—and had then taken the lead in pressing Blake. Lefebvre, reduced to his original force—the 13,000 men of Sebastiani and Leval, followed as far as the end of the defile of El Berron, and then turned off by a flanking road which reaches the upper valley of the Ebro at Medina de Pomar. He intended to strike

---

[1] I gather from a comparison of the muster-rolls of the Galician army in October and in December, that four battalions rejoined Blake and six escaped towards Santander.

[2] He had originally (see the table on p. 403)—

Galician troops (four divisions and two brigades) .	23,313
The Asturian Division of Acevedo	7,633
La Romana's troops from the Baltic (the infantry only)	5,294
Cavalry and artillery (400 and 1,000 respectively) .	1,400
	37,640

From this have to be deducted—

Losses in battle and by desertion	6,000
The cavalry, all the artillery save one battery, and two battalions guarding the same, all still to the rear towards Reynosa	2,400
Two battalions of regiment Del Rey with Malaspina, at Villarcayo	1,000
Part of the 4th Division, cut off and retreating on Santander	2,200
	11,600

This leaves 26,040 available at Espinosa; the real figure was probably somewhat smaller.

at Villarcayo and Reynosa, and to intercept Blake's retreat at
one of these two points. If he arrived there before the Galicians,
who would be delayed by the necessity of fighting continual rearguard actions with Victor, he hoped that the whole of the Spanish
army might be surrounded and captured.

In this expectation he was disappointed, for matters came to a
head before he was near enough to exercise any influence on the
approaching battle. On November 10 Blake turned to bay: his
rearguard, composed of the troops from the Baltic, had been so
much harassed and detained by the incessant attacks of Victor's
leading division, that its commander, the Conde de San Roman,
sent to the general to ask for aid. Unless supported by more
troops he would be surrounded and cut off. Tempted by the
strong defensive position in front of the picturesque old town of
Espinosa de los Monteros, Blake directed the rearguard to take
post there, and brought up the whole of the rest of his army into
line with them. At this point the high-road along the river
Trueba, after passing through a small plain (the Campo de Pedral-
va), reaches a defile almost blocked by the little town of Espinosa,
for steep hills descending from each flank narrow the breadth of
the passage to half a mile. Here Blake occupied a semicircular
position of considerable strength. The troops of San Roman took
post at its southern end, on a hill above the high-road, and close
to the river's edge. The line was prolonged to the north of them,
across the narrow space of level ground, by the Vanguard Brigade
(Mendizabel) and the 3rd Division (Riquelme). Where the ground
begins to rise again lay the 1st Division (Figueroa), and on the
extreme left, far to the north, the Asturians of Acevedo occupied
a lofty ridge called Las Peñuccas. Here they were so strongly
placed that it seemed unlikely that they could either be turned or
dislodged by a frontal attack. The rest of the army formed a
second line: the Reserve Brigade (Mahy) was in the rear of the
centre, in the suburb of Espinosa. The 2nd Division (Martinengo)
and the small remains of the 4th Division lay behind San Roman,
near the Trueba, to support the right wing, along the line of the
high-road. The whole amounted to something between 22,000
and 23,000 men, but there were only six guns with the army—the
same light battery which had fought at Zornoza. They were
posted on the right-centre, with Mendizabel's brigade, in a position
from which they could sweep the level ground in front of Espinosa.

Blake also called up to his aid the one outlying force that was within reach, a brigade under General Malaspina, which lay at Villarcayo, guarding the dépôt which had been there established. But these 2,500 men and the six guns which they had with them were prevented, as we shall see, from reaching the field[1].

The position of Espinosa was most defensible: its projecting wings were each strong, and its centre, drawn far back, could not prudently be attacked as long as the flanking heights were in the hands of the Spaniards. But the pursuing French were under the impression that the Galician army was so thoroughly demoralized, and worn out by hunger and cold, that it would not stand. Victor had with him the infantry of his own corps, some 21,000 strong: Villatte's division, which led the pursuit, dashed at the enemy as soon as it came upon the field. Six battalions drew up opposite the Spanish centre, to contain any sally that it might make, while the other six swerved to the left and made a desperate attack on the division from the Baltic, which held the heights immediately above the banks of the Trueba[2]. San Roman's troops, the pick of the Spanish army, made a fine defence, and after two hours of hard fighting retained their position.

At this moment—it was about three o'clock in the short winter afternoon—Victor himself came on the scene, bringing with him his other two divisions, the twenty-two battalions of Ruffin and Lapisse. The Marshal was anxious to vindicate himself from the charge of slackness which his master had made against him for his conduct on November 5, and pushed his men hastily to the front. Nine fresh battalions—a brigade of Ruffin's and a regiment of Lapisse's division—attacked again the heights from which Villatte had been repulsed[3]. There followed a very fierce fight, and Blake only succeeded in holding his ground by bringing up to the aid of the regiments from the Baltic the whole of his 3rd Division and part of his 2nd. At dusk the heights were still in Spanish hands, and Victor's corps was obliged to draw back into the woods at the foot of the position.

This engagement was most creditable to Blake's army: the lie

---

[1] Malaspina had two battalions of Del Rey, and the Betanzos and Monterrey militia. (Journal of Blake's Operations in the *Vaughan Papers*.)

[2] Puthod's brigade of Villatte's division, the 94th and 95th of the Line.

[3] The 9th Léger and 24th of the Line from Ruffin's division, and the 54th from that of Lapisse, each three battalions strong.

of the ground was in their favour, but considering their fatigue and semi-starvation they did very well in repulsing equal numbers of the best French troops. They were aided by the reckless manner in which Villatte and Victor attacked: it was not consonant with true military principles that the van should commit itself to a desperate fight before the main body came up, or that a strong position should be assailed without the least attempt at a preliminary reconnaissance.

Next day the Marshal, taught caution by his repulse, resumed the action in a more scientific fashion. He came to the conclusion that Blake would have been induced by the battle of the previous day, to strengthen his right, and in this he was perfectly correct. The Spaniard had shifted all his reserves towards the high-road and the banks of the Trueba, expecting to be attacked on the same ground as on the previous day. But Victor, making no more than a demonstration on this point, sent the greater part of Lapisse's division to attack the extreme left of Blake's line—the Asturian troops who held the high ridge to the north of Espinosa. Here the position was very strong, but the troops were not equal in quality to the veteran battalions from the Baltic [1]. When the French pressed up the hill covered by a thick cloud of skirmishers, the Asturians fell into disorder. Their general, Acevedo, and his brigadiers, Quiros and Valdes, were all struck down while trying to lead forward their wavering troops. Finally the whole division gave way and fled down the back of the hill towards Espinosa. Their rout left the enemy in possession of the high ground, which completely commanded the Spanish centre, and General Maison, who had led the attack, fully used his advantage. He fell upon the Galician 1st Division from the flank, while at the same moment Victor ordered his entire line to advance, and assailed the whole of Blake's front. Such an assault could not fail, and the Spaniards gave way in all directions, and escaped by fording the Trueba and flying over the hillsides towards Reynosa. They had to abandon their six guns and the whole of their baggage, which lay parked behind Espinosa. The losses in killed and wounded were not very heavy—indeed many more were hurt in the hard fighting of November 10 than in the rout of November 11: it is probable that

---

[1] It is fair to the Asturians to mention that eight of their ten battalions were raw levies; there were among them only one regular and one militia battalion of old formation.

the whole of the Spanish casualties did not exceed 3,000 men : nor were many prisoners captured, for formed troops cannot pursue fugitives who have broken their ranks and taken to the hills. The main loss to Blake's army came from straggling and desertion after the battle, for the routed battalions, when once scattered over the face of the country, did not easily rally to their colours. When Blake reassembled his force at Reynosa he could only show some 12,000 half-starved men out of the 23,000 who had stood in line at Espinosa. The loss in battle had fallen most heavily on the division from the Baltic—their commander, San Roman, with about 1,000 of his men had fallen in their very creditable struggle on the first day of the fight[1]. Victor's triumph had not been bloodless : in the repulse of the tenth the fifteen battalions which had tried to storm the heights had all suffered appreciable losses : the total of French casualties on the two days cannot have fallen below 1,000 killed and wounded.

To complete the story of Blake's retreat, it is only necessary to mention that the detached brigade under Malaspina, which he had called up from Villarcayo to Espinosa, was never able to rejoin. On its way it fell in with Marshal Lefebvre's corps, marching to outflank the retreat of the Galician army. Attacked by Sebastiani's division, Malaspina had to turn off and make a hasty and isolated retreat, sacrificing his six guns. The driving away of his small force was the only practical work done in this part of the campaign by the 4th Corps : its long turning movement was rendered useless by Blake's rapid retreat across its front to Reynosa.

[1] It is necessary to protest against the groundless libel upon this corps in which Napier indulges (i. 257) when he says : ' It has been said that Romana's soldiers died Spartan-like, to a man, in their ranks ; yet in 1812 Captain Hill of the Royal Navy, being at Cronstadt to receive Spaniards taken by the Russians during Napoleon's retreat, found the greater portion were Romana's men captured at Espinosa ; they had served Napoleon for four years, passed the ordeal of the Moscow retreat, and were still 4,000 strong.' This is ludicrous : the eight battalions of the Baltic division landed in Spain 5,294 strong ; a month after Espinosa they still figured for 3,953 in the muster-rolls of the army of Galicia (see the morning state in Arteche, iv. 532). Only 1,300 were missing, so Victor, clearly, cannot have taken 4,000 prisoners. Captain Hill's (or Napier's) mistake lies in not seeing that the Russian prisoners of 1812 belonged to the 5,000 men of La Romana's army (regiments of Guadalajara, Asturias, and the Infante) which did not succeed in escaping from Denmark in 1808, and remained perforce in Napoleon's ranks.

NAPOLEON CROSSES THE EBRO: THE ROUT OF GAMONAL: SOULT'S PURSUIT OF BLAKE

AFTER resting for only thirty-six hours at Bayonne the Emperor, as we have already seen, pushed on to Vittoria, where he arrived on November 6. He found in and about that ancient city the bulk of the Imperial Guard, his brother Joseph's reserves, the light cavalry of Beaumont and Franceschi, and the heavy cavalry of Latour-Maubourg and Milhaud. The divisions of Marchand and Bisson, which were to complete the corps of Ney, were close behind him, so that he had under his hand a mass of at least 40,000 men. The 2nd Corps, which Bessières had so long commanded, was in front of him at Pancorbo, just beyond the Ebro. Victor and Lefebvre, very busy with Blake, lay on his right hand with some 35,000 men. The troops which had hitherto been under Ney, with Moncey's 3rd Corps, were on his right—the former at Logroño, the latter at Caparrosa and Lodosa. They were in close touch with the armies of Castaños and Palafox.

All was ready for the great stroke, and on the day of his arrival the Emperor gave orders for the general advance, bidding Bessières (whose corps formed his vanguard) to march at once on Burgos and sweep out of it whatever troops he might find in his front. Napoleon imagined that the force in this section of the Spanish line would turn out to be Pignatelli's ' Army of Castile,' but that very untrustworthy body had ceased to exist, and had been drafted into the ranks of the army of Andalusia [1]. It was really with the newly arrived army of Estremadura that the 2nd Corps had to deal.

Everything seemed to promise a successful issue to the Emperor's plan: the enemy had only a trifling force in front of him at Burgos. Palafox and Castaños were still holding their dangerous advanced positions at Sanguesa and Calahorra. Blake was being pursued by

---

[1] See pp. 393-4, and *Nap. Corresp.*, 14,443.

Victor, while Lefebvre was marching to intercept him. The only *contretemps* that had occurred was the temporary check to Villatte's division on November 5, which had been caused by the carelessness of the Duke of Dantzig and the unaccountable timidity of the Duke of Belluno. But by the seventh their mistakes had been repaired, and Blake was once more on the run, with both marshals in full cry behind him. The Emperor found time to send to each of them a letter of bitter rebuke [1], but told them to push on and catch up the army of Galicia at all hazards. Upon Moncey, on the other hand, he imposed the duty of keeping absolutely quiet in his present position : his share in the game would only begin when Castaños and Palafox should have been turned and enveloped by troops detached from the central mass of the army.

The total stay of the Emperor in Vittoria covered parts of four days. All this time he was anxiously expecting decisive news from Victor and Lefebvre, but it had not yet arrived when he set forth. He waited, also in vain, for the news that Bessières had occupied Burgos : but that marshal did not show the decision and dash which Napoleon expected from him: finding that there was infantry in the place, he would not risk an action without his master's presence, and merely contented himself with pushing back the Spanish outposts, and extending his cavalry on both flanks. It is possible that his slackness was due to chagrin on receiving the intelligence that he was about to be superseded in command of the 2nd Corps by Soult, whom the Emperor had summoned out of Germany, and who was due at the front on the ninth. Bessières was to be compensated by being given the command of the reserve-cavalry of the army, five splendid divisions of dragoons, of which four were already on the Ebro. But this post, which would always keep him at the Emperor's heels, was probably less attractive to him than the more independent position of chief of a corps complete in all arms. He was probably loth to leave the divisions with which he had won the victory of Medina de Rio Seco. Be this as it may, he was told to attack Burgos on the sixth, and on the ninth he had not yet done so. On the morning of that day Soult arrived, alone and on a jaded post-horse, having outridden even his aides-de-camp [2], who did not join him till twenty-four

[1] That to Victor will be found in *Nap. Corresp.*, 14,445.

[2] For details of their ride against time, see the *Mémoires* of St. Chamans, his senior aide-de-camp (p. 107).

hours later. He at once took over command of the 2nd Corps, and proceeded next day to carry out the Emperor's orders by attacking the enemy.

The supersession of Bessières was not the only change which was made during the few days while the Emperor lay at Vittoria. He rearranged the internal organization of several of the corps, altered the brigading of that of Moncey, and turned over to other corps most of the troops which had hitherto served under Ney, leaving to that marshal little more than the two newly arrived divisions from Germany (those of Lagrange and Marchand).

The troops destined for the march on Burgos counted some 70,000 men, but only the 2nd Corps and the cavalry of Milhaud and Franceschi were in the front line. These 18,000 bayonets and 6,500 sabres were amply sufficient for the task. Behind followed fourteen battalions of the Imperial Guard and the cavalry of that corps, the two divisions of Ney's 6th Corps, the division of Dessolles from King Joseph's reserve, and two and a half divisions of reserve cavalry—an enormous mass of troops, of which nearly 20,000 were veteran cavalry from Germany, a force invaluable for the sweeping of the great plains of Old Castile [1].

When we turn to enumerate the forces opposed to the Emperor

---

[1] The figures here given are mainly those indicated by Napoleon in his dispatch of Nov. 8 (*Nap. Corresp.*, 14,456), supplemented from the morning state of the army on Oct. 10 :—

2nd Corps (Marshal Soult) :

Division Mouton (Merle)	6,000
Division Bonnet	4,500
Division Merle (Verdier)	7,000
Cavalry of Lasalle	2,000

6th Corps (Marshal Ney) :

Division Marchand . . ⎫	17,000
Division Lagrange (late Bisson) ⎭	
Cavalry of Colbert (detached at this moment) . .	2,000
From King Joseph's Reserve, Division Dessolles . .	6,000
Imperial Guard ⎧ fourteen battalions of infantry . .	8,000
⎩ cavalry	3,500
Cavalry Brigade (Beaumont) belonging to the 1st Corps .	1,200
Latour-Maubourg's Division of Dragoons (six regiments) .	3,700
Milhaud's Division of Dragoons (three regiments) . .	2,500
Franceschi's Light Cavalry (four regiments) . . .	2,000
Lahoussaye's Division of Dragoons (four regiments) . .	2,000
Total . . .	67,400

at Burgos, the disproportion between the two armies appears ludicrous. Down to November 6 the only Spanish troops in that ancient city consisted of two battalions, one from the reserves of the army of Galicia, the other from the army of Castile [1]. They numbered 1,600 men, and had four guns with them. If Bessières had attacked on the sixth, he would have found no more than this miserable detachment to oppose him. But on November 7 there arrived from Madrid the 1st Division of the army of Estremadura under the Conde de Belvedere, 4,000 foot and 400 horse with twelve guns. On the next day there came up the greater part of the 2nd Division of the same army, about 3,000 infantry and two regiments of hussars. On the tenth, therefore, when Soult attacked, Belvedere —who took the command as the senior general present—had about 8,600 bayonets, 1,100 sabres, and sixteen guns under his orders.

Down to November 2 the army of Estremadura had been commanded by Don Joseph Galuzzo, Captain-General of that province —the officer who had given so much trouble to Dalrymple by his refusal to desist from the futile siege of Elvas. He had been repeatedly ordered to bring his army up to Madrid, but did not arrive till the end of October. On the twenty-ninth of that month he marched for Burgos, his three divisions, 13,000 men in all, following each other at intervals of a day. But on November 2 he received orders to lay down his command and return to Aranjuez, to answer some charges brought against him by the Supreme Junta. No successor was nominated to replace him, and hence the conduct of the army fell into the hands of the Conde de Belvedere, the chief of the 1st Division, a rash and headstrong young aristocrat with no military experience whatever. His family influence had made him a general at an age when he might reasonably have expected to lead a company, and he found himself by chance the interim commander of an army : hence came the astonishing series of blunders that led to the combat of Gamonal.

Belvedere's army was still incomplete, for his 3rd Division had only reached Lerma, thirty miles back on the Madrid road, when the French cavalry came forward and began to press in his outposts. Clearly a crisis was at hand, and the Count had to consider how he would face it. Isolated with 10,000 men on the edge of the great plain of Old Castile, and with an enemy of unknown

---

[1] These battalions were those of Tuy and Benavente, the first a militia battalion, the second a new volunteer corps.

strength in front of him, he should have been cautious. If he
attempted a stand, he should at least have taken advantage of the
ancient fortifications of Burgos and the broken ground near the
city. But with the most cheerful disregard of common military
precautions, the Count marched out of Burgos, advanced a few
miles, and drew up his army across the high-road in front of the
village of Gamonal. He was in an open plain, his right flank ill
covered by the river Arlanzon, which was fordable in many places,
his left completely 'in the air,' near the village of Vellimar. In
front of the line was a large wood, which the road bisects: it gave
the enemy every facility for masking his movements till the last
moment. Belvedere had ranged his two Estremaduran batteries
on the centre: he had six battalions in his first line, including two
of the Royal Guards—both very weak [1]—with a cavalry regiment
on each flank. His second line was formed of four battalions—two
of them Galician: two more battalions, the four Galician guns,
and his third cavalry regiment were coming up from the rear, and
had not yet taken their post in the second line when the short and
sudden battle was fought and lost [2].

[1] Each mustered less than 400 bayonets.

[2] To show how strange is Napier's statement (i. 254) that the army of
Estremadura consisted of 'the best troops then in Spain,' and that it was
therefore disgraceful that they 'fought worse than the half-starved peasants
of Blake,' we may perhaps give the list of Belvedere's little force: it consisted of—

 1st Division (General de Alos) :
  *4th battalion of the Spanish Guards . . . . ⎫
  One battalion of Provincial Grenadiers of Estremadura ⎪
  *Regiment of Majorca (two batts.) . . . . ⎬ 4,160
  *2nd Regiment of Catalonia (one batt.) . . . ⎪
  One company of Sharpshooters . . . . . ⎭
 2nd Division (General Henestrosa) :
  *4th battalion of the Walloon Guards . . . . ⎫
  Volunteers of Badajoz (two batts.) . . . . ⎪
  Volunteers of Valencia de Alcantara (one batt.) . . ⎬ 3,300
  Volunteers of Zafra (one batt.) . . . . ⎭
 Galician troops: Battalions of Tuy and Benavente . . 1,600
 Cavalry : 2nd, 4th, and 5th Hussars (called respectively
  'Lusitania,' 'Volunteers of Spain,' and 'Maria Luisa') 1,100
 Artillery : two and a half batteries 250
 Sappers : one battalion 550
       Total . . . 10,960

Only the cavalry and the five battalions marked with a star were regulars.

Soult came on the scene during the hours of the morning, with the light-cavalry division of Lasalle deployed in his front. Then followed the dragoons of Milhaud, and three infantry divisions of the 2nd Corps—Mouton in front, then Merle, then Bonnet bringing up the rear. When he came upon the Spaniards, arrayed on either side of the road, the Marshal was able with a single glance to recognize the weakness of their numbers and their position. He did not hesitate for a moment, and rapidly formed his line of battle, under cover of the wood which lay between the two armies. Milhaud's division of dragoons rode southward and formed up on the banks of the Arlanzon, facing the Spanish right : Lasalle's four regiments of light cavalry composed the French centre : the twelve battalions of Mouton's division deployed on the left, and advanced through the wood preceded by a crowd of tirailleurs. There was no need to wait for Merle and Bonnet, who were still some way to the rear.

The engagement opened by a discharge of the two Spanish batteries, directed at those of Mouton's men who were advancing across the comparatively open ground on each side of the high-road. But they had hardly time to fire three or four salvos before the enemy was upon them. The seven regiments of cavalry which formed the left and centre of the French army had delivered a smashing charge at the infantry opposed to them in the plain. The regiment of Spanish hussars which covered their flank was swept away like chaff before the wind, and the unfortunate Estremaduran and Galician battalions had not even time to throw themselves into squares before this torrent of nearly 5,000 horsemen swept over them. They received the attack in line, with a wavering ill-directed fire which did not stop the enemy for a moment. Five battalions were ridden down in the twinkling of an eye, their colours were all taken, and half the men were hewn down or made prisoners [1]. The remnant fled in disorder towards Burgos. Then Milhaud's dragoons continued the pursuit, while Lasalle's chasseurs swerved inwards and fell upon the flank of the surviving half of Belvedere's army. At the same moment the infantry of Mouton attacked them vigorously from the front. The inevitable result was the complete rout and dispersion of the whole : only the

[1] As ill luck would have it four of these five battalions in the plain were raw levies, the Volunteers of Badajoz (two batts.) and of Tuy and Benavente. They had not skill enough even to form square.

battalion of Walloon Guards succeeded in forming square and going off the field in some order. The rest broke their ranks and poured into Burgos, in a stream of fugitives similar to that which was already rushing through the streets from the other wing. The sixteen Spanish guns were all captured on the spot, those of the second line before they had been unlimbered or fired a single shot.

Belvedere, who was rash and incompetent but no coward, made two desperate attempts to rally his troops, one at the bridge of the Arlanzon, the other outside the city; but his men would not halt for a moment: their only concern was to get clear of the baggage-train which was blocking the road in the transpontine suburb. A little further on the fugitives met the belated battalions of Valencia and Zafra, which had been four or five miles from the field when the battle was lost. The Commander-in-chief tried to form them across the road, and to rally the broken troops upon them: but they cried 'Treason,' pretended that their cartridge-boxes were empty, broke their ranks, and headed the flight. Ere night they had reached Lerma, thirty miles to the rear, where the 3rd Division of Estremadura had just arrived.

Napoleon was probably using less than his customary exaggeration when he declared in his *Bulletin* that he had won the combat of Gamonal at the cost of fifteen killed and fifty wounded. It is at any rate unlikely that his total of casualties exceeded the figure of 200. The army of Estremadura on the other hand had suffered terribly: considering that its whole right wing had been ridden down by cavalry, and that the pursuit had been urged across an open plain for nine miles, it may well have lost the 2,500 killed and wounded and the 900 prisoners spoken of by the more moderate French narrators of the fight[1]. It is certain that it left behind twelve of the twenty-four regimental standards which it carried to the field, and every one of its guns[2].

The French army celebrated its not very glorious victory in the

[1] It is fair to say, however, that Jourdan asserts that their loss was only about 1,500 (*Mémoires*, p. 85). There is no Spanish estimate of any authority. Napoleon in his *Bulletin* claimed 3,000 killed and 3,000 prisoners, one of his usual exaggerations.

[2] There were only sixteen field-guns with the army, yet Napoleon says that he took twenty-five (*Nap. Corresp.*, 14,478). If this figure is correct (which we may doubt) there must have been some guns of position taken in the city of Burgos. But of the twelve flags there is no question: they were forwarded to Paris two days later (*Nap. Corresp.*, 14,463).

usual fashion by sacking Burgos with every attendant circumstances
of misconduct. They were so much out of hand that the house
next to that in which the Emperor had taken up his quarters for
the night was pillaged and set on fire, so that he had to shift
hastily into another street [1].

The night of the tenth was devoted to plunder, but on the following morning Bonaparte resumed without delay the execution
of his great plan, and hurried out to the south the heavy masses of
cavalry which were to sweep the plains of Old Castile. Lasalle's
division pushed on to Lerma, from which the shattered remnants
of the army of Belvedere hastily retired. Milhaud's dragoons were
directed on Palencia, Franceschi's light cavalry more to the west,
along the banks of the Urbel and the Odra. Nowhere, save at
Lerma, was a single Spanish soldier seen, but it is said that some
of Milhaud's flying parties obtained vague information of the
advance of Sir John Moore's English army beyond the frontier
of Portugal. His vanguard was reported to be at Toro, an utter
mistake, for the expeditionary force had not really passed Salamanca on the day when the rumour was transmitted to the
Emperor [2]. There is no sign in his dispatches of any serious
expectation of a possible British diversion.

On the same day on which the cavalry poured down into the
plains of Castile, the Emperor began also to execute the great
flanking movements which were to circumvent the armies of Blake
and Castaños and to drive the one into the Bay of Biscay and the
other against the Pyrenees. On the afternoon of the eleventh
Soult, with the three divisions of Mouton, Merle, and Bonnet, and
Debelle's cavalry brigade [3], was directed to make forced marches
upon Reynosa, by the hilly road that passes by Urbel and Olleros [4].

---

[1] *Mémoires* of St. Chamans (Soult's senior aide-de-camp), p. 110. Compare
the *Journal* of Fantin des Odoards (p. 189) for the scenes of horror in and
about the town. The scattered corpses of Spaniards, cut down as they fled,
covered the road for half-a-day's march beyond Burgos.

[2] *Nap. Corresp.*, 14,496, contains this false report.

[3] This brigade did not properly belong to the 2nd Corps, but to Franceschi's
division of reserve cavalry. Lasalle, with the proper cavalry division of the
2nd Corps, was being employed elsewhere.

[4] This was done on November 11, and not (as Arteche says) on the thirteenth.
The proof may be found in the itinerary given by St. Chamans in his
Mémoires (p. 110). On the thirteenth the Marshal was already at Canduelas,
close to Reynosa.

It was hoped that he might reach Reynosa before Blake, whose retreat towards the west was being closely pressed by Victor and Lefebvre. If he failed to catch the army of Galicia, the Marshal was to push on across the mountains, and occupy the important harbour-town of Santander, where it was known that British stores had been landed in great quantities. Milhaud was to co-operate in this movement by sending from Palencia one of his brigades of dragoons, to cut the road from Reynosa to Saldaña, by which the Emperor considered it likely that Blake would send off his heavy baggage and guns when he heard of Soult's approach[1]. Two days after dispatching Soult to the north-west, the Emperor gave orders for the other great turning movement, which was destined to cut off the army of Castaños. On the thirteenth Marshal Ney, with one division of his own corps (that of Marchand) and with the four regiments of Dessolles from the central reserve, together with the light cavalry of Beaumont, had marched from Burgos, in the wake of Lasalle's advance. On the sixteenth he reached Aranda de Duero, and, having halted there for two days, was then directed to turn off from the high-road to Madrid, and march by Osma and Soria so as to fall upon the rear of Castaños, who was still reported to be in the neighbourhood of Tudela[2]. If he could succeed in placing himself at Tarazona before the enemy moved, the Emperor considered that the fate of the Spanish ' Army of the Centre' was sealed.

While the movements of Soult and Ney were developing, Napoleon remained at Burgos. He stayed there in all for ten days, while his army passed by, each corps that arrived pressing forward along the high-road to Madrid by Lerma as far as Aranda. His advance on the Spanish capital was not to begin till he was certain how Blake and Castaños had fared, and whether there was any considerable body of the enemy interposed between him and the point at which he was about to strike. Meanwhile his correspondence shows a feverish activity devoted to subjects of the most varied kind. A good many hours were devoted to drawing up a scheme for the restoration of the citadel of Burgos : it was the Emperor's own brain which planned the fortifications that proved such an obstacle to Wellington four years later in September, 1812.

---

[1] *Nap. Corresp.*, 14,467 and 14,477. Napoleon to Bessières, Nov. 13 (at two, midnight), and to Milhaud, Nov. 16 (at three, midnight).

[2] These orders will be found in *Nap. Corresp.*, 14,489.

It was in these days also that Napoleon dictated the last reply sent to Canning with regard to the peace negotiations that had been started at Erfurt. At the same moment he was commenting on the *Code Napoléon*, organizing the grand-duchy of Berg, ordering the assembly of Neapolitan troops for a descent on Sicily, regulating the university of Pisa, and drawing up notes on the internal government of Spain for the benefit of his brother Joseph [1]. But the most characteristic of all his actions was a huge piece of 'commandeering' of private property. Burgos was the great distributing centre for the wool-trade of Spain : here lay the warehouses of the flock-masters, who owned the great herds of merino sheep that feed upon the central plateaux of Castile. There were 20,000 bales of wool in the city, not government stores but purely private accumulations. The Emperor seized it all and sold it in France, gloating over the fact that it was worth more than 15,000,000 francs [2].

Neither of the flanking expeditions which the Emperor sent out quite fulfilled his expectations, but that of Soult was worked far more successfully than that of Ney. The Duke of Dalmatia's corps marched sixty miles over bad Spanish roads in three days—a great feat for infantry—and reached Canduelas close to Reynosa on November 13. If Blake had not already been flying for his life before Victor, he must have been intercepted. But he had made such headlong speed that he had already reached Reynosa only twenty-four hours after his defeat at Espinosa. He had hoped to refit and reorganize his army by means of the vast accumulation of stores collected there, for he had left both Victor and Lefebvre far behind, and calculated on getting several days' rest. His first act was to begin to evacuate his artillery, baggage, and wounded on to Leon by the road of Aguilar del Campo and Saldaña. He intended to follow with the infantry [3], but on the morning of November 14 Soult's advanced cavalry came upon the flank of the great slow-moving convoy, and captured a considerable part of it. The Asturian general, Acevedo, lying wounded in his

---

[1] *Nap. Corresp.*, 14,465, 14,488–91, 14,472, 14,482, 14,503, and 14,499 respectively.

[2] For this barefaced robbery see the *Sixth Bulletin of the Army of Spain*, published at Madrid on December 14, and also Jourdan's *Mémoires*, pp. 85, 86 ; cf. Arteche, iii. 325.

[3] Leith, Nov. 16, from Cabezon de Sal (in the Record Office).

carriage, was slain, it is said, by Debelle's dragoons, along with
many other unfortunates.   Much of the artillery and all the
baggage was taken.   The news of this disaster showed Blake that
his only road into the plain was cut: no retreat on Leon was any
longer possible.   At the same moment the approach of Victor
along the Espinosa road and of Lefebvre along the Villarcayo road
was reported to him.   It seemed as if he was doomed to destruction
or capture, for all the practicable roads were cut, and the army,
though a little heartened up by two days of regular rations at
Reynosa, was in the most disorganized condition.   But making a
desperate appeal to the patriotism of his men, Blake abandoned
all his stores, all his wheeled vehicles, even his horses, and struck
up by a wild mountain track into the heart of the Asturian hills.
He went by the gorge of Cabuerniga, along the rocky edge of the
Saja torrent, and finally reached the sea near Santillana.   This
forced march was accomplished in two days of drenching rain, and
without food of any kind save a few chestnuts and heads of maize
obtained in the villages of this remote upland.   If anything was
needed to make Blake's misery complete it was to be met, at
Renedo [1] [November 15], by the news that he was superseded by
La Romana, who came with a commission from the Junta to take
command of the army of Galicia.   After the receipt of the
intelligence of Zornoza, the Government had disgraced the Irish
general, and given his place to the worthy Marquis.   But the
latter did not assume the command for some days, and it was left
to Blake to get his army out of the terrible straits in which it now
lay.   On nearing the coast he obtained a little more food for his
men from the English vessels that had escaped from Santander [2],
waited for his stragglers to come up, and, when he had 7,000 men
collected, resumed his march.   He sent the wrecks of the Asturian
division back to their own province, but resolved to return with
the rest of his army to the southern side of the Cantabrian
Mountains, so as to cover the direct road from Burgos to Galicia.
He had quite shaken off his pursuers, and had nothing to fear save
physical difficulties in his retreat.   But these were severe enough
to try the best troops, and Blake's men, under-fed, destitute of
great-coats and shoes, and harassed by endless marching, were in a

---

[1] Not Arnedo as in Napier (i. 257).

[2] See letter of General Leith (dated from San Vincente de la Barquera,
Nov. 17), in the Record Office.

piteous state: although they had not thrown away their muskets, very few had a dry cartridge left in their boxes[1]. An English officer who accompanied them described them as 'a half-starved and straggling mob, without officers, and all mixed in utter confusion[2].' The snow was now lying deep on the mountains, and the road back to the plains of Leon by Potes and Pedrosa was almost as bare and rough as that by which the troops had saved themselves from the snare at Reynosa. Nevertheless Blake's miserable army straggled over the defile across the Peñas de Europa, reached the upper valley of the Esla, and at last got a few days of rest in cantonments around Leon. Here La Romana took up the command, and by December 4 was at the head of 15,000 men. This total was only reached by the junction of outlying troops, for there had come into Leon a few detachments from the rear, and that part of the artillery and its escort which had escaped Soult's cavalry at Aguilar del Campo. Of Blake's original force, even after stragglers had come up, there were not 10,000 left: that so many survived is astonishing when we consider the awful march that they had accomplished[3]. Between November 1 and 23 they had trudged for three hundred miles over some of the roughest country in Europe, had crossed the watershed of the Cantabrian Mountains thrice[4] (twice by mere mule-tracks), wading through rain and snow for the greater part of the time, for the weather had been abominable. For mere physical difficulty this retreat far exceeded Moore's celebrated march to Corunna, but it is fair to remember that Blake had shaken off his pursuers at Reynosa, while the English general was chased by an active enemy from first to last.

While the unhappy army of Galicia was working out its salvation

[1] General Leith to Sir John Moore, from Renedo on Nov. 15 (in the Record Office).

[2] It is from that officer's dispatches alone that we glean some details of this miserable retreat. There is nothing of the kind in Toreño, Arteche, or any other Spanish authority that I have found.

[3] Of La Romana's army of 15,626 men (Dec. 4) about 5,000 belonged to regiments which had not been present at Espinosa, including the battalions of Tuy, Betanzos, Monterrey, Santiago, Salamanca, the 3rd Volunteers of Galicia, and the *Batallon del General*, the artillery reserve, and a number of detached companies that had been left behind at Reynosa, Astorga, and Sahagun before Blake marched on Bilbao on October 11.

[4] Once between Valmaceda and Espinosa, once between Reynosa and Renedo, once between Potes and Pedrosa.

over these rough paths, Soult's corps had fared comparatively well. On reaching Reynosa on November 14 the Duke of Dalmatia had come into possession of an enormous mass of plunder, the whole of the stores and munitions of Blake's army. Among the trophies were no less than 15,000 new English muskets and thirty-five unhorsed field-guns. The food secured maintained the 2nd Corps for many days: it included, as an appreciative French consumer informs us, an enormous consignment of excellent Cheshire cheese, newly landed at Santander[1]. At Reynosa Soult's arrival was followed by that of Victor and Lefebvre, who rode in at the head of their corps the day after the place had been occupied [November 15]. There was no longer any chance of catching Blake, and the assembly of 50,000 men in this quarter was clearly unnecessary. The Emperor sent orders to Victor to march on Burgos and join the main army, and to Lefebvre to drop down into the plains as far as Carrion, from whence he could threaten Benavente and Leon[2]. Soult, whose men were much less exhausted than those of the other two corps, was charged with the occupation of Santander and the pursuit of Blake. He marched by the high-road to the sea, just in time to see seventeen British ships laden with munitions of war sailing out of the harbour[3]. But he captured, nevertheless, a large quantity of valuable stores, which were too heavy to be removed in a hurry [November 16].

The Marshal left Bonnet's division at Santander, with orders to clear the surrounding district and to keep open the road to Burgos. With the rest of his troops he marched eastward along the coast, trying to get information about Blake's movements. At San Vincente de la Barquera he came upon the wrecks of the Asturian division which Blake had left behind him when he turned south again into the mountains. They fled in disorder the moment that they were attacked, and the principality seemed exposed without any defence to the Marshal's advance. But Soult did not intend to lose touch with his master, or to embark on any unauthorized expedition. When he learnt that the Galician army had returned to the plains he followed their example, and crossed the Cantabrian Mountains by a track over the Sierras Albas from Potes to Cervera, almost as impracticable as the parallel defile over

---

[1] *Mémoires* of Gen. St. Chamans, p. 111.
[2] *Nap. Corresp.*, 14,496 (Napoleon to Berthier, from Burgos, Nov. 20).
[3] Leith mentions this in his letter from Cabezon de Sal, Nov. 16.

which Blake had escaped.   Coming down on to the upper valley of the Pisuerga he reached Saldaña, where he was again in close communication with Lefebvre.

Blake and his army might now be considered as being out of the game; they were so dispersed and demoralized that they required no more attention.   But there was as yet no news of Ney, who had been sent to execute the turning movement against Castaños, which corresponded to the one that Soult had carried out against the Galicians.   Meanwhile more troops continued to come up to Burgos, ready for the Emperor's great central march on Madrid.   King Joseph and his Guards had arrived there as early as the twelfth; Victor came down from Reynosa on the twenty-first[1], and on the same day appeared the division of dragoons commanded by Lahoussaye[2].   The belated corps of Mortier and Junot were reported to be nearing Bayonne: both generals received orders to march on Burgos, after equipping their men for a serious winter campaign.   Independent of the large bodies of men which were still kept out on the two flanks under Soult and Lefebvre, Moncey and Ney, there would soon be 100,000 bayonets and sabres ready for the decisive blow at the Spanish capital.

[1] *Nap. Corresp.*, 14,502 : on the twenty-first the 1st Corps was at Tardajos, outside Burgos.

[2] *Nap. Corresp.*, 14,501.

SECTION VII: CHAPTER V

TUDELA

HAVING narrated the misfortunes of Blake and of Belvedere, we must now turn to the eastern end of the Spanish line, where Castaños and Palafox had been enjoying a brief and treacherous interval of safety, while their friends were being hunted over the Cantabrian Mountains and the plains of Old Castile. From October 26-27—the days when Ney and Moncey drove Castaños' advanced troops back over the Ebro—down to November 21, the French in Navarre made no further movement. We have seen that it was essential to Napoleon's plan of campaign that the armies of Andalusia and Aragon should be left unmolested in the dangerous advanced position which they were occupying, till measures should have been taken to cut them off from Madrid and to drive them back against the roots of the Pyrenees. The Emperor had left opposite to them the whole of Moncey's corps, one division of Ney's corps (that of Lagrange), and the cavalry of Colbert and Digeon [1]—in all about 27,000 bayonets and 4,500 sabres. They had strict orders to act merely as a containing force: to repel any attack that the Spaniards might make on the line of the Ebro or the Aragon, but not to advance till they should receive the orders from head quarters.

The initiative therefore had passed back to the Spanish generals: it was open to them to advance once more against the enemy, if they chose to be so foolish. Their troops were in very bad order for an offensive campaign. Many of them (like Blake's men) had never received great-coats or winter clothing, and were facing the November frosts and the incessant rain with the light linen garments in which they had marched up from the south. An English observer, who passed through the camps of Palafox and Castaños at this moment, reports that while the regulars and the Valencian troops seemed fairly well clad, the Aragonese, the Castilians, and the Murcians were suffering terribly from exposure.

[1] Colbert's brigade belonged to Ney's corps; Digeon's dragoons were part of the reserve-cavalry of Latour-Maubourg.

The Murcians in especial were shivering in light linen shirts and pantaloons, with nothing but a striped *poncho* to cover them against the rain [1]. Hence came a terrible epidemic of dysentery, which thinned the ranks when once the autumn began to melt into winter. The armies of Castaños and Palafox should have counted 53,000 men at least when the fighting at last began. It seems doubtful whether they actually could put much over 40,000 into the field. Castaños claims that at Tudela his own 'Army of the Centre' had only 26,000 men in line, and the Aragonese about 16,000. It is probable that the figures are almost correct.

Nevertheless, the generals assumed the responsibility of ordering a general advance. We have shown in an earlier chapter that after the arrival of the three deputies from Madrid, and the stormy council of war at Tudela on November 5, a new plan of offensive operations was adopted. It was not quite so mad as the scheme that had been drafted in October, for seizing the passes of the Pyrenees and surrounding the whole French army. Castaños and Palafox, it will be remembered, were to mass the bulk of their forces between Tudela and Caparrosa, cross the Aragon, and deliver a frontal attack upon the scattered fractions of the corps of Moncey at Peralta, Falces, and Lodosa. There would have been something to say for this plan if it had been proposed in September, or early in October; but on November 5 it was hopeless, for it ignored the fact that 80,000 French troops had entered Biscay and Navarre since the middle of October, and that Napoleon himself had reached Vittoria. To advance now was to run into the lion's mouth.

The armies of Andalusia and Aragon were just beginning to concentrate when, on November 8, a dispatch came in from Blake announcing his disaster at Zornoza, and his hurried retreat beyond Bilbao. The same day there arrived a correct report of the arrival of the Emperor and great masses of French troops at Vittoria, with an inaccurate addition to the effect that they were being directed on Logroño and Lodosa, as if about to cross the Central Ebro and fall upon the left flank of the army of Andalusia [2].

Castaños, in his *Vindication*, published to explain and defend his

---

[1] Unpublished diary of Sir Charles Vaughan, then riding with the staff of Palafox.

[2] The best picture of Castaños' head quarters at this time is to be found in the diary of General Graham, printed in his *Life* by Delavoye.

Battle of ESPINOSA. November 11th. 1808

Madrid in 1808.

Battle of Tudela. November 23. 1808.

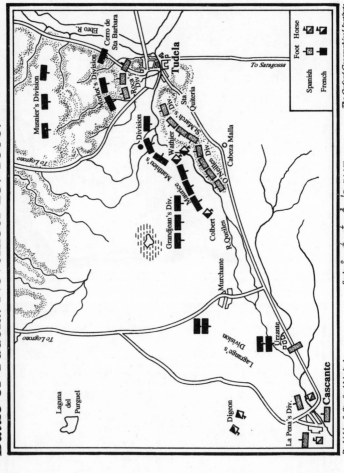

To Saragossa

Ebro R.

Cerro de Sta Barbara

Maurice's Division

Morlot's Division

Roca's Div.

Tudela

To Logroño

Sta. Quiteria

St. March's Div.

Wathier

St. March's Div.

Division

Mathieu's Division

O'Neille's Div.

Cabeza Malla

Maurice's Div.

Colbert

R. Queiles

Grandjean's Div.

Murchante

Laguna del Purguel

To Logroño

Lagrange's Division

Urzante

Digeon

La Peña's Div.

Cascante

movements during this campaign, stated that his first impulse was
to march by Logroño and Haro to meet the enemy, or to hasten
by Agreda and Soria to interpose himself between the Emperor
and Madrid. But, on second thoughts, he resolved that it was
more necessary to endeavour to beat the French in his immediate
front, and that it would be better to persevere in the plan, drawn
up on November 5, for a blow at Moncey. A sharp thrust delivered
on this point would distract the attention of the Emperor from
Blake, and draw him off the direct road to Madrid. Meanwhile,
however, on November 11 Castaños fell ill, and took to his bed at
Cintruenigo. While he was thus disabled, the deputy Francisco
Palafox took the astounding step of issuing orders in his own name
to the divisional generals both of the Andalusian and the Aragonese
armies. Nothing like this had been seen since the days in the
French Revolutionary War, when the 'Representatives on Mission'
used to overrule the commands of the unhappy generals of the
Republic. Before the concentration of the armies was complete,
the Deputy ordered the assumption of the offensive at all points in
the line: he directed O'Neille, whom he incorrectly supposed to be
already at Caparrosa, to attack Moncey at once; bade Grimarest,
with the 2nd Andalusian division, to cross the Ebro at Calahorra;
La Peña to threaten Milagro; and Cartaojal, with a small flanking
brigade, to demonstrate against the French troops who lay at
Logroño. These orders produced utter confusion, for some of
the generals obeyed, while others sent the answer that they would
not move without the permission of their proper chiefs, Castaños
and Joseph Palafox. The former got his first notice of the Deputy's
presumptuous action by letters from La Peña, delivered to his bed-
side, in which he was asked whether he had given his sanction to the
project for crossing the Ebro [1]. As a matter of fact only Grimarest
and Cartaojal moved: the former was sharply repulsed at the fords
opposite Calahorra: the latter, more fortunate, skirmished with
Lagrange's division, in front of Logroño, without coming to any
harm [November 13].

It was now three days since the Emperor had routed Belvedere
at Gamonal and entered Burgos, and two days since Blake had
been beaten at Espinosa. The conduct of the generals who had

---

[1] See Graham's *Diary*, p. 280. This is far the best authority for the chaotic
movements of the Spaniards during these weeks. Some allowance, perhaps,
should be made for Graham's dislike for the Palafox brothers.

charge of the last intact army that Spain possessed, seems all the
more insane when we reflect on the general condition of affairs.
For on the fourteenth the mad advance which Francisco Palafox
advocated was resumed, Castaños on his sick bed not having had
sufficient energy to lay an embargo on the moving forward of his
own troops.   On the fourteenth O'Neille arrived at Caparrosa and
drove out of it Moncey's advanced posts, while Grimarest and La
Peña received new instructions—to push up the Ebro and attack
Lodosa, which O'Neille was at the same moment to assail from the
other side of the stream.   Thus the great river was to be placed
between the two halves of the army, which had no communication
except by the bridge of Tudela, far to the rear of both.   'This
seems rather a hazardous undertaking,' wrote Graham in his diary,
'affording the enemy an opportunity of attacking on whichever
side of the river he chooses with superior force.'   But the only
thing that prevented it from being attempted was the sudden
refusal of O'Neille to advance beyond Caparrosa unless he were
provided with 50,000 rations of biscuit, and reinforced at once
with 6,000 bayonets from the Army of the Centre [November 18].
As if the situation were not already sufficiently complicated,
Castaños had on the preceding day received unofficial intelligence [1]
from Madrid, to the effect that the Central Junta had determined
to depose him, and to appoint the Marquis of La Romana general-
in-chief of the Army of the Centre as well as of the Army of Galicia.
This really made little difference, as the Marquis was at this moment
with Blake's corps (he had joined it at Renedo on the fifteenth), so
that he could not issue any orders for the troops on the Ebro, from
whom he was separated by the whole French army.   Castaños
remained at the head of the Andalusians till he was formally
superseded, and it was he who was destined to fight the great
battle that was now impending.   It is hard to say what might
have happened had the French held back for a few days more, for
now, at the last moment, Joseph Palafox suddenly harked back to
his old plan for an advance on Pampeluna and the roots of the
Pyrenees, and proposed to Castaños that the whole of the Andalusian
army save La Peña's division should assist him [2].   Castaños and

[1] By a letter from Lord William Bentinck, at Madrid (see Graham's *Diary*,
p. 281).

[2] It is most difficult to unravel all these projects and counter-projects :
I have followed Graham, who was always at the side of Castaños, supplement-
ing him with that general's own vindication, and with Butron's narrative.

Coupigny strongly opposed this mad idea, and submitted an entirely different scheme to the Captain-General of Aragon, inviting him to bring all his forces to Calahorra, and to join the Army of the Centre in taking up a defensive position behind the Ebro.

The two plans were being hotly debated, when news arrived which proved decisive. The French were at last on the move, and their columns were pouring out of Logroño and Lodosa along the southern bank of the Ebro, heading for Calahorra and Tudela [November 21]. On the same day a messenger arrived from the Bishop of Osma, bearing the intelligence that a French corps (he called it that of Dessolles, but it was really Ney) had marched up the head-waters of the Douro to Almazan, and was heading for Soria and Agreda, with the obvious intention of falling upon the rear of the Army of the Centre. If Castaños remained for a moment longer at Calahorra, he would clearly be caught between the two French armies. He should have retired at once in the direction of Saragossa, before Ney could reach him : but instead he took the dangerous half-measure of falling back only as far as the line Tudela—Tarazona. This was a safer position than that of Calahorra—Arnedo, but still sufficiently perilous, for the enveloping corps from the south could still reach his rear by a long turning movement through Xalon and Borja.

If the position from Tudela, on the banks of the Ebro, to Tarazona at the foot of the Sierra de Moncayo was to be held, the army of Castaños needed strong reinforcements, for the line was ten miles long, and there were but 26,000 men to occupy it. The Army of Aragon must be brought up also, and Castaños wrote at once to O'Neille at Caparrosa, inviting him to hasten to cross the Ebro and occupy Tudela and its immediate vicinity. The dispatch reached the Irish general late on the afternoon of the twenty-first, but he refused to obey without the permission of his own commander, Joseph Palafox. Thus the night of November 21–22 was lost, but next morning the Aragonese Captain-General appeared from Saragossa, and met Castaños and Coupigny. They besought him to bid O'Neille join the Army of the Centre, but at first he refused, even when the forward march of Moncey and the flanking movement of Ney had been explained to him. He still clung to his wild proposal for a blow at Pampeluna, 'talking,' says Colonel Graham, 'such nonsense as under the present circumstances ought only to have come from a madman [1].' But at the last moment he yielded, and at noon on the twenty-second wrote orders to O'Neille to bring his two divisions to Tudela, and to form up on the right of the Army of Andalusia. When the Aragonese host at last got under weigh, the hour was so late that darkness was falling before the bridge of Tudela was passed. O'Neille then had an unhappy inspiration: he ordered his men to defer the crossing of the Ebro till the following morning, and to cook and encamp on the northern bank. Half of the line which Castaños intended to hold next day was still ungarnished with troops when the dawn broke, and soon it was discovered that the French were close at hand.

The approaching enemy were not, as Castaños and Palafox supposed, under the command of Moncey and Ney. The latter was carrying out his turning movement by Soria: the former was for the moment superseded. The Emperor regarded the Duke of Conegliano as somewhat slow and overcautious, and for the sudden and smashing blow which he had planned had chosen another instrument. This was Marshal Lannes, who had crossed the Pyrenees with the 'Grand Army,' but had been detained for a fortnight at Vittoria by an accident. His horse had fallen with him over a precipice, and he had been so bruised and shaken that his life was despaired of. It appears that the celebrated surgeon Larrey cured him by the strange device of sewing up his battered frame in the skin of a newly flayed sheep [2]. By November 20 he was again fit for service, and set out from Logroño with Lagrange's division of Ney's corps, Colbert's light cavalry, and Digeon's dragoons. Moncey joined him by the bridge of Lodosa, bringing his whole corps—four divisions of infantry and one of cavalry. The protection of Navarre had been handed over to General Bisson, the governor of Pampeluna.

Lannes met with no opposition whatever in his march to Tudela, and easily reached Alfaro on the twenty-second. Here he learnt that the Spaniards were awaiting him beyond the river Queiles, drawn up on a very long front between Tudela and Tarazona. On the morning of the twenty-third he came in sight of them, and deployed for an attack: the state of utter disorder in which the enemy lay gave the best auguries for the success of the imperial arms.

Castaños had placed the troops under his immediate command

[1] Graham's *Diary*, p. 284.
[2] See Larrey's *Mémoires de Chirurgie Militaire*.

at Tarazona and Cascante, which were destined to form the left
and centre of his position : the remainder of it, from Cascante to
Tudela, was allotted to the Aragonese and to the Murcian division
of the Army of Andalusia, which had been across the Ebro in
O'Neille's company, and was now returning with him. Till they
came up Castaños had only under his hand two complete divisions
of his 'Army of the Centre,' and some small fragments of two
others. The complete divisions were those of Grimarest (No. 2)
and La Peña (No. 4), each of which had been increased in numbers
but not in efficiency by having allotted to it some of the battalions
of the 'Army of Castile,' which had been dissolved for its bad
conduct at Logroño on October 26. There had at last begun to
arrive at the front a considerable part of the other two Andalusian
divisions, which had first been detained beyond the Sierra Morena
by the Junta of Seville, and then kept some time in Madrid to
complete their equipment. Two battalions of these belated troops
had at last appeared on October 30, and ten more had since come
up [1]. But the bulk of the 1st and 3rd Divisions was still absent,
and no more than 5,500 men from them had been added to
Castaños' army. The mixed brigade formed from these late
arrivals seems to have been under General Villariezo, of the 1st
Division. The whole force amounted to about 28,000 men, of whom
3,000 were horsemen, for the army of Andalusia was stronger in the
cavalry arm than any other of the Spanish hosts. But of these
the Murcian and Valencian division of Roca (formerly that of
Llamas) was with O'Neille, and had not yet reached the field ; while
five battalions, from the dissolved Castilian army, were far away
on the left in the mountains of Soria, whither Castaños had detached
them under General Cartaojal, with orders to observe the French
corps which was coming up on his rear.

The other half of the Spanish army consisted of the missing
division of the Army of the Centre—that of Roca—and the two
divisions belonging to Palafox—those of O'Neille and Saint March
—the former composed mainly of Aragonese [2], the latter almost
entirely of Valencian troops. None of the Aragonese reserves from

---

[1] Of the 1st Division there seem to have arrived one battalion each of the
regiments Reina, Jaen, Irlanda, and Barbastro, and the Jaen Militia. Of the
3rd Division one battalion each of Campo Mayor, Volunteers of Valencia, and
the Militia of Plasencia, Guadix, Lorca, Toro, and Seville (No. 1).

[2] But with one Valencian and two Murcian battalions : see Appendix.

the great camp at Saragossa had yet come upon the scene. But the two divisions in the field were very strong—they must have had at least 17,000 men in their ranks. On November 1 they were more than 18,000 strong, and, two months after—when they had passed through the disaster of Tudela, and had endured ten days of the murderous siege of Saragossa—they still showed 14,000 bayonets. We cannot calculate them at less than 17,000 men for the battle of November 23. On the other hand, there were hardly 600 cavalry in the whole corps.

It would appear then that Castaños must have had some 45,000 men in line, between Tarazona and Tudela, when Lannes came up against him [1]. The French marshal, on the other hand, had about 34,000. On the difference in quality between the two armies we have no need to dilate: even the two divisions of the conscripts of 1807, which served in Moncey's corps, were old soldiers compared to

[1] The troops should have numbered—

2nd Division of the Army of Andalusia [Grimarest] (five battalions of regulars, four of militia, and four of new levies) about	6,000
4th Division of the Army of Andalusia [La Peña] (seven battalions of regulars, three of militia, and three of new levies) about	7,500
Mixed brigade of the 1st and 3rd Divisions [Villariezo] (six battalions of regulars and six of militia) about . .	5,500
5th Division (Murcians and Valencians) [Roca] (eight battalions of regulars, two of militia, and seven of new levies)	6,500
Castilian battalions distributed between the other divisions, or detached on the left [Cartaojal]	8,000
O'Neille's Division of the Army of Aragon (three battalions of regulars, five battalions of Aragonese, and three of Valencian and Murcian new levies)	9,000
Saint March's Division of the Army of Aragon (three battalions of regulars, one of militia, and ten of Valencian new levies)	8,000
Cavalry (3,000 Andalusians, 600 Aragonese) . . .	3,600
Artillery	1,800
	55,900
Minus the detachment of Cartaojal, about 3,000 . .	3,000
Total . . .	52,900

But we must make large deductions for sickness (which had fallen heavily on the ill-clothed men), for loss in previous actions, desertion, and detachments ; e. g. some of Roca's division were on the Lower Ebro.

the armies of Aragon and Castile, or a great part of that of Andalusia. Moreover, as in all the earlier battles of the Peninsular War, the Spaniards were hopelessly outmatched in the cavalry arm. There was no force that could stop the 4,500 or 5,000 horsemen of Colbert, Digeon, and Wathier [1].

The position Tudela—Tarazona, which Castanos intended to hold, is of enormous length—about ten and a half miles in all. Clearly 45,000 men in the close order that prevailed in the early nineteenth century were inadequate to hold it all in proper strength. Yet if the points on which the French were about to attack could be ascertained in good time, the distances were not so great but that the army could concentrate on any portion of the line within three hours. But to make this practicable, it was necessary firstly that Castaños should keep in close touch with the enemy by means of his cavalry—he had quite enough for the purpose—and secondly that he should have all his men massed at suitable points, from which they could march out to the designated fighting-ground at short notice. The Spanish troops were, now as always, so slow at manœuvring that the experiment would be a dangerous one, but this was the only way in which the chosen position could possibly be held. The ground was not unfavourable; it consisted of a line of gentle hills along the south bank of the river Queiles, which commanded a good view over the rolling plain across which the French had to advance. On the extreme right was the town

[1] The French army consisted of—

Moncey's Corps :

Maurice Mathieu's Division (twelve battalions) . .		7,000
Musnier's Division (eight battalions)		5,500
Morlot's Division (six battalions)		4,000
Grandjean's (late Frère's) Division (eight battalions) .		5,000
Cavalry of Wathier (three regiments)		1,600

Ney's Corps :

Lagrange's Division		6,000
Colbert's Cavalry (three regiments)		2,200

Reserve Cavalry :

Digeon's Brigade of Dragoons (two regiments) . .		1,200
Artillery, &c.		1,200
Total		33,700

These figures are mainly taken from Napoleon's dispatch, No. 14,456, of Nov. 8. They do not include the Irish, Prussian, and Westphalian battalions of Moncey's corps garrisoning Pampeluna and San Sebastian.

of Tudela, covered by a bold hill—the Cerro de Santa Barbara—
which overhangs the Ebro. Thence two long ridges, the hills of
Santa Quiteria and Cabezo Malla, extend for some two and a half
miles in a well-marked line : this section formed the right of the
position. From the left of the Cabezo Malla as far as the little
town of Cascante—four miles—the ground is less favourable ;
indeed, it is fairly flat, and the line is indicated mainly by the
Queiles and its irrigation-cuts, behind which the Spanish centre
was to form[1]. From Cascante westward as far as Tarazona—a
distance of four miles or a little over—the position is better
marked, a spur of the Sierra de Moncayo coming down in a gentle
slope all along the southern bank of the little Queiles. The centre,
between the Cabezo Malla and Cascante, was obviously the weak
point in the position, as the only obstacle to the enemy's advance
was the river, which was fordable by all arms at every point along
this dangerous four miles.

The disaster which Castaños was to suffer may be ascribed to
two mistakes, one of which was entirely within his own control,
while the other was due to the stupidity of O'Neille. With 3,000
cavalry in hand, the Commander-in-chief ought to have known of
every movement of the French for many hours before they drew
near to the position. It would then have been in his power to
concentrate on those parts of the line where the attack was about
to be delivered. But instead of sending out his horse ten miles to
the front, Castaños kept them with the infantry[2], and the first
notice of the approach of Lannes was only given when, at nine in
the morning, a regiment of Wathier's cavalry rode right up to the
town of Tudela, driving in the outposts and causing great confusion.
To the second cause of disaster we have already had occasion to
allude : on the night of the twenty-second O'Neille had (contrary
to his orders) encamped north of the Ebro. His 17,000 men began

[1] The town and the hill, unlike the rest of the position, are on the *north*
bank of the Queiles.

[2] It is impossible to acquit Castaños of the charge of carelessness on this
point. Doyle's letter of the night of Nov. 22 is conclusive : ' Not one soldier
has been left to observe the motions of the enemy, or to check the progress
of his advanced guard, common pickets excepted, which are pushed a little
outside the town. I confess I have not a shade of doubt that the enemy will
attack at daybreak, and confusion must naturally ensue ' (Doyle's correspondence in the Record Office). It is seldom that a military prophecy is so
exactly fulfilled.

to defile over the bridge next morning in a leisurely fashion, and were still only making their way to their designated positions when Lannes attacked. In fact the Spanish line of battle was never formed as had been planned: the various brigades of the Army of Aragon were hurried one after another on to the heights south-west of Tudela, but entirely without system or order: the lower ground to the left of the Cabezo Malla was never occupied at all, and remained as a gap in the centre of the line all through the battle.

Lannes, who was aware that the Spaniards were intending to fight at Tudela, had marched at dawn from his camps in front of Alfaro in two columns. One, composed of Moncey's corps, with Wathier's cavalry at its head, came by the high-road near the Ebro. The other, composed of the two independent cavalry brigades of Colbert and Digeon, and of Lagrange's division, was more to the west, and headed for Cascante. The Marshal had no intention of attacking the left of the Spanish line in the direction of Tarazona, which he left entirely to itself. He met not a single Spanish vedette till Wathier's cavalry ran into the pickets immediately outside Tudela.

Castaños was in the town, engaged in hurrying the march of the Aragonese troops across the great bridge of the Ebro, when the fusillade broke out. The unexpected sound of musketry threw the troops into great excitement, for they were jammed in the narrow mediaeval lanes of Tudela when the sounds of battle came rolling down from the Cerro de Santa Barbara. The Commander-in-chief himself was caught between two regiments and could not push his way out to the field for some time. But the men were quite ready to fight, and hurried to the front as fast as they were able. Roca's Valencian division (the 5th of the Andalusian army) had been the first to cross the Ebro: it was pushed up to the Cerro de Santa Barbara, and reached its summit just in time to beat off the leading brigade, one from Morlot's division, which was ascending the hill from the other side. Saint March's battalions, who had crossed the bridge next after Roca, were fortunate enough to be able to deploy and occupy the hill of Santa Quiteria before they were attacked. But O'Neille's Aragonese and Murcians were less lucky: they only succeeded in seizing the Cabezo Malla ridge after driving off the skirmishers of Maurice Mathieu's French division, which had come up next in succession to Morlot, and was just preparing to mount the slope. But the position was just saved, and the Army of Aragon was by ten o'clock formed up along the hills, with its right overhanging the Ebro and its left—quite in the air—established on the Cabezo Malla. The front was somewhat over two miles in length, and quite defensible; but the troops were in great disorder after their hurried march, and the generals were appalled to find that the Army of the Centre had not moved up to join them, and that there was a gap of three miles between the Cabezo Malla and the nearest of the Andalusian divisions. Castaños perceived this fact and rode off, too late, to bring up La Peña from Cascante to fill the void. Palafox was not on the field: he had gone off at daybreak (still in high dudgeon that his scheme for an attack by Pampeluna had been overruled) and was far on the road to Saragossa.

It is clear that Lannes' first attack was unpremeditated and ill-arranged: he had been tempted to strike when his vanguard only had come up, because he saw the Spanish position half empty and the Aragonese divisions struggling up in disorder to occupy it. Hence came his first check: but the preliminary skirmish had revealed to him the existence of the fatal gap between the two Spanish armies, and he was now ready to utilize it. While Castaños was riding for Cascante, the divisions of Musnier, Grandjean, and Lagrange were coming upon the field, and Lannes was preparing for a second and more serious attack.

Meanwhile the fortune of the day was being settled on the left. When the army of Lannes appeared in the plain, La Peña at Cascante should have marched at once towards the Aragonese, and Grimarest and Villariezo from Tarazona should have moved on Cascante to replace La Peña's division at that place. Neither of them stirred, though the situation was obvious, and though they presently received orders from Castaños to close in to their right. La Peña was the most guilty, for the whole battle-field was under his eye: he would not move because he had before him Digeon's and Colbert's cavalry, and was afraid to march across their front in the open plain, protected only by the shallow Queiles. He had 8,000 or 9,000 Andalusian and Castilian infantry, and 1,500 horse, but allowed himself to be neutralized by two brigades of dragoons. All that he did in response to the summons to move eastward was to send two battalions to occupy the hamlet of Urzante, a mile to his right. There was still a space of three miles between him and Saint March. This scandalous and cowardly inaction is in keeping

with the man's later career : it was he who in 1811 betrayed
Graham at Barossa, and fled back into safety instead of stopping
to assist his allies.   On this occasion he lay for four hours motion-
less, while he watched the French forming up for a second attack
on the Army of Aragon.   Cowed by the 3,000 dragoons in his
front, he made no attempt to march on the Cabezo Malla to
O'Neille's assistance.   Grimarest's conduct was almost equally
bad : he was further from the scene of fighting, and could not,
like La Peña, see the field : but it is sufficient to say that he
received Castaños' order to march on Cascante at noon, and that
he did not reach that place—four miles distant—till dusk.

The Commander-in-chief himself was most unlucky : he started
for Cascante about noon, intending to force his divisional generals
to draw near the battle-field.   But as he was crossing the gap
between O'Neille and La Peña he was sighted by some French
cavalry, who were cautiously pushing forward through the unoccupied ground.   He and his staff were chased far to the rear by
this reconnoitring party, and only shook them off by riding hard
and scattering among the olive groves.   Unable to reach Cascante,
he was returning towards Tudela, when he received a hasty note
from General Roca to the effect that the right wing of the army
had been broken, and the heights of Santa Barbará lost.

When his three belated divisions had appeared Lannes had
drawn up his army in two lines, and flung the bulk of it against
the Aragonese, leaving only Colbert's and Digeon's dragoons and
the single division of Lagrange to look after La Peña and the rest
of the Army of Andalusia.

Instead of sending forward fresh troops, Lannes brought up to
the charge for a second time the regiments of Maurice Mathieu
and Morlot.   Behind the latter Musnier deployed, behind the
former Grandjean, but neither of these divisions, as it turned out,
was to fire a shot or to lose a man.   While Morlot with his six
battalions once more attacked the heights above the city, Maurice
Mathieu with his twelve attempted both to push back O'Neille
and to turn his flank by way of the Cabezo Malla.   After a short
but well-contested struggle both these attacks succeeded.   Morlot,
though his leading brigade suffered heavily, obtained a lodgement
on top of the Cerro de Santa Barbara, by pushing a battalion
up a lateral ravine, which had been left unwatched on account of
its difficulty.   Others followed, and Roca's division broke, poured

down the hill into Tudela, and fled away by the Saragossa road.
Almost at the same moment O'Neille's troops were beaten off the
Cabezo Malla by Maurice Mathieu, who had succeeded in slipping
a battalion and a cavalry regiment round their left flank, on the
side of the fatal gap. Seeing the line of the Aragonese reeling
back, General Lefebvre-Desnouettes, to whom Lannes had given
the chief command of his cavalry, charged with three regiments of
Wathier's division at the very centre of the hostile army. He
burst through between O'Neille and Saint March's troops, and
then wheeling outward attacked both in flank. This assault was
decisive. The whole mass dispersed among the olive groves, irrigation-cuts, and stone fences which cover the plain to the south of
Tudela. A few battalions kept their ranks and formed a sort of
rearguard, but the main part of Roca's, Saint March's, and
O'Neille's levies fled straight before them till the dusk fell, and far
into the night. Some of them got to Saragossa next day, though
the distance was over fifty miles.

Meanwhile La Peña's futile operations in front of Cascante had
gone on all through the afternoon. He had at first nothing but
cavalry in front of him, but about three o'clock Lagrange's division,
which had been the last to arrive on the field of all the French
army, appeared in his direction. Its leading brigade marched into
the gap, wheeled to its right, and drove out of Urzante the two
isolated battalions which La Peña had placed there in the morning.
They made a gallant resistance [1], but had to yield to superior
numbers and to fall back on the main body at Cascante [2]. Here
they found not only La Peña but also Grimarest, and Villariezo's
mixed brigade, for these officers had at last deigned to obey
Castaños' orders and to close in to the right. There was now an
imposing mass of troops collected in this quarter, at least 18,000
foot and 3,000 horse, but they allowed themselves to be 'contained'
by Lagrange's single division and Digeon's dragoons. Colbert,
with the rest of the cavalry, had ridden through the gap and gone
off in pursuit of the Aragonese. The remaining hour of daylight

---

[1] Graham witnessed this and reports in his *Diary* (p. 285) that ' the two
regiments that had been sent down into the plain behaved uncommonly
well.'

[2] I agree with Schepeler and the Spanish witnesses in holding that on this
side the French did very little ; their great advance, as Schepeler says, ' ist
nur Bulletinformel und weiter nichts.'

was spent in futile skirmishing with Lagrange, and after dark La Peña and Grimarest retired unmolested to Borja, by the road which skirts the foot of the Sierra de Moncayo. They were only disturbed by a panic caused by the blowing up of the reserve ammunition of the Army of the Centre. Some of the troops took the explosion for a sudden discharge of French artillery, broke their ranks, and were with difficulty reassembled.

It is impossible to speak too strongly of the shameful slackness and timidity of La Peña and his colleagues. If they had been tried for cowardice, and shot after the manner of Admiral Byng, they would not have received more than their deserts. That 20,000 men, including the greater part of the victors of Baylen, should assist, from a distance of four miles only, at the rout of their comrades of the Army of Aragon, was the most deplorable incident of all this unhappy campaign.

From the astounding way in which the Andalusian army had been mishandled, it resulted that practically no loss—200 killed and wounded at the most—was suffered in this quarter, and the troops marched off with their artillery and wagons, after blowing up their reserve ammunition and abandoning their heavy baggage in their camps [1]. The Aragonese had, of course, fared very differently. They lost twenty-six guns—apparently all that they had brought to the field—over 1,000 prisoners, and at least 3,000 killed and wounded [2]. That the casualties were not more numerous was due to the fact that the plain to the south of Tudela was covered with olive-groves, and irrigation-cuts, which checked the French cavalry and facilitated the flight of the fugitives.

Lannes, it is clear, did not entirely fulfil Napoleon's expectations. He did not take full advantage of the gap between O'Neille and La Peña, and wasted much force in frontal attacks which might have been avoided. If he had thrust two divisions and all his horse between the fractions of the Spanish army, before ordering the second attack of Maurice Mathieu and Morlot, the victory would have been far more decisive, and less costly. The loss of

---

[1] The 3,000 men of Cartaojal's troops, which had been detached to watch Ney in the direction of Agreda, were cut off from the rest of the Army of the Centre, and ran great risks. But they ultimately escaped and rejoined the main body.

[2] Only Saint March's casualties are preserved. They amounted to 1,328. Roca and O'Neille must have suffered in proportion.

the 3rd Corps was 44 killed and 513 wounded ; that of Lagrange's division and the dragoons has not been preserved, but can have been but small—probably less than 100 in all—though Lagrange himself received a severe hurt in the arm. The only regiment that suffered heavily was the 117th, of Morlot's division, which, in turning Roca off the Cerro de Santa Barbara, lost 303 killed and wounded, more than half the total casualties of the 3rd Corps.

Lannes had carried out indifferently well the part of the Emperor's great plan that had been entrusted to him ; but this, as we have seen, was only half of the game. When Castaños and the Aragonese were routed, they ought to have found Marshal Ney at their backs, intercepting their retreat on Saragossa or Madrid. As a matter of fact he was more than fifty miles away on the day of the battle, and arrived with a tardiness which made his flanking march entirely futile. The orders for him to march from Aranda on Soria and Tarazona had been issued on November 18 [1], and he had been warned that Lannes would deliver his blow on the twenty-second. But Ney did not receive his instructions till the nineteenth, and only set out on the twentieth. When once he was upon the move he made tremendous marches, for on the twenty-first he had reached Almazan, more than sixty miles from his starting-point : by dusk on the twenty-second he had pushed on to Soria [2], where he halted for forty-eight hours on account of the utter exhaustion of his troops. He had pushed them forward no less than seventy-eight miles in three days, a rate which cannot be kept up. Hence he was obliged to let them spend the twenty-third and twenty-fourth in Soria : at dawn on the twenty-fifth they set out again, and executed another terrible march. It is thirty miles from Soria to Agreda, in the heart of the Sierra de Moncayo, where the 6th Corps slept on that night, and every foot of the way was over villainous mountain roads. Hence Ney only reached Tarazona early on the twenty-sixth, three days after the battle ; yet it cannot be said that he had been slow : he had covered 121 miles in six and a half days, even when the halt at Soria is included. This is very fair marching for infantry, when the difficulties of the country are considered. Napoleon ungenerously ascribed the escape of Castaños to the fact that 'Ney had allowed himself to be imposed upon by the Spaniards,

---

[1] *Nap. Corresp.*, 14,489.   [2] Ibid., 14,504.

and rested for the twenty-second and twenty-third at Soria, because he chose to imagine that the enemy had 80,000 men, and other follies. If he had reached Agreda on the twenty-third, according to my orders, not a man would have escaped[1].' But, as Marshal Jourdan very truly remarks in his *Mémoires*, 'Calculating the distance from Aranda to Tarazona via Soria, one easily sees that even if Ney had given no rest to his troops, it would have been impossible for him to arrive before the afternoon of the twenty-fourth, that is to say, twenty-four hours after the battle. It is not he who should be reproached, but the Emperor, who ought to have started him from Aranda two days earlier[2].'

Blind admirers of Bonaparte have endeavoured to make out a case against Ney, by accusing him of having stopped at Soria for three days in order to pillage it—which he did not, though he made a requisition of shoes and cloth for great-coats from the municipality. If he is really to blame, it is rather for having worked his men so hard on the twentieth to the twenty-second that they were not fit to march on the twenty-third: he had taken them seventy-eight miles on those three days, with the natural result that they were dead beat. If he had contented himself with doing sixteen or eighteen miles a day, he would have reached Soria on the twenty-third, but his men would have been comparatively fresh, and could have moved on next morning. Even then he would have been late for the battle, as Jourdan clearly shows: the fact was that the Emperor asked an impossibility of him when he expected him to cover 121 miles in four days, with artillery and baggage, and a difficult mountain range to climb[3].

Meanwhile the routed forces of O'Neille, Roca, and Saint March joined at Mallen, and retreated along the high-road to Saragossa, accompanied for part of the way by Castaños; while those of La Peña, Grimarest, and Villariezo marched by Borja to La Almunia on the Xalon, where their General-in-chief joined them and directed them to take the road to Madrid, not that which led to the Aragonese capital. On the night of the twenty-fifth the

---

[1] Napoleon to Joseph Napoleon, from Aranda, Nov. 27 (*Nap. Corresp.*, 14,518).

[2] Jourdan's *Mémoires*, p. 92.

[3] Ney's march and its difficulties can be studied in the *Mémoires* of Rocca, then a captain in the 2nd Hussars, who shared this march with the 6th Corps.

Army of Andalusia, minus the greater part of the wrecks of Roca's division [1], was concentrated at Calatayud, not much reduced in numbers, but already suffering from hunger—all their stores having been lost at Cascante and Tarazona—and inclined to be mutinous. The incredible mismanagement at Tudela was put down to treachery, and the men were much inclined to disobey their chiefs. It was at this unhappy moment that Castaños received a dispatch from the Central Junta dated November 21, which authorized him to incorporate the divisions of O'Neille and Saint March with the army of Andalusia, leaving only the Aragonese under the control of Palafox. This order, if given a month earlier, would have saved an enormous amount of wrangling and mismanagement. But it was now too late : these divisions had retired on Saragossa, and the enemy having interposed between them and Castaños, the authorization remained perforce a dead letter.

Lannes had directed Maurice Mathieu, with the divisions of Lagrange and Musnier, to follow the Andalusians by Borja, while Morlot and Grandjean pursued the Aragonese on the road of Mallen. The chase does not seem to have been very hotly urged, but on each road a certain number of stragglers were picked up. Ney, reaching Borja on the twenty-sixth with the head of his column, found himself in the rear of Maurice Mathieu, and committed to the pursuit of Castaños. Their vanguard reached Calatayud on the twenty-seventh, and learnt that the Army of the Centre had evacuated that city on the same morning, and was pressing towards Madrid, with the intention of taking part in the defence of the capital.

Ney, taking with him Lagrange's infantry and Digeon's and Colbert's cavalry from the troops which fought at Tudela, and adding them to the two divisions of Marchand and Dessolles, which had formed his turning column, urged the pursuit as fast as he was able. Twice he came up with the Spanish army : on each occasion Castaños sacrificed his rearguard, which made a long stand and was terribly mauled, while he pushed ahead with his main body. At this cost the army was saved, but it arrived in New Castile half starved and exhausted, and almost as much demoralized as if it had been beaten in a pitched battle. A few days later many of the battalions burst into open mutiny, when they were ordered to retire into the mountains of Cuenca. But at least

---

[1] Only 1,500 of them, with Roca himself, followed Castaños.

they had escaped from Ney by rapid marching, and still preserved the form and semblance of an army.

Meanwhile Napoleon, on his side, had begun to operate against Madrid with a speed and sureness of stroke that made futile every attempt of the Spaniards to intervene between him and his goal. The moment that the news of Tudela reached him (November 26) he had hurled his main body upon the capital, and within eight days it was in his hands. The march of the army of Andalusia to cover Madrid was (though Castaños could not know it) useless from the first. By hurrying to the aid of the Junta, through Siguenza and Guadalajara, he was merely exposing himself for a second time to destruction. His troops were destined to escape from the peril in New Castile, by a stroke of fortune just as notable as that which had saved them from being cut off on the day after Tudela. But he, meanwhile, was separated from his troops, for on arriving at Siguenza he was met by another dispatch from the Junta, which relieved him of the command of the army of the Centre, and bade him hasten to Head Quarters, where his aid was required by the Central Committee for War. Handing over the troops to the incapable La Peña, Castaños hastened southward in search of the Junta, whose whereabouts in those days of flight and confusion it was not easy to find.

SECTION VII: CHAPTER VI

PASSAGE OF THE SOMOSIERRA: NAPOLEON AT MADRID

AFTER completing his arrangements for the two sweeping flank-movements that were destined to entrap Blake and Castaños, the Emperor moved forward from Burgos on November 22, along the great road to Madrid by Lerma and Aranda de Duero. His advance was completely masked by the broad screen of cavalry which had gone on in front of him. Lasalle was ahead, Milhaud on the right flank, and covered by them he moved with ease across the plain of Old Castile. He brought with him a very substantial force, all the Imperial Guard, horse and foot, Victor and his 1st Corps, and the reserve-cavalry of Latour-Maubourg and Lahoussaye. King Joseph and his household troops were left behind at Burgos, to preserve the line of communication with Vittoria and Bayonne. The flanks were quite safe, with Ney and Moncey lying out upon the left, and Soult and Lefebvre upon the right. In a few days—supposing that the armies of Blake and Castaños fell into the snare, or were at least broken and scattered—the Emperor hoped to be able to draw in both Ney and Lefebvre to aid in his enveloping attack upon Madrid. Nor was this all: the corps of Mortier and Junot were now approaching the Pyrenees, and would soon be available as a great central reserve. The whole force put in motion against Madrid was enormous: the Emperor had 45,000 men under his own hand: Ney and Lefebvre could dispose of 40,000 more: Mortier and Junot were bringing up another 40,000 in the rear. Omitting the troops left behind on the line of communication and the outlying corps of Soult and Moncey, not less than 130,000 men were about to concentrate upon Madrid.

The Emperor halted at Aranda from November 23 to 28, mainly (as it would seem) to allow the two great flanking operations to work themselves out. When Soult reported that Blake's much-chased army had dissolved into a mere mob, and taken refuge in the fastnesses of the Asturias, and when Lannes sent in the news of Tudela, the Emperor saw that it was time to move. On the twenty-eighth he marched on Madrid, by the direct high-road that crosses the long and desolate pass of the Somosierra.

Meanwhile the Spaniards had been granted nineteen days since the rout of Gamonal in which to organize the defence of their capital—a space in which something might have been done had their resources been properly applied and their commanders capable. It is true that even if every available man had been hurried to Madrid, the Emperor must still have prevailed: his numbers were too overwhelming to be withstood. But this fact does not excuse the Junta for not having done their best to hold him back. It is clear that when the news of Gamonal reached them, on the morning of the twelfth, orders should have been sent to Castaños to fall back on the capital by way of Calatayud and Siguenza, leaving Palafox and the Aragonese to 'contain' Moncey as long as might be possible. Nothing of the kind was done, and the army of the Centre—as we have seen—was still at Tudela on the twenty-third. There was another and a still more important source of aid available: the English army from Portugal had begun to arrive at Salamanca on November 13: its rearguard had reached that city ten days later. With Sir John Moore's designs and plans of campaign we shall have to deal in another chapter. It must suffice in this place to say that he was now within 150 miles of Madrid by a good high-road: the subsidiary column under Hope, which had with it nearly the whole of the British artillery, was at Talavera, still nearer to the capital. If the Junta had realized and frankly avowed the perils of the situation, there can be no doubt that they would have used every effort to bring Moore to the defence of Madrid. Seven or eight good marches could have carried him thither. But the Spaniards did nothing of the kind: refusing to realize the imminence of the danger, they preferred to urge on Mr. Frere, the newly arrived British minister, a scheme for the union of Moore's forces with Blake's broken 'Army of the Left[1].' They suggested that Hope's division might be

---

[1] Mr. Frere to General Moore (from Aranjuez, Nov. 25) ; compare the letter of Martin de Garay (secretary of the Junta) to Mr. Frere, dated Nov. 24 : 'If the English troops form a junction with the Army of the Left, we compose a formidable body of 70,000 infantry and 6,000 cavalry, a force with which we shall be certain of our blow, which we never could be by any different conduct.'

brought up to reinforce the capital, but that the rest of the British troops should operate in the valley of the Douro. This proposition was wholly inadmissible, for Hope had with him all Moore's cavalry and most of his guns. To have separated him from his chief would have left the latter incapable of any offensive movement. Hope declined to listen to the proposal, and marched via the Escurial to join the main army[1].

The fact was that the Junta still persisted in the foolish belief that Napoleon had no more than 80,000 men disposable in Northern Spain, instead of the 250,000 who were really at his command. They looked on the French advance to Burgos as a mere reconnaissance in force made by a single corps, and in this notion the imbecile Belvedere did his best to confirm them, by stating in his dispatch that the force which had routed him amounted to no more than 3,000 horse and 6,000 infantry[2]. Instead of calling in Castaños and making a desperate appeal for aid to Moore, the Junta contented themselves with endeavouring to reorganize the wrecks of the army of Estremadura, and pushing forward the belated fragments of the 1st and 3rd Andalusian divisions, which still lingered in Madrid, as well as the few Castilian levies that were now available for service in the field. Nothing can show their blind self-confidence more clearly than their proclamation of November 15, put forward to attenuate the ill effects on the public mind of the news of the rout of Gamonal. 'The Supreme Junta of Government'—so runs the document—'in order to prevent any more unhappy accidents of this kind, has already taken the most prudent measures; it has nominated Don Joseph Heredia to the command of the army of Estremadura: it has ordered all the other generals of the Army of the Right to combine their movements: it has given stringent orders for the prompt reinforcement of the above-named army . . . There is every hope that the enemy, who now boasts of having been able to advance as far as Burgos, will soon be well chastised for his temerity. And if it is certain—as the reports from the frontier assure us—that the Emperor of the French has come in person to inspect the conduct

---

[1] Morla used many arguments to induce Hope to direct his men on Madrid, when the English general rode in from Talavera to discuss the situation with the Spanish authorities. Hope, of course, pleaded the duty of obedience to his chief.

[2] Belvedere's dispatch to the Junta (*Madrid Gazette* of Nov. 15).

of his generals and his troops in Spain, we may hope that the valiant defenders of our fatherland may aspire to the glory of making him fly, with the same haste with which they forced his brother Joseph to abandon the throne and the capital of which he vainly thought that he had taken possession [1].'

Since they systematically undervalued the number of Napoleon's host, and refused to believe that there was any danger of a serious attack on Madrid during the next few days, it was natural that the Junta should waste, in the most hopeless fashion, the short time of respite that was granted to them between the rout of Gamonal and Napoleon's advance from Aranda. They hurried forward the troops that were close at hand to hold the passes of the watershed between Old and New Castile, and then resumed their usual constitutional debates.

The forces available for the defence of Madrid appear absurdly small when we consider the mighty mass of men that Bonaparte was leading against them. Nearly half of the total was composed of the wrecks of the Estremaduran army. Belvedere, as it will be remembered, had brought back to Lerma the remains of his 1st and 2nd Divisions, and rallied them on his intact 3rd Division. The approach of Lasalle's cavalry on November 11 scared them from Lerma, and the whole body, now perhaps 8,000 or 9,000 strong, fell back on Aranda. From thence we should have expected that they would retire by the high-road on Madrid, and take post in the pass of the Somosierra. But the Estremaduran officers decided to retreat on Segovia, far to the left, leaving only a handful of men [2] to cover the main line of access to the capital. It looks as if a kind of 'homing instinct' had seized the whole army, and compelled them to retire along the road that led to their own province. The only explanation given by their commanders was that they hoped to pick up in this direction many of the fugitives who had not rallied to their main body (one cannot say to their colours, for most of them had been captured by the

---

[1] Proclamation of the Supreme Junta, published in the *Madrid Gazette* of Nov. 15, 1808.

[2] Arteche says that 'all the intact troops,' i. e. the whole 3rd Estremaduran division, fell back on the Somosierra. But this is incorrect, for a dispatch of General Trias (*Madrid Gazette* of November 22) shows that he only took two or three battalions to the pass, and even some of these must afterwards have gone on to Segovia, for only one Estremaduran corps (the Badajoz Regiment) is found in the list of San Juan's little army (Arteche, iii. 496).

French) on the day after Gamonal[1].   At Segovia the unhappy
Belvedere was superseded by Heredia, whom the Junta had sent
down from Aranjuez to reorganize the army.

The other troops available for the defence of Madrid consisted
mainly of the belated fractions of the army of Andalusia, which
Castaños had summoned so many times to join him on the Ebro,
but which were still, on November 15, in or about Madrid.   They
were supposed to be completing their clothing and equipment, and
to be incorporating recruits.   But considering the enormous space
of time that had elapsed since Baylen, it is not unfair to believe
that the true reason for their detention in the capital had been
the Junta's wish to keep a considerable body of troops in its own
immediate neighbourhood.   It was convenient to have regiments
near at hand which had not passed under the control of any of the
generals commanding the provincial armies.   There were in Madrid
no less than nine battalions of the original division of Reding—all
regulars and all corps who had distinguished themselves at Baylen[2].
Of the 3rd Division there were two regular and two old militia
battalions[3].   The remainder of the available force in the capital
consisted of four battalions of new levies raised in the capital (the
1st and 2nd Regiments of the 'Volunteers of Madrid'), of one new
corps from Andalusia (the 3rd Volunteers of Seville), and of fragments
of four regiments of cavalry[4].   The whole division, twelve thousand
strong, was placed under the charge of General San Juan, a veteran
of good reputation[5].   But he was only a subordinate: the supreme

---

[1] See Arteche, iii. 321.   The fugitives fled so far and wide that Blake
rallied 157 of the regiment of Tuy at Leon!   Leith Hay found them all over
the country-side on November 15.

[2] These corps were the Walloon Guards (3rd batt.), Reina (two batts.), Jaen
(two batts.), Corona (two batts.), Irlanda (two batts.)—much the larger half of
the original 1st Division of Andalusia, and all old corps (see the lists in
Arteche, iii. 496).

[3] The regiment of Cordova (two batts.) and the provincial militia of
Alcazar and Toledo.

[4] Two squadrons each of 'Principe' and 'Voluntarios de Madrid,' one each
of Alcantara and Montesa.   The whole amounted to no more than 600
sabres.

[5] Napier's description of the 'Army of Reserve' is very incomplete: he
says that 'Belvedere's army rallied part in the Somosierra and part on the
side of Segovia.   The troops which had been detained in Madrid from Castaños' army were forwarded to the Somosierra; those left behind from
Cuesta's levies (the Castilians) went to Segovia' (i. 259).   But, as we have

command in Madrid was at this moment in dispute between General Eguia, who had just been appointed as head of the whole 'Army of Reserve,' and the Marquis of Castelar, Captain-General of New Castile. The existence of two rival authorities on the spot did not tend to facilitate the organization of the army, or the formation of a regular plan of defence. Eguia, succeeding at last in asserting his authority, ordered San Juan with his 12,000 men to defend the Somosierra, while Heredia with the 9,000 Estremadurans was to hold the pass of the Guadarrama, the alternative road from Old Castile to Madrid via Segovia and San Ildefonso. These 21,000 men were all that could be brought up to resist Napoleon's attack, since the Junta had neglected to call in its more distant resources. It is clear that from the first they were doomed to failure, for mountain chains are not like perpendicular walls: they cannot be maintained merely by blocking the roads in the defiles. Small bodies of troops, entrenched across the actual summit of the pass, can always be turned by an enemy of superior numbers; for infantry can easily scramble up the flanking heights on each side of the high-road. These heights must be held by adequate forces, arranged in a continuous line for many miles on each side of the defile, if the position is not to be outflanked. Neither Heredia nor San Juan had the numbers necessary for this purpose.

It was open to Napoleon to attack both the passes, or to demonstrate against one while concentrating his main force on the other, or to completely ignore the one and to turn every man against the other. He chose the last-named alternative: a few cavalry only were told off to watch the Estremadurans at Segovia, though Lefebvre and the 4th Corps were ultimately sent in that direction. The main mass of the army marched from Aranda against the Somosierra. San Juan had not made the best of his opportunities: he had done no more than range his whole artillery across the pass at its culminating point, with a shallow earthwork to protect it. This only covered the little plateau at the head of the defile: the flanking heights on either side were not prepared or entrenched. They were steep, especially on the right side of the road, but nowhere inaccessible to infantry moving in skirmishing order. At the northern foot of the pass lies the little town of

seen, only one regiment of Belvedere's men went to the Somosierra, and the Castilians (Madrid Volunteers) marched thither and not to Segovia.

Sepulveda, which is reached by a road that branches off from the Madrid *chaussée* before it commences to mount the defile. To this place San Juan pushed forward a vanguard, consisting of five battalions of veteran line troops[1], a battery, and half his available cavalry. It is hard to see why he risked the flower of his little army in this advanced position: they were placed (it is true) so as to flank any attempt of the French to advance up the high-road. But what use could there be in threatening the flank of Napoleon's 40,000 men with a small detached brigade of 3,500 bayonets? And how were the troops to join their main body, if the Emperor simply 'contained' them with a small force, and pushed up the pass?

Napoleon left Aranda on November 28: on the twenty-ninth he reached Boceguillas, near the foot of the mountains, where the Sepulveda road joins the great *chaussée*, at the bottom of the pass. After reconnoitring the Spanish position, he sent a brigade of fusiliers of the Guard, under Savary, to turn the enemy out of Sepulveda. Meanwhile he pushed his vanguard up the defile, to look for the position of San Juan. Savary's battalions failed to dislodge Sarden's detachment before nightfall: behind the walls of the town the Spaniards stood firm, and after losing sixty or seventy men Savary drew off. His attack was not really necessary, for the moment that the Emperor had seized the exit of the defile, the force at Sepulveda, on its cross-road, was cut off from any possibility of rejoining its commander-in-chief, and stood in a very compromised position. Realizing this fact, Colonel Sarden retreated in the night, passed cautiously along the foot of the hills, and fell back on the Estremaduran army at Segovia. The only result, therefore, of San Juan's having made this detachment to threaten the Emperor's flank, was that he had deprived himself of the services of a quarter of his troops—and those the best in his army —when it became necessary to defend the actual pass. He had now left to oppose Napoleon only six battalions of regulars, two of militia, and seven of raw Castilian and Estremaduran levies: the guns which he had established in line across the little plateau, at the crest of the pass, seem to have been sixteen in number. The Emperor could bring against him about five men to one.

[1] One battalion of Walloon Guards, two each of the regiments of Jaen and Irlanda, and three squadrons of the regiments of Montesa and Alcantara, with six guns, all under Colonel Sarden (colonel of the Montesa Regiment).

The high-road advances by a series of curves up the side of the mountain, with the ravine of the little river Duraton always on its right hand. The ground on either flank is steep but not inaccessible. Cavalry and guns must stick to the *chaussée*, but infantry can push ahead with more or less ease in every direction. There were several rough side-tracks on which the French could have turned San Juan's position, by making a long circling movement. But Bonaparte disdained to use cautious measures: he knew that he had in front of him a very small force, and he had an exaggerated contempt for the Spanish levies. Accordingly, at dawn on the thirtieth, he pushed up the main defile, merely taking the precaution of keeping strong pickets of infantry out upon the flanking heights.

When, after a march of about seventeen miles up the defile, the French reached the front of San Juan's position, the morning was very far spent. It was a dull November day with occasional showers of rain, and fogs and mists hung close to the slopes of the mountains. No general view of the ground could be obtained, but the Emperor made out the Spanish guns placed across the high-road, and could see that the heights for some little way on either hand were occupied. He at once deployed the division of Ruffin, belonging to Victor's corps, which headed his line of march. The four battalions of the 96th moved up the road towards the battery: the 9th Léger spread out in skirmishing order to the right, the 24th of the Line to the left. They pressed forward up the steep slopes, taking cover behind rocks and in undulations of the ground: their progress was in no small degree helped by the mist, which prevented the Spaniards from getting any full view of their assailants. Presently, for half a mile on each flank of the high-road, the mountain-side was alive with the crackling fire of the long lines of tirailleurs. The ten French battalions were making their way slowly but surely towards the crest, when the Emperor rode to the front. He brought up with him a battery of artillery of the Guard, which he directed against the Spanish line of guns, but with small effect, for the enemy had the advantage in numbers and position. Bonaparte grew impatient: if he had waited a little longer Ruffin's division would have cleared the flanking heights without asking for aid. But he was anxious to press the combat to a decision, and had the greatest contempt for the forces in front of him. His main idea

at the moment seems to have been to give his army and his
generals a sample of the liberties that might be taken with Spanish
levies. After noting that Victor's infantry were drawing near
the summit of the crest, and seemed able to roll back all that
lay in front of them, he suddenly took a strange and unexpected
step. He turned to the squadron of Polish Light Horse, which
formed his escort for the day, and bade them prepare to charge
the Spanish battery at the top of the pass. It appeared a perfectly insane order, for the Poles were not 100 strong[1]: they could
only advance along the road four abreast, and then they would
be exposed for some 400 yards to the converging fire of sixteen
guns. Clearly the head of the charging column would be vowed
to destruction, and not a man would escape if the infantry supports
of the battery stood firm. But Bonaparte cared nothing for the
lives of the unfortunate troopers who would form the forlorn hope,
if only he could deliver one of those theatrical strokes with which
he loved to adorn a *Bulletin*. It would be tame and common-
place to allow Victor's infantry to clear the heights on either side,
and to compel the retreat of the Spanish guns by mere outflanking.
On the other hand, it was certain that the enemy must be growing
very uncomfortable at the sight of the steady progress of Ruffin's
battalions up the heights: the Emperor calculated that San
Juan's artillerymen must already be looking over their shoulders
and expecting the order to retire, when the crests above them
should be lost. If enough of the Poles struggled through to the
guns to silence the battery for a moment, there was a large chance
that the whole Spanish line would break and fly down hill to
Buitrago and Madrid. To support the escort-squadron he ordered
up the rest of the Polish regiment and the *chasseurs à cheval* of
the Guard: if the devoted vanguard could once reach the guns
1,000 sabres would support them and sweep along the road. If,
on the other hand, the Poles were exterminated, the Guard cavalry
would be held back, and nothing would have been lost, save the
lives of the forlorn hope.

[1] Seven officers and eighty men, to be exact (see Ségur, *Mémoires*, iii. 282).
It does not seem to be generally known that the Poles were not yet lancers.
They were only armed with the lance three months later (see *Nap. Corresp.*,
14,819, giving the order to that effect), and were at this moment properly
styled *Chevaux-Légers Polonais* only. Almost every narrative of the Somosierra that I have read calls them lancers ; Napier is an exception.

General Montbrun led the Polish squadron forward for about half the distance that separated them from the guns: so many saddles were emptied that the men hesitated, and sought refuge in a dip of the ground where some rocks gave them more or less cover from the Spanish balls. This sight exasperated the Emperor: when Walther, the general commanding the Imperial Guard, rode up to him, and suggested that he should wait a moment longer till Victor's tirailleurs should have carried the heights on each side of the road, he smote the pommel of his saddle and shouted, 'My Guard must not be stopped by peasants, mere armed banditti [1].' Then he sent forward his aide-de-camp, Philippe de Ségur, to tell the Poles that they must quit their cover and charge home. Ségur galloped on and gave his message to the *chef d'escadron* Korjietulski: the Emperor's eye was upon them, and the Polish officers did not shrink. Placing themselves at the head of the survivors of their devoted band they broke out of their cover and charged in upon the guns, Ségur riding two horses' lengths in front of the rest. There were only 200 yards to cross, but the task was impossible; one blasting discharge of the Spanish guns, aided by the fire of infantry skirmishers from the flanks, practically exterminated the unhappy squadron. Of the eighty-eight who charged four officers and forty men were killed, four officers (one of them was Ségur) and twelve men wounded [2]. The foremost of these bold riders got within thirty yards of the guns before he fell.

Having thus sacrificed in vain this little band of heroes, Bonaparte found himself forced, after all, to wait for the infantry. General Barrois with the 96th Regiment, following in the wake of the lost squadron, seized the line of rocks behind which the Poles had taken refuge before their charge, and began to exchange a lively musketry fire with the Spanish battalions which flanked and guarded the guns. Meanwhile the 9th and 24th Regiments on either side had nearly reached the crest of the heights. The

---

[1] All this narrative comes from Philippe de Ségur, who must be followed in preference to the 13th *Bulletin* and all the witnesses who allege that the Poles did reach the battery. He, if any one, knew what really happened (*Mémoires*, iii. 281–5). His account of the whole business is in close accord with that of De Pradt, who was also an eye-witness.

[2] The frightful proportion of killed to wounded came, of course, from the fact that the casualties were caused by artillery fire.

enemy were already wavering, and falling back before the advance of Barrois' brigade, whose skirmishers had struggled to the summit just to the right of the grand battery on the high-road, when the Emperor ordered a second cavalry charge. This time he sent up Montbrun with the remaining squadrons of the Polish regiment, supported by the *chasseurs à cheval* of the Guard. The conditions were completely changed, and this second attack was delivered at the right moment: the Spaniards, all along the line, were now heavily engaged with Victor's infantry. When, therefore, the horsemen rode furiously in upon the guns, it is not wonderful that they succeeded in closing with them, and seized the whole battery with small loss. The defenders of the pass gave way so suddenly, and scattered among the rocks with such speed, that only 200 of them were caught and ridden down. The Poles pursued those of them who retired down the road as far as Buitrago, at the southern foot of the defile, but without inflicting on them any very severe loss; for the fugitives swerved off the path, and could not be hunted down by mounted men among the steep slopes whereon they sought refuge. The larger part of the Spaniards, being posted to the left of the *chaussée*, fled westward along the side of the mountain and arrived at Segovia, where they joined the army of Estremadura. With them went San Juan, who had vainly tried to make his reserve stand firm behind the guns, and had received two sword-cuts on the head from a Polish officer. Only a small part of the army fled to the direct rear and entered Madrid.

The story of the passage of the Somosierra has often been told as if it was an example of the successful frontal attack of cavalry on guns, and as if the Poles had actually defeated the whole Spanish army. Nothing of the kind occurred: Napoleon, as we have seen, in a moment of impatience and rage called upon the leading squadron to perform an impossibility, and caused them to be exterminated. The second charge was quite a different matter: here the horsemen fell upon shaken troops already closely engaged with infantry, and broke through them. But if they had not charged at all, the pass would have been forced none the less, and only five minutes later than was actually the case[1]. In short, it

---

[1] The real course of events is best given by Ségur (iii. 295), who writes as follows: 'Pendant que notre charge avait attiré sur elle les feux de l'ennemi, le général Barrois avait profité de cette diversion. Il s'était avancé jusqu'à

was Ruffin's division, and not the cavalry, which really did the work. Napoleon, with his habitual love of the theatrical and his customary disregard of truth, wrote in the 13th *Bulletin* that the charge of the Polish Light Horse decided the action, and that they had lost only eight killed and sixteen wounded! This legend has slipped into history, and traces of its influence will be found even in Napier[1] and other serious authors.

The combat of the Somosierra, in short, is only an example of the well-known fact that defiles with accessible flank-slopes cannot be held by a small army against fourfold numbers. To state the matter shortly, fifteen battalions of Spaniards (five of them regular battalions which had been present at Baylen) were turned off the heights by the ten battalions of Ruffin: the cavalry action was only a spectacular interlude. The Spanish infantry, considering that there were so many veteran corps among them, might have behaved better. But they did not suffer the disgrace of being routed by a single squadron of horse as Napoleon asserted ; and if they fought feebly their discouragement was due, we cannot doubt, to the fact that they saw the pass packed for miles to the rear with the advancing columns of the French, and knew that Ruffin's division was only the skirmishing line (so to speak) of a great army.

On the night of November 30, Napoleon descended the pass and fixed his head quarters at Buitrago. On the afternoon of December 1 the advanced parties of Latour-Maubourg's and Lasalle's cavalry rode up to the northern suburbs of Madrid : on

le rocher, notre point de départ. Là, poussés en avant par l'empereur pour recommencer ma charge, treize de ses grenadiers avaient été abattus par le feu de la redoute. Alors, rétrogradant derrière le roc, il avait envoyé quelques compagnies à l'escalade des hauteurs à notre droite, puis lui-même, à la tête de sa brigade, y était monté. . . . Les Espagnols, se voyant près d'être abordés, avaient déchargé leurs armes, et, se débandant aussitôt, ils s'étaient mis a fuir à toutes jambes. Au même moment à sa gauche le bruit de la canonnade avait cessé. C'était alors que le régiment entier de lanciers Polonais, recommençant la charge prématurée de notre escadron détruit, avait achevé, sans autre perte, d'enlever la position. Les canons, quelques officiers et 150 à 200 Espagnols seulement purent être atteints, tant la dispersion de l'armée devant les quatre bataillons de Barrois avait été subite et rapide.'

[1] He describes it as if 'a position nearly impregnable, and defended by 12,000 men, had been abandoned to the wild charge of a few squadrons, whom two companies of steady infantry could have stopped ' (i. 268).

the second the French appeared in force, and the attack on the city began.

The Spanish capital was, and is, a place incapable of any regular defence. It had not even, like Valencia and Saragossa, the remains of a mediaeval wall: its development had taken place in the sixteenth century, when serious fortifications had gone out of date. Its streets were broad and regular, unlike the tortuous lanes which had been the real strength of Saragossa. Nothing separates the city from its suburbs save ornamental gates, whose only use was for the levy of octroi duties. Madrid is built in a level upland, but there is a rising ground which dominates the whole place: it lies just outside the eastern limit of the city. On it stood the palace of the Buen Retiro (which gives its name to the height), and several other public buildings, among them the Observatory and the royal porcelain manufactory, known as La China. The latter occupied the more commanding and important section of the summit of the hill. Between the Retiro and the eastern side of the city lies the public park known as the Prado, a low-lying open space laid out with fountains, statues, and long avenues of trees. Three broad and handsome streets [1] run eastward and terminate in the Prado, just opposite the Retiro, so that cannon planted either by the palace or by La China can search them from end to end. This was so obvious that Murat, during his occupation of Madrid in April and May, had built three redoubts, one large and two small, facing down into the city and armed with guns of position. The inhabitants of Madrid had partly dismantled them after the departure of the French—and did themselves no harm thereby, for these earthworks were useless for defence against an enemy from without: they could be employed to overawe the city but not to protect it [2].

Ever since the rout of Gamonal, those members of the Junta who were gifted with ordinary foresight must have realized that it was probable that the Emperor would appear ere long before the gates of the capital. But to avoid alarming the excitable populace, the fact was concealed as long as possible, and it was given out that Madrid would be defended at the impregnable Somosierra. It was not till November 25 that any public measures for the fortification of the capital were spoken of. On that day the

---

[1] The Calle de Alcala, Calle de Atocha, and Carrera de San Geronimo.

[2] This description is mainly from Vaughan's unpublished diary (p. 230).

Junta issued a proclamation placing the charge of the capital in the hands of the Marquis of Castelar, Captain-General of New Castile, and of Don Tomas de Morla, the officer who had won a name by bombarding and capturing the French fleet at Cadiz in June. Under their directions, preparations were begun for putting the city in a state of defence. But the military men had a strong and well-founded belief that the place was indefensible, and that all efforts made to fortify it were labour thrown away: the fight must be made at the Somosierra, not at the gates of Madrid. It was not till the news of the rout of San Juan's army on the thirtieth came to hand, that any very serious work was executed. But when this disaster was known there was a sudden and splendid outburst of energy. The populace, full of vindictive memories of May 2, were ready and willing to fight, and had no conception of the military weakness of their situation. If Saragossa had defended itself street by street, why, they asked, should not Madrid do the same? Their spirits were so high and their temper so ferocious, that the authorities realized that they must place themselves at the head of the multitude, or be torn to pieces as traitors. On December 1 a Junta of Defence was formed, under the presidency of the Duke of Infantado, in which Morla and Castelar were given a large and heterogeneous mass of colleagues—magistrates, officers, and prominent citizens forming an unwieldy body very unfit to act as an executive council of war. The military resources at their disposal were insignificant: there was a handful of the fugitives from the Somosierra—Castelar estimated them as not more than 300 or 400 in all [1]—and two battalions of new levies from the south, which had arrived only on the morning of December 1. The organized forces then were not more than 2,500 or 3,000 in all. But there was a vast and unruly mob of citizens of Madrid and of peasants, who had flocked into the city to aid in its defence. Weapons rather than men were wanting, for when 8,000 muskets from the Arsenal had been served out, the supply ran short. All private persons owning firearms of any description were invited to hand them in to the Junta: but this resource soon failed, and finally pikes were served out, and even mediaeval weapons from the royal armoury and the family collections of certain grandees. How many men, armed in one way or another,

---

[1] This must have been an under-estimate. More than 1,500 of the Somosierra troops had joined the army of Infantado by the New Year.

took part in the defence of Madrid will never be known—it cannot have been less than 20,000, and may have amounted to much more.

Not merely the combatants, but the whole population of both sexes turned themselves with absolute frenzy to the work of fortification. In the two days which they had at their disposal they carried out an enormous and ill-compacted scheme for surrounding the whole city with lines. In front of each of the gates a battery was established, formed of earth reveted with paving-stones: to connect these a continuous wall was made, by joining together all the exterior houses of the town with earthworks, or with piles of stones and bricks pulled down from buildings in the suburbs. On several fronts ditches were excavated: the more important streets were blocked with barricades, and the windows and doors of exposed buildings were built up. There were very few engineers at the disposal of the Junta of Defence, and the populace in many places worked not under skilled guidance but by the light of nature, executing enormous but perfectly useless works. 'The batteries,' wrote a prominent Spanish witness, 'were all too small: they were so low that they did not prevent the gates and streets which they defended from being enfiladed: the guns being placed *en barbette* were much exposed, and were dominated by the artillery which the enemy afterwards placed on the high ground [i. e. the Retiro heights]. The low parapets and the want of proportion between them and their banquettes left the infantry unsheltered: indeed they were harmed rather than helped by the works, for the splinters of the paving-stones which formed the parapets proved more deadly to the garrison than did the enemy's cannon-balls. The batteries were too low at the flanks, and placed so close to the buildings in their rear that the guns could not easily be worked nor the infantry supports move freely. The gates behind being all of hewn stone, every ball that struck them sent such a shower of fragments flying that the effect was like grape: it forced the defenders to lie flat, and even then caused terrible loss [1].' It may be added that not only were the works unscientifically executed, but that the most tiresome results were produced by the misguided energy of persons who threw up barricades, or dug cuttings, behind them, so that it was

[1] Report on the defences of Madrid, by the Duke of Infantado, quoted in Arteche (iii. 400, 401).

very hard to send up reinforcements, and quite impossible to withdraw the guns from one battery for use in another.

It was natural that these self-taught engineers should neglect the one most important point in the defences of Madrid. The Retiro heights were the key of the city: if they were lost, the whole place lay open to bombardment from the dominating ground. But nothing was done here, save that the old French works round the factory of La China were repaired, the buildings of the palace, barracks, and hospital in the vicinity barricaded, and a low continuous earthwork constructed round the summit of the hill. It should have been turned into a regular entrenched camp, if the city was really to be defended.

The Junta of Defence did its best to preserve order and introduce discipline: all the armed men were paraded in the Prado, told off into bands, and allotted their posts around the circumference of the city. But there were many idle hands, and much confusion: it was inevitable that mobs should collect, with the usual consequences. Cries of 'Treason' were raised, some houses were sacked, and at least one atrocious murder was committed. The Marquis of Perales was president of the sub-committee which the Junta had appointed to superintend the manufacture and distribution of ammunition. Among the cartridges given out to the people some were found in which sand had been substituted for powder—probably they were relics of some petty piece of peculation dating back to the times of Godoy. When this was discovered, a furious mob ran to the house of the marquis, beat him to death, and dragged his corpse through the streets on a hurdle [1].

If the populace of Madrid was full of blind self-confidence, and imagined that it had the power to beat off the assault of Napoleon, its leaders were in a much more despondent frame of mind. Morla was one of those who had joined the patriotic party merely

[1] Napier calls Perales 'a respectable old general'; but as Toreño remarks (i. 305), he was neither old, nor a military officer of any rank, nor respectable. He was a man of fashion noted for his licentious life, and the mob which murdered him is said to have been headed by his discarded mistress. Arteche suggests that the sand-cartridges were constructed for the purpose of ruining him, and that the whole business was a piece of private vengeance. The marquis had once been a very popular character among the lower classes, but had lost credit by showing politeness to Murat.

because he thought it was the winning side: he was deeply
disgusted with himself, and was already contemplating the
traitorous desertion to the enemy which has covered his name
with eternal disgrace. Castelar seems to have been weak and
downhearted. The Duke of Infantado was enough of a soldier to
see the hopeless inefficiency of the measures of defence which had
been adopted. The only chance of saving Madrid was to hurry up
to its aid the two field-armies which were within touch—the old
Andalusian divisions (now under La Peña), which, by orders of the
Supreme Junta, were marching from Calatayud on the capital,
and the routed bands of Heredia and San Juan at Segovia. Urgent
appeals were sent to both of these hosts to press forward without
delay: Infantado himself rode out to meet the army of the Centre,
which on this day [Dec. 1] had not long passed Siguenza in its
retreat, and was still nearly eighty miles from the capital. He
met it at Guadalajara on the next day, in very bad condition, and
much reduced by long marches and starvation: with the colours
there were only 9,000 foot and 2,000 horse, and these were in
a state of half-developed mutiny. The rest of the 20,000 men who
had escaped from Tudela were ranging in small bands over the
country-side, in search of food, and were not rallied for many days.
There was not much to be hoped for from the army of the Centre,
and it was evident that it could not reach Madrid till December 3 or 4. The troops of San Juan and Heredia were not so far
distant, but even they had fifty-five miles to march from Segovia,
and—as it turned out—the capital had fallen before either of the
field-armies could possibly come to its aid. Still more fruitless
were the attempts made at the last moment to induce Sir John
Moore to bring up the British expeditionary force from Salamanca
—he was 150 miles away, and could not have arrived before
December 7, three days after the capitulation had been signed.

Napoleon dealt with the insurgents of Madrid in a very summary
manner. On December 1—as we have already seen—his vedettes
appeared before the city: on the morning of the second the
dragoons of Lahoussaye and Latour-Maubourg came up in force
and invested the northern and eastern fronts of the city. At noon
the Emperor himself appeared, and late in the afternoon the
infantry columns of Victor's corps. December 2 was one of Bonaparte's lucky days, being the anniversary of Austerlitz, and he
had indulged in a faint hope that an open town like the Spanish

capital might do him the courtesy of surrendering without a blow, like Vienna in 1805, or Berlin in 1806. Accordingly he sent a summons to the Junta in the afternoon; but the Spaniards were in no mood for yielding. General Montbrun, who rode up to the gates with the white flag, was nearly mobbed by enraged peasants, and the aide-de-camp who took the dispatch into the city was only saved from certain death by the exertions of some Spanish officers of the line. The Junta sent him back with the haughty reply that 'the people of Madrid were resolved to bury themselves under the ruins of their houses rather than to permit the French troops to enter their city.'

Since the 'sun of Austerlitz' was not destined to set upon the triumphal entry of the Emperor into the Spanish capital, it became necessary to prepare for the use of force. As a preliminary for an attack on the following morning, Lapisse's division of Victor's corps was sent forward to turn the Spaniards out of many isolated houses in front of their line of entrenchments, which were being held as advanced posts. The ground being cleared, preparations could be made for the assault. The moment that Bonaparte cast eyes on the place, he realized that the heights of the Retiro were the key of the position. Under cover of the night, therefore, thirty guns were ranged in line opposite the weak earthworks which crowned the eminence. Artillery in smaller force was placed in front of several of the northern and eastern gates of the city, to distract the attention of the garrison from the critical point. Before dawn the Emperor sent in another summons to surrender, by the hands of an artillery officer who had been captured at the Somosierra. It is clear that he wished, if possible, to enter Madrid without being obliged to deliver up the city to fire and sword: it would be unfortunate if his brother's second reign were to begin under such unhappy conditions. But it is hard to understand how he could suppose that the warlike frenzy of the Spaniards would have died down between the afternoon of December 2 and the dawn of December 3. All the reply that he obtained was a proposal from the Captain-General Castelar, that there should be a suspension of arms for twelve hours. The sole object of this delay was to allow the Spanish field-armies time to draw nearer to Madrid. Recognizing the fact—which was obvious enough—the Emperor gave orders for an immediate assault. A cannonade was opened against the gates of Los Pozos, the Recoletos, Fuencarral, and several others on the northern and eastern sides of the city. Considerable damage was done to the Spanish defences, but these attacks were all subsidiary. The real assault was delivered against the Retiro heights. The heavy cannonade which was directed against the Spanish works soon opened several breaches. Then Villatte's division of Victor's corps was sent in to storm the position, a feat which it accomplished with the greatest ease. The garrison of this all-important section of the defences consisted of a single battalion of new levies—the Regiment of Mazzaredo—and a mass of armed citizens. They were swept out of their works, and pursued downhill into the Prado. Pressing onward among the avenues and fountains, Villatte's division took in the rear the defenders of the three neighbouring gates, and then, pushing in among the houses of the city, made a lodgement in the palace of the Duke of Medina Celi, and several other large buildings. There was now nothing between the French army and the heart of Madrid save the street-barricades, which the populace had thrown up behind the original lines of defence.

If Napoleon had chosen to send into the fight the rest of Victor's corps, and had pushed forward the whole of his artillery to the edge of the captured heights, with orders to shell the city, there can be little doubt that Madrid might have been stormed ere nightfall. Its broad streets did not give the facilities of defence that Saragossa had possessed, and the Emperor had at his disposal not a weak and heterogeneous army, such as Verdier had commanded, but more than 40,000 veteran troops. His artillery, too, had on the Retiro a vantage-ground such as did not exist outside the Aragonese capital. Nevertheless the Emperor did not press the attack, and once more sent in a demand for the surrender of the place, at about eleven in the morning of December 3.

The populace of Madrid did not yet recognize its own forlorn state, and was keeping up a vigorous fusillade at the gates and behind the barricades. It had suffered severe loss from the French artillery, owing to the unscientific construction of the defences, but was not yet ready to yield. But the Junta was in a very different frame of mind: the military men thoroughly understood the situation, and were expecting to see a hundred guns open from the crest of the Retiro within the next few minutes. Their civilian colleagues, the magistrates, and local notables were looking forward with no enviable feelings to the conflagration and the general sack that seemed to be at hand. In short the idea of rivalling

Saragossa was far from their thoughts. When Napoleon's letter,
offering 'pardon to the city of Madrid, protection and security for
the peaceful inhabitants, respect for the churches and the clergy,
oblivion for the past,' was delivered to the Junta, the majority
decided to treat with him. They sent out as negotiators General
Morla, representing the military element, and Don Bernardo Iriarte[1],
on behalf of the civil authorities. Napoleon treated these delegates
to one of those scenes of simulated rage which he was such an adept
at producing—his harangue was quite in the style of the famous
allocutions to Lord Whitworth and to Metternich. It was necessary, he thought, to terrify the delegates. Accordingly he let loose
on Morla a storm of largely irrelevant abuse, stringing together
accusations concerning the bombardment of the French fleet at
Cadiz, the violation of the Convention of Baylen, the escape of
La Romana's troops from the Baltic, and (strangest of all!) the
misconduct of the Spanish troops in Roussillon during the war of
1793-5. He ended by declaring that unless the city had been
surrendered by six o'clock on the following morning, every man
taken in arms should be put to the sword.

Morla was a very timid man[2], moreover he was already meditating submission to King Joseph : he returned to the Junta in a state
of absolute collapse, and gave such a highly coloured account of
the Emperor's wrath, and of the number of the French army, that
there was no further talk of resistance. The main difficulty was
to stop the promiscuous firing which was still going on at the
outposts, and to induce the more exasperated section of the mob
to quit the city or to lay down their arms. Many of them took
the former alternative : the Marquis of Castelar, resolved to avoid
captivity, got together his handful of regular troops, and fled in
haste by the road towards Estremadura : he was followed by some
thousands of peasants, and by a considerable number of persons
who thought themselves too much compromised to be able to
remain behind. Having got rid of the recalcitrants, the Junta
drew up a form of capitulation in eleven articles, and sent it out
to the French camp. Napoleon, anxious above all things to get
possession of the city as soon as possible, accepted it almost
without discussion, though it contained many clauses entirely in-

[1] Not 'another military officer,' as Napier says.
[2] 'Hombre de corazon pusilánime, aunque de fiera y africana figura,' says
Toreño (i. 307).

appropriate to such a document. As he did not intend to observe any of the inconvenient stipulations, he did not care to waste time in discussing them [1]. Morla and Fernando de Vera, governor of the city, came back with the capitulation duly ratified by Berthier, and next morning the gates were opened, a division under General Belliard marched in, and the Spaniards gave up their artillery and laid down their muskets without further trouble. After the spasmodic burst of energy which they had displayed during the last four days, the citizens showed a melancholy apathy which surprised the conquerors. There was no riot or confusion, nor were any isolated attempts at resistance made. Hence the occupation of Madrid took place without any scenes of bloodshed or pillage, the Emperor for his part keeping a very stern hand upon the soldiery, and sending in as small a garrison as could safely be allotted to the task.

Madrid having fallen after no more than two days of resistance, the two Spanish field-armies which were marching to its aid were far too late to be of any use. The army of the Centre under La Peña had reached Guadalajara at nightfall on December 2: there it was met by the Duke of Infantado, who had come out from Madrid to hurry on the troops. At his solicitation the wearied and disorganized host, with Ney's corps pressing hard on its heels, marched for San Torcaz and Arganda, thus placing itself in a most dangerous position between the Emperor and the corps that was in pursuit. Fortunately La Peña got early news of the capitulation, and swerving southward from Arganda, made for the passage of the Tagus at Aranjuez. But Bonaparte had sent out part of Victor's corps to seize that place, and when the army of the Centre drew near, it found French troops in possession [December 6]. With Ney behind, Victor in front, and Bessières' cavalry ranging all over the plain of New Castile, the Spaniards were in grave danger. But they escaped by way of Estremera, crossed the ferries on the Upper Tagus, and finally rallied—in a

---

[1] The first clause of the Capitulation was to the effect that no religion save the Catholic Apostolic Roman faith should be tolerated! The second provided that all government officials should be continued in the tenure of their offices. Clearly such articles were absurd in a military capitulation, and the second was impossible to execute, as the conqueror must necessarily place in office such persons as he could trust. But the amnesty articles (Nos. 4 and 11) could have been observed, and were not.

most miserable and disorganized condition—at Cuenca. The
artillery, unable to leave the high-road, had been sent off three
days before, from Guadalajara towards the kingdom of Murcia,
almost without an escort: by a piece of extraordinary luck it
escaped without seeing an enemy.

The doings of the disorganized divisions of San Juan and
Heredia, which had marched from Segovia on December 2, were much
more discreditable.   Late on the third they reached the Escurial,
some thirty miles from Madrid, and were met by fugitives from
the capital, who reported that the Retiro had been stormed, and that
the Junta of Defence was debating about a surrender.   The two
commanders were doubting whether they ought not to turn back,
when their troops broke out into mutiny, insisting that the march
on Madrid must be continued.   After a scene of great disorder
the generals gave in, and resumed their advance on the morning
of the fourth, just at the moment when Morla was opening the
gates to Napoleon.   They had only gone a few miles when certain
news of the capitulation was received.   There followed a disgraceful
scene; the cry of treason ran down the ranks: some battalions
disbanded themselves, others attacked their own officers, and the
whole mass dissolved and went off in panic to Talavera, leaving its
artillery abandoned by the wayside.   They had not even seen
a French vedette, or fired a single shot, yet they fled in utter
rout for sixty miles, and only halted when they could run no
further.   Seven or eight thousand men out of the two armies were
got together at Talavera, on the sixth; but when, next morning,
San Juan attempted to take up the command again, they raised
the idiotic cry that he wished to lead them forward into the midst
of Napoleon's armies in order to force them to surrender!   The
unfortunate general was hunted down, shot as he was trying to
escape from a window, and hung from a large elm-tree just outside the town.   This was the most disgraceful scene of the whole
campaign in 1808.   It was not for some days later that the remnants of this miserable army were reduced to some shadow of
discipline, and consented to march under the command of new
generals.

It is clear that even if Madrid had held out for a day or two
more, by dint of desperate street-fighting, it would have got no
effective aid from the armies in the field.   We cannot therefore
say that the Junta of Defence did much harm by its tame sur-

render. From the military point of view Madrid was indefensible: on the other hand it was eminently desirable, from the political point of view, that Napoleon should not enter the place unopposed, to be received, as at Vienna or Berlin, by obsequious deputations mouthing compliments, and bearing the keys of the city on silver salvers. It was far better, in the long run, for Spain and for Europe that he should be received with cannon-balls, and forced to fight his way in. This simple fact made all his fictions to the effect that he was only opposed by the rabble, the monks, and the agents of England appear absurd. He could not, after this, pretend to introduce his brother Joseph as a legitimate sovereign quietly returning to his loyal capital. So much was secured by the two days' resistance of Madrid: on the other hand, when once the French were inside the city, and further resistance would have ended merely in general pillage and conflagration, it would have required more than Spartan resolution for the Junta to go on fighting. If Madrid had been burnt like Moscow, the moral effect on Spain and on Europe would, no doubt, have been enormous. But the heterogeneous council of war, composed of dispirited officers and local notables trembling for their homes, could hardly be expected to see this. They yielded, considering that they had already done enough by way of protest—and even with Saragossa in our mind we should be loth to say that their capitulation was culpable. The one shameful thing about the surrender was that within a few days both Morla, the military head of the defence, and several of the chief civil officials, swore allegiance to Joseph Bonaparte, and took service under him. Such treason on the part of prominent men did more to encourage the invader and to dishearten Spain and her allies than the loss of half a dozen battles. For, when once desertion begins, no one knows where it will stop, and every man distrusts his neighbour as a possible traitor. Madrid, as we have already said, was not a true national capital, nor was its loss a fatal blow; but that its chief defenders should shamelessly throw over the cause of their country, and join the enemy, was a symptom of the most dire and deadly sort. But, fortunately, the fate of the country was not in the hands of its corrupt bureaucracy, but in those of its much-enduring people.

CHAPTER I

NAPOLEON AT MADRID

FROM December 4 to December 22 the Emperor remained fixed in the neighbourhood of Madrid. He did not settle down in the royal palace, and it would seem that he made no more than one or two hurried visits of inspection to the city[1]. He established himself outside the gates, at Chamartin, a desolate and uncomfortable country house of the Duke of Infantado, and devoted himself to incessant desk-work[2]. It was here that he drew up his projects for the reorganization of the kingdom of Spain, and at the same time set himself to the task of constructing his plans of campaign against those parts of the Peninsula which still remained unsubdued. In seventeen days, uninterrupted by the cares of travel, Bonaparte could get through an enormous amount of business. His words and deeds at this period are well worth studying, for the light that they throw alike on his own character and on his conceptions of the state and the needs of Spain.

His first act was to annul the capitulation which he had granted to the inhabitants of Madrid. Having served its purpose in inducing the Junta to yield, it was promptly violated. 'The Spaniards have failed to carry it out,' he wrote, 'and I consider

---

[1] Not, as the Spaniards whispered, because he feared the stiletto of some fanatical monk, but because he wished to leave the place clear for his brother Joseph. For the curious story of his visit to the royal palace, and long study of the portrait of Philip II, see Toreño, i. 309.

[2] For the discomforts of Chamartin see the *Mémoires sur la Révolution d'Espagne* of De Pradt. Though belonging to one of the richest nobles of Spain, it had not a single fireplace, and the imperial courtiers and aides-de-camp had to shiver in the ante-rooms over miserable *braseros*.

the whole thing void[1].' Looking at the preposterous clauses which he had allowed to be inserted in the document, there can be no doubt that this was his intention at the very moment when he ratified it. It was a small thing that he should break engagements, such as those in which he had promised not to quarter troops in the monasteries (Article 7), or to maintain all existing officials in their places (Article 2). But having guaranteed security for their life and property, freedom from arrest, and free exit at their pleasure, to such persons as chose to remain behind in the city, it was shameless to commence his proceedings with a proscription and a long series of arrests. The list of persons declared traitors and condemned to loss of life and goods was not very long: only ten persons were named, and seven of these were absent from Madrid. But the three others, the Prince of Castelfranco, the Marquis of Santa Cruz, and the Count of Altamira, were seized and dispatched into France, sentenced to imprisonment for life.

The arrests were a much more serious matter. In flagrant contravention of the terms of surrender, Bonaparte put under lock and key all the members of the Council of the Inquisition on whom he could lay hands, irrespective of what their conduct had been during the reign of the Supreme Junta. He also declared all the superior officers of the army resident in Madrid, even retired veterans, to be prisoners of war, and liable to answer with their necks for the safety of the captives of Dupont's corps. Among them was discovered an old French *émigré*, the Marquis de Saint-Simon, who had entered the service of Charles IV as far back as 1793, and had taken part in the last campaign. The Emperor refused to consider him as a Spaniard, declared that he was one of his own subjects, had him tried by court-martial, and condemned him to death. All this was to lead up to one of those odious comedies of magnanimity which Bonaparte sometimes practised for the benefit of the editor of the *Moniteur*. Saint-Simon's daughter was admitted to the imperial presence to beg for her father's life, and the master of the world deigned to com-

---

[1] 'La capitulation, n'ayant pas été tenue par les habitants de Madrid, est nulle,' Napoleon to Belliard, Dec. 5 (*Nap. Corresp.*, 14,534). He scolds Belliard for having allowed the document to be printed and placarded on the walls. Every copy was to be torn down at once. In what respect the Spaniards had broken the treaty he does not state. He may have referred to the evasion of Castelar's troops.

mute the punishment of the 'traitor' to imprisonment for life
in the mountain-fortress of Joux [1]. This was a repetition of the
Hatzfeldt affairs at Berlin, and Saint-Simon was treated even worse
than the unfortunate Prussian nobleman of 1806. Truly the
tender mercies of the wicked are cruel!

Among other persons who were arrested were Don Arias Mon,
president of the Council of Castile, the Duke of Sotomayor, and
about thirty other notables: some were ultimately sent away to
France, others allowed to go free after swearing allegiance to
Joseph Bonaparte.

All these measures were designed to strike terror into the hearts
of the Spaniards. But at the same time the Emperor issued a
series of decrees—in his own name and not in that of his brother,
the titular king—which were intended to conciliate them by
bestowing upon them certain tangible benefits. He knew that
there existed the nucleus of a Liberal party in Spain, and hoped
to draw it over to his side by introducing certain much-needed
reforms in the administration of the country. With this object
he removed the tiresome inter-provincial octroi duties, abolished
all feudal dues and all rights of private jurisdiction, declared that
all monopolies should be annulled, and forbade all assignments
of public revenues to individuals. Such measures would have
seemed excellent to many good Spaniards, if they had been introduced by a legitimate ruler: but coming from the hand of a foreign
conqueror they were without effect. Moreover there was hardly
a square mile of Spanish territory, outside Madrid and the other
towns held by the French, where Napoleon's writs could run.
Every village which was unoccupied was passively or actively dis-
obedient. The reforms, therefore, were but on paper. Another
series of decrees, which appeared at the same time, were in themselves quite as justifiable as those which were concerned with
administrative changes, but were certain to offend nine-tenths of
the Spanish nation. They dealt with the Church and its ministers.
The most important was one which declared (with perfect truth)
that there were far too many monasteries and nunneries in Spain, and
that it was necessary to cut them down to one-third of their existing
number. The names of those which were destined to survive were
published: to them the inmates of the remaining institutions were

---

[1] Cf. *Nap. Corresp.*, 14,708, with De Pradt (p. 205–6) and Arteche (iii. 432).

to be transferred, as vacancies arose. The suppressed convents were to become the property of the state. Part of their revenues was to be devoted to raising the salaries of the secular clergy, so that every parish priest should have an income of 2,400 reals (about £25). Monks or nuns who might choose to leave the monastic life were to be granted a small pension [1]. At the same time the Inquisition was abolished 'as dangerous to the crown and to civil authority,' and all its property confiscated. In Madrid there was seized 2,453,972 reals in hard cash—about £25,000; the smallness of the amount much surprised the French, who had vague ideas concerning the fabulous wealth of the institution [2].

The only results of these measures were that every Spaniard was confirmed in his belief that Napoleon was a concealed atheist and an irreconcilable enemy of all religion. Could anything else be expected of one who (in spite of his *Concordats* and *Te Deums*) was after all a child of the Revolution? The man who had persecuted the Pope in January, 1808, would naturally persecute the monks of Spain in December. As to the Inquisition, its fate inspired no rejoicing: it had been effete for many years: there was not a prisoner in any of its dungeons. Indeed it had enjoyed a feeble popularity of late, for having refused to lend itself as a tool to Godoy. The only result of Napoleon's decree for its abolition was that it acquired (grotesque as the idea may seem) considerable credit in the eyes of the majority of the Spanish people, as one of the usurper's victims. Never was work more wasted than that which the Emperor spent on his reforms of December, 1808. They actually tended to make old abuses popular with the masses, merely because he had attempted to remove them. As to the possibility of conciliating the comparatively small body of Liberals, he was equally in error: they agreed with the views of Jovellanos: reforms were necessary, but they must come from within, and not be imposed by force from without. They were Spaniards first and reformers afterwards. The only recruits whom Bonaparte succeeded in enrolling for his brother's court were the purely selfish bureaucrats who would accept any government—who would serve Godoy, Ferdinand, Joseph, a red republic, or the Sultan of Turkey

---

[1] For details see the decree in *Nap. Corresp.*, 14,528. The last-named clause curiously resembles a provision of Henry VIII of England, at the Dissolution of 1536.

[2] Cf. *Nap. Corresp.*, 14,563, and De Pradt, *Mémoires*, &c., p. 205.

with equal equanimity, so long as they could keep their places or gain better ones.

The Emperor had a curious belief in the power of oaths and phrases over other men, though he was entirely free himself from any feebleness of the kind. He took considerable pains to get up a semblance of national acceptance of his brother's authority, now that his second reign was about to begin. Joseph had appeared at Chamartin on December 2[1] : but he was not allowed [to re-enter Madrid for many days. The Emperor told him to stay outside, at the royal palace of the Pardo, till things were ready for his reception. This was not at all to the mind of the King, who took his position seriously, and was deeply wounded at being ordered about in such an arbitrary fashion. He sent in a formal protest against the publication of the decrees of December 4 : his own name, he complained, not that of his brother, ought to have appeared at the bottom of all these projects of reform. He had never coveted any crown, and least of all that of Spain : but having once accepted the position he could not consent to be relegated into a corner, while all the acts of sovereignty were being exercised by his brother. He was ready to resign his crown into the hands from which he had received it : but if he was not allowed to abdicate, he must be allowed to reign in the true sense of the word. It made him blush with shame before his subjects[2] when he saw them invited to obey laws which he had never seen, much less sanctioned. Napoleon refused to accept this abdication : he looked at matters from an entirely different point of view. He was master of Spain, as he considered, not merely by the cession made at Bayonne, but by the new title of conquest. He intended to restore Joseph to the throne, but till he had done so he saw no reason why he should not exercise all the rights of sovereignty at Madrid. If, in a moment of pique, he said that his brother might exchange the crown of Spain for that of Italy, or for the position of lieutenant of the Emperor in France during his own numerous absences, there is clear evidence that these were empty words. His dispatches show not the least sign of any project for

---

[1] Napier (i. 273) makes a curious blunder in saying that he remained at Burgos.

[2] This odd phrase is used by Joseph himself in his letter of Dec. 8, sent from the Pardo, after he had received the decrees issued on Dec. 4 by his brother.

the future of Spain other than the restoration of Joseph; and while the latter was at the Pardo he was continually receiving notes concerning the reorganization of the Spanish army and finances, which presuppose his confirmation on the throne within the next few days[1].

It would seem that Napoleon's real object in keeping his brother off the scene, and acting as if he intended to annex Spain to France as a vassal province, was merely to frighten the inhabitants of Madrid into a proper frame of mind. If they remained recalcitrant, and refused to come before him with petitions for pardon, they were to be threatened with a purely French military government. If they bowed the knee, they should have back King Joseph and the mockery of liberal and constitutional monarchy which he represented. So much we gather from the Emperor's celebrated proclamation of December 7, and his allocution to the Corregidor and magistrates of Madrid two days later. Both of these addresses are in the true Napoleonesque vein. In the first we read that if the people of Spain prefer 'the poisons which the English have ministered to them' to the wholesome régime introduced from France, they shall be treated as a conquered province, and Joseph shall be removed to another throne. 'I will place the crown of Spain on my own brow, and I will make it respected by evil-doers, for God has given me the strength and the force of will necessary to surmount all obstacles.' In the second, which is written in a mood of less rigour, the inhabitants of Madrid are told that nothing could be easier than to cut up Spain into provinces, each governed by a separate viceroy. But if the clergy, nobles, merchants, and magistrates of the capital will swear a solemn oath upon the Blessed Sacrament to be true and loyal for the future to King Joseph, he shall be restored to them and the Emperor will make over to him all his rights of conquest. We

---

[1] There is a complete *catena* of letters and dispatches from Dec. 4 to Dec. 22, in which the retention of Joseph as king is presupposed : (1) 14,531 [Dec. 5] advises him to raise a Spanish army ; (2) 14,537 [Dec. 7] advises the Spaniards to 'make their King certain of their love and confidence'; (3) 14,543 [Dec. 9], the allocution to the Corregidor, bids the Madrileños swear fidelity on the Sacrament to their King ; (4) 14,558 [Dec. 13] speaks of the knitting up again of the bonds which attach Joseph's subjects to their sovereign; (5) 14,593 [Dec. 18] gives the King advice as to the reorganization of his finances. None of them could have been written if there had been any real intention of ousting Joseph from the throne.

cannot stop to linger over the other details of these addresses : one of the most astounding statements in them is that the quarrel between King Charles and King Ferdinand had been hatched by the English ministry [1], and that the Duke of Infantado, acting as their tool, was plotting to make Spain England's vassal, 'an insensate project which would have made blood run in torrents'! But this mattered little, as within a few weeks every English soldier would have been cast out of the Peninsula, and Lisbon no less than Saragossa, Valencia, and Seville would be flying the French flag [2].

In accordance with the Emperor's command, the notables of Madrid, civil and ecclesiastical, were compelled to go through the ceremony of swearing allegiance to King Joseph on the Holy Sacrament, which was exposed for several days in every church for this purpose. Apparently a very large number of persons were induced, by terror or despair, to give in their formal submission to the intrusive King. Three pages of the *Madrid Gazette* for December 15 are filled with the names of the deputies of the ten quarters and sixty-four *barrios* of the city, who joined in the formal petition for the restoration to them of 'that sovereign who unites so much kindness of heart with such an interest in the welfare of his subjects, and whose presence will be their joy.'

Satisfied with this declaration, and pretending to take it as the expression of the wishes of every Spaniard who was not the paid agent of England or the slave of the Inquisition, the Emperor was graciously pleased to restore Joseph to all his rights. Great preparations were made for his solemn entry, which was celebrated with considerable state in the month of January.

But his plans for the reorganization of Spain only formed a part of the Emperor's work at Chamartin. He was also busied in the reconcentration of his armies, for the purpose of overrunning those parts of the Peninsula which still remained unconquered. On the very morrow of the fall of Madrid he had pushed out detachments

---

[1] *Nap. Corresp.*, 14,547, p. 108.

[2] Napier (i. 273) prints Bonaparte's allocution in full, with the astonishing comment that it ' was an exposition of the principles upon which Spain was to be governed, and it forces reflection upon the passionate violence with which men resist positive good, to seek danger, misery, and death rather than resign their prejudices.' Is the desire for national independence a prejudice? And should it be easily resigned for 'positive good,' e. g. administrative reform?

in all directions, to cover all the approaches to the capital, and to
hunt down any remnants of the Spanish armies which might still
be within reach [1].   He was particularly hopeful that he might catch
the army of the Centre, which, with Ney and Maurice Mathieu at
its heels, was coming in from the direction of Siguenza and Calatayud.
To intercept it the fusiliers of the Guard marched for Alcala, one of
Victor's divisions for Guadalajara, and another for Aranjuez; while
Bessières with the Guard cavalry, and one of Latour-Maubourg's
brigades of dragoons, swept all the country around the Tajuna and
the Tagus.   But, as we have already seen, La Peña's famishing men
ultimately got away in the direction of Cuenca.   When it was
certain that they had escaped from the net, Napoleon rearranged
his forces on the eastern side of Madrid.   Bessières, with Latour-
Maubourg's whole division of dragoons [2], occupied cantonments
facing at once towards Cuenca and towards La Mancha: the
Marshal's head quarters, on December 11, were at Tarancon.   Of
Victor's infantry, one division (Ruffin) marched on Toledo, which
opened its gates without resistance; another, that of Villatte, remained at Aranjuez with an advanced guard at Ocaña, a few miles
further south.   The third division of the 1st Corps, that of Lapisse,
remained at Madrid.   Ney's troops were also at hand in this
quarter: when La Peña had finally escaped from him, he was told
to leave the division of Dessolles at Guadalajara and Siguenza.
These forces were destined to keep open the communications between
Madrid and Aragon, where the siege of Saragossa was just about
to begin.   With his other two divisions, those of Marchand and
Maurice Mathieu [3], Ney was directed to march into Madrid: he
was to form part of the mass of troops which the Emperor was
collecting, in and about the capital, for new offensive operations.
For this same purpose the 4th Corps, that of Lefebvre, was brought
up from Old Castile: the Marshal with his two leading divisions,
those of Sebastiani and Leval, arrived in Madrid on December 9:
his third division, that of Valence, composed of Poles, was some
way to the rear, having only reached Burgos on December 1.   But

---

[1] *Nap. Corresp.*, 14,525.

[2] I cannot speak for certain as to the moment at which Digeon's brigade of
dragoons, which had been lent to Lannes for the Tudela campaign, rejoined
Latour-Maubourg.   But probably it came across with Ney, as it was with its
division by Dec. 28 (Jourdan's *Mémoires*, p. 138).

[3] The latter had taken over Lagrange's division after Tudela.

by the thirteenth the whole corps was concentrated at Madrid.
A few days later the divisions of Sebastiani and Valence were
pushed on to Talavera, as if to form the advanced guard of an
expedition against Estremadura, while that of Leval remained in
Madrid[1]. Talavera had been occupied, before the Duke of Dantzig's
arrival, by the cavalry of Lasalle and Milhaud, who drove out of
it without difficulty the demoralized troops that had murdered
San Juan. This mob, now under the orders of Galluzzo, the
Captain-General of Estremadura, fled behind the Tagus and barricaded the bridges of Arzobispo and Almaraz, to cover its front.

It will thus be seen that the troops of Victor, Lefebvre, and
Dessolles, with the cavalry of Latour-Maubourg, Lasalle, and
Milhaud thrown out in front of them, formed a semicircle pro-
tecting Madrid to the east, the south, and the south-west. On the
north-west, in the direction of the Guadarrama and the roads
towards the kingdom of Leon, the circle was completed by a
brigade of Lahoussaye's division of dragoons, who lay in and
about Avila[2]. In the centre, available for a blow in any direction,
were the whole of the Imperial Guard (horse and foot), Ney's corps,
Lapisse's division of Victor's corps, and Leval's division of Lefebvre's
corps, besides King Joseph's Guards—a total of at least 40,000 men.
It only needed the word to be given, and these troops (after deducting a garrison for Madrid) could march forward, either to join
Lefebvre for a blow at Lisbon, or Victor for a blow at Seville.

Meanwhile there were still reinforcements coming up from the
rear: the belated corps of Mortier, the last great instalment of the
army of Germany, had at last reached Vittoria, accompanied by
the division of dragoons of Lorges. The Marshal was directed to
take his corps to Saragossa, in order to assist Lannes and Moncey
in the siege of that city; but the dragoons were sent to Burgos on
the road to Madrid. Moreover Junot's corps, after having been
refitted and reorganized since its return from Portugal, was also
available. Its leading division, that of Delaborde, had crossed the
Bidassoa on December 4, and had now reached Burgos. The other
two divisions, those of Loison and Heudelet (who had replaced
Travot at the head of the 3rd Division) were not far behind. They

---

[1] This division was incomplete, having left behind in Biscay two Dutch
and one German battalions.

[2] The other brigade was astray near Toledo, contrary to the Emperor's
intention : *Nap. Corresp.*, 14,594, orders it to march on Talavera.

could all be brought up to Madrid by the first day of January. The last division of reserve cavalry, Millet's four regiments of dragoons, was due a little later, and had not yet crossed the frontier.

That the Emperor believed that there was no serious danger to be apprehended from the side of Leon and Old Castile, is shown by the fact that he allotted to these regions only the single corps of Soult. Nor had the Duke of Dalmatia even the whole of his troops in hand, for the division of Bonnet was immobilized in Santander, and only those of Merle and Mermet were near his head quarters at Carrion. The cavalry that properly belonged to his corps were detached, under Lasalle, in New Castile. Instead of them he had been assigned the four regiments forming the division of Franceschi[1]. He was promised the aid of Millet's dragoons when they should arrive, but this would not be for some three weeks at the least. Nevertheless, with the 15,000 foot and 1,800 or 2,000 light cavalry at his disposal, Soult was told that he commanded everything from the Douro to the Bay of Biscay, and that he might advance at once into Leon, as there was nothing in his way that could withstand him[2]. As far as the Emperor knew, the only hostile force in this direction was the miserable wreck of Blake's army, which had been rallied by La Romana on the Esla. In making this supposition he was gravely mistaken, and if Soult had obeyed his orders without delay, and advanced westward from Carrion, he would have found himself in serious trouble; for, as we shall presently see, the English from Salamanca were in full march against him at the moment when the Emperor dispatched these instructions. It was in the valley of the Douro, and not (as Bonaparte intended) in that of the Tagus that the next developments of the winter campaign of 1808 were to take place.

It remains only to speak of the north-east. The Emperor was determined that Saragossa should pay dearly for the renown that

---

[1] 8th Dragoons, 22nd Chasseurs, 1st Supplementary regiment of Chasseurs, and Hanoverian Chasseurs.

[2] Cf. *Nap. Corresp.*, 14,581 (of Dec. 10, 1808, but wrongly dated Dec. 17 in the collection), the rough draft of the dispatch to be sent to Soult, with the full document, which was fortunately captured on its way to Carrion, and fell into the hands of Sir John Moore. It is printed in the original French in James Moore's account of his brother's campaign (London, 1809). The documents tally accurately, but Berthier has expanded, as was his wont, Napoleon's short phrases.

it had won during its first siege. He directed against it not only Moncey's force, the troops which had won Tudela, but the whole of Mortier's 5th Corps. One of its divisions was to take post at Calatayud, relieving Musnier's eight battalions at that point, and to keep open (with the aid of Dessolles) the road from Saragossa to Madrid: but the rest would be available to aid in the siege. More than 40,000 men were to be turned against Palafox and the stubborn Aragonese. With Catalonia we need not deal in this place: the operations in the principality had little or no connexion with those in the rest of Spain. St. Cyr and Duhesme, with the 7th Corps, had to work out their own salvation. They were not to expect help from the Emperor, nor on the other hand were they expected to assist him for the present, though it was hoped that some day they might invade Aragon from the side of Lerida.

Looking at the disposition of the French troops on December 15–20, we can see that the Emperor had it in his power to push the central mass at Madrid, supported by the oncoming reserves under Junot and Lorges, either to support Lefebvre on the road to Lisbon, or Victor on the road to Seville. As a matter of fact there can be no doubt that the former was his intention. He was fully under the impression that the English army was at this moment executing a hasty retreat upon Portugal, and he had announced that his next move was to hurl them into the sea. 'Tout porte à penser que les Anglais sont en pleine marche rétrograde,' he wrote to Soult on December 10. On December 12 he issued in his *Bulletin* the statement that the 'English are in full flight towards Lisbon, and if they do not make good speed the French army may enter that capital before them [1].' If anything was wanted to confirm the Emperor in his idea that the English were not likely to be heard of in the north, it was the capture by Lasalle's cavalry of eight stragglers belonging to the King's German Legion near Talavera. 'When we catch Hanoverians the English cannot be far off,' he observed [2], and made all his arrangements on the hypothesis that

[1] See the statement in the *Madrid Gazette* for Dec. 12 (p. 1576). It is not in the *Correspondance de Napoléon,* and contains invaluable details as to the placing of the French army on that day.

[2] 'Le général Lasalle a pris huit Hanovriens . . . Puisqu'il a pris des Hanovriens, cela sent la proximité des Anglais' (*Nap. Corresp.,* 14,551, Dec. 12). These must have been stragglers from Hope's division, which had passed Talavera at least a fortnight before. The Germans with it were the 3rd Light Dragoons, K.G.L.

Moore would be met in the valley of the Tagus, and not in that of
the Douro. In so doing he was breaking one of his own precepts,
that censuring generals 'qui se font des tableaux' concerning their
enemy's position and intentions, before they have sufficient data
upon which to form a sound conclusion. All that he really knew
about Moore and his army was that they had reached Salamanca
in the middle of November, and had been joined towards the end
of the month by Hope's column that marched—as we shall presently
relate—via Badajoz and the Escurial. Of the existence of this last
division we have clear proof that Bonaparte was aware, for he
inserted a silly taunt in the *Bulletin* of December 5 to the effect
that 'the conduct of the British had been dishonourable. Six
thousand of them were at the Escurial on November 20 : the
Spaniards hoped that they would aid in the defence of the capital
of their allies. But they did not know the English : as soon as the
latter heard that the Emperor was at the Somosierra they beat
a retreat, joined the division at Salamanca, and retired towards the
sea-coast.' There is also no doubt that the Emperor had received
intelligence of a more or less definite sort concerning the landing
of Baird's division at Corunna. It is vaguely alluded to in the
10th *Bulletin*, and clearly spoken of in the *Madrid Gazette* of
December 17 [1]. But though aware of the existence of all the three
fractions of the British army, Bonaparte could draw no other
deduction from the facts at his disposal than that the whole of
them would promptly retreat to Portugal, when the passage of the
Somosierra and the fall of Madrid became known to their commander-in-chief. Lisbon, he thought, must be their base of
operations, and on it they must retire : he had forgotten that one
of the advantages of sea-power is that the combatant who possesses
it can transfer his base to any port that he may choose. So far
from being tied to Lisbon was Moore, that he at one moment
contemplated making Cadiz his base, and finally moved it to
Corunna.

[1] Napoleon seems to have got the knowledge of Baird's arrival from the
London newspapers. An English brigantine, called the *Ferret*, ran into
Santander, under the impression that it was still in Spanish hands. On
board were many journals, with details about the Cintra Court of Inquiry,
and about the reinforcements for Spain. Long extracts from them were
reprinted in the *Madrid Gazette* for the second half of December. The
danger of the press already existed !

With preconceived ideas of this sort in his head, the Emperor was preparing to push on his main body in support of the advanced troops under Lefebvre and Lasalle on the road to Estremadura and Portugal. Victor meanwhile was to guard against the unlikely chance of any move being made on Madrid by the shattered 'Army of the Centre' from Cuenca, or by new Andalusian levies. Already Lasalle's horsemen were pushing on to Truxillo and Plasencia, almost to the gates of Badajoz and to the Portuguese frontier, when unexpected news arrived, and the whole plan of campaign was upset.

Instead of retiring on Lisbon, Sir John Moore had pushed forward into the plains of Old Castile, and was advancing by forced marches to attack the isolated corps of Marshal Soult. Bonaparte was keenly alive, now as always, to the danger of a defeat in the valley of the Douro. Moreover the sight of a British army in the field, and within striking distance, acted on him as the red rag acts upon the bull. No toil or trouble would be too great that ended in its destruction, and looking at his maps the Emperor thought that he saw the way to surround and annihilate Moore's host. Throwing up without a moment's delay the whole plan for the invasion of Portugal, he marched for the passes of the Guadarrama with every man that was disposable at Madrid. His spirits were high, and the event seemed to him certain. He sent back to his brother Joseph the command to put in the Madrid newspapers and circulate everywhere the news that 36,000 English troops were surrounded and doomed to destruction[1]. Meanwhile, with 50,000 men at his back, he was marching hard for Arevalo and Benavente.

---

[1] I know no better way of displaying the Napoleonesque method than the printing opposite each other of his dispatches 14,620 and 14,626, both addressed to Joseph Bonaparte. For the benefit of the newspapers the English army was to be overstated by 10,000 or 12,000 men!

14,620.	14,626.
Faites mettre dans les journaux et répandre partout que 36,000 Anglais sont cernés. Je suis sur leurs derrières tandis que le maréchal Soult est devant eux.	Leur force *réelle* est de 20,000 à 21,000 infanterie, et de 4,000 à 5,000 de cavalerie avec une quarantaine de pièces de canon.

SECTION VIII: CHAPTER II

MOORE AT SALAMANCA

IT will be remembered that on October 6, 1808, the command of the British forces in Portugal had passed into the hands of Sir John Moore, to the entire satisfaction of Wellesley and the other officers who had served under those slow and cautious generals Sir Hew Dalrymple and Sir Harry Burrard. The moment that the news of Vimiero was received, and long before the details of the Convention of Cintra could come to hand, the Government had determined to send on the victorious British army into Spain, and to assist it with heavy reinforcements from home. Dalrymple was even informed that he might cross the frontier at once, if he chose, without waiting for any detailed instructions from the War Office[1]. Wellesley, as we have seen, thought that his chief should have done so without delay, and observed that if *he* had charge of affairs the army would be at Madrid by October 1[2].

Yet when Moore took over the command, he found that little or nothing had been done to carry out this design. The delay was partly occasioned by the tardy evacuation of Portugal by Junot's troops : the last of them, as we have seen[3], did not leave the Tagus till the month of October had begun. But it was still more due to the leisurely and feeble management of Dalrymple, who would not march without detailed and definite orders from home. He might well have begun to move his brigades eastward

---

[1] Castlereagh to Dalrymple, Sept. 2, 1808 : ' As circumstances may come to your knowledge which might render the immediate employment of your disposable forces in the north of Spain of the utmost importance to the common cause, without waiting for orders from hence, I am to inform you that you should not consider the present instructions as depriving you of the latitude of discretion which you now possess, without waiting for express orders from hence.'

[2] See p. 274.

[3] See p. 283, dealing with the garrison of Elvas.

long before the last small detachments of the French had disappeared. But when on October 6 Dalrymple's successor looked
around him, he found that the whole army was still concentrated
in the neighbourhood of Lisbon, save Hope's two brigades, and
these had been sent forward to the frontier not so much for the
purpose of entering Spain, as for that of bringing moral force to
bear on General Galluzzo, and compelling him to abandon his
ridiculous siege of Elvas. Two things had been especially neglected
by Dalrymple—the exploration of the roads that lead from Portugal into Spain, and the pressing on of the formation of a proper
divisional and regimental transport for the army. It is strange
to find that he had remembered the existence of both of these
needs : his dispatches speak of his intention to send officers both
towards Badajoz and into Beira, and he asserts that 'the army
is in high order and fit to move when required[1].' Yet his
successor had to state that as a matter of fact no body of information about the routes and resources of Portugal and Spain had
been collected, and that the scheme for moving and feeding the
army had not been drawn up. 'When I shall pass the frontier
of Portugal,' wrote Moore to Castlereagh, 'it is impossible for me
at this instant to say : it depends on a knowledge of the country
which I am still without, and on commissariat arrangements yet
unmade[2].' We may grant that Dalrymple had been somewhat
handicapped by the fact that his army had been landed, in the
old haphazard British fashion, without any proper military train.
We may also concede that no one could have foreseen that the
Portuguese and Spanish governments would be unable to supply
any useful information concerning the main roads and the resources
of their own countries. But the whole month of September had
been at the disposal of the late commander-in-chief, and he, with
his quartermaster-general, Murray, must take the blame of having
failed to accomplish in it all that might have been done. Within
a fortnight after the Convention of Cintra had been signed, British
officers ought to have explored every road to the frontier, and to
have reported on their facilities. Yet on October 6 Moore could
not find any one who could tell him whether the roads Lisbon—
Sabugal—Almeida, and Lisbon—Abrantes—Castello Branco were
or were not practicable for artillery ! And this was in spite of the

[1] Dalrymple to Castlereagh, Sept. 27.
[2] Moore to Castlereagh from Lisbon, Oct. 9, 1808.

fact that a British detachment had actually marched from Lisbon
to Almeida, in order to receive the surrender of the garrison of
that fortress.   The fact would seem to be that Dalrymple had
placed his confidence in the native governments of the Peninsula.
He vainly imagined that the Portuguese engineers could supply
him with accurate details concerning the roads and resources of
Beira and the Alemtejo.   He sent a very capable officer—Lord
William Bentinck—to Madrid, and entered into communication
with the Spanish government.   From them he hoped that he
might get some account of the plan of campaign in which his
army was to join, a list of the routes which it would be convenient
for him to use, and details as to the way in which he could collect
and carry provisions.   As a matter of fact he could only obtain
a quantity of vague and generally useless suggestions, some of
which argued an astonishing ignorance of military affairs in those
who made them.   If there had been a Spanish commander-in-chief,
Dalrymple might have extracted from him his views about the
campaign that must shortly begin.   But the Junta had steadfastly
refused to unite the charge of their many armies in the hands of
a single general: they told Lord William that he might make
inquiries from Castaños: but the Andalusian general could only
speak for himself.   It was not he, but a council of war, that would
settle the plan of operations: he could only give Bentinck the
conclusions that had been arrived at after the abortive meeting
of generals that had taken place on September 5.   In answer to
a string of questions administered to him by Dalrymple's emissary,
as to the routes that the British army had better follow, and the
methods of supply that it had better adopt, he could only reply
that he was at present without good maps, and could not give
the necessary information in detail.   He could only refer Bentinck
to the newly formed Commissariat Board (*Junta de Víveres*), which
ought to be able to designate the best routes with reference to the
feeding of the army and the establishment of magazines [1].   Of
course this board turned out to know even less than Castaños
himself.   Nothing whatever was done for the British army, with
the exception that a certain Colonel Lopez was sent to its head
quarters to act as the representative of the *Junta de Víveres*.   It
does not seem that he was able to do anything for the expeditionary

---

[1] The very interesting (and sometimes very sensible) replies of Castaños to
Bentinck will be found in the latter's letter to Dalrymple (Oct. 2).

force that they could not have done for themselves. In this way
the whole time that Dalrymple had at his disposal had been wasted
in the long correspondence with Madrid, and not a soldier had
passed the frontier when Moore took up the command.

Meanwhile, it ought at least to have been possible to make
preparations in Portugal, even if nothing could be done in Spain.
But the question of transport and commissariat was a very difficult
one. The British army had struggled from Mondego Bay to
Lisbon with the aid of the small ox-wagons of the country-side,
requisitioned and dismissed from village to village. But clearly
a long campaign in Spain could not be managed on these lines.
A permanent provision of draught and pack animals was required,
and natives must be hired to drive them. The few regular enlisted
men of the Royal Wagon Train who had reached Portugal were
only enough to take care of the more important military stores.
Moreover their wagons turned out to be much too heavy for the
roads of the Peninsula, and had to be gradually replaced by
country carts[1]. The great mass of the regimental baggage and
the food had always to be transported on mules, or vehicles bought
or hired from the peasantry. The Portuguese did not care to
contract to take their animals over the frontier, and it was most
difficult to collect transport of any kind, even with the aid of the
local authorities. When once Moore's dreadful retreat began, his
drivers and muleteers deserted their wagons and beasts, and fled
home, resolved that if they must lose their property they would
not lose their lives also[2].

In later years Wellington gradually succeeded in collecting a large
and invaluable army of Spanish and Portuguese employés, who—in
their own fashion—were as good campaigners as his soldiery, and
served him with exemplary fidelity even when their pay was many
months in arrear. But in 1808 this body of trained camp-followers
did not exist, and Moore had the greatest difficulty in scraping
together the transport that took him forward to Salamanca. As
to commissariat arrangements, he found that even though he

---

[1] Moore to Castlereagh from Salamanca, Dec. 10, 1808.
[2] A good account of the difficulties of transport in Moore's army will be
found in Quartermaster Surtees's *Twenty-five Years in the Rifle Brigade*. Placed
in charge of the baggage and beasts of the 2/95th, he found it absolutely
impossible to keep the native drivers from absconding, even when they had
to sacrifice their beasts to do so (pages 81–82).

divided his army into several small columns, and utilized as many separate routes as possible, it was not easy for the troops to live. The commissariat officers, sent on to collect magazines at the various halting-places, were so inexperienced and so uniformly ignorant of the Portuguese tongue, that even where they were energetic they had the greatest difficulty in catering for the army. Wellesley, as we have already seen [1], had been complaining bitterly of their inefficiency during the short Vimiero campaign. Moore, more gracious in his phrases, wrote that 'we have a Commissariat extremely zealous, but quite new and inexperienced in the important duties which it falls to their lot to perform.' This was but one of the many penalties which England had to pay for her long abstention from continental warfare on a large scale. It is easy to blame the ministry, the permanent officials in London, or the executive officials on the spot [1]. But in reality mere want of knowledge of the needs of a great land-war accounts for most of the mistakes that were committed. To lavish angry criticism on individuals, as did the Opposition papers in England at the time, was almost as unjust as it was useless. The art of war, in this as in its other branches, had to be learnt; it was not possible to pick it up by intuition. Nothing can be more interesting than to look through the long series of orders and directions drawn up by the quartermaster-general's department between 1809 and 1813, in which the gradual evolution of order out of chaos by dint of practical experience can be traced. But in October, 1808, the process was yet in its infancy.

It was with the greatest difficulty, therefore, that Moore got his army under weigh. He found it, as he wrote to Castlereagh, 'without equipment of any kind, either for the carriage of the light baggage of regiments, artillery stores, commissariat stores, or any other appendage of an army, and without a magazine formed on any of the routes by which we are to march [2].' Within ten days, however, the whole force was on the move. The heavy impedimenta were placed in store in Lisbon: it was a thousand pities that the troops did not leave behind their women and children, whose presence with the regiments was destined to cause so many harrowing scenes during the forced marches of the ensuing winter. They were offered a passage to England, but the greater part

[1] See p. 231.   [2] Moore to Castlereagh, Oct. 9, 1808.

refused it, and the colonels (from mistaken kindness) generally allowed them to march with their corps.

The direction in which the army was to move had been settled in a general way by the dispatches sent from Castlereagh to Dalrymple in September [1]. It was to be held together in a single mass and sent forward to the Ebro, there to be put in line with Blake and Castaños. An attempt on the part of the Junta to distract part of it to Catalonia had been firmly and very wisely rejected. The French were still on the defensive when the plan was drawn out, and Burgos had been named as the point at which the British troops might aim. It was very close to the enemy, but in September neither English nor Spanish statesmen were taking into consideration the probability of the advent of the Emperor, and his immediate assumption of the offensive. They were rather dreaming of an advance towards the Pyrenees by the allied armies. If the large reinforcements which were promised to Moore were destined to land at Corunna, rather than at Gihon or Santander, it was merely because these latter ports were known to be small and destitute of resources, not because they were considered to be dangerously near to the French. La Romana's division, it will be remembered, was actually put ashore at Santander: it is quite possible that Sir David Baird's troops might have been sent to the same destination, but for the fortunate fact that it was believed that it would be impossible to supply him with transport from the bare and rugged region of the Montaña. Corunna was selected as the landing-place for all the regiments that were to join Moore, partly on account of its safe and spacious port, partly because it was believed that food and draught animals could be collected with comparative ease from Galicia.

More than 12,000 men, including three regiments of cavalry (the arm in which the force in Portugal was most deficient) and a brigade of the Guards, had been drawn from the home garrisons. The charge of this fine division had been given to Sir David Baird [2], an officer with a great Indian reputation, but comparatively un-

---

[1] Castlereagh to Dalrymple, Sept. 2, 1808.

[2] It is fair to this distinguished officer to state that his dispatches and letters show no trace whatever of the irascible and impracticable temper that has been attributed to him. They are most sensible, cautious, and prudent, and not at all what might have been expected from the hero of the story of 'the lad that was chained to our Davie.'

practised in European warfare. They were embarked at Harwich, Portsmouth, Ramsgate, and Cork at various dates during September and October, and on the thirteenth of the latter month the main body of the force reached Corunna. By some stupid mismanagement at home the cavalry, the most important part of the expedition, were shipped off the last, and did not arrive till three weeks [1] after the rest of the troops had reached Spain.

By October 18 Moore reported that the greater part of his troops were already in motion, and as Baird's infantry had reached Corunna on the thirteenth, it might have been expected that the junction of their forces would have taken place in time to enable them to play a part in the defensive campaign against Napoleon which ended in the fall of Madrid on December 4. If the troops had marched promptly, and by the best and shortest routes, they might have easily concentrated at Salamanca by the middle of November : Napier suggests the thirteenth [2] as a probable day, and considering the distances the date seems a very reasonable one. At that moment Gamonal and Espinosa had only just been fought and lost: Tudela was yet ten days in the future: sixteen days were to elapse before the Somosierra was forced. It is clear that the British army, which at Salamanca would have been only seven marches (150 miles) from Madrid, and four marches (eighty miles) from Valladolid, might have intervened in the struggle : whether its intervention might not have ended in disaster, considering the enormous forces of the French [3], is another matter. But the British Government intended that Moore and Baird should take part in the campaign : the Junta had been told to expect their help : and for the consolidation of the alliance between the two nations it was desirable that the help should be given in the most prompt and effective fashion.

There is no possibility of asserting that this was done. Moore and Baird did not join till December 20 : no British soldier fired a single shot at a Frenchman before December 12 [4]. The whole

[1] The 7th and 10th Hussars apparently on Nov. 7, the 15th Hussars on Nov. 12. See Baird to Castlereagh, Nov. 8 and 13, 1808.

[2] Napier, i. 347.

[3] It is to be remembered that Baird's cavalry would not have been up till Nov. 20-25, owing to its tardy start from England. Nothing could have been more unlucky.

[4] At the skirmish at Rueda on that date.

army was so much out of the campaign that Bonaparte never could learn what had become of it, and formed the most erroneous hypotheses concerning its position and intentions. We may frankly say that not one of his movements, down to the fall of Madrid, was in the least influenced by the fact that there was a British force in Spain.

That this circumstance was most unfortunate from the political point of view it would be childish to deny. It gave discontented Spaniards the opportunity of asserting that they had been deserted and betrayed by their allies[1]. It afforded Bonaparte the chance, which he did not fail to take, of enlarging upon the invariable selfishness and timidity of the British[2]. It furnished the critics of the ministry in London with a text for declamations against the imbecility of its arrangements. It is true that after the fall of Madrid Moore was enabled, by the new situation of affairs, to make that demonstration against the French lines of communication in Castile which wrecked Napoleon's original plan of campaign, and saved Lisbon and Seville. But this tardy though effective intervention in the struggle was a mere afterthought. Moore's original plan had been to make a tame retreat on Lisbon, when he discovered that he was too late to save Madrid. It was a mere chance that an intercepted dispatch and an unfounded rumour caused him to throw up the idea of retiring into Portugal, and to strike at the Emperor's flank and rear by his famous march on Sahagun. Without this piece of good fortune he would never have repaired the mischief caused by the lateness of his original arrival on the scene. How that late arrival came to pass it is now our duty to investigate.

As far as Moore's own army was concerned, the loss of time may be ascribed to a single cause—a mistake made in the choice of the roads by which the advance into Spain was conducted. It was the original intention of the British general to march on Almeida and Ciudad Rodrigo by three parallel routes, those by Coimbra and Celorico, by Abrantes, Castello Branco, and Guarda, and by Elvas, Alcantara, and Coria[3]. He was compelled to utilize

[1] See the letters from Spanish officers in the *Madrid Gazette* for Dec. 19, 1808.

[2] See the Dec. 5 *Bulletin*, and the inspired articles in the *Madrid Gazette* for Dec. 14.

[3] Moore to Castlereagh, Oct. 9: 'The march from this will be by the three roads Coimbra, Guarda, and Alcantara.'

the last-named road, which was rather circuitous and notoriously bad, by the fact that Dalrymple had left Hope's two brigades at Elvas, and that any advance from that place into the kingdom of Leon could only be directed across the bridge of Alcantara. If Moore had stuck to this original resolve, and used none but these three roads, his army might have been concentrated at Salamanca on or about November 13. This could have been done with ease if all the reserve artillery and heavy baggage had taken the Coimbra—Celorico road, the easiest of the three, and nothing but an irreducible minimum had been allowed to follow the columns which went by the other routes. It would have been necessary also to move the troops in masses of not less than a brigade, and to keep them well closed up.

Moore had the best intentions: he cut down the baggage to what he considered the smallest practicable bulk, and started off the leading regiments on the Coimbra route as easily as October 11, two days after he had taken over the command[1]. 'I am sufficiently aware,' he wrote, ' of the importance of even the name of a British army in Spain, and I am hurrying as much as possible[2].' Then followed an irreparable mistake: it was all-important to find out which of the roads was most suitable for artillery and heavy baggage. Moore consulted the available officers of the old Portuguese army, and received from them the almost incredibly erroneous information that neither the Coimbra—Celorico—Almeida road nor the Abrantes—Guarda—Almeida road was practicable for artillery. It would seem that he also sought information from the officers whom Dalrymple had sent out into the province of Beira, and that their answers tallied with those of the Portuguese[3], for he wrote to Castlereagh that 'every information agreed that neither of them was fit for artillery or could be recommended for cavalry.' General Anstruther, then in command at Almeida, must take a considerable share in the blame that has to be distributed to those who failed to give the Commander-in-chief accurate information,

---

[1] Moore to Castlereagh, Oct. 9.

[2] Ibid., Oct. 11.

[3] Moore also consulted Colonel Lopez, the Spanish officer who had been sent to his head quarters by the Junta, as being specially skilled in roads and topography. But Lopez disclaimed any knowledge, and could only say that Junot's artillery had been nearly ruined by the roads between Ciudad Rodrigo and Abrantes.

for he more than any one else had been given the chance of trying
these roads. But whatever may be the proportion in which the
censure must be distributed, a certain amount must be reserved
for Moore himself. He ought on first principles to have refused
to believe the strange news that was brought to him. It might
have occurred to him to ask how heavy guns of position had found
their way to the ramparts of Almeida, the second fortress of
Portugal, if there was no practicable road leading to it. A few
minutes spent in consulting any book dealing with Portuguese
history would have shown that in the great wars of the Spanish
Succession, and again in that of 1762[1], forces of all arms had
moved freely up and down the Spanish frontier, in the direction
of Celorica, Guarda, Sabugal, and Castello Branco. Even a glance
at Dumouriez's *Account of the Kingdom of Portugal*, the one
modern military book on the subject then available, would have
enabled Moore to correct the ignorant reports of the natives.
Strangest of all, there seems to have been no one to tell him that,
only four months before, Loison, in his campaign against the
insurgents of Beira, had taken guns first from Lisbon to Almeida,
then from Almeida to Pezo de Ragoa and Vizeu, and finally from
Almeida to Abrantes[2]. It is simply astounding that no one seems
to have remembered this simple fact. In short, it was not easily
pardonable in any competent general that he should accept as
possible the statement that there was no road for artillery connecting the capital of Portugal and the main stronghold of its
north-eastern frontier. Moore did so, and in a fortnight was
bitterly regretting his credulity. 'If anything adverse happens,'
he wrote to his subordinate Hope, 'I have not necessity to plead:
the road we are now travelling [Abrantes—Villa Velha—Guarda]
is practicable for artillery': the brigade under Wilmot has already
reached Guarda, and as far as I have already seen the road presents few obstacles, and those easily surmounted. This knowledge
was only acquired by our own officers: when the brigade was at
Castello Branco, it was still not certain that it could proceed[3].'

[1] e.g. in 1706 Lord Galway took over forty guns, twelve of which were
heavy siege-pieces, from Elvas by Alcantara and Coria to Ciudad Rodrigo.
In 1762 the Spaniards took no less than ninety guns from Ciudad Rodrigo by
Celorico and Sabugal to Castello Branco, and thence back into Spain.

[2] Napier does not seem to know this, and distinctly states (i. 102) that
Loison had no guns.

[3] Moore to Hope, from Almeida, Nov. 8.

What made the case worse was that another of the three roads, the one by Coimbra and Celorico, was far easier than that by Guarda. Both Wellesley and Masséna took enormous trains of artillery and baggage over it in 1810, without any particular difficulty[1].

Misled by the erroneous reports as to the impracticability of the Portuguese roads, Moore took the unhappy step of sending six of the seven batteries of his corps, his only two cavalry regiments, and four battalions of infantry to act as escort[2], by the circuitous high-road from Elvas to Madrid. In order to reach Salamanca they were to advance almost to the gates of the Spanish capital, only turning off at Talavera, in order to take the route by the Escurial, Espinar, and Arevalo. To show the result of this lamentable divagation, it is only necessary to remark that from Lisbon to Salamanca via Coimbra is about 250 miles: from Lisbon to Salamanca via Elvas, Talavera, and Arevalo is about 380 miles: i. e. it was certain that the column containing all Moore's cavalry and nearly all his guns would be at least seven or eight days late at the rendezvous, in a crisis when every moment was of vital importance. As a matter of fact the head of the main column reached Salamanca on November 13 : the cavalry and guns turned up on December 4. It would not be fair, however, to say that the absence of Hope's column delayed the advance of the whole army for so much as three weeks. It was only the leading regiments from Lisbon that appeared on November 13. However carefully the march of the rest had been arranged, the rear could not have come in till several days later: indeed the last brigade did not appear till the twenty-third: this delay, however, was owing to bad arrangements and preventable accidents. But it cannot be denied that the twelve days Nov. 23—Dec. 4 were completely sacrificed by the non-arrival of the cavalry and guns, without which Moore very wisely refused to move forward. If the army had been concentrated—Baird could easily have arrived from Corunna ere this—it would have been able to advance on November 23, and the campaign would undoubtedly have been modified

---

[1] In endeavouring to excuse Moore, Napier takes the strange course of making out that the Guarda road, though usable, as experience showed, was 'in a military sense, non-practicable' from its difficulties. This will not stand in face of Moore's words quoted above. Of the Coimbra—Celorico road he omits all mention (i. 345).

[2] These were the 2nd, 36th, 71st, and 92nd Foot.

in its character, for the Emperor would have learnt of the arrival of Moore upon the scene some days before he crossed the Somo-sierra and started on his march for Madrid.   There can be no doubt that he would have changed his plans on receiving such news, for the sight of a British army within striking distance would have caused him to turn aside at once with a large part of his army.   Very probably he might have directed Lefebvre, Victor, and the Imperial Guard—all the disposable forces under his hand—against Moore, and have left Madrid alone for the present as a mere secondary object.   It is impossible to deny that disaster to the British arms might have followed: on the other hand Moore was a cautious general, as his operations in December showed.   He would probably have retired at once to the mountains, and left the Emperor a fruitless stern-chase, such as that which actually took place a month later.   But whether he would have fallen back on the route to Portugal, or on the route to Galicia, it is impossible to say: everything would have depended on the exact development of Napoleon's advance, but the first-named alternative is the more probable[1].

[1] Napier has a long note, in justification of Moore, to the effect that if the concentration point of the British army had been Burgos instead of Salamanca, Hope's detour would have cost no waste of time, and would have been rather profitable than otherwise.   But Moore distinctly looked upon the movement as a deplorable necessity, not as a proper strategical proceeding. ' It is a great round,' he wrote to Castlereagh on October 27, when announcing this modification of his original plan, ' and will separate the corps, for a time, from the rest of the army : *but there is no help for it.*'   Moreover he stated, in this same letter, that he would not move forward an inch from Salamanca till Hope should have reached Espinar, on the northern side of the Guadar-rama Pass.   At a later date he announced that he should not advance till Hope had got even nearer to him, and made his way as far as Arevalo [letter of Nov. 24].   He was too good a general to dream of a concentration at Burgos, when once he had ascertained the relative positions of the Spanish and the French armies, for that place was within a couple of marches of the enemy's outposts at Miranda and Logroño.   There is, in short, no way of justifying Hope's circular march, when once it is granted that the roads of Northern Portugal were not impracticable for artillery.   Moore knew this perfectly well, as his letter to Hope, which we have quoted on p. 495 shows. No arguments are worth anything in his justification when he himself writes ' if anything adverse happens, I have not necessity to plead.'   This is the language of an honest man, conscious that he has made a mistake, and prepared to take the responsibility.   Napier's apology for him (i. 345-7) is but ingenious and eloquent casuistry.

The erroneous direction given to Moore's cavalry and guns, however, was not the only reason for the late appearance of the British army upon the theatre of war. Almost as much delay was caused by a piece of egregious folly and procrastination, for which the Spaniards were wholly responsible. When Sir David Baird and the bulk of his great convoy arrived in the harbour of Corunna on October 13, he was astonished to find that the Junta of Galicia raised serious objections to allowing him to land. Their real reason for so doing was that they wished the British troops to disembark further east, at Gihon or Santander. They did not realize the military danger of throwing them ashore in places so close to the French army, nor did it affect them in the least when they were told that the equipment of Baird's force in those barren regions would be almost impossible. All that they cared for was to preserve Galicia from the strain of having to make provisions for the feeding and transport of a second army, when all its resources had been sorely tried in supplying (and supplying most indifferently) the troops of Blake. They did not, however, make mention of their real objections to Baird's disembarkation in their correspondence with him, but assumed an attitude of very suspicious humility, stating that they considered their functions to have come to an end now that the Central Junta had met, and that they thought it beyond their competence to give consent to the landing of such a large body of men without explicit directions from Aranjuez. Baird could not offer to land by force, in face of this opposition. He did not, however, move off to Santander (as the Galicians had hoped), but insisted that an officer should be promptly dispatched to the Supreme Junta. This was done, but the delay in receiving an answer was so great that thirteen days were wasted: the Galician officer bearing the consent of the central government travelled (so Moore complained) with the greatest deliberation, as if he were carrying an unimportant message in full time of peace [1]. The first regiments, therefore, only landed on October 26, and it was not till November 4 that all the infantry were ashore. Thus they were certain to be late at the rendezvous in the plains of Leon. Nor was this all: the Supreme Junta had suggested that, in order to facilitate the feeding of the division, Baird should send it forward not in large masses but in bodies of 2,000 men, with a considerable interval between them.

---

[1] Moore to Bentinck from Salamanca, Nov. 13, 1808.

The advice was taken, and in consequence the troops were soon spread out over the whole length of road between Corunna and Astorga. The greatest difficulty was found in equipping them for the march: Galicia, always a poor country, had been almost stripped of mules and carts to supply Blake. It was absolutely impossible to procure a sufficient train for the transport of Baird's food and baggage. He was only able to gather enough beasts to carry his lighter impedimenta from stage to stage, by the offer of exorbitant rates of hire. He vainly hoped to complete his equipment when he should have reached the plains. Part of his difficulties was caused by lack of money: the Government at home had not realized that only hard cash would circulate in Spain: dollars in abundance were to come out in the *Tigre* frigate in a few weeks: meanwhile it was expected that the Spaniards would gladly accept British Government bills. But so little was paper liked in the Peninsula that only £5,000 or £6,000 in dollars could be raised at Corunna [1]: without further resources it would have been impossible to begin to push the army forward. The feat was only accomplished by borrowing 92,000 dollars from the Galician Junta. For this act, carefully ignored by Napier, they deserve a proper recognition: it shows a much better spirit than might have been expected after their foolish behaviour about the disembarkation. Shortly after, Baird succeeded in getting £40,000 from Mr. Frere, the new minister to Madrid, who chanced to arrive at Corunna with £410,000 in cash destined for the Spanish government. Finally on November 9 the expected ship came in with the 500,000 dollars that had been originally intended to be divided between Corunna and Lisbon, and Baird had as much money as he could possibly require, even when mules and draught-oxen had risen to famine prices in Galicia [2]. If he still found it hard to move, it was because this poor and desolate province was really drained dry of resources [3].

[1] Baird to Castlereagh, Oct. 14, 1808.

[2] Napier knew the correspondence of Baird by heart. It is therefore most unfair in him to suppress the loan made by the Galician Junta, which appears in Sir David's letters of Oct. 22, 29, and Nov. 13, as also the receipt of the 500,000 dollars sent by the British Government in the *Tigre*, which is acknowledged in the letter of Nov. 9. He implies that the only sums received were £40,000 from Mr. Frere and £8,000 from Sir John Moore. The simple fact is that no good act done by a Spanish Junta or a Tory minister is ever acknowledged by Napier.

[3] After reading Sir Charles Vaughan's diary, showing how hard he and

But what between the Junta's folly in hindering the landing of the troops, and the unfortunate lack of money in the second half of October, all-important time was lost. Baird ought to have been near Salamanca by November 13: as a matter of fact he had only reached Astorga with three brigades of infantry and some artillery, but without a single mounted man to cover his march, on November 22. There he received, to his infinite dismay, the news that Blake had been routed at Espinosa on November 11, and Belvedere at Gamonal on November 10. There was now no Spanish army between him and the French : the latter might be advancing, for all he knew, upon Leon. He heard of Soult being at Reynosa, and Lefebvre at Carrion : if they continued their advance westward, they would catch him, with the 9,000 infantry of the Corunna column, marching across their front on the way to Salamanca. Appalled at the prospect, he halted at Astorga, and, after sending news of his situation to Moore, began to prepare to retreat on Corunna, if the marshals should continue their movement in his direction. This, as we have already seen, they did not : Napoleon had no knowledge of the position of the British troops, and instead of ordering the dukes of Dalmatia and Dantzig to push westward, moved them both in a southerly direction. Soult came down to Sahagun and Carrion : Lefebvre, on being relieved by the 2nd Corps, moved on Madrid by way of Segovia. Thus Baird, left entirely unmolested, was in the end able to join Moore.

It is time to turn to the movements of that general. After sending off Sir John Hope on his unhappy circular march by Badajoz and the Escurial, he set out from Lisbon on October 26. He took with him the whole force in Portugal, save a single division which was left behind to protect Lisbon, Elvas, and Almeida while a new native army was being reorganized. This detachment was to be commanded by Sir John Cradock, who was just due from England : it comprised four battalions of the German Legion, a battalion each of the 9th, 27th, 29th, 31st, 40th, 45th, and 97th Foot, the wrecks of the 20th Light Dragoons, and six batteries of artillery—about 9,000 men in all. The rest,

Mr. Stuart found it to procure enough draught animals to take their small party from Corunna to Madrid, in September, 1808, I cannot doubt that by October the collecting of the transport for a whole army was an almost impossible task in Galicia.

twenty-five battalions of infantry, two cavalry regiments and seven batteries, marched for Spain. Two brigades under Beresford took the good road by Coimbra and Celorico to Almeida: three under Fraser went by Abrantes and Guarda, taking with them the single battery which Moore had retained with his main body, in order to try whether the roads of Eastern Portugal were as bad as his advisers had reported. Two brigades under General Paget, starting from Elvas, not from Lisbon, separated themselves from Hope and marched on Ciudad Rodrigo by Alcantara and Coria. The general himself followed in the track of Fraser, whom he overtook and passed in the neighbourhood of Castello Branco [1].

The march was a most unpleasant one, for the autumn rains surprised the troops in their passage through the mountains. Moreover some of the regiments were badly fed, as Sataro, the Portuguese contractor who had undertaken to supply them with meat, went bankrupt at this moment and failed to fulfil his obligations. Nevertheless the advance was carried out with complete success: the men were in good heart, marched well, and generally maintained their [2] discipline. On November 13 the leading

---

[1] It may perhaps be worth while to give the composition and brigading of Moore's army on the march from Lisbon and Elvas to Salamanca.

There marched by Coimbra and Almeida, Beresford [1/9th, 2/43rd, 2/52nd] and Fane [1/38th, 1/79th, 2/95th]. By Abrantes and Guarda went Bentinck [1/4th, 1/28th, 1/42nd, and four companies 5/60th] and Hill [1/5th, 1/32nd, 1/91st]: this column took with it one battery: it was followed by two isolated regiments, the 1/6th and 1/50th. The corps which marched from Elvas by Alcantara, under Paget, was composed of the brigades of Alten (1st and 2nd Light Battalions of the K. G. L.) and Anstruther 20th, 1/52nd, 1/95th. The 3rd Regiment joined the army from Almeida, where it was in garrison, and the 1/82nd came up late from Lisbon. It was originally intended that Bentinck and Beresford should form a division under Fraser, Anstruther and Alten a division under Paget. Of the troops which reached Salamanca the 3rd and 5/60th were sent back to Portugal.

The original brigading of Baird's force was:—Cavalry Brigade (Lord Paget) 7th, 10th, and 15th Hussars. 1st Brigade (Warde) 1st and 3rd batts. of the 1st Foot Guards. 2nd Brigade (Manningham) 3/1st, 1/26th, 2/81st. 3rd Brigade (Leith) 51st, 2/59th, 76th. Light Brigade (R. Crawfurd) 2/43rd, 1/95th, 2/95th (detachments). The 2/14th and 2/23rd were also present, perhaps as a brigade under Mackenzie.

All these arrangements were temporary, and at Sahagun, as we shall see, the whole army was recast. A complete table of Moore's army, with its final organization, force, and losses, will be found in the Appendix.

[2] Moore names one regiment only as an exception.

regiments began to file into Salamanca, whither the Commander-in-chief had already preceded them. The concentration would have been a little more rapid but for a strange mistake of General Anstruther, commanding at Almeida, who detained some of the troops for a few days, contrary to the orders which had been sent him. But by the twenty-third the three columns had all joined at Salamanca [1], where Moore now had 15,000 infantry and the solitary battery that had marched with Fraser's division. The guns had met with some tiresome obstacles, but had surmounted them with no great difficulty, and Moore now saw (as we have already shown) that he might have brought the whole of his artillery with him, if only he had been given correct information as to the state of the roads.

On November 23, then, the British commander-in-chief lay at Salamanca, with six infantry brigades and one battery. Baird lay at Astorga, with four brigades and three batteries : a few of his battalions were still on the march from Galicia. Hope, with Moore's cavalry and guns, was near the Escurial. Lord Paget with Baird's equally belated cavalry, which had left Corunna on the fifteenth, was between Lugo and Astorga. The situation was deplorable, for it was clear that the army would require ten days more to concentrate and get into full fighting order, and it was by no means certain that those ten days would be granted to it. Such were the unhappy results of the false direction given to Hope's column, and of the enforced delay of Baird at Corunna, owing to the folly of the Galician Junta.

It may easily be guessed that Moore's state of mind at this moment was most unenviable. He had received, much at the same time as did Baird, the news of Gamonal and Espinosa. He was aware that no screen of Spanish troops now lay between him and the enemy. He had heard of the arrival of Milhaud's dragoons at Valladolid, and of Lefebvre's corps at Carrion, and he expected every moment to hear that they were marching forward against himself. Yet he could not possibly advance without cavalry or guns, and if attacked he must fly at once towards Portugal, for it would be mad to attempt to fight in the plains with no force at his disposition save a mass of foot-soldiery. If the French moved forward from Valladolid to Zamora on the one side, or to Avila on the other, he would inevitably be cut off from Baird and Hope.

[1] Save two stray battalions, which had started last from Lisbon.

There was no serious danger that any one of the three columns might be caught by the enemy, if they halted at once, for each had a clear and safe line of retreat, on Lisbon, Corunna, and Talavera respectively. But if they continued their movement of concentration the case was otherwise. To any one unacquainted with Bonaparte's actual design of throwing all his forces on Madrid by the Somosierra road, it looked not only possible, but probable, that the enemy would advance westward as well as southward from his present positions, and if he did so the game was up. The British army, utterly unable to concentrate, must fly in three separate directions. Moore and Hope might ultimately unite in front of Lisbon: Baird might he shipped round from Corunna to the same point. But this movement would take many weeks, and its moral effect would be deplorable. What would be thought of the general who marched forward till he was within eighty miles of the French, and then ordered a precipitate retreat, without even succeeding in concentrating his army or firing a single shot? The thought filled Moore's heart with bitterness: must he, with all his ability and with his well-earned reputation, swell the list of the failures, and be reckoned with the Duke of York, Dalrymple, and Hutchinson among the generals who were too late—who had their chance of fame, and lost it by being an hour, or a week, or a month behind the decisive moment? But on one point he was clear: he must run no unnecessary risk with the forces committed to him: they were, as was once remarked, not *a* British field-army, but the only British field-army. Supposing they were destroyed, no such second host existed: it would take years to make another. There were still many regiments on home service, but those which now lay at Salamanca and Astorga were the pick of the whole, the corps chosen for foreign service because they were the fittest for it.

The question, then, which Moore had to put to himself was whether he should persist in attempting to complete the concentration of his army, and in case of success take an active part in the campaign, or whether he should simply order each fraction of the British forces to retreat at once towards some safe base. The way in which the question should be answered depended mainly on two points — what would be the movements of the French during the next few days, and what Spanish troops existed to co-operate with the British army, in case it were determined to commence active operations. For clearly the 30,000 men of Moore and Baird could

not hope to struggle unaided against the whole French army in
Spain.

To explain Moore's action, it is necessary to remember that he
started with a strong prejudice against trusting the British army
to the mercy of Spanish co-operation.   He had been receiving very
gloomy reports both from Mr. Stuart, the temporary representative
of the British Government at Aranjuez, and from Lord William
Bentinck, the military agent whom Dalrymple had sent to Madrid.
The latter was one of the few British officers who (like Wellesley)
foresaw from the first a catastrophe whenever the French reinforcements should cross the Ebro [1].   Moreover the character of Moore's
correspondence with the Central Junta, before and during his
advance, had conspired with the reports of Stuart and Bentinck to
give him a very unfavourable idea of the energy and administrative
capacity of our allies.   He had been vexed that the Junta refused
to put him in direct communication with the Spanish generals [2].
He complained that he got from them tardy, unfrequent, and
inaccurate news of the enemy's movements.   He was disgusted
that Lopez, the officer sent to aid him in moving his troops, turned
out to know even less about the roads of the Spanish frontier than
he did himself.   But above all he professed that he was terrified by
the apathy which he found both among the officials and the people
of the kingdom of Leon and Old Castile.   He had been politely
received by the authorities both at Ciudad Rodrigo and at Salamanca, but he complained that he got little but empty compliments from them.

There was some truth in this allegation, though certain facts
can be quoted against it [3], even from Moore's own correspondence.

[1] There is an undertone of gloom in most of Bentinck's very capable letters,
which contrasts sharply with the very optimistic views expressed by Doyle
and most of the other military agents.   On Oct. 2 he 'feels the danger
forcibly' of the want of a single commander for the Spanish armies.   On
Sept. 30 he remarks that 'the Spanish troops consider themselves invincible,
but that the Spanish Government ought not to be deluded by the same
opinion.'   On Nov. 14 'he must not disguise that he thinks very unfavourably of the affairs of Spain : the Spaniards have not the means to repel the
danger that threatens' : most of his letters are in more or less the same
strain.

[2] Except with Castaños, from whom some sensible but rather vague advice
was procured.

[3] e.g. in his letter of Nov. 19 Moore speaks of the town of Salamanca as
doing its best for him : the clergy were exerting themselves, and a convent

Leon and Old Castile had, as we have already had occasion to remark, been far less energetic than other parts of the Peninsula in raising new troops and coming forward with contributions to the national exchequer. They had done no more than furnish the 10,000 men of Cuesta's disorderly 'Army of Castile,' a contingent utterly out of proportion with their population and resources. Nor did they seem to realize the scandal of their own sloth and procrastination. Moore had expected to see every town full of new levies undergoing drill before marching to the Ebro, to discover magazines accumulated in important places like Ciudad Rodrigo and Salamanca, to find the military and civil officials working busily for the armies at the front. Instead he found an unaccountable apathy. Even after the reports of Espinosa and Gamonal had come to hand, the people and the authorities alike seemed to be living in a sort of fools' paradise, disbelieving the gloomy news that arrived, or at least refusing to recognize that the war was now at their own doors. Moore feared that this came from want of patriotism or of courage.

As a matter of fact, the people's hearts were sound enough[1], but they had still got 'Baylen on the brain': they simply failed to

of nuns had promised him £5,000. In his *Journal* he has a testimonial to the fidelity with which the people of Tordesillas protected an English officer from a raiding party of French cavalry. There are some similar notes in British memoirs : e.g. 'T. S.' of the 71st expresses much gratitude for the kindness of the people of Peñaranda, who, when Hope's division arrived in a drenched and frozen condition, rolled out barrels of spirits into the streets and gave every man a good dram before the regiments marched on. Some towns, e.g. Zamora and Alba de Tormes, behaved well in opposing (though without any hope of success) the French, when they did appear.

[1] As to the conduct of the Spaniards I think that the best commentary on it is that of Leith Hay (i. 80–1), who was riding all over Castile and Leon in these unhappy weeks. 'Thus terminated a journey of about 900 miles, in which a considerable portion of the country had been traversed, under circumstances which enabled me to ascertain the sincere feeling of the people. It is but justice to say that I met with but one sentiment as to the war : that I was everywhere treated with kindness. I mention this as a creditable circumstance to the inhabitants of the Peninsula, and in contradiction to the statements often recorded, unjustly in my opinion, as to the want of faith, supineness, and perfidy of the Spanish people. . . . Their conduct was throughout distinguished by good faith, if it was at the same time rendered apparently equivocal from characteristic negligence, want of energy, and the deficiency of that moral power that can alone be derived from free institutions and an enlightened aristocracy.'

recognize the full horror of the situation. That their armies
were not merely beaten but dispersed, that the way to Madrid was
open to Bonaparte, escaped them. This attitude of mind enraged
Moore. 'In these provinces,' he wrote, 'no armed force whatever
exists, either for immediate protection or to reinforce the armies.
The French cavalry from Burgos, in small detachments, are overrunning the province of Leon, and raising contributions to which
the inhabitants submit without the least resistance : the enthusiasm
of which we heard so much nowhere appears. Whatever good-will
there is (and among the lower orders I believe there is a good deal)
is taken no advantage of. I am at this moment in no communication with any of their generals. I am ignorant of their plans, or
those of their government [1].' And again, he adds in despair, ' I hope
a better spirit exists in the southern provinces : here no one stirs—
and yet they are well inclined [2].' While Leon and Old Castile
were in this state of apathy, it was maddening to Moore to receive
constant appeals from the Supreme Junta, begging that the British
army might move forward at once. Their dispatches were accompanied by representations, which Moore knew to be inaccurate,
concerning the numbers and enthusiasm of the Spanish armies
still in the field, and by misrepresentations of the force of the
French. They were also backed by urgent letters from Mr. Frere,
the new ambassador at Madrid, urging him to give help at all
costs.

These appeals were intolerable to a man who dared not advance
because his army (partly by his own fault, partly owing to circumstances that had not been under his control) was not concentrated.
From the point of view of policy, Moore knew that it was all-important that he should take the field : but, from the point of view
of strategy, he saw that an advance with the 15,000 men that he
had at Salamanca might very probably lead to instant and complete
disaster. He refused to move, but all the time he knew that his
refusal was having the worst effect, and would certainly be represented by his critics as the result of timidity and selfishness. It
was this consciousness that caused him to fill his dispatches with
the bitterest comments on the Spanish government and people.
He had been induced to advance to Salamanca, he said, by false
pretences. He had been told that there was a large army in front
of him, ready to cover his concentration. He had been informed

---

[1] Moore to Castlereagh from Salamanca, Nov. 24.   [2] Ibid., Dec. 8.

that the whole country-side was full of enthusiasm, that he might look for ready help from every official, that when once he had crossed the frontier transport and food would be readily provided for him. Instead, he found nothing but apathy and disasters. 'Had the real strength and composition of the Spanish armies been known, and the defenceless state of the country, I conceive that Cadiz, not Corunna, would have been chosen for the disembarkation of the troops from England : and Seville or Cordova, not Salamanca, would have been selected as the proper place for the assembling of this army[1].' Thus he wrote to Castlereagh : to Frere, in response to constant invitations to strike a blow of some sort in behalf of Spain, he replied in more vigorous terms[2]. 'Madrid is threatened; the French have destroyed one army (Blake's), have passed the Ebro, and are advancing in superior numbers against another (Castaños'), which from its composition promises no resistance, but must retire or be overwhelmed. No other armed force exists in this country : I perceive no enthusiasm or determined spirit among the people. This is a state of affairs quite different from that conceived by the British Government, when they determined to send troops to the assistance of Spain. It was not expected that these were to cope alone with the whole force of France : as auxiliaries they were to aid a people who were believed to be enthusiastic, determined, and prepared for resistance. It becomes therefore a question whether the British army should remain to be attacked in its turn, or should retire from a country where the contest, from whatever circumstances, is become unequal.'

All that Moore wrote was true : yet, granting the accuracy of every premise, his conclusion that he ought to retire to Portugal was not necessarily correct. The British Government had undoubtedly over-estimated the power and resources of Spain : the Supreme Junta had shown no capacity for organization or command : most of the Spanish generals had committed gross military blunders. But none of these facts were enough to justify Moore in washing his hands of the whole business, and marching out of Spain without firing a shot. He had not been sent to help the patriots only if they were powerful and victorious, to desert them if they proved weak and unlucky. If these had been the orders

---

[1] Moore to Castlereagh from Salamanca, Nov. 24.
[2] Moore to Frere from Salamanca, Nov. 27.

issued to him by Castlereagh, all Bonaparte's taunts about the selfishness and timidity of the British Government would have been
justified.   It was true that on his arrival at Salamanca he found
the aspect of the war very different from what he had expected at
the moment of his quitting Lisbon.   Instead of aiding the victorious
Spanish armies to press up to the Pyrenees, he would have to cover
their retreat and gain time for the reorganization of the scattered
remnants of their first line of defence.   To reject this task because
the Supreme Junta had been incapable, or Blake and Palafox rash
and unskilful, would have been unworthy of a man of Moore's
talents and courage.

Yet in a moment of irritation at the mismanagement that he
saw before him, and of anger at the continual importunities that
he was receiving from the Central Junta and from Mr. Frere,
Moore nearly committed this fault.   The last piece of news which
broke down his resolution and drove him to order a retreat was the
account of the battle of Tudela.   If he had been forced to wait for
the notification of this disaster through Spanish official sources, he
might have remained ignorant of it for many days.   But Charles
Vaughan, the secretary of Mr. Stuart, had been in the camp of
Palafox, and had ridden straight from Tudela to Madrid, and from
Madrid to Salamanca—476 miles in six days [1].   He brought the
intelligence of Castaños' defeat to the English commander-in-chief
on the night of November 28.   Moore lost not a moment in
dictating orders of retreat to the whole army.   In the few hours
that elapsed before midnight he gave his own troops directions to

---

[1] The notes and diaries of this ancient member of my own College have
been of enormous use to me for side-lights on Spanish politics during 1808.
His summary of his great ride from Caparrosa in Navarre to Corunna, between
November 21 and December 2, is perhaps worth quoting. ' From Caparrosa
to Madrid and from Madrid to Salamanca, with the dispatches for Sir John
Moore, containing the defeat of the army commanded by General Castaños,
I rode post. I stayed the night at Salamanca, and at two o'clock on the
following day (Nov. 29) I set out for Astorga with dispatches for Sir D. Baird,
and with Sir J. Moore's dispatches for England. I was detained only six
hours at Astorga, and after riding two days and two nights on end arrived
at Corunna the evening of Dec. 2. The post-horses at every relay in Spain
were at this time so overworked that the journey was tiresome and painful.
I had ridden 790 miles from Caparrosa to Corunna in eleven days (Nov. 21 to
Dec. 2). I had a night's rest at Agreda, Cetina, and Salamanca, and two at
Madrid.' Deducting two days in Madrid, the ride was really one of 790 miles
in nine days.

prepare to retire on Portugal, sent Hope a dispatch bidding him turn off on to cross-roads and move by Peñaranda on Ciudad Rodrigo and Almeida, and wrote to Baird that he must return to Corunna, re-embark his army, and bring it round by sea to Lisbon.

The spirit in which Moore acted is shown by the wording of his letter to Hope:—'I have determined to give the thing up, and to retire. It was my wish to have run great risks to fulfil what I conceive to be the wishes of the people of England, and to give every aid to the Spanish cause. But they have shown themselves equal to do so little for themselves, that it would only be sacrificing this army, without doing any good to Spain, to oppose it to such numbers as must now be brought against us. A junction with Baird is out of the question, and with you, perhaps, problematical. ... This is a cruel determination for me to make—I mean to retreat: but I hope you will think the circumstances such as demand it[1].'

To Moore, weighed down by the burden of responsibility, and worried by the constant pressure of the Spaniards at Madrid, 'who expected every one to fly but themselves,' this resolve to retreat seemed reasonable, and even inevitable. But it was clearly wrong: when he gave the order he was overwrought by irritation and despondency. He was sent to aid the Spaniards, and till he was sure that he could do absolutely nothing in their behalf, it was his duty not to abandon them. The British army was intended to be used freely in their cause, not to be laid up—like the talent in the napkin—lest anything might happen to it. Its mere presence at Salamanca was valuable as an encouragement to the Spaniards, and a check on the free movement of the French. Above all, it was not yet proved that the concentration with Baird and Hope was impossible: indeed, the events of the last few days were rendering it more and more likely that the junction might, after all, take place. The French cavalry which had appeared at Valladolid had gone off southward, without any attempt to move in the direction of Salamanca. Soult and Lefebvre were also moving in a direction which would not bring them anywhere near the British army. Hope had crossed the Guadarrama unhindered, and was now near Villacastin, only seventy miles from Moore's head quarters. Under these circumstances it was most impolitic

[1] Moore to Hope from Salamanca, Nov. 28.

to order an instant retreat. What would have been thought of Moore if this movement had been carried out, and if after the British columns had reached Corunna and Almeida the news had come that no French infantry had ever been nearer than fifty miles to them, that their concentration had been perfectly feasible, and that Napoleon had possessed no knowledge of their where-abouts? All these facts chanced to be true—as we have seen. The Emperor's advance on Madrid was made without any reference to the British army, by roads that took him very far from Sala-manca : he was marching past Moore's front in serene unconscious-ness of his proximity. If, at the same moment, the British had been hurrying back to Portugal, pursued only by phantoms hatched in their general's imagination, it is easy to guess what military critics would have said, and what historians would have written. Moore would have been pronounced a selfish and timid officer, who in a moment of pique and despondency deliberately abandoned his unhappy allies.

Fortunately for his own reputation and for that of England, his original intentions of the night of November 28 were not fully carried out. Only Baird's column actually commenced its retrograde movement. That general received Moore's letter from Vaughan on the thirtieth, and immediately began to retire on Galicia. Leaving his cavalry and his light brigade at Astorga, to cover his retreat, he fell back with the rest of his division to Villafranca, fifty miles on the road towards Corunna. Here (as we shall see) he received on December 6 a complete new set of orders, counter-manding his retreat and bidding him return to the plains of Leon.

Hope also had heard from Moore on the thirtieth, had been informed that the army was to retire on Portugal, and was told to make forced marches by Peñaranda and Ciudad Rodrigo to join his chief—unless indeed he were forced to go back by the way that he had come, owing to the appearance of French troops in his path. Fortunately no such danger occurred : Hope arranged his two cavalry regiments as a screen in front of his right, in the direction of Arevalo and Madrigal. He hurried his infantry and guns by Fontiveros and Peñaranda, along the road that had been pointed out to him. The cavalry obtained news that patrols of French dragoons coming from the north had pushed as far as Olmedo and La Nava—some sixteen or eighteen miles from their outposts—but did not actually see a single hostile vedette. This

was lucky, as, if Napoleon had heard of a British force hovering
on the flank of his advancing columns, he would certainly have
turned against it the troops that were covering the right flank
of his advance on Madrid—Lefebvre's corps and the dragoons of
Milhaud. But, as it chanced, Hope was entirely unmolested: he
moved, as was right, with his troops closed up and ready for
a fight: on the night of the thirtieth his infantry actually slept
in square without piling arms: during the ensuing thirty-six
hours they marched forty-seven miles before they were allowed to
encamp at Peñaranda. There they were practically in safety:
slackening the pace for the exhausted infantry and for the over-
driven oxen of the convoy, Hope drew in to Alba de Tormes, where
he was only fifteen miles from Salamanca[1]. Here he received
orders not to push for Ciudad Rodrigo, but to turn northward
and join the main body of the army, which was still—as it turned
out—in its old positions. Thus on December 3 Moore could
at last dispose of his long-lost cavalry and guns, and possessed
an army of 20,000 men complete in all arms. This very much
changed the aspect of affairs for him, and removed one of his
main justifications for the projected retreat on Portugal. Hope
also brought information as to the movements of the French which
was of the highest importance. He reported that their columns
were all trending southward, none of them to the west of Segovia.
He had also heard of the infantry of the 4th Corps, and could
report that it had marched by Valladolid and Olmedo on Segovia,
evidently with the intention of driving Heredia's Estremaduran
troops out of the last-named city, and of opening the Guadarrama
Pass[2]. There was no sign whatever of any movement of the

---

[1] There is a good, but short, account of this forced march, in bitter cold, to
be found in the memoir of 'T. S.' of the 71st, one of Hope's four infantry
regiments. He speaks of a curious fact that I have nowhere else seen
mentioned, viz. that at Peñaranda the artillery horses were so done up that
Hope buried six guns, and turned their teams to help the other batteries.
Apparently they were dug up a few days after by troops sent out from
Salamanca, as the tale of batteries is complete when Moore resumed his
march.

[2] I think that Napier (i. 287–8) somewhat exaggerates the danger which
Hope ran in his march from Villacastin to Alba de Tormes. Of course if
Lefebvre had been marching on Salamanca, the situation would have been
dangerous: but as a matter of fact he was marching on the Guadarrama,
which Hope had safely passed on the twenty-eighth. Every mile that the

French in this quarter towards Salamanca. Thus the Emperor's plan for a concentration of his whole army on Madrid became clear to Moore's discerning eyes.

British moved took them further from Lefebvre's route : his infantry was never within fifty miles of Hope's convoy : and supposing his brigade of cavalry had got in touch with the British, it could have done nothing serious against a force of all arms in the hands of a very capable general. The ' 4,000 cavalry' of which Napier speaks were in reality only 1,500.

SECTION VIII : CHAPTER III

MOORE'S ADVANCE TO SAHAGUN

MOORE'S determination to retreat on Portugal lasted just seven days. It was at midnight on November 28–29 that he wrote his orders to Baird and Hope, bidding the one to fall back on Corunna and the other on Ciudad Rodrigo. On the afternoon of December 5 he abandoned his scheme, and wrote to recall Baird from Galicia : on the tenth he set out on a very different sort of enterprise, and advanced into the plains of Old Castile with the object of striking at the communications of the French army. We have now to investigate the curious mixture of motives which led him to make such a complete and dramatic change in his plan of campaign.

Having sent off his dispatches to Hope and Baird, the Commander-in-chief had announced next morning to the generals who commanded his divisions and brigades his intention of retreating to Portugal. The news evoked manifestations of surprise and anger that could not be concealed. Even Moore's own staff did not succeed in disguising their dismay and regret[1]. The army was looking forward with eagerness to another campaign against the French under a general of such well-earned reputation as their present chief : a sudden order to retreat, when the enemy had not even been seen, and when his nearest cavalry vedettes were still three or four marches away, seemed astounding. There would have been remonstrances, had not Moore curtly informed his subordinates that 'he had not called them together to request their counsel, or to induce them to commit themselves to giving any opinion on the subject. He was taking the whole responsibility entirely upon himself : and he only required that they would immediately prepare to carry it into effect.' In face of this speech there could be no argument or opposition : but there was

---

[1] See James Moore's memoir of his brother, p. 72 ; compare Napier, i. 292, and Lord Londonderry's account of his own observations at Salamanca, in his *History of the Peninsular War*, i. 220, 221.

murmuring in every quarter: of all the officers of the army of
Portugal Hope is said to have been the only one who approved
of the Commander-in-chief's resolve.   The consciousness of the
criticism that he was undergoing from his own subordinates did
not tend to soften Moore's temper, which was already sufficiently
tried by the existing situation of affairs.

After announcing this determination, it might have been expected that Moore would fall back at once on Almeida.   But
while beginning to send back his stores and his sick [1], he did not
move his fighting-men: the reason (as he wrote to Castlereagh [2])
was that he still hoped that he might succeed in picking up Hope's
division, if the French did not press him.   Accordingly he lingered
on, waiting for that general's approach, and much surprised that
the enemy was making no advance in his direction.   It was owing
to the fact that he delayed his departure for five days, on the
chance that his lost cavalry and guns might after all come in, that
Moore finally gained the opportunity of striking his great blow and
saving his reputation.

During this period of waiting and of preparation to depart,
appeals from many quarters came pouring in upon Moore, begging
him to advance at all costs and make his presence felt by the
French.   The first dispatches which he received were written before
his determination to retreat was known: after it was divulged, his
correspondents only became the more importunate and clamorous.
Simultaneous pressure was brought to bear upon him by the British
ambassador at Aranjuez, by the Supreme Junta, by the general
who now commanded the wrecks of the Spanish army of Galicia,
and by the military authorities at Madrid.   Each one of them
had many and serious considerations to set before the harassed
Commander-in-chief.

Moore had been so constantly asserting that Blake's old ' Army of
the Left ' had been completely dispersed and ruined, that it must
have been somewhat of a surprise to him when the Marquis of
La Romana wrote from Leon, on November 30, to say that he was
now at the head of a considerable force, and hoped to co-operate in
the oncoming campaign.   The Galicians had rallied in much greater

---

[1] The heavy ammunition and all the sick who could be moved were sent off
on Dec. 5, under the escort of the 5/60th.   See Moore's ' General Orders' for
that day, and Ormsby, ii. 54.

[2] Moore to Castlereagh, from Salamanca, Nov. 29.

numbers than had been expected: their losses in battle had not
been very great, and the men had dispersed from sheer want of food
rather than from a desire to desert their colours. Their equipment
was in the most wretched condition, and their shoes worn out:
but their spirit was not broken, and if they could get food and
clothing, they were quite prepared to do their duty. La Romana
enclosed a dispatch of Soult's which had been intercepted, and
remarked that the news in it (apparently a statement of the
marshal's intention to move westward) made it advisable that
the English and Spanish armies should at once concert measures
for a junction[1].

All that the Marquis stated was perfectly true: his army was
growing rapidly, for his muster-rolls of December 4 showed that
he had already 15,600 men with the colours, exclusive of sick and
wounded: ten days later the number had gone up to 22,800[2].
This was a force that could not be entirely neglected, even though
the men were in a dire state of nakedness, and were only just
recovering from the effects of their dreadful march from Reynosa
across the Cantabrian hills. Moore had always stated, in his
dispatches to Castlereagh, that there was no Spanish army with
which he could co-operate. He was now offered the aid of 15,000
men, under a veteran officer of high reputation and undoubted
patriotism. The proposal to retreat on Portugal seemed even less
honourable than before, when it involved the desertion of the
Marquis and his much-tried host.

Not long after the moment at which La Romana's dispatch
came to hand, there arrived at Salamanca two officers deputed
by the Central Junta to make a final appeal to Moore. These
were Don Ventura Escalante, Captain-General of the kingdom
of Granada, and the Brigadier-General Augustin Bueno. They
had started from Aranjuez on November 28, and seem to have
arrived at the British head quarters on December 3 or 4. They
brought a letter from Don Martin de Garay, the secretary to the
Junta, stating that they were authorized to treat with Moore
for the drawing up of a plan of campaign, 'by which the troops of
his Britannic Majesty may act in concert with those of Spain,
accelerating a combined movement, and avoiding the delays that

---

[1] La Romana to Moore, from Leon, Nov. 30.

[2] See the 'morning states' for the army of Galicia on Dec. 4 and Dec. 14,
in Arteche (iv. 532, 533).

are so prejudicial to the noble enterprise in which the two nations are engaged[1].' The proposal that the two generals made would appear to have been that Moore should march on Madrid by the Guadarrama Pass, picking up Hope's division on the way, and ordering Baird to follow as best he could. They wished to demonstrate to their despondent ally that it was possible to concentrate for the defence of Madrid a force sufficient to hold the Emperor at bay. If the British came up, they hoped even to be able to repulse him with decisive effect. They alleged that Castaños had escaped from Tudela with the Andalusian divisions almost intact, and must now be at Guadalajara, quite close to the capital, with 25,000 good troops. Heredia, with the rallied Estremaduran army, was at Segovia, and had 10,000 bayonets : San Juan with 12,000 men was occupying the impregnable Somosierra. Andalusian and Castilian levies were coming in to Madrid every day—they believed that 10,000 men must already be collected. This would constitute when united a mass of nearly 60,000 men : if Moore brought up 20,000 British troops all must go well, for Napoleon had only 80,000 men in the north of Spain. After deducting the army sent against Saragossa, and the detachments at Burgos and in Biscay, as also the corps of Soult, he could not have much more than 20,000 men concentrated for the attack on Madrid. All this ingenious calculation was based on the fundamental misconception that the French armies were only one-third of their actual strength—which far exceeded 200,000 men. But on this point Moore was as ill informed as the Spaniards themselves, and the causes which he alleged for refusing to march on Madrid had nothing to do with statistics. He informed them that his reasons for proposing to retreat on Portugal were that the Spanish armies were too much demoralized to offer successful resistance to the Emperor, and that the road to the capital was now in the possession of the French. He then introduced Colonel Graham, who had just returned from a meeting with San Juan, and had heard from him the story of the forcing of the Somosierra on November 29. Of this disaster Escalante and Bueno were still ignorant : they had to learn from English lips that the French were actually before the gates of Madrid, that Heredia and San Juan were in flight, and that their junction with Castaños (wherever that general might now be) had become

[1] Martin de Garay to Moore, from Aranjuez, Nov. 28, 1808.

impossible. This appalling news deeply affected Escalante and
Bueno, but they then turned to urging Moore to unite with
La Romana, and march to the relief of Madrid. The British
general replied that he did not believe that the Marquis had
5,000 men fit to take the field along with the British[1], and that
any such scheme would be chimerical. His whole bearing towards
the emissaries of the Junta seems to have been frigid to the verge
of discourtesy. How much they irritated him may be gathered from
the account of the interview which he sent to Mr. Frere two days
later. In language that seems very inappropriate in an official
dispatch—destined ere long to be printed as a 'Parliamentary
Paper'—he wrote: 'The two generals seemed to me to be two weak
old men, or rather women, with whom it was impossible for me to
concert any military operations, even had I been so inclined. Their
conferences with me consisted in questions, and in assertions with
regard to the strength of different Spanish corps, all of which
I knew to be erroneous. They neither knew that Segovia or the
Somosierra were in the hands of the enemy. I shall be obliged
to you to save me from such visits, which are very painful[2].'

It is clear that the mission of Escalante and Bueno had no great
share in determining Sir John to abandon his projected retreat on
Portugal, though it may possibly have had some cumulative effect
when taken in conjunction with other appeals that were coming
in to him at the same moment. It was quite otherwise with the
dispatches which he received from the authorities at Madrid, and
from the British ambassador at Aranjuez: in them we may find
the chief causes of his changed attitude. The Madrid dispatch
was written by Morla and the Prince of Castelfranco—the two
military heads of the Junta of Defence which had been created
on December 1—in behalf of themselves and their colleagues. It
was sent off early on December 2, before Napoleon had begun to
press in upon the suburbs, for it speaks of the city as menaced,
not as actually attacked by the enemy. It amounted to an appeal
to Moore to do something to help Madrid—not necessarily (as has
been often stated) to throw himself into the city, but, if he judged

[1] This answer is recorded in the despairing appeal which Escalante wrote
to Moore from Calzada de Baños on Nov. 7, after having started back to join
the Junta. The rest of Moore's arguments can be gathered from his own
dispatches.
[2] Moore to Frere, from Salamanca, Dec. 6, 1808.

it best, to manœuvre on the flank and rear of the Emperor's army, so as to distract him from his present design.   The writers stated, in much the same terms that Escalante and Bueno had used, that Castaños with 25,000 men from Tudela and San Juan with 10,000 men from the Somosierra were converging on the capital, and added that the Junta had got together 40,000 men for its defence.   With this mass of new levies they thought that they could hold off for the moment the forces that Napoleon had displayed in front of them ; but when his reserves and reinforcements came up the situation would be more dangerous.   Wherefore they made no doubt that the British general would move with the rapidity that was required in the interests of the allied nations. They supposed it probable that Moore had already united with La Romana's army, and that the two forces would be able to act together.

There is no reason to think, with Napier and with Moore's biographer [1], that this dispatch was written by Morla with the treacherous intent of involving the British army in the catastrophe that was impending over the capital.   Morla ultimately betrayed his country and joined King Joseph, but there is no real proof that he contemplated doing so before the fall of Madrid.   The letter was signed not only by him but by Castelfranco, of whose loyalty there is no doubt, and who was actually arrested and imprisoned by Bonaparte.   Moreover, if it had been designed to draw Moore into the Emperor's clutches, it would not have given him the perfectly sound advice to fall upon the communications of the French army after uniting with La Romana—the precise move that the British general made ten days later with such effect. It would have begged him to enter Madrid, without suggesting any other alternative.

Moore had always stated that his reluctance to advance into Spain had been due, in no small degree, to the apathy which he had found there : but now the capital, as it seemed, was about to imitate Saragossa and to stand at bay behind its barricades. He had no great confidence in its power to hold out.   'I own,' he wrote to Castlereagh, 'that I cannot derive much hope from the resistance of one town against forces so formidable, unless the

---

[1] See James Moore (p. 86-7), where he vilely mistranslates the letter—even rendering *corte* by ' country ' ; and Napier (i. 291), where the same accusation is formulated.

spark catches and the flame becomes pretty general [1].' But he could realize the dishonour that would rest upon his own head if, as now seemed possible, Madrid were to make a desperate resistance, and at the same moment the British army were to be seen executing unmolested a tame retreat on Portugal. The letter of Morla and Castelfranco he might perhaps have disregarded, suspecting the usual Spanish exaggerations, if it had stood alone. But it was backed up by an appeal from the most important British sources. Mr. Stuart, whose forecasts Moore had always respected because they were far from optimistic [2], had written him to the effect that 'the retrograde movements of the British divisions were likely to produce an effect not less serious than the most decisive victory on the part of the enemy.' Frere, the newly arrived ambassador to the Central Junta, launched out into language of the strongest kind. He had already discovered that his opinions were fundamentally opposed to those of Moore: this was but natural, as the general looked upon the problem that lay before him from a military point of view, while the ambassador could only regard its political aspect. Any impartial observer can now see that the advance of the British army into Spain was likely to be a hazardous matter, even if Hope and Baird succeeded in joining the main body at Salamanca. On the other hand, it is quite clear that the Spanish government would have every reason to regard itself as having been abandoned and betrayed, if that advance were not made. Balancing the one danger against the other, it seems evident that Frere was right, and that it was Moore's duty to make a diversion of some sort against the French. Executed on any day before Madrid fell, such a movement would have disturbed Bonaparte and distracted him from his main plan of operations. Nor would the operation have been so hazardous as Moore supposed, since his junction with Hope had become certain when that general reached Peñaranda, while Baird had never had any French troops in his neighbourhood. The retreat on Galicia was always open: that on Portugal was equally available till the moment when the capitulation of Madrid set free great masses of Bonaparte's central reserve.

In his earlier epistles to Moore Frere had deprecated the idea of a retreat, and had suggested that if for military reasons an advance

---

[1] Moore to Castlereagh, from Salamanca, Dec. 5.
[2] Stuart to Moore, from Madrid, Nov. 30.

should be impracticable, it would at least be possible that the British army might remain on Spanish ground. He had soon learnt that the general entertained very different views, and his penultimate letter, that of November 30, shows signs of pique at the small impression that his arguments had made upon his correspondent [1]. Now on December 3 he wrote from Talavera, whither he had followed the Supreme Junta in their flight, to try his last effort. To his previous arguments he had only one more to add, the fact that on December 1–2 the people of Madrid were showing that spirit of fanatical patriotism which Moore had sought in vain hitherto among the Spaniards. The populace, as he had learnt, was barricading the streets and throwing up batteries: 30,000 citizens and peasants were now under arms. Considering their spirit, he had no hesitation in taking upon himself the responsibility of representing the propriety, not to say the necessity, of doing something in their behalf. The fate of Spain depended absolutely, for the moment, on some help being given by the British army. Frere had first-hand evidence of the enthusiasm which was reigning in Madrid on the first day of December, having spoken to several persons who had just left the capital, including a French *émigré* colonel, one Charmilly, to whose care he entrusted his last letter to the Commander-in-chief. But so convinced was he that no argument of his would affect Sir John Moore, that he took a most improper step, and endeavoured to appeal to the public opinion of the army over the head of its general. He entrusted Charmilly with a second letter, which he was only to deliver if Moore refused to countermand his retreat after reading the first. This document was a request that in case Sir John remained fixed in his original determination, he would allow the bearer of these letters to be examined before a Council of War. Frere thought that Charmilly's account of what was going on in Madrid would appeal to the Brigadiers, if it had no effect on the Lieutenant-General—and probably he was not far wrong. Such a plan struck at the roots of all military obedience: it could only have occurred to a civilian. If anything could have made the matter worse, it was that the document should be entrusted not

---

[1] 'I do not know that I can in any way express with less offence the entire difference of our opinions on this subject, than by forwarding what I had already written, in ignorance of the determination [to retreat] which you had already taken' (Aranjuez, Nov. 30).

to a British officer but to a foreign adventurer, a kind of person to whom the breach between the civil and military representatives of Great Britain ought never to have been divulged. Moreover Charmilly (though Frere was not aware of this fact) chanced to be personally known to Moore, who had a very bad opinion of him [1]. The *émigré* was said to have been implicated in the San Domingo massacres of 1794, and to have been engaged of late in doubtful financial speculations in London. To send him to Salamanca with such an errand seemed like a deliberate insult to the Commander-in-chief. Frere was innocent of this intention, but the whole business, even without this aggravation, was most unwise and improper.

Charmilly handed in his first document on the evening of December 5, a few hours after Morla's messenger had delivered the appeal from Madrid. Moore received him in the most formal way, dismissed him, and began to compare Frere's information with that of the Junta of Defence, of the emissaries from Aranjuez, and of his other English correspondents. Putting all together, he felt his determination much shaken: Madrid, as it seemed, was really about to defend itself: the preparations which were reported to him bore out the words of Morla and Castelfranco. His own army was seething with discontent at the projected retreat: Hope being now only one march away, at Alba de Tormes, he could no longer plead that he was unable to advance because he was destitute of cavalry and guns. Moreover, he was now so far informed as to the position—though not as to the numbers—of the French, that he was aware that there was no very serious force in front of himself or of Baird: everything had been turned on to Madrid. Even the 4th Corps, of which Hope had heard during his march, was evidently moving on Segovia and the Guadarrama.

Contemplating the situation, Moore's resolution broke down: he knew what his army was saying about him at the present moment: he guessed what his government would say, if it should chance that Madrid made a heroic defence while he was retreating unpursued on Lisbon and Almeida. A man of keen ambition and soldierly feeling, he could not bear to think that he might be sacrificing

---

[1] He had called on Sir John a few days before, while on his way to Madrid to solicit a military post from the Junta. Moore wrote on Nov. 27 to Mr. Stuart, to say that he had seen him and that ' he never could help having a dislike to people of this description.'

his life's work and reputation to an over-conscientious caution.
Somewhere between eight o'clock and midnight on the night of
December 5 he made up his mind to countermand the retreat. He
dashed off a short note to Castlereagh, and a dispatch to Baird,
and the thing was done.   To the war-minister he wrote that
'considerable hopes were entertained from the enthusiastic manner
in which the people of Madrid resist the French.' This hope he
did not share himself, but 'in consequence of the general opinion,
which is also Mr. Frere's, I have ordered Sir David Baird to
suspend his march [to Corunna] and shall myself continue at this
place until I see further, and shall be guided by circumstances.'
To Madrid he would not go till he was certain that the town was
making a firm defence, and that the spirit of resistance was spreading
all over Spain : but the plan of instant retreat on Portugal was
definitely abandoned [1]. The dispatch to Baird shows even more
of the General's mind, for he and his subordinate were personal
friends, and spoke out freely to each other. The people of Madrid,
Moore wrote, had taken up arms, refused to capitulate, and were
barricading their streets—they said that they would suffer anything rather than submit.   Probably all this came too late, and
Bonaparte was too strong to be resisted.   'There is, however, no
saying, and I feel myself the more obliged to give it a trial,
as Mr. Frere has made a formal representation, which I received
this evening.   All this appears very strange and unsteady—but if
the spirit of enthusiasm *does* arise in Spain, and the people *will* be
martyrs, there is no saying what our force may do.'   Baird therefore
was to stay his march on Corunna, to make arrangements to return
to Astorga, and to send off at once to join the main army one of
his three regiments of hussars [2].   All this was written ere midnight :
at early dawn Moore's mind was still further made up.   He sent
to Sir David orders to push his cavalry to Zamora, his infantry,
brigade by brigade, to Benavente, in the plains of Leon.   'What
is passing at Madrid may be decisive of the fate of Spain, and we
must be at hand to take advantage of whatever happens.   The
wishes of our country and our duty demand it of us, with whatever
risk it may be attended. . . . But if the bubble bursts, and Madrid
falls, we shall have a run for it. . . . Both you and me, though we
may look big, and determine to get everything forward, yet we must

---

[1] Moore to Castlereagh, from Salamanca, Dec. 5.
[2] Moore to Baird, from Salamanca, Dec. 5.

never lose sight of this, that at any moment affairs may take the turn that will render it necessary to retreat[1].'

If only Moore had discovered on November 13, instead of on December 5, that events at Madrid were important, and that his country's wishes and his duty required him to take a practical interest in them, the winter campaign of 1808 would have taken —for good or evil—a very different shape from that which it actually assumed. Meanwhile his resolve came too late. Madrid had actually capitulated thirty-six hours before he received the letters of Morla and of Frere. Moreover the offensive could not be assumed till Baird should have retraced his steps from Villa-franca, and returned to the position at Astorga from which his wholly unnecessary retreat had removed him.

A painful and rather grotesque scene had to be gone through on the morning of December 6. Colonel Charmilly had been received by Moore on the previous night in such a dry and formal manner, that it never occurred to him that the letter which he had delivered was likely to have had any effect. Accordingly he presented himself for the second time next morning, with Frere's supplementary epistle, taking it for granted that retreat was still the order of the day, and making the demand for the assembly of a Council of War. Moore, fresh from the severe mental struggle which attended the reversal of all his plans, was in no mood for politeness. Righteously indignant at what seemed to him both a deliberate personal insult, and an intrigue to undermine his authority with his subordinates, he burst out into words of anger and contempt, and told his provost-marshal to expel Charmilly from the camp without a moment's delay[2]. When this had been done, he sat down to write a dispatch to Frere, in which his conscientious desire to avoid hard words with a British minister struggled in vain with his natural resentment. He began by justifying his original resolve to retreat; and then informed his correspondent that 'I should never have thought of asking your opinion or advice, as the determination was founded on circumstances with which you could not be acquainted, and was a question

---

[1] Moore to Baird, from Salamanca, Dec. 6. The strange grammar would seem to show that the letter was dashed off in a hurry, and never revised.

[2] Charmilly, greatly indignant, published a narrative of the whole, in which he justified himself and his character. It does not alter the main facts of the case.

purely military, of which I thought myself the best judge.' When
he made up his mind, the army had been hopelessly divided into
fractions, and there was good reason at that moment to fear
that the French would prevent their concentration. But as the
resistance made by the people of Madrid had deterred Bonaparte
from detaching any corps against him, and the junction of the
British divisions now seemed possible, the situation was changed.
'Without being able to say exactly in what manner, everything
shall be done for the assistance of Madrid, and the Spanish cause,
that can be expected from an army such as I command.' But
Moore would not move till Baird came up, and even then, he said,
he would only have 26,000 men fit for duty[1]. Believing that
Frere's conduct had been inspired by a regard for the public
welfare, he should abstain from any comment on the two letters
brought by Colonel Charmilly. But he must confess that he
both felt and expressed much indignation at a person of that sort
being made the channel of communication between them. 'I have
prejudices against all that class, and it is impossible for me to put
any trust in him. I shall therefore thank you not to employ him
in any communication with me[2].'

Moore had kept his temper more in hand than might have been
expected, considering the provocation that he had received: the
same cannot be said for Frere, whose next letter, written from
Truxillo on December 9, ended by informing the general that 'if
the British army had been sent abroad for the express object of
doing the utmost possible mischief to the cause of Spain, short
of actually firing upon the Spanish troops, they would have most
completely fulfilled their purpose by carrying out exactly the
measures which they have taken[3].' This was unpardonable language from one official writing a state paper to another, and it is
regrettable to find that Frere made no formal apology for it in
his later dispatches. Even when he discovered that Moore was
actually executing a diversion against the communications of the
French army, he only wrote that he was 'highly gratified' to find
that they were at last agreed on the advisability of such a

---

[1] His muster-rolls show 33,000 troops in all, with 29,000 actually present
with the colours, but Leith's brigade and the 82nd, 2,539 men, were not up.

[2] Moore to Frere, Dec. 6. The version presented to Parliament has been
somewhat expurgated : I quote from that given by James Moore.

[3] Frere to Moore, from Truxillo, Dec. 9.

move [1]. Frere's uncontrolled expressions showed that he was entirely
unfit for a diplomatic post, and cannot be too strongly reprobated.
At the same time we are forced to concede that his main thesis
was perfectly true: nothing could have been more unhappy than
that the aid of a British army of 33,000 men should have been
promised to Spain: that the army should have marched late, in
isolated divisions and by the wrong roads: that after its van had
reached Salamanca on November 13, it should not have taken one
step in advance up to December 5: that just as Madrid was
attacked it should tamely begin to retreat on Corunna and Lisbon.
Moore was only partly responsible for all this: but it is certain
that the whole series of movements had in truth been calculated
to do the utmost possible mischief to the cause of Spain and of
England. If Moore had died or been superseded on December 4,
1808, he would have been written down as wellnigh the worst
failure in all the long list of incompetent British commanders since
the commencement of the Revolutionary War.

It is, therefore, with all the greater satisfaction that we now
pass on to the second part of the campaign of the British army in
Spain, wherein Moore showed himself as resourceful, rapid, and
enterprising as he had hitherto appeared slow and hesitating.
Having once got rid of the overcaution which had hitherto
governed his movements, and having made up his mind that it
was right to run risks, he showed that the high reputation which
he enjoyed in the British army was well deserved.

Moore's first intention, as is shown by his orders to Baird and
his letters to Castlereagh, was merely to disturb the French communications by a sudden raid on Valladolid, or even on Burgos.
If Madrid was really holding out, the Emperor would not be able
to send any large detachment against him, unless he made up his
mind to raise the siege of the capital. It was probable that
Bonaparte would consider the destruction of an English army of
even more importance than the prosecution of the siege, and that
he would come rushing northward with all his army. In that
case, as Moore wrote to Baird, 'we shall have a run for it,' but
Madrid would be saved. In short, Napoleon was to be treated
like the bull in the arena, who is lured away from a fallen adversary
by having a red cloak dangled before his eyes. Supposing that
the main force of the French were turned upon him, Moore was

[1] Frere to Moore, from Merida, Dec. 14.

perfectly well aware that his line of retreat on Portugal would
be cut, for troops marching from the neighbourhood of Madrid,
via the Guadarrama Pass, might easily seize Salamanca.   But it
is one of the privileges of the possessor of sea-power that he can
change his base whenever he chooses, and Moore wrote to Castlereagh to request that transports might be massed at Corunna
for the reception of his army.   If forced to fall back on that
place he intended to sail round to Lisbon or to Cadiz, as circumstances might dictate.

In the unlikely event of Bonaparte's persisting in the siege of
Madrid, and sending only small detachments against the British
army, Moore thought that he would be strong enough to make
matters very unpleasant for the enemy in Old Castile.   If he beat
the forces immediately opposed to him, and seized Valladolid and
Burgos, the Emperor would be compelled to come north, whether
he wished it or no.

All these plans were perfectly reasonable and well concerted,
considering the information that was at Moore's disposition on
December 6.   But that information was based on two false
premises : the one was that Madrid was likely to hold out for
some little time—Moore never supposed that it could be for very
long, for he remained fixed in his distrust of Spanish civic virtues :
the second was that the French army in the north of Spain did
not amount to more than 80,000 or 100,000 men, an estimate
which had been repeated to him by every Spaniard with whom
he had communicated, and which had been confirmed, not only
by Frere, but by Stuart and other English correspondents in whom
he had some confidence.   If he had known that the French had
entered Madrid on December 4, and that they numbered more
than 250,000 bayonets and sabres, his plans would have been
profoundly modified [1].

---

[1] Moore's plans between Dec. 6 and 10, the day on which he got news of
the fall of Madrid, must be gathered from his rather meagre dispatches to
Castlereagh of midnight, Dec. 5, and of Dec. 8 ; from his much more explicit
letters to Frere on Dec. 6 and 10 ; from that to La Romana on Dec. 8 ; and
most of all from the very interesting and confidential letters to Baird on
Dec. 6 and 8.

His doubts as to the permanence of the outburst of enthusiasm in Madrid
are plainly expressed in nearly every one of these epistles.   The terrible
under-estimate of Napoleon's disposable forces is to be found in that to
Castlereagh on Dec. 12, where he writes that 'the French force in Spain

Moore's original intention was to move on Valladolid, a great centre of roads, and a sort of halfway-house between Burgos and Madrid. Meanwhile, Baird was to come down from Astorga via Benavente, and to converge on the same point. A cavalry screen in front of the combined force was formed, by pushing the two regiments which belonged to Moore's own corps towards Alaejos and Tordesillas, on the south bank of the Douro; while Baird's cavalry brigade, under Lord Paget, made a forced march from Astorga to Toro, and extended itself north of the river. Moore's infantry was not to move till the tenth, but that of Baird was already returning as fast as it could manage from Villafranca to Astorga. The unfortunate orders of retreat, issued on November 29, had cost Sir David six marches, three from Astorga to Villafranca and three from Villafranca to Astorga—time lost in the most miserable and unnecessary fashion. One of his brigades, that of General Leith [1], was now so far off that it never managed to overtake the army, and was out of the game for something like a fortnight. But the rest, which had only to return from Villafranca [2], succeeded in joining the main body in much better time than might have been expected. The fact was that the news of an advance had restored the high spirits of the whole army, and the men stepped out splendidly through the cold and rainy winter days, and easily accomplished their twenty miles between dawn and dusk.

Moore, meanwhile, was occupied at Salamanca in making the last preparations for his advance. He had already sent back into Portugal one large convoy on December 5, escorted by the fifth battalion of the 60th Regiment. He now dispatched another which marched by Ciudad Rodrigo, where it picked up the 3rd Foot, who guarded it back to Portugal [3]. The two between them contained all his heavy baggage, and all the sick from his base hospital who could bear transport—probably more than 1,500 invalids: for the total number of the sick of the army was very nearly 4,000, and the larger half of them must have belonged to Moore's own corps,

may fairly be set down at 80,000 men, besides what is in Catalonia.' Acting upon this hypothesis, it is no wonder that he was convinced that Bonaparte could not both besiege Madrid and hunt the British army.

[1] Consisting of the 51st Regiment, 59th (2nd batt.), and 76th.

[2] Except the 'Light Brigade' of Baird's army which had never left Astorga, having been intended to act with the cavalry as a rearguard.

[3] The 3rd had been at Ciudad Rodrigo since Oct. 29 guarding communications.

which was in worse trim than that of Baird. The loss of the
regiments sent off on escort duty was partly made up a few days
later by the arrival of the 82nd, which came up by forced marches
from Oporto, and reached Benavente on December 26. It was
the leading battalion of a brigade which the government had
resolved to add to Moore's force from the slender division of
Cradock: the other two battalions of the brigade were too far
behind, and never succeeded in joining the field-army[1]. Allowing
for these final changes we find that Moore and Baird started forth
with 29,946 effective sabres and bayonets—in which are included
1,687 men on detachment: they left behind them nearly 4,000
sick[2]. If we deduct 2,539 for Leith's brigade, which was still far
beyond Villafranca, and for the belated 82nd, the actual force which
carried out the great raid into the plain of Old Castile must have
been just over 25,000 strong: of these 2,450 were cavalry, and
there were 1,297 artillery gunners and drivers with sixty-six guns.

Moore had, of course, given notice to La Romana of his change
of plan: in response to his letter of December 6 the Marquis
expressed his pleasure at the prospect of the union of the allied
armies, and his wish to co-operate to the best of his power[3]. He
had now collected 20,000 men—a formidable army on paper—and
was certain to do his best, but what that might amount to was
very doubtful. It was well known that a great part of his troops
were not fit to move: but it was not till a few days later that
Moore received definite intelligence as to the exact amount of
military aid that might be furnished by the army of the Left.

The British troops were fully committed to their new plan of
campaign—Baird was hastening back to Astorga, the sick and the
convoys had started for Portugal, the cavalry had pushed well
to the front—when Moore suddenly received a piece of intelligence
which profoundly modified the situation. Madrid had fallen into

[1] They were the 45th (1st batt.) and the 97th.

[2] See the tables in the Appendix. It seems to result that the gross total
who marched from Corunna and Lisbon was 33,884, that the deduction of
3,938 sick leaves 29,946. Leith's battalions and the 82nd were 2,539 strong,
the men on detachment 1,687: this leaves 25,720 for the actual marching
force.

[3] As Arteche very truly observes, the letter of La Romana cannot be safely
quoted (after the fashion of James Moore on his p. 122) as approving of the
retreat on Portugal. He is answering the dispatch of Dec. 6, not that of
Nov. 28.

the hands of Bonaparte: the news was brought by Colonel Graham, who had been sent off with the reply to Morla and Castelfranco. Forced to make a long detour, because all the direct roads were known to be in the hands of the French, he had fallen in at Talavera with the fugitive army from the Escurial, and had almost witnessed the murder of San Juan. From information given him by various persons, and especially by two belated members of the Central Junta, he learnt that Napoleon had stormed the Retiro and the Prado, and that Morla had signed a capitulation. The populace were said to be still in possession of their arms, and it was supposed that there would be much trouble in pacifying the city; but there was no doubt that, from a military point of view, it was in the Emperor's power [1].

Considering Moore's earlier doubts and hesitations, we should almost have expected that this news would have induced him to throw up his whole plan for an advance into Old Castile, and once more to order a retreat on Almeida. But he evidently considered that he was now committed to the raid on Bonaparte's lines of communication, and thought that, even if he could not save Madrid, he could at least distract the enemy from an attempt to push further south, and give the Spanish armies time to rally. There was a chance, as he wrote to Castlereagh [2], that he might effect something, and he should take it, committing himself to Fortune: 'If she smiles we may do some good: if not, we shall still I hope have the merit of having done all that we could. The army, for its numbers, is excellent, and is (I am confident) quite determined to do its duty.'

On December 11 the infantry at last began to move forward from Salamanca—a month all but two days had elapsed since its vanguard reached that city. On that day the reserve division, under General E. Paget, and Beresford's brigade of Fraser's division marched for Toro, where they found Lord Paget with Baird's cavalry, ready to cover their advance. These troops were to form the left-hand column of the advance on Valladolid. On the next day Hope's detachment from Alba de Tormes, and the brigades of Bentinck, Fane, Hill, and Charles Alten from Salamanca, which formed the right-hand column, marched for Alaejos and Tordesillas. In front of them was Charles Stewart's cavalry brigade,

[1] Graham to Moore, from Talavera, Dec. 7–8.
[2] Moore to Castlereagh, from Salamanca, Dec. 10.

which, on the same evening (December 12), fell upon a French cavalry patrol at Rueda and captured it whole, only one man escaping. The prisoners turned out to belong to the 22nd Chasseurs of Franceschi's cavalry division, which, as it was discovered, lay at Valladolid without any infantry supports[1]. They expressed the greatest surprise at finding themselves assailed by English cavalry, as they were under the impression that Moore had retired on Lisbon some days before. This side-light on the general ignorance prevailing in the French army as to the position and designs of the British was very valuable : the first meeting with the enemy, trifling as was the success, promised well for the future.

On the thirteenth Moore himself came up from Salamanca to Alaejos, where he overtook the infantry. Stewart's cavalry meanwhile pushed on to Tordesillas and Medina del Campo, without coming across any traces of the French. At Tordesillas they found themselves in touch with Lord Paget's horsemen on the other side of the Douro, who had also met with no opposition whatever. On the fifteenth the whole army would have converged on Valladolid, if Moore's original intention had been carried out. But a fortunate accident intervened to prevent this march, which would have placed the British troops nearer to Madrid and to the Emperor than did the route which they finally adopted.

There was brought to Moore at Alaejos an intercepted dispatch from Berthier to Soult, containing the most valuable information. The officer bearing it had been sent off from Madrid without an escort, according to the Emperor's usual habit—a habit that cost the lives of some scores of unfortunate aides-de-camp during the first year of the Peninsular War. It was only by experience that Napoleon and his marshals learnt that isolated officers travelling in this fashion were devoted in Spain to probable death and possible torture, as Marbot (after a personal experience of the kind) bitterly observed. The bearer of this particular dispatch had been murdered by peasants at the post-house of Valdestillos, near Segovia.

The document was full of invaluable facts and details. It informed Soult that with his existing force—the two infantry divisions of Merle and Mouton, and the four cavalry regiments of

---

[1] There were thirty of these dragoons : with them were fifty infantry, apparently a belated detail or foraging party from Lefebvre's corps.

Franceschi's division [1]—he was strong enough to march straight before him from Saldaña, and to overrun the whole kingdom of Leon. He was to seize the towns of Leon, Zamora, and Benavente, and to sweep the débris of the army of Galicia into its native mountains. He would find nothing else to oppose him; for the English, as all accounts agreed, were in full retreat on Lisbon. They had last been heard of at Salamanca and the Escurial. A knowledge of this plan was valuable to Moore, but still more so was what followed —a sketch of the position of the French army at the moment when the dispatch was written. The advanced guard of the 'Grand Army' (Lefebvre's corps) was at Talavera, and would shortly be at Badajos: Bessières was chasing Castaños beyond the Upper Tagus, on the road to Valencia. Mortier's and Junot's corps had reached Spain: the former had been ordered off to aid in the siege of Saragossa: the latter was on the march to Burgos, and its leading division had reached Vittoria. The chief omission was that Berthier did not mention the Imperial Guard or the corps of Ney, which were in or about Madrid when he wrote, and were probably destined to follow Lefebvre's march on Badajos and Lisbon. The dispatch ends with the curious note that 'His Majesty is in the best of health. The city of Madrid is quite tranquil: the shops are open, theatrical amusements have been resumed, and you would never suppose that our first addresses to the place had been emphasized by 4,000 cannon-balls [2].'

Moore was thus placed in possession of the Emperor's plan of campaign, and of the dislocation of the greater part of his army. Most important of all, he discovered that his own position and designs were wholly unsuspected. His mind was soon made up: Soult, as it seemed, with his 15,000 or 16,000 men at Saldaña and Carrion, was about to move forward into Leon. He would thus be placed at an enormous distance from the Emperor, and would have no solid supports save the leading division of Junot's corps, which must now be drawing near to Burgos. If he advanced, the whole British army, aided by whatever troops La Romana could produce, might be hurled upon him. The results could not be

---

[1] Berthier speaks as if Mouton were still commanding one of Soult's divisions, but he was now gone, and Mermet's name ought to appear.

[2] This dispatch, though often published, has been deliberately omitted (like some others) in the *Correspondance de Napoléon*, vol. xviii, probably because it shows the Emperor in one of his least omniscient moods.

doubtful, and a severe defeat inflicted on the 2nd Corps would shake the hold of the French on Northern Spain, and ruin all the Emperor's plans.   Moreover the region where Soult might be looked for, about Carrion, Sahagun, and Mayorga, was far more remote from Madrid than the Valladolid country, where Moore was originally intending to strike his blow, so that several days would be gained before the Emperor could interfere.

Accordingly, on December 15, the whole army suddenly changed its direction from eastward to northward.   The left-hand column of the infantry crossed the Douro at Zamora, the right-hand column at Toro.   The cavalry, screening the march of both, went northward from Tordesillas to the banks of the Sequillo, pushing its advanced parties right up to Valladolid, and driving back the dragoons of Franceschi, several of whose detachments they cut off, capturing a colonel and more than a hundred men.   They inter-cepted the communications between Burgos and Madrid to such effect that Bonaparte believed that the whole British army was moving on Valladolid, and drew up his first plan of operations under that hypothesis[1].

Meanwhile four good marches [December 16–20] carried Moore's infantry from Zamora and Toro by the route Villalpando—Valderas to Mayorga.   The weather was bitterly cold, which in one way favoured the movement, for the frost hardened the country roads, which would otherwise have been mere sloughs of mud.   A little snow fell from time to time, but not enough to incommode the troops.   They marched well, kept their discipline, and left few sick or stragglers behind.   This was the result of good spirits, for they had been told that they would meet the French before the week was out.   At Mayorga the junction with Baird's column was safely effected.

When the army had thus completed its concentration, Sir John Moore, for reasons which it is not quite easy to understand, re-arranged all its units.   He formed it into four divisions and two

---

[1] It is clear from *Nap. Corresp.*, 14,614, 14,616–7, that Franceschi actually evacuated Valladolid and retired northwards.   Napoleon at first believed that Moore had occupied the place : but 14,620 mentions that no more happened than that 100 hussars swooped down on it on Dec. 19, and carried off the intendant of the province and 300,000 reals (£3,000) from the treasury. This exploit is omitted by nearly every English writer.   Only Vivian mentions it in his diary, and says that the lucky captors belonged to the 18th Hussars (*Mémoirs*, p. 94).   What became of the money ?

independent light brigades. The 1st Division was given to Sir
David Baird, the 2nd to Sir John Hope, the 3rd to General Fraser,
the 4th (or Reserve) to General E. Paget. The two light brigades
were under Charles Alten and Robert Crawfurd (now as always
to be carefully distinguished from Catlin Crawfurd, who commanded
a brigade of Hope's division). All the old arrangements of the
army of Portugal were broken up: Baird was given three regiments
which had come from Lisbon : on the other hand he had to make
over four of his Corunna battalions to Hope and two to Fraser.
Apparently the idea of the Commander-in-chief was to mix the
corps who had already had experience of the French in Portugal
with the comparatively raw troops who had landed in Galicia.
Otherwise it is impossible to understand the gratuitous divorce of
regiments which had been for some time accustomed to act together.
The cavalry was formed as a division of two brigades under Lord
Paget : the three hussar regiments from Corunna formed one, under
General Slade ; the two corps from Lisbon the other, under Charles
Stewart, the brother of Lord Castlereagh. Of the whole army
only the 82nd and Leith's brigade were still missing : the former
had not yet reached Benavente. The belated regiments of the latter
were still on the further side of Astorga, and never took any part
in the advance.

During this march Moore at last got full information as to the
state of La Romana's troops, and the aid that might be expected
from them. The Marquis himself, writing to contradict a false
report that he was retiring on Galicia, confessed that two-thirds of
his 20,000 men wanted reclothing from head to foot, and that
there was a terrible want of haversacks, cartridge-boxes, and shoes.
He complained bitterly that the provinces (i. e. Asturias and
Galicia) were slack and tardy in forwarding him supplies, and laid
much of the blame on them[1]. But he would move forward the
moment he could be assisted by Baird's troops in pressing the
French in his front. He reported that Soult had 10,000 infantry

[1] Toreño, being an Asturian, is rather indignant at Romana's reflection on
the Junta of his province, and observes (i. 324) that the Marquis did not
take the trouble to ask for help from them, only writing them a single letter
during his stay at Leon. But they sent him some tents, and took in some
of his sick. From Galicia there was coming for him an enormous convoy
with 100 wagons of English boots and clothes : but it was three weeks too
late, and had only reached Lugo by Jan. 1.

at Saldaña, Carrion, and Almanza, with cavalry out in advance at Sahagun : he dared not move across their front southward, for to do so would uncover the high-road through Leon to the Asturias. But the appearance of Baird on the Benavente—Palencia road should be the signal for him to advance against the French in conjunction with his allies [1].

Romana's description of his army did not sound very promising. But a confidential report from an English officer who had visited his cantonments gave an even less favourable account of the Galicians. Colonel Symes had seen four of the seven divisions which formed the ' Army of the Left.' He wrote that the soldiers were ' in general, stout young men, without order or discipline, but not at all turbulent or ferocious. Their clothing was motley, and some were half-naked. Their manœuvres were very confusedly performed, and the officers were comparatively inferior to the men. The equipment was miserable : of sixteen men of General Figueroa's guard only six had bayonets. The springs and locks of the muskets often did not correspond. A portion of them—at least one-third —would not explode, and a French soldier could load and fire his piece with precision thrice, before a Spaniard could fire his twice.' Of the three divisions which he saw reviewed at Leon, one (the 5th, the old troops from the Baltic) seemed superior to the rest, and was armed with good English firelocks : there was also a corps of light troops, 1,000 men in uniform, who might be called respectable [2]. . . . Without undervaluing the spirit of patriotism of the Spaniards, which might in the end effect their deliverance, the writer of the report could only say that they were not, and for a very long time could not be, sufficiently improved in the art of war to be coadjutors in a general action with the British : if any reliance were placed on Spanish aid in the field, terrible disappointment must result : ' we must stand or fall through our own means [3].' Colonel Symes doubted whether La Romana would even dare to take his troops into the field at all—wherein he did the Marquis grave injustice : he had every intention of doing his best—though that best turned

---

[1] Romana to Moore, from Leon, Dec. 14.

[2] Possibly the two light infantry battalions (Catalonia and Barcelona) of the Baltic division.

[3] Symes to Baird, from Leon, Dec. 14. Baird, of course, forwarded the letter to Moore. I have cut down the report to one-third of its bulk, by omitting the less important parts.

out to be merely the bringing to the front of the 7,000 or 8,000 men out of his 22,000, who were more or less armed and equipped, while the rest were left behind as wholly unserviceable.

With this document before him, Moore must have found a certain grim humour in the perusal of a letter from the Supreme Junta, which reached him at Toro on December 16, informing him that La Romana would join him with 14,000 'picked men,' and that within a month 30,000 more Asturian and Galician levies should be at his disposal. This communication was brought to him by Francisco Xavier Caro, the brother of the Marquis, who was himself a member of the Junta. With him came Mr. Stuart, as an emissary from the British minister, bringing the last of those unhappy epistles which Frere had written before he knew that the plan of retreating on Portugal had been given up. We have already quoted one of its insulting phrases on page 524 : the rest was in the same strain. Fortunately, it could be disregarded, as Moore was actually advancing on the enemy, with a definite promise of help from La Romana. Caro professed to be much delighted that the Junta's hopes were at last obtaining fruition. Stuart expressed surprise and grief at the tone of Frere's letters, and 'seemed not much pleased at his mission [1].' This was the last of the many troubles with the British and Spanish civil authorities which were destined to harass the Commander-in-chief. For the future it was only military cares that were to weigh upon his mind.

On December 20 the army had concentrated at Mayorga. Somewhat to his disappointment Moore discovered that Soult had not begun the advance on Leon which Berthier's intercepted dispatch had ordered. Either no duplicate of it had been received by the Marshal, or he had been disconcerted by the report that the English were on the move for Valladolid. That they were coming against his own force he can as yet hardly have guessed. He was still in his old position, one infantry division at Saldaña, the other at Carrion. Debelle's light-cavalry brigade lay in front as a screen, with its head quarters at Sahagun, only nine miles from the English advanced pickets, which had reached the abbey of Melgar Abaxo.

The proximity of the enemy led Lord Paget, who showed himself throughout the campaign a most admirable and enterprising cavalry commander, to attempt a surprise. Marching long ere

[1] Moore's diary, quoted in his brother's memoir of him, pp. 141, 142.

dawn with the 10th and 15th Hussars, he reached the vicinity of
Sahagun without being discovered.   Debelle had no outlying
vedettes, and his main-guard on the high-road was suddenly surrounded and captured before it was aware that an enemy was near.
Only a single trooper escaped, but he aroused the town, and Paget,
hearing the French trumpets sounding in the streets, saw that he
must lose no time.   He sent General Slade with the 10th Hussars
by the straight road into Sahagun, while he himself galloped
around it with the 15th to cut off the enemy's retreat.   As he
reached the suburb he found Debelle forming up his two regiments
—the 8th Dragoons and the 1st Provisional Chasseurs—among
the snow-covered stumps of a vineyard.   Nothing could be seen of
the 10th, which was scouring the town, but Paget formed up the
15th for a charge.   His first movement was checked by an unexpected ditch ; but moving rapidly down it he crossed at a place
where it was practicable, and found Debelle changing front to meet
him.   Catching the French before they had begun to move—their
new formation was not yet quite completed—Paget charged into
them without hesitation, though they outnumbered him by nearly
two to one.   He completely rode down the front regiment, the
provisional chasseurs, and flung it back on to the dragoons, who
broke and fled.   The chasseurs, who were commanded by Colonel
Tascher, a cousin of the Empress Josephine, were half destroyed :
two lieutenant-colonels, eleven other officers, and 157 men were
taken prisoners, twenty were killed, many were wounded [1].   The
regiment indeed was so mauled that Bonaparte dissolved it soon
after, and replaced it in Franceschi's division by the 1st Hussars,
which had just arrived from France.

This was perhaps the most brilliant exploit of the British cavalry
during the whole six years of the war.   When the Peninsular
medals were distributed, nearly forty years after, a special clasp
was very rightly given for it, though many combats in which a
much larger number of men were engaged received no such notice.
While reading the records of later stages of the war the historian
must often regret that Wellington never, till Waterloo, had the
services of Paget as commander of his light cavalry.   There were
unfortunate personal reasons which rendered the presence of the

---

[1] Compare Lord Londonderry (a participator in the charge), Vivian, Adam
Neale, and on the French side, Colonel St. Chamans, Soult's aide-de-camp.
The British lost only 14 men (Vivian, p. 97).

victor of Sahagun and Benavente impossible in the camp of the victor of Vimiero [1].

The scared survivors of Debelle's brigade rode back to give Soult notice that the enemy was upon him, and might close in on the very next day. Meanwhile Moore's infantry, following in the wake of Paget's horse, reached Sahagun on the evening of the twenty-first. It was to be almost their last step in advance. The general allowed one day's rest to enable the rear divisions to close up to the van, so that all might advance on Saldaña and Carrion in a compact mass. He intended to deliver his much-desired blow at Soult upon the twenty-third.

The Duke of Dalmatia, though he had heard nothing as yet of the British infantry, made the right inference from the vigorous way in which his cavalry had been driven in, and concluded that Moore was not far off. He drew down his second infantry division from Saldaña to Carrion, thus concentrating his corps, and sent aides-de-camp to Burgos and Palencia to hurry up to his support every regiment that could be found. The disposable troops turned out to be Lorges's division of dragoons, and Delaborde's division of the 8th Corps, which were both on their way from Burgos to Madrid. The rest of Junot's infantry was two days off, on the road from Vittoria to Burgos. The brigade of Franceschi's cavalry which had evacuated Valladolid, was also heard of on the Palencia road. No news or orders had been received from Madrid, with which place communication was now only possible by the route of Aranda, that by Valladolid being closed.

If Moore, allowing his infantry the night of the twenty-first and the morning of the twenty-second to recruit their strength, had marched on Carrion on the afternoon of the latter day, he would have caught Soult at a disadvantage at dawn on the twenty-third, for none of the supporting forces had yet got into touch with the Marshal. If the latter had dared to make a stand, he would have been crushed: but it is more probable that—being a prudent general—he would have fallen back a march in the direction of Burgos. But, as it chanced, Moore resolved to give his men forty-eight hours instead of thirty-six at Sahagun—and twelve hours

[1] After his return from Spain in January, 1809, Paget eloped with the wife of Henry Wellesley, the younger brother of Wellington. Naturally they could not be placed together for many years, and Paget lost his chance of seeing any more of the war. But at Waterloo he gloriously vindicated his reputation as the best living British cavalry-officer.

often suffice to change the whole situation. The army was told to rest as long as daylight lasted on the twenty-third, and to march at nightfall, so as to appear in front of the bridge of Carrion at dawn on the twenty-fourth. Attacked at daybreak, the Marshal would, as Moore hoped, find no time to organize his retreat and would thus be forced to fight.

While waiting at Sahagun for the sun to set, Moore received a dispatch from La Romana to say that, in accordance with his promise, he had marched from Leon to aid his allies. But he could only put into the field some 8,000 men and a single battery —with which he had advanced to Mansilla, with his vanguard at Villarminio, on the road to Saldaña. He was thus but eighteen miles from Sahagun, and though he had only brought a third of his army with him, could be utilized in the oncoming operations.

But this was not the only news which reached Moore on the afternoon of the twenty-third. Only two short hours before he received the dispatch from Mansilla, another note from La Romana had come in, with information of very much greater importance. A confidential agent of the Marquis, beyond the Douro, had sent him a messenger with news that all the French forces in the direction of the Escurial were turning northward and crossing the Guadarrama. Putting this intelligence side by side with rumours brought in by peasants, to the effect that great quantities of food and forage had been ordered to be collected in the villages west of Palencia, Moore drew the right inference. What he had always expected had come to pass. Napoleon had turned north from Madrid, and was hastening across the mountains to overwhelm the British army [1].

Without losing a moment, Moore countermanded his advance on Carrion. The orders went out at nine o'clock, when the leading brigades had already started. As the men were tramping over the frozen snow, in full expectation of a fight at dawn, they were suddenly told to halt. A moment later came the command to turn back by the road that they had come, and to retire to their bivouacs of the previous day. Utterly puzzled and much disgusted the troops returned to Sahagun.

---

[1] From Moore's dispatch to La Romana, written on the twenty-third, we gather that the letter with the news about the French movements came in about six p.m., and the second one with the report that the Spaniards had reached Mansilla about eight. The latter is acknowledged in a postscript to Moore's reply to the former. The resolve to retreat was made between six and eight o'clock.

SECTION VIII: CHAPTER IV

NAPOLEON'S PURSUIT OF MOORE: SAHAGUN TO ASTORGA

WE have many times had occasion in this narrative to wonder at the extreme tardiness with which news reached the Spanish and the English generals. It is now at the inefficiency of Napoleon's intelligence department that we must express our surprise. Considering that Moore had moved forward from Salamanca as far back as December 12, and had made his existence manifest to the French on that same day by the successful skirmish at Rueda, it is astonishing to find that the Emperor did not grasp the situation for nine days. Under the influence of his pre-conceived idea that the British must be retiring on Lisbon, he was looking for them in every other quarter rather than the banks of the Upper Douro. On the seventeenth he was ordering reconnaissances to be made in the direction of Plasencia [1] in Estremadura (of all places in the world) to get news of Moore, and was still pushing troops towards Talavera on the road to Portugal. The general tendency of all his movements was in this direction, and there can be no doubt that in a few days his great central reserve would have followed in the wake of Lasalle and Lefebvre, and started for Badajoz and Elvas. On the nineteenth he reviewed outside Madrid the troops that were available for instant movement—the Imperial Guard, the corps of Ney, the divisions of Leval and Lapisse—about 40,000 men with 150 guns, all in excellent order, and with fifteen days' biscuit stored in their wagons [2]. Of the direction they were to take we can have no doubt, when we read in the imperial

---

[1] *Nap. Corresp.*, 14,577 [Dec. 17], orders Lasalle's cavalry to push for Plasencia in order to get news of the British army.

[2] Napier (i. 304) says that there were 60,000 men present, but it is hard to see how such a number could have been collected on that day at Madrid; and the official account of the review in the *Madrid Gazette* for Dec. 23 says that 40,000 men appeared, ' all in beautiful order, and testifying their enthusiasm by their shouts as His Majesty rode past the front of each regiment.' The Emperor never understated his forces on such occasions: the tendency was the other way.

correspondence orders for naval officers to be hurried up to reorganize the arsenal of Lisbon [1], and a private note to Bessières—
the commander-in-chief of the cavalry—bidding him start his spare
horses and his personal baggage for Talavera [2].

The Emperor's obstinate refusal to look in the right direction
is very curious when we remember that Moore's cavalry was
sweeping the plains as far as Valladolid from December 12 to 16,
and that on the eighteenth Franceschi had abandoned that important city, while Soult had got news of Moore's being on the
move two days earlier. Clearly either there was grave neglect in
sending information on the part of the French cavalry generals
in Old Castile, or else the Emperor had so convinced himself that
the British were somewhere on the road to Lisbon, that he did
not read the true meaning of the dispatches from the north. Be
this as it may, it is evident that there was a serious failure in the
imperial intelligence department, and that a week or more was
wasted. Bonaparte ought to have been astir two or three days
after Stewart and Paget drove in Franceschi's screen of vedettes.
As a matter of fact it was nine days before any move was made
at the French head quarters: yet Rueda is only ninety-five miles
from Madrid.

The first definite intelligence as to the English being on the
move in Old Castile reached the Emperor on the evening of
December 19. Yet it was only on the twenty-first that he really
awoke to the full meaning of the reports that reached him from
Soult and Franceschi [3]. But when he did at last realize the
situation, he acted with a sudden and spasmodic energy which
was never surpassed in any of his earlier campaigns. He hurled
on to Moore's track not only the central reserve at Madrid, but
troops gathered in from all directions, till he had set at least
80,000 men on the march, to encompass the British corps which
had so hardily thrown itself upon his communications. Moore
had been perfectly right when he stated his belief that the sight
of the redcoats within reach would stir the Emperor up to such
wrath, that he would abandon every other enterprise and rush
upon them with every available man.

On the evening of the twenty-first the French troops from every

---

[1] *Nap. Corresp.*, 14,514, to Admiral Decrés.   Cf. De Pradt, p. 211.

[2] *Nap. Corresp.*, 14,553, to Bessières, Dec. 12.

[3] In *Nap. Corresp.* there is no trace of movement till the twenty-second.

camp around Madrid were pouring out towards the Escurial and the two passes over the Guadarrama. The cavalry of Ney's corps and of the Imperial Guard was in front, then came the masses of their infantry. Lapisse's division fell in behind: an express was sent to Dessolles, who was guarding the road to Calatayud and Saragossa, to leave only two battalions and a battery behind, and to make forced marches on the Escurial with the rest of his men. Another aide-de-camp rode to set Lahoussaye's division of dragoons on the move from Avila[1]. Finally messengers rode north to bid Lorges's dragoons, and all the fractions of Junot's corps, to place themselves under the orders of Soult. Millet's belated division of dragoons was to do the same, if it had yet crossed the Ebro.

The Emperor, once more committing the error of arguing from insufficient data, had made up his mind that the English were at Valladolid[2]. He had no news from that place since Franceschi had abandoned it, and chose to assume that Moore, or at any rate some portion of the British army, was there established. Under this hypothesis it would be easy to cut off the raiders from a retreat on Portugal, or even on Galicia, by carrying troops with extreme speed to Tordesillas and Medina de Rio Seco. This comparatively easy task was all that Napoleon aimed at in his first directions. Villacastin, Arevalo, Olmedo, and Medina del Campo are the points to which his orders of December 21 and 22 require that the advancing columns should be pushed.

For the maintenance of Madrid, and the 'containing' of the Spanish armies at Cuenca and Almaraz, the Emperor left nothing behind but the corps of Lefebvre, two-thirds of the corps of Victor, and the three cavalry divisions of Lasalle, Milhaud, and Latour-Maubourg—8,000 horse and 28,000 foot in all, with ninety guns[3].

---

[1] All this can be studied in *Nap. Corresp.*, 14,609, 14,611, 14,614. The march out towards the Escurial is fixed, by the *Madrid Gazette* of Dec. 23, as having begun late on the twenty-first.

[2] This error appears in *Nap. Corresp.*, 14,614 [Dec. 22], 'si les Anglais veulent tenir à Valladolid'; 14,616 [Dec. 23] says, 'Les Anglais paraissent être à Valladolid, probablement avec une avant-garde.' It is only on Dec. 27 that he writes to King Joseph that they had never been there at all, save with a flying party of 100 light cavalry.

[3] This is Napoleon's own estimate (*Nap. Corresp.*, 14,615). Marshal Jourdan, who was more or less in charge of the whole, as chief of the staff to King Joseph, says that there were in reality only 30,000 men in all

King Joseph was left in nominal command of the whole. Such a force was amply sufficient to hold back the disorganized troops of Galluzzo and Infantado, but not to advance on Seville or on Lisbon. It was impossible that any blow should be dealt to the west or the south, till the Emperor should send back some of the enormous masses of men that he had hurled upon Moore. Thus the English general's intention was fully carried out: his raid into Old Castile had completely disarranged all Bonaparte's plans. It gave the Spaniards at least two months in which to rally and recover their spirits, and it drew the field-army of the Emperor into a remote and desolate corner of Spain, so that the main centres of resistance were left unmolested.

Napoleon had guessed part, but by no means all, of Moore's design. 'The manœuvre of the English is very strange,' he wrote to his brother Joseph; 'it is proved that they have evacuated Salamanca. Probably they have brought their transports round to Ferrol, because they think that the retreat on Lisbon is no longer safe, as we could push on from Talavera by the left bank of the Tagus and shut the mouth of the river. . . . Probably they have evacuated Portugal and transferred their base to Ferrol, because it offers advantages for a safe embarkation. But while retreating, they might hope to inflict a check on the corps of Soult, and may not have made up their mind to try it till they had got upon their new line of retreat, and moved to the right bank of the Douro. They may have argued as follows: " If the French commit themselves to a march on Lisbon, we can evacuate on Oporto, and while doing so are still on our line of communications with Ferrol. Or, possibly, they may be expecting fresh reinforcements. But whatever their plan may be, their move will have a great influence on the end of this whole business."'

The Emperor thought therefore that Moore's main object had been to change an unsafe base at Lisbon for a safe one in Galicia, and that the demonstration against Soult was incidental and secondary. It does not seem to have struck him that the real design was to

(*Mémoires Militaires*, p. 130). Not only was Victor's corps short of the division of Lapisse (which the Emperor had carried off), but Lefebvre's was also incomplete, as two Dutch and one German battalions of Leval's division were behind in Biscay, garrisoning Bilbao and other points. King Joseph's Guards had also left some detachments behind, and up to full strength (*Nap. Corresp.*, 14,615).

lure the central field-army of the French from Madrid, and to postpone the invasion of the south. Many of his apologists and admirers have excused his blindness, by saying that Moore's plan was so rash and hazardous that no sensible man could have guessed it. But this is a complete mistake: the plan, if properly carried out, was perfectly sound. Sir John knew precisely what he was doing, and was prepared to turn on his heel and go back at full speed, the instant that he saw the least movement on the side of Madrid. It was in no rash spirit that he acted, but rather the reverse: 'I mean to proceed bridle in hand,' he said; 'and if the bubble bursts, we shall have a run for it.' And on this principle he acted: three hours after he got notice that Napoleon was on the march, he started to 'make a run for it' to Astorga, and his promptness was such that his main body was never in the slightest danger from the Emperor's rush on Benavente, fierce and sudden though it was. The disasters of the second part of the retreat were not in the least caused by Napoleon's intercepting movement, which proved an absolute and complete failure.

But to proceed: Ney's corps, which led the advance against Moore, crossed the Guadarrama on the night of December 21, and had arrived safely at Villacastin, on the northern side of the passes, on the morning of the twenty-second. As if to contradict the Emperor's statement—made as he was setting out—that 'the weather could not be better,' a dreadful tempest arose that day. When Bonaparte rode up from Chamartin, to place himself at the head of his Guard, which was to cross the mountains on the twenty-second, he found the whole column stopped by a howling blizzard, which swept down the pass with irresistible strength and piled the snow in large drifts at every inconvenient corner of the defile. It is said that several horsemen were flung over precipices by the mere force of the wind. The whole train of cannon and caissons stuck halfway up the ascent, and could neither advance nor retreat. Violently irritated at the long delay, Napoleon turned on every pioneer that could be found to clear away the drifts, set masses of men to trample down the snow into a beaten track, forced the officers and all the cavalry to dismount and lead their horses, and unharnessed half the artillery so as to give double teams to the rest. In this way the Guard, with the Emperor walking on foot in its midst, succeeded at last in crawling through to Villacastin by the night of December 23.

---

[1] Moore to Baird, from Salamanca, Dec. 6.

A considerable number of men died of cold and fatigue, and the passage had occupied some sixteen hours more than had been calculated by the Emperor. The troops which followed him had less trouble in their passage, the tempest having abated its fury, and the path cleared by the Guard being available for their use.

At the very moment at which Moore was countermanding the advance on Sahagun—about seven o'clock on the evening of the twenty-third — Napoleon was throwing himself on his couch at Villacastin, after a day of fatigue which had tried even his iron frame. For the next week the two armies were contending with their feet and not their arms, in the competition which the French officers called the 'race to Benavente[1].' Napoleon was at last beginning to understand that he had not before him the comparatively simple task of cutting the road between Valladolid and Astorga, but the much harder one of intercepting that between Sahagun and Astorga. For the first three days of his march he was still under some hopes of catching the English before they could cross the Esla—and if any of them had been at Valladolid this would certainly have been possible. On December 24 he was at Arevalo: on Christmas Day he reached Tordesillas, where he waited twenty-four hours to allow his infantry to come up with his cavalry. On the twenty-seventh he at last understood—mainly through a letter from Soult—that the English were much further north than he had at first believed. But he was still in high spirits: he did not think it probable that Moore also might have been making forced marches, and having seized Medina de Rio Seco with Ney's corps, he imagined that he was close on the flank of the retreating enemy. 'To-day or to-morrow,' he wrote to his brother Joseph on that morning, 'it is probable that great events will take place. If the English have not already retreated they are lost: even if they have already moved they shall be pursued to the water's edge, and not half of them shall re-embark. Put in your newspapers that 36,000 English are surrounded, that I am at Benavente in their rear, while Soult is in their front[2].' The announcement was duly made in the *Madrid Gazette*, but the Emperor had been deceived as to the condition of affairs, which never in actual fact resembled the picture that he had drawn for himself[3].

---

[1] The phrase will be found in De Pradt, p. 211.

[2] *Nap. Corresp.*, 14,620 (Napoleon to King Joseph, Dec. 27).

[3] Oddly enough Joseph had anticipated his brother's orders, by putting in

Sir John had commenced his retreat from Sahagun on the twenty-fourth, with the intention of retiring to Astorga, and of taking up a position on the mountains behind it that might cover Galicia. He did not intend to retire any further unless he were obliged[1]. If Soult should follow him closely, while the Emperor was still two or three marches away, he announced his intention of turning upon the Marshal and offering him battle. He wrote to La Romana asking him to hold the bridge of Mansilla (the most northerly passage over the Esla) as long as might be prudent, and then to retire on the Asturias, leaving the road to Galicia clear for the English army[2].

At noon on the twenty-fourth Moore started off in two columns: Baird's division marched by the northern road to Valencia de Don Juan, where the Esla is passable by a ford and a ferry: Hope and Fraser took the more southern route by Mayorga and the bridge of Castro Gonzalo. The reserve division under E. Paget, and the two light brigades, remained behind at Sahagun for twenty-four hours to cover the retreat. The five cavalry regiments were ordered to press in closely upon Soult, and to keep him as long as possible in doubt as to whether he was not himself about to be attacked.

This demonstration seems to have served its purpose, for the Marshal made no move either on the twenty-fourth or the twenty-fifth. Yet by the latter day his army was growing very formidable, as all the corps from Burgos and Palencia were reporting themselves to him: Lorges's dragoons had reached Frechilla, and Delaborde with the head of the infantry of Junot's corps was at Paredes, only thirteen miles from Soult's head quarters at Carrion. Loison and Heudelet were not far behind. Yet the English columns marched for two days wholly unmolested.

On the twenty-sixth Baird crossed the Esla at Valencia: the ford was dangerous, for the river was rising: a sudden thaw on the twenty-fourth had turned the roads into mud, and loosened the snows. But the guns and baggage crossed without loss, as did

the *Madrid Gazette* of that very day a notice that a British corps was in the most critical position, that its retreat was cut off, and that ' London, so long insensible to the woes of Spain, will soon grieve over a disaster that is her own and not that of another.'

Moore to La Romana, from Sahagun, night of Dec. 23-4.

[2] Moore to La Romana, from Sahagun, Dec. 24.

also some of the infantry, the rest using the two ferry-boats[1].
Hope and Fraser, on the Mayorga road, had nothing but the
badness of their route to contend against. The soil of this part
of the kingdom of Leon is a soft rich loam, and the cross-roads
were knee-deep in clay: for the whole of the twenty-sixth it
rained without intermission: the troops plodded on in very surly
mood, but as yet there was no straggling. It was still believed
that Moore would fight at Astorga, and, though the men grumbled
that 'the General intended to march them to death first and to
fight after[2],' they still kept together.

But already signs were beginning to be visible that their discipline was about to break down. A good deal of wanton damage
and a certain amount of plunder took place at the halting-places
for the night—Mayorga, Valderas, and Benavente. A voice from
the ranks explains the situation. 'Our sufferings were so great
that many of the men lost their natural activity and spirits, and
became savage in their dispositions. The idea of running away,
without even firing a shot, from the enemy we had beaten so
easily at Vimiero, was too galling to their feelings. Each spoke
to his fellow, even in common conversation, with bitterness: rage
flashed out on the most trifling occasion of disagreement. The
poor Spaniards had little to expect from such men as these, who
blamed them for their inactivity. Every man found at home was
looked upon as a traitor to his country. "Why is not every
Spaniard under arms and fighting? The cause is not ours: are
we to be the only sufferers?" Such was the common language,
and from these feelings pillage and outrage naturally arose[3].'
The men began to seize food in the towns and villages without
waiting for the regular distribution, forced their way into houses,
and (the country being singularly destitute of wood) tore down
sheds and doors to build up their bivouac fires. The most deplorable mischief took place at Benavente, where the regiment
quartered in the picturesque old castle belonging to the Duchess of
Ossuna burnt much of the mediaeval furniture, tore down the
sixteenth-century tapestry to make bed-clothes, and lighted fires

---

[1] There is a good account of this dangerous passage in Adam Neale's
Spanish Campaign of 1808.

[2] Memoir of 'T. S.' of the 71st Highlanders, p. 53.

[3] I am again quoting from the admirable narrative of 'T. S.', the private in
the 71st.   Compare Ormsby's *Letters*, ii. 92–3, for the wanton plundering.

on the floors of the rooms, to the destruction of the porcelain friezes and alcoves [1]. Moore issued a strongly-worded proclamation against these excesses on December 27, blaming the officers for not keeping an eye upon the men, and pointing out that 'not bravery alone, but patience and constancy under fatigue and hardship were military virtues [2].' Unfortunately, such arguments had little effect on the tired and surly rank and file. Things were ere long to grow much worse.

The infantry, as we have seen, accomplished their march to Benavente without molestation, and all, including the rearguard, were across the Esla by the twenty-seventh. Paget's cavalry, however, had a much more exciting time on the last two days. Finding that he was not attacked, Soult began to bestir himself on the twenty-sixth: he sent Lorges's dragoons after the British army, in the direction of Mayorga, while with Franceschi's cavalry and the whole of his infantry he marched by the direct road on Astorga, via the bridge of Mansilla.

Lorges's four regiments were in touch with the rearguard of Paget's hussars on the twenty-sixth and twenty-seventh, but they were not the only or the most important enemies who were now striving to drive in Moore's cavalry screen. The advanced guard of the Emperor's army had just come up, and first Colbert's brigade of Ney's corps and then the cavalry of the Guard began to press in upon Paget: Lahoussaye's dragoons arrived on the scene a little later. It is a splendid testimonial to the way in which the British horsemen were handled, that they held their own for three days against nearly triple forces on a front of thirty miles [3]. No better certificate could be given to them than the fact that the Emperor estimated them, when the fighting was over, at 4,000 or 5,000 sabres, their real force being only 2,400. He wrote, too, in a moment of chagrin when Moore's army had just escaped from him, so that he was not at all inclined to

---

[1] The French did worse, as they burnt the whole castle when they occupied it during the first days of the new year. But that is no justification for the conduct of the British. For a description of the damage done see Ormsby, ii. 102, 103.

[2] General Order, issued at Benavente on Dec. 27.

[3] Five regiments (7th, 10th, and 15th Hussars, 18th Light Dragoons, 3rd K. G. L.) were being pressed by thirteen French regiments—four each of Lorges's and Lahoussaye's, two of Colbert's, and three of the Guard.

exaggerate their numbers, and as a matter of fact rated the
infantry too low.

But under the admirable leading of Paget the British cavalry
held its own in every direction.   Moore was not exaggerating
when he wrote on the twenty-eighth that 'they have obtained
by their spirit and enterprise an ascendency over the French which
nothing but great superiority of numbers on their part can get the
better of[1].'   The 18th Light Dragoons turned back to clear their
rear six times on December 27, and on each occasion drove in the
leading squadrons of their pursuers with such effect that they
secured themselves an unmolested retreat for the next few miles.
At one charge, near Valencia de Don Juan, a troop of thirty-eight
sabres of this regiment charged a French squadron of 105 men, and
broke through them, killing twelve and capturing twenty.   The
10th Hussars, while fending off Lorges's dragoons near Mayorga,
found that a regiment of the light cavalry of Ney had got into
their rear and had drawn itself up on a rising ground flanking
the high-road.   Charging up the slope, and over soil deep in the
slush of half-melted snow, they broke through the enemy's line,
and got off in safety with 100 prisoners.   Every one of Paget's
five regiments had its full share of fighting on the twenty-sixth
and twenty-seventh, yet they closed in on to Benavente in perfect
order, with insignificant losses, and exulting in a complete consciousness of their superiority to the enemy's horse.   Since the
start from Salamanca they had in twelve days taken no less than
500 prisoners, besides inflicting considerable losses in killed and
wounded on the French.   They had still one more success before
them, ere they found themselves condemned to comparative use-
lessness among the mountains of Galicia.

On the twenty-eighth Robert Crawfurd's brigade had waited
behind in the mud and rain, drawn up in front of the bridge of
Castro Gonzalo, 'standing for many hours with arms posted, and
staring the French cavalry in the face, while the water actually ran
out of the muzzles of their muskets[2].'   At last our hussars retired,
and Crawfurd blew up two arches of the bridge when Paget had
passed over, and moved back on Benavente, after some trifling
skirmishing with the cavalry of the Imperial Guard, who had
come up in force and tried to interrupt his work.   The inde-

[1] Moore to Castlereagh, from Benavente, Dec. 28.
[2] *Recollections of Rifleman Harris*, p. 171.

fatigable British horsemen left pickets all along the river on each
side of the broken bridge, ready to report and oppose any attempt
to cross.

After resting for a day in Benavente Moore had sent on the divisions of Fraser and Hope to Astorga, by the highway through La
Baneza. The division of Baird, marching from Valencia by villainous
cross-roads, converged on the same point, where the three corps
met upon December 29. Their march was wholly unmolested by
the French, who were being successfully held back by Moore's rearguard under the two Pagets—the cavalry general and the commander
of the reserve division—and by Crawfurd and Alten's light brigades.
On the same morning that the main body reached Astorga, the
infantry of the rearguard marched out of Benavente, leaving
behind only the horsemen, who were watching all the fords, with
their supports three miles behind in the town of Benavente. Seeing
that all the infantry had disappeared, Lefebvre-Desnouettes, who
commanded the cavalry of the Guard, thought it high time to
press beyond the Esla : it was absurd, he thought, that the mass
of French horsemen, now gathered opposite the broken bridge of
Castro Gonzalo, should allow themselves to be kept in check by a
mere chain of vedettes unsupported by infantry or guns. Accordingly he searched for fords, and when one was found a few hundred
yards from the bridge, crossed it at the head of the four squadrons
of the chasseurs of the Guard, between 500 and 600 sabres [1]. The
rest of his troops, after vainly seeking for other passages, were
about to follow him. The moment that he had got over the
water Lefebvre found himself withstood by the pickets, mainly
belonging to the 18th Light Dragoons, who came riding in
from their posts along the river to mass themselves opposite to
him. When about 130 men were collected, under Colonel Otway,
they ventured to charge the leading squadrons of the chasseurs, of course with indifferent success. After retiring a few
hundred yards more, they were joined by a troop of the 3rd
Dragoons of the King's German Legion, under Major Burgwedel,
and again turned to fight. At this second clash the front line of
the pursuers was broken for a moment, and the dragoons who had
burst through the gap had a narrow escape of being surrounded

---

[1] Napoleon (*Nap. Corresp.*, 14,623) says that the regiment of chasseurs was
only 300 strong, and their loss only sixty. But the splendid regiments of the
Guard cavalry had not yet fallen to this small number of sabres.

and captured by the second line, but finally fought their way out of the *mêlée* with no great loss. Charles Stewart, their brigadier, now came up and rallied them for the second time : he retired towards the town in good order, without allowing himself to be cowed by Lefebvre's rapid advance, for he knew that supports were at hand. Lord Paget, warned in good time, had drawn out the 10th Hussars under cover of the houses of the southern suburb of Benavente. He waited till the chasseurs drew quite near to him, and were too remote from the ford they had crossed to be able to retire with ease : then he suddenly sallied out from his cover and swooped down upon them. The pickets at the same moment wheeled about, cheered, and charged. The enemy, now slightly outnumbered—for the 10th were fully 450 sabres strong, and the pickets at least 200—made a good fight. A British witness observes that these ' fine big fellows in fur caps and long green coats' were far better than the line regiments with which the hussars had hitherto been engaged. But in a few minutes they were broken, and chased for two miles right back to the ford by which they had crossed. Lefebvre himself was captured by a private of the 10th named Grisdale, his wounded horse having refused to swim the river [1]. With him there were taken two captains and seventy unwounded prisoners. The chasseurs left fifty-five men dead or hurt upon the field, and many of those who got away were much cut about [2]. The British casualties were fifty, almost all from the men who had furnished the pickets, for the 10th suffered little : Burgwedel, who had led the Germans of the 3rd K. G. L., was the only officer hurt [3].

The remnant of the chasseurs crossed the river, and were immediately supported by other regiments, who (after failing to find another ford) had come down to that which Lefebvre had used.

---

[1] He was sent to England, and long lived on parole at Cheltenham. While he was there Charles Vaughan called on him, and got from him some valuable information about the first siege of Saragossa, whose history he was then writing. In 1811 Lefebvre broke his parole and escaped to France, where Napoleon welcomed him and restored him to command.

[2] Larrey, the Emperor's surgeon, commenting on sabre-wounds, says that no less than seventy wounded of the chasseurs came under his care on this occasion.

[3] In James Moore's book this gallant officer appears under the English disguise of Major Bagwell, under which I did not at first recognize him (p. 181). Oddly enough Adam Neale makes the same mistake (p. 179).

They showed some signs of attempting a second passage, but Lord Paget turned upon them the guns of Downman's horse-battery, which had just galloped up from Benavente. After two rounds the enemy rode off hastily from the river, and fell back inland. They had received such a sharp lesson that they allowed the British cavalry to retreat without molestation in the afternoon. Napoleon consoled himself with writing that the British were 'flying in panic' —a statement which the circumstances hardly seemed to justify [1]— and gave an exaggerated account of the disorders which they had committed at Valderas and Benavente, to which he added an imaginary outrage at Leon [2]. But there is no more talk of Moore's corps being surrounded—wherefore it suddenly shrinks in the Emperor's estimation, being no longer 36,000 strong, but only '21,000 infantry, with 4,000 or 5,000 horse.' Lefebvre's affair he frankly owned, when writing to King Joseph, was disgusting : 'by evening I had 8,000 horse on the spot, but the enemy was gone [3].'

Paget indeed was so effectively gone, that though French cavalry by the thousand crossed the ford that night they could do nothing. And Crawfurd had so thoroughly destroyed the bridge of Castro Gonzalo—he had blown up the central pier, and not merely cut the crowns of the arches—that infantry and guns could not cross till the thirtieth. It was only on that day that the heads of Ney's corps and of the Imperial Guard came up: Lapisse's division was still far behind, at Toro. All that the rapid forced marches of the Emperor had brought him was the privilege of assisting at Paget's departure, and of picking up in Benavente some abandoned carts, which Moore had caused to be broken after burning their contents.

Napoleon still consoled himself with the idea that it was possible that Soult might have been more fortunate than himself, and might perhaps already be attacking the English at Astorga. This was not the case : after learning that Moore had disappeared from his front, the Duke of Dalmatia had taken the road Sahagun—Mansilla, as the shortest line which would bring him to Astorga, the place

[1] *Nap. Corresp.*, 14,623 (Napoleon to Josephine, from Benavente, Dec. 31), 'Les Anglais fuient épouvantés.'

[2] *Nap. Corresp.*, 14,626 (Napoleon to King Joseph). Joseph is to insert in the Madrid papers letters·written from these three places with descriptions of the brigandage practised by the English—'à Leon ils ont chassé les moines.' No English troops had ever been within thirty miles of Leon !

[3] 'Cette affaire m'a coûté une soixantaine de mes chasseurs. Vous sentez combien cela m'a été désagréable' (ibid.).

where any army intending to defend Galicia would make its first stand. This choice brought him upon the tracks of La Romana's army, not of the British. The Marquis, when Moore retired, had moved back on Leon, but had sent to his ally a message to the effect that he could not accept the suggestion to make the Asturias his base, and would be forced, when the enemy advanced, to join the British at Astorga. It was absolutely impossible, he said, to repair to the Asturias, for the pass of Pajares, the only coach-road thither, was impassable on account of the snow[1]. La Romana left as a rearguard at the all-important bridge of Mansilla, his 2nd Division, 3,000 strong, with two guns. Contrary to Moore's advice he would not blow up the bridge, giving as his reason that the Esla was fordable in several places in its immediate neighbourhood. This was a blunder; but the officer in command of the 2nd Division committed a greater one, by drawing up his main body in front of the bridge and not behind it—a repetition of Cuesta's old error at Cabezon. Soult did not come in contact with the Spanish rear-guard till four days after he had left Carrion: so heavy had been the rain, and so vile the road, that it took him from the twenty-sixth to the twenty-ninth to cover the forty-five miles between Carrion and Mansilla. But on the morning of December 30 he delivered his attack: a tremendous cavalry-charge by the chasseurs and dragoons of Franceschi broke the Spanish line, and pursuers and pursued went pell-mell over the bridge, which was not defended for a moment. The French captured 1,500 men—who were cut off from re-crossing the river—two guns, and two standards. Hearing of this disaster La Romana at once evacuated Leon, which Soult seized on the thirty-first. The place had been hastily fortified, and there had been much talk of the possibility of defending it[2]; but at the first summons it opened its gates without firing a shot. The Marquis—leaving 2,000 sick in the hospitals, and a considerable accumulation of food in his magazines—fell back on Astorga, much to the discontent of Moore, who had not desired to see him in that direction. Soult at Leon was only twenty-five miles from Astorga: he was now but one march from Moore's rearguard, and in close touch with the Emperor, who coming up from the south reached La Baneza on the same day—the last of the old year, 1808.

[1] Symes to Moore, from La Romana's camp at Mansilla, Dec. 25.
[2] Ibid.

The divisions of Baird, Hope, and Fraser, as we have already seen, had reached Astorga on the twenty-ninth, the reserve division and the light brigades (after a most fatiguing march from Benavente) on the thirtieth, while the cavalry was, as always, to the rear, keeping back the advancing squadrons of Bessières. Thus on the thirtieth the English and Spanish armies were concentrated at Astorga with every available man present—the British still 25,000 strong; for they had suffered little in the fighting, and had not yet begun to straggle—but Romana with no more than 9,000 or 10,000 of the nominal 22,000 which had been shown in his returns of ten days before. His 2nd Division had been practically destroyed at Mansilla: he had left 2,000 sick at Leon, and many more had fallen out of the ranks in the march from that place— some because they wished to desert their colours, but more from cold, disease, and misery; for the army was not merely half naked, but infected with a malignant typhus fever which was making terrible ravages in its ranks [1].

Moore had told La Romana on the twenty-fourth that he hoped to make a stand at Astorga. The same statement had been passed round the army, and had kept up the spirits of the men to some extent, though many had begun to believe that 'Moore would never fight [2].' There were magazines of food at Astorga, and much more considerable ones of military equipment: a large convoy of shoes, blankets, and muskets had lately come in from Corunna, and Baird's heavy baggage had been stacked in the place before he marched for Sahagun. The town itself was surrounded with ancient walls, and had some possibilities of defence: just behind it rises the first range of the Galician mountains, a steep and forbidding chain pierced only by the two passes which contain the old

---

[1] All witnesses agree that the army of Galicia was in a most distressing condition. 'This army was literally half naked and half starved,' says Adam Neale. 'A malignant fever was raging among them, and long fatigues, privation, and this mortal distemper made them appear like spectres issuing from a hospital rather than an army' (p. 181). 'T.S.' describes them as 'looking more like a large body of peasants driven from their homes, and in want of everything, than a regular army' (p. 56). The men fit for service are described as being no more than 5,000 strong.

[2] 'We all wished it, but none believed it,' writes 'T.S.' 'We had been told the same at Benavente, but our movement had no appearance of a retreat in which we were to face about and make a stand: it was more like a shameful flight' (p. 56). This undoubtedly was the prevailing view in the ranks.

and the new high-roads to Corunna. The former—the shorter, but by far the more rugged—is called the defile of Foncebadon; the latter—longer and easier—is the defile of Manzanal.

The question was at once raised as to whether the position in rear of Astorga should not be seriously defended. The town itself would naturally have to be given up, if the French chose to press on in force; but the two defiles might be fortified and held against very superior numbers. To turn 25,000 British troops out of them would have been a very serious task, and the Spaniards meanwhile could have been used for diversions on the enemy's flank and rear. La Romana called upon Moore, at the moment of the latter's arrival at Astorga, and proposed that they should join in defending the passes. To give them up meant, he said, to give up also the great upland valley behind them—the Vierzo—where lay his own dépôts and his park of artillery at Ponferrada, and where Moore also had considerable stores and magazines at Villafranca. The proposal was well worthy of being taken into account, and was far from being—as Napier calls it—'wilder than the dreams of Don Quixote!' for the positions were very strong, and there was no convenient route by which they could be turned. The only other way into Galicia, that by Puebla de Senabria, is not only far away, but almost impassable at midwinter from the badness of the road and the deep snow. Moreover it leads not into the main valley of the Minho, but into that of the Tamega on the Portuguese frontier, from which another series of difficult defiles have to be crossed in order to get into the heart of Galicia. La Romana thought that this road might practically be disregarded as an element of danger in a January campaign.

The suggestion of the Marquis deserved serious consideration. Moore's reasons for a summary rejection of the proposal are not stated by him at any length [1]. He wrote to Castlereagh merely that there was only two days' bread at Astorga, that his means of carriage were melting away by the death of draught beasts and the desertion of drivers, and that he feared that the enemy might use the road upon his flank—i.e. the Puebla de Senabria route—to turn his position. He purposed therefore to fall back at once to the coast as fast as he could, and trusted that the French, for want of food, would not be able to follow him further than Villafranca. To these reasons may be added another, which Moore cited in his

[1] Moore to Castlereagh, from Astorga, Dec. 31, 1808.

conversation with La Romana, that the troops required rest, and could not get it in the bleak positions above Astorga [1].

Some of these reasons are not quite convincing : though there were only two days' rations at Astorga, there were fourteen days' at Villafranca, and large dépôts had also been gathered at Lugo and Corunna. These could be rendered available with no great trouble, if real energy were displayed, for there was still (as the disasters of the retreat were to show) a good deal of wheeled transport with the army. The flanking road by Puebla de Senabria was (as we have said) so difficult and so remote that any turning corps that tried it would be heard of long before it became dangerous. There would be great political advantage in checking Bonaparte at the passes, even if it were only for a week or ten days. Moreover, to show a bold front would raise the spirits of the army, whose growing disorders were the marks of discontent at the retreat, and whose one wish was to fight the French as soon as possible. As to the rest which Moore declared to be necessary for the troops, this could surely have been better given by halting them and offering to defend the passes, than by taking them over the long and desolate road that separated them from Corunna. The experiences of the next eleven days can hardly be called ' rest.'

Though clearly possible, a stand behind Astorga may not have been the best policy. Napoleon had a vast force in hand after his junction with Soult, and he was a dangerous foe to brave, even in such a formidable position as that which the British occupied. But it is doubtful whether this fact was the cause of Moore's determination to retreat to the sea. If we may judge from the tone of his dispatches, his thought was merely that he had promised to make a diversion, under strong pressure from Frere and the rest ; that he had successfully carried out his engagement, and lured the Emperor and the bulk of the French forces away from Madrid ; and that he considered his task completed. In his letter of December 31 to Castlereagh, he harks back once more to his old depreciation of the Spaniards—they had taken no advantage of the chance he had given them, they were as apathetic as ever, his exertions had been wasted, and so forth [2]. In so writing he made a mistake : his

---

[1] This plea is not to be found in any of Moore's dispatches, but only in La Romana's account of the interview which he sent to the Junta.

[2] ' Abandoned from the beginning by everything Spanish, we were equal to nothing by ourselves. From a desire to do what I could, I made the

campaign was so far from being wasted that he had actually saved Spain. He had caused the Emperor to lose the psychological moment for striking at Seville and Lisbon, when the spirits of the patriots were at their lowest, and had given them three months to rally. By the time that the southward move from Madrid was once more possible to the French, Spain had again got armies in the field, and the awful disasters of November and December, 1808, had been half forgotten.

It seems improbable, from Moore's tone in his dispatch of December 31, that he ever had any serious intention of standing behind Astorga. He had fallen back upon his old desponding views of the last days of November, and was simply set on bringing off the British army in safety, without much care for the fate of the Spaniards whom he so much disliked and contemned. The only sign of his ever having studied the intermediate positions between Astorga and Corunna lies in a report addressed to him on December 26, by Carmichael Smith of the Royal Engineers. This speaks of the Manzanal—Rodrigatos position as presenting an appearance of strong ground, but having the defect of possessing a down-slope to the rear for six miles, so that if the line were forced, a long retreat downhill would be necessary in face of the pursuing enemy. The engineer then proceeded to recommend the position of Cacabellos, a league in front of Villafranca, as being very strong and safe from any turning movement. But Moore, as we shall see, refused to stand at the one place as much as at the other, only halting a rearguard at Cacabellos to keep off the pursuing horse for a few hours, and never offering a pitched battle upon that ground. It is probable that nothing would have induced him to fight at either position, after he had once resolved that a straight march to the sea was the best policy.

So little time did Moore take in making up his mind as to the desirability of holding the passes above Astorga, that he pushed on Baird's, Fraser's, and Hope's divisions towards Villafranca on

movement against Soult. As a diversion it has answered completely : but as there is nothing to take advantage of it, I have risked the loss of an army to no purpose. I find no option now but to fall down to the coast as fast as I am able. . . . The army would, there cannot be a doubt, have distinguished itself, had the Spaniards been able to offer any resistance. But from the first it was placed in situations in which, without the possibility of doing any good, it was itself constantly risked ' (Moore to Castlereagh, from Astorga, Dec. 31).

the thirtieth, while Paget's reserve with the two light brigades followed on the thirty-first. The whole British army was on the other side of Astorga, and across the passes, when Soult and Bonaparte's columns converged on La Baneza. Their infantry did not enter Astorga till the first day of the new year, thirty-six hours after Moore's main body had evacuated the place.

But this easy escape from the Emperor's clutches had been bought at considerable sacrifices. Astorga was crammed with stores of all kinds, as we have already had occasion to mention : food was the only thing that was at all short. But there was not sufficient transport in the place, and the retreating army was already losing wagons and beasts so fast that it could not carry off much of the accumulated material that lay before it. A hasty attempt was made to serve out to the troops the things that could be immediately utilized. La Romana's Spaniards received several thousand new English muskets to replace their dilapidated weapons, and a quantity of blankets. Some of the British regiments had shoes issued to them ; but out of mere hurry and mismanagement several thousand pairs more were destroyed instead of distributed, though many men were already almost barefoot. There were abandoned all the heavy baggage of Baird's division (which had been stacked at Astorga before the march to Sahagun), an entire dépôt of entrenching tools, several hundred barrels of rum, and many scores of carts and wagons for which draught animals were wanting. A quantity of small-arms ammunition was blown up. But the most distressing thing of all was that those of the sick of the army who could not bear to be taken on through the January cold in open wagons had to be left behind : some four hundred invalids, it would seem, were abandoned in the hospital and fell into the hands of the French [1].

The most deplorable thing about these losses was that all the evacuation and destruction was carried out under difficulties, owing to the gross state of disorder and indiscipline into which the army was falling. The news that they were to retreat once more without fighting had exasperated the men to the last degree. Thousands of them got loose in the streets, breaking into houses, maltreating the inhabitants, and pillaging the stores, which were to be aban-

[1] Compare Moore to Castlereagh (from Astorga, Dec. 31) with *Nap. Corresp.*, 14,637, and with James Moore's memoir (p. 184), and ' T. S.'s autobiography (p. 57).

doned, for their private profit. The rum was naturally a great attraction, and many stragglers were left behind dead drunk, to be beaten out of the place by the cavalry when they left it on the night of the thirty-first. La Romana had to make formal complaint to Moore of the misbehaviour of the troops, who had even tried to steal his artillery mules and insulted his officers. There can be no doubt that if the rank and file had been kept in hand many valuable stores could have been distributed instead of destroyed, and the straggling which was to prove so fatal might have been nipped in the bud. But the officers were as discontented as the men, and in many regiments seem to have made little or no effort to keep things together. Already several battalions were beginning to march with an advanced guard of marauders and a rearguard of limping stragglers, the sure signs of impending trouble.

By the thirty-first, however, Astorga was clear of British and Spanish troops. Moore marched by the new high-road, the route of Manzanal: La Romana took the shorter but more rugged defile of Foncebadon. But he sent his guns along with the British, in order to spare the beasts the steeper ascents of the old *chaussée*. The terrible rain of the last week was just passing into snow as the two columns, every man desperately out of heart, began their long uphill climb across the ridge of the Monte Teleno, towards the uplands of the Vierzo.

NOTE

THIS account of the retreat from Sahagun is constructed from a careful comparison of the official documents with the memoirs and monographs of the following British eye-witnesses :—Robert Blakeney (of the 28th), Rifleman Harris and Sergeant Surtees (of the 2/95th), Lord Londonderry, and Lord Vivian of the Cavalry Brigade, Leith Hay (Aide-de-Camp to General Leith), Charles and William Napier, T.S. of the 71st, Steevens of the 20th, the Surgeon Adam Neale, and the Chaplain Ormsby. Bradford, another chaplain, has left a series of admirable water-colour drawings of the chief points on the road as far as Lugo, made under such difficulties as can be well imagined. Of French eye-witnesses I have used the accounts of St. Chamans, Fantin des Odoards, Naylies, De Gonneville, Lejeune, and the detestably inaccurate Le Noble.

SECTION VIII: CHAPTER V

SOULT'S PURSUIT OF MOORE: ASTORGA TO CORUNNA

WHEN he found that Moore had escaped from him, Napoleon slackened down from the high speed with which he had been moving for the last ten days. He stayed at Benavente for two nights, occupying himself with desk-work of all kinds, and abandoning the pursuit of the British to Bessières and Soult. The great *coup* had failed: instead of capturing the expeditionary force he could but harass it on its way to the sea. Such a task was beneath his own dignity: it would compromise the imperial reputation for infallibility, if a campaign that had opened with blows like Espinosa, Tudela, and the capture of Madrid ended in a long and ineffectual stern-chase. If Bonaparte had continued the hunt himself, with the mere result of arriving in time to see Moore embark and depart, he would have felt that his prestige had been lowered. He tacitly confessed as much himself long years after, when, in one of his lucubrations at St. Helena, he remarked that he would have conducted the pursuit in person, if he had but known that contrary winds had prevented the fleet of British transports from reaching Corunna. But of this he was unaware at the time; and since he calculated that Moore could be harassed perhaps, but not destroyed or captured, he resolved to halt and turn back. Soult should have the duty of escorting the British to the sea: they were to be pressed vigorously and, with luck, the Emperor trusted that half of them might never see England again. But no complete success could be expected, and he did not wish to appear personally in any enterprise that was but partially successful.

Other reasons were assigned both by Napoleon himself and by his admirers for his abandonment of the pursuit of Moore. He stated that Galicia was too much in a corner of the world for him to adventure himself in its mountains—he would be twenty days journey from Paris and the heart of affairs. If Austria began to move again in the spring, there would be an intolerable delay before he could receive news or transmit orders [1]. He wished to take in hand the reorganization of his armies in Italy, on the Rhine, and beyond the Adriatic. All this was plausible enough, but the real reason of his return was that he would not be present at a fiasco or a half-success. It would seem, however, that there may have been another operating cause, which the Emperor never chose to mention; the evidence for it has only cropped up of late years [2]. It appears that he was somewhat disquieted by secret intelligence from Paris, as to obscure intrigues among his own ministers and courtiers. The Spanish War had given new occasions to the malcontents who were always criticizing the Empire. Not much could be learnt by the French public about the affair of Bayonne, but all that had got abroad was well calculated to disgust even loyal supporters of the Empire. The talk of the *salons*, which Napoleon always affected to despise, but which he never disregarded, was more bitter than ever. It is quite possible that some hint of the conspiracy of the ' Philadelphes,' which four months later showed its hand in the mysterious affair of D'Argenteau, may have reached him. But it is certain that he had disquieting reports concerning the intrigues of Fouché and Talleyrand. Both of those veteran plotters were at this moment in more or less marked disgrace. For once in a way, therefore, they were acting in concert. They were relieving their injured feelings by making secret overtures in all directions, in search of allies against their master. Incredible as it may appear, they had found a ready hearer in Murat, who was much disgusted with his brother-in-law for throwing upon him the blame for the disasters of the first Spanish campaign. Other notable personages were being drawn into the cave of malcontents, and discourses of more than doubtful loyalty were being delivered. Like many other cabals of the period, this one was destined to shrink into nothingness at the reappearance of the master at Paris [3]. But while he was away

---

[1] These reasons will be found set forth at length in *Nap. Corresp.*, 14,684 (to King Joseph, Jan. 11), and 14,692 (to Clarke, Jan. 13).

[2] There is a distinct allusion to the matter, however, in Fouché's *Mémoires* (i. 385).

[3] For a long account of all this intrigue see the *Mémoires* of Chancellor Pasquier (i. 355, &c.). He says that it was discovered by Lavalette, the Postmaster-General, who sent information to the Viceroy of Italy, in consequence of which a compromising letter from Caroline Bonaparte (at Naples) to Talley-

his agents were troubled and terrified: they seem to have sent
him alarming hints, which had far more to do with his return to
France than any fear as to the intentions of Austria [1].

An oft-repeated story says that the Emperor received a packet
of letters from Paris while riding from Benavente to Astorga on
January 1, 1809, and, after reading them by the wayside with
every sign of anger, declared that he must return to France. If
the tale be true, we may be sure that the papers which so moved
his wrath had no reference to armaments on the Danube, but
were concerned with the intrigues in Paris. There was absolutely
nothing in the state of European affairs to make an instant
departure from Spain necessary. On the other hand, rumours of
domestic plots always touched the Emperor to the quick, and
it must have been as irritating as it was unexpected to discover
that his own sister and brother-in-law were dabbling in such
intrigues, even though ostensibly they were but discussing what
should be done if something should happen in Spain to their
august relative.

Already ere leaving Benavente the Emperor had issued orders
which showed that he had abandoned his hope of surrounding and
crushing Moore. He had begun to send off, to the right and to
the left, part of the great mass of troops which he had brought
with him. On December 31 he wrote to Dessolles, and ordered him
to give his division a short rest at Villacastin, and then to return to
Madrid, where the garrison was too weak. On January 1, the whole
of the Imperial Guard was directed to halt and return to Benavente,
from whence it was soon after told to march back to Valladolid.
Lapisse's division of Victor's corps, which had got no further than
Benavente in its advance, was turned off to subdue the southern
parts of the kingdom of Leon. To the same end were diverted
D'Avenay's [2] and Maupetit's [3] brigades of cavalry. Quite contrary

rand was seized. The reproaches which he puts into Napoleon's mouth must,
I fancy, be taken as about as authentic as an oration in Thucydides.

[1] There was also at this moment a slight recrudescence of the old agitation
of the *chouans* in the west of France. Movable columns had to be sent
out in the departments of the Mayenne and Sarthe. See *Nap. Corresp.*,
14,871-2.

[2] This was a temporary brigade, made up of the 3rd Dutch Hussars and
a provisional regiment of dragoons.

[3] 5th Dragoons and part of the regiment of Westphalian *Chevaux-Légers*;
they belonged to the corps-cavalry of Lefebvre.

to Moore's expectations and prophecies, the people of this part of Spain displayed a frantic patriotism, when once the enemy was upon them. Toro, an open town[1], had to be stormed: Zamora made a still better resistance, repulsed a first attack, and had to be breached and assaulted by a brigade of Lapisse's division. The villagers of Penilla distinguished themselves by falling upon and capturing a battery of the Imperial Guard, which was passing by with an insufficient escort. Of course the guns were recovered, and the place burnt, within a few days of the exploit[2].

Having sent off the Guards, Lapisse, Dessolles, and Maupetit's and D'Avenay's cavalry, the Emperor had still a large force left in hand for the pursuit of Moore. There remained Soult's and Ney's corps, the horsemen of Lahoussaye, Lorges, and Franceschi, and the greater part of Junot's 8th Corps. The Emperor had resolved to break up this last-named unit: it contained many third-battalions belonging to regiments which were already in Spain: they were directed to rejoin their respective head quarters. When this was done, there remained only enough to make up two rather weak divisions of 5,000 men each. These were given to Delaborde and Heudelet, and incorporated with Soult's 2nd Corps. Loison's division, the third of the original 8th Corps, was suppressed[3]. Junot himself was sent off to take a command under Lannes at the siege of Saragossa. When joined by Delaborde and Heudelet, Soult had a corps of exceptional strength— five divisions and nearly 30,000 bayonets. He could not use for the pursuit of Moore Bonnet's division, which had been left to garrison Santander. But with the remainder, 25,000 strong, he pressed forward from Astorga in pursuance of his master's orders. His cavalry force was very large in proportion: it consisted of 6,000 sabres, for not only were three complete divisions of dragoons with him, but Ney's corps-cavalry (the brigade of Colbert) was up at the front and leading the pursuit. Ney himself, with his two infantry divisions, those of Maurice Mathieu and Marchand, was a march or two to the rear, some 16,000 bayonets strong. If Soult

[1] The defence of Toro was headed by a stray English officer. The place was taken by D'Avenay, not by Maupetit as Arteche says. See the *Mémoires* of De Gonneville, i. 207.

[2] For information on these rather obscure operations consult the *Mémoires* of De Gonneville (of D'Avenay's brigade) and *Nap. Corresp.*, 14,685.

[3] There were only two battalions remaining with Loison by Jan. 10.

should suffer any check, he was sure of prompt support within
three days. Thus the whole force sent in chase of Moore mustered
some 47,000 men [1].

The head of the pursuing column was formed by Lahoussaye's
dragoons and Colbert's light cavalry : in support of these, but
always some miles to the rear, came Merle's infantry. This formed
the French van : the rest of Soult's troops were a march behind,
with Heudelet's division for rearguard. All the 2nd Corps followed
the English on the Manzanal road: only Franceschi's four regiments
of cavalry turned aside, to follow the rugged pass of Foncebadon,
by which La Romana's dilapidated host had retired. The exhausted
Spaniards were making but slow progress through the snow and
the mountain torrents. Franceschi caught them up on January 2,
and scattered their rearguard under General Rengel, taking a
couple of flags and some 1,500 men : the prisoners are described
as being in the last extremity of misery and fatigue, and many
of them were infected with the typhus fever, which had been
hanging about this unfortunate corps ever since its awful experience
in the Cantabrian hills during the month of November [2].

Moore's army, as we have already seen, had marched out from
Astorga—the main body on December 30, the rearguard on the
thirty-first. After determining that he would not defend the passes
of Manzanal and Foncebadon, the general had doubted whether
he should make his retreat on Corunna by the great *chaussée*,
or on Vigo, by the minor road which goes via Orense and the
valley of the Sil. It is strange that he did not see that his mind
must be promptly made up, and that when once he had passed the
mountains he must commit himself to one or the other route.
But his dispatches to Castlereagh show that it was not till he had

---

[1] A month after the pursuit of Moore had ended, and the battle of Corunna
had been fought, the four infantry divisions of Soult's corps which were in
Galicia had still 19,000 effective bayonets for the invasion of Portugal. The
three cavalry divisions were some 5,300 strong. Ney's corps, which had
hardly been engaged, had 16,000 infantry and 1,000 cavalry. There were
still, therefore, 41,300 men in hand of the two corps. It is impossible to
make the losses from the long pursuit in the snow and the battle of Corunna
less than 4,500 or 5,000 men, when we reflect that Moore lost 6,000, of whom
only 2,000 were prisoners, and that Soult suffered at least 1,500 casualties in
the Corunna fighting.

[2] *Nap. Corresp.*, 14,662. ' Les hommes pris sur La Romana étaient hor-
ribles à voir,' says Napoleon, who saw them at Astorga.

reached Lugo that he finally decided in favour of the main road[1]. He must have formed the erroneous conclusion that the French would not pursue him far beyond Astorga[2]: he thought that they would be stopped by want of provisions and by fatigue. Having formed this unsound hypothesis, he put off the final decision as to his route till he should reach Lugo. Meanwhile, to protect the side-road to Vigo he detached 3,500 of his best troops, Robert Crawfurd's light brigade [the 43rd (1st batt.), 52nd (2nd batt.), and 95th (2nd batt.)], and Alten's brigade of the German Legion. They diverged from the main road after leaving Astorga, and marched, by Ponferrada and La Rua, on Orense. How much they suffered on the miserable bypaths of the valley of the Sil may be gathered in the interesting diaries of Surtees and Harris: but it was only with the snow and the want of food that they had to contend. They never saw a Frenchman, embarked unmolested at Vigo, and were absolutely useless to Moore during the rest of the campaign. It is impossible to understand how it came that they were sent away in this fashion, and nothing can be said in favour of the move. Unless the whole army were going by the Orense road, no one should have been sent along it: and the difficulties of the track were such that to have taken the main body over it would have been practically impossible. As it was, 3,500 fine soldiers were wasted for all fighting purposes. The duty of covering the rear of the army, which had hitherto fallen to the lot of Crawfurd, was now transferred to General Paget and the 'Reserve Division[3].' One regiment of hussars [the 15th] was left with them: the other four cavalry corps pushed on to the front, as there was no great opportunity for using them, now that the army had plunged into the mountains.

[1] This is made absolutely certain by his letter of Jan. 13, in which he says that 'at Lugo I became sensible of the impossibility of reaching Vigo, which is at too great a distance.' On starting from Astorga, then, he still thought that he might be able to embark at that port. A glance at the map shows that the march Astorga—Lugo—Vigo is two sides of a triangle. If the Vigo route was to be taken, the only rational places to turn on to it are Astorga and Ponferrada.

[2] 'After a time the same difficulties which affect us must affect him [Soult]: therefore the rear once past Villafranca, I do not expect to be molested' (Moore to Castlereagh, from Astorga, Dec. 31).

[3] Consisting of the 20th Foot, and the first battalions of the 28th, 52nd, 91st, and 95th.

Colbert and Lahoussaye took some little time, after leaving Astorga, before they came upon the rear of Moore's army. But they had no difficulty in ascertaining the route that the English had taken: the steep uphill road from Astorga into the Vierzo was strewn with wreckage of all kinds, which had been abandoned by the retreating troops. The long twelve-mile incline, deeply covered with snow, had proved fatal to a vast number of draught animals, and wagon after wagon had to be abandoned to the pursuers, for want of sufficient oxen and mules to drag them further forward. Among the derelict baggage were lying no small number of exhausted stragglers, dead or dying from cold or dysentery.

The whole *morale* of Moore's army had suffered a dreadful deterioration from the moment that the order to evacuate Astorga was issued. As long as there was any prospect of fighting, the men—though surly and discontented—had stuck to their colours. Some regiments had begun to maraud, but the majority were still in good order. But from Astorga onward the discipline of the greater part of the corps began to relax. There were about a dozen regiments[1] which behaved thoroughly well, and came through the retreat with insignificant losses: on the other hand there were many others which left from thirty to forty per cent. of their men behind them. It cannot be disguised that the enormous difference between the proportion of 'missing' in battalions of the same brigade, which went through exactly identical experiences, was simply due to the varying degrees of zeal and energy with which the officers kept their men together. Where there was a strong controlling will the stragglers were few, and no one fell behind save those who were absolutely dying. The iron hand of Robert Crawfurd brought the 43rd and 95th through their troubles with a loss of eighty or ninety men each. The splendid discipline of the Guards brigade carried them to Corunna with even smaller proportional losses. There is no mistaking the coincidence when we find that the battalion which Moore denounced at Salamanca as being the worst commanded and the worst disciplined in his force, was also the one which left a higher percentage of stragglers behind than any other corps. The fact was that the toils of the

[1] The reader should note, in the Appendix dealing with the numbers of Moore's army, the very small proportional losses suffered by the two battalions of the Guards, the 43rd (1st batt.), 4th, 42nd, 71st, 79th, 92nd, 95th (2nd batt.), and the cavalry.

retreat tried the machinery of the regiments to the utmost, and that where the management was weak or incompetent discipline broke down. It was not the troops who had the longest marches or the most fighting that suffered the heaviest losses: those of Paget's division, the rearguard of the whole army, which was constantly in touch with the French advance, compare favourably with those of some corps which never fired a shot between Benavente and Corunna. It is sad to have to confess that half the horrors of the retreat were due to purely preventible causes, and that if the badly-managed regiments had been up to the disciplinary standard of the Guards or the Light Brigade, the whole march would have been remembered as toilsome but not disastrous. Moore himself wrote, in the last dispatch to which he ever set his hand, that 'he would not have believed, had he not witnessed it, that a British army would in so short a time have been so completely demoralized. Its conduct during the late marches was infamous beyond belief. He could say nothing in its favour but that when there was a prospect of fighting the men were at once steady, and seemed pleased and determined to do their duty[1].' This denunciation was far too sweeping, for many corps kept good order throughout the whole campaign: but there was only too much to justify Moore's anger.

The serious trouble began at Bembibre, the first place beyond the pass of Manzanal, where Hope's, Baird's, and Fraser's divisions had encamped on the night of the thirty-first. The village was unfortunately a large local dépôt for wine: slinking off from their companies, many hundreds of marauders made their way into the vaults and cellars. When the divisions marched next morning they left nearly a thousand men, in various stages of intoxication, lying about the houses and streets. The officers of Paget's Reserve, who came up that afternoon, describe Bembibre as looking like a battle-field, so thickly were the prostrate redcoats strewn in every corner. Vigorous endeavours were made to rouse these bad soldiers, and to start them upon their way; but even next morning there were multitudes who could not or would not march[2].   When

---

[1] I quote from the original in the Record Office, not from the mutilated version printed in the *Parliamentary Papers* and elsewhere.

[2] Blakeney, of the 28th, says : ' We employed the greater part of Jan. 1 in turning or dragging the drunken men out of the houses into the streets, and sending forward as many as could be moved. Yet little could be effected with men incapable of standing, much less of marching' (p. 50).

the Reserve evacuated the place on January 2, it was still full of
torpid stragglers. Suddenly there appeared on the scene the
leading brigade of Lahoussaye's dragoons, pushing down from the
pass of Manzanal, and driving before them the last hussar picket
which Paget had left behind. The noise of the horsemen roused
the lingerers, who began at last to stagger away, but it was
too late: 'the cavalry rode through the long line of these
lame defenceless wretches, slashing among them as a schoolboy
does among thistles[1].' Most of the stragglers, it is said, were
still so insensible from liquor that they made no resistance, and
did not even get out of the road[2]. A few, with dreadful cuts
about their heads and shoulders, succeeded in overtaking the
Reserve. Moore had the poor bleeding wretches paraded along
the front of the regiments, as a warning to drunkards and
malingerers.

Meanwhile Baird and Hope's divisions had reached Villafranca
on the first, and scenes almost as disgraceful as those of Bembibre
were occurring. The town was Moore's most important dépôt: it
contained fourteen days' rations of biscuit for the whole army, an
immense amount of salt-beef and pork, and some hundreds of
barrels of rum. There was no transport to carry off all this
valuable provender, and Moore ordered it to be given to the
flames. Hearing of this the troops broke into the magazines,
and began to load themselves with all and more than they could
carry, arguing, not unnaturally, that so much good food should
not be burnt. Moore ordered one man—who was caught breaking
into the rum store—to be shot in the square. But it was no use;
the soldiers burst loose, though many of their officers cut and
slashed at them to keep them in the ranks, and snatched all that
they could from the fires. Some forced open private houses and
plundered, and in a few cases maltreated, or even murdered, the
townsfolk who would not give them drink. A great many got
at the rum, and were left behind when the divisions marched on
January 3[3].

While these orgies were going on at Villafranca, Paget and
the Reserve had been halted six miles away, at Cacabellos, where

---

[1] 'T. S.' of the 71st (*Journal*, p. 58).

[2] Adam Neale, p. 188. Both he and 'T. S.' mention the parading of the
wounded men along the lines.

[3] Cf. Blakeney, Neale, Londonderry, and James Moore.

the high-road passes over the little river Cua[1]. There was here a position in which a whole army could stand at bay, and Moore's engineers had pointed it out to him as the post between Astorga and Lugo where there was the most favourable fighting-ground. It is certain that if he had chosen to offer battle to Soult on this front, the Marshal would have been checked for many days—he could not have got forward without calling up Ney from Astorga, and there is no good road by which the British could have been outflanked. But Moore had no intention of making a serious defence: he was fighting a rearguard action merely to allow time for the stores at Villafranca to be destroyed.

The forces which were halted at Cacabellos consisted of the five battalions of the Reserve (under Paget), the 15th Hussars, and a horse-artillery battery. A squadron of the cavalry and half of the 95th Rifles were left beyond the river, in observation along the road towards Bembibre: the guns were placed on the western side of the Cua, commanding the road up from the bridge. The 28th formed their escort, while the other three battalions of the division were hidden behind a line of vineyards and stone walls parallel with the winding stream[2].

About one o'clock in the afternoon the French appeared, pushing cautiously forward from Bembibre with Colbert's cavalry brigade of Ney's corps now at their head, while Lahoussaye's division of dragoons was in support. The infantry were not yet in sight. Colbert, a young and very dashing officer, currently reputed to be the most handsome man in the whole French army, was burning to distinguish himself. He had never before met the British, and had formed a poor opinion of them from the numerous stragglers and drunkards whom he had seen upon the road. He thought that the rearguard might be pushed, and the defile forced with little loss. Accordingly he rode forward at the head of his two regiments[3], and fell upon the squadron of the 15th Hussars which was observing him. They had to fly in hot haste, and, coming in suddenly to the bridge, rode into and over the last two companies of the 95th Rifles, who had not yet crossed the

[1] Not the Guia, as the English generally call it.

[2] I take my account of the skirmish mainly from Blakeney, whose narrative is admirable. Those of Londonderry, Napier, and Neale do not give so many details.

[3] They were the 15th Chasseurs and the 3rd Hussars.

stream. Colbert, sweeping down close to their heels, came upon the disordered infantry and took some forty or fifty prisoners before the riflemen could escape across the water [1]. But, seeing the 28th and the guns holding the slope above, he halted for a moment before attempting to proceed further.

Judging however, from a hasty survey, that there were no very great numbers opposed to him, the young French general resolved to attempt to carry the bridge of Cacabellos by a furious charge, just as Franceschi had forced that of Mansilla five days before. This was a most hazardous and ill-advised move: it could only succeed against demoralized troops, and was bound to fail when tried against the steady battalions of the Reserve division. But ranging his leading regiment four abreast, Colbert charged for the bridge: the six guns opposite him tore the head of the column to pieces, but the majority of the troopers got across and tried to dash uphill and capture the position. They had fallen into a dreadful trap, for the 28th blocked the road just beyond the bridge, while the 95th and 52nd poured in a hot flanking fire from behind the vineyard walls on either side. There was no getting forward: Colbert himself was shot as he tried to urge on his men [2], and his aide-de-camp Latour-Maubourg fell at his side. After staying for no more than a few minutes on the further side of the water, the brigade turned rein and plunged back across the bridge, leaving many scores of dead and wounded behind them.

Lahoussaye's dragoons now came to the front: several squadrons of them forded the river at different points, but, unable to charge among the rocks and vines, they were forced to dismount and to act as skirmishers, a capacity in which they competed to no great advantage against the 52nd, with whom they found themselves engaged. It was not till the leading infantry of Merle's division came up, not long before dusk, that the French were enabled to make any head against the defenders. Their voltigeurs bickered with the 95th and 52nd for an hour, but when the formed columns tried to cross the bridge, they were so raked by the six guns opposite them that they gave back in disorder. After dark the firing ceased, and Moore, who had come up in person from Villa-

---

[1] Forty-eight is the number given in Cope's excellent *History of the Rifle Brigade*.

[2] He was shot by Tom Plunket, a noted character in the 95th, from a range that seemed extraordinary to the riflemen of that day.

franca at the sound of the cannon, had no difficulty in withdrawing
his men under cover of the night. In this sharp skirmish each
side lost some 200 men: the French casualties were mainly in
Colbert's cavalry, the British were distributed unequally between
the 95th (who suffered most), the 28th, and 52nd: the other two
regiments present (the 20th and 91st) were hardly engaged [1].

Marching all through the night of 3rd–4th of January the
Reserve division passed through Villafranca, where stores of all
kinds were still blazing in huge bonfires, and did not halt till they
reached Nogales, eighteen miles further on. They found the road
before them strewn with one continuous line of wreckage from
the regiments of the main body. The country beyond Villafranca
was far more bare and desolate than the eastern half of the Vierzo :
discipline grew worse each day, and the surviving animals of the
baggage-train were dying off wholesale from cold and want of
forage. The cavalry horses were also beginning to perish very
fast, mainly from losing their shoes on the rough and stony
road. As soon as a horse was unable to keep up with the regiment, he was (by Lord Paget's orders) shot by his rider, in order
to prevent him from falling into the hands of the French. Many
witnesses of the retreat state that the incessant cracking of the
hussars' pistols, as the unfortunate chargers were shot, was the
thing that lingered longest in their memories of all the sounds of
these unhappy days.

Beyond Villafranca the Corunna road passes through the picturesque defile of Piedrafita, by which it reaches the head waters of
the Nava river, and then climbing the spurs of Monte Cebrero comes
out into the bleak upland plain of Lugo. This fifty miles contained the most difficult and desolate country in the whole of
Moore's march, and was the scene of more helpless and undeserved
misery than any other section of the retreat. It was not merely
drunkards and marauders who now began to fall to the rear, but
steady old soldiers who could not face the cold, the semi-starvation,
and the forced marches. Moore hurried his troops forward at a
pace that, over such roads, could only be kept up by the strongest

---

[1] Napoleon's not very convincing account of the combat (*Nap. Corresp.*,
14,647) runs as follows : ' Trois mille Ecossais, voulant défendre les gorges
de Picros près de Villafranca, pour donner le temps à beaucoup de choses à
filer, ont été culbutés. Mais le général Colbert pétillant de faire avancer
sa cavalerie, une balle l'a frappé au front, et l'a tué.'

men. On January 5 he compelled the whole army to execute a forced march of no less than thirty-six continuous hours, which was almost as deadly as a battle. This haste seems all the less justifiable because the district abounded with positions at which the enemy could be held back for many hours, whenever the rear-guard was told to stand at bay. At Nogales and Constantino, where opposition was offered, the French were easily checked, and there were many other points where similar stands could have been made. It would seem that Moore, shocked at the state of indiscipline into which his regiments were falling, thought only of getting to the sea as quickly as possible. Certainly, the pursuit was not so vigorous as to make such frantic haste necessary. Whenever the Reserve division halted and offered battle, the French dragoons held off, and waited, often for many hours, for their infantry to come up.

'All that had hitherto been suffered by our troops was but a prelude to this time of horrors,' wrote one British eye-witness. 'It had still been attempted to carry forward our sick and wounded: here (on Monte Cebrero) the beasts which dragged them failed, and they were left in their wagons, to perish among the snow. As we looked round on gaining the highest point of these slippery precipices, and observed the rear of the army winding along the narrow road, we could see the whole track marked out by our own wretched people, who lay expiring from fatigue and the severity of the cold—while their uniforms reddened in spots the white surface of the ground. Our men had now become quite mad with despair: excessive fatigue and the consciousness of dis-grace, in thus flying before an enemy whom they despised, excited in them a spirit which was quite mutinous. A few hours' pause was all they asked, an opportunity of confronting the foe, and the certainty of making the pursuers atone for all the miseries that they had suffered. Not allowed to fight, they cast themselves down to perish by the wayside, giving utterance to feelings of shame, anger, and grief. But too frequently their dying groans were mingled with imprecations upon the General, who chose rather to let them die like beasts than to take their chance on the field of battle. That no degree of horror might be wanting, this unfortunate army was accompanied by many women and children, of whom some were frozen to death on the abandoned baggage-wagons, some died of fatigue and cold, while their infants were seen vainly sucking at their clay-cold breasts[1].' It is shocking to have to add that the miserable survivors of these poor women of the camp were abominably maltreated by the French[2].

Not only was the greater part of the baggage-train of the army lost between Villafranca and Lugo, but other things of more importance. A battery of Spanish guns was left behind on the crest of Monte Oribio for want of draught animals, and the military chest of the army was abandoned between Nogales and Cerezal. It contained about £25,000 in dollars, and was drawn in two ox-wagons, which gradually fell behind the main body as the beasts wore out. General Paget refused to fight a rearguard action to cover its slow progress, and ordered the 28th Regiment to hurl the small kegs containing the money over a precipice. The silver shower lay scattered among the rocks at the bottom : part was gathered up by Lahoussaye's dragoons, but the bulk fell next spring, when the snow melted, into the hands of the local peasantry [Jan. 4].

On the further side of the mountains, between Cerezal and Constantino, the army was astounded to meet a long train of fifty bullock-carts moving southward. It contained clothing and stores for La Romana's army, which the Junta of Galicia, with incredible carelessness, had sent forward from Lugo, though it had heard that the British were retreating. A few miles of further advance would have taken it into the hands of the French. Very naturally, the soldiery stripped the wagons and requisitioned the beasts for their own baggage. The shoes and garments were a godsend to those of the ragged battalions who could lay hands on them, and next day at Constantino many of the Reserve fought in whole- or half-Spanish uniforms.

The skirmish at Constantino, on the afternoon of January 5, was the most important engagement, save that of Cacabellos, during the whole retreat. It was a typical rearguard action to cover a

---

[1] From Adam Neale's *Spanish Campaign of 1808*, pp. 190, 191.

[2] For French evidence of this see the journal of Fantin des Odoards of the 31st Léger : ' Plusieurs jeunes Anglaises devenues la proie de nos cavaliers étaient mises à l'encan en même temps que les chevaux pris avec elles. J'ai vu, à mon grand scandale, qu'elles n'avaient pas toujours la préférence' (p. 196). Cf. the miserable story of Mrs. Pullen in the *Recollections of Rifleman Harris*, p. 142.

bridge : the British engineers having failed in their endeavour to blow up the central arch, Paget placed his guns so as to command the passage, extended the 28th and the 95th along the nearer bank of the deep-sunk river, and held out with ease till nightfall.   Lahoussaye's dragoons refused, very wisely, to attempt the position. Merle's infantry tried to force the passage by sending forward a regiment in dense column, which suffered heavily from the guns, was much mauled by the British light troops ranged along the water's edge, and finally desisted from the attack, allowing Paget to withdraw unmolested after dark.   The French were supposed to have lost about 300 men—a figure which was probably exaggerated: the British casualties were insignificant.

On January 6 Paget and the rearguard reached Lugo, where they found the main body of the army drawn out in battle order on a favourable position three miles outside the town.   The fearful amount of straggling which had taken place during the forced marches of the fourth and fifth had induced Moore to halt on his march to the sea, in order to rest his men, restore discipline, and allow the laggards to come up.   A tiresome *contretemps* had made him still more anxious to allow the army time to recruit itself.   He had made up his mind at Herrerias (near Villafranca) that the wild idea of retiring on Vigo must be given up.   The reports of the engineer officers whom he had sent to survey that port, as well as Ferrol and Corunna, were all in favour of the last-named place.   Accordingly he had sent orders to the admiral at Vigo, bidding him bring the fleet of transports round to Corunna.   At the same time Baird was directed to halt at Lugo, and not to take the side-road to Vigo via Compostella. Baird duly received the dispatch, and should have seen that it was sent on to his colleagues, Hope and Fraser.   He gave the letter for Fraser to a private dragoon, who got drunk and lost the important document.   Hence the 3rd Division started off on the Compostella road, a bad bypath, and went many miles across the snow before it was found and recalled.   Baird's negligence cost Fraser's battalions 400 men in stragglers, and having marched and countermarched more than twenty miles, they returned to Lugo so thoroughly worn out that they could not possibly have resumed their retreat on the sixth [1].

Moore had found in Lugo a dépôt containing four or five days'

---

[1] The whole of this story may be found in Londonderry (i. 272), Ormsby (ii. 140), James Moore (p. 190), as well as in Napier.

provisions for the whole force, as well as a welcome reinforcement —Leith's brigade of Hope's division, which had never marched to Astorga, and had been preceding the army by easy stages in its retreat. Including these 1,800 fresh bayonets, the army now mustered about 19,000 combatants. Since it left Benavente it had been diminished by the strength of the two Light Brigades detached to Vigo (3,500 men), by 1,000 dismounted cavalry who had been sent on to Corunna, by 500 or 600 sick too ill to be moved, who had been left in the hospitals of Astorga and Villafranca, and by about 2,000 men lost by the way between Astorga and Lugo. Moore imagined that the loss under the last-named head had been even greater: but the moment that the army halted and the news of approaching battle flew round, hundreds of stragglers and marauders flocked in to the colours, sick men pulled themselves together, and the regiments appeared far stronger than had been anticipated. The Commander-in-chief issued a scathing ' General Order ' to the officers commanding corps with regard to this point. ' They must be as sensible as himself of the complete disorganization of the army. If they wished to give the troops a fair chance of success, they must exert themselves to restore order and discipline. The Commander of the Forces was tired of giving orders which were never attended to : he therefore appealed to the honour and feelings of the army : if those were not sufficient to induce them to do their duty, he must despair of succeeding by any other means. He had been obliged to order military executions, but there would have been no need for them if only officers did their duty. It was chiefly from their negligence, and from the want of proper regulations in the regiments, that crimes and irregularities were committed [1].'

The Lugo position was very strong: on the right it touched the unfordable river Minho, on the left it rested on rocky and inaccessible hills. All along the front there was a line of low stone walls, the boundaries of fields and vineyards. Below it there was a gentle down-slope of a mile, up which the enemy would have to march in order to attack. The army and the general alike were pleased with the outlook : they hoped that Soult would fight, and knew that they could give a good account of him.

The Marshal turned out to be far too circumspect to run his head against such a formidable line. He came up on the sixth,

[1] General Orders (Lugo, Jan. 6, 1809).

with the dragoons of Lahoussaye and Franceschi and Merle's infantry. On the next morning Mermet's and Delaborde's divisions and Lorges's cavalry appeared. But the forced marches had tried them no less than they had tried the British. French accounts say that the three infantry divisions had only 13,000 bayonets with the eagles, instead of the 20,000 whom they should have shown, and that the cavalry instead of 6,000 sabres mustered only 4,000. Some men had fallen by the way in the snow, others were limping along the road many miles to the rear : many were marauding on the flanks, like the British who had gone before them. Heudelet's whole division was more than two marches to the rear, at Villafranca.

On the seventh, therefore, Soult did no more than feel the British position. He had not at first been sure that Moore's whole army was in front of him, and imagined that he might have to deal with no more than Paget's Reserve division, with which he had bickered so much during the last four days. He was soon undeceived : when he brought forward a battery against Moore's centre, it was immediately silenced by the fire of fifteen guns. A feint opposite the British right, near the river, was promptly opposed by the Brigade of Guards. A more serious attack by Merle's division, on the hill to the left, was beaten back by Leith's brigade, who drove back the 2nd Léger and 36th of the Line by a bayonet-charge downhill, and inflicted on them a loss of 300 men.

On the eighth many of Soult's stragglers came up, but he still considered himself too weak to attack, and sent back to hurry up Heudelet's division, and to request Ney to push forward his corps to Villafranca. He remained quiescent all day, to the great disappointment of Moore, who had issued orders to his army warning them that a battle was at hand, and bidding them not to waste their fire on the tirailleurs, but reserve it for the supporting columns. As the day wore on, without any sign of movement on the part of the French, the British commander began to grow anxious and depressed. If Soult would not move, it must mean that he had resolved to draw up heavy reinforcements from the rear. It would be mad to wait till they should come up : either the Marshal must be attacked at once, before he could be strengthened, or else the army must resume its retreat on Corunna before Soult was ready. To take the offensive Moore considered very doubtful policy—the French had about his own numbers, or perhaps even

more, and they were established in a commanding position almost
as strong as his own.   Even if he beat them, they could fall back
on Heudelet and Ney, and face him again, in or about Villafranca.   To win a second battle would be hard work, and, even
if all went well, the army would be so reduced in numbers that
practically nothing would remain for a descent into the plains of
Leon.

Accordingly Moore resolved neither to attack nor to wait to be
attacked, but to resume his retreat towards the sea.   It was not
a very enterprising course ; but it was at least a safe one ; and since
the troops were now somewhat rested, and (as he hoped) restored
to good spirits, by seeing that the enemy dared not face them, he
considered that he might withdraw without evil results.   Accordingly the evening of the eighth was spent in destroying impedimenta
and making preparations for retreat.   Five hundred foundered
cavalry and artillery horses were shot, a number of caissons knocked
to pieces, and the remainder of the stores of food destroyed so far
as was possible.   At midnight on January 8-9 the army silently
slipped out of its lines, leaving its bivouac fires burning, so as to
delude the enemy with the idea that it still lay before him.
Elaborate precautions had been taken to guide each division to
the point from which it could fall with the greatest ease into the
Corunna road.   But it is not easy to evacuate by night a long
position intersected with walls, enclosures, and suburban bypaths.
Moreover the fates were unpropitious : drenching rain had set in,
and it was impossible to see five yards in the stormy darkness.
Whole regiments and brigades got astray, and of all the four
divisions only Paget's Reserve kept its bearings accurately and
reached the *chaussée* exactly at the destined point.   For miles on
each side of the road stray battalions were wandering in futile
circles when the day dawned.   Instead of marching fifteen miles
under cover of the night, many corps had got no further than four
or five from their starting-point.   Isolated men were scattered all
over the face of the country-side, some because they had lost their
regiments, others because they had deliberately sought shelter from
the rain behind any convenient wall or rock.

Continuing their retreat for some hours after daybreak, the
troops reached the village of Valmeda, where their absolute exhaustion made a halt necessary.   The more prudent commanders
made their men lie down in their ranks, in spite of the downpour,

and eat as they lay.   But Baird, from mistaken kindness, allowed
his division to disperse and to seek shelter in the cottages and
barns of neighbouring hamlets : they could not be got together
again when the time to start had arrived, and Bentinck and Manningham's brigades left an enormous proportion of their men behind.
The same thing happened on a smaller scale with Hope's and
Fraser's divisions : only Paget's regiments brought up the rear in
good order.   But behind them trailed several thousand stragglers,
forming a sort of irregular rearguard.   There was more dispersion,
disorder, and marauding in this march than in any other during
the whole retreat.   The plundering during this stage seems to
have been particularly discreditable : the inhabitants of the villages
along the high-road had for the most part gone up into the hills,
in spite of the dreadful weather.   The British seem to have imputed
their absence to them as a crime, and to have regarded every empty
house as a fair field for plunder.   As a matter of fact it was not
with the desire of withholding aid from their friends that the Galicians had disappeared, but from fear of the French.   If they had
remained behind they would have been stripped and misused by
the enemy.   But the unreasoning soldiery chose to regard the
unfortunate peasants as hostile[1] : they wantonly broke up doors

---

[1] In defence of the unfortunate Galicians, whose patriotism and good faith
has been impugned by so many English narrators of the retreat, it is only
necessary to quote the reflections of two dispassionate eye-witnesses.   Leith Hay
(i. 132) writes : ' To expect that the peasantry were to rush from their houses,
and supply the wants of our soldiers with the only provision that they
possessed for their own families—who might in consequence be left in the
midst of the mountains, at midwinter, to starve—was imagining friendly
feeling carried to an unnatural extent, and just as likely to happen as it
would have been if, Napoleon having invaded Britain, an English yeoman
should have earnestly requested one of our own soldiers to accept the last
morsel of bread he had the means of obtaining for his children.'   Ormsby
(ii. 162) says, to much the same effect : ' As to their inhospitable reception
of us, and the concealment of provisions, in candour I must be their apologist,
and declare my conviction that the charge in many instances is unfounded
and in others exaggerated.   Do those who are most loud in their complaints
honestly think that an army of 30,000 Spaniards would be better received in
England than we were in Spain ?   I doubt it much.   The people, dispirited
and alarmed, began to look to self-preservation as the primary or sole object
of their care.   Add to this the horror and dismay which the excesses of our
soldiers struck, and you will not be surprised that villages and houses were
frequently deserted.   Is it a matter of astonishment that the peasantry fled

and furniture, and stole all manner of useless household stuff. Even worse outrages occasionally happened: where the inhabitants, in outlying farms and hamlets, had remained behind, they turned them out of their houses, robbed them by force, and even shot those who resisted. In return, it was but natural that isolated marauders should be killed by the angry country-folk. But the good spirit of the Galicians was displayed in many places by the way in which they fed stragglers [1], and saved them from the French by showing them bypaths over the hills. No less than 500 men who had lost their way were passed on from village to village by the peasants, till they reached Portugal.

What between deliberate marauding for food or plunder [2], and genuine inability to keep up with the regiment on the part of weakly men, Moore's main body accomplished the march from Lugo to Betanzos in the most disorderly style. Paget's rearguard kept their ranks, but the troops in front were marching in a drove, without any attempt to preserve discipline. An observer counted one very distinguished regiment in Manningham's brigade of Baird's division, and reports that with the colours there were only nine officers, three sergeants, and three privates when they reached the gates of Betanzos [3].

Fortunately for Moore, the French pursued the retreating army with the greatest slackness. It was late on the morning of the ninth before Soult discovered that the British were gone: the drenching rain which had so incommoded them had at least screened their retreat. After occupying Lugo, which was full of dead horses,

into the recesses of their mountains, intimidated by our presence and confounded by our crimes?'

[1] For instances of kindness shown by the peasantry see Ormsby (ii. 139). On the other hand the educated classes were often sulky, and even insolent, because they thought that Moore was deliberately abandoning Spain from cowardice. See in Ormsby the anecdotes of the Alcalde of Pinhalla (ii. 79) and the Alcalde of Villafranca (ii. 127), as also of the abuse which he got from a ' furious canon of Lugo,' on whom he was billeted (ii. 147, 148).

[2] Outside Betanzos Paget halted, stopped the marauding stragglers, and had them stripped of their plunder. Blakeney of the 28th saw 1,500 men searched. ' It is impossible to enumerate the different articles of plunder which they had crammed into their packs and haversacks—brass candlesticks bent double, bundles of common knives, copper saucepans, every kind of domestic utensil, without regard to weight or value' (p. 92).

[3] Adam Neale, p. 196. The same battalion could show 500 bayonets for the battle of Corunna, so the men were not far off, as it would seem.

broken material, and spoiled provisions, the Marshal pushed on Franceschi's cavalry in pursuit. But he had lost twelve hours, and Moore was far ahead: only stragglers were captured on the road, and the British rearguard was not sighted till the passage of the Ladra, nearly halfway from Lugo to Betanzos [1]. This was late in the day, and Paget was not seriously molested, though the engineers who accompanied him failed to blow up the bridges over the Ladra and the Mendeo, partly because their powder had been spoilt by the rain, partly (as it would seem) from unskilful handiwork.

The fatiguing retreat was continued through part of the night of January 9–10, and on the following morning all the regiments reached Betanzos, on the sea-coast. The indefatigable Reserve division took up a position on a low range of heights outside the town, to cover the incoming of the thousands of stragglers who were still to the rear. From this vantage-ground they had the opportunity of witnessing a curious incident which few of the narrators of the retreat have failed to record. Franceschi's cavalry had resumed the pursuit, and after sweeping up some hundreds of prisoners from isolated parties, came to the village at the foot of the hills where the stragglers had gathered most thickly. At the noise of their approach, a good number of the more able-bodied men ran together, hastily formed up in a solid mass across the road, and beat off the French horsemen by a rolling fire. This had been done more by instinct than by design: but a sergeant of the 43rd, who assumed command over the assembly, skilfully brought order out of the danger [2]. He divided the men into two parties, which retired alternately down the road, the one facing the French while the other pushed on. The chasseurs charged them several times, but could never break in, and the whole body escaped to the English lines [3]. They had covered the retreat of

---

[1] Le Noble (*Campagne du Maréchal Soult*, p. 24) says that Franceschi made a 'charge' here and took 500 prisoners. The number of prisoners is very probably correct, but it is hardly a 'charge' when isolated stragglers are picked up. The rearguard was never molested, and retired without having to fire a shot.

[2] This sergeant's name was William Newman. He was rewarded by an ensign's commission in the 1st West India Regiment.

[3] I think that it must be to this combat that one of the reminiscences of 'T. S.' of the 71st relates, though he is vague in his dates. 'Sleep was stealing over me when I perceived a bustle around me. It was an advanced

many other stragglers, who ran in from all sides while the combat was going on.   Yet in spite of this irregular exploit, the army lost many men: on this day and the preceding ninth, more than 1000 were left behind—some had died of cold and fatigue, some had been cut down by the French.   But the majority had been captured as they straggled along, too dazed and worn out even to leave the road and take to the hillside when the cavalry got among them [1].

Soult had as yet no infantry to the front, and Moore remained for a day at Betanzos, observed by Franceschi's and Lahoussaye's cavalry, which dared not molest him.   On January 11 he resumed his march to Corunna, with his army in a far better condition than might have been expected.   The weather had turned mild and dry, and the climate of the coastland was a pleasant change from that of the mountains [2].   The men had been well fed at Betanzos with food sent on from Corunna, and, marching along the friendly sea with their goal in sight, recovered themselves in a surprising manner.   Their general was not so cheerful: he had heard that the fleet from Vigo had failed to double Cape Finisterre, and was still beating about in the Atlantic.   He had hoped to find it already in harbour, and was much concerned to think that he might have to stand at bay for some days in order to allow it time to arrive.

party of the French.   Unconscious of my action I started to my feet, levelled my musket, which I still retained, fired and formed with the other stragglers. There were more of them than of us, but the action and the approach of danger in a shape which we could repel roused our downcast feelings. . . . While we ran they pursued, the moment we faced about they halted.   We never fought but with success, never were attacked but we forced them to retire ' (p. 60).

[1] The stragglers' battle in front of Betanzos is described by Adam Neale (p. 196), Blakeney (pp. 90, 91), and Steevens of the 20th (p. 70), as well as by Napier and the other historians.   I find no account of it in Le Noble or the other French narrators, such as Naylies, St. Chamans, or Fantin des Odoards.   Le Noble gives instead a wholly fictitious account of an engagement of Franceschi with English *cavalry*, in which the latter lost a thousand men and five guns (p. 34).   As the cavalry had marched for Corunna before Franceschi came up, and lost only about 200 men in the whole campaign, I am quite at a loss to understand what can be the foundation of this romance.

[2] Fantin des Odoards gives a vivid and picturesque account of the relief caused to the pursuers, by the sudden plunge into fine spring-like weather, on descending from the snows of the interior (p. 198).

At Betanzos more sacrifices of war-material were made by the retiring army. Moore found there a large quantity of stores intended for La Romana, and had to spike and throw into the river five guns and some thousands of muskets. A considerable amount of food was imperfectly destroyed, but enough remained to give a welcome supply to the famishing French. It had been intended to blow up Betanzos bridge, but the mines were only partially successful, and the 28th Regiment from Paget's Reserve division had to stay behind and to guard the half-ruined structure against Franceschi's cavalry, till the main body had nearly reached Corunna, and the French infantry had begun to appear.

On the night of the eleventh, the divisions of Hope, Baird, and Fraser reached Corunna, while that of Paget halted at El Burgo, four miles outside the town, where the *chaussée* crosses the tidal river Mero. Here the bridge was successfully blown up: it was only the second operation of the kind which had been carried out with efficiency during the whole retreat. Another bridge at Cambria, a few miles further up the stream, was also destroyed. Thus the French were for the moment brought to a stand. On the twelfth their leading infantry column came up, and bickered with Paget's troops, across the impassable water, for the whole day [1]. But it was not till the thirteenth that Franceschi discovered a third passage at Celas, seven miles inland, across which he conducted his division. Moore then ordered the Reserve to draw back to the heights in front of Corunna. The French instantly came down to the river, and began to reconstruct the broken bridge. On the night of the thirteenth infantry could cross: on the fourteenth the artillery also began to pass over. But Soult advanced with great caution: here, as at Lugo, he was dismayed to see how much the fatigues of the march had diminished his army: Delaborde's division was not yet up: those of Merle and Mermet were so thinned by straggling that the Marshal resolved not to put his fortune to the test till the ranks were again full.

This delay gave the British general ample time to arrange for his departure. On the thirteenth, he blew up the great stores of powder which the Junta of Galicia had left stowed away in a magazine three miles outside the town. The quantity was not much less than 4,000 barrels, and the explosion was so powerful that wellnigh every window in Corunna was shattered.

[1] There is a good account of the bickering in Blakeney, pp. 102–5.

On the afternoon of the fourteenth the long-expected transports at last ran into the harbour, and Moore began to get on board his sick and wounded, his cavalry, and his guns. The horses were in such a deplorable state that very few of them were worth re-shipping: only about 250 cavalry chargers and 700 artillery draught-cattle were considered too good to be left behind[1]. The remainder of the poor beasts, more than 2,000 in number, were shot or stabbed and flung into the sea. Only enough were left to draw nine guns, which the general intended to use if he was forced to give battle before the embarkation was finished. The rest of the cannon, over fifty in number, were safely got on board the fleet. The personnel of the cavalry and artillery went on shipboard very little reduced by their casualties in the retreat. The former was only short of 200 men, the latter of 250: they had come off so easily because they had been sent to the rear since Cacabellos, and had retreated to Corunna without any check or molestation. Along with the hussars and the gunners some 2,500 or 3,000 invalids were sent on board. A few hundred more, too sick to face a voyage, were left behind in the hospitals of Corunna. Something like 5,000 men had perished or been taken during the retreat; 3,500 had embarked at Vigo, so that about 15,000 men, all infantry save some 200 gunners, remained behind to oppose Soult. Considering all that they had gone through, they were now in very good trim: all the sick and weakly men had been sent off, those who remained in the ranks were all war-hardened veterans. Before the battle they had enjoyed four days of rest and good feeding in Corunna. Moreover, they had repaired their armament: there were in the arsenal many thousand stand of arms, newly arrived from England for the use of the Galician army. Moore made his men change their rusty and battered muskets for new ones, before ordering the store to be destroyed. He also distributed new cartridges, from an enormous stock found in the place. The town was, in fact, crammed with munitions of all sorts. Seeing that there would be no time to re-embark them, Moore utilized what he could, and destroyed the rest.

---

[1] I obtain these figures from the *Parliamentary Returns* of 1809.

Battle of Corunna. January 16. 1809.

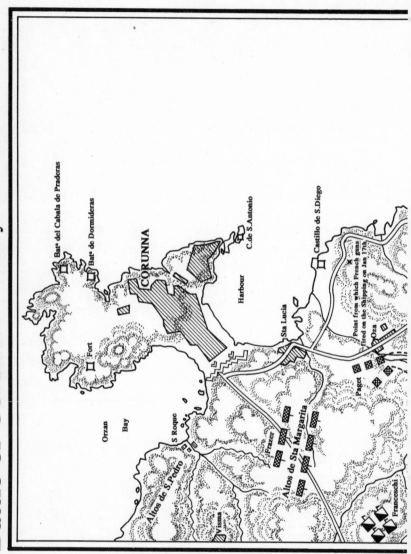

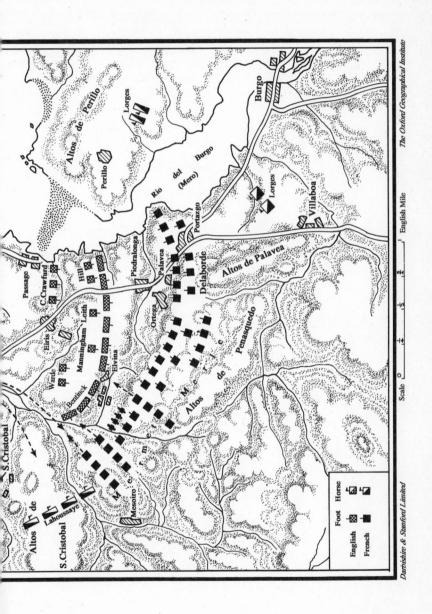

Scale   0   1   2   3   4   English Mile

Legend:

Foot   Horse

English

French

Burgo

Villaboa

Lorges

Altos de Palavea

Penasquedo

Altos de Perillo

Perillo

Rio del (Mero) Burgo

Piedralonga

Portazgo

Ortega

Palavea

Delaborde

Altos de Mero

Mesoiro

S. Cristobal

Altos de S. Cristobal

Lahoussaye

Bentinck

Warde

Manningham

Leith

Elvina

Biris

C. Crawfurd

Passage

Hill

SECTION VIII: CHAPTER VI

THE BATTLE OF CORUNNA

WHEN Sir John Moore found that the transports were not ready on the twelfth, he had recognized that he might very probably have to fight a defensive action in order to cover his retreat, for two days would allow Soult to bring up his main-body. He refused to listen to the timid proposal of certain of his officers that he should negotiate for a quiet embarkation, in return for giving up Corunna and its fortifications unharmed [1]. This would have been indeed a tame line of conduct for a general and an army which had never been beaten in the field. Instead he sought for a good position in which to hold back the enemy till all his impedimenta were on shipboard. There were no less than three lines of heights on which the army might range itself to resist an enemy who had crossed the Mero. But the first two ranges, the Monte Loureiro just above the river, and the plateaux of Palavea and Peñasquedo two miles further north, were too extensive to be held by an army of 15,000 men. Moore accordingly chose as his fighting-ground the Monte Moro, a shorter and lower ridge, only two miles outside the walls of Corunna. It is an excellent position, about 2,500 yards long, but has two defects: its western and lower end is commanded at long cannon-range by the heights of Peñasquedo. Moreover, beyond this extreme point of the hill, there is open ground extending as far as the gates of Corunna, by which the whole position can be turned. Fully aware of this fact, Moore told off more than a third of his army to serve as a flank-guard on this wing, and to prevent the enemy from pushing in between the Monte Moro and the narrow neck of the peninsula on which Corunna stands.

Soult, even after he had passed the Mero and repaired the bridges, was very circumspect in his advances. He had too much

---

[1] There can be no doubt that this strange suggestion was made, as Moore himself mentions it in his dispatch of Jan. 13, the last which he wrote.

respect for the fighting power of the English army to attack before he had rallied his whole force. When Delaborde's division and a multitude of stragglers had joined him on the fifteenth, he at last moved forward and seized the heights of Palavea and Peñasquedo, overlooking the British position. There was some slight skirmishing with the outposts which had been left on these positions, and when the French brought down two guns to the lower slopes by Palavea, and began to cannonade the opposite hill, Colonel McKenzie, of the 5th Regiment, made an attempt to drive them off, which failed with loss, and cost him his life.

As the French pressed westward along these commanding heights, Moore saw that he might very possibly be attacked on the following day, and brought up his troops to their fighting-ground, though he was still not certain that Soult would risk a battle. The divisions of Hope and Baird were ranged along the upper slopes of the Monte Moro : the ten battalions of the former on the eastern half of the ridge, nearest the river, the eight battalions of the latter on its western half, more towards the inland. Each division had two brigades in the first line and a third in reserve. Counting from left to right, the brigades were those of Hill and Leith from Hope's division, and Manningham and Bentinck from Baird's. Behind the crest Catlin Crawfurd supported the two former, and Warde's battalions of Guards the two latter. Down in the hollow behind the Monte Moro lay Paget's division, close to the village of Eiris [1]. He was invisible to the French, but so placed that he could immediately move out to cover the right wing if the enemy attempted a turning movement. Lastly, Fraser's division lay under cover in Corunna, ready to march forth to support Paget the moment that fighting should begin [2]. Six of the nine guns (small six-pounders), which Moore had left on shore, were distributed in pairs along the front of Monte Moro : the other three were with Paget's reserve.

After surveying the British position from the Peñasquedo heights, Soult had resolved to attempt the manoeuvre which Moore had thought most probable—to assault the western end of the line, where the heights are least formidable, and at the same moment to turn the Monte Moro by a movement round its extreme right through the open ground. Nor had it escaped

---

[1] Paget had just lost his senior brigadier, Anstruther, who died of dysentery in Corunna that day. His second brigade was commanded by Disney.

[2] His two brigadiers were Beresford and Fane.

him that the ground occupied by Baird's division was within cannon-shot of the opposite range.   He ordered ten guns to be dragged up to the westernmost crest of the French position, and to be placed above the village of Elvina, facing Bentinck's brigade. The rest of his artillery was distributed along the front of the Peñasquedo and Palavea heights, in situations that were less favourable, because they were more remote from the British lines. The hills were steep, no road ran along their summit, and the guns had to be dragged by hand to the places which they were intended to occupy.   It was only under cover of the night that those opposite Elvina were finally got to their destination.

Soult's force was now considerably superior to that which was opposed to him, sufficiently so in his own estimation to compensate for the strength of the defensive positions which he would have to assail.   He had three infantry divisions with thirty-nine battalions (Heudelet was still far to the rear), and twelve regiments of cavalry, with about forty guns [1].   The whole, even allowing for stragglers

---

[1] The force stood as follows :—

Infantry—1st Division, Merle (Brigades Reynaud, Sarrut, Thomières).

2nd Léger (three batts.) 4th Léger (four batts.) 15th of the Line (three batts.) 36th of the Line (three batts.)	Each of Merle's regiments (of which three were originally two battalions and one three battalions strong) had received an additional battalion from the dissolved corps of Junot, before leaving Astorga.

2nd Division, Mermet (Brigades Gaulois, Jardon, Lefebvre).

31st Léger (four batts.) 47th of the Line (four batts.) 122nd of the Line (four batts.) 2nd Swiss Regiment (two batts.) 3rd Swiss Regiment (one batt.)	The 47th had received two, and the 31st Léger and 2nd Swiss each one battalion from Junot's corps. The 122nd was a new regiment, consolidated from six battalions of the 'Supplementary Legions of Reserve.'

3rd Division, Delaborde (Brigades Foy and Arnaud).

17th Léger (three batts.) 70th of the Line (four batts.) 86th of the Line (three batts.) 4th Swiss Regiment (one batt.)	The 70th and 86th, from Portugal, had each received a battalion from Merle's division, where they had been serving in the autumn. The 17th Léger had been transferred from the 6th Corps to the 2nd.

Cavalry—Lahoussaye's Division of Dragoons (Brigades Marisy and Caulaincourt).

17th, 18th, 19th, and 27th Dragoons—four regiments.   [See over.]

still trailing in the rear, and for men who had perished in the snows of the mountains, must have been over 20,000 strong. The cavalry had 4,500 sabres, and the infantry battalions must still have averaged over 500 men, for in November they had nearly all been up to 700 bayonets, and even the toilsome march in pursuit of Moore cannot have destroyed so much as a third of their numbers: only Merle's division had done any fighting. It is absurd of some of the French narrators of the battle to pretend that Soult had only 13,000 infantry—a figure which would only give 330 bayonets to each battalion [1].

Soult's plan was to contain the British left and centre with two of his divisions—those of Delaborde and Merle—while Mermet and the bulk of the cavalry should attack Moore's right, seize the western end of Monte Moro, and push in between Baird's flank and Corunna. If this movement succeeded, the British retreat would be compromised: Delaborde and Merle could then assail Hope and prevent him from going to the rear: if all went right, two-thirds of the British army must be surrounded and captured.

The movement of masses of infantry, and still more of cavalry and guns, along the rugged crest and slopes of the Peñasquedo heights, was attended with so much difficulty, that noon was long passed before the whole army was in position. It was indeed so late in the day, that Sir John Moore had come to the conclusion that Soult did not intend to attack, and had ordered Paget's division, who were to be the first troops to embark, to march down to the harbour [2]. The other corps were to retire at dusk, and go on shipboard under cover of the night.

But between 1.30 and 2 o'clock the French suddenly took the offensive: the battery opposite Elvina began to play upon Baird's division, columns descending from each side of it commenced to pour down into the valley, and the eight cavalry regiments of Lahoussaye

Lorges's Division of Dragoons (Brigades Vialannes and Fournier).
13th, 15th, 22nd, and 25th Dragoons—four regiments.

Franceschi's Mixed Division (Brigades Debelle and Girardin [?]).
1st Hussars, 8th Dragoons, 22nd Chasseurs, and Hanoverian Chasseurs—four regiments.

Artillery—600 men (?): exact figures not available.

[1] e. g. Le Noble in his *Campagne du Maréchal Soult, 1808–9*, p. 41.
[2] Blakeney, p. 114.

and Franceschi, pushing out from behind the Peñasquedo heights, rode northward along the lower slopes of the hills of San Cristobal, with the obvious design of cutting in between the Monte Moro and Corunna.

Moore welcomed the approach of battle with joy: he had every confidence in his men and his position, and saw that a victory won ere his departure would silence the greater part of the inevitable criticism for timidity and want of enterprise, to which he would be exposed on his return to England. He rode up to the crest of his position, behind Baird's division, took in the situation of affairs at a glance, and sent back orders to Paget to pay attention to the French turning movement, and to Fraser to come out from Corunna and contain any advance on the part of the enemy's cavalry on the extreme right.

For some time the English left and centre were scarcely engaged, for Merle and Delaborde did no more than push tirailleurs out in front of their line, to bicker with the skirmishers of Hill, Leith, and Manningham. But Bentinck's brigade was at once seriously assailed: not only were its lines swept by the balls of Soult's main battery, but a heavy infantry attack was in progress. Gaulois and Jardon's brigades of Mermet's division were coming forward in great strength: they turned out of the village of Elvina the light company of the 50th, which had been detached to hold that advanced position, and then came up the slope of Monte Moro, with a dense crowd of tirailleurs covering the advance of eight battalion columns. Meanwhile the third brigade of Mermet's division was hurrying past the flank of Bentinck's line, in the lower ground, with the obvious intention of turning the British flank. Beyond them Lahoussaye's dragoons were cautiously feeling their way forward, much incommoded by walls and broken ground.

All the stress of the first fighting fell on the three battalions of Bentinck, on the hill above Elvina. Moore was there in person to direct the fight: Baird, on whom the responsibility for this part of the ground would naturally have fallen, was wounded early in the day, by a cannon-ball which shattered his left arm [1], and was borne to the rear. When the French came near the top of the slope, driving in before them the British skirmishing line, the Commander-in-chief ordered the 42nd and 50th to charge down

---

[1] His dispatch to Castlereagh, of Jan. 18, proves that he was wounded before Moore fell.

upon them.   The 4th, the flank regiment of the whole line, could
not follow them : it was threatened by the encircling movement of
the French left, and Moore bade it throw back its right wing so as
to form an angle *en potence* with the rest of the brigade, while still
keeping up its fire.   The manœuvre was executed with such precision as to win his outspoken approval—'That is exactly how it
should be done,' he shouted to Colonel Wynch, and then rode off
to attend to the 50th and 42nd, further to his left.

Here a very heavy combat was raging.   Advancing to meet the
French attack, these two battalions drove in the tirailleurs with
the crushing fire of their two-deep line, and then became engaged
with the supporting columns on the slopes above Elvina.   For
some time the battle stood still, but Moore told the regiments
that they must advance to make their fire tell, and at last Colonel
Sterling and Major Charles Napier led their men over the line of
stone walls behind which they were standing, and pressed forward.
The head of the French formation melted away before their volleys,
and the enemy rolled back into Elvina.   The 42nd halted just
above the village, but Napier led the 50th in among the houses,
and cleared out the defenders after a sharp fight.   He even passed
through with part of his men, and became engaged with the French
supports on the further side of the place.   Presently Mermet sent
down his reserves and drove out the 50th, who suffered very heavily :
Charles Napier was wounded and taken, and Stanhope the junior
major was killed [1].   While the 50th was reforming, Moore brought up
the divisional reserve, Warde's two magnificent battalions of Guards,
each of which, in consequence of their splendid discipline during
the retreat, mustered over 800 bayonets.   With these and the 42nd
he held the slope above Elvina in face of a very hot fire, not only
from the enemy's infantry but from the battery on the opposite
heights, which swept the ground with a lateral and almost an
enfilading fire.   It was while directing one of the Guards' battalions
to go forward and storm a large house on the flank of the village
that Moore received a mortal wound.   A cannon-ball struck him
on the left shoulder, carrying it away with part of the collar-bone,
and leaving the arm hanging only by the flesh and muscles above

---

[1] Every student of the Peninsular War should read Charles Napier's vivid
and thrilling account of the storm of Elvina.   William Napier reprinted
it in vol. i of his brother's biography.   Charles was within an ace of being
murdered after surrender, and was saved by a gallant French drummer.

the armpit [1]. He was dashed from his horse, but immediately raised himself on his sound arm and bade his aide-de-camp Hardinge see that the 42nd should advance along with the Guards. Then he was borne to the rear, fully realizing that his wound was mortal: his consciousness never failed, in spite of the pain and the loss of blood, and he found strength to send a message to Hope to bid him take command of the army. When his bearers wished to unbuckle his sword, which was jarring his wounded arm and side, he refused to allow it, saying 'in his usual tone and with a very distinct voice, "It is well as it is. I had rather that it should go out of the field with me."' He was borne back to Corunna in a blanket by six men of the Guards and 42nd. Frequently he made them turn him round to view the field of battle, and as he saw the French line of fire rolling back, he several times expressed his pleasure at dying in the moment of victory, when his much-tried army was at last faring as it deserved.

While Bentinck's brigade and the Guards were thus engaged with Mermet's right, a separate combat was going on more to the west, where Edward Paget and the Reserve division had marched out to resist the French turning movement. The instant that Moore's first orders had been received, Paget had sent forward the 95th Rifles in extended order to cover the gap, half a mile in breadth, between the Monte Moro and the heights of San Cristobal. Soon afterwards he pushed up the 52nd into line with the riflemen. The other three battalions of the division moved out soon after. Paget had in front of him a brigade—five battalions—of Mermet's division, which was trying to slip round the corner of Monte Moro in order to take Baird in the flank. He had also to guard against the charges of Lahoussaye's cavalry more to his right, and those of Franceschi's chasseurs still further south. Fortunately the ground was so much cut up with rough stone walls, dividing the fields of the villages of San Cristobal and Elvina, that Soult's cavalry were unable to execute any general or vigorous advance. When the British swept across the low ground, Lahoussaye's dragoons made two or three attempts to charge, but, forced to advance among walls and ravines, they never even compelled Paget's battalions to form square, and were easily driven off by a rolling fire. The Reserve division steadily advanced, with the 95th and 52nd in its front, and the horsemen gave back. It was in vain

---

[1] Letter of his aide-de-camp Hardinge in James Moore's *Life*, p. 220.

that Lahoussaye dismounted the 27th Dragoons and ranged them as *tirailleurs* along the lower slopes of the heights of San Cristobal. The deadly fire of Paget's infantry thinned their ranks, and forced them back. It would seem that the 95th, 28th, and 91st had mainly to do with Lahoussaye, while the 52nd and 20th became engaged with the infantry from the division of Mermet, which was bickering with the 4th Regiment below the Monte Moro, and striving to turn its flank. In both quarters the advance was completely successful, and Paget pushed forward, taking numerous prisoners from the enemy's broken infantry. So far did he advance in his victorious onslaught that he approached from the flank the main French battery on the heights of Peñasquedo, and thought that (if leave had been given him) he would have been able to capture it: for its infantry supports were broken, and the cavalry had gone off far to the right. But Hope sent no orders to his colleague, and the Reserve halted at dusk at the foot of the French position.

Franceschi's horsemen meanwhile, on the extreme left of the French line, had at first pushed cautiously towards Corunna, till they saw Fraser's division drawn up half a mile outside the gates, on the low ridge of Santa Margarita, covering the whole neck of the peninsula. This checked the cavalry, and presently, when Paget's advance drove in Lahoussaye, Franceschi conformed to the retreat of his colleague, and drew back across the heights of San Cristobal till he had reached the left rear of Soult's position, and halted in the upland valley somewhere near the village of Mesoiro.

We left Bentinck's and Warde's brigades engaged on the slopes above Elvina with Mermet's right-hand column, at the moment of the fall of Sir John Moore. The second advance on Elvina had begun just as the British commander-in-chief fell: it was completely successful, and the village was for the second time captured. Mermet now sent down his last reserves, and Merle moved forward his left-hand brigade to attack the village on its eastern side. This led to a corresponding movement on the part of the British. Manningham's brigade from the right-centre of the British line came down the slope, and fell upon Merle's columns as they pressed in towards the village. This forced the French to halt, and to turn aside to defend themselves: there was a long and fierce strife, during the later hours of the afternoon, between Manningham's two right-hand regiments (the 3/1st and 2/81st) and the 2nd Léger and 36th of the Line of Reynaud's brigade. It was prolonged till the

2/81st had exhausted all its ammunition, and had suffered a loss of 150 men, when Hope sent down the 2/59th, the reserve regiment of Leith's brigade, to relieve it. Soon afterwards the French retired, and the battle died away at dusk into mere distant bickering along the bottom of the valley, as a few skirmishers of the victorious brigade pursued the retreating columns to the foot of their position.

Further eastward Delaborde had done nothing more than make a feeble demonstration against Hope's very strong position on the heights above the Mero river. He drove in Hill's pickets, and afterwards, late in the afternoon, endeavoured to seize the village of Piedralonga [1], at the bottom of the valley which lay between the hostile lines. Foy, who was entrusted with this operation, took the voltigeur companies of his brigade, and drove out from the hamlet the outposts of the 14th Regiment. Thereupon Hill sent down Colonel Nicholls with three more companies of that corps, supported by two of the 92nd from Hope's divisional reserve. They expelled the French, and broke the supports on which the voltigeurs tried to rally, taking a few prisoners including Foy's brigade-major. Delaborde then sent down another battalion, which recovered the southern end of the village, while Nicholls held tightly to the rest of it. At dusk both parties ceased to push on, and the firing died away. The engagement at this end of the line was insignificant : Foy lost eighteen killed and fifty wounded from the 70th of the Line, and a few more from the 86th. Nicholls's casualties were probably even smaller [2].

Soult had suffered such a decided reverse that he had no desire to prolong the battle, while Hope—who so unexpectedly found himself in command of the British army—showed no wish to make

[1] Erroneously called in most British and French accounts Palavea Abaxo. The latter village is at the foot of the French line, a little to the north.

[2] For an account of this combat from the French side see Foy's report to Delaborde, printed in Girod de l'Ain's *Vie militaire du Général Foy* (appendix), where the losses of the brigade are given. On the English side the 92nd lost three killed and five wounded (see Gardyne's *History of the 92nd Regiment*). The 14th do not separate their battle-losses from those of the retreat in their casualty-returns. They had sixty-six dead and missing in the whole campaign, and put on board at Corunna seventy-two sick and wounded. Probably not more than ten of the former and thirty of the latter were hit in the battle ; if the casualties were any larger on January 16 the losses in the retreat must have been abnormally small in the 14th Regiment.

a counter-attack, and was quite contented to have vindicated his position. He claimed, in his dispatch, that at the end of the engagement the army was holding a more advanced line than at its commencement: and this was in part true, for Elvina was now occupied in force, and not merely by a picket, and Paget on the right had cleared the ground below the heights of San Cristobal, which Lahoussaye had been occupying during the action. Some of the French writers have claimed that Soult also had gained ground[1]: but the only fact that can be cited in favour of their contention is that Foy was holding on to the southern end of Piedralonga[2]. All the eye-witnesses on their side concede that at the end of the action the marshal's army had fallen back to its original position[3].

English critics have occasionally suggested that the success won by Paget and Bentinck might have been pressed, and that if the division of Fraser had been brought up to their support, the French left might have been turned and crushed[4]. But considering that Soult had fourteen or fifteen intact battalions left, in the divisions of Merle and Delaborde[5], it would have been well in his power to fight a successful defensive action on his heights, throwing back his left wing, so as to keep it from being encircled. Hope was right to be contented with his success: even if he had won a victory he could have done no more than re-embark, for the army was not in a condition to plunge once more into the Galician highlands in pursuit of Soult, who would have been joined in a few days by Heudelet, and in a week by Ney.

The losses suffered by the two armies at the battle of Corunna

[1] Of course the untrustworthy Le Noble does so, and falsifies his map accordingly.

[2] Foy's brigade engaged two battalions of the 70th Regiment, besides three companies of *voltigeurs* of the 86th ; this was all that Delaborde sent forward. There were two *chefs de bataillon* among the wounded.

[3] 'Chaque armée resta sur son terrain,' says St. Chamans, Soult's senior aide-de-camp (the man who so kindly entreated Charles Napier, as the latter's memoirs show). 'A la nuit, qui seule a pu terminer cette lutte opiniâtre, nous nous sommes retrouvés au point d'où nous étions partis à 3 heures,' says Fantin des Odoards, of Mermet's division (p. 200). 'Nos troupes furent obligées, par des forces supérieures, de rentrer dans leurs premiers postes,' says Naylies, of Lahoussaye's dragoons (p. 46).

[4] Blakeney urges this very strongly (pp. 117, 118) ; Graham also.

[5] It would seem that only the 2nd Léger and 36th of the Line of Merle, and the 70th of Delaborde, had been seriously engaged.

are not easy to estimate. The British regiments, embarking on the day after the fight, did not send in any returns of their casualties till they reached England. Then, most unfortunately, a majority of the colonels lumped together the losses of the retreat and those of the battle. It is lucky, however, to find that among the regiments which sent in proper returns are nearly all those which fought the brunt of the action. The 50th and 42nd of Bentinck's brigade were by far the most heavily tried, from the prolonged and desperate fighting in and about Elvina. The former lost two officers killed and three wounded, with 180 rank and file: the Highland battalion thirty-nine rank and file killed and 111 (including six officers) wounded. The Guards' brigade, on the other hand, which was brought up to support these regiments, suffered very little; the first battalion of the 1st Regiment had only five, the second only eight killed, with about forty wounded between them. In Manningham's brigade the 81st, with its loss of three officers and twenty-seven men killed, and eleven officers and 112 men wounded, was by far the heaviest sufferer: the Royals may also have had a considerable casualty-list, but its figures are apparently not to be found, except confused with those of the whole retreat. Paget's division in its flank march to ward off the French turning movement suffered surprisingly little: of its two leading regiments the 1/95th had but twelve killed and thirty-three wounded, the 1/52nd five killed and thirty-three wounded. The other three battalions, which formed the supports, must have had even fewer men disabled. Hope's division, with the exception of the 14th and the 59th, was not seriously engaged: the few battalions which sent in their battle-losses, apart from those of the retreat, show figures such as six or ten for their casualties on January 16. Fraser's whole division neither fired a shot nor lost a man. It is probable then that Hope, when in his dispatch he estimated the total loss of the British army at 'something between 700 and 800,' was overstating rather than understating the total.

Soult's losses are even harder to discover than those of Moore's army. His chronicler, Le Noble [1], says that they amounted to no more than 150 killed and 500 wounded. The ever inaccurate Thiers reduces this figure to 400 or less. On the other hand Naylies, a combatant in the battle, speaks of 800 casualties; and

---

[1] Belmas gives the same number, probably copying Le Noble.

Marshal Jourdan, in his *précis* of the campaign, gives 1,000 [1]. But all these figures must be far below the truth. Fantin des Odoards has preserved the exact loss of his own corps, the 31st Léger, one of the regiments of Mermet's division, which fought in Elvina. It amounted to no less than 330 men [2]. The other four regiments of the division were not less deeply engaged, and it is probable that Mermet alone must have lost over 1,000 in killed and wounded. Two of his three brigadiers went down in the fight: Gaulois was shot dead, Lefebvre badly hurt. Of Merle's division, one brigade was hotly engaged in the struggle with Manningham's battalions, in which our 2/81st lost so heavily. The French cannot have suffered less, as they were the beaten party. Lahoussaye's dragoons must also have sustained appreciable loss: that of Delaborde (as we have already seen) was limited to about eighteen killed and fifty wounded. Of unwounded prisoners the British took seven officers and 156 men. If we put the total of Soult's casualties at 1,500, we probably shall not be far wrong. All the later experience of the war showed that, when French troops delivered in column an uphill attack on a British position and failed, they suffered twice or thrice the loss of the defenders: we need only mention Vimiero and Busaco. On this occasion there was the additional advantage that Moore's army had new muskets and good ammunition, while those of Soult's corps were much deteriorated. A loss of 1,500 men therefore seems a fair and rational estimate. The impression left by the battle on Soult's mind was such that, in his first dispatch to the Emperor, he wrote that he could do no more against the English till he should have received large reinforcements [3]. But two days later, when Hope had evacuated Corunna, he changed his tone and let it be understood that he had gained ground during the battle, and had so far established an advantage that his position forced the English to embark. This allegation was wholly without foundation. Hope simply carried out the arrangements which Moore had made for sending off the army to England, and his resolve was dictated by the condition of his troops, who urgently needed reorganization and repose, and not by any fear of what the Marshal could do against him.

[1] Jourdan's *Mémoires*, p. 126.   [2] Fantin des Odoards, p. 201.

[3] See Marshal Jourdan's very judicious remark on Soult's bulletins in his *Mémoires militaires* (p. 127). 'His first dispatch was not that of a general who imagined that he had been successful.'

Moore, borne back to his quarters in Corunna, survived long enough to realize that his army had completely beaten off Soult's attack, and had secured for itself a safe departure. In spite of his dreadful wound he retained his consciousness to the last. Forgetful of his own pain, he made inquiries as to the fate of his especial friends and dependants, and found strength to dictate several messages, recommending for promotion officers who had distinguished themselves, and sending farewell greetings to his family. He repeatedly said that he was dying in the way he had always desired, on the night of a victorious battle. The only weight on his mind was the thought that public opinion at home might bear hardly upon him, in consequence of the horrors of the retreat. 'I hope the people of England will be satisfied,' he gasped; 'I hope my country will do me justice.' And then his memory wandered back to those whom he loved: he tried in vain to frame a message to his mother, but weakness and emotion overcame him, and a few minutes later he died, with the name of Pitt's niece (Lady Hester Stanhope) on his lips. Moore had expressed a wish to be buried where he fell, and his staff carried out his desire as far as was possible, by laying him in a grave on the ramparts of Corunna. He was buried at early dawn on the seventeenth, on the central bastion that looks out towards the land-side and the battle-field. Hard by him lies General Anstruther, who had died of dysentery on the day before the fight. Soult, with a generosity that does him much credit, took care of Moore's grave, and ordered a monument to be erected over the spot where he fell[1]. La Romana afterwards carried out the Marshal's pious intentions.

Little remains to be said about the embarkation of the army. At nine o'clock on the night of the battle the troops were withdrawn from the Monte Moro position, leaving only pickets along its front. Many regiments were embarked that night, more on the morning of the seventeenth. By the evening of that day all were aboard save Beresford's brigade of Fraser's division, which remained to cover the embarkation of the rest.

Soult, when he found that the British had withdrawn, sent up some field-pieces to the heights above Fort San Diego, on the southern end of the bay. Their fire could reach the more outlying transports, and created some confusion, as the masters hastily

---

[1] The inscription was to run: ' Hic cecidit Iohannes Moore dux exercitus Britannici, in pugna Ianuarii xvi, 1809, contra Gallos a duce Dalmatiae ductos.'

weighed anchor and stood out to sea. Four vessels ran on shore, and three of them could not be got off: the troops on board were hastily transferred to other ships, with no appreciable loss: from the whole army only nine men of the Royal Wagon Train are returned as having been 'drowned in Corunna harbour,' no doubt from the sinking of the boat which was transhipping them. General Leith records, in his diary, that on the vessel which took him home there were fragments of no less than six regiments: we can hardly doubt that this must have been one of those which picked up the men from the stranded transports.

Beresford's brigade embarked from a safe point behind the citadel on the eighteenth, leaving the town in charge of the small Spanish garrison under General Alcedo, which maintained the works till all the fleet were far out to sea, and then rather tamely surrendered. This was entirely the doing of their commander, a shifty old man, who almost immediately after took service with King Joseph [1].

The returning fleet had a tempestuous but rapid passage: urged on by a raging south-wester the vessels ran home in four or five days, and made almost every harbour between Falmouth and Dover. Many transports had a dangerous passage, but only two, the *Dispatch* and the *Smallbridge*, came to grief off the Cornish coast and were lost, the former with three officers and fifty-six men of the 7th Hussars, the latter with five officers and 209 men of the King's German Legion [2]. So ended the famous 'Retreat from Sahagun.'

Moore's memory met, as he had feared, with many unjust aspersions when the results of his campaign were known in England. The aspect of the 26,000 ragged war-worn troops, who came ashore on the South Coast, was so miserable that those who saw them were shocked. The state of the mass of 3,000 invalids, racked with fever and dysentery, who were cast into the hospitals was eminently distressing. It is seldom that a nation sees its troops returning straight from the field, with the grime and sweat of battle and march fresh upon them. The impression made was

[1] St. Chamans calls him ' un vieux faible et sans moyens, mené par une espèce de courtisane.' Mr. Stuart (in a note to Vaughan) describes him as an ' unscrupulous old rascal.'

[2] Cf. for their losses the *Parliamentary Papers for 1809* (pp. 8, 9), and Beamish's *History of the German Legion*.

a very unhappy one, and it was easy to blame the General. Public discontent was roused both against Moore and against the ministry, and some of the defenders of the latter took an ungenerous opportunity of shifting all the blame upon the man who could no longer vindicate himself. This provoked his numerous friends into asserting that his whole conduct of the campaign had been absolutely blameless, and that any misfortunes which occurred were simply and solely the fault of maladministration and unwise councils at home. Moore was the hero of the Whig party, and politics were dragged into the discussion of the campaign to a lamentable extent. Long years after his death the attitude of the critic or the historian, who dealt with the Corunna retreat, was invariably coloured by his Whig or Tory predilections.

The accepted view of the present generation is (though most men are entirely unacquainted with the fact) strongly coloured by the circumstance that William Napier, whose eloquent history has superseded all other narratives of the Peninsular War, was a violent enemy of the Tory ministry and a personal admirer of Moore. Ninety years and more have now passed since the great retreat, and we can look upon the campaign with impartial eyes. It is easy to point out mistakes made by the home government, such as the tardy dispatch of Baird's cavalry, and the inadequate provision of money, both for the division which started from Lisbon and for that which started from Corunna. But these are not the most important causes of the misfortunes of the campaign. Nor can it be pleaded that the ministry did not support Moore loyally, or that they tied his hands by contradictory or over-explicit orders. A glance at Castlereagh's dispatches is sufficient to show that he and his colleagues left everything that was possible to be settled by the General, and that they approved each of his determinations as it reached them without any cavilling or criticism [1].

Moore must take the main responsibility for all that happened. On the whole, the impression left after a study of his campaign is very favourable to him. His main conception when he marched from Salamanca—that of gaining time for the rallying of the Spanish armies, by directing a sudden raid upon the Emperor's communications in Castile—was as sound as it was enterprising. The French critics who have charged him with rashness have never

---

[1] In fairness to the government Castlereagh's dispatches, 92–105 in the *Parliamentary Papers for 1809*, should be carefully studied.

read his dispatches, nor realized the care with which he had thought out the retreat, which he knew would be inevitable when his movement became known at Madrid. He was never for a moment in any serious danger of being surrounded by the Emperor, because he was proceeding (as he himself wrote) 'bridle in hand,' and with a full knowledge that he must 'have a run for it' on the first receipt of news that Napoleon was upon the march. His plan of making a diversion was a complete success: he drew the Emperor, with the 70,000 men who would otherwise have marched on Lisbon, up into the north-west of the Peninsula, quite out of the main centre of operations. Napoleon himself halted at Astorga, but 45,000 men marched on after the British, and were engulfed in the mountains of Galicia, where they were useless for the main operations of the war. Spain, in short, gained three months of respite, because the main disposable field-army of her invaders had been drawn off into a corner by the unexpected march of the British on Sahagun. 'As a diversion the movement has answered completely,' wrote Moore to Castlereagh from Astorga[1], and with justice. That the subsequent retreat to Corunna was also advisable we must concede, though the arguments in favour of attempting a defence of Galicia were more weighty than has generally been allowed[2].

But when we turn to the weeks that preceded the advance from Salamanca, and that followed the departure from Astorga, it is only a very blind admirer of Moore who will contend that everything was arranged and ordered for the best. That the army, which began to arrive at Salamanca on November 13, did not make a forward move till December 12 is a fact which admits of explanation, but not of excuse. The main governing fact of its inactivity was not, as Moore was always urging, the disasters of the Spaniards, but the misdirection of the British cavalry and artillery on the roundabout route by Elvas, Talavera, and the Escurial. For this the British general was personally responsible: we have already shown that he had good reasons for distrusting the erroneous reports on the roads of Portugal which were sent in to him, and that he should not have believed them[3]. He ought to have marched on Almeida, with his troops distributed between the three available roads, and should have had a compact

---

[1] Moore to Castlereagh, from Astorga, Dec. 31, 1808.
[2] See the arguments stated on pp. 554–5.
[3] See the facts stated on pp. 493–5.

force of all arms concentrated at Salamanca by November 15.
Even without Baird he could then have exercised some influence
on the course of events. As it was, he condemned himself—by the
unmilitary act of separating himself from his guns and his horsemen—to a month of futile waiting, while the fate of the campaign
was being settled a hundred and fifty miles away.

The chance that Napoleon turned his whole army upon Madrid,
and did not send a single corps in search of the British, gave
Moore the grand opportunity for striking at the French communications, which he turned to such good account in the middle
of December. But, though he so splendidly vindicated his reputation by this blow, we cannot forget the long hesitation at
Salamanca by which it was preceded, nor the unhappy project
for instant retreat on Portugal, which was so nearly put into
execution. If it had been carried out, Moore's name would have
been relegated to a very low place in the list of British commanders,
for he would undoubtedly have evacuated Lisbon, just as he had
prepared to evacuate Corunna on the day before he was slain. We
have his own words to that effect. On November 25 he put on
paper his opinion as to the defence of Portugal. ' Its frontier,' he
wrote, ' is not defensible against a superior force. It is an open
frontier, all equally rugged, but all equally to be penetrated. If the
French succeed in Spain, it will be vain to attempt to resist them in
Portugal. The British must in that event immediately take steps
to evacuate the country[1].' It is fortunate that Sir Arthur
Wellesley was not of this opinion, or the course of the Peninsular
War, and of the whole struggle between Bonaparte and Britain,
might have been modified in a very unhappy fashion.

So much must be said of Moore's earlier faults. Of his later
ones, committed after his departure from Astorga, almost as much
might be made. His long hesitation, as to whether he should
march on Vigo or on Corunna, was inexcusable: at Astorga his
mind should have been made up, and the Vigo road (a bad cross-
route on which he had not a single magazine) should have been
left out of consideration. By failing to make up his mind, and
taking useless half-measures, Moore deprived himself of the services
of Robert Crawfurd and 3,500 of the best soldiers of his army.
But, as we have shown elsewhere, the hesitation was in its origin
the result of the groundless hypothesis which Moore had formed—

_____
[1] Moore to Castlereagh, from Salamanca, Nov. 25.

one knows not from what premises—that the French would not be able to pursue him beyond Villafranca.

Still more open to criticism is the headlong pace at which Moore conducted the last stages of the retreat. Napier has tried to represent that the marches were not unreasonable: 'in eleven days,' he wrote, 'a small army passed over a hundred and fifty miles of good road [1].' But we have to deduct three days of rest, leaving an average of about seventeen miles a day; and this for January marching, in a rugged snow-clad country, is no trifle. For though the road was 'good,' in the sense that it was well engineered, it was conducted over ridge after ridge of one of the most mountainous lands in Europe. The desperate uphill gradients between Astorga and Manzanal, and between Villafranca and Cerezal, cannot be measured in mere miles when their difficulty is being estimated. The marching should be calculated by hours, and not by miles. Moreover, Moore repeatedly gave his men night-marches, and even two night-marches on end. Half the horrors of the dreadful stage between Lugo and Betanzos came from the fact that the army started at midnight on January 8–9, only rested a few hours by day, and then marched again at seven on the evening of the ninth, and through the whole of the dark hours between the ninth and tenth. Flesh and blood cannot endure such a trial even in good weather, and these were nights of hurricane and downpour. Who can wonder that even well-disposed and willing men lagged behind, sank down, and died by hundreds under such stress?

All this hurry was unnecessary: whenever the rearguard turned to face the French, Soult was forced to wait for many hours before he could even begin an attempt to evict it. For his infantry was always many miles to the rear, and he could not effect anything with the horsemen of his advanced guard against Paget's steady battalions—as Cacabellos sufficiently showed. Napier urges that any position that the British took up could be turned by side-roads: this is true, but the flanking movement would always take an inordinate time, and by the moment that the French had started upon it, the British rearguard could have got off in safety, after having delayed the enemy for the best part of a day. If, instead of offering resistance only at Cacabellos, Constantino, and Lugo, Moore had shown fight at three or four other places—e.g. at

[1] Napier, i. 349.

the narrow pass of Piedrafita, the passage of the Ladra, and the defile of Monte Falqueiro—he need not have hurried his main body beyond their strength, and left the road strewn with so many exhausted stragglers. French and English eye-witnesses alike repeatedly express their surprise that such positions were left undefended. While not disguising the fact that a great proportion of the British losses were due to mere want of discipline and sullen discontent on the part of the rank and file, we cannot fail to see that this was not the sole cause of the disasters of the retreat. The General drove his men beyond their strength, when he might, at the cost of a few rearguard skirmishes, have given them four or five days more in which to accomplish their retreat. Moore arrived at Corunna on January 11: it was January 16 before Soult had so far collected his army that he could venture to attack. At any other point, the result of offering battle would have been much the same. No excuse for Moore can be made on the ground of insufficient supplies: at Villafranca, Lugo, and Betanzos he destroyed enormous quantities of food, and often so imperfectly that the French succeeded in living for several days on what they could save from the flames.

In making these criticisms we are not in the least wishing to impugn Moore's reputation as a capable officer and a good general. He was both, but his fault was an excessive sense of responsibility. He could never forget that he had in his charge, as was said, 'not *a* British army, but *the* British army'—the one efficient force that the United Kingdom could put into the field. He was loth to risk it, though ultimately he did so in his admirably conceived march on Sahagun. He had also to think of his own career: among his numerous friends and admirers he had a reputation for military infallibility which he was loth to hazard. Acting under a strong sense of duty he did so, but all the while he was anxiously asking himself 'What will they say at home?' It was this self-consciousness that was Moore's weak point. Fortunately he was a man of courage and honour, and at the critical moment recovered the confidence and decision which was sometimes wanting in the hours of doubt and waiting.

Few men have been better loved by those who knew them best. To have served in the regiments which Moore had trained at Shorncliffe in 1803–5, was to be his devoted friend and admirer for life and death. Handsome, courteous, just, and benevolent, unsparing to himself, considerate to his subordinates, he won all hearts. 'He was a very king of men,' wrote Charles Napier; and Charles's more eloquent brother has left him a panegyric such as few generals have merited and fewer still obtained [1].

[1] 'Thus ended the career of Sir John Moore, a man whose uncommon capacity was sustained by the purest virtue, and governed by a disinterested patriotism, more in keeping with the primitive than the luxurious age of a great nation. His tall graceful person, his dark searching eyes, strongly defined forehead, and singularly expressive mouth indicated a noble disposition and a refined understanding. The lofty sentiments of honour habitual to his mind were adorned by a subtle playful wit, which gave him in conversation the ascendency which he always preserved by the decisive vigour of his action. He maintained the right with a vehemence bordering on fierceness, and every important transaction in which he was engaged increased his reputation for talent, and confirmed his character as a stern enemy to vice, a steadfast friend to merit, a just and faithful servant of his country. The honest loved him, the dishonest feared him; he did not shun, but scorned and spurned the base, and, with characteristic propriety, they spurned at him when he was dead. . . . If glory be a distinction, for such a man death is not a leveller!' (*Peninsular War*, i. 333.)

APPENDICES

I

GODOY'S PROCLAMATION OF OCT. 5, 1806

ESPAÑOLES!

E<small>N</small> circunstancias menos arriesgadas que las presentes han procurado los vasallos leales auxiliar á sus soberanos con dones y recursos anticipados á las necesidades ; pero en esta prevision tiene el mejor lugar la generosa accion de súbdito hácia su señor. El reino de Andalucía privilegiado por la naturaleza en la produccion de caballos de guerra ligeros ; la provincia de Extremadura que tantos servicios de esta clase hizo al señor Felipe V. ¿ verán con paciencia que la caballería del rey de España esté reducida é incompleta por falta de caballos? No, no lo creo ; antes sí espero que del mismo modo que los abuelos gloriosos de la generacion presente sirvieron al abuelo de nuestro rey con hombres y caballos, asistan ahora los nietos de nuestro suelo con regimientos ó compañías de hombres diestros en el manejo del caballo, para que sirvan y defiendan á su patria todo el tiempo que duren las urgencias actuales, volviendo despues llenos de gloria y con mejor suerte al descanso entre su familia. Entonces sí que cada cual se disputará los laureles de la victoria ; cual dirá deberse á su brazo la salvacion de su familia ; cual la de su gefe ; cual la de su pariente ó amigo, y todos á una tendrán razon para atribuirse á sí mismos la salvacion de la patria. Venid pues, amados compatriotas, venid á jurar bajo las banderas del mas benéfico de los soberanos : venid y yo os cubriré con el manto de la gratitud, cumpliéndoos cuanto desde ahora os ofrezco, si el Dios de las victorias nos concede una paz tan feliz y duradera cual le rogamos. No, no os detendrá el temor, no la perfidia : vuestros pechos no abrigan tales vicios, ni dan lugar á la torpe seduccion. Venid pues y si las cosas llegasen á punto de no enlazarse las armas con las de nuestros enemigos, no incurriréis en la nota de sospechosos, ni os tildaréis con un dictado impropio de vuestra lealtad y pundonor por haber sido omisos á mi llamamiento.

Pero si mi voz no alcanzase á despertar vuestros anhelos de gloria, sea la de vuestros inmediatos tutores ó padres del pueblo á quienes me dirijo, la que os haga entender lo que debeis á vuestra obligacion, á vuestro honor, y á la sagrada religion que profesais.

E<small>L PRÍNCIPE DE LA</small> P<small>AZ.</small>

San Ildefonso, 5 de octubre de 1806.

II

THE TREATY OF FONTAINEBLEAU

TRAITÉ SECRET ENTRE S.M.I. NAPOLÉON, EMPEREUR DES FRANÇAIS, ROI D'ITALIE, ETC., ET SA MAJESTÉ CATHOLIQUE CHARLES IV, ROI D'ESPAGNE, ETC.

Art. 1er. La province entre Minhô et Duero, la ville d'Oporto y comprise, sera donnée en toute propriété et souveraineté à S. M. le roi d'Etrurie, avec le titre de roi de la Lusitanie septentrionale.

2. La province d'Alentéjo, et le royaume des Algarves, seront donnés en toute propriété et souveraineté au prince de la Paix, dont il jouira avec le titre de prince des Algarves.

3. Les provinces de Beira, Tras-los-Montes et de l'Estramadure portugaise, resteront en dépôt jusqu'à la paix générale, et alors on disposera d'elles selon les circonstances, et conformément à ce qui sera convenu entre les deux hautes parties contractantes.

4. Le royaume de la Lusitanie septentrionale sera possédé par les descendans de S. M. le roi d'Etrurie, héréditairement et suivant les lois de succession qui sont en usage dans la famille régnante de S. M. le roi d'Espagne.

5. La principauté des Algarves sera possédée par les descendans du prince de la Paix, héréditairement et d'après les lois de succession qui sont en usage dans la famille régnante de S. M. le roi d'Espagne.

6. A défaut de descendans ou héritiers légitimes du roi de la Lusitanie septentrionale ou du prince des Algarves, ces pays seront donnés moyennant l'investiture par S. M. le roi d'Espagne, pourvu qu'ils ne puissent jamais être réunis sous une seule personne, ni à la couronne d'Espagne.

7. Le royaume de la Lusitanie septentrionale, et la principauté des Algarves, reconnaîtront comme protecteur S. M. le roi d'Espagne, et les souverains de ces pays ne pourront jamais faire la paix ni la guerre sans le consentement du roi catholique.

8. Si les provinces de Beira, de Tras-los-Montes et de l'Estramadure portugaise, restant en dépôt, étaient rendues au tems de la paix générale à la maison de Bragance, en échange de Gibraltar, la Trinité, et d'autres colonies que les Anglais ont conquises sur l'Espagne et ses alliés, le nouveau souverain de ces provinces aurait à l'égard de S. M. C. le roi d'Espagne les mêmes soumissions que le roi de la Lusitanie septentrionale, et le prince des Algarves, et il possédera sous les mêmes conditions.

9. S. M. le roi d'Etrurie cède en toute propriété et souveraineté le royaume d'Etrurie à S. M. l'empereur des Français, roi d'Italie.

10. Quand l'occupation définitive des provinces du Portugal sera effectuée, les différens princes qui doivent les posséder nommeront d'accord les commissaires pour fixer les limites naturelles.

11. S. M. l'empereur des Français, roi d'Italie, garantit à S. M. C. le roi d'Espagne la possession de ses états du continent d'Europe, situés au midi des Pyrénées.

12. S. M. l'empereur des Français, roi d'Italie, s'oblige à reconnaître S. M. C. le roi d'Espagne comme empereur des deux Amériques quand tout

sera prêt, afin que S. M. puisse prendre ce titre, ce qui pourra arriver au tems de la paix générale, ou le plus tard, d'ici à trois ans.

13. Les hautes puissances contractantes accorderont les moyens de faire à l'amiable une division égale des îles, colonies et autres propriétés d'outre-mer du Portugal.

14. Le présent traité restera secret, il sera ratifié, et les ratifications seront échangées à Madrid dans vingt jours.

Fait à Fontainebleau, le 27 octobre 1807.

Duroc.

Eugenio Izquierdo.

CONVENTION SECRÈTE.

Art. 1er. Un corps de troupes impériales françaises, de vingt-cinq mille hommes d'infanterie et de trois de cavalerie, entrera en Espagne, il fera sa jonction avec un corps de troupes espagnoles, composé de huit mille hommes d'infanterie, trois mille de cavalerie, et trente pièces d'artillerie.

2. Au même tems, une division de troupes espagnoles de dix mille hommes prendra possession de la province d'entre Minhô et Duero, et de la ville d'Oporto, et une autre division de six mille hommes, composée pareillement de troupes espagnoles, prendra possession de l'Alentéjo et du royaume des Algarves.

3. Les troupes françaises seront nourries et entretenues par l'Espagne, et leur solde payée par la France pendant tout le temps de leur passage en Espagne.

4. Depuis le moment où les troupes combinées seront entrées en Portugal, les provinces de Beira, Tras-los-Montes et l'Estramadure portugaise (qui doivent rester en dépôt), seront administrées et gouvernées par le général commandant des troupes françaises, et les contributions qui leur seront imposées seront au profit de la France. Les provinces qui doivent composer le royaume de la Lusitanie septentrionale et la principauté des Algarves seront administrées et gouvernées par les généraux commandant les divisions espagnoles qui en prendront possession, et les contributions qui leur seront imposées resteront au bénéfice de l'Espagne.

5. Le corps du centre sera sous les ordres du commandant des troupes françaises, aussi bien que les troupes espagnoles qui lui seront réunies. Cependant, si le roi d'Espagne ou le prince de la Paix trouvaient convenable et jugeaient à propos de s'y rendre, le général commandant des troupes françaises et elles-mêmes seront soumises aux ordres du roi d'Espagne ou du prince de la Paix.

6. Un autre corps de quarante mille hommes de troupes françaises sera réuni à Bayonne le 20 novembre prochain ou avant ce temps-là, et il devra être prêt à marcher sur le Portugal, en passant par l'Espagne, si les Anglais envoient des renforts et menacent d'attaquer le premier. Cependant, ce nouveau corps de troupes n'entrera que quand les deux hautes parties contractantes se seront mises d'accord pour cet effet.

7. La présente convention sera ratifiée, et l'échange des ratifications sera faite au même temps que le traité d'aujourd'hui.

Fait à Fontainebleau, le 27 octobre 1807.

Duroc.

Eugenio Izquierdo.

III

PAPERS RELATING TO THE 'AFFAIR OF THE ESCURIAL'

LETTER OF CHARLES IV TO NAPOLEON.

MONSIEUR MON FRÈRE,

Dans le moment où je ne m'occupais que des moyens de.coopérer à la destruction de notre ennemi commun ; quand je croyais que tous les complots de la ci-devant reine de Naples avaient été ensevelis avec sa fille, je vois avec une horreur qui me fait frémir, que l'esprit d'intrigue le plus horrible a pénétré jusque dans le sein de mon palais. Hélas ! mon cœur saigne en faisant le récit d'un attentat si affreux ! mon fils aîné, l'héritier présomptif de mon trône, avait formé le complot horrible de me détrôner ; il s'était porté jusqu'à l'excès d'attenter contre la vie de sa mère ! Un attentat si affreux doit être puni avec la rigueur la plus exemplaire des lois. La loi qui l'appelait à la succession doit être révoquée : un de ses frères sera plus digne de le remplacer et dans mon cœur et sur le trône. Je suis dans ce moment à la recherche de ses complices pour approfondir ce plan de la plus noire scélératesse ; et je ne veux perdre un seul moment pour en instruire V. M. I. et R., en la priant de m'aider de ses lumières et de ses conseils.

Sur quoi je prie Dieu, mon bon frère, qu'il daigne avoir V. M. I. et R. en sa sainte et digne garde.

CHARLES.

A St.-Laurent, ce 29 octobre 1807.

LETTER OF PRINCE FERDINAND TO CHARLES IV.

SEÑOR :

Papá mio : he delinquido, he faltado á V. M. como rey y como padre ; pero me arrepiento, y ofrezco á V. M. la obediencia mas humilde. Nada debia hacer sin noticia de V. M. ; pero fui sorprendido. He delatado á los culpables, y pido á V. M. me perdone por haberle mentido la otra noche, permitiendo besar sus reales pies á su reconocido hijo.

FERNANDO.

San Lorenzo, 5 de noviembre de 1807.

PROCLAMATION OF CHARLES IV, PARDONING THE PRINCE.

REAL DECRETO.

La voz de la naturaleza desarma el brazo de la venganza, y cuando la inadvertencia reclama la piedad, no puede negarse á ello un padre amoroso. Mi hijo ha declarado ya los autores del plan horrible que le habian hecho concebir unos malvados : todo lo ha manifestado en forma de derecho, y todo consta con la escrupulosidad que exige la ley en tales pruebas : su arrepentimiento y asombro le han dictado las representaciones que me ha dirigido.

En vista de ellos y á ruego de la reina mi amada esposa perdono á mi hijo, y le volveré á mi gracia cuando con su conducta me dé pruebas de una verdadera reforma en su frágil manejo ; y mando que los mismos jueces que han entendido en la causa desde su principio la sigan, permitiéndoles asociados si los necesitaren, y que concluida me consulten la sentencia ajustada á la ley, segun fuesen la gravedad de delitos y calidad de personas en quienes recaigan; teniendo por principio para la formacion de cargos las respuestas dadas por el príncipe á las demandas que se le han hecho ; pues todas estan rubricadas y firmadas de mi puño, asi como los papeles aprehendidos en sus mesas, escritos por su mano ; y esta providencia se comunique á mis consejos y tribunales, circulándola á mis pueblos, para que reconozcan en ella mi piedad y justicia, y alivien la afliccion y cuidado en que les puso mi primer decreto ; pues en él verán el riesgo de su soberano y padre que como á hijos los ama, y asi me corresponden. Tendreislo entendido para su cumplimiento.

San Lorenzo, 5 de noviembre de 1807.

Yo EL REY.

IV

ABDICATION OF CHARLES IV

Como los achaques de que adolezco no me permiten soportar por mas tiempo el grave peso del gobierno de mis reinos, y me sea preciso para reparar mi salud gozar en un clima mas templado de la tranquilidad de la vida privada, he determinado despues de la mas seria deliberacion abdicar mi corona en mi heredero y mi muy caro hijo el príncipe de Asturias. Por tanto es mi real voluntad que sea reconocido y obedecido como rey y señor natural de todos mis reinos y dominios. Y para que este mi real decreto de libre y espontánea abdicacion tenga su éxito y debido cumplimiento, lo comunicareis al consejo y demas á quien corresponda.

Dado en Aranjuez, á 19 de marzo de 1808.

Yo EL REY. A Don Pedro Cevallos.

V

THE SPANISH ARMY IN 1808

[Mainly from the table in Arteche, vol. i, Appendix 9.]

N.B.—The numbers are taken from returns made on various days between March and June, 1808. They include only rank and file. The officers should have been ninety-eight to a regiment of guards, seventy to a line regiment, forty-one to a light battalion, thirty-four to a militia battalion, forty-two to a cavalry regiment. But most corps were under strength in officers, no less than in men, in June, 1808, and Arteche, giving every regiment of infantry a complete staff of officers, is clearly over-estimating them. He gives e. g. 2,450 officers of line infantry, the possible maximum, while the *Estado Militar* for 1808 gives only 1,521 present ; so with the militia he gives 1,887 officers, while apparently there were only 1,230 actually existing. It would seem that his gross total of 7,222 officers ought to be cut down to 5,911. For the rank and file we get :—

ROYAL GUARD.

CAVALRY.			INFANTRY.		
Numbers.		*Quartered in*	*Numbers.*		*Quartered in*
Life Guards .	615	} Old Castile and Madrid.	Halberdiers (one compy.)	152	} Madrid.
Royal Carabineers. . .	540		Spanish Guards (three batts.)	3,294	} 1, 2 Barcelona. 3 New Castile.
Total	1,155		Walloon Guards (three batts.) . .	2,583	} 1 Madrid. 2 Barcelona. 3 Portugal.
			Total	6,029	

INFANTRY OF THE LINE.

N.B.—Each regiment had three battalions of four companies, and should have numbered 2,186 bayonets.

Numbers.		*Quartered in*	*Numbers.*		*Quartered in*
			Forward 24,171		
Africa . . .	898	{ 1, 3 Andalusia. 2 S. Sebastian.	Navarre . .	822	Galicia.
America . .	808	{ 1 New Castile. 2, 3 Valencia.	Ordenes Militares . .	708	} 1 Estremadura. 2, 3 Andalusia.
Aragon . .	1,294	Galicia.	Princesa . .	1,969	Denmark.
Asturias . .	2,103	Denmark.	Principe . .	1,267	Galicia.
Borbon . .	1,544	Balearic Isles.	Reina . . .	1,530	Andalusia.
Burgos . .	1,264	Andalusia.	Rey. . . .	1,353	{ 1 S. Sebastian. 2 Portugal. 3 Galicia.
Cantabria . .	1,024	Ceuta (Africa).			
Ceuta . . .	1,235	,, ,,			
Cordova . .	793	Andalusia.	Saragossa . .	1,561	{ 1, 2 Portugal. 3 Andalusia.
Corona . .	902	,,	Savoia . . .	936	Valencia.
España . .	1,039	Ceuta (Africa).	Seville . . .	1,168	Galicia.
Estremadura .	770	Catalonia.	Soria . . .	1,311	Balearic Isles.
Granada . .	1,113	Balearic Isles.	Toledo . . .	1,058	{ 1, 2 Galicia. 3 Portugal.
Guadalajara .	2,069	Denmark.	Valencia . .	923	Murcia.
Jaen . . .	1,755	{ 1,2 Andalusia. 3 Ceuta (Africa).	Volunteers of Castile . .	1,487	} ,,
Leon . . .	1,195	Galicia.	Voluntarios de la Corona .	1,296	} 1 Portugal. 2, 3 Galicia.
Majorca . .	1,749	{ 1, 2 Portugal. 3 Estremadura.	Voluntarios del Estado . .	742	} Madrid.
Malaga . .	854	Andalusia.	Zamora . .	2,096	Denmark.
Murcia . .	1,762	{ 1, 2 Portugal. 3 Andalusia.			
Forward	24,171		Total	44,398	

LIGHT INFANTRY.

N.B.—The regiment had only a single battalion of six companies. It should have numbered 1,200 bayonets.

	Numbers.	Quartered in		Numbers.	Quartered in
1st of Aragon	1,305	Madrid and Saragossa.	Forward	8,474	
2nd of Aragon	1,225	Balearic Isles.	2nd of Catalonia . .	685	Galicia.
Barbastro . .	1,061	½ Andalusia. ½ Portugal.	Gerona . .	1,149	½ Portugal. ½ Andalusia.
1st of Barcelona . . .	1,266	Denmark.	Tarragona .	1,142	½ Pampeluna. ½ Estremadura.
2nd of Barcelona . . .	1,300	Balearic Isles.	Volunteers of Navarre .	963	½ Portugal. ½ Galicia.
Campo Mayor	1,153	½ Portugal. ½ Andalusia.	Volunteers of Valencia .	1,242	½ Portugal. ½ Andalusia.
1st of Catalonia . .	1,164	Denmark.			
Forward	8,474		Total	13,655	

FOREIGN INFANTRY.

N.B.—The Swiss Regiments had two battalions, the others three.

	Numbers.	Quartered in	No.	Numbers.	Quartered in
IRISH.			Forward	2,004	
Irlanda . .	513	1 Estremadura. 2, 3 Andalusia.	SWISS. 1. Wimpfen	2,079	Catalonia.
Hibernia . .	852	1 Asturias. 2, 3 Galicia.	2. Reding Senior .	1,573	New Castile.
Ultonia . .	351	Gerona.	3. Reding Junior .	1,809	Andalusia.
ITALIAN.			4. Beschard .	2,051	Balearic Isles.
Naples . . .	288	Galicia.	5. Traxler .	1,757	Murcia.
			6. Preux . .	1,708	Madrid.
Forward	2,004		Total	12,981	

MILITIA.

N.B.—The four grenadier regiments had two battalions each, and should have been 1,600 strong; the rest one battalion, 600 strong.

	Numbers.	Quartered in		Numbers.	Quartered in
Prov. Gren. of			Forward	5,825	
Old Castile	1,605	Portugal.	Alcazar . .	595	Andalusia.
New Castile	1,430	Portugal.	Avila . . .	574	Valencia.
Andalusia .	1,413	Andalusia.	Badajos . .	589	Andalusia.
Galicia . .	1,377	1 Galicia. 2 Portugal.	Betanzos . .	599	Galicia.
			Burgos . .	577	Andalusia.
Forward	5,825		Forward	8,759	

	Numbers.	Quartered in		Numbers.	Quartered in
Forward	8,759		Forward	19,580	
Bujalance . .	594	Andalusia.	Mondoñedo .	591	Galicia.
Chinchilla .	558	,,	Monterrey .	591	,,
Ciudad Real .	575	,,	Murcia . .	564	Murcia.
Ciudad Rodrigo	585	,,	Orense . .	584	Galicia.
Compostella .	599	Galicia.	Oviedo . .	543	Asturias.
Cordova . .	584	Andalusia.	Plasencia . .	593	Andalusia.
Cuenca . .	596	,,	Pontevedra .	568	Galicia.
Ecija . . .	589	,,	Ronda . . .	574	Andalusia.
Granada . .	553	,,	Salamanca .	600	Galicia.
Guadix . . .	588	,,	Santiago . .	596	,,
Jaen . . .	584	,,	Segovia . .	591	,,
Jerez . . .	574	,,	Seville . . .	547	Andalusia.
Laredo . . .	571	Santander.	Siguenza . .	579	,,
Leon . . .	591	Galicia.	Soria . . .	582	Valencia.
Logroño . .	558	Andalusia.	Toledo . . .	579	Andalusia.
Lorca . . .	562	,,	Toro . . .	553	,,
Lugo . . .	589	Galicia.	Truxillo . .	567	,,
Majorca . .	570	Balearic Isles.	Tuy . . .	583	Galicia.
Malaga . .	401	Andalusia.	Valladolid .	562	,,
Forward	19,580		Total	30,527	

CAVALRY.

N.B.—Each regiment had five squadrons, and should have numbered about 700 sabres.

1. HEAVY CAVALRY.

Regiment.	Numbers.	Quartered in	Regiment.	Numbers.	Quartered in
1st Rey . .	634	Denmark.	Forward	2,623	
2nd Reina .	668	Old Castile.	7th Alcantara	589	Portugal.
3rd Principe .	573	New Castile.	8th España .	553	Andalusia.
4th Infante .	615	Denmark.	9th Algarve .	572	Denmark.
5th Borbon .	616	Catalonia.	10th Calatrava	670	Andalusia.
6th Farnesio .	517	Andalusia.	11th Santiago	549	Portugal.
			12th Montesa	667	Andalusia.
Forward	2,623		Total	7,232	

2. LIGHT CAVALRY.

CAZADORES.	Numbers.	Quartered in		Numbers.	Quartered in
1st Rey . .	577	Madrid.	Forward	3,546	
2nd Reina .	581	Portugal.	HUSSARS.		
3rd Almanza .	598	Denmark.	1st Numancia	630	Valencia.
4th Pavia . .	663	Andalusia.	2nd Lusitania	554	Madrid.
5th Villaviciosa	628	Denmark.	3rd Olivenza .	558	Portugal.
6th Sagunto .	499	Andalusia.	4th Voluntarios de España	548 }	New Castile.
			5th Maria Luisa	680	Estremadura.
			6th Españoles	692	Balearic Isles.
Forward	3,546		Total	7,208	

A scheme was on foot for converting eight of the light regiments into dragoons. Several of them are designated sometimes as dragoons, sometimes as cazadores or hussars.

N.B.—The 14,440 troopers had only 9,526 horses!

ARTILLERY.

1. FIELD.

	Numbers.	Quartered in		Numbers.	Quartered in
1st Regiment	1,143	Catalonia.	Forward	2,289	
2nd ,,	1,146	Valencia and Murcia.	3rd Regiment	1,078	Andalusia.
			4th ,,	1,043	Galicia.
Forward	2,289		Total	4,410	

Each regiment consisted of ten batteries; of the whole forty, six were horse-artillery. 477 men (four batteries) were in Denmark.

2. GARRISON.

Two 'Brigades' and fifteen 'Compañias Fijas' at various places, in all 1,934.

Adding general staff, &c., the total of the artillery, field and garrison, was 292 officers and 6,679 men.

ENGINEERS.

169 officers and a battalion of sappers. The latter was quartered at Alcala de Henares, and had a strength of 922 men, besides 127 detached in Denmark.

GENERAL TOTAL (Rank and File only).

	Infantry.	Cavalry.	Artillery.	Engineers.
Royal Guard . .	6,029	1,155		
Infantry of the Line .	44,398			
Light Infantry . .	13,655			
Foreign Infantry .	12,981			
Militia . . .	30,527			
Cavalry . . .		14,440		
Artillery . . .			6,679	
Engineers . . .				1,049
	107,590	15,595	6,679	1,049 = 130,913

Add 5,911 officers, and we get a gross total of 136,824.

VI

THE FIRST FRENCH 'ARMY OF SPAIN'

1. '1st CORPS OF OBSERVATION OF THE GIRONDE' [ARMY OF PORTUGAL].

Commander, General Junot.   Chief of the Staff, General Thiébault.

Men.

1st Division, General Delaborde (Brigades Avril and Brennier) :
15th of the Line (3rd batt.), 1,033 ; 47th ditto (2nd batt.), 1,210 ;
70th ditto (1st and 2nd batts.), 2,299 ; 86th ditto (1st and 2nd
batts.), 2,116 ; 4th Swiss (1st batt.), 1,190.

Total, seven battalions   .   .   .   7,848

2nd Division, General Loison (Brigades Charlot and Thomières) :
2nd Léger (3rd batt.), 1,255 ;   4th ditto (3rd batt.), 1,196 ;
12th ditto (3rd batt.), 1,302 ; 15th ditto (3rd batt.), 1,314 ;
32nd of the Line (3rd batt.), 1,265 ; 58th ditto (3rd batt.),
1,394 ; 2nd Swiss (2nd batt.), 755.   Total, seven battalions   8,481

3rd Division, General Travot (Brigades Graindorge and Fusier) :
31st Léger (3rd batt.), 653 ;   32nd ditto (3rd batt.) 983 ; 26th of
the Line (3rd batt.), 537 ; 66th ditto (3rd and 4th batts.), 1,004 ;
82nd ditto (3rd batt.), 861 ; *Légion du Midi* (1st batt.), 797 ;
Hanoverian Legion, 703.   Total, eight battalions   5,538

Cavalry Division, General Kellermann (Brigades Margaron and
Maurin) :
26th Chasseurs, 244 ; 1st Dragoons, 261 ; 3rd ditto, 236 ; 4th
ditto, 262 ; 5th ditto, 249 ; 9th ditto, 257 ; 15th ditto, 245   .   1,754

Artillery, Train, &c.   1,297

Total of the Corps (twenty-two battalions, seven squadrons)   24,918

2. '2nd CORPS OF OBSERVATION OF THE GIRONDE.'

Commander, General Dupont.   Chief of the Staff, General Legendre.

Men.

1st Division, General Barbou (Brigades Pannetier and Chabert) :
Garde de Paris (2nd batts. of 1st and 2nd Regiments), 1,454 ;
3rd Legion of Reserve (1st and 2nd batts.), 2,057 ; 4th ditto
(1st, 2nd, and 3rd batts.), 3,084 ; Marines of the Guard, 532 ;
4th Swiss (2nd batt.), 709.   Total, nine battalions   7,836

2nd Division, General Vedel (Brigades Poinsot and Cassagne) :
1st Legion of Reserve (three batts.), 3,011 ; 5th ditto (three batts.),
2,695 ; 3rd Swiss (1st batt.), 1,178.   Total, seven battalions   6,884

3rd Division, General Frere (Brigades Laval and Rostolland) :
15th Leger (2nd batt.), 1,160 ; 2nd Legion of Reserve (three
batts.), 2,870 ; 2nd Swiss (1st batt.), 1,174.

Total, five battalions   .   .   .   5,204

Cavalry Division, General FRESIA (Brigades Rigaud and Dupré) : **Men.**
1st Provisional Cuirassiers, 778 ; 2nd ditto, 681 ; 1st Provisional
Chasseurs, 556 ; 2nd ditto, 662 ; 6th Provisional Dragoons, 623.
Total, fifteen squadrons . . .   3,300

Artillery, Train, &c.   1,204

Total of the Corps (twenty-one battalions, fifteen squadrons)   24,428

3. 'CORPS OF OBSERVATION OF THE OCEAN COAST.'

Commander, Marshal MONCEY. Chief of the Staff, General Harispe.
Men.

1st Division, General MUSNIER (Brigades Brun and Isemburg) :
1st Provisional Regiment of Infantry (four batts.), 2,088 ; 2nd
ditto, 2,183 ; 3rd ditto, 2,118 ; 4th ditto, 2,232 ; Westphalian
battalion, 1,078.   Total, seventeen battalions   9,699

2nd Division, General GOBERT (Brigades Lefranc and Dufour) :
5th Provisional Regiment (four batts.), 2,095 ; 6th ditto, 1,851 ;
7th ditto, 1,872 ; 8th ditto, 1,921 ; Irish Legion, 654.
Total, seventeen battalions . . .   8,393

3rd Division, General MORLOT (Brigades Bujet and Lefebvre) :
9th Provisional Regiment (four batts.), 2,448 ; 10th ditto, 2,146 ;
11th ditto, 2,062 ; Prussian battalion, 493.
Total, thirteen battalions . . .   7,149

Cavalry Division, General GROUCHY (Brigades Privé and Wathier) :
1st Provisional Dragoons, 660 ; 2nd ditto, 872 ; 1st Provisional
Hussars, 597 ; 2nd ditto, 721.   Total, twelve squadrons   2,850

Artillery, Train, &c.   1,250

Total of the Corps (forty-seven battalions, twelve squadrons)   29,341

4. 'CORPS OF OBSERVATION OF THE PYRENEES.'

Commander, Marshal BESSIÈRES. Chief of the Staff, General Lefebvre-
Desnouettes.
Men.

1st Division, General MERLE (Brigades Darmagnac and Gaulois) :
47th of the Line (1st batt.), 1,235 ; 86th ditto (two companies),
231 ; 3rd Swiss (2nd batt.), 721 ; 1st *Régiment de Marche* (two
batts.), 965 ; 1st Supplementary Regiment of the Legions of
Reserve (two batts.), 2,096.   Total, six and a quarter battalions   5,248

2nd Division, General VERDIER (Brigades Sabathier and Ducos) :
17th Provisional Regiment (four batts.), 2,110 ; 18th ditto, 1,928 ;
13th ditto, 2,185 ; 14th ditto, 2,295.   Total, sixteen battalions   8,518

Cavalry Division, General LASALLE :
10th Chasseurs, 469 ; 22nd ditto, 460 ; *Escadron de Marche* of
Cuirassiers, 153.   Total, seven squadrons   1,082

Artillery, Train, &c.   408

Men.

Detached troops belonging to the Corps of Bessières.

(1) Garrison of Pampeluna, General D'Agoult :
   15th of the Line (4th batt.), 435 ; 47th ditto (3rd batt.), 297 ;
   70th ditto (3rd batt.), 488 ; 5th *Escadron de Marche* of Cuirassiers, 329 ; Artillery, 63 1,612

(2) Garrison of San Sebastian, General Thouvenot :
   2nd Supplementary Regiment of the Legions of Reserve (4th
   batt.), 890 ; Dépôt Battalion, 1,240 ; Cavalry Dépôt, 60 ;
   Artillery, 28 2,218

Total of the Corps (twenty-seven and a quarter battalions, nine
   squadrons) 19,086

5. 'CORPS OF OBSERVATION OF THE EASTERN PYRENEES.'

Commander, General Duhesme.   Chief of the Staff, Colonel Fabre.

Men.

1st Division, General Chabran (Brigades Goulas and Nicolas).
   2nd of the Line (3rd batt.), 610 ; 7th ditto (1st and 2nd batts.),
   1,785 ; 16th ditto (3rd batt.), 789 ; 37th ditto (3rd batt.), 656 ;
   56th ditto (4th batt.), 833 ; 93rd ditto (3rd batt.), 792 ; 2nd
   Swiss (3rd batt.), 580.   Total, eight battalions 6,045

2nd Division, General Lecchi (Brigades Milosewitz and ?) :
   2nd Italian Line (2nd batt.), 740 ; 4th ditto (3rd batt.), 587 ;
   5th ditto (2nd batt.), 806 ; Royal *Vélites* (1st batt.), 519 ;
   1st Neapolitan Line (1st and 2nd batts.), 1,944.
                            Total, six battalions . . . 4,596

Cavalry Brigade, General Bessières :
   3rd Provisional Cuirassiers, 409 ; 3rd Provisional Chasseurs, 416 825

Cavalry Brigade, General Schwartz :
   Italian Chasseurs of the Prince Royal, 504 ; 2nd Neapolitan
   Chasseurs, 388 892

Artillery, Train, &c. 356

Total of the Corps (fourteen battalions, nine squadrons) 12,714

6. IMPERIAL GUARD.

Commander, General Dorsenne.

Men.

1st Fusiliers (three batts.), 1,570 ; 2nd ditto, 1,499 ; Marines of
   the Guard [detached to Dupont's Corps].   Total, six battalions . 3,069

Dragoons, 252 ; Chasseurs and Mamelukes, 321 ; *Gendarmes
   d'élite*, 304 ; Polish Light Horse, 737 ; Guard of the Duke of
   Berg, 148 1,762

Artillery, &c.. 1,581

Total (six battalions, nine squadrons) 6,412

7. TROOPS WHICH ENTERED SPAIN AFTER THE OUTBREAK OF THE WAR, IN JUNE, JULY, AND AUGUST.

	Men.
Division MOUTON (Brigades Rey and Reynaud): 2nd Léger (1st and 2nd batts.); 4th ditto (1st, 2nd, and 4th batts.); 12th ditto (1st and 2nd batts.); 15th of the Line (1st and 2nd batts.); *Garde de Paris* (one batt.)	5,100
Brigade of General BAZANCOURT: 14th of the Line (1st and 2nd batts.), 1,488; 44th ditto (1st and 2nd batts.), 1,614	3,102
Polish Brigade (Colonel Chlopiski): 1st, 2nd, and 3rd of the Vistula (each of two batts.) . . .	3,951
Four *Bataillons de Marche* (Nos. 4, 5, 6, 7)	2,281
Division of General REILLE at Perpignan [for details see p. 320] .	8,370
Division of General CHABOT ('Reserve of Perpignan') . . .	2,667
Portuguese Troops, before Saragossa (two batts.)	553
National Guards of the Pyrenees, before Saragossa (two batts.) .	971
General Dépôt at Bayonne	7,659
Battalions, companies, and smaller drafts sent to join their corps in June—August	8,687
Escadrons de Marche, Polish Lancers, Cavalry of the Imperial Guard	3,911
Artillery, drafts	851
Engineers, ditto	101
Total . . .	48,204

GENERAL TOTAL.

	Men.
Junot's Corps	24,918
Dupont's Corps	24,428
Moncey's Corps	29,341
Bessières' Corps	19,086
Duhesme's Corps	12,714
Imperial Guard	6,412
Troops which entered Spain in June, July, and August	48,204
	165,103

N.B.—The organization and the greater part of the figures come from the table at the end of vol. iv of Foy's history of the Peninsular War. But a few corrections are made where more detailed information is available, especially in the seventh section, where Foy is incomplete (e.g. he omits one of Mouton's brigades).

VII

PAPERS RELATING TO THE TREACHERY AT BAYONNE

PROTEST OF CHARLES IV AGAINST HIS ABDICATION.

Protesto y declaro que todo lo que manifiesto en mi decreto del 19 de marzo, abdicando la corona en mi hijo, fue forzado por precaver mayores males y la efusion de sangre de mis queridos vasallos, y por tanto de ningun valor.

Yo EL REY.

Aranjuez, 21 de marzo de 1808.

LETTER OF NAPOLEON TO FERDINAND VII.

MON FRÈRE,

J'ai reçu la lettre de V. A. R. Elle doit avoir acquis la preuve, dans les papiers qu'elle a eu du roi son père, de l'intérêt que je lui ai toujours porté. Elle me permettra, dans la circonstance actuelle, de lui parler avec franchise et loyauté. En arrivant à Madrid, j'espérais porter mon illustre ami à quelques réformes nécessaires dans ses Etats, et à donner quelque satisfaction à l'opinion publique. Le renvoi du prince de la Paix me paraissait nécessaire pour son bonheur et celui de ses peuples. Les affaires du Nord ont retardé mon voyage. Les événemens d'Aranjuez ont eu lieu. Je ne suis point juge de ce qui s'est passé, et de la conduite du prince de la Paix ; mais ce que je sais bien, c'est qu'il est dangereux pour les rois d'accoutumer les peuples à répandre du sang et à se faire justice eux-mêmes. Je prie Dieu que V. A. R. n'en fasse pas elle-même un jour l'expérience. Il n'est pas de l'intérêt de l'Espagne de faire du mal à un prince qui a épousé une princesse du sang royal, et qui a si long-temps régi le royaume. Il n'a plus d'amis ; V. A. R. n'en aura plus, si jamais elle est malheureuse. Les peuples se vengent volontiers des hommages qu'ils nous rendent. Comment, d'ailleurs, pourrait-on faire le procès au prince de la Paix, sans le faire à la reine et au roi votre père ? Ce procès alimentera les haines et les passions factieuses ; le résultat en sera funeste pour votre couronne ; V. A. R. déchire par là ses droits. Qu'elle ferme l'oreille à des conseils faibles et perfides. Elle n'a pas le droit de juger le prince de la Paix : ses crimes, si on lui en reproche, se perdent dans les droits du trône. J'ai souvent manifesté le désir que le prince de la Paix fût éloigné des affaires. L'amitié du roi Charles m'a porté souvent à me taire, et à détourner les yeux des faiblesses de son attachement. Misérables hommes que nous sommes ! faiblesse et erreur, c'est notre devise. Mais tout cela peut se concilier. Que le prince de la Paix soit exilé d'Espagne, et je lui offre un refuge en France. Quant à l'abdication de Charles IV, elle a eu lieu dans un moment où mes armées couvraient les Espagnes ; et, aux yeux de l'Europe et de la postérité, je paraîtrais n'avoir envoyé tant de troupes que pour précipiter du trône mon allié et mon ami. Comme souverain voisin, il m'est permis de vouloir connaître, avant de reconnaître, cette abdication. Je le dis à V. A. R., aux Espagnols, au monde entier : Si l'abdication du roi Charles est de pur mouvement, s'il n'y a pas été forcé par l'insurrection et l'émeute d'Aranjuez, je ne fais aucune difficulté de l'admettre, et je reconnais V. A. R. comme roi d'Espagne. Je désire donc causer avec elle sur cet objet. La circonspection que je porte depuis un mois dans ces affaires doit lui être garant de l'appui qu'elle trouvera en moi, si, à son tour, des factions, de quelque nature qu'elles soient, venaient à l'inquiéter sur son trône.

Quand le roi Charles me fit part de l'événement du mois d'octobre dernier, j'en fus douloureusement affecté, et je pense avoir contribué, par des insinuations que j'ai faites, à la bonne issue de l'affaire de l'Escurial. V. A. R. avait bien des torts ; je n'en veux pour preuve que la lettre qu'elle m'a écrite, et que j'ai constamment voulu oublier. Roi à son tour, elle saura combien les droits du trône sont sacrés. Toute démarche près d'un souverain étranger, de la part d'un prince héréditaire, est criminelle. V. A. R. doit se défier des écarts et des émotions populaires.

On pourra commettre quelques meurtres sur mes soldats isolés, mais la ruine de l'Espagne en serait le résultat. J'ai déjà vu avec peine qu'à Madrid on ait répandu des lettres du capitaine-général de la Catalogne, et fait tout ce qui pouvait donner du mouvement aux têtes. V. A. R. connaît ma pensée toute entière : elle voit que je flotte entre diverses idées qui ont besoin d'être fixées. Elle peut être certaine que, dans tous les cas, je me comporterai avec elle comme avec le roi son père. Qu'elle croie à mon désir de tout concilier, et de trouver des occasions de lui donner des preuves de mon affection et de ma parfaite estime.

Sur ce, je prie Dieu qu'il vous ait en sa sainte et digne garde.

NAPOLÉON.

Bayonne, le 16 avril 1808.

SECOND ABDICATION OF CHARLES IV.

Art. Ier. S. M. le roi Charles, n'ayant en vue pendant toute sa vie que le bonheur de ses sujets, et constant dans le principe, que tous les actes d'un souverain ne doivent être faits que pour arriver à ce but ; les circonstances actuelles ne pouvant être qu'une source de dissensions d'autant plus funestes que les factions ont divisé sa propre famille, a résolu de céder, comme il cède par le présent, à S. M. l'empereur Napoléon, tous ses droits sur le trône des Espagnes et des Indes, comme au seul qui, au point où en sont arrivées les choses, peut rétablir l'ordre : entendant que ladite cession n'ait lieu qu'afin de faire jouir ses sujets des deux conditions suivantes :

1º. L'intégrité du royaume sera maintenue. Le prince que S. M. l'empereur Napoléon jugera devoir placer sur le trône d'Espagne sera indépendant, et les limites de l'Espagne ne souffriront aucune altération.

2º. La religion catholique, apostolique et romaine sera la seule en Espagne. Il ne pourra y être toléré aucune religion réformée, et encore moins infidèle, suivant l'usage établi jusqu'aujourd'hui.

II. Tous actes faits contre ceux de nos fidèles sujets, depuis la révolution d'Aranjuez, sont nuls et de nulle valeur, et leurs propriétés leur seront rendues.

III. Sa majesté le roi Charles ayant ainsi assuré la prospérité, l'intégrité et l'indépendance de ses sujets, Sa Majesté l'Empereur s'engage à donner refuge dans ses états au roi Charles, à la reine, à sa famille, au prince de la Paix, ainsi qu'à ceux de leurs serviteurs qui voudront les suivre, lesquels jouiront en France d'un rang équivalent à celui qu'ils possédaient en Espagne.

The remaining seven articles have reference to the estates and revenues in France, which the Emperor makes over to Charles IV and his family.

RESIGNATION OF HIS RIGHTS BY FERDINAND VII.

Art. I. Son Altesse Royale le prince des Asturies adhère à la cession faite par le roi Charles, de ses droits au trône d'Espagne et des Indes, en faveur de Sa Majesté l'Empereur des Français, roi d'Italie, et renonce, en tant que de besoin, aux droits qui lui sont acquis, comme prince des Asturies, à la couronne des Espagnes et des Indes.

II. Sa Majesté l'Empereur des Français, roi d'Italie, accorde en France à Son Altesse Royale le prince des Asturies le titre d'Altesse Royale, avec tous les honneurs et prérogatives dont jouissent les princes de son rang. Les descendans de Son Altesse Royale le prince des Asturies conserveront le titre de prince et celui d'Altesse Sérénissime, et auront toujours le même rang en France, que les princes dignitaires de l'Empire.

The remaining five articles have reference to the estates and revenues in France, which the Emperor makes over to Ferdinand.

VIII

THE CAPITULATION OF BAYLEN

1. ORGANIZATION OF THE ARMY OF CASTAÑOS

N.B.—* marks an old regiment of the regular army ; † a militia regiment ; ‡ a regiment of new levies.

Commander-in-chief, Lieut.-General FRANCISCO XAVIER CASTAÑOS.
Chief of the Staff, Major-General Tomas Moreno.

1st Division, General TEODORO REDING : *Men.*
 * Walloon Guards (3rd batt.), 852 ; *Reina, 795 ; *Corona, 824 ;
 *Jaen, 922 ; *Irlanda, 1,824 ; *3rd Swiss, 1,100 ; *Barbastro
 (half batt.), 331 ; †Jaen, 500 ; ‡1st of Granada, 526 ; ‡Caza-
 dores of Antequera, 343 ; ‡Tejas, 436. Total 8,453

Cavalry attached to the 1st Division :
 *Montesa, 120 ; *Farnesio, 213 ; *Dragones de la Reina, 213 ;
 *Numancia, 100 ; *Olivenza, 140 ; ‡Lancers of Utrera and
 Jerez, 114. Total 900

Men.

One horse-battery (six guns), one field-battery (four guns) . . 200
Two companies of sappers 166

Total of the Division . . 9,719

2nd Division, Major-General Marquis COUPIGNY :
   *Ceuta, 1,208 ; *Ordenes Militares, 1,909 ; †Granada, 400 ;
   †Truxillo, 290 ; †Bujalance, 403 ; †Cuenca, 501 ; †Ciudad
   Real, 420 ; ‡2nd of Granada, 450 ; ‡3rd of Granada, 470 ;
   ‡Volunteers of Catalonia, 1,178.   Total   7,229
Cavalry attached to 2nd Division :
   *Borbon, 401 ; *España, 120.   Total   521
One horse-battery (six guns) 100
One company of sappers 100

Total of the Division . . 7,950

3rd Division, Major-General FELIX JONES :
   *Cordova, 1,106 ; *Light Infantry of Valencia (half batt.), 359 ;
   *ditto of Campo-Mayor, 800 ; †Burgos, 415 ; †Alcazar, 400 ;
   †Plasencia, 410 ; †Guadix, 459 ; †Lorca, 490 ; †Seville, 267.
          Total   4,706

Cavalry attached to 3rd Division :
   *Calatrava, 222 ; *Santiago, 86 ; *Sagunto, 101 ; *Principe, 300.
          Total   709

Total of the Division . . 5,415

4th Division (Reserve), Lieut.-General MANUEL LA PENA :
   *Africa, 525 ; *Burgos, 2,089 ; *Saragossa (3rd batt.), 822 ;
   *Murcia (3rd batt.), 420 ; *2nd Swiss, 243 ; *Marines, 50 ;
   †Provincial Grenadiers of Andalusia, 912 ; †Siguenza, 502.
          Total   5,563
Cavalry attached to 4th Division :
   *Pavia, 541 541
Artillery, two horse-batteries (twelve guns) . . . . . (?) 302
Sappers, one company 100

Total of the Division . . 6,506

Total of the army, 29,590 : viz. infantry, 25,951 ; cavalry, 2,671 ; artillery,
602 ; sappers, 366, with twenty-eight guns.

N.B.—The force of the two flying columns of Col. Cruz-Murgeon and the
Conde de Valdecañas is not ascertainable. They were both composed of new
levies : Arteche puts the former at 2,000 foot, and the latter at 1,800 foot and
400 horse.   Other authorities give Cruz-Murgeon 3,000 men.

   It should be noted that Castaños' field-army does not comprise the whole
number of men under arms in Andalusia. Most of the regular regiments had
left behind their third battalion, which was being completed with recruits,
and was not fit to take the field. Of all the regiments only Burgos, Irlanda,
and Ordenes Militares seem to have gone forward three battalions strong.

2. CORRESPONDENCE OF THE FRENCH GENERALS.

(*a.*) GENERAL DUPONT TO GENERAL VEDEL.

Je vous prie, mon cher général, de vous porter le plus rapidement possible sur Baylen, pour y faire votre jonction avec le corps qui a combattu aujourd'hui à Mengibar et qui s'est replié sur cette ville. Le sixième régiment provisoire et deux escadrons, l'un de dragons et l'autre de chasseurs, sont réunis à votre division.

J'espère que l'ennemi sera rejeté demain sur Mengibar, au delà du fleuve, et que les postes de Guarraman et de la Caroline resteront en sûreté ; ils sont d'une grande importance.

Lorsque vous aurez obtenu ce succès, je désire que vous réunissiez à Andujar une partie de vos forces, afin de combattre l'ennemi qui se trouve devant nous. Vous ne laisserez à Baylen que ce qui sera nécessaire pour sa défense.

Si l'ennemi occupe Baëza, il faut l'en chasser.

Recevez mes assurances d'amitié.

Le général DUPONT.

Andujar, le 16 juillet 1808.

(*b.*) GENERAL VEDEL TO GENERAL DUPONT.

Mon général,

Il est huit heures et demie. J'arrive à Baylen, où je n'ai trouvé personne. Le général Dufour en est parti à minuit et a marché sur Guarraman. Comme il n'a laissé personne pour m'instruire des motifs de cette démarche, je ne puis rien dire de positif à cet égard ; mais le bruit commun étant que les troupes ennemies, qui ont attaqué hier le général Belair, se sont dirigées avec celles qui étaient à Ubeda, vers les gorges, par Linharès et Sainte-Hélène, on doit penser que le général Dufour s'est mis à leur poursuite, afin de les combattre.

Comme les instructions de Votre Excellence portent que je dois faire ma jonction avec le corps qui s'était replié sur Baylen, quoique harassé et fatigué, je partirai d'ici pour me rendre encore aujourd'hui à Guarraman, afin de regagner la journée que l'ennemi a sur moi, l'atteindre, le battre, et déjouer ainsi ses projets sur les gorges.

Je vais écrire au général Dufour, pour l'informer de mon mouvement, savoir quelque chose de positif sur sa marche et sur les données qu'il peut avoir de celle de l'ennemi.

. . . .

Le général de division,

VEDEL.

Baylen, le 17 juillet 1808.

(*c.*) GENERAL DUPONT TO GENERAL VEDEL.

J'ai reçu votre lettre de Baylen ; d'après le mouvement de l'ennemi, le général Dufour a très-bien fait de le gagner de vitesse sur la Caroline et sur Sainte-Hélène, pour occuper la tête des gorges ; je vois avec plaisir que vous

vous hâtez de vous réunir à lui, afin de combattre avec avantage, si l'ennemi se présente. Mais, au lieu de se rendre à Sainte-Hélène, l'ennemi peut suivre la vieille route, qui de Baëza va à Guëmada, et qui est parallèle à la grande route ; s'il prend ce parti, il faut le gagner encore de vitesse au débouché de cette route, afin de l'empécher de pénétrer dans la Manche. D'après ce que vous me dites, ce corps ne serait que d'environ dix mille hommes, et vous êtes en mesure de la battre complétement ; s'il est plus considérable, manœuvrez pour suspendre sa marche, ou pour le contenir dans les gorges, en attendant que j'arrive à votre appui.

. . . .

Si vous trouvez l'ennemi à la Caroline, ou sur tout autre point de la grande route, tâchez de le battre, pour me venir rejoindre et repousser ce qui est devant Andujar.

. . . .

Mille amitiés.

Le général DUPONT.

Andujar, le 17 juillet 1808.

N.B.—It will be seen that by letter (a) Dupont deliberately divides his army into two halves. By letter (b) Vedel shows that he made no reconnaissances, but acted merely on ' le bruit commun.' By letter (c) Dupont accepts Vedel's erroneous views without suspicion, and authorizes him to go off on the wild-goose chase which he was projecting.

3. CAPITULATION.

Leurs Excellences MM. le comte de Casa Tilly et le général don Francisco Xavier Castaños, commandant en chef l'armée d'Espagne en Andalousie, voulant donner une preuve de leur haute estime à Son Excellence M. le général comte Dupont, grand aigle de la Légion d'honneur, commandant en chef le corps d'observation de la Gironde, ainsi qu'à l'armée sous ses ordres, pour la belle et glorieuse défense qu'ils ont faite contre une armée infiniment supérieure en nombre, et qui les enveloppait de toutes parts ; sur la demande de M. le général de brigade Chabert, commandant de la Légion d'honneur, et chargé des pleins pouvoirs de Son Excellence le général en chef de l'armée française, en présence de Son Excellence M. le général comte Marescot, grand aigle de la Légion d'honneur et premier inspecteur du génie, ont arrêté les conventions suivantes :

Art. 1er. Les troupes françaises sous les ordres de Son Excellence M. le général Dupont sont prisonnières de guerre, la division Vedel et les autres troupes françaises en Andalousie exceptées.

2. La division de M. le général Vedel, et généralement toutes les troupes françaises en Andalousie, qui ne sont pas dans la position de celles comprises dans l'article 1er, évacueront l'Andalousie.

3. Les troupes comprises dans l'article 2 conserveront généralement tous leurs bagages, et, pour éviter tout sujet de trouble pendant la marche, elles remettront leur artillerie, train et autres armes, à l'armée espagnole, qui s'engage à les leur rendre au moment de leur embarquement.

4. Les troupes comprises dans l'article 1er du traité sortiront de leur camp

avec les honneurs de la guerre ; chaque bataillon ayant deux canons en tête ; les soldats armés de leurs fusils, qui seront déposés à quatre cents toises du camp.

5. Les troupes de M. le général Vedel et autres, ne devant pas déposer les armes, les placeront en faisceaux sur le front de bandière ; elles y laisseront aussi leur artillerie et leur train. Il en sera dressé procès-verbal par des officiers des deux armées, et le tout leur sera remis ainsi qu'il est convenu dans l'article 3.

6. Toutes les troupes françaises en Andalousie se rendront à San-Lucar et à Rota, par journées d'étape, qui ne pourront excéder quatre lieues de poste, avec les séjours nécessaires, pour y être embarquées sur des vaisseaux ayant équipage espagnol, et transportées en France au port de Rochefort.

7. Les troupes françaises seront embarquées aussitôt après leur arrivée. L'armée espagnole assure leur traversée contre toute agression hostile.

8. MM. les officiers généraux, supérieurs et autres, conserveront leurs armes, et les soldats leurs sacs.

9. Les logements, vivres et fourrages, pendant la marche et la traversée, seront fournis à MM. les officiers généraux et autres y ayant droit, ainsi qu'à la troupe, dans la proportion de leur grade, et sur le pied des troupes espagnoles en temps de guerre.

10. Les chevaux de MM. les officiers généraux, supérieurs et d'état-major, dans la proportion de leur garde, seront transportés en France, et nourris sur le pied de guerre.

11. MM. les officiers généraux conserveront chacun une voiture et un fourgon ; MM. les officiers supérieurs et d'état-major, une voiture seulement, sans être soumis à aucun examen, *mais sans contrevenir aux ordonnances et aux lois du royaume.*

12. Sont exceptées de l'article précédent les voitures prises en Andalousie, dont l'examen sera fait par M. le général Chabert.

13. Pour éviter la difficulté d'embarquer les chevaux des corps de cavalerie et d'artillerie, compris dans l'article 2, lesdits chevaux seront laissés en Espagne, et seront payés, d'après l'estimation de deux commissaires français et espagnol, et acquittés par le gouvernement espagnol.

14. Les blessés et malades de l'armée française, laissés dans les hôpitaux, seront traités avec le plus grand soin, et seront transportés en France sous bonne et sûre escorte, aussitôt après leur guérison.

15. Comme, en diverses rencontres et particulièrement à la prise de Cordoue, plusieurs soldats, au mépris des ordres des généraux et malgré les efforts des officiers, se sont portés à des excès qui sont inévitables dans les villes qui opposent encore de la résistance au moment d'être prises, MM. les généraux et autres officiers prendront les mesures nécessaires pour retrouver les vases sacrés qu'on pourrait avoir enlevés, et les restituer, s'ils existent.

16. Tous les employés civils, attachés à l'armée française, ne sont pas considérés comme prisonniers de guerre ; ils jouiront cependant, pour leur transport en France, de tous les avantages de la troupe, dans la proportion de leur emploi.

17. Les troupes françaises commenceront à évacuer l'Andalousie le 23

juillet, à quatre heures du matin. Pour éviter la grande chaleur, la marche des troupes s'effectuera de nuit, et se conformera aux journées d'étape qui seront réglées par MM. les officiers d'état-major français et espagnols, en évitant le passage des villes de Cordoue et de Séville.

18. Les troupes françaises, pendant leur marche, seront escortées par la troupe de ligne espagnole, à raison de trois cents hommes d'escorte par colonne de trois mille hommes, et MM. les officiers généraux seront escortés par des détachements de cavalerie et d'infanterie de ligne.

19. Les troupes, dans leur marche, seront toujours précédées par des commissaires français et espagnols, qui devront assurer les logements et les vivres nécessaires, d'après les états qui leur seront remis.

20. La présente capitulation sera portée de suite à Son Excellence M. le duc de Rovigo, commandant en chef les troupes françaises en Espagne, par un officier français qui devra être escorté par des troupes de ligne espagnoles.

21. Il est convenu par les deux armées qu'il sera ajouté, comme articles supplémentaires, à la capitulation, ce qui peut avoir été omis et ce qui pourrait encore augmenter le bien-être des troupes françaises pendant leur séjour en Espagne, et pendant la traversée.

Signé,

Xavier Castaños.	Marescot, Général de Division.
Conde de Tilly.	Chabert, Général de Brigade.

Ventura Escalante, Capitan-General de Granada.

SUPPLEMENTARY ARTICLES OF AUGUST 6.

Art. 1er. On a déjà sollicité du roi d'Angleterre et de l'amirauté anglaise des passe-ports pour la sûreté du passage des troupes françaises.

2. L'embarquement s'effectuera sur des vaisseaux de l'escadre espagnole, ou sur tous autres bâtiments de transport qui seront nécessaires pour conduire le total des troupes françaises, au moins par division, à commencer par celle du général Dupont, et immédiatement après, celle du général Vedel.

3. Le débarquement s'effectuera sur les côtes du Languedoc ou de Provence, ou bien au port de Lorient, selon que le voyage sera jugé plus commode et plus court.

4. On embarquera des vivres pour un mois et plus, afin de prévenir tous les accidents de la navigation.

5. Dans le cas qu'on n'obtînt pas de l'Angleterre les passe-ports de sûreté qu'on a demandés, alors on traitera des moyens les plus propres pour le passage par terre.

6. Chaque division des troupes françaises sera cantonnée sur différents points, dans un rayon de huit à dix lieues, en attendant que le susdit embarquement ait son effet.

Ainsi fait à Séville, le 6 août 1808.

Signé,

Xavier Castaños.

LETTER OF THE CAPTAIN-GENERAL OF ANDALUSIA, REPUDIATING THE CAPITULATION.

Monsieur le général Dupont,

Je n'ai jamais eu ni de mauvaise foi, ni de fausse dissimulation : de là vient ce que j'écrivis à V. E., sous la date du 8, dicté, d'après mon caractère, par la plus grande candeur, et je suis fâché de me voir obligé, par votre réponse en date d'hier, de répéter en abrégé ce que j'eus l'honneur de dire alors à V. E., et ce qui certainement ne peut manquer de se vérifier.

Ni la capitulation, ni l'approbation de la junte, ni un ordre, exprès de notre souverain chéri, ne peuvent rendre possible ce qui ne l'est pas ; il n'y a point de bâtiments, ni de moyens de s'en procurer pour le transport de votre armée. Quelle plus grande preuve que celle de retenir ici très-dispendieusement les prisonniers de votre corps, pour n'avoir point de quoi les transporter sur d'autres points hors du continent ?

Lorsque le général Castaños promit d'obtenir des Anglais des passe-ports pour le passage de votre armée, il ne put s'obliger à autre chose qu'à les demander avec instance, et c'est ce qu'il a fait. Mais comment V. E. put-elle croire que la nation britannique accéderait à la laisser passer, certaine qu'elle allait lui faire la guerre sur un autre point, ou peut-être sur le même ?

Je me persuade que ni le général Castaños, ni V. E. ne crurent que ladite capitulation pût être exécutée : le but du premier fut de sortir d'embarras, et celui de V. E. d'obtenir des conditions qui, quoique impossibles, honorassent sa reddition indispensable. Chacun de vous obtint ce qu'il désirait, et maintenant il est nécessaire que la loi impérieuse de la nécessité commande.

Le caractère national ne permet d'en user avec les Français que d'après cette loi, et non d'après celle des représailles ; V. E. m'oblige de lui exprimer des vérités qui doivent lui être amères. *Quel droit a-t-elle d'exiger l'exécution impossible d'une capitulation avec une armée qui est entrée en Espagne sous le voile de l'alliance intime et de l'union, qui a emprisonné notre roi et sa famille royale, saccagé ses palais, assassiné et volé ses sujets, détruit ses campagnes et arraché sa couronne ?* Si V. E. ne veut s'attirer de plus en plus la juste indignation des peuples, que je travaille tant à réprimer, qu'elle cesse de semblables et d'aussi intolérables réclamations, et qu'elle cherche, par sa conduite et sa résignation, à affaiblir la vive sensation des horreurs qu'elle a commises récemment à Cordoue. V. E. croit bien assurément que mon but, en lui faisant cet avertissement, n'a d'autre objet que son propre bien : le vulgaire irréfléchi ne pense qu'à payer le mal par le mal, sans apprécier les circonstances, et je ne peux m'empêcher de rendre V. E. responsable des résultats funestes que peut entraîner sa répugnance à ce qui ne peut manquer d'être.

Les dispositions que j'ai données à D. Juan Creagh, et qui ont été communiquées à V. E., sont les mêmes que celles de la junte suprême, et sont, en outre, indispensables dans les circonstances actuelles : le retard de leur exécution alarme les peuples et attire des inconvénients : déjà ledit Creagh m'a fait part d'un accident qui me donne les plus grandes craintes. *Quel stimulant pour la populace, de savoir qu'un seul soldat était porteur de 2,180 livres tournois !*

C'est tout ce que j'ai à répondre à la dépêche de V. E., et j'espère que celle-ci sera la dernière réponse relative à ces objets, demeurant, sur toute autre chose, dans le désir de lui être agréable, étant son affectionné et sincère serviteur,

MORLA.

IX

THE CONVENTION OF CINTRA

1. DEFINITIVE CONVENTION FOR THE EVACUATION OF PORTUGAL BY THE FRENCH ARMY.

The Generals commanding-in-chief of the British and French armies in Portugal having determined to negotiate and conclude a treaty for the evacuation of Portugal by the French troops, on the basis of the agreement entered into on the 22nd instant for a suspension of hostilities, have appointed the undermentioned officers to negotiate the same in their names : viz. on the part of the General-in-chief of the British army, Lieut.-Col. Murray, Quartermaster-General, and on the part of the French army, M. Kellermann, General of Division, to whom they have given authority to negotiate and conclude a Convention to that effect, subject to their ratification respectively, and to that of the Admiral commanding the British fleet at the entrance of the Tagus. These two officers, after exchanging their full powers, have agreed upon the articles which follow :—

I. All the places and forts in the kingdom of Portugal occupied by the French troops shall be delivered up to the British army in the state in which they are at the moment of the signature of the present Convention.

II. The French troops shall evacuate Portugal with their arms and baggage: they shall not be considered prisoners of war : and on their arrival in France they shall be at liberty to serve.

III. The English Government shall furnish the means of conveyance for the French army, which shall be disembarked in any of the ports of France between Rochefort and L'Orient inclusively.

IV. The French army shall carry with it all its artillery of French calibre, with the horses belonging to it, and the tumbrils supplied with sixty rounds per gun. All other artillery arms and ammunition, as also the military and naval arsenals, shall be given up to the British army and navy, in the state in which they may be at the period of the ratification of the Convention.

V. The French army shall carry away with it all its equipment, and all that is comprehended under the name of property of the army, that is to say its military chest, and the carriages attached to the field commissariat and field hospital, or shall be allowed to dispose of such part of the same on its account, as the Commander-in-chief may judge it unnecessary to embark. In like manner all individuals of the army shall be at liberty to dispose of all their private property of every description, with full security hereafter for the purchasers.

VI. The cavalry are to embark their horses, as also the Generals and other officers of all ranks : it is, however, fully understood that the means of conveyance[1] for horses at the disposal of the British Commander-in-chief are very limited : some additional conveyance may be procured in the port of Lisbon.

VII. In order to facilitate the embarkation, it shall take place in three divisions, the last of which will be principally composed of the garrisons of the places, of the cavalry and artillery, the sick, and the equipment of the army. The first division shall embark within seven days from the ratification of the Convention, or sooner if possible.

VIII. The garrisons of Elvas, Peniche, and Palmella will be embarked at Lisbon ; that of Almeida at Oporto, or the nearest harbour. They will be accompanied on their march by British commissaries, charged with providing for their subsistence and accommodation.

IX. All the French sick and wounded who cannot be embarked are entrusted to the British army. . . . The English Government shall provide for their return to France, which shall take place by detachments of 150 or 200 men at a time[2].

X. As soon as the vessels employed to carry the army to France shall have disembarked it . . . every facility shall be given them to return to England without delay : they shall have security against capture until their arrival in a friendly port[2].

XI. The French army shall be concentrated in Lisbon, or within a distance of about two leagues from it. The British army will approach to within three leagues of the capital, so as to leave about one league between the two armies.

XII. The forts of St. Julian, the Bugio, and Cascaes shall be occupied by the British troops on the ratification of the Convention. Lisbon and its forts and batteries, as far as the Lazaretto or Trafaria on one side, and the Fort St. Joseph on the other inclusively, shall be given up on the embarkation of the second division, as shall be also the harbour and all the armed vessels in it of every description, with their rigging, sails, stores, and ammunition. The fortresses of Elvas, Almeida, Peniche, and Palmella shall be given up so soon as British troops can arrive to occupy them : in the meantime the British General-in-chief will give notice of the present Convention to the garrisons of those places, as also to the troops in front of them, in order to put a stop to further hostilities.

XIII. Commissaries shall be appointed on both sides to regulate and accelerate the execution of the arrangements agreed upon.

XIV. Should there arise any doubt as to the meaning of any article, it shall be explained favourably to the French army.

XV. From the date of the ratification of the present Convention, all arrears

---

[1] Of transports fitted for carrying horses Dalrymple only had at this moment those which had brought 180 horses for the 20th Light Dragoons, 300 of the Irish commissariat, and 560 of the 3rd Light Dragoons of the German Legion, which had just arrived with Moore.

[2] These articles are shortened of some unimportant verbiage and details.

of contributions, requisitions, and claims of the French Government against the subjects of Portugal, or other individuals residing in this country, founded on the occupation of Portugal by the French troops since December, 1807, which may not have been paid up are cancelled ; and all sequestrations laid upon their property, movable or immovable, are removed, and the free disposal of the same is restored to their proper owners.

XVI. All subjects of France, or of powers in friendship or alliance with France, domiciliated in Portugal, or accidentally in this country, shall be protected. Their property of every kind, movable and immovable, shall be respected, and they shall be at liberty either to accompany the French army or to remain in Portugal. In either case their property is guaranteed to them with the liberty of retaining or disposing of it, and of passing the sale[1] of it into France or any other country where they may fix their residence, the space of one year being allowed them for that purpose.

It is fully understood that shipping is excepted from this arrangement ; only, however, as regards leaving the port, and that none of the stipulations above mentioned can be made the pretext of any commercial speculation.

XVII. No native of Portugal shall be rendered accountable for his political conduct during the period of the occupation of this country by the French army. And all those who have continued in the exercise of their employments, or who have accepted situations under the French Government, are placed under the protection of the British commanders. They shall suffer no injury in their persons or property, it not having been at their option to be obedient or not to the French Government. They are also at liberty to avail themselves of the stipulations of the sixteenth article.

XVIII. The Spanish troops detained on board ship in the port of Lisbon shall be given up to the General-in-chief of the British army, who engages to obtain of the Spaniards to restore such French subjects, either military or civil, as may have been detained[2] in Spain, without having been taken in battle or in consequence of military operations, but on the occasion of the occurrences of the 29th of May last, and the days immediately following.

XIX. There shall be an immediate exchange established for all ranks of prisoners made in Portugal since the commencement of the present hostilities.

XX. Hostages of the rank of field-officers shall be mutually furnished on the part of the British army and navy, and on that of the French army, for the reciprocal guarantee of the present Convention.

The officer representing the British army to be restored on the completion

---

[1] The meaning of this odd and crabbed phrase is shown by the French duplicate of the Convention—' d'en faire passer le produit en France.' Murray should have written ' the proceeds ' instead of ' the sale.'

[2] Murray's English does not here translate Kellermann's French : the latter has ' détenus en Espagne,' i. e. ' at present prisoners in Spain,' not ' who may have been detained in Spain.' For the persons intended were primarily General Quesnel, his staff, and escort, who had been seized in Portugal and then taken into Spain. The clause also covered some French officers and commissaries who had been seized at Badajoz and elsewhere while making their way to Lisbon, at the moment when the insurrection broke out.

of the articles which concern the army, and the officer of the navy on the disembarkation of the French troops in their own country. The like is to take place on the part of the French army [1].

XXI. It shall be allowed to the General-in-chief of the French army to send an officer to France with intelligence of the present Convention. A vessel will be furnished by the British Admiral to carry him to Bordeaux or Rochefort.

XXII. The British Admiral will be invited to accommodate His Excellency the Commander-in-chief [2] and the other principal French officers on board of ships of war.

Done and concluded at Lisbon this thirteenth day of August, 1808.

GEORGE MURRAY, Quar.-Mas.-Gen.
KELLERMANN, Général de Division.

Three unimportant supplementary articles were added, one stipulating that French civilian prisoners in the hands of the English or Portuguese should be released, another that the French army should subsist on its own magazines till it embarked, a third that the British should allow the free entry of provisions into Lisbon after the signature of the Convention.

2. REPORT OF THE COURT OF INQUIRY.

On a consideration of all circumstances, as set forth in this Report, we most humbly submit our opinion, that no further military proceeding is necessary on the subject. Because, howsoever some of us may differ in our sentiments respecting the fitness of the Convention in the relative situation of the two armies, it is our unanimous declaration, that unquestionable zeal and firmness appear throughout to have been exhibited by Lieut.-Generals Sir Hew Dalrymple, Sir Harry Burrard, and Sir Arthur Wellesley, as well as that the ardour and gallantry of the rest of the officers and soldiers, on every occasion during this expedition, have done honour to the troops, and reflected lustre on Your Majesty's arms.

All which is most dutifully submitted.

(Signed)

DAVID DUNDAS, General.	HEATHFIELD, General.	G. NUGENT, Lieut.-Gen.
MOIRA, General.	PEMBROKE, Lieut.-Gen.	OL. NICHOLLS, Lieut.-Gen.
PETER CRAIG, General.		

Dec. 22, 1808.

3. LORD MOIRA'S ' OPINION.'

I feel less awkwardness in obeying the order to detail my sentiments on the nature of the Convention, because that I have already joined in the tribute of applause due in other respects to the Officers concerned. My

---

[1] The hostage for the English army was Col. Donkin. I cannot find out who was the naval hostage.

[2] i. e. Junot and his chief officers preferred the hospitalities of a man of war to the hard fare of a transport.

opinion, therefore, is only opposed to theirs on a question of judgment, where their talents are likely to have so much more weight, as to render the profession of my difference, even on that point, somewhat painful.   Military duty is, however, imperious on me not to disguise or qualify the deductions which I have made during this investigation.

An Armistice simply might not have been objectionable, because Sir Hew Dalrymple, expecting hourly the arrival of Sir John Moore's division, might see more advantage for himself in a short suspension of hostilities, than what the French could draw from it.   But as the Armistice involved, and in fact established, the whole principle of the Convention, I cannot separate it from the latter.

Sir Arthur Wellesley has stated that he considered his force, at the commencement of the march from the Mondego river, as sufficient to drive the French from their positions on the Tagus.   That force is subsequently joined by above 4,000 British troops, under Generals Anstruther and Acland.   The French make an attack with their whole disposable strength, and are repulsed with heavy loss, though but a part of the British army is brought into action. It is difficult to conceive that the prospects which Sir Arthur Wellesley entertained could be unfavourably altered by these events, even had not the certainty of speedy reinforcements to the British army existed.

It is urged, that, had the French been pushed to extremity, they would have crossed the Tagus, and have protracted the campaign in such a manner as to have frustrated the more important view of the British Generals, namely, sending succours into Spain.

This measure must have been equally feasible for the French if no victory had been obtained over them ; but I confess that the chance of such an attempt seems to me assumed against probability.   Sir Hew Dalrymple notices what he calls ' the critical and embarrassed state of Junot,' before that General has been pressed by the British army ; and, in explanation of that expression, observes, that the surrender of Dupont, the existence of the victorious Spanish army in Andalusia, which cut off the retreat of the French in that direction, and the universal hostility of the Portuguese, made the situation of Junot one of great distress.   No temptation for the translation of the war into Alentejo presents itself from this picture ; nor does any other representation give ground to suppose, that Junot could have contemplated the measure, as holding forth any prospect but ultimate ruin, after much preliminary distress and disgrace.   The strongest of all proofs as to Junot's opinion, arises from his sending the very morning after the battle of Vimiera, to propose the evacuation of Portugal ; a step which sufficiently indicated that he was satisfied he could not only make no effectual defence, but could not even prolong the contest to take the chance of accidents.   He seems, indeed, to have been without any real resource.

I humbly conceive it to have been erroneous to regard the emancipation of Portugal from the French, as the sole or the principal object of the expedition.—Upon whatever territory we contend with the French, it must be a prominent object in the struggle to destroy their resources, and to narrow their means of injuring us, or those whose cause we are supporting.

This seems to have been so little considered in the Convention, that the terms appear to have extricated Junot's army from a situation of infinite distress, in which it was wholly out of play, and to have brought it, in a state of entire equipment, into immediate currency, in a quarter too, where it must interfere with our most urgent and interesting concerns.

Had it been impracticable to reduce the French army to lay down its arms unconditionally, still an obligation not to serve for a specified time might have been insisted upon, or Belleisle might have been prescribed as the place at which they should be landed, in order to prevent the possibility of their reinforcing (at least for a long time) the armies employed for the subjugation of Spain. Perhaps a stronger consideration than the merit of those terms presents itself. Opinion relative to the British arms was of the highest importance, as it might influence the confidence of the Spaniards, or invite the nations groaning under the yoke of France, to appeal to this country, and co-operate with it for their deliverance. The advantages ought, therefore, to have been more than usually great, which should be deemed sufficient to balance the objection of granting to a very inferior army, hopeless in circumstances, and broken in spirit, such terms as might argue, that, notwithstanding its disparity in numbers, it was still formidable to its victors. No advantages seem to have been gained that would not have equally followed from forcing the enemy to a more marked submission. The gain of time as to sending succours into Spain cannot be admitted as a plea; because it appears that no arrangements for the reception of our troops in Spain had been undertaken previous to the Convention; and this is without reasoning on subsequent facts.

I trust that these reasons will vindicate me from the charge of presumption, in maintaining an opinion contradictory to that professed by so many most respectable Officers; for, even if the reasons be essentially erroneous, if they are conclusive to my mind (as I must conscientiously affirm them to be), it is a necessary consequence that I must disapprove the Convention.

MOIRA, General.

December 27, 1808.

X

THE CENTRAL JUNTA OF REGENCY

LIST OF THE MEMBERS.

N.B.—The notes as to individuals are extracted from Arguelles.
1. For ARAGON. Don Francisco PALAFOX, Brigadier-General [younger brother of Joseph Palafox, the Captain-General]. Don Lorenzo CALVO DE ROZAS [Intendant-General of the Army of Aragon, long a banker in Madrid].
2. For ASTURIAS. Don Gaspar JOVELLANOS [Councillor of State, sometime Minister of Justice]. The Marquis of CAMPO SAGRADO, Lieut.-General.
3. For the CANARY ISLANDS. The Marquis of VILLANUEVA DEL PRADO.

4. For OLD CASTILE. Don Lorenzo BONIFAZ [Prior of Zamora]. Don Francisco Xavier CARO [a Professor of the University of Salamanca].

5. For CATALONIA. The Marquis of VILLEL [Grandee of Spain]. The Baron de SABASONA.

6. For CORDOVA. The Marquis DE LA PUEBLA [Grandee of Spain]. Don Juan RABE [a merchant of Cordova].

7. For ESTREMADURA. Don Martin GARAY [Intendant-General of Estremadura]. Don Felix OVALLE [Treasurer of the Army of Estremadura].

8. For GALICIA. The Conde de GIMONDE. Don Antonio ABALLE [an advocate].

9. For GRANADA. Don Rodrigo RIQUELME [Regent of the Chancellery]. Don Luis FUNES [Canon of Santiago].

10. For JAEN. Don Francisco CASTANEDO [Canon of Jaen]. Don Sebastian JOCANO [Accountant-General].

11. For LEON. Don Antonio VALDES [Bailiff of the Knights of Malta, sometime Minister of Marine]. The Visconde de QUINTANILLA.

12. For MADRID. The Marquis of ASTORGA [Grandee of Spain]. Don Pedro SILVA [Patriarch of the Indies].

13. For the BALEARIC ISLES. Don Tomas VERI [Lieut.-Col. of Militia]. The Conde de AYAMANS.

14. For MURCIA. The Conde de FLORIDA-BLANCA [sometime Secretary of State]. The Marquis DEL VILLAR.

15. For NAVARRE. Don Miguel BALANZA and Don Carlos AMATRIA [formerly representatives in the Cortes of Navarre].

16. For SEVILLE. The Archbishop of LAODICEA [Coadjutor-Bishop of Seville]. The Conde de TILLY.

17. For TOLEDO. Don Pedro RIVERO [Canon of Toledo]. Don José Garcia LATORRE [an advocate].

18. For VALENCIA. The Conde de CONTAMINA [Grandee of Spain]. The Principe PIO [Grandee of Spain and a Lieut.-Col. of Militia].

XI

THE SPANISH ARMIES, OCT.—NOV. 1808

N.B.—* signifies an old line or light regiment ; † a militia battalion ; ‡ a newly raised corps.

1. THE ARMY OF GALICIA [RETURN OF OCT. 31].

General BLAKE.

	Officers.	Men.
Vanguard Brigade, General MENDIZABAL :		
*2nd Catalonian Light Infantry (one batt.) ; *Volunteers of Navarre (one batt.) ; *two batts. of United Grenadiers ; *Saragossa (one batt.) ; *one company of sappers . .	87	2,797
1st Division, General FIGUEROA :		
*Rey (two batts.) ; *Majorca (one batt.) ; *Hibernia (one batt.) ; *one batt. of united light companies ; †Mondoñedo ; ‡Batallon Literario ; *one company of sappers .	86	3,932

Officers.   Men.

2nd Division, General MARTINENGO :

  *Navarre (two batts.) ; *Naples (two batts.) ; †Pontevedra ;
†Segovia ; ‡'Volunteers of Victory' (one batt.) ; sappers,
one company ; Cavalry : *Reina (two squadrons) ; *Montesa (one squadron) ; and one detachment of mixed regiments. [The cavalry was 302 sabres in all.] .   . . 117   4,949

3rd Division, General RIQUELME :

  *Gerona Light Infantry (one batt.) ; *Seville (two batts.) ;
*Marines (three batts.) ; †Compostella (one batt.) ; one
company of sappers 119   4,677

4th Division, General CARBAJAL :

  *Barbastro Light Infantry (one batt.); *Principe (two batts.);
*Toledo (two batts.) ; *two batts. of United Grenadiers ;
*Aragon (one batt.) ; †Lugo ; †Santiago .   . . 143   3,388

5th Division [from Denmark], General Conde de SAN ROMAN :

  *Zamora (three batts.) ; *Princesa (three batts.) ; *1st Barcelona Light Infantry (one batt.) ; *1st Catalonian Light
Infantry (one batt.) ; one company of sappers . . 159   5,135

Asturian Division : General ACEVEDO :

  *Hibernia (two batts.) ; † Oviedo ; ‡Castropol ; ‡Grado ;
‡Cangas de Onis ; ‡Cangas de Tineo ; ‡Lena ; ‡Luarca ;
‡Salas ; ‡Villaviciosa 233   7,400

Reserve Brigade, General MAHY :

  *Volunteers of the Crown (one batt.) ; *United Grenadiers
(one batt.) ; †Militia Grenadiers (two batts.) ; ‡*Batallon
del General* (one batt.) 90   2,935

Detached Troops on the line of communications—Reynosa,
Burgos, Astorga :

  *Saragossa (one batt.) ; *Buenos Ayres (one batt.) ; *Volunteers of the Crown (one batt.) ; †Santiago ; †Tuy ; †Salamanca ; ‡*Batallon del General* (one batt.) ; and seven
detached companies of various corps . . . 181   5,577

Detached troops left with the Artillery Reserve :

  †Betanzos ; †Monterrey 40   900

  Artillery Reserve (thirty-eight guns) 33   1,000

                       Total . . .1,288 42,690

N.B.—The four cavalry regiments from Denmark, Rey, Infante, Villaviciosa, and Almanza did not join Blake, being without horses, but marched on foot to Estremadura to get mounted. They had 147 officers and 2,252 men.

2. THE ARMY OF ARAGON.

General Joseph PALAFOX.

1st Division, General O'NEILLE :

  *Spanish Guards (one batt.), 609 ; *Estremadura (one batt.), 600 ;
*1st Volunteers of Aragon (one batt.), 1,141 ; ‡1st Light

Men.

Infantry of Saragossa, 614 ; ‡4th Tercio of Aragon, 1,144 ; ‡2nd of Valencia, 869 ; ‡1st Volunteers of Murcia, 1,029 ; ‡2nd ditto, 968 ; ‡Huesca, 1,219 ; ‡Cazadores de Fernando VII (Aragonese), 386 ; ‡Suizos de Aragon, 825 ; ‡Escopeteros de Navarra, 227 ; *Dragoons ' del Rey,' 169 ; artillery, 79 ; sappers, 47.

Total . . 9,926

[From a return of Nov. 1, 1808, in the English Record Office.]

2nd Division, General SAINT MARCH :
*Volunteers of Çastile (three batts.) ; †Soria ; ‡Turia (three batts.) ; ‡Volunteers of Borbon (one batt.) ; ‡Alicante (three batts.) ; ‡Chelva (one batt.) ; ‡Cazadores de Fernando VII (Valencian) (one batt.) ; ‡Segorbe (one batt.) ; *Dragoons of Numancia (620 sabres) ; one company of sappers. Total 9,060
[This total is from Vaughan's diary. He was present when Palafox reviewed the division on Nov. 1, and took down the figures.]

3rd Division, General Conde de LAZAN [detached to Catalonia, Nov. 10] :
‡1st Volunteers of Saragossa, 638 ; ‡3rd Volunteers of Aragon, 593 ; ‡Fernando VII de Aragon, 648 ; ‡Daroca, 503 ; ‡La Reunion, 1,286 ; ‡Reserva del General, 934 ; artillery, 64 ; one troop of cavalry (Cazadores de Fernando VII), 22. Total 4,688
[The figures are from a table in Arteche, iii. 469.]

Reserve at Saragossa :
There was a mass of troops in the Aragonese capital which had not yet been brigaded, and in part had not even been armed or clothed in October. They included the following regiments *at least* : 2nd Volunteers of Aragon ; 1st, 2nd, 3rd, and 5th Tercios of Aragon ; 2nd Light Battalion of Saragossa ; and the battalions of Calatayud, Doyle, Barbastro, Jaca, Tauste, Teruel, and Torrero ; besides (in all probability) some eight or ten other corps which are found existing in December, when the second siege began, though they cannot be proved to have existed in October. In that month, however, there must have been at least 10,000 armed men in the Aragonese reserve, perhaps as many as 15,000.

Total of the Army of Aragon, *at least* 33,674 men, of which only 789 were cavalry.

3. ARMY OF ESTREMADURA.

General GALLUZZO [afterwards the Conde de BELVEDERE].

Men.

1st Division, Conde de BELVEDERE : [afterwards General DE ALOS]
*Spanish Guards (4th batt.) ; *Majorca (two batts.) ; *2nd Light Infantry of Catalonia (one batt.) ; †Provincial Grenadiers (one batt.) ; one company of tirailleurs 4,160

Men.

Cavalry, * 4th Hussars (' Volunteers of Spain') 360

Sappers, two companies; artillery, two batteries 408

2nd Division, General HENESTROSA :

* Walloon Guards (4th batt.); ‡ Badajoz (two batts.); ‡Valencia
de Alcantara ; ‡Zafra 3,300

Cavalry, 5th Hussars (Maria Luisa) 298

Sappers, two companies ; artillery, two batteries 440

3rd Division, General TRIAS :

† Badajoz ; ‡Truxillo (one batt.) ; ‡Merida ; ‡La Serena . . 3,580

Cavalry, 2nd Hussars (Lusitania) 300

Total of the Army, 12,846, of which 958 were cavalry.

[N.B.—From the *Madrid Gazette* of Oct. 21, 1808, compared with the
table in Arteche, iii. 496.]

4. ARMY OF THE CENTRE.

General CASTAÑOS.

Men.

1st Division, Conde de VILLARIEZO :

* Walloon Guards (two batts.) ; * Reina (three batts.) ; * Corona
(two batts.) ; * Jaen (three batts.) ; * Irlanda (three batts.) ;
* Barbastro (one batt.) ; †Jaen . . . . . (about) 8,500

Out of these fifteen battalions nine were detached to the rear in
or about Madrid, and were not present on the Ebro.

2nd Division, General GRIMAREST :

* Ceuta (two batts.) ; Ordenes Militares (three batts.) ; †Truxillo ;
† Bujalance ; †Cuenca ; †Ciudad Real ; ‡Tiradores de España ;
‡ Volunteers of Catalonia ; ‡Tiradores de Cadiz ; ‡Carmona (about) 6,000

3rd Division, General RENGEL :

* Cordova (two batts.) ; * Volunteers of Valencia (one batt.) ;
* Campo Mayor (one batt.) ; †Toledo ; †Burgos ; †Alcazar ;
†Plasencia ; †Guadix ; †Seville no. 1 ; †Lorca ; †Toro.

Out of these thirteen battalions four were detached to the rear, and
were not present on the Ebro . . . . (about) 6,500

4th Division, General LA PEÑA :

* Africa (two batts.) ; * Burgos (two batts.) ; * Saragossa (one batt.) ;
* Murcia (two batts.) ; †Provincial Grenadiers of Andalusia
(two batts.) ; †Siguenza ; ‡Navas de Tolosa ; ‡Baylen ; ‡5th
Battalion of Seville . . . . (about) 7,500

5th [Murcian-Valencian] Division, General ROCA [*vice* General LLAMAS] :

* Savoya (two batts.) ; * Valencia (three batts.) ; * America (three
batts.) ; †Murcia ; †Avila ; ‡Liria ; ‡Cazadores de Valencia
(three batts.) ; ‡Orihuela (two batts.) ; Tiradores of Xativa and
Cartagena (two companies) ; ‡Penas de San Pedro . . (about) 8,000

[One regiment was left at Aranjuez as guard to the Junta, with General
Llamas in command.]

'Army of Castile,' General Pignatelli [after Oct. 30, General Cartaojal] :

Men.

 * Cantabria (two batts.); † Leon Militia; ‡ Grenadiers ' del General';
 ‡ Cazadores de Cuenca ; ‡ 1st, 2nd, and 3rd Volunteers of Leon ;
 ‡ 1st, 2nd, and 3rd Tercios of Castile ; ‡ Tiradores de Castilla ;
 ‡ Volunteers of Benavente; ‡ Volunteers of Zamora; ‡ Volunteers
 of Ledesma . . . . Total (about) 11,000

The first-named four corps were made into a detached brigade
under Cartaojal on Oct. 30 : the others (except ‡ Benavente in
garrison at Burgos) were dispersed among the Andalusian divisions
for misbehaviour at Logroño on Oct. 26.

 Cavalry : * Farnesio ; * Montesa ; * Reina ; * Olivenza; * Borbon ;
 * España ; * Calatrava; * Santiago ; * Sagunto ; * Principe ;
 * Pavia ; * Alcantara. Very few of these regiments had more
 than three squadrons at the front, some only one. The total
 was not more than 3,500 sabres, even including one or two
 newly raised free-corps, of insignificant strength . . .

             (about) 3,500

Total of the Army of the Centre, about 51,000 men, of whom only about
42,000 were on the Ebro : the remaining 9,000 were in or about Madrid,
and were incorporated in San Juan's ' Army of Reserve.'

5. ARMY OF CATALONIA.

[Morning state of Nov. 5, 1808.]

General Vives.

                Men.

Vanguard Division, Brigadier-General Alvarez :
 * Ultonia, 300; * Borbon (one batt.), 500 ; * 2nd of Barcelona,
 1,000 ; 1st Swiss (Wimpfen) (one batt.), 400 ; ‡ 1st Tercio of
 Gerona, 900 ; ‡ 2nd ditto, 400 ; ‡ Tercio of Igualada, 400 ; ‡ ditto
 of Cervera, 400; ‡ 1st ditto of Tarragona, 800; ‡ ditto of Figueras,
 400 5,500
 Cavalry, ‡ Hussars of San Narciso 100

1st Division, General Conde de Caldagues :
 * 2nd Walloon Guards (one batt.), 314 ; * Soria (two batts.), 780 ;
 * Borbon (detachment), 151 ; * 2nd of Savoia (two batts.), 1,734 ;
 * 2nd Swiss (detachment), 270 ; ‡ Tercio of Tortosa, 984;
 ‡ Igualada and Cervera (detachments), 245 ; * sappers, 50 . . 4,528
 Cavalry : * Husares Españoles (two squadrons), 220 ; ‡ Cazadores
 de Cataluña, 180 400
 Artillery, one battery (six guns) 70

2nd Division, General Laguna :
 † Provincial Grenadiers of Old Castile (two batts.), 972 ; † ditto of
 New Castile (two batts.), 924 ; ‡ Volunteers of Saragossa, 150 ;
 sappers, 30 2,076

	Men.
Cavalry, * Husares Españoles	200
Artillery, one battery (seven guns)	84

3rd Division, General LA SERNA :
* Granada (two batts.), 961 ; ‡2nd Tercio of Tarragona, 922 ;
　‡' Division of Arzu,' 325 ; ‡Compañias Sueltas, 250 . . . **2,458**

4th Division, General MILANS :
‡1st Tercio of Lerida, 872 ; ‡ditto of Vich, 976 ; ‡ditto of Man-
　resa, 937 ; ‡ditto of Vallés, 925 . . . . . . **3,710**

Reserve :

* Spanish Guards, 60; * Grenadiers of Soria, 188; * ditto of Wimpfen, 169; General's bodyguard, 340; sappers, 20 . .	777
Cavalry, * Husares Españoles	80
Artillery (four guns)	50

Total of the Army, 20,033, of which 780 are cavalry.

These five armies formed the front line. Their total strength was 151,243,
if the 9,000 men left behind at Madrid are deducted.

TROOPS IN THE SECOND LINE.

1. ARMY OF GRANADA [MARCHING TOWARDS CATALONIA].

General REDING.

　　　　　　　　　　　　　　　　　　　　　　　　　　Men.

1st Division :
* 2nd Swiss (Reding), 1,000 ; ‡1st Regiment of Granada [alias
　Iliberia](two batts.), 2,400 ; ‡Baza(two batts.), 2,400; ‡Almeria,
　(two batts.), 2,400 . . . . **8,200**

2nd Division :

‡Santa Fé (two batts.), 2,400 ; ‡Antequera (one batt.), 1,200 ; ‡Loxa (two batts.), 2,400	6,000
Cavalry, ‡Hussars of Granada	670
Artillery (six guns)	130
Total of the Army . . .	15,000

N.B.—This return is from a dispatch from Granada in the *Madrid Gazette*
of Oct. 28, corroborated by another of Nov. 5, announcing the arrival of the
force at Murcia.

2. GALICIAN RESERVES.

	Officers.	Men.
Detached Troops in garrison in Galicia :		
* Majorca (one batt.) ; * Leon (one batt.) ; * Aragon (one batt.)	77	2,010
etached troops on the Portuguese frontier :		
* Leon (one batt.) ; †Orense ; and four detached companies .	48	1,600
	125	3,610

3. ASTURIAN RESERVES.

[N.B.—This force is exclusive of the troops under Acevedo in the Army of Blake. The numbers are from a morning state of December.]

Men.

‡Covadonga, 360; ‡Don Carlos, 335; ‡Ferdinand VII, 316; ‡Gihon, 586; ‡Infiesto, 489; ‡Llanes, 420; ‡Luanco, 400; ‡Navia, 528; ‡Pravia, 581 ; ‡Riva de Sella, 685 ; ‡Siero, 585.   Total   5,285

4. ARMY OF RESERVE OF MADRID.

N.B.—This force, which fought at the Somosierra, consisted of parts of the Armies of Andalusia and Estremadura ; its numbers have already been counted among the troops of those armies.

General SAN JUAN.

Men.

From the 1st Division of Andalusia :
  *Walloon Guards (one batt.), 500 ; *Reina (two batts.), 927 ;
  *Jaen (two batts.), 1,300 ; *Irlanda (two batts.), 1,186 ; *Corona
  (two batts.), 1,039   4,952

From the 3rd Division of Andalusia :
  *Cordova (two batts.), 1,300 ; †Toledo, 500 ; †Alcazar, 500 ;
  ‡3rd of Seville, 400   2,700

From the Army of Estremadura :
  ‡Badajoz (remains of two batts.)   566

Castilian Levies :
  ‡1st Volunteers of Madrid (two batts.), 1,500 ; ‡2nd ditto, 1,500 .   3,000

Cavalry : *Principe, 200 ; *Alcantara, 100 ; *Montesa, 100 ;
  ‡Volunteers of Madrid, 200   600

Artillery (twenty-two guns)   300

                                Total . . .   12,118

N.B.—Of this force the following battalions fled to Madrid, and afterwards joined the Army of the Centre :—1st Volunteers of Madrid, Corona, half 3rd of Seville, Reina, Alcazar. The following fled to Segovia, and joined the Army of Estremadura :—Jaen, Irlanda, Toledo, Badajoz, 2nd Volunteers of Madrid, Walloon Guards, and half 3rd of Seville.

5. ESTREMADURAN RESERVES.

[Left in garrison at Badajoz, when the three divisions of Galluzzo marched to Madrid.]

Men.

‡Leales de Fernando VII (three batts.), 2,256 ; ‡Plasencia (one
  batt.), 1,200 ; ‡Badajoz (one batt.), 752   4,208

Cavalry : ‡Cazadores of Llerena, 200 ? Cazadores of Toledo, 200 ?   400

                                Total   4,608

[For these forces compare *Madrid Gazette* of Oct. 21, giving organization of the Army of Estremadura, with the list of troops which marched forward to Burgos in first section of this Appendix. The above regiments remained behind, and are found in existence in Cuesta's army next spring. See Appendix to vol. ii giving his forces.]

6. BALEARIC ISLES.

There apparently remained in garrison in the Balearic Isles, in November, the following troops:—

Men.

*4th Swiss (Beschard) (two batts.), 2,121; * Granada (one batt.), 222; *Soria (one batt.), 413; †Majorca, 604. Total 3,360

7. MURCIAN AND VALENCIAN RESERVES.

[Mostly on the march to Saragossa in November, 1808. The figures mainly from a return of Jan. 1 are too low for the November strength.]

Men.

* 5th Swiss (Traxler), 1,757; ‡1st Tiradores de Murcia, 813; ‡2nd ditto, 124; ‡3rd Volunteers of Murcia, 1,151; ‡5th ditto, 1,077; ‡ Florida-Blanca, 352; ‡3rd of Valencia (figures wanting; ? 500). Total 5,774

8. ANDALUSIAN RESERVES.

Men.

*España (three batts.), 1,039; †Jerez, 574; †Malaga, 401; †Ronda, 574; †Ecija, 589. Total 3,177

‡2nd of Seville, 500; ‡4th ditto, 433; ‡Cazadores of Malaga (one batt.), 1,200; ‡Velez Malaga (three batts.), 2,400; ‡2nd of Antequera (one batt.), 1,200; ‡Osuna (two batts.), 1,061. Total 6,794

In addition, the following regular regiments had each, as it would seem, left the *cadre* of one battalion behind in Andalusia to recruit, before marching to the Ebro to join Castaños:—Africa, Burgos, Cantabria, Ceuta, Corona, Cordova, Murcia. What the total of their numbers may have been in November and December, it is impossible to say—perhaps 400 each may be allowed, giving a total of 2,800. Of cavalry regiments there must have been in existence in Andalusia the nucleus of the following new regiments:— ‡Tejas; ‡Montanas de Cordova; ‡Granada. Their force was trifling—a single squadron, or at most two. If we give them 600 men in all, we shall probably be not far wrong. Several regular cavalry regiments had left the *cadre* of one or two squadrons behind.

The existence of all these regiments in November—December can be proved. The 2nd and 4th of Seville reached Madrid in time to join in its defence against Napoleon, and then fled to join the Army of the Centre. The figures given are their January strengths, when they had already suffered severely. The Malaga regiment's figure is from *Madrid Gazette* of Nov. 29, recording its march out to Granada. The militia battalions Jerez, Malaga, Ronda, Ecija were all in existence in June, they did not march to the Ebro, and are found in the Army of the Centre in the spring of 1809. España was apparently in garrison at Ceuta, and only brought up to the front early in 1809. Velez Malaga, 2nd of Antequera, and Osuna are first heard of under Del Palacio in January, 1809. They must have been raised by December at the latest.

The total of the Andalusian reserves accounted for in this table is 13,371, but no such number could have been sent forward in December, as many of the battalions were not properly armed, much less uniformed. But some of the volunteers, all the militia, and the regular regiment España—perhaps 6,000 or 7,000 in all—should have been at Madrid by Dec. 1. Only 1,000 bayonets actually reached it before Napoleon's arrival.

It would seem then that the second line of the Spanish Army consisted of something like the following numbers :—

	Men.
Army of Reserve of Madrid	12,118
Reding's Granadan Divisions	15,000
Galician Reserves	3,610
Asturian Reserves	5,285
Estremaduran Reserves	4,608
Balearic Isles Reserves	3,360
Murcian and Valencian Reserves . . .	5,774
Andalusian Reserves	13,371
Cavalry from Denmark, in march for Estremadura	2,252
Total	65,378

Some of the battalions (e. g. the Valencians and Murcians who went to Saragossa) must have been much stronger in December ; on the other hand, others (e. g. the Estremadurans) are probably over-estimated : they showed no such figures as those given above, when they took the field early in 1809.

N.B.—In several armies, notably in those of Aragon and the Centre, there are doubtful points. It is impossible to speak with certainty of the number of battalions which some corps took to the front. It will be noted that all the numbers given are much larger than those attributed by Napier (i. 504) to the Spanish armies. I have worked from detailed official figures, the greater part of which seem perfectly trustworthy.

XII

THE FRENCH ARMY OF SPAIN

IN NOVEMBER, 1808.

N.B.—The distribution of the regiments is that of November. The detailed strength of the corps, however, comes from an October return, and there had been several changes at the end of that month.

1st Corps. Marshal Victor, Duke of Belluno.

1st Division (Ruffin) :
9th Léger, three batts.
24th of the Line, three batts.
96th   ,,   four batts.

2nd Division (Lapisse) :
16th Léger, three batts.
8th of the Line, three batts.
45th   ,,   three batts.
54th   ,,   three batts.

3rd Division (Villatte) :
27th Léger, three batts.
63rd of the Line, three batts.
94th   ,,   three batts.
95th   ,,   three batts.

Corps Cavalry (Brigade Beaumont) :
2nd Hussars.
26th Chasseurs.

The gross total of this corps on Oct. 10 was 33,937 men, of whom 2,201 were detached, and 2,939 in hospital. The 4th Hussars, originally belonging to this corps, was transferred to the 3rd Corps by November.

2nd Corps. Marshal Bessières : after Nov. 9, Marshal Soult.

1st Division (Mouton, afterwards Merle) :
2nd Léger, three batts.
4th   ,,   three batts.
15th of the Line, three batts.
36th   ,,   three batts.
[Garde de Paris, one batt.]

2nd Division (Merle, afterwards Mermet) :
31st Léger, three batts.
47th of the Line, two batts.
70th   ,,   one batt.
86th   ,,   one batt.
1st Supply. Regt. of the Legions of Reserve } = 122nd of the Line, four batts.
2nd ditto
2nd Swiss Regiment, one batt.
3rd   ,,   ,,   one batt.

3rd Division (Bonnet) :
13th Prov. Regt. } = 119th of the
14th   ,,   } Line, four batts.
17th   ,,   } = 120th of the
18th   ,,   } Line, four batts.

Corps Cavalry (Division Lasalle) :
9th Dragoons (transferred from Milhaud).
10th Chasseurs.
22nd   ,,

Lasalle, with the 9th Dragoons and 10th Chasseurs, was detached after Gamonal (Nov. 10) and replaced by Franceschi's division. The corps received in January a reinforcement of twenty-two battalions from the dissolved 8th Corps, which formed two new divisions under Delaborde and Heudelet.

The gross total of this corps on Oct. 10 was 33,054 men, of whom 7,394 were detached and 5,536 in hospital.

3RD CORPS. Marshal MONCEY, Duke of Conegliano.

1st Division (Maurice Mathieu, afterwards Grandjean):
14th of the Line, four batts.
44th ,, three batts.
70th ,, one batt.
2nd of the Vistula, two batts.
3rd ,, two batts.

2nd Division (Musnier):
1st Prov. Regt. } = 114th of the
2nd ,, } Line, four batts.
3rd ,, } = 115th of the
4th ,, } Line, four batts.
[One Westphalian batt.]

3rd Division (Morlot):
5th Prov. Regt. { = 116th of the
{ Line, two batts.
9th ,, } = 117th of the
10th ,, } Line, four batts.
[One Prussian batt.]
[One Irish batt.]

4th Division (Grandjean):
5th Léger, three batts.
2nd Legion of Reserve, four batts.
1st of the Vistula, two batts.

Corps Cavalry (Brigade Wathier):
1st Provisional Cuirassiers (= 13th Cuirassiers).   1st Provisional Hussars.
2nd Provisional Light Cavalry (Hussars and Chasseurs).

Grandjean's division (No. 4) was afterwards absorbed in Morlot's [December], with the exception of the 1st of the Vistula, sent to join Musnier. The cavalry was afterwards strengthened by the 4th Hussars from the 1st Corps. The 121st of the Line (four batts.) arrived in December, and joined Morlot. The battalions in square brackets were left behind in the garrisons of Biscay and Navarre.

The gross total of the corps on Oct. 10 was 37,690 men, of whom 11,082 were detached in garrisons, &c. and 7,522 in hospital.

4TH CORPS. Marshal LEFEBVRE, Duke of Dantzig.

1st Division (Sebastiani):
28th of the Line, three batts.
32nd ,, three batts.
58th ,, three batts.
75th ,, three batts.

2nd Division (Leval):
Nassau Contingent, two batts.
Baden ,, two batts.
Hesse-Darmstadt ,, two batts.
Frankfort ,, one batt.
Dutch ,, two batts.

3rd Division (Valence):
4th of the Vistula, two batts.
7th ,, two batts.
9th ,, two batts.

Corps Cavalry (Brigade Maupetit):
5th Dragoons.
3rd Dutch Hussars.
Westphalian *Chevaux-Légers*.

The gross total of this corps on Oct. 10 was 22,895 men, of whom 955 were detached and 2,170 in hospital.

5TH CORPS. Marshal MORTIER, Duke of Treviso.

1st Division (Suchet):
17th Léger, three batts.
34th of the Line, four batts.
40th   ,,   three batts.
64th   ,,   three batts.
88th   ,,   three batts.

2nd Division (Gazan):
21st Léger, three batts.
28th   ,,   three batts.
100th of the Line, three batts.
103rd   ,,   three batts.

Corps Cavalry (Brigade Delaage):
10th Hussars.   21st Chasseurs.

The gross total of this corps on Oct. 10 was 24,552 men, of whom 188 were detached and 1,971 in hospital.

6TH CORPS. Marshal NEY, Duke of Elchingen.

1st Division (Marchand):
6th of the Line, three batts.
39th   ,,   three batts.
69th   ,,   three batts.
76th   ,,   three batts.

2nd Division (Lagrange, afterwards
     Maurice Mathieu):
25th Léger, four batts.
27th of the Line, three batts.
50th   ,,   four batts.
59th   ,,   three batts.

Corps Cavalry (Brigade Colbert):
3rd Hussars.   15th Chasseurs.

The gross total on Oct. 10 was 38,033 men, of whom 3,381 were detached and 5,051 in hospital. This total, however, includes a division under Mermet, whose battalions were transferred to the 2nd and 3rd Corps, when the campaign began in November. The 6th Corps, including its cavalry and artillery, had probably not more than 20,000 net when it took the field in its final form.

7TH CORPS. General GOUVION ST. CYR.

1st Division (Chabran):
2nd of the Line, one batt.
7th   ,,   two batts.
10th   ,,   one batt.
37th   ,,   one batt.
56th   ,,   one batt.
93rd   ,,   one batt.
2nd Swiss, one batt.

2nd Division (General Lecchi):
2nd Italian Line Regt., one batt.
4th   ,,   ,,   one batt.
5th   ,,   ,,   one batt.
Italian Chasseurs (*Velites*), one batt.
1st Neapolitan Line Regt., two batts.

3rd Division (Reille):
32nd Léger, one batt.
16th of the Line, one batt.
56th   ,,   one batt.
113th   ,,   two batts.
Prov. Regt. of Perpignan, four batts.
5th Legion of Reserve, one batt.
Chasseurs des Montagnes, one batt.
Battalion of the Valais, one batt.

4th Division (Souham):
1st Léger, three batts.
3rd   ,,   one batt.
7th of the Line, two batts.
42nd   ,,   three batts.
67th   ,,   one batt.

5th Division (Pino) :
  1st Italian Light Regt., three batts.
  2nd   ,,   ,,   three batts.
  4th Italian Line Regt., two batts.
  5th   ,,   ,,   one batt.
  6th   ,,   ,,   three batts.
  7th   ,,   ,,   one batt.

6th Division (Chabot) :
  2nd Neapolitan Line Regt., two batts.
  Chasseurs of the Pyrénées Orientales, one batt.

Corps Cavalry :
  Brigade Bessières :
  3rd Provisional Cuirassiers.
  3rd   ,,   Chasseurs.

  Brigade Schwartz :
  Italian Chasseurs of the Prince Royal.
  2nd Neapolitan Chasseurs.

  Brigade Fontane :
  Italian Royal Chasseurs.
  7th Italian Dragoons.

  Unattached Regiment :
  24th Dragoons.

The gross total of this corps on Oct. 10 was 42,382 men, of whom 1,302 were detached and 4,948 in hospital. But this does not include several regiments which did not join St. Cyr from Italy till long after the date of the return. In January, 1809, he had 41,386 men present with the colours, and 6,589 in hospital, besides 543 prisoners. There had also been considerable losses in the fighting. Probably the corps in November–December was well over 50,000 strong.

8TH CORPS. General JUNOT, Duke of Abrantes.

Dissolved in December, 1808. The troops were drafted as follows :—
1st Division (Delaborde) :
  15th of the Line, one batt., drafted to join its regt. in Merle's Div., 2nd Corps.
  47th   ,,   two batts.   ,,   Mermet's   ,,
  70th   ,,   three batts., received one more batt. from Mermet's Div.
  86th   ,,   two batts.   ,,   ,,   ,,
  4th Swiss, one batt.
This division, therefore, in January, 1809, consisted of four battalions 70th, three battalions 86th, and one battalion 4th Swiss. It was sent to join Soult, and strengthened by three battalions of the 17th Léger, thus having eleven battalions at Corunna.

2nd Division (Loison) :
  2nd Léger, one batt., drafted to join its regt. in Merle's Div., 2nd Corps.
  4th   ,,   one batt.   ,,   ,,   ,,   ,,
  12th ,,   one batt.   ,,   ,,   Dessolles' Div.
  15th ,,   one batt.
  32nd of the Line, one batt., drafted to join its regt. in Sebastiani's Div., 4th Corps.
  58th   ,,   one batt.   ,,   ,,   ,,   ,,
  2nd Swiss, one batt., drafted to join the batt. in Mermet's Div., 2nd Corps.
The remaining battalion of this division, that of the 15th Léger, was drafted to join Heudelet's Division, and became part of the 2nd Corps.

3rd Division (Heudelet) :

31st Léger, one batt., drafted to join its regt. in Mermet's Div. of 2nd Corps.

32nd ,, one batt.	82nd of the Line, one batt.
26th of the Line, two batts.	*Légion du Midi*, one batt.
66th ,, two batts.	Hanoverian Legion, one batt.

N.B.—The last-named eight battalions, afterwards joined by one from Loison's Division, were formed into the 4th Division of the 2nd Corps.

The whole corps cavalry of the 8th Corps was composed of provisional regiments, which were dissolved, and sent to join their units.

The 8th Corps on Oct. 10 had a gross total of 25,730 men, of whom 2,137 were detached, and 3,523 in hospital.

RESERVE.

(1) Independent Reserve Division (General Dessolles) :

12th Léger, three batts.	51st of the Line, three batts.
43rd of the Line, three batts.	55th ,, three batts.

(2) Guards of the King of Spain (General Saligny) :

Four battalions of Infantry.	One regiment of Cavalry.

(Two regiments, mainly Spanish deserters, were added in January.)

The total is confused in the return of Oct. 10 with that of the Imperial Guard, and includes also some regiments left in garrison in the north, e. g. the 118th of the Line ; including these the Reserve amounted to 13,000 men.

RESERVE OF CAVALRY.

Division of Dragoons, Latour-Maubourg :

Brigades Oldenbourg, Perreimond, Digeon.

1st, 2nd, 4th, 14th, 20th, and 26th Dragoons.

The gross total of the division on Oct. 10 was 3,695 sabres.

Division of Dragoons, Milhaud :

The 12th, 16th, and 21st Dragoons.

(The 5th and 9th Dragoons, originally belonging to this division, were transferred to Lefebvre and Lasalle respectively.)

The gross total of the division on Oct. 10 was 2,940 sabres, probably including one of the transferred regiments.

Division of Dragoons, Lahoussaye :

Brigades D'Avenay and Marisy. (On D'Avenay being transferred to an independent provisional brigade, Caulaincourt replaces him.)

17th, 18th, 19th, and 27th Dragoons.

The gross total of this division on Oct. 10 was 2,020 sabres.

Division of Dragoons, Lorges :

Brigades Vialannes and Fournier.

13th, 15th, 22nd, and 25th Dragoons.

The gross total of this division on Oct. 10 was 3,101 sabres.

Division of Dragoons, Millet (Kellermann after Jan. 1809) :

3rd, 6th, 10th, and 11th Dragoons.

The gross total of this division on Oct. 10 was 2,903 sabres.

Division of Light Cavalry, FRANCESCHI :
Brigades Debelle and Girardin (?).

| 8th Dragoons. | 'Supplementary Regiment' of |
| 22nd *Chasseurs à Cheval.* | *Chasseurs à Cheval.* |

Hanoverian *Chevaux-Légers.*

The Provisional Chasseurs were dissolved in Jan. 1809, and replaced by the 1st Hussars. The 22nd belonged to the original corps-cavalry of Soult.

The numbers of this division (which had not yet been put together on October 10) seem unobtainable, save that the 1st Hussars was 712 strong. Probably Franceschi's total would be about 2,400 sabres.

IMPERIAL GUARD.

Infantry :

Two regiments of Grenadiers (four batts.), two regiments of Chasseurs (four batts.), two regiments of Fusiliers (six batts.).

Cavalry :

One regiment each of *Chasseurs à Cheval*, Grenadiers, Dragoons, *Gendarmes d'élite*, Polish Light Horse, one squadron of Mamelukes. 36 guns.

The total was about 8,000 infantry and 3,500 horse, with 600 gunners.

N.B.—A few late-coming regiments, and a few units not attached to any division, are not included in the above tables, e. g. the 118th, 121st, and 122nd Regiments of the Line, and the 27th Chasseurs. Nor are there included the dépôt of undistributed conscripts at Bayonne, nor the battalions of National Guards forming movable columns inside the French frontier. But the 19,371 artillery of the army are included in the corps, divisions, and brigades.

GROSS TOTAL OF THE WHOLE ON OCTOBER 10.

	Total.	Detached.	Hospital or missing.	Effective present.
1st Corps	33,937	2,201	2,939	28,797
2nd Corps	33,054	7,394	5,536	20,124
3rd Corps	37,690	11,082	7,522	19,086
4th Corps	22,895	955	2,170	19,770
5th Corps	24,552	188	1,971	22,393
6th Corps	38,033	3,381	5,051	29,601
7th Corps	42,382	1,302	4,948	36,132
8th Corps	25,730	2,137	3,523	20,070
Reserve Cavalry . . .	17,059 ⎫			
Imperial Guard . . .	12,100 ⎬ 3,533	3,945	34,801
Reserve of Infantry (Dessolles, Joseph's Guards, &c.) . .	13,120 ⎭			
Troops on the march from Germany not distributed to the corps	5,200	363	74	4,763
Columns inside the French frontier (National Guards) . .	8,860	107	165	8,588
	314,612	32,643	37,844	244,125

Exclusive of the dépôt of conscripts at Bayonne.

XIII

SIR JOHN MOORE'S ARMY:

ITS STRENGTH AND ITS LOSSES.

N.B.—The first column gives the strength of each of Baird's regiments on Oct. 2, and of Moore's regiments on Oct. 15, deducting from the latter men left behind in Portugal. The second column gives the men present with the colours on Dec. 19, but not those in hospital or ' on command ' on that day. These last amounted on Dec. 19 to 3,938 and 1,687 respectively. The third column gives the numbers disembarked in England in January.

	Total strength in Oct. 1808.	Effective strength present on Dec.19,1808.	Disembarked in England in Jan. 1809.	Deficiency.
Cavalry (Lord Paget).				
7th Hussars	672	497	575	97[1]
10th ,, ...	675	514	651	24
15th ,, ...	674	527	650	24
18th Light Dragoons .	624	565	547	77
3rd ,, ,, K.G.L.	433	347	377	56
	— 3,078	— 2,450	— 2,800	— 278
1st Division (Sir D. Baird).				
Warde's Brigade :				
1st Foot Guards, 1st batt.	1,340	1,300	1,266	74
,, ,, 2nd batt.	1,102	1,027	1,036	66
Bentinck's Brigade :				
4th Foot, 1st batt. . .	889	754	740	149
42nd ,, 1st batt. . .	918	880	757	161
50th ,, 1st batt. . .	863	794	599	264
Manningham's Brigade:				
1st Foot, 3rd batt. . .	723	597	507	216
26th ,, 1st batt. . .	870	745	662	208
81st ,, 2nd batt. . .	719	615	478	241
	— 7,424	— 6,712	— 6,045	— 1,379
2nd Division (Sir J. Hope).				
Leith's Brigade :				
51st Foot	613	516	506	107
59th ,, 2nd batt. . .	640	557	497	143
76th ,, ...	784	654	614	170
Hill's Brigade :			[Estimate][2]	
2nd Foot	666	616	461	205
5th ,, 1st batt. . .	893	833	654	239
14th ,, 2nd batt. . .	630	550	492	138
32nd ,, 1st batt. . .	806	756	619	187
	— 5,032	— 4,482	— 3,843	— 1,189
Carried forward . .	15,534	13,644	12,688	2,846

[1] Includes fifty-six men drowned on return voyage to England.

[2] The 76th Regiment failed to send in its disembarkation return, so that its loss has to be averaged.

	Total strength on Oct. 1808.	Effective strength present on Dec.19,1808.	Disembarked in England in Jan. 1809.	Deficiency.
Brought forward .	15,534	13,644	12,688	2,846
Catlin Crawfurd's Brigade :				
36th Foot, 1st batt. . .	804	736	561	243
71st ,, 1st batt. . .	764	724	626	138
92nd ,, 1st batt. . .	912	900	783	129
	—— 2,480	—— 2,360	—— 1,970	—— 510
3rd Division (Lt.-Gen. Fraser).				
Beresford's Brigade :				
6th Foot, 1st batt. . .	882	783	491	391
9th ,, 1st batt. . .	945	607	572	373
23rd ,, 2nd batt. . .	590	496	418	172
43rd ,, 2nd batt. . .	598	411	368	230
Fane's Brigade :				
38th Foot, 1st batt. . .	900	823	757	143
79th ,, 1st batt. . .	932	838	777	155
82nd ,, 1st batt. . .	830	812	602	228
	—— 5,677	—— 4,770	—— 3,985	—— 1,692
Reserve Division (Maj.-Gen. E. Paget).				
Anstruther's Brigade:				
20th Foot	541	499	428	113
52nd ,, 1st batt. . .	862	828	719	143
95th ,, 1st batt. . .	863	820	706	157
Disney's Brigade :				
28th Foot, 1st batt. . .	926	750	624	302
91st ,, 1st batt. . .	746	698	534	212
	—— 3,938	—— 3,595	—— 3,011	—— 927
1st Flank-Brigade (Col. R. Crawfurd).				
43rd Foot, 1st batt. . .	895	817	810	85
52nd ,, 2nd batt. .	623	381	462	161
95th ,, 2nd batt. .	744	702	648	96
	—— 2,262	—— 1,900	—— 1,920	—— 342
2nd Flank-Brigade (Brig.-Gen. C. Alten).				
1st Lt. Batt. K.G.L. .	871	803	708	163[1]
2nd ,, ,, .	880	855	618	262[2]
	—— 1,751	—— 1,658	—— 1,326	—— 425
Artillery, &c. . . .	1,455	1,297	1,200	255[3]
Staff Corps	137	133	99	38
Total . .	33,234	29,357	26,199	7,035

[1] Includes twenty-two men drowned on return voyage to England.

[2] Includes 187 men drowned on return voyage to England.

[3] Includes twenty-two drowned on return voyage to England, and nine drowned in Corunna harbour.

It will be noted that if to the 29,357 of the second column there are added the 3,938 sick and the 1,687 men 'on command,' the gross total of the army on Dec. 19 must have been 34,982, a figure which exceeds that at the bottom of the first column. It would seem, therefore, that about 1,748 men in small detachments joined the army at Salamanca and elsewhere before Dec. 19. They must represent drafts and convoy-escorts coming up from Portugal. The apparent deficiency for the campaign therefore is 8,783. But it must not be supposed that these 8,783 men were all lost between Salamanca and Corunna : from them we must deduct (1) the 296 casualties by shipwreck while returning to England ; (2) 589 rank and file who escaped individually to Portugal, and were then enrolled (along with the convalescent sick left behind by Moore's regiments) in the two 'battalions of detachments' which fought at Talavera ; (3) the number of sick discharged from Salamanca on to Portugal in the convoys escorted by the 5/60th and 3rd Regiments. I can nowhere find the number of these invalids stated, but it must have been large, as the total of the sick belonging to the whole army was nearly 4,000 in December. It will be a very modest estimate if we give 1,500 for those of them who were at Salamanca, the head-quarters hospital of the army, and were capable of being moved back to Portugal.

We may therefore deduct under these three heads about 2,385 men. This figure taken from 8,783 leaves 6,398 for the real loss in the campaign.

But even from this total 400 more must be deducted, for 400 British convalescents were released by the Galician insurgents from French captivity and sent back to Lisbon in the spring of 1809. ['Further papers relative to Spain and Portugal,' p. 7 in *Parliamentary Papers* for 1809.]

On the whole, then, about 5,998 men were actually lost. Napier's estimate of 3,233 (i. 502) for the total loss is certainly too low. Of these 2,189 were prisoners sent to France. [Schepeler, 'Table of prisoners sent to France, 1809-13' on p. 150.] The remaining 3,809 perished in battle, by the road, or in hospital.

INDEX

Acevedo, general, commands division under Blake, 408 ; wounded at Espinosa, 415; murdered by the French, 426.

Acland, brigadier-general, arrives at Peniche, 241 ; at Vimiero, 249–58 ; gives evidence before the Court of Inquiry, 294.

Afrancesados, party of the, in Spain, 97.

Alagon, Palafox defeated at, 145.

Alcedo, general, governor of Corunna, surrenders to Soult, 596.

Alcolea, combat of, 129.

Alexander, Emperor of Russia, his meeting with Napoleon at Erfurt, 377.

Andalusia, province of, rises against the French, 69 ; its geography, 74, 80.

Anstruther, brigadier-general, arrives in Portugal, 248 ; at Vimiero, 250–61 ; in command at Almeida, 494 ; dies at Corunna, 595.

Antonio, Don, brother of Charles IV, appointed head of the Junta of Regency, 48 ; goes to Bayonne, 62 ; at Valençay, 56.

Army, the Spanish, its character and organization, 89–95 : see also Tables and Appendices v, viii, &c.

Army of Spain, the French, character of the first, 103–7 ; of the second, 107–13 : see also Tables and Appendices vi, &c.

Artillery, the, of the Spanish army, 94, 95 ; of the French army, 112 ; tactics of the, 120–2.

Asturias, Prince of the : see Ferdinand.

Asturias, province of the, declares war on France, 65 ; sends emissaries to England, 66 ; sends troops to Blake's army, 382, 384.

Baget, Juan, leader of Catalan *miqueletes*, 318, 322, 328.

Baird, Sir David, general, lands at Corunna, 484, 491, 498 ; advances to Astorga, 500 ; joins Moore at Mayorga, 532 ; wounded at Corunna, 584, 589.

Barcelona, treacherously seized by Duhesme, 36 ; operations round, 302, 318.

Baylen, battle of, 187–92 ; Convention of, 197–9 ; text of the Convention, Appendix, 621–3.

Bayonne, French troops at, 6–12, 34 ; treachery of Napoleon at, 51–6.

Beauharnais, Marquis of, French ambassador at Madrid, his negotiations with Ferdinand, Prince of the Asturias, 19, 20; refuses to acknowledge Ferdinand as King, 43, 46.

Belesta, general, joins Blake with his division, 208.

Belvedere, Conde de, defeated at Gamonal, 421–3.

Bembibre, the British at, 566.

Benavente, combat of, 549–51.

Bentinck, Lord William, British military representative in Madrid, 365 ; endeavours to get information from the Junta, 488 ; his correspondence with Moore, 504 ; at Corunna, 584.

Bernadotte, Jean Baptiste, marshal, Prince of Ponte Corvo, in command on the Baltic, 368 ; tricked by La Romana, 373.

Bessières, Jean Baptiste, marshal, Duke of Istria, leads a *corps d'armée* into Spain, 40 ; his first operations, 125, 126 ; operations in Northern Spain, 140, 142, 166–72 ; victory at Medina de Rio Seco, 169–72 ; represses rising in Biscay, 356 ; superseded by Soult, 418 ; pursues Infantado, 470.

Bessières, general, leads French cavalry in Catalonia, 309, 318.

Betanzos, the stragglers' battle at, during Moore's retreat, 579.

Bilbao, taken and sacked by Merlin, 356 ; taken by Blake, 383 ; taken by Lefebvre, 400.

Biscay, rising in, 355, 356.

Blake, Joachim, captain-general of the province of Galicia, 163 ; his differences with Cuesta, 165 ; defeated at Medina de Rio Seco, 168–72 ; his operations in Biscay, 382, 384, 400 ; defeated at Zornoza, 407 ; at Valmaceda, 411 ; at Espinosa, 413–6 ; escapes into the Asturian hills, 427 ; superseded by La Romana, 427.

Bonaparte, Joseph : see Joseph Napoleon.

Bonaparte, Louis, King of Holland, refuses the crown of Spain, 46.

Bonnet, general, at Gamonal, 422 ; occupies Santander, 429.

Bowes, general, B. F., commands brigade under Wellesley, 232 ; at Roliça, 237 ; at Vimiero, 249–59.

Brennier, general, at Roliça, 239 ; at Vimiero, 253–9.

Burgos, taken and sacked by Napoleon, 424.

Burrard, Sir Harry, second in command of British troops in Portugal, 226 ; arrives at Maceira Bay, 250 ; assumes command at Vimiero and refuses to advance, 260, 261 ; joins in negotiations for the Convention of Cintra, 268 ; summoned before the Court of Inquiry, 294.

Cabezon, combat of, 141.

Cacabellos, combat of, 567–9.

Caldagues, Count of, leader of Catalan levies, 327 ; relieves Gerona, 328–30.

Canning, George, Foreign Secretary, gives assistance to the Asturians, 66 ; permits the embarkation of Dupont's troops after Baylen, 202 ; his speech on the Spanish insurrection, 222 ; sends Robertson to La Romana, 371 ; his replies to the Notes of France and Russia, 378, 379.

Caraffa, general, arrested by Junot, 208, 209 ; released by Convention of Cintra, 273.

Carlos, Don, brother of Ferdinand VII, sent to Bayonne to meet Napoleon, 47, 48 ; confined at Valençay, 55.

Castaños, general, in command of Andalusian army, 127 ; opposes Dupont at Andujar, 177 ; receives capitulation of Dupont, 197 ; marches on Madrid, 346 ; commands the 'Army of the Centre,' 385–431 ; defeated at Tudela, 441–4 ; his retreat, 447–9; superseded, 449.

Castelar, Marquis of, defends Madrid against Napoleon, 463–9.

Castlereagh, Robert, Stewart, viscount, his policy, 221, 223, 224 ; his confidence in Wellesley, 225 ; commends Wellesley to Dalrymple, 263 ; receives

Wellesley's report on the Spanish War, 289, 290 ; his correspondence with Moore, 487, 493, 506, 518, 522, 529, 548, 554, 597, 599.

Castro Gonzalo, combat of, 548.

Catalonia, province of, revolts against the French, 70 ; geography of, 82, 303–6 ; the struggle in, 301–33.

Cavalry, tactics of, in the Peninsular War, 117–20 ; the Spanish, its weakness, 92, 93, 120 ; the French, 105.

Cervellon, Conde de, captain-general of Valencia, his incapacity, 134–9.

Cevallos, Don Pedro, minister of Foreign Affairs, accompanies Ferdinand VII to Bayonne, 48 ; his interview with Napoleon, 51, 52 ; takes office under Joseph, 174 ; reappointed minister by the Supreme Junta, 359.

Chabert, general, at Baylen, 187, 189 ; negotiates terms of surrender, 196, 197.

Chabran, general, his expedition to Tarragona, 309 ; recalled by Duhesme, 312 ; checked at Granollers, 319.

Charles IV, King of Spain, his character, 13 ; arrests Ferdinand, Prince of the Asturias, for high treason, 21 ; pardons him, 23 ; compelled to disgrace Godoy, 41 ; abdicates in favour of Ferdinand, 42 ; withdraws his abdication, 45 ; summoned to Bayonne by Napoleon, 53 ; abdicates in favour of Napoleon, 55.

Charlot, general, at Vimiero, 254, 255.

Charmilly, colonel, emissary sent by Frere to Moore, 520–3.

Cintra, Convention of, 268–72 ; its terms, 272–8 ; Court of Inquiry on, 291–300.

Claros, Don Juan, leader of Catalan miqueletes, 321, 328.

Cochrane, Lord, harasses Duhesme's troops, 324, 331 ; blockades Barcelona, 327.

Colbert, general, at Tudela, 441–4 ; slain at Cacabellos, 569.

Colli, Baron, his attempt to release Ferdinand from Valençay, 18.

Collingwood, Lord, commanding Mediterranean Fleet, refuses to allow embarkation of Dupont's troops, 201.

Constantino, combat of, 572–3.

Cordova, sack of, by Dupont's troops, 130.

Cortes, proposal to summon the, 362.

Corunna, Baird lands at, 484, 491, 498 ; arrival of Moore at, 581 ; battle of, 583–95.

Cotton, admiral, resents the terms of the Convention of Cintra, 271, 272 ;

THE
NAPOLEONIC LIBRARY
Published by Greenhill Books

SIR CHARLES OMAN:
Studies in the Napoleonic Wars

Wellington's Army

F. LORAINE PETRE:
Napoleon's Campaign in Poland, 1806–1807

Napoleon's Conquest of Prussia, 1806

**Napoleon and the Archduke Charles: A History
of the Franco-Austrian Campaign in the Valley
of the Danube in 1809**

Napoleon's Last Campaign in Germany, 1813

Napoleon at Bay, 1814

JAC WELLER:
Wellington in India

Wellington in the Peninsula

Wellington at Waterloo

**Adventures with the Connaught Rangers,
1809–1814**
by William Grattan

A Boy in the Peninsular War
by Robert Blakeney

**A British Rifleman:
Journal and Correspondence during
the Peninsular War**
by Major George Simmons

The Campaign of 1812 in Russia
by General Carl von Clausewitz
Introduction by George F. Nafziger

The Campaign of Waterloo
by the Hon. Sir John Fortescue

History of the Waterloo Campaign
by Captain William Siborne

In the Peninsula with a French Hussar:
Memoirs of the War of the French in Spain
by Albert Jean Michel de Rocca

Journal of the Waterloo Campaign
by General Cavalié Mercer

Life in Napoleon's Army:
The Memoirs of Captain Elzéar Blaze
Commentary by Lt. Gen. Charles Napier
Introduction by Philip Haythornthwaite

Memoirs of a French Napoleonic Officer:
Jean-Baptiste Barrès, Chasseur of the Imperial Guard
Edited by Maurice Barrès

The Memoirs of Baron de Marbot, volume 1
The Memoirs of Baron de Marbot, volume 2

Napoleon and Iberia: The Twin Sieges of Ciudad
Rodrigo and Almeida, 1810
by Donald D. Horward

Napoleon and Waterloo: The Emperor's Campaign
with the Armée du Nord, 1815
by A. F. Becke

Napoleon's Army:
The Military Memoirs of Charles Parquin
Translated and edited by B. T. Jones

The Notebooks of Captain Coignet
by Captain Jean-Roche Coignet

The Peninsular Journal, 1808–1817
by Major-General Sir Benjamin D'Urban

Waterloo Letters
Edited by Major-General H. T. Siborne

**With the Guns in the Peninsula: The Peninsular War
Journal of Captain William Webber**
Edited by Richard Henry Wollocombe